Christopher G. Beehner

Spirituality, Sustainability, and Success

Concepts and Cases

Second Edition

palgrave
macmillan

Christopher G. Beehner
Seminole State College of Florida
Heathrow, FL, USA

ISSN 2662-3668 ISSN 2662-3676 (electronic)
Palgrave Studies in Workplace Spirituality and Fulfillment
ISBN 978-3-031-47642-6 ISBN 978-3-031-47643-3 (eBook)
https://doi.org/10.1007/978-3-031-47643-3

Cover illustration: Kotenko Oleksandr/shutterstock.com

This Palgrave Macmillan imprint is published by the registered company Springer Nature Switzerland AG
The registered company address is: Gewerbestrasse 11, 6330 Cham, Switzerland

Paper in this product is recyclable.

Foreword

The very valuable and outstanding contribution of Chris Beehner, through this unique book, is that he manages to not only make visible the nexus between sustainability and spirituality but also clarifies its relevance to individuals and organizations. Beehner's work clarifies and offers examples and concrete arguments on the benefits of nurturing spirituality at the individual and workplace level for individual and organizational success. Making this visible is certainly key in helping individuals, managers, and business leaders understand why and how to move forward, from their contexts, in a way that accelerates the much needed and urgent transition toward more sustainable societies. Beehner can reflect and speak about that with authority given his years of experience not only in the private sector but also in the teaching of management and business in higher education.

For many, the conventional approach to the sustainability concept is envisioned when the social, environmental, and economic dimensions are brought together and when decisions are made from that intersection. Similarly, the triple bottom line lens of business highlights the need to balance the interests of people, planet, and profit, which should be reflected in the planning and reporting of enterprises. For others, the political, cultural, spiritual, and ethical factors cannot be outside the sustainability equation and must be considered in a broader view of the concept of sustainability. In fact, exploring the idea of sustainability, including its spiritual dimension, can help us expand our vision to see the higher purpose and roots of "what" and "why" of sustainability. Given that through spirituality we can see and feel a deep sense of connectedness, interdependence and therefore of empathy and care for the whole.

Humans are inherently spiritual, despite the fact that this has become quite fuzzy in mainstream society and taken away from many contexts where materialism is increasingly taken over. However, our spirituality can be awakened and nurtured through our spirit of service being put into action, our experience and connection with nature and capacity to contemplate and understand the close connection between our inner and outer world including with the universe (practices that are fading away from the predominant fast pace urban societies, and we could even say shallow). A unique international document that can help and inspire us to search to higher purpose and meaning of life and that, given its language and tone, can help us expand our understanding of sustainability including its spiritual dimension is The Earth Charter.

The Earth Charter is known for offering a broad and comprehensive ethical foundation for a more just, sustainable, and peaceful global society. Stressing the close relationship between the quest for enduring peace, social justice, and environmental protection, it emphasizes our interdependence and responsibility with the well-being of the human family and the large living world. In other words, it makes clear that we can only ensure lasting peace when ecological protection and a healthy environment are ensured and when the challenges of social injustices are addressed. Through its preamble and sixteen principles, The Earth Charter offers an ethical framework based on scientific knowledge and principles from international law with a strong spiritual language that helps us recalibrate the human/nature relationship. Hence, it can be used (and has been used) as a valuable instrument for individuals and organizations, as we navigate the foggy weather and turbulent waters in which many decisions need to be made. After more than two decades since its launch, The Earth Charter involves a document, a global movement that involves individuals and organizations from all regions of the world that have embraced the Earth Charter and are using it in different ways, and also an international secretariat that coordinates this movement and an education center.

It invites us to move away from the focus on material life to nurture our being and responsibility to contribute to the common good when it states, "We must realize that when basic needs have been met, human development is primarily about being more, not having more". It also encourages us to see "Earth's vitality, diversity, and beauty" as a sacred trust, as well as to live "with reverence for the mystery of being, gratitude for the gift of life, and humility regarding the human place in nature".

Changing the course of things is not only necessary, but urgent. And it is not only the task of governments or the United Nations. Moving in the direction of sustainability with resolve and a deep sense of urgency, connection, interdependence, and responsibility must be in the hands, minds, and hearts of individuals and business leaders. The spark of this change starts with a new consciousness. We are entering a phase that requires clearer and expanded consciousness, resilience, strength, and balance between our inner and outer world. Awakening our spirituality and understanding of a broad sense of sustainability will make us more effective.

This book offers important insights and inspiration to make this happen.

Dr. Mirian Vilela
Executive Director
Earth Charter International
San Jose, Costa Rica

Preface

I first encountered the concept of workplace spirituality while preparing for my doctoral dissertation. The degree specialization of my Doctor of Business Administration was organizational leadership, and I was seeking to "make my mark" in that field. The idea of incorporating spirituality into the workplace was not only intriguing, but seemed appropriate. Thinking back to this time, I recall the quote attributed to French Jesuit priest Pierre Teilhard de Chardin: "We are not human beings having a spiritual experience. We are spiritual beings having a human experience".

I have been passionate about nature and the environment since childhood, and during my business career I often promoted green and sustainable business ideas to my employers, often with mixed response. Near the end of my doctoral dissertation journey, I left industry and accepted a full-time business faculty position at Seminole State College of Florida. While primarily teaching traditional business topics, I was encouraged by my dean to develop and teach a course entitled *Sustainable Business Strategies*. That course provided a new trajectory for my academic career and the foundation for the first edition of this book.

In early 2017, Dr. Satinder Dhiman of Woodbury University contacted me about writing a chapter in a major research work entitled *Handbook of Engaged Sustainability*. During email exchanges about the chapter, Satinder queried whether I would have an interest in writing a book about both spirituality and sustainability. Over a period of several months, and numerous email exchanges, the first edition of *Spirituality, Sustainability, and Success: Concepts and Cases* was conceived and came to fruition. This second edition expands the conversation to include Indigenous and post-pandemic perspectives about the topics.

This book is written for doctoral students, scholars, policymakers, and management practitioners who are interested in better understanding how spirituality and sustainability are beneficial for individual and organizational success. The book is organized into fourteen chapters. The first three chapters introduce the fundamentals of spirituality and workplace spirituality. Chapter 4 is new to this edition and explores the topic of Indigenous spirituality. Chapter 5 is also new and explores spirituality in the post-pandemic era. Chapter 6 covers sustainability and success from an individual perspective, and Chapter 7 explores the topic of sustainable business. Chapter 8 is new to this edition and explores the topic of Indigenous sustainability. Chapter 9 is also new and explores sustainability in the post-pandemic era. The chapters that follow demonstrate how each of the constructs are beneficial in achieving individual and organizational success. The remaining chapters build the case for the proposition that a combination of spirituality and sustainability can produce individual and organizational success. The final chapter summarizes the previous chapters and offers future recommendations. Each chapter includes a chapter case, personal interview, reflection topic, or reflection questions to stimulate critical thinking, and provide instructional tools for academic use and practical application.

I approached the topics of Indigenous spirituality and sustainability with great reverence and some apprehension. As a non-Native, I am not capable of truly understanding Indigenous cosmologies. My approach has been academic, as an outsider, and I apologize if I did not fully represent every important aspect of these time-tested concepts in the limited space available in these pages. There are countless Indigenous cultures, traditions, and worldviews, all of whom deserve respect and inclusion in any dialogue about spirituality and sustainability. Sadly, I was able to summarize only a handful in this manuscript. However, I trust that my book opens the door to the critical contributions of the Indigenous Peoples globally and stimulates further interest on the part of the readers to humbly quest for further knowledge and understanding of these traditional ways.

I would like to acknowledge Satinder Dhiman for introducing me to the Palgrave Macmillan organization, and Marcus Ballenger at Palgrave Macmillan for his continued support with my writing efforts. I would like to thank Hugh Moore, retired Dean of the Center for Business, Legal Studies, and Entrepreneurship at Seminole State College of Florida for supporting and encouraging my sustainable business endeavors. Last, but most important, I am indebted to my wife Corene, and my sons, Logan, and Erik for supporting me during my doctoral studies and career change, and for providing influence and encouragement in the sustainability-focused direction in which my career is moving.

Heathrow, USA
Christopher G. Beehner

Contents

List of Figures

1

Introduction: The Nexus of Spirituality and Sustainability

1.1 Introduction

During the past few decades, the topics of spirituality and sustainability have received considerable interest from both industry and academia, influenced by the increase in corporate scandals, and industry-related environmental disasters. Scholars have suggested spirituality and sustainability are mutually interdependent, with spirituality enhancing efforts to act in a sustainably responsible manner, and sustainability reinforcing the connectedness of all life (Marques et al., 2010). However, both topics are frequently misunderstood, or even eschewed by some members of both communities. While spirituality and religion share common ingredients, these two terms are not synonymous. However, conversations about spirituality are often assumed to be religious, and discussion of spirituality at the workplace is frequently stifled. Likewise, conversations about sustainability are frequently alleged to be the domain of government, nonprofits, and environmentalists, not capitalist business enterprises. I join Holthaus (2012) in lamenting that business acquaintances perceive sustainability as a radical environmentalist threat to commerce, fully convinced the free-market system should guide human endeavors, and

C. G. Beehner, *Spirituality, Sustainability, and Success*, Palgrave Studies in Workplace Spirituality and Fulfillment, https://doi.org/10.1007/978-3-031-47643-3_1

that continual economic growth is the only feasible path to successful society.

In this chapter, spirituality will be examined from a secular perspective, and sustainability from a pragmatic business perspective. The systems perspective will be introduced to support the interconnectedness of spirituality and sustainability within the context of traditional and nontraditional religious doctrine, and contemporary thought. This foundation of the nexus of spirituality and sustainability will provide a foundation upon which the remaining chapters will build, demonstrating that spirituality and sustainability are beneficial for individual and organizational success. The remaining chapter themes and topics will also be summarized.

The premise of this book is that spirituality (individual and workplace), and sustainability are beneficial for individual (and organizational) success. The focus of this text will be the examination of spirituality from a secular, non-sectarian perspective, and the examination of sustainability from a holistic, yet pragmatic perspective. The framework for each will be broad, interdisciplinary, non-religious, and non-political to be inclusive of a broad readership. Religious content is intended to provide historical and contextual perspectives for spirituality and sustainability, and not to endorse religiosity, or any specific religion as necessary for spirituality or sustainability practice. Equipped with an understanding that spirituality is not the same as religion, business leaders and academics may be more likely to engage in conversation about the role of spirituality in workplace and organizational settings. Moreover, when sustainability is understood to be a viable business and organizational concept and model, and not simply "tree hugging", business and organizational leaders and academics may be more likely to engage in conversation about sustainable business.

The reader may query why and how two seemingly unrelated terms are being discussed within the same text. This author hopes to demonstrate spirituality and sustainability to be more related than they seem, and that both engender success at individual and organizational levels. Throughout the chapters of this text, similarities and overlaps between spirituality and sustainability will be identified. Each chapter will conclude with a chapter case, personal interview summary, or reflection questions to stimulate critical thinking, and provide instructional tools for academic use and practical application.

This text combines two contemporary topics in a practical manner as legitimate tools for individual and organizational or business success. While existing texts examine the individual or organizational benefits of either spirituality or sustainability, few texts incorporate the two constructs in an examination of the relationship between both constructs and individual and organizational success. The overall benefits proposed by this text include an understanding of the benefits of incorporating spirituality and sustainability in both personal and career success, and in business or organizational success; and, examples and resources to assist readers in practical application of these principles, and in educating others about benefits and practical application.

The expanding interest in both spirituality and sustainability partially originates from the increase in corporate scandals, and industry-related environmental disasters in recent decades. Beginning in 2001, numerous Fortune 500 company executives were accused of major ethical misconduct from financial misstatement to intentional fraud. The crisis was not unique to the United States, with German automobile manufacturer Volkswagen admitting to intentionally tampering with emission systems to falsify performance data. Sustainability-minded drivers were stunned to learn their environmentally friendly vehicles were emitting pollution at unsafe and illegal levels. The 1989 Exxon Valdes oil spill, and the 2010 BP Deepwater Horizon oil rig explosion reinforce the magnitude of industrial accidents on the environment.

Spirituality and sustainability are interrelated, both invoking a higher sense of purpose and meaning among individuals and organizations embracing either or both concepts. Næss (1989) suggested humanity is inseparable from nature: if humanity harms nature, we are harming ourselves. Chavez (2010) noted the dissection of sustainability and spirituality into two separate parts to be arbitrary, reflective of the materialistic reductionist framework of contemporary society. To address the problems faced by humankind, we must reunite the concepts of spirituality and sustainability from a systems perspective—both are interconnected and must be considered and embraced collectively. However, prior to exploring the nexus of spirituality and sustainability, a summary description of spirituality and sustainability is appropriate.

1.2 Brief Summary of Spirituality

This section begins with an examination of the definition and description of spirituality from a secular perspective. Some of the religious influence on spirituality will be examined in the section about the nexus spirituality and sustainability. The Merriam-Webster dictionary contains multiple definitions for the term spirituality, the more secular being "the quality or state of being spiritual". In turn, of the five definitions of spiritual, the more secular ones include relating to, consisting of, or affecting the spirit, and related or joined in the spirit. When we get to the core term spirit, we find a total of fourteen definitions of spiritual. Again, choosing the secular ones, we find several options: "an animating or vital principle held to give life to physical organisms"; "the immaterial intelligent or sentient part of a person"; "a special attitude or frame of mind"; and, "the feeling, quality, or disposition characterizing something". Clearly spirituality has multiple meanings outside of religion, adding puzzlement to the topic.

Some scholars suggest any definition of spirituality must contain as criteria the feelings, thoughts, experiences, and behavior emanating from the quest for the Sacred, characterized as a divine entity, object, truth, or reality (Hill et al., 2000). Chavez (2010) noted that the Sacred, unknown, or unknowable entity is part of the foundation of most spiritual doctrines. Mitroff defined spirituality as "the desire to find ultimate purpose in life, and to live accordingly" (Cavanagh, 1999, p. 186). Vaill (1996) described spirituality as "the feeling individuals have about the fundamental meaning of who they are, what they are doing, [and] the contributions they are making" (p. 218). The meaning of life has four characteristics: when individuals consider their lives to be meaningful, they are committed to a meaningful life; the commitment to meaningful life provides the framework for the interpretation of life events, and for the foundation of purpose; if individuals believe their lives are meaningful, they see themselves as fulfilling their purpose in life; and, the process of achieving purpose in life proves that life is existentially significant (Battlista & Almond, 1973).

Numerous secular definitions of spirituality have emanated in recent organizational science literature (Dent et al., 2005), ranging from the process of seeking a relationship with a higher power believed to influence the order of things, that is broader than any one religion (Zellars & Perrewe, 2003), to the process of placing value on the non-material characteristics of life (Krishnan, 2008). LaPierre (1994) summarized the components of spirituality to be: quest for meaning in life; transcendental encounter; sense of community; search for conclusive truth or highest value; respect for and appreciation of the mystery of nature; and, a personal transformation. A person's spirit is considered the animating principle or life force providing motivation in the quest for meaning, purpose, and a sense of worth (Baldacchino, 2017). According to Cowan (1993), "Spirituality is like gravity. It must be taken into account because it is there. Ignore it and you are ignoring the most central fact of any human situation" (61).

1.3 Brief Summary of Sustainability

While there are countless definitions of sustainability, most related to specific fields of study, the focus of the chapters in this book are sustainability within the context of business and development. A commonly accepted definition of sustainable development is drawn from the World Commission on Environment and Development (WCED), commonly known as the Brundtland Report: "Sustainable development is the development that meets the needs of the present without compromising the ability of future generations to meet their own needs" (WCED, 1987). While academia strives for consistent terminology usage, the terms green and sustainable (or sustainability) are sometimes used interchangeably (Collins et al., 2016). However, in business, the term green is increasingly applied to products and processes, while sustainability is applied to systems and enterprises (Yanarella et al., 2009). Hence, because the focus of several chapters of this book are with examining sustainability within the context of individual and organizational success, we will consider sustainability as referring to actions and processes undertaken by individuals and organizations to ensure present needs are met without compromising the ability of future individuals and organizations to meet their needs in similar fashion.

While traditional definitions of sustainability have been environmental in nature, Orr (2002) emphasizes sustainability should not only be concerned with ecological integrity, but also social and economic justice, nonviolence, democracy, and peace (McDaniel, 2002). While the traditional business model described a company providing shareholder return on investment (Balestrero & Udo, 2014), the emerging sustainable business model incorporates the environmental definition, suggesting a sustainable business provides goods and services of value to the current generation while ensuring goods and services can also be provided to future generations (Beehner, 2017).

The WCED concept of sustainability is often characterized by the "triple bottom line" of economy, environment, and society (Elkington et al., 2007), referred to colloquially as the three Ps—profits, planet, and people (Seghezzo, 2009). One objection to the triple bottom line approach is whether incorporating environmental sustainability into the business model will be perceived as a legitimate function of capitalist organizations (Springett & Kearins, 2001; Thomas, 2005). Holthaus (2012) also questioned the triple bottom line image, as represented in some workshops as a three-legged stool. Holthaus believes the three-component image is detrimental to the sustainability cause, because when the environment, society, and the economy are partitioned into three categories, we are separating humans from nature, and the economy from both humans and nature as if it were equal to and independent of the natural and social environments. However, the economy is not only dependent upon and interconnected with both the natural and social environments, and the complex relationship among the three components cannot be simplified. As an alternative to the three-legged stool metaphor, Holthaus proposes the reintegration of the three categories into a one-legged stool representation.

We currently live in the sixth millennium of recorded civilization. While the expansion of civilization, commerce, and population was slow and methodical for the first 57 centuries, the last three centuries witnessed population increase 22-fold, per capita income increase 855%, and global income increase 300-fold (Targowski, 2012). Indeed per capita income increased 800%, and population increased 500% in the 1820–1998 time frame (Maddison, 2001). At present rates of consumption, it will take the resources of three Earths to allow the Chinese and Indian population to achieve American consumption levels, and another six Earths to allow the remaining population to achieve those levels (Targowski, 2012). This calculus suggests the existing rate of consumption is unsustainable.

1.4 Sacredness of Sustainability

The interconnectedness of spirituality and sustainability find common denominators in traditional and nontraditional religious doctrine. Therefore, analysis of the nexus of spirituality and sustainability should begin with a secular review of the religious principles related to both constructs. Due to space limitations, only the doctrine of the major religions will be examined to the extent such information is relevant to understanding the spirituality and sustainability nexus. In addition, separate chapters exploring Indigenous spirituality and sustainability have been added to this edition. The section concludes with a summary of contemporary thought to help prepare the foundation of how a spiritual and sustainable mindset is beneficial for individuals, organizations, and society.

The earliest religious scripture supporting sustainability appears in the book of Genesis, common to two of the Abrahamic religious scriptures: the Christian Holy Bible, and the Jewish Torah. Judaism, Christianity, and Islam are the major Abrahamic religions because all three recognize Abraham as their first prophet, although there are several other religions which share this common attribute (e.g., Bahá'í Faith, Druzism, Samaratianism, Rastafari, and Mandaeism). Chapter 1 of Genesis describes heaven and Earth as having been created by God, with humankind given dominion over Creation (Genesis 1:26–28). The Genesis Creation account provides a religious understanding of the position humans occupy within the environment, with the first chapter portraying humankind as master over nature, and the second chapter portraying humankind as steward over nature (Benstein, 2006). The term stewardship is frequently used to describe this interdependent relationship between humanity and nature (Hui, 2008). It is also important to note that in the Genesis narrative, humankind was described as having been created in God's image.

A similar Creation story appears in the Islamic Quran. The Quran makes it clear that humankind has been given authority to protect, care for, and maintain God's creation, referring to a human as God's Calipha or khilafah (steward or guardian; Fagan, 2015). Humankind bears the burden of moral responsibility for utilizing natural resources with due respect, because God has provided these resources to meet our every need (Mahdi, 2006). Sustainability is firmly entrenched within Islam, with humankind the appointed custodians of nature, destined to coexist harmoniously with all other living things (Bsoul et al., 2022). Allah created a perfectly balanced world based on sustainability and circularity which must be maintained by acting with moderation, thoughtfulness, and justice. Waste, pollution, and destruction are qualities despised by Allah (GreenIftar, n.d.).

Several chapters later in Genesis Chapter 9, the author describes an apocalyptic flood, an event common among several major religions. In the Genesis account, Noah is instructed by God to build a large boat for the transportation and salvation of all species, including the members of his family. The impending flood is considered the result of poor human behavior dooming the planet. After the flood, the Genesis flood narrative reinforces the interdependence of humankind and the environment because after the flood, God made a covenant to not destroy the Earth again in such manner. However, the agreement is not made with Noah, but with all of the creation (Benstein, 2006). The story of the Great Flood is also included in the Islamic Quran, in Sura 11 and Sura 71, with the key character named Nuh.

The sustainability analogy is clear—man and nature are interdependent, not only sharing the planet, but figuratively speaking, sharing the same boat. Ironically, while God promised Noah to never destroy the Earth again, humans have reached the point in which we possess (and are exercising) the ability to disrupt the natural order on Earth, leading to the potential destruction of life on Earth (Benstein, 2006). Perhaps the Abrahamic God promised not to destroy the Earth again by flood knowing that we would attempt to do so ourselves in the future through sea level rise resulting from human-induced climate change.

The Judeo-Christian case for sustainability can be summarized with five faith-based principles: honoring God (as creator of all, including humankind in the image of God; honoring neighbors (showing respect and passion for others and their property); honoring creations (stewardship of nature as service to God); honoring commissions (love God and love neighbors as you would yourself); and, the everlasting principle (because God is everlasting and transcends creation, humankind should maintain stewardship of nature all of the time; Hui, 2008). Unfortunately, there are many reasons Christians ignore the Biblical call to sustainability. Dr. J. Matthew Sleeth left his career as an emergency room director to write, preach, and teach about Christian faith and environmentalism. In his book, *Serve God, Save the planet*, Sleeth (2007) describes the primary reasons Christians ignore God's call for environmental stewardship:

- There is no need to worry about nature because God will renew everything after the rapture [the prophetic return, or second coming of Jesus].
- Material wealth and possessions are God's reward to believers.
- Driving a large sports utility vehicle (SUV) will keep a family safe in an accident.
- Not having time to worry about the environment.
- No need to care about the planet because other people don't care.
- This generation will be gone when all the environmental problems play out.
- Not wanting to associate with tree huggers who worship nature.
- Science will find a solution.
- It is the role of government to protect us.
- God lives in heaven, so it is not necessary to care about plants and animals on Earth.

Echoing Carson's (1962) concern about the effects of environmental degradation on planetary health, Sleeth contemplated the effects of environmental degradation on human health, as witnessed from his career treating cancer patients.

In a 2015 encyclical, Pope Francis called for an "ecological conversion" recognizing that "the world is God's loving gift" (Vatican Insider, 2015). In his second encyclical, *Laudato si'* (Praise Be to You) the pope criticized consumerism and irresponsible development, deplored environmental degradation and global warming, and called upon all humankind to take "swift and unified global action". Pope Francis further suggested Christian spirituality "encourages a prophetic and contemplative lifestyle, one capable of deep enjoyment free of the obsession with consumption", and proposes spiritual growth symbolized by moderation and the ability to find happiness with little. Pope Francis suggests the proposed ecological conversion consists of actions such as inviting others to learn how to contemplate the "mystical meaning" offered by leaves, mountain trails, dewdrops, or the faces of the poor. This encyclical is unique in being the first occasion in which a Muslim writer, Ali al-Khawas was quoted in a footnote, as the Pope concluded his encyclical by recommending two prayers, one "for our earth" and one "in union with creation" (Vatican Insider, 2015).

Much of the previous argument for a Christian obligation to environmental sustainability may be equally relevant to Judaism because both religions share most of the sacred scripture, including the Genesis text. Benstein (2006) further suggests a Judaic sustainability obligation through the concept of *tikkun*, characterized by the restoration or repair of nature. Moreover, Jewish scripture required the practice of sustainable agriculture, as described in Shemot [Exodus], 23:10–11. "And six years you shall sow your land, and you shall gather in its produce. And the seventh year you shall release it from work and abandon it, and the poor among your people will eat".

Islam shares a common lineage with Christianity and Judaism, because all three religions identifying Abraham as the patriarch. The traditional cosmological models of the Abrahamic traditions each share the principle of transcendentalist dualism, visualizing a divine creator and a human soul as non-physical (spiritual) beings existing separately and distinguished from physical nature (Reuter, 2015). The three religions likewise enjoy common religious figures, with Islam considering Jesus and other Biblical characters to be prophets. However, the three religions embrace divergent doctrines, with limited overlapping acceptance of sacred texts.

The Qur'an is the sacred text governing Muslim life including prohibition of actions harmful to the body, mind, soul, or society (Baines, 2018). The prohibition of everything that is harmful suggests a Muslim case for sustainability. The spiritual themes within the Qur'an (Renard, 1996) suggesting a notion of sustainability include inner discipline, gratitude, generosity, personal responsibility, and the struggle for justice. Specifically, Matali identified several sustainability principles and guidelines highlighted within the Holy Quran: *Adl* (justice)—governs human relationships and other living creatures; *Mizan* (balance)—governs human social, economic, and environmental relationships, especially with regard to equilibrium with nature, including natural resource use, and species life cycles; *Wasat* (middleness)—selection of the middle path in economic planning, social conduct, scientific pursuits, ideological views, and resource consumption; *Rahmah* (mercy)—governs all aspects of human relationships and treatment of all living organisms; *Amanah* (trustworthiness and custodianship)—humankind is a trustee of all earthly resources, appointed by the Creator; *Taharah* (spiritual purity and physical cleanliness)—contentment through spiritual purity, conscious of the presence of the Creator, resulting in a balanced society, harmonious with the environment, devoid of air and water pollution, and generating an economy devoid of usury and dishonesty; *Haq* (truthfulness and rights)—honesty in all dealings, and respect for the rights of all living organisms; and, *Ilm Nafi'* (usefulness of knowledge and science)—theological, scientific, and technical knowledge must be beneficial to all living organisms, present and future (Matali, 2012).

While there are five pillars of Islamic faith (Baines, 2018), two of the Islamic pillars imply support for sustainability: charity and fasting (which includes not only refraining from food, drink, and sexual activity, but also refraining from any negative behaviors). Marinova et al. (2008) suggest "a sustainable lifestyle requires a moral unity of humankind", and that the religious, moral, and social teachings of Islam can be a powerful unifying force. Sufism is the spiritual path of Islam leading followers to divine knowledge, characterized as a selfless, tolerant, peaceful spiritual journey of transformation (Akman, 2008). According to Sufism, God created the universe in harmony, and we should recognize that harmony individually and in the collective groups and organizations in which we participate (Akman, 2008).

The concept of sustainability is not unique to the Abrahamic denominations, with major religions Buddhism and Hinduism both promoting environmental stewardship. Kovacs (2014) criticized Western materialism from a Buddhist perspective for having brought humans out of nature to become the dominant species, only to pollute and consume the planetary resources in support of an anthropocentric model. Kovacs suggests the Buddhist Four Noble Truths offer the solution to the planetary degradation resulting from the unbridled economic growth of contemporary society. According to the First Noble Truth, the true nature of sentient beings is misery or suffering, with the Second Noble Truth proclaiming the pervasive unbridled appetite for the transitory experiences while on Earth of the impermanent world to be the origin of that suffering. The Third Noble Truth declares the mitigation of suffering occurs through elimination of attachment and greed, accomplished as explained by the Fourth Noble Truth by following the Noble Eightfold Path. This lifestyle advice leads to the ultimate goal of Buddhism: alleviating suffering through the eradication of greed, hatred, and deception. The highest Buddhist virtue regarding the environment is "*non-harming*" (Kovacs, 2014).

The focus of Buddhist spirituality is with the elimination of suffering through enlightened understanding of reality, and the cultivation of wisdom and compassion (Muesse, 2002). Buddhist spiritual life is lived in pursuit of these ideals, through practice, not belief, or doctrine. Practicing Buddhist spirituality does not require subscription to a particular dogma, or belief in the existence of God (Muesse, 2002). The foundation of Buddhist spirituality training is the "Noble Path", consisting of eight interrelated, simultaneously sought disciplines intended to assist adherents in recovering their essential natures. Four disciplines are focused with moral behavior and the practice of compassion: wholesome action, speech, livelihood, and effort. The remaining four disciplines are focused on nurturing wisdom: wholesome concentration, mindfulness, thinking, and understanding. In contemporary life, Buddhist spirituality promotes a lifestyle providing an alternative to modern-day stress, prescribing awareness, contemplation, quietness, and tranquility as antidotes to the haste, hurry, noise, and confusion of contemporary society. Buddhism is focused on the current state, not a future-oriented, other-worldly lifestyle (Muesse, 2002).

The Buddhist teachings represent an approach to mitigation of actions leading to the destruction of life. While Buddhism promotes the rejection of actions and attitudes that are destructive, it also promotes participation in positive actions and attitudes such as compassion, gratitude, and love. These positive values are to be directed at all living beings, as well as trees, mountains, lakes, and rivers. Kovacs (2014) underscores the Buddhist lifestyle is exemplified by contentment, moderation, and simplicity, all of which demonstrate a sustainable lifestyle. In Buddhism, sustainability is an outcome, not a goal (Kovacs, 2014).

Hinduism comprises a diversity of spiritual and traditional ideas, absent a unified sectarian order, indisputable religious authorities, governing bodies, prophets, or mandatory sacred scriptures (Lipner, 2009). Hindus "need not be religious in the minimal sense described to be accepted as a Hindu by Hindus or describe oneself perfectly validly as Hindu. One may be polytheistic or monotheistic, monistic, or pantheistic, even an agnostic, humanist, or atheist, and still be considered a Hindu" (Lipner, 2009, p. 8). Hinduism considers the material world to be subordinate and subsequent to universal consciousness (Haigh, 2010). The Hindu beliefs most related to sustainability are: belief that all creatures are one universal consciousness (Haigh, 2010); belief in a Supreme Being that is the creator of everything; *karma*, the law of cause and effect by which one creates one's destiny through thoughts, words, and actions; and, most importantly, belief that all of life is to be loved and revered as sacred, requiring the practice of *ahimsa*, or non-injury, in thought, word, and action (Himalayan Academy, 2018).

The Sanskrit word for spirituality, *adhyatma* means pertaining to soul (Hindu Janajagruti Samiti, n.d.). The focus of Hindu spirituality is with the nature of the soul, and information related to the present and future spiritual condition of the adherent. Hinduism proposes every living being continuously aspires, and constantly attempts to acquire the supreme quality of happiness. Happiness, which is continual, and of the highest quality is called Bliss, and the curriculum for its acquisition is the science of Spirituality (Hindu Janajagruti Samiti, n.d.). Hinduism describes the desire to go from the impermanent to the permanent, as the process of reincarnation. Aspects of Hindu spirituality include: disdain for material things; distrust of intellect; yearning for divine edification; charity; purity of heart; humility; meekness; and, communion with God (Age-of-the-sage.org, n.d.).

Following Hindu tradition, Gandhi believed attachment to material possessions, and obsession with never-ending growth were the source of most of society's problems, long before the emergence of the Western Green movement (Haigh, 2010). The *Srimad Bhagavad Gita* unquestionably links materialism with *asuric* (demoniac) tendencies that cause humans to become a burden to the planet (Prabhupada, 1993). Gandhi's formula for social and ecological justice was to live simply so that others can simply live (Haigh, 2010). *Sarvodaya,* the Gandhian political system inspired by his six-concept version of education for sustainability (Richards, 1982), sought balance, emphasizing stability instead of growth (Doctor, 1967). Similar to contemporary sustainability movements, *Sarvodaya* emphasized sustainable local production over unsustainable long distance product transportation, and quality over quantity. Gandhi is frequently quoted: "The world has enough for everyone's need, but not enough for everyone's greed".

Less traditional religions such as the Wiccan, Native American, and Inuit traditions emphasize a connection and oneness with nature, with the latter often referred to as a nature-worshipping religion. Wicca, also referred to as witchcraft is a contemporary Pagan religion claiming origins predating Christianity and most major religions. Wicca was formally founded in England between 1921 and 1950 with followers claiming to be adherents of a surviving pagan religion (Doyle White, 2016). Many Christians insist that Wiccans are really Satanists, worshipping the Christian devil, or Satan, a claim Wiccans reject (Sunshine, 2020), citing no reference to a devil or Satan in their tradition. Followers practice in groups or solitary with no formal doctrine or hierarchical structure common to most major religions. Common Wiccan beliefs include the duo theistic worship of both a god and goddess, respect for (and in some traditions, worship of) nature, and the recognition of natural cycles (solar, lunar, seasonal, etc.; Doyle White, 2016). The Wiccan Rede succinctly describes the responsibility to others as "an [if] it harm none, do what you will" (Holzer, 1971).

Native American and Inuit cultures present models of sustainability, further recognizing a link between subsistence, sustainability, and spirituality (Holthaus, 2012). The late nineteenth-century environmentalist and cofounder of the Sierra Club, John Muir, frequently implied Native Americans were closely connected with nature, observing that for countless centuries, Natives lived among the hills of the Sierra while leaving minimal visible impact on the land (Wakefield, 1994). Muir noted the Native American trails appeared in sharp contrast to what one might expect if Western inhabitants occupied the land for a similar length of time. Muir likewise admired the natural roads and structures which bore little resemblance to the monumental infrastructures of the European colonial settlers. According to Muir, "[Native Americans] walk softly and they hurt the landscape hardly more than the birds and squirrels..." (Wakefield, 1994). Indigenous spiritualities will be explored further in Chapter 4 and Indigenous sustainability will be explored further in Chapter 8.

In the Earth-focused cultural and religious traditions, the separation of sustainability and spirituality would be unimaginable, because Gods and spiritual beings are embodied in the Earth, and in all living entities (Chavez, 2010). In these nature-based cosmologies, natural resource malfeasance may result in material consequences from actors within the spirit world. Chavez (2010) identified seven tenets or "common threads" to stimulate a newer, deeper framework for spiritual, sustainable action. These common threads are: the preservation of life; awakening; compulsive consumption as a disorder; oneness (we are all connected) change starts within; awe; and, purity, and will be discussed further in Chapter 9.

1.5 The Nexus of Spirituality and Sustainability

A "green revolution" is currently underway, transforming the cosmological foundation of religion and spirituality globally (Horstmann & Reuter, 2009). An increasing number of forward-thinking religious and spiritual groups appear to be engaged in efforts to meet the challenges presented by the global ecological crisis (Reuter, 2015). The more significant development underway is a shift toward a more environmentally friendly religious viewpoint in the major global religions, including the two largest, Islam and Christianity (Reuter, 2015). Yale University Senior Lecturer and Research Scholar Mary Evelyn Tucker acknowledges "[t]here is growing recognition that cultural and religious values have a significant role to play in helping to shape a sustainable future" (Tucker, 2012, p. 2). The major global religions possess tremendous potential for advocating sustainability (Haigh, 2010), with Christianity having 2.1 billion adherents, followed by Islam with 1.5 billion, Hinduism with 900 million, and Buddhism with 400 million (Adherents.com, 2010).

It can be argued that one's inner and outer world are not only interconnected, but reflections of each other. "Spiritual teachings have celebrated and consecrated our ties with the non-human world, reminding us of our delicate and inescapable partnership with air, land, water, and other living beings" (Mebratu, 1998). As such, individuals at least partially embody the whole universe and must therefore reflect cosmic order in their lives (Carroll, 2004). This interconnectedness is so intense that the human community is incomprehensible when considered absent the entire planetary community, suggesting the proper role of human intelligence is to elevate and not exploit the natural world (Carroll, 2004). Albert Einstein's colleague David Bohm believed quantum theory described the wholeness of the universe—*separate without separateness* (Dhiman, 2017). Hence, an interconnected system necessitates all members recognize their relationship with the whole and interact with other members accordingly.

Heaton (2016) suggests the sustainability threats confronting humankind, and the subsequent limited ability to overcome the sustainability challenge stems from the limited level of consciousness achieved by most humankind. Solving the disruptive environmental problems caused by human activity will require a different level of consciousness than the level at which they were created (Coates, 2012; Heaton, 2016). The magnitude of the sustainability challenge requires a significant shift in our mindset in which we reevaluate the how and why of our existence, and our relationship with the planet which we inhabit (Ehrenfeld & Hoffman, 2013). Heaton further argues the potential range of human consciousness development includes higher states of awareness of and interconnectedness with the holistic model of nature. These higher states of consciousness create conditions of holistic awareness, concern, and action through which life on Earth not only survives but thrives (Ehrenfeld & Heaton, 2016; Hoffman, 2013). This higher state, described as flourishing invokes a positive image of a planet working and operating for the health and benefit of all inhabitants (Ehrenfeld & Heaton, 2016; Hoffman, 2013), enabling humankind to both overcome the sustainability challenge, and progress to a more favorable model of individual and collective quality of life (Heaton, 2016).

To exist in a more restorative, prosperous relationship with nature, humankind must develop higher states of consciousness to understand the complexity of nature, thereby operating in tune with nature, and not creating unintended adverse conditions. Heaton (2016) suggests sustainability-as-flourishing may be developed through the higher states of consciousness advocated in the writings of Maharishi Mahesh Yogi (1995). The Vedic spiritual tradition provides practical tools to enhance an experience of wholeness with natural law, further enhancing the capacity for sustainability-as-flourishing (Heaton, 2016). Sustainability is a phenomenon of holistic enlightenment, not in the complex minutiae of components and relationships, but in the simple experience of the holistic creative intelligence existing within one's own Transcendental Consciousness. Maharishi identifies Transcendental Consciousness as the spiritual essence of life, transcending space, time, and all relative, changing experience (Heaton, 2016). The consciousness development movement is focused on integrated understanding and inclusive relationships (Heaton, 2016), consistent with the perspective of sustainability considering the integration and interrelatedness of all people and things. Kumar and Giri (2020) suggested a strong interconnectedness between

Indian spirituality and the UN SDGs because Indian spirituality and philosophy provide the underlying structure necessary to offset ambiguity with the current sustainable development agenda and develop organic awareness for sustainable development goals (Kumar & Giri, 2020).

Aldo Leopold (1949), considered by many to be one of the founders of the modern environmentalism movement, suggested the humankind embrace a more spiritual perspective of their relationship with nature, and each other through the adoption of the "land ethic" (Stead & Stead, 2014). Leopold's conception of a land ethic consisted of a moral code of conduct based upon an interconnected caring relationship between humankind and land, wherein caring for the inhabitants cannot be separated from caring for the land (The Aldo Leopold Foundation, 2018). Ecological economist Daly (1977) suggested the sustainability process begins with humankind's appreciation of the natural world, resulting in improved quality of life and spiritual ambitions (Stead & Stead, 2014).

Sustainability is deeply rooted in the sacredness of humankind and nature, and as such necessitates the construction of spiritual capabilities or competencies requiring spiritual capital and spiritual intelligence (Stead & Stead, 2014). These spiritual capabilities appeal directly to the human quest for meaning and value in all aspects of their lives, and the longing to be a part of a greater purpose (Stead & Stead, 2014). Senge (1990) suggested the creation of a shared vision to be essential to the formation of spiritual intelligence, which then becomes the cultural foundation that binds organizational members together (Stead & Stead, 2014). The development of organizational spiritual capabilities is antecedent to the development of successful triple bottom line strategies, which reinforce sustainability-based core competencies, thereby creating a difficult-to-imitate competitive advantage (Stead & Stead, 2014).

If spirituality is indeed necessary to address the environmental challenge of our era, it would provide support if sustainability seekers were found to be concurrently seeking spirituality in their lives. This notion is supported by the findings of a study of adult sustainable education students in which the majority reported being simultaneously engaged in spiritual exploration (Lange, 2008). Students reported being engaged in one of the following types of spiritual explorations:

> Seeking places of sanctuary, especially within nature;
> Seeking a deeper awareness and increased sense of connectedness;
> Expressing a spiritual orientation or seeking new spiritual practices; and,
> Shifting toward a spiritually oriented lifestyle (Lange, 2008, p. 217)

Most participants expressed participation in the course reaffirmed their feelings about spiritual exploration, providing them with the courage to act on their feelings.

Bouckaert (2014) supported a spiritual approach to business ethics and responsibility, suggesting sustainability characterized by "caring for future generations" exhibits a spiritual commitment that prepares for, and makes possible every declaration of rights, transforming the economy according to those rights. The cultivation of spirituality is deemed essential for business to succeed in the development of a sustainable and flourishing world (Laszlo et al., 2014). Levinas (1996) and Jonas (1979) developed a notion of responsibility from the contextual understanding of the vulnerability of life leading to an ethic of compassion and responsibility. Confronted with the global impact of contemporary technology and lifestyles we should recognize our planet and the lives of future generations are threatened (Bouckaert, 2014).

1.6 Interconnectedness of Spirituality and Sustainability

While ancient and Indigenous traditions recognize the interconnectedness of spirituality and sustainability, contemporary science has mostly separated the two concepts. However, scholars have begun recognizing and integrating the two concepts in research and practice. Leal Filho et al. (2022) found general agreement about the relationship between spirituality and sustainability and the usefulness of including spiritual conditions in sustainability education and research. However, this application is limited by lack of a common definition of spirituality and insufficient training to spiritual concerns in education and research (Kamppinen & Jakonen, 2015). Ecosystems have a "logic" of their own, independent of the demands and requirements of humankind (Knippenberg, 2010). Humankind is much more dependent on ecosystems and other creatures than they are dependent on humankind. We are beginning to recognize how deeply we are embedded in nature, yet we still behave as if nature and the other species only exist for our use, possession, and control (Knippenberg, 2010).

Spirituality is a conceptual framework for viewing everything as interconnected, where individual components are infused by the same intelligible logic or elements out of which different presences are made (Kamppinen & Jakonen, 2015). Therefore, systems thinking forms the basis for spirituality in one form or another. Systems thinking is a general worldview about the nature of reality viewing the world as a collection of systems, and all entities linked with other entities (Kamppinen & Jakonen, 2015). It is a tool of thought used in several science, management, and futures research disciplines (Bunge, 1979) typically influenced by science and ontological materialism (Kamppinen & Jakonen, 2015). Systems thinking and spirituality are endeavors to understand the world in terms of interconnectedness, wholes, and components. Regardless of whether it is based on materialistic or idealistic ontology, systems thinking offers tools for analyzing and linking the differences between the ideal and reality (Kamppinen & Jakonen, 2015). Elkins et al. (1988) described spirituality as a form of knowledge based on a conceptual framework that categorizes the world into "reality" and "appearance". Spirituality invites individuals to seek legitimate connections between the perceived phenomena and reality upholding appearances and regulates the dynamics of the reality.

According to Wilber (2000), there are two sides to spirituality: it exists within humans as a psychological capability and attitude about the world; and, it exists in the systemic character of the world, the *systemicity* that makes the integrated attitude believable. Wilber (2007) identified four definitions of spirituality, all of which should be considered when examining or developing spirituality:

1. Spirituality describes the higher levels of cognition, interpersonal relations, and appreciating the aesthetic beauty in the world.
2. Spirituality is a separate developmental line with its own intelligence, different from aesthetic, musical, kinesthetic, or other intelligence.
3. Spirituality is a state of consciousness.
4. Spirituality is a special attitude, existing at any of the structures of consciousness.

Another aspect of spirituality embraced by Wilber is that the cognitive components unfolding in spirituality consider the world as a systemic whole, an interconnected supersystem that is permeated by the Spirit (Kamppinen & Jakonen, 2015). Experiencing the wholeness and interconnectedness of the world can only occur if the world possesses those properties. Spirit manifests in the design or organization of matter when material entities become connected (Kamppinen & Jakonen, 2015).

While spirituality and systems thinking have been explored from the theoretical or scholarly perspective, attempting to explain and comprehend their codependency, the practical approach is completely different (Kamppinen & Jakonen, 2015). According to Wilber (1989), in both Eastern and Western worldviews, there are two approaches to spirituality—that of the scholar and the practitioner. The scholar pragmatically examines spirituality as one might examine insects, rocks, or fossils (Kamppinen & Jakonen, 2015) without considering the notion of practicing spiritual or religious rituals (Wilber, 1989). Although practitioners of spirituality and scientists share some common tools of systems thinking, spiritual practitioners are generally committed to idealistic ontology and reasonable methodologies, while scientists are committed to materialistic ontology and meticulous tests and examinations (Kamppinen & Jakonen, 2015). Systems thinking is explored in Chapter 12 within the context of system leadership as a method of combining spirituality and sustainability to achieve meaningful success.

1.7 Chapter Summaries

This introductory chapter has provided a foundation of the definition, characteristics, and framework of both spirituality and sustainability. The nexus of spirituality and sustainability was examined through both religious and secular lenses to better understand the relationship between the two constructs. The intent of this chapter was to prepare a starting point from which to better understand how spirituality and sustainability are interconnected. The remaining chapters will expand the foundation, building a structure for individual and organizational success through the integration of spirituality and sustainability.

In Chapter 2, spirituality will be examined in greater detail, including the theoretical framework, and literature summary of spirituality. The framework will be broad, interdisciplinary, and non-religious, with spirituality defined as a mental phenomenon taking place in the mind and spirit, and as such, transcendent of religion or culture. Spirituality will be discussed both within and absent religion, and secular spiritual models will be examined, including Targowski's concept of universal spirituality, or Spirituality 2.0. In Chapter 2 the argument will be made for spirituality as an individual level success factor. In line with the broad, interdisciplinary, and non-religious framework of the text, the individual benefits of spirituality will be examined from a secular perspective. Existing literature will be synthesized to demonstrate the benefits, along with interviews, reflective questions, and/or exercises to assist with practical application of workplace spirituality. The role of ethics in individual spirituality will be examined. The chapter includes a synthesis of literature explaining the growing interest in spirituality, and spirituality as a calling, which is followed by explorations of the relationship, and importance of spirituality in individual success, and the benefits of spirituality. The chapter concludes with reflective questions designed to stimulate further thought and conversation concerning individual spirituality.

Chapter 3 will expand upon the spirituality discussion by introducing and examining the concept of workplace spirituality and organizational spirituality, including the definition, theoretical framework, and literature summary of workplace spirituality. The framework will be broad, interdisciplinary, and non-religious. The benefits, limitations, and potential risks of workplace spirituality are discussed. The common themes (which are related to the topics of this text) emerging from examination of the workplace spirituality are identified. The role of ethics in workplace spirituality will be examined. The servant, authentic, spiritual, and values leadership styles and models will be examined within the context of workplace spirituality. The chapter concludes with reflective questions designed to stimulate further thought and conversation concerning workplace spirituality and spiritual workplaces.

Chapter 4 is new to this edition and explores Indigenous spirituality. While contemporary society has been established on a foundation of humanmade institutions and structures, most Indigenous cultures recognize the interconnectedness of nature and humankind, and that we cannot live and survive outside of nature. Indigenous spirituality is often characterized by a holistic, comprehensive way of living. Although spiritual beliefs vary among the millions of Indigenous cultures, commonalities exist between many of the dominant Indigenous cultures. Common Indigenous cultures and their respective spiritual beliefs and practices will be explored within the context of the role of spirituality in individual and collective success. The similarities and differences of these Indigenous cultures will be examined to develop a better understanding of their role and importance in achieving spirituality. The absence of a spiritual-secular binary in Indigenous cultures will add an important perspective to the discussion about spirituality.

Chapter 5 is also new to this edition and includes research and perspectives on spirituality in the post-pandemic era. While religious affiliation and participation began declining decades before the COVID-19 pandemic, the pandemic stimulated inward reflection in many individuals and cultures. Many individuals were reminded of their mortality and used time working at home and loss of friends and loved ones as opportunities to find meaning and spirituality in their lives. The concept that spirituality exists both within and absent religious institutions became more evident as churches were closed or provided services virtually. The role of spirituality in the post-pandemic era will be examined within the context of individual and organizational success. The content and case study will provide perspective on the role of spirituality during and after unexpected global crises.

In Chapter 6 I introduce the definition, theoretical framework, and literature summary of sustainability, expanding upon the content provided in Chapter 1. The sustainability framework will be broad, interdisciplinary, and non-political. While concepts such as climate change are accepted by most members of the academic community, sustainability is examined in a broader context of individual and organizational responsibility and citizenship for the planet in general. The history of the sustainability movement is followed by examination of contemporary issues and perspectives on sustainability, and the relevance and importance of sustainability in business. The chapter concludes with reflective questions designed to stimulate further thought and conversation about sustainability and sustainable business. In Chapter 6 the argument will be made for sustainability as an individual level success factor. A review of the literature examines sustainable lifestyles and careers, and sustainable management and leadership. The chapter concludes with a personal interview summary of an individual who has incorporated sustainability into their career, resulting in individual success.

The topic of Chapter 7 is sustainable business. The emerging sustainable business model is compared with the traditional business models. While many have argued that capitalism may be the cause of our current environmental state, others argue capitalism is a powerful means to create value while solving our environmental problems. The systems perspective and the stakeholder approach will be discussed to support the necessity for achieving and the interconnectedness of the UN sustainable development goals (SDGs). The transition from capitalism solely as a means for profit maximization to newer models of conscious capitalism, the circular economy, environmental social and governance (ESG) investing, and social entrepreneurship will be explored. The role, benefits, and challenges of business achieving sustainability will be explored in this chapter. The chapter's case study will illustrate the dark side of integrating spirituality and performative attempts at greening.

Chapter 8 is new to this edition and explores Indigenous sustainability. While contemporary society is established on a foundation of humanmade institutions and structures, Indigenous cultures recognize the interconnectedness of nature and humankind, and that we cannot live and survive outside of nature. Creation is conceived as a living process wherein all inhabitants are members of a living universe. Most Indigenous traditions and belief systems regard nature with deep respect. They have a strong sense of place and belonging which sustains knowledge and ways of life that promote nature conservation and sustainable natural resource use. Common Indigenous cultures and their respective spiritual beliefs and practices will be explored within the context of the role of sustainability in individual and collective success. The absence of a spiritual-secular binary in Indigenous cultures will add an important perspective to the discussion about sustainability.

Chapter 9 is also new to this edition and includes research and perspectives on sustainability in the post-pandemic era. The increase in work from home (WFH) employment during and following the COVID-19 pandemic demonstrated that many business and organizational activities can be performed remotely, in a more sustainable manner. The brief pause in atmospheric CO2 rise gave hope that meaningful climate change mitigation was possible. This chapter will explore sustainability research, initiatives, and topics in the aftermath of the COVID-19 pandemic to provide perspective on achieving sustainability during, or despite unexpected global crises.

In Chapter 10 the argument will be made for workplace spirituality and organizational spirituality as organizational level success factors. In line with the broad, interdisciplinary, and non-religious framework of the text, the business and organizational benefits of workplace spirituality will be examined from a secular perspective. The chapter begins with the examination of the organizational benefits of workplace spirituality, followed by a review of the characteristics and attributes of spiritual organizations. Moreover, the potential risks, challenges, and controversies surrounding both spiritual organizations and workplace spirituality will be discussed. Spiritual intelligence is briefly examined because the development of organizational spiritual capabilities is an antecedent to the development of successful triple bottom line strategies. Finally, the Spiritual Incorporated Argument (SIA) is introduced as a method of providing intrinsic justification for the incorporation of spirituality into business management. The contributions and roles of religious and spiritual NGOs and IGOs will also be examined. The benefits and successes of workplace spirituality programs, suggestions for the implementation of workplace spirituality, and a case study examining a business that has implemented workplace spirituality conclude the chapter.

In Chapter 11 the argument will be made for sustainability as an organizational level success factor. Existing literature will be synthesized to demonstrate the benefits of sustainable business, along with methods and models for implementing sustainability within an organization. Examples of businesses that have achieved success by implementing and incorporating sustainability are identified, and the chapter concludes with a case study designed to stimulate further thought and conversation about the relationship between sustainability and organizational success. The contributions and roles of sustainability NGOs and IGOs will be examined.

In Chapter 12 we will examine the integration of spirituality and sustainability for individual level success. This chapter will argue that the combination of spirituality and sustainability are beneficial for individual success. Because limited existing literature examines both variables in terms of individual success, much of the content of this chapter addresses the theoretical and conceptual framework for the proposed hypothesis. Spiritual and sustainable lifestyles such as voluntary simplicity and flourishing, and corresponding benefits will be examined. Systems thinking, Holistic Model of Wellness, Vocational Souljourn, and complexity theory are introduced as frameworks through which to understand the individual-level benefits of combined spirituality and sustainability. Spiritual intelligence, sustainable leadership, eco-spirituality, and ecologism are discussed within the context of individual spirituality, sustainability, and success. The chapter concludes with personal interview summaries of individuals who have applied both spirituality and sustainability to achieve personal success.

In Chapter 13 we will examine the integration of spirituality and sustainability for organizational level success. This chapter will argue that the combination of workplace spirituality and sustainability are beneficial for business and organizational success. Existing literature will be synthesized to demonstrate the benefits of workplace spirituality and sustainability on a business/organizational level. Because limited existing literature examines both variables in terms of organizational success, much of the content of this chapter addresses the theoretical and conceptual framework for the proposed hypothesis. Systems thinking, the Quadruple Bottom Line for Sustainability, and Man-Environment-Organism (M-E-O) are introduced as frameworks through which to understand the proposed relationship. Flourishing, conscious capitalism, and spiritual entrepreneurship are introduced within the context of the chapter theme. The chapter concludes with an examination of Laloux's proposed model of organizational evolution, and the emerging evolutionary "teal" organization. The chapter includes a continuation of the personal interview summaries from Chapter 12, of two individual who have applied both spirituality and sustainability to achieve success in their organizations.

Chapter 14 completes our journey with a summary of the key themes of previous chapters. In this final chapter I reiterate the position taken in Chapters 12 and 13, that the commonalities of, and interconnection between spirituality (both individual and workplace), and sustainability support the hypothesis: ***A combination of spirituality and sustainability positively impacts both individual and organizational success***. The social, political, economic, and environmental challenges faced by humankind may benefit from contemporary alternatives to existing systems and models such as the circular economy and Spirituality 2.0. Recommendations are included for future research, and future trends and applications of workplace spirituality and sustainability in personal and business/organizational success are identified.

1.8 Concluding Thoughts

In this introductory chapter, I have prepared a foundation from which to better understand how spirituality and sustainability are interconnected. The human spiritual condition has the capacity to orient our practical, worldly undertakings in the accomplishment of positive social consequences, while mitigating the environmental impact of consumerism

(Walker, 2013). The spiritual competencies supporting sustainability are obviously intangible (Stead & Stead, 2014). Humankind currently exists in the sixth millennium of civilization. While human progress has resulted in astronomical financial wealth, eradicated many diseases, and accomplished monumental scientific achievements, the current state of natural resource consumption is unsustainable. A course of action is necessary which ensures individual and organizational success, while guaranteeing opportunities for success to future inhabitants. The proposed course of action is both spiritual and sustainable in nature.

Reflection Questions

1. Do you agree that similarities exist between spirituality and sustainability? Explain why or why not.
2. Do you agree that spirituality and sustainability have a viable role in contributing to individual and organizational success? Explain why or why not.
3. Can spirituality exist within an organization or institution that is not primarily religious or spiritual in nature?

References

Adherents.com. (2010). *Major religions of the world ranked by number of adherents*. http://www.adherents.com/Religions_By_Adherents.html

Age-of-the-sage.org. (n.d.). *Vedic-Hindu spirituality quotations and quotes*. http://www.age-of-the-sage.org/mysticism/vedic_hindu_spirituality.html

Akman, K. (2008). Sufism, spirituality and sustainability: Rethinking Islamic mysticism through contemporary sociology. *Comparative Islamic Studies, 4*(1/2), 1–15. https://doi.org/10.1558/cis.v4i4.1-4.2.1

Baines, W. (2018). *Islam at a glance: A religion, demystified*. http://www.beliefnet.com

Baldacchino, D. (2017). Spirituality in the Healthcare Workplace. *Religions, 8*(12), 260. https://doi.org/10.3390/rel8120260

Balestrero, G., & Udo, N. (2014). *Organizational survival: Profitable strategies for a sustainable future*. McGraw-Hill Education.

Battlista, J., & Almond, R. (1973). The development of meaning in life. *Psychiatry, 36*, 409–427. https://doi.org/10.1080/00332747.1973.11023774

Beehner, C.G. (2017, January). Teaching sustainability to a traditional business audience. In *Conference Proceedings of the International Academy of Business and Public Administration Discipline, 14(1).* Paper presented at IABPAD Conference: Orlando, FL (pp. 298–308).

Benstein, J. (2006). *The way into Judaism and the environment*. Jewish Lights Publishing.

Bouckaert, L. (2014). Spirituality: The missing link in business ethics. In L. Zsolnai (Ed.) *The spiritual dimension of business ethics and sustainability management* (pp. 15–26). Springer. https://doi.org/10.1007/978-3-319-11677-8_20

Bsoul, L., Omer, A., Kucukalic, L., & Archbold, R. H. (2022). Islam's perspective on environmental sustainability: A conceptual analysis. *Social Sciences, 11*(6), 228. https://doi.org/10.3390/socsci11060228

Bunge, M. (1979). *A world of systems.* Reidel Publishing.

Carson, R. (1962). *Silent spring*. Houghton Mifflin Company.

Carroll, J.E. (2004). *Sustainability and spirituality.* State University of New York Press.

Cavanagh, G. (1999). Spirituality for managers: Context and critique. *Journal of Organizational Change Management, 12*(3), 186–195. https://doi.org/10.1108/09534819910273793

Chavez, F. I. (2010). Sustainability & spirituality: Common threads. Originally published in the *Green MBA Journal, 6*(1). Dominican University of California. http://feliciachavez.com

Coates, J. (2012). Prisoners of the story: A role for spirituality in thinking and living our way to sustainability. In J. Groen, D. Coholic, & J. R. Graham (Eds.), *Spirituality in social work and education: Theory, practice, and pedagogies* (pp. 57–76). Wilfrid Laurier University Press.

Collins, D., Junghans, A., & Haugen, T. (2016). Green and sustainable—How are these terms reflected in the context of facilities management? *CFM Second Nordic Conference 29–30 August 2016 Technical University of Denmark.*

Cowan, J. (1993). *The common table: Reflections and meditations on community and spirituality in the workplace.* Harper Business.

Daly, H. E. (1977). *Steady state economics*. Freeman.

Dent, E. B., Higgins, M. E., & Wharff, D. M. (2005). Spirituality and leadership: An empirical review of definitions, distinctions, and embedded

assumptions. *The Leadership Quarterly, 16*(5), 625–653. https://doi.org/10.1016/j.leaqua.2005.07.002
Dhiman, S. (2017). *Holistic leadership: A new paradigm for today's leaders*. Palgrave Macmillan.
Doctor, A. H. (1967). *Sarvodaya: A political and economic study*. Asia Books.
Doyle White, E. (2016). *Wicca: History, belief, and community in modern pagan witchcraft*. Sussex Academic Press.
Ehrenfeld, J., & Hoffman, A. J. (2013). *Flourishing: A frank conversation about sustainability*. Stanford University Press.
Elkington, J., Tickell, S., & Lee, M. (2007). *SustainAbility. 20 Years of global leadership [online]*. London: SustainAbility. http://www.sustainability.com
Elkins, D. N., Hedström, L. J., Hughes, L. L., Leaf, J. A., & Saunders, C. (1988). Toward a humanistic-phenomenological spirituality: Definition, description, and measurement. *Journal of Humanistic Psychology, 28*(4), 5–18. https://doi.org/10.1177/0022167888284002
Fagan, H. (2015). *What does Islam teach about ecology?* PlantingSeeds Projects. https://www.ps.org.au/content/articles/2015/12/23/islam#:~:text=God%20is%20the%20Owner%20and,steward%2C%20deputy%2C%20guardian
Green Iftar. (n.d.) *Islam and sustainability*. https://www.greeniftar.com/en/islam-and-sustainability/
Haigh, M. (2010). Education for a sustainable future: Strategies of the New Hindu religious movements. *Sustainability, 2*(11), 3500–3519. https://doi.org/10.3390/su2113500
Heaton, D. (2016). Higher consciousness for sustainability-as-flourishing. In S. Dhiman & J. Marques (Eds.), *Spirituality and sustainability: New horizons and exemplary approaches* (pp. 121–137). Springer International Publishing.
Hill, P. C., Pargament, K. I., Hood, R. W., McCullough, M. E., Jr., Swyers, J. P., Larson, D. B., & Zinnbauer, B. J. (2000). Conceptualizing religion and spirituality: Points of commonality, points of departure. *Journal for the Theory of Social Behaviour, 30*(1), 51–77. https://doi.org/10.1111/1468-5914.00119
Himalayan Academy. (2018). *Nine beliefs of Hinduism*. Author. https://www.himalayanacademy.com/readlearn/basics/nine-beliefs
Hindu Janajagruti Samiti. (n.d.). *Why is man interested in spirituality?* https://www.hindujagruti.org/hinduism/knowledge/article/why-is-man-interested-in-spirituality.html
Holthaus, G. (2012). *Learning native wisdom: What traditional cultures teach us about subsistence, sustainability, and spirituality*. University Press of Kentucky.
Holzer, H. (1971). *The truth about witchcraft*. Doubleday.

Horstmann, A., & Reuter, T. A. (2009). The post-modern shift. *Asian Journal of Social Science, 37*, 853–856. https://doi.org/10.1163/156848409X12526657425145

Hui, L. T. (2008). Combining faith and CSR: A paradigm of corporate sustainability. *International Journal of Social Economics, 35*(6), 449–465. https://doi.org/10.1108/03068290810873429

Jonas, H. (1979). *Das Prinzip Verantwortung: Versuch einer Ethik für die technologische Zivilisation.* Suhrkamp, Frankfurt am Main (*The Imperative of Responsibility: In Search of an Ethics for the Technological Age*. 1984). Chicago University Press.

Kamppinen, M., & Jakonen, J. P. (2015). Systems thinking, spirituality and Ken Wilber: Beyond new age. *Approaching Religion, 5*(2), 3–14. https://doi.org/10.30664/ar.67570

Knippenberg, L. (2010). Chasing God: The idea of sustainable development and its implications. In F. Wijsen & S. Marcos (Eds.), *Indigenous Voices in the sustainability discourse. Spirituality and the struggle for a better quality of life* (pp. 31–48). LIT Verlag.

Kovacs, G. (Ed.). (2014). Buddhist spiritual orientation to nature and sustainability. In L. Zsolnai (Ed.), *The spiritual dimension of business ethics and sustainability management* (pp. 57–68). Springer. https://doi.org/10.1007/978-3-319-11677-8_20

Krishnan, V. (2008). The impact of transformational leadership on followers' duty orientation and spirituality. *Journal of Human Values, 14*(1), 11–22. https://doi.org/10.1177/097168580701400103

Kumar, S., & Giri, T. K. (2020). Interconnectedness between spirituality and sustainable development goals: Evidence from an Indian perspective. *International Journal of Indian Culture and Business Management, 20*(1), 133–149. https://doi.org/10.1504/IJICBM.2020.105553

Lange, E. (2008). Re-enchantment to escape empire: Spirituality, sustainability, critical transformative learning. In *Proceedings of the 27th National Conference of the Canadian Association for Studies in Adult Education Conference,* University of British Columbia.

LaPierre, L. L. (1994). A model for describing spirituality. *Journal of Religion and Health, 33*(2), 153–161. https://doi.org/10.1007/BF02354535

Laszlo, C., Saillant, R., Pose, I. B., & Brown, J. S. (2014). *Flourishing enterprise: The new spirit of business.* Stanford University Press.

Leal Filho, W., Salvia, A. L., Ulluwishewa, R., Abubakar, I. R., Mifsud, M., LeVasseur, T. J., Correia, V., Consorte-McCrea, A., Paço, A., Fritzen, B., Ray, S., Gordon, N., Luetz, J.M., Borsari, B., Venkatesan, M., Mukul, S.A.,

Carp, R.M., Begum, H., Nunoo, E.K., ... Farrugia, E. (2022). Linking sustainability and spirituality: A preliminary assessment in pursuit of a sustainable and ethically correct world. *Journal of Cleaner Production, 380*, e135091. https://doi.org/10.1016/j.jclepro.2022.135091

Leopold, A. (1949). *A sand county almanac*. Random House.

Levinas, E. (1996). *Basic philosophical writings* (A. T. Peperzak, S. Critchley, & R. Bernasconi, Eds.). Indiana University Press.

Lipner, J. J. (2009). *Hindus: Their religious beliefs and practices* (2nd ed.). Routledge.

Maddison, A. (2001). *The world economy, a millennial perspective* (pp. 17–31). OECD.

Mahdi, A. R. (2006). *The creation of an environmental conscience (part 2 of 4): Man—God's steward on the Earth*. The Religion of Islam. https://www.islamreligion.com/articles/334/creation-of-an-environmental-conscience-part-2/

Marinova, D., Hossain, A., & Hossain-Rhaman, P. (2008). Islam in sustainability. *International Journal of Environmental, Cultural, Economic, and Social Sustainability, 4*(5), 123–130. https://espace.curtin.edu.au/handle/20.500.11937/29819

Marques, J., Dhiman, S., & King, R. (2010). Exploring the link between spirituality and sustainability. *Business Renaissance Quarterly, 5*(1), 19. https://www.proquest.com

Matali, Z. H. (2012). Sustainability in Islam. In R. Clugston & S. Holt (Eds.), *Exploring synergies between faith values and education for sustainable development* (pp. 35–38). Earth Charter International and Earth Charter Center for Education for Sustainable Development at UPEACE.

McDaniel, J. (2002). Spirituality and sustainability. *Conservation Biology, 16*(6), 1461–1464. http://www.jstor.org/stable/3095400

Mebratu, D. (1998). Sustainability and sustainable development: Historical and conceptual review. *Environmental Impact Assessment Review, 18*(6), 493–520. https://doi.org/10.1016/S0195-9255(98)00019-5

Muesse, M. W. (2002). *What does it mean to lead a spiritual life? A Buddhist perspective*. Center for Spiritual Growth Tennessee. http://www.explorefaith.org/steppingstones_SpiritualLife_Buddhist.htm

Næss, A. (1989). *Ecology, community and lifestyle. Outline of an ecosophy*. (D. Rothenberg, Trans. & Rev.). Cambridge University Press.

Orr, D. (2002). Four challenges of sustainability. *Conservation Biology, 16*(6), 1457–1460. https://doi.org/ https://doi.org/10.1046/j.1523-1739.2002.01668.x

Prabhupada, A. B. S. (1993). *Bhagavad-Gita as it is: With the original Sanskrit text, Roman transliteration, English equivalents, translation and elaborate purports*. Bhaktivedanta Book Trust.

Renard, J. (1996). *Seven doors to Islam: Spirituality and the religious life of Muslims*. University of California Press.

Reuter, T. A. (2015). The green revolution in the world's religions: Indonesian examples in international comparison. *Religions, 6*(4), 1217–1231. https://doi.org/10.3390/rel6041217

Richards, G. (1982). *Philosophy of Gandhi*. Curzon Press.

Seghezzo, L. (2009). The five dimensions of sustainability. *Environmental Politics, 18*(4), 539–556. https://doi.org/10.1080/09644010903063669

Senge, P. M. (1990). *The fifth discipline: The art and practice of the learning organization*. Doubleday/Currency.

Sleeth, J. M. (2007). *Serve God, Save the planet*. Zondervan.

Springett, D., & Kearins, K. (2001). Gaining legitimacy? Sustainable development in business school curriculum. *Sustainable Development, 9*, 213–221. https://doi.org/10.1002/sd.164

Stead, J. G., & Stead, W. E. (2014). Building spiritual capabilities to sustain sustainability-based competitive advantages. *Journal of Management, Spirituality & Religion, 11*(2), 143–158. https://doi.org/10.1080/14766086.2013.832359

Sunshine, G. (2020). *Wicca and eclectic neo-paganism: Beliefs and practices, emerging worldviews*. Colson Center. https://breakpoint.org/wicca-and-eclectic-neo-paganism-beliefs-and-practices-emerging-worldviews-22/

Targowski, A. (2012). Spirituality 2.0—A condition for a wise civilization. *Dialogue and Universalism, 22*(2), 133–143. https://www.ceeol.com

The Aldo Leopold Foundation. (2018). *The land ethic*. Author. https://www.aldoleopold.org/about/the-land-ethic/

Thomas, T. E. (2005). Are business students buying it? A theoretical framework for measuring attitudes toward the legitimacy of environmental sustainability. *Business Strategy and the Environment, 14*(3), 186–197. https://doi.org/10.1002/bse.446

Tucker, M. E. (2012). World religions, the Earth Charter, and sustainability. In R. Clugston & S. Holt (Eds.), *Exploring synergies between faith values and education for sustainable development* (pp. 1–3). Earth Charter International and Earth Charter Center for Education for Sustainable Development at UPEACE.

Vaill, P. B. (1996). *Learning as a way of being*. Jossey-Bass.

Vatican Insider. (2015). *Pope Francis' encyclical: This "wounded world" needs "an ecological conversion"*. The Vatican. http://www.lastampa.it/2015/06/17/vaticaninsider/eng/the-vatican/pope-francis-encyclical-this-wounded-world-needs-an-ecological-conversion-VIDiWxrhCcCwmSDen1R9yI/pagina.html

Wakefield, R. (1994, Winter). Muir's early Indian views: Another look at *My First Summer in The Sierra. The John Muir Newsletter, 5*(1). https://vault.sierraclub.org/john_muir_exhibit/john_muir_newsletter/wakefield_indian_views.aspx

Walker, A. G. (2013). The relationship between the integration of faith and work with life and job outcomes. *Journal of Business Ethics, 112*(3), 453–461. https://doi.org/10.1007/s10551-012-1271-0

Wilber, K. (1989). Foreword. In G. Feuerstein & K. Wilber (Eds.), *Yoga: The technology of ecstasy*. Tarcher.

Wilber, K. (2000). *Integral psychology: Consciousness, spirit, psychology, therapy.* Shambhala.

Wilber, K. (2007). *Integral spirituality: A startling new role for religion in the modern and postmodern world*. Shambhala Publications.

World Commission on Environment and Development. (1987). *Our common future*. Oxford University Press.

Yanarella, E. J., Levine, R. S., & Lancaster, R. W. (2009). Research and solutions: "Green" vs. sustainability: From semantics to enlightenment. *Sustainability: The Journal of Record, 2*(5), 296–302. https://doi.org/10.1089/SUS.2009.9838

Yogi, M. (1995). *Maharishi University of Management: Wholeness on the move.* Maharishi University of Management Press.

Zellars, K. L., & Perrewe, P. L. (2003). The role of spirituality in occupational stress and well-being. In R. A. Giacalone & C. J. Jurkiewicz (Eds.), *Handbook of workplace spirituality and organizational performance* (pp. 300–313). M. E. Sharpe.

2 Individual Spirituality and Success

2.1 Introduction

This chapter will introduce the definition, theoretical framework, and literature summary of spirituality. The framework will be broad, interdisciplinary, and non-religious, with spirituality defined as a mental phenomenon taking place in the mind and spirit, and as such, transcendent of religion or culture. However, the influence of major religions on spirituality is so profound that a summary of the spiritual aspects of each major religion is included. Contemporary spirituality movements such as alternative spiritualities, occulture, Lifestyles of Health and Sustainability (LOHAS), and Spirituality 2.0 will be explored. The spirituality discourse concludes with an examination of spiritual capital, spiritual intelligence, and the general benefits of spirituality.

The focus of the latter portion of the chapter will be spirituality and success, with a primary focus on career success. Popular interest in spirituality has increased with the rise of secularism, and popular disillusionment with, and declining confidence in religious institutions. Concurrent with the increasing interest in spirituality, more employees are seeking avenues for spiritual expression in the workplace and career. Career theory and holistic models of spirituality and career development

C. G. Beehner, *Spirituality, Sustainability, and Success*, Palgrave Studies in Workplace Spirituality and Fulfillment, https://doi.org/10.1007/978-3-031-47643-3_2

are explored. Because spirituality can be expressed in entrepreneurial pursuits, whereby individuals seek to incorporate individual morals and values directly into a business venture, spiritual entrepreneurship will also be explored. The role of ethics in individual spirituality will be examined. The chapter concludes with an examination of the individual benefits of spirituality in terms of career, health, and relationships.

Spirituality has been compared to an iceberg: Only a small tip of an iceberg is visible from above the surface (Heintzman, 2009). In this chapter we will look below the surface to obtain a better understanding of spirituality at the individual level. Although the context of spirituality within this chapter and book is secular, because spirituality is commonly associated with religion, the religious roots of spirituality will be examined, along with the spirituality religiosity dichotomy. Contemporary spirituality movements will be explored, and the development and importance of spiritual capital and spiritual intelligence will also be considered. The benefits of spirituality will be examined in this chapter.

2.2 Recent Interest in Spirituality

Many scholars have been reluctant to study spirituality, either assuming spirituality cannot be scientifically studied, or that it should not be studied (Miller & Thoresen, 2003). However, research on spirituality and religiosity increased beginning in the latter decades of the previous century (Zinnbauer et al., 1997). Historically, there was no differentiation between spirituality and religion or religiosity until the rise of secularism in the latter-half of the twentieth century (Turner et al., 1995), and a popular disillusionment with and declining confidence in religious institutions (Roof, 1993; Turner et al., 1995; Twenge et al., 2016). The declining interest in religion will be examined later in this chapter.

Spirituality refers to a broad spectrum of ideas, experiences, and customs pertinent to individual and group well-being, and considered to have a positive impact on all aspects of life (Walker, 2013). Research findings suggest individual spirituality may be analogous to a human relationship: Within this relationship, an individual forms attachment with a higher power or entity, providing feelings of support and love (Duffy, 2006; Rowatt & Kirkpatrick, 2002; Sim & Loh, 2003). While spirituality is often considered at the individual level, a common spiritual dimension exists in communities and societies, providing a unique distinguishing characteristic of humanity that will progressively become more manifest in the future human progression to a more sustainable global society (Dahl, 1996). However, because the spiritual journey begins at the individual level, there cannot be collective spiritual order without individual order (Dhiman, 2017).

Spirituality is accepted as a participating consciousness requiring the identification of humans with an environment in which all natural elements and creatures are perceived as living (Berman, 1981). Participative consciousness is a sense of being an active participant within the cosmos, because we are not outside observers, but rather engaged in a conscious, active relationship with the cosmos (Berman, 1981). The most fundamental human assumptions are preserved in cosmologies, which can be religious, or secular, or a synthesis of both (Reuter, 2015). Cosmologies offer a context for life after death with either practical exercises to prepare for the afterlife, or a model of the non-physical dimensions one could expect to experience in the afterlife (Chavez, 2010).

Spirituality is identified with peace, joy, justice, and a combined sense of body, mind, and soul, and is closely affiliated with imagination, creativity, relationships, and notions of a transcendent reality existing outside scientifically verifiable evidence (Walker, 2013). All major spiritual traditions are vested in the transformation of individuals from a self-centered worldview to an internalized understanding of our location in and connectedness to all things (Walker, 2013). The term spirituality has often been used so proximately that one researcher labeled it a "fuzzy" concept that "embraces obscurity with passion" (Spilka, 1993, p. 1). Not surprisingly, spirituality is frequently described as an elusive construct requiring empirical foundation and operationalization (Hood et al., 1996; Spilka, 1993; Spilka & McIntosh, 1996).

Spirituality is not dichotomous: it is not a quality that is either present or absent in an individual (Miller & Thoresen, 2003). Spirituality and religiousness can be described as latent constructs—basic conceptual entities not observed directly but can be understood from observation of some of their elemental dimensions. Latent constructs are complex and usually complicated, with no single aspect or measure capable of capturing the essential meaning. Most individuals desire better health, reduced disease, greater inner peace, and a fuller sense of meaning, purpose, and satisfaction, conditions which have not materialized with increasing levels of affluence and materialism (Myers, 2000).

Definitions of religion and spirituality frequently incorporate traditional concepts of the sacred, such as God, Christ, and the Church (Zinnbauer et al., 1997). Spirituality encompasses an awareness of a divine presence and a search for meaningful answers to existential questions (Dhiman, 2017). However, because the spirituality label has conceptually separated from religion, it has been adopted by diverse groups of believers, suggesting different meanings may have been associated with these terms (Zinnbauer et al., 1997). Therefore, researchers must recognize the numerous meanings attributed to spirituality and religiosity by various religious and cultural groups, and the diverse ways these groups consider themselves to be religious and/or spiritual (Zinnbauer et al., 1997).

In examining contemporary spirituality, four types of geography have been identified that dominate spiritual climate (Bartolini et al., 2017): personal; niche spaces; retreats and spirituality communities; and, transcendental spaces. Personal geographies comprise notions such as the personal journey, and which have been the focus of most geographers. Niche spaces describe locations normally reserved for other functions, where individuals and groups temporarily participate in alternative spiritual practices, such as coffee shops, library meeting rooms, or living rooms. Retreats and spiritual communities are locations where planned spiritual events occur. Finally, transcendental spaces are spaces of the mind and "beyond".

2.3 The Spirituality Religion Dichotomy

Walker (2013) suggested the term *spirituality* originates from the Christian tradition, although contemporary usage is common to most religions. All major religious traditions understand that the individual spiritual core must be developed through a personal inner striving (Walker, 2013). The need for individual self-realization and understanding of a more profound, higher reality is nearly universal among religions (Walker, 2013). While the focus of spirituality in this text is secular, the influence of major religions on spirituality cannot be ignored and was discussed in Chapter 1.

The current disillusionment with religion is confirmed by survey results indicating fewer Americans believe in God, identify as religious, and are less likely to pray (Twenge et al., 2016). Americans reporting a lack of confidence in organized religion declined from 14% in the early 1970s to 24% in 2014, with those reporting "a great deal" of confidence fell more than 50%, from 41 to 20% during the same period (Twenge et al., 2016). American adults in the 2010s reported being less religious than a similar population in previous decades, when measured by church attendance, belief in God, regular prayer, and believing the Bible is the word of God. The most significant change was with regular prayer, with the number of Americans who never pray increased five-fold from 1988 to 2014, and eight-fold for adults aged 18–29 during the same period (Twenge et al., 2016). This defection from religion supports findings from an earlier study of Baby Boomers, wherein Roof (1993) noted increased interest in "new religions" emphasizing direct spiritual experience over institutional religions.

Further supporting the changing conception of spirituality and religiosity in the United States, the Zinnbauer et al. (1997) study findings indicated the terms religiousness and spirituality describe different concepts, although not entirely independent concepts. While 93% of respondents identified as spiritual, and 78% identified as religious, there were collective differences in self-rated religiousness and spirituality, and varying definitions of both terms (Zinnbauer et al., 1997). Spirituality and religiousness were both described a belief in, and often having a relationship with a God or higher power. However, consistent with more recent scholarly definitions (Spilka & McIntosh, 1996), spirituality was most often described in personal or experiential terms, while definitions of religiousness encompassed organizational or institutional beliefs and practices such as church membership, church attendance, and commitment to organized religious doctrine (Zinnbauer et al., 1997). Spirituality and religious participation in the pandemic and post-pandemic era will be explored in Chapter 5.

Religion has become negatively associated with traditional, restrictive demands (Turner et al., 1995), while spirituality has become positively associated with personal experiences of transcendence (Spilka & McIntosh, 1996). During the latter-half of the previous century, spirituality began to acquire a more distinct, secular meaning, viewed more favorably than religion (Turner et al., 1995; Zinnbauer et al., 1997). Since the 1960s, interest in spirituality has increased considerably (Roof, 1993), and American religious life has transformed to include elements traditionally defined as spiritual. However, more recent findings suggest identification as a spiritual person may be declining, although overall, Americans reported being more spiritual in 2014 compared with 1998 (Twenge et al., 2016).

Spirituality is described as existing independent of institutionalized religion. While the focus of religion is external, characterized by rites and rituals, the focus of spirituality is internal, characterized by self-reflection about "the kingdom within" (Marques et al., 2005). Hicks (2002) best defined the bifurcation of religion and spirituality as religion having more of an external focus, while spirituality has an inward focus, making spirituality accessible to everyone, regardless and irrespective of religion. Further, Dent and colleagues (2005) maintained that a person can be religious without ever experiencing spirituality, and likewise, a person can be spiritual without ever participating in a religion. Most researchers have defined spirituality as a secular construct, and not as a religious construct (Geigle, 2012). However, others suggested ideologies, activities, and lifestyles cannot be spiritual unless they include contemplation of the Sacred (Hill et al., 2000).

The recent schism between religion and spirituality may be the result of the rise of secularism and the growing disillusionment with organized religion (Hill et al., 2000), along with the historical-cultural events affecting people's perception of God (Sheldrake, 1992). However, some scholars suggest characterizing religion and spirituality as incongruous opposites contradicts the experiences of many who appear to incorporate both constructs into their lives (Hill et al., 2000). Moreover, both spirituality and religion embrace a process of inquiry because neither spirituality nor religion are automatically known, and with neither construct does the desired outcome impose itself on others (Hill et al., 2000).

Helminski (2007) warned that absent a spiritual reality, religion degenerates into intellectualism, formalism, legalism, and authoritarian extremism. Holthaus (2012) speaks of a paradox in which religions are expanding globally, with some fundamentalist adherents willing to sacrifice their own lives, and the lives of others to foster beliefs driven by power, vengeance, and violence, yet do not promote genuine spiritual awareness. This paradox occurs in contrast with the doctrine of all major religions and philosophies admonishing power, vengeance, and violence to be spiritual inhibitors, distracting from the core doctrines of caring for our weak, poor, and neighbors.

While many scholars question whether a place exists for religion in a modern, secular society, concluding both religion and spirituality now exist outside of modern society, Bartolini et al. (2017) challenged the presumption that modern society is anti-religious or anti-spiritual. Wilford (2010) argued the natural scales for religion are the individual, family, and community, and may exist in or alongside modern society. However, many scholars suggest religion must necessarily endure on islands in the great ocean of modernity (Bartolini et al., 2017). According to Wilford, religion survives as a premodern enchantment of a less than enchanting modern life. However, Cloke and Beaumont (2013) see religion providing a profound critique of modern society, and a collection of practices alleviating the excesses of the neoliberal crisis. Cloke and Beaumont characterized religion as a system of mobile, shifting networks and discourses. The ideal location for these interconnected networks is the modern city, which is a cosmopolitan hub for numerous secular and non-secular networks (Bartolini et al., 2017).

The coexistence of multiple ideas of faith, belief, and spirit in contemporary society, has been seen as a problem for religion, with each struggling to assert control over and above the truths of other (competing) doctrines. However, this is not only a problem for religion, but likewise for science and reason, which can be categorized as options among multiple alternatives, which can also be accepted or rejected. Once religion, science, and superstition are provided equal footing (with neither able to sustain claims of absolute authority), the modern city becomes an incubator for new faiths and belief systems (Bartolini et al., 2017). Nevertheless, the collective, often conflicting, and contradictory systems of religion, spirituality, superstition, magic, science, and reason may be considered the building blocks that constructed modern society (Bartolini et al., 2017). Holloway profoundly concluded the boundary between the religious and the non-religious has become "increasingly fuzzy and fluid" (2012, p. 204).

2.4 Contemporary Spirituality Movements

Study findings suggest Christianity has been declining for decades, ushering in an era of increasing influence of a postsecular society (Heelas & Woodhead, 2005). However, in the argument between the secularization of modern society (e.g., Wilford, 2010), and the importance of religion in a postsecular society (Cloke & Beaumont, 2013), two types of spiritualties are not only overlooked (Bartolini et al., 2017), but may be motivated by the disillusionment with traditional religion: alternative spirituality, and occulture (a blend of the occult and culture). Some scholars proposed the rise of postsecular society is influenced by wider social trends. Heelas and Woodhead (2005) carefully position the rise of alternative New Age spiritualities within the context of increasing consumerism, and a transition from industrial capitalism further in the direction of soft capitalism (Thrift, 1997). Moreover, the increasing concern for personal well-being, happiness, mental and emotional states, and bodily experiences, defined as subjectivization, must also be considered. Heelas and Woodward (2005) suggest the outcome of discontent with consumerism and the rise of subjectivization to be the dramatic increase in alternative spiritualities promoting individual well-being, health, and happiness (Bartolini et al., 2017).

These alternative spiritualities offer a dialogue of spiritual abundance, happiness, and peace that appears beyond the reach of contemporary science and government (Bartolini et al., 2017). Holloway (2003) suggested that perhaps modern society is not as disenchanted and secular as is commonly assumed, with modern spirituality more commonplace, no longer occurring in discrete spaces, such as churches, mosques, and synagogues, but rather in quite ordinary spaces, such as living rooms, kitchens, coffee shops, boutiques, public meeting rooms, sports clubs, schools, and town halls (MacKian, 2012). Alternative spiritualities and occulture mark a fundamental shift in popular culture, with paranormal belief increasing in contemporary Western societies (Hill, 2011). Details of occulture and the paranormal in popular culture transpose the conclusion that modern society is becoming emancipated from divine, spiritual, mystical, supernatural, superstitious ideas. Instead of existing outside modern society, occulture is a description of modernity, both as a form and a lived experience (Bartolini et al., 2017). While some scholars suggest some kind of mini-spiritual revolution may be occurring, and that occulture may now be or soon become the dominant form of culture (Heelas & Woodhead, 2005), Bartolini et al. (2017) are hesitant to exaggerate claims that a fundamental spiritual transformation is taking place in contemporary society.

Outside the realm of religion, and the previously discussed areas of occulture and alternative spiritualities, secular spiritual movements have emerged during the contemporary era. One such movement, Lifestyles of Health and Sustainability (LOHAS) emerged as a method of achieving balance of both health and sustainability (Emerich, 2011). According to Emerich, LOHAS has evolved into what Besecke (2013) describes as reflexive spirituality, in which spirituality is injected into consumer decisions (Emerich, 2011). Purchases are analyzed in terms of whether it will provide benefit or suffering, thereby engaging in seeking transcendent meaning in a rational consumer society.

In his diagnosis of contemporary civilization, Targowski (2012) characterized the present state of civilization by multiple ideological conflicts, and lack of common wisdom, resulting in the decline of contemporary civilization. The development of civilization has been significantly influenced by religions, many of which are currently engaged in structural and perennial conflict, with conflict resolution only feasible when religions achieve solidarity, an unlikely event under current conditions (Targowski, 2012). Mitigating the decay of civilization requires promotion of a wise, universal complementary civilization. The proposed control mechanism for this evolutionary, universal system is Spirituality 2.0, a binding collection of complementary values, drawn from the key contemporary civilizations.

Spirituality 2.0 was introduced as a practical solution to the current state of religious conflict and disagreement, offering an overlaying platform of shared values, encouraging religious tolerance. Spirituality 2.0 forms an amalgamation of existing religious and cultural values, which may limit the need to develop an all-encompassing Universal-Complementary Civilization (UCC). The Spirituality 2.0 values include: ancestral spiritual contact (African); morality, based on harmony with the Universe and all inhabitants (Buddhist); sacredness of elders and family (Chinese); moderation in desire and appetite gratification (Hinduism); awareness that crime will be punished (Islam); cooperation with and worship of nature (Japanese); devotion and sacrifice inspired by a sense of participation in the collective community (Eastern); free election, tolerance, technology based on discovery and application of nature laws (Western); human rights, international law, free flow of ideas, people, goods, and services, respect for other viewpoints (Global); and, wisdom, integrity, conditional forgiveness, equality, and sustainability (Universal Complementary).

Spirituality 2.0 is not a replacement for any or all existing Religions 1.0, because such an ambition would be heretical, revolutionary, impossible to win, unnecessary, and harmful. Spirituality 2.0 would grow globally, rather than in localized pockets, teaching a complementary morality, based upon the most essential values of each Religion 1.0 (Targowski, 2012). Targowski admits the likelihood of enforcing a new, wise civilization through Spirituality 2.0 is low, but feasible, requiring several generations to implement (Targowski, 2012).

2.5 Spiritual Capital

Sociologists use the term religious capital to refer to the level of investment or commitment of an individual to their religious faith. More recently, social scientists have considered the term spiritual capital to be reflective of the level of investment or commitment in spirituality. Spiritual capital is defined as the collection of values, ethical viewpoints and visions for change held by both individuals and organizations. Spiritual capital is fashioned by traditions, systems, and engagement broadly defined relationships, and the sense of meaning and purpose derived from activities. The characteristics of spiritual capital include: belief in, and commitment to a higher moral order, manifested in commitment to values such as truth, self-knowledge, right action, and purpose in life; connection to extensive relationships in far-reaching communities where the individual feels like he or she "fits in"; and, a sense of meaning and purpose in work or vocation (Baker et al., 2011).

Bourdieu identified three conditions of religious capital: embodied, objectified, and institutionalized (1986). Likewise, spiritual capital can be categorized within these three conditions (Verter, 2003). In the embodied state, spiritual capital is a measure of both position and disposition, including spiritual knowledge, abilities, and credentials. In the objectified state, spiritual capital is a measure of material and symbolic objects, theologies, and ideologies. Finally, in the institutionalized state, spiritual capital is measured by the power organizations exercise to legitimize and promote spirituality, and to qualify organizational members to exercise spiritual authority. Institutionalized spiritual capital is more relevant to the concept of workplace spirituality and will be further discussed in Chapter 3.

Capital may be acquired through the exchange of other forms of capital. Spiritual capital may be acquired through socialization, education, or other investment of temporal or financial capital (Verter, 2003). Likewise, because spiritual capital may be translated into other forms of capital, when strategically invested, spiritual capital may bring social and economic improvement (Verter, 2003). However, spiritual capital that is poorly invested may lead to social and economic failure. The advantage of spiritual capital over religious capital lies in the independent nature of the former. An individual may acquire spiritual capital in whatever form through the exchange of other forms of capital, independent of any religion or religious leader.

2.6 Spiritual Intelligence

Vaughan (2002) suggests spiritual intelligence is one of several types of intelligence and can be developed relatively independently. Spiritual intelligence is defined as a collection of mental capacities contributing to the awareness, integration, and adaptive application of the intangible and transcendent characteristics of one's existence, resulting in the following outcomes: deep existential reflection, meaning enhancement, recognition of a transcendent self, and spiritual environment mastery (King, 2008). An extensive literature review supports four core components of spiritual intelligence: (1) critical existential thinking, (2) personal meaning development, (3) transcendental awareness, and (4) conscious state enlargement (King & DeCicco, 2009). Spiritual intelligence calls for multiple approaches to knowing, and integration of the inner life of mind and spirit with the outer life of work. It may be developed through inquiry, practice, and spiritual experiences, depending on the context and method of integration. Spiritual intelligence becomes manifest through wisdom and compassionate action, and provides critical judgment psychological well-being, and healthy human development decision-making (Vaughan, 2002).

Zohar and Marshall (2000) introduced the concept of a spiritual quotient (SQ) as a measurement of the spiritual intelligence (SI) of a person. Akhtarand and colleagues (2015) argued that SI may be the means to reduce unethical behavior within organizations, which in the first decade of the twenty-first century caused multiple high-profile business failures. Sustainability is deeply rooted in the sacredness of humankind and nature, and as such necessitates the construction of spiritual capabilities or competencies requiring spiritual capital and spiritual intelligence (Stead & Stead, 2014). These spiritual capabilities appeal directly to the human quest for meaning and value in all aspects of their lives, and the longing to be a part of a greater purpose

(Stead & Stead, 2014). Senge (1990) suggested the creation of a shared vision to be essential to the formation of spiritual intelligence, which then becomes the cultural foundation that binds organizational members together (Stead & Stead, 2014). The development of organizational spiritual capabilities is antecedent to the development of successful triple bottom line strategies, which reinforce sustainability-based core competencies, thereby creating a difficult to imitate competitive advantage (Stead & Stead, 2014).

Emmons (2000a) provided support for Gardner's (1983) spiritual intelligence foundation, proposing five essential abilities: capacity for transcendent awareness (of a divine being or oneself); ability to enter spiritual states of consciousness; ability to consecrate everyday experiences; the ability to utilize spirituality in problem solving; and, capacity to engage in virtuous behaviors. The capacity to engage in virtuous behaviors has been removed (Emmons, 2000b) due to its more accurate interpretation as preferred behavior (Mayer, 2000). Noble (2000) agreed with Emmons' (2000a) interpretation of spiritual intelligence, further adding two additional critical abilities: (1) "the conscious recognition that physical reality is embedded within a larger, multidimensional reality" (p. 46); and, (2) "the conscious pursuit of psychological health, not only for ourselves but for…the global community" (p. 46). The first ability closely resembles Emmons' (2000a) capacity for transcendent awareness, while the second ability mirrors Emmons' preferred behavior capacity.

2.7 Recent Career Interest in Spirituality

Americans have reported increased interest in spirituality, frequently at the expense of religion. Scholars cited disillusionment with established religion, and the desire for spiritual communion absent a religious intermediary or institution. This contemporary spirituality is in some circumstances secular in nature, with adherents recognizing a higher calling to serve a purpose greater than success as measured by status or wealth accumulation. Harman (1992) suggested business is reflecting a "change of mind" in competitive, exploitive materialism and consumerism will be replaced by a new business paradigm with alternative values of relationship quality, the oneness of humanity, cooperation, caring, nurturing, and spiritual values.

To respond to the spiritual needs of employees to empower them to become successful, managers must embrace the principles of the new business paradigm (Ashar & Lane-Maher, 2004). Because employees want to succeed at work, and perceive spirituality as a component of success, employees desire to disclose their spirituality at work (Ashar & Lane-Maher, 2004). Adults spend a significant portion of waking hours at work, likewise, obtaining a significant amount of their social identity from work (Duchon & Plowman, 2005). Because participation in the traditional sources of community, such as neighborhoods, civic organizations, and religious institutions have been declining, workers have increasingly been seeking community within the context of the workplace (Duchon & Plowman, 2005). The desire for community at work has increased the desire for wholeness and connectedness at the workplace (Duchon & Plowman, 2005).

While Industrial Era careers were characterized by income and advancement, the evolution of the post-industrial economy is becoming characterized by a shift to postmaterialism (Inglehart, 2008). Recent literature suggests a growing contemporary focus of employment as a secular spiritual calling. The shift from an industrial-based to a knowledge-based society is characterized by a focus on self-expression, subjective well-being, and individual spirituality versus survival values (Pettersson, 2003). Early Protestant Work Ethic (PWE) literature (Hill & Smith, 2010; Weber, 1958) suggested that Calvinist Protestants were more likely than other religious adherents to view work as a calling. However, more recently, Davidson and Caddell (1994) suggested individuals with less-developed religious self-concepts or who participate less in religious activities are likely to view work more secularly as employment, and less likely as a calling. Other researchers identified the distinction that a job is associated with the material benefits of work, with interests and ambitions expressed primarily during leisure activities, a career is associated with a deeper personal investment in work intended to achieve advancement, and a calling is associated with morally and socially significant work resulting in personal fulfillment (Dries, 2011; Wrzesniewski et al., 1997).

Although the teachings of Buddhism differ from those of Christianity, similar themes are identified in literature on Buddhism and work (Dries, 2011). According to Buddhism, the essence of life exists in the purification of human character, a goal partially achieved through work. Buddhism divides work into three functions (Dries, 2011; Schumacher, 2003): providing opportunity to utilize and develop individual capabilities; overcoming self-centeredness by working with others toward a common goal; and, generating the goods and services necessary for subsistence. An important career guide for Buddhists is the Noble Eightfold Path (Inoue, 1997), with the path of Right Livelihood indicating individuals should avoid careers that, directly or indirectly, harm other living beings. Consequently, the path of Right Livelihood has significant implications for Buddhist career selection (Dries, 2011).

While capitalism and communism are frequently portrayed as ideological rivals, according to Lucas and colleagues (2006), both ideologies serve a surprisingly similar purpose, promoting conceptualization of career and career success benefiting the prevailing socio-political system at the possible expense of individual members (Van Buren, 2003). The American Dream promotes individual career pursuits most likely to preserve the capitalist system, further fostering nationwide economic growth. Failure is a result of individual limitations or lack of responsibility and not the fault of the system. Likewise, communist rhetoric under Chairman Mao suspended individual critical thinking, and restricted career choice, to conceal worker, work, and power inequality, with complaining nearly nonexistent (Dries, 2011; Lucas et al., 2006).

The concept of a boundaryless career has received considerable attention in contemporary career literature (Dries, 2011). The boundaryless career challenges traditional employment concepts of continuous single-employer service, upward mobility focus, separation of work and personal life (Arthur & Rousseau, 1996), and weakened employee-employer connection (Arnold & Cohen, 2008). However, despite the boundaryless career having become a mainstream topic career literature, some researchers suggest the theoretical career approach is not entirely accommodative to actual individual career experiences (e.g., Briscoe &

Finkelstein, 2009), and critics note boundaryless career literature disregards the contributions and requirements of unskilled workers (Dries, 2011). According to Dany (2003), individual career definitions are continuously shaped throughout life, changing whenever personal life changes influence priorities.

Considering less than 1% of employees globally attain the highest positions within their organizations (Buzzanell & Goldzwig, 1991), and that, at some point in their careers, many employees are terminated, laid-off, or otherwise required to take a backward career step due to (unexpected) personal events (Bright et al., 2009), it is reasonable conjecture that most employees have unsuccessful careers (Dries, 2011). Moreover, the impact of gender, race, and social class barriers (the glass ceiling) on career success is frequently underestimated, further contributing to perceptions that individuals are at fault when they experience career setbacks or failures (Brown, 2002; Lucas et al., 2006).

Researchers suggested a necessity of including the recognition, validation, and discussion of spirituality in career planning, because individuals desiring career success also require resources and support that respond to their holistic needs (Royce-Davis & Stewart, 2000). The primary focus of the limited contemporary research in spirituality, religion, and career development has been understanding the degree to which spirituality and religiousness affect individual navigation of career-specific tasks (Duffy, 2006). Duffy and Blustein (2005) found no significant relationship among spirituality, religiousness, and career choice commitment. However, spirituality and religiousness were found to be significant positive predictors of career decision self-efficacy, suggesting individual connection with a higher power may provide similar benefits to connections with other people. Career development research has demonstrated positive relationships with friends and family provide support in performance of career development tasks (Blustein et al., 1991; O'Brien, 1996; Schultheisset al., 2002). Two categories of career-related spirituality issues have been identified: spiritual struggles, with their resolution cited as an important career need; and, spiritual growth, signified by a specific moment when spiritual development was identified as significant for career direction (Royce-Davis & Stewart, 2000). In their study of spirituality and success, Ashar and Lane-Maher (2004) found three definitions of success reported by study participants: sense of accomplishment, work-family balance, and contributions to the community.

2.8 Work as a Calling

There are distinct differences between religious and secular spiritual callings. While a religious calling originates from a set of beliefs in an external God or higher being (Weiss et al., 2003), a secular calling originates internally (Dobrow, 2004). While research findings on religious calling often indicate a desire for service to others, secular calling highlights the derivation of meaning from serving self, community, or the greater good of society (Dobrow, 2004). A calling that originates from a relationship with God or a higher being typically reflects purpose through the process of "discernment", which describes learning how to hear one's own voice, further enhancing the ability to act with authenticity (Weiss et al., 2003). In contrast, a calling that originates from within identifies a vocation of self-exploration, including methods such as self-examination, reflection, meditation, and relational activities. Finally, an individual pursuing a religious calling finds meaning in the belief that the calling is part of God's greater plan, while an individual pursuing a secular calling finds meaning through personal fulfillment.

Hall and Chandler (2005) suggested a calling can arise from a set of religious beliefs or from an individual's sense of self and meaningfulness, and as such is a more expansive or generalized concept that may transcend religious significance (Hall & Chandler, 2005). When employment becomes a calling, it provides an individual with greater meaning and identity (Moore, 1992), and when individuals find meaning and identity through employment, it becomes a calling (Thompson, 2001). When unique talents are aligned with the needs of the greater society, work transcends from being a job to a vocation or calling (Leider, 1997). This may be an appropriate place to recall the quote attributed to Confucius: "Choose a job you love, and you will never have to work a day in your life".

In viewing work as a calling, spirituality can be applied within the context of almost any career path. For example, employment as a customer service representative offers greater meaning and satisfaction when performed within the context of improving other people's satisfaction and well-being. Any job or position becomes a calling when the actor finds meaning and purpose in contributing to a cause that is greater than the contributor. Spirituality becomes a worldview through which employment evolves from a means of income to a means of service to a greater cause.

There are numerous careers that more closely align with a spiritual worldview than others, including social worker, minister, healthcare worker, police officer or firefighter, and nonprofit manager to name a few. Careers such as these require an inner desire to serve others, with individuals who follow these paths without an inner, transcending motivation likely to find dissatisfaction in undertaking such a career direction absent a true calling. It may seem second nature that spirituality might be relevant in the healthcare field, because several studies indicate nurses are drawn to the occupation by perceptions or experiences demonstrating the importance of compassion and caring within this profession (Tietjen, 2013) (Baldacchino, 2017). Individuals employed in human resources are likewise motivated by a desire to assist others in securing employment that is suitable, rewarding, and perhaps fulfills the desire for a calling or vocation. However, any career can be spiritual when it is pursued as a calling or vocation, and not solely for employment or income.

2.9 Career Theory

Spirituality and individual success may be examined through the lens of career theory, proponents of which suggest individuals express spirituality within the context of personal life meaning as well as the organizational context in which they are achieved (Lips-Wiersma, 2002). While the premise of psychological career theory is with a personally constructed reality, assuming individuals have a degree of career direction control, the premise of sociological career theory is that institutions influence career direction within a socially constructed reality (Hotchkiss & Borrow, 1990). Lips-Wiersma (2002) found the achievement of spirituality to be the result of a positive relationship between individual spirituality and the organizational environment in which it is achieved. Individuals often change careers when they determine they are no longer authentically achieving their life purposes, supporting the argument that spirituality influences work behavior. Career theory will be discussed in greater detail in Chapter 6.

2.10 Holistic Models of Spirituality and Career Development

In addition to Career Theory, several holistic models exist with which to examine spirituality and career development (Duffy, 2006). The common theme among spirituality and career development theories is that spirituality, religiosity, and career issues are connected by means of an overall developmental or holistic system. Although theorists regard the integration of spirituality and career decision-making as advisable, all recognize that this integration does not occur within every individual (Duffy, 2006). The Holistic Model of Wellness, developed by Witmer and Sweeney (1992) consists of five basic individual life tasks: spirituality, self-regulation, work, friendship, and love. Consistent with other holistic approaches, each of the five basic tasks builds upon the others and based on the emphasis given to a given task, guides the other four tasks. The focal point of Witmer and Sweeney's model is spirituality, which is not connected with religious beliefs or a higher power, but to "life enhancing beliefs about human dignity, human rights, and reverence for life" (p. 141). Spirituality serves as the primary instrument of value development, in turn guiding work behavior, and may provide purpose and meaning, further impacting the other four life tasks. While the Holistic Model of Wellness is not empirically supported, the proposition that spirituality influences values and purpose, thereby influencing work, is supported in limited empirical research.

The Lifecareer, or Life-is-Career model developed by Miller-Tiedeman (1994), proposed that individuals let life experience and values direct their career paths. This model deviates from traditional career theory by encouraging individuals to learn as they go, exercise flexibility and openness with new career paths, and develop their own individual theory about career decision-making, instead of worrying about making the correct career decisions in a timely manner. Miller-Tiedeman advocated the focus of life should not be finding the right career, but rather finding the right life, with a career acting as a complementary, not a primary goal. Spiritual and religious aspects may serve a significant purpose in this model, because for some individuals spirituality and religion represent governing life ingredients and values that substantially influence career choice.

According to Brewer's Vocational Souljourn (2001) model, an individual's life is prescribed by three fundamental principles: meaning, being, and doing. Meaning describes the "what" of life and defines individual values, being describes who the individual is, and doing describes the action or "how" of life (Brewer, 2001). Brewer classified work into four categories: job, occupation, career, and vocation. The Souljourn model depicts work as a spectrum, with a job at one end of the spectrum, characterized as temporary, financially driven activity, and a vocation at the other end, characterized as a personally significant path serving as the highest expression of work. For Brewer, a vocation is something individuals are called by the Creator to do as an expression of their true selves rather than in pursuit of fame or money. Brewer suggested that for stability to occur in an individual's life, the three principles of meaning, being, and doing must be in equilibrium. Brewer applied Jungian (1954) precepts of energy to demonstrate that when these three principles are in disequilibrium, excessive energy is expended trying to correct this imbalance. However, when these three principles align, contradictory boundaries between work and non-work are abolished, resulting in a free flow of energy throughout the system.

Bloch (2004, 2005) developed a theory concerning the connection between spirituality and career development founded in complexity theory, which posits that in any system, each component is directly or indirectly affected by the other components. In complexity theory, each system contains a specific amount of energy to be shared among all components in a constant state of flux. Within this system, spirituality and work are connected through principles originally developed by Bloch and Richmond (1998), including: viewing work as a calling; recognizing work has a purpose beyond financial reward; working in an environment consistent with personal values; and, experiencing community and connection at work. Bloch (2004) suggested people who consider work to be spiritual also consider their contribution to the world, avoid self-centeredness, and integrate their work and personal lives. Bloch (2004) urged career counselors to discuss with clients the types of careers that are most aligned, not only with their skills and interests, but also with individual values and sense of self. Moreover, career counselors should encourage clients to not only consider the types of careers they find attractive, but also the reasons behind these feelings, to better assist clients with discerning true calling, instead of determining the most convenient or lucrative career option.

2.11 Entrepreneurship and Spirituality

Morris and Schindehutte (2005) suggested entrepreneurship is a values-driven endeavor. Entrepreneurs often place greater focus on personal meaning in entrepreneurial pursuits and are primarily driven by internal values (Kinjerski & Skrypnek, 2004), such as spirituality (Baloget al., 2014). An examination of entrepreneurial integration of spirituality and work provides a unique perspective of individual workplace behavior, and a better understanding of relationships with employees, customers, and the community (Kauanui et al., 2008). While the primary focus of entrepreneurship research has been economic growth and wealth, several entrepreneurship studies have found financial gain is not the primary motivator for launching a new business venture (Amit et al., 2001; Katz, 1992). Entrepreneurs often seek meaning in their work and seek personal happiness by pursuing enjoyable work to become "whole persons" (King et al., 2003), and find an overwhelming sense of personal fulfillment and satisfaction (King-Kauanui et al., 2010). Spiritual entrepreneurs view their businesses as a faithful vocation and seek to incorporate personal morals and values directly into the business (Nwankwo et al., 2012), often seeing a connection with the "big picture", and the integration of social concerns with economic concerns (King-Kauanui et al., 2005). In the contemporary competitive business environment, an increasing number of individuals are embracing entrepreneurship as an occupation providing meaning and purpose (King-Kauanui et al., 2005).

While most traditional entrepreneurship literature has ignored spirituality when examining motivation, one study identified two groups of entrepreneurs: those who combine mind, body, and soul with their work, and those who do not (Kauanui et al., 2008). These two groups have been further broken down into five modalities. The "make me whole" who are internally motivated, are engaged in work that they love and in which they find meaning and purpose, and who fully engage spirituality at work. The soul seekers do not fully integrate spirituality or religion in their work, struggle with a definition of spirituality, and consider work to be rewarding, with financial security as the primary motivation. The "conflicting goals" perceive a relationship between spirituality and entrepreneurship, but struggle to integrate the two, considering work to be a means of achieving success and goal or dream gratification. The "mostly business" group may perceive a connection between spirituality and work, but do not apply that connection in practice, considering work as "a means to an end". The "strictly business" group are not spiritual, separate business from personal life, and consider work to acquire wealth which is the measure of success (Kauanui et al., 2008).

2.12 Ethics and Individual Spirituality

Ethics prescribes behaviors that are considered appropriate and what is considered right in living one's life (Chippendale, 2001). An individual with spiritual principles and values may have a better understanding of the ethical problems which exist in business (Kumari, 2014). Spirituality serves a vital role in guiding ethical behaviors of both leaders and followers. According to Sulmasy (2013), every system of ethics requires stories and narratives to address fundamental questions and inspirations such as the nature of the universe, and the meaning of life. Creighton-Smith et al. (2017) suggested the forces in the realm of spirituality or religiosity may be one of the most effective determinants of ethical behavior. Edginton and Kangas (2014) claimed spirituality is one of the most significant influences impacting humankind and guides most societal beliefs, cultures, practices, and decisions.

Researchers have demonstrated that spirituality and religiosity contributed to ethical behavior, social responsibility, sustainability, ecological principles, environmental mindsets, pro-environmental behavior, and ecologically/socially conscious consumer behavior (Göçen & Özğan, 2018). Researchers demonstrated that spirituality influences ethical decisions and low spirituality contributes to unethical behavior (Rodriguez-Rad & Ramos-Hidalgo, 2018). According to Lowery et al. (2014), individuals who are more spiritual may be less likely to engage in manipulative work acts, unethical behaviors, and unethical activities. Ananthram and Chan (2016) found that religious virtues, ethical virtues, and secular spirituality contributed to ethical decision-making. Some participants reported that integrity, courage, and conscientiousness were a result of ethical virtues. The relationship between spirituality, religion, and ethical behavior can vary across groups and cultural belief systems (Kalafatoğlu, 2022). Consumers with higher spiritual awareness are more likely to be ethically inclined (Vitell et al., 2016). Spirituality may be a predictor of green consumer behavior (Chairy, 2012), and ethical decision-making combined with spirituality influences buying habits which may directly or indirectly impact the planet (Göçen & Özğan, 2018).

Spirituality and ethics may contribute to the well-being of an individual and society (Göçen & Özğan, 2018). Dhiman (2016) identified ethics as a balancing force, suggesting that the absence of a spiritual dimension may result in self-centered and greedy behavior. Zsolnai (2010) added that spiritual experiences transcend an individual's narrow self-concepts and create empathy. From a spiritual and ethical perspective, the well-being of all communities and ecosystems are dependent upon care, empathy, and respect (Göçen & Özğan, 2018).

Greene (2013) considered science, economics, and self-interest to be inadequate for achieving sustainable development or maintaining world order suggesting ethics, spirituality, and values must be applied to achieve sustainability. Humankind is facing major challenges and changes, and individuals who make decisions with spirit and ethics are needed to lead the next era of humanity (Göçen & Özğan, 2018; Greene, 2013). Only individual lives which are based on moral and spiritual awareness and live in harmony with nature can protect the planet (Dhiman, 2016).

The current decline in ethics will create problems that will be further exacerbated by the proliferation of the Internet in households, through minimization of daily regular contact and social bonds (Göçen & Özğan, 2018). While science and technology have contributed significantly to human social development, they have also contributed significant problems, some of which may be the result of declining spiritual values in ethical and holistic decision-making (Pillai, 2016). Spirituality can contribute to sustainability and global problem solving, and spirituality and ethics will become essential for the well-being of individuals and humanity on a greater scale in the coming decades (Göçen & Özğan, 2018).

2.13 Individual Benefits of Spirituality

All wisdom traditions uphold the importance of self-knowledge as a prelude to the pursuit of happiness and fulfillment (Dhiman, 2017). Research findings suggest spirituality is likely to produce positive satisfaction, increased feelings of fulfillment, and a better quality of life (Dierendonck & Mohan, 2006; Mohan, 2001; WHOQOL SRPB Group, 2006). Considerable research findings indicate religious and spiritual factors contribute to adolescent and adult psychological well-being (Paloutzian & Park, 2013; Pargament et al., 2013). Higher spirituality levels were associated with a more positive life perspective, greater perceived social support, higher stress resilience, and lower anxiety levels (Pardini et al., 2000).

Spirituality was shown to directly affect purpose in life, and indirectly affect academic engagement, suggesting students who are searching for meaning and purpose may not become academically engaged unless or until they find purpose in life (Greenway, 2006). Spirituality was shown to support academic success in African American students through providing: an entity with whom students could discuss issues; inspiration for excellence; life purpose, which reassured students of their academic plans; an ability to overcome barriers; and, reduced relational distractions (Wood & Hilton, 2012).

Spiritual exercises and activities such as meditation, mindfulness, and prayer have been found to produce positive emotional, mental, and physical health benefits. Substantial research literature suggests meditation is not only beneficial to mental health (Baer et al., 2008; Carmody & Baer, 2008; Shapiro, 1992), but has been proven effective in eliminating perceived stress and corresponding symptoms (Carmody & Baer, 2008; Chang et al., 2004). Personal spiritual awareness and reflection may be associated with holistic healing presence resulting from the therapeutic use of self, developed through nurturing inner power (Watson, 1999). Research suggests personal spirituality and healthy attitudes in care are predictors of both effective care and personal relationships (Grant et al., 2004; Van Leeuwen et al., 2006).

Historically, religion, spirituality, and medical practice have been interwoven (Mueller et al., 2001). Contemporary healthcare worker spirituality was determined to be beneficial for both caregivers and patients (Boero et al., 2005; Cobb, 2004; Ross et al., 2015). Nurse individual spirituality appears to be incorporated within spiritual care delivery through demonstration of positive attitudes and mutual respect experienced during caregiver-patient interactions (Formosa & Baldacchino, 2010; Ross et al., 2014). Most individuals indicate having a spiritual life, and most patients regard spiritual and physical health to be equally important (Mueller et al., 2001).

Numerous studies indicated spirituality favorably impacts recovery from illness, and contributes to improved well-being (Cigrang et al., 2003; Meraviglia, 2004; Peselow et al., 2014), and reduced levels of depression (Konkoly et al., 2013; Peselow et al., 2014). Several studies have shown religious coping strategies, like prayer and feeling God's presence, alleviate anxiety and apprehension in patients with multiple myeloma, and alleviate some physical symptoms in patients with cancer; however, there are inconclusive results regarding the positive impact of spirituality (Sherman et al., 2009; Tarakeshwar et al., 2006). The positive individual and community health benefits attributed to spirituality necessitate further attention be paid to religious and spiritual beliefs as a topic of patient-caregiver conversation (Levin et al., 1996). Likewise, increased effort should be encouraged regarding the importance of spiritual awareness with respect to treatment and hygienic services (Levin et al., 1996).

There are many avenues for individual and collective practice of religion and spirituality, including: prayer; meditation; mindfulness; intentionality; service to others; fasting; worship; and, music. Prayer is a key element of most major faith traditions (Levin, 2001). Four mechanisms have been identified through which prayer may affect individual health and well-being: relaxation response; placebo; positive emotional expression; and, supernatural intervention channel (Jantos & Kiat, 2007). The health benefits of prayer are the result of the positive emotions engendered by prayer, with both silent and spoken prayer associated with increased cerebral activity, manifest in the form of higher beta frequencies (Levin, 2001). The possibility of the existence of a Creator-God willingly choosing to answer (or not answer) petitionary prayers through an unexplainable method may be the most held belief of people who are concerned for self or for others health and well-being.

Meditation contributes to both cognitive and emotional function regulation (Baeret al., 2006; Segal et al., 2002). Practicing meditation can enhance emotional intelligence (EI), tolerance, friendliness, empathy, positive states of mind, positive values, happiness, joy, and positive thinking (Baer et al., 2006; Beddoe & Murphy, 2004; Chang et al., 2004; Lutz et al., 2008; Shapiro, 1992), and has been demonstrated to decrease anger, anxiety, hostility, depression, and depression relapses (Dua & Swinden, 1992; Hayes, 2004; Segal et al., 2002, 2007). Meditation has been found to improve psychological health, and psychological well-being through accumulation of high EI, and cultivation of a positive attitude toward perceived stress, with longer durations of meditation resulting in greater improvements in EI level, and increased reductions in perceived stress, and negative mental health (Chu, 2010).

Mindfulness is commonly defined as the state of being attentive to and aware of what is occurring at the present, further defined by Hanh (1976) as "keeping one's consciousness alive to the present reality" (p. 11). Mindfulness is an aspect of consciousness that has received considerable attention with respect to well-being (Brown & Ryan, 2003). Numerous philosophical, spiritual, and psychological traditions emphasize the importance of consciousness for the maintenance and enrichment of well-being (Wilber, 2000). Moreover, research indicates favorable employee benefits such as reduced emotional exhaustion and increased job satisfaction (Hülsheger et al., 2013).

Intentionality suggests behavior that is deliberate or purposive, including a mental state in which beliefs and thoughts are directed at an object or state. Henry David Thoreau wrote about living life deliberately, suggesting living intentionally required active participation with whatever an individual is currently experiencing. The spiritual practice of intentionality can bring about career success by harnessing the energy of the mind to produce successful goal setting, job seeking, and work performance skills (Bloch & Richmond, 1997). While intentionality does not replace the importance of networking, resumes, and interviewing, it does enhance individual ability to successfully complete these career tasks (Bloch & Richmond, 1997).

Service to others is a common practice of spiritual and religious traditions. Study findings suggest individuals given money to purchase gifts for others reported higher levels of happiness than individuals given money to purchase gifts for themselves (Dunn et al., 2008). For many people, fasting for a period of times is a spiritual, or health practice intended to "purify" the mind, body, or senses, much as washing of feet has been a tradition in several wisdom traditions. Fasting and washing can be either practical, symbolic, or both, invoked in reference to one's state of consciousness, referring to a mind free from distractions or impurities (Chavez, 2010). According to Levin (2001), the practice of worship produces similar health benefits as those achieved through prayer, resulting from the positive emotions engendered during worship. The idea that music is beneficial should not be surprising since the physical, mental, and social benefits of music have been documented since as early as 4000 BC (Spintge & Droh, 1992). Music has been used in various medical therapies and treatments because music is pervasive, emotional, engaging, distracting, physical, ambiguous, social, and communicative, and affects behavior and identities (MacDonald et al., 2012).

2.14 Concluding Thoughts

Interest in spirituality has increased during the past few decades (Zinnbauer et al., 1997), likely motivated by popular disillusionment with and declining confidence in religious institutions (Roof, 1993; Turner et al., 1995; Twenge et al., 2016). However, a secondary trend may be influencing the spirituality quest. Technology may be influencing the spirituality movement on two fronts. First, technology has made individuals and society more "technologically" social, through social media and videoconferencing. Prior to the current technological era, socialization required face-to-face contact. Lesser social means of communication included printed media, and later audio telecommunication. Today, individuals may communicate instantaneously across the globe (and even beyond the globe, with relatives and friends residing on the International Space Station). This increased socialization reduces the necessity for physical interaction, perhaps threatening the viability of traditional social organizations such as churches, mosques, temples, and synagogues. Second, this rapid, impersonal mode of communication may present a feeling of emptiness or a missing component in our lives. We must stop to question, are we really socializing with our loved ones when we are unable to share a physical embrace? Are we really engaged in personal communion and fellowship when we post our deepest thoughts, or share a photo of our lunch on social media?

The spiritual ramifications of social media and technology are profound. The chronology of religious communication from a Judeo-Christian context began with early oral communication, followed by instructions written in stone (Ten Commandments), then hand-written on papyrus and parchment, followed by the printing press, television, the Internet, and now social media. The rapid technological advancement in communication raises several questions about the impact of and relationship of technology with spirituality. Evangelical Christian churches in the United States have successfully formed communities over significant distances, reaching thousands of adherents, through telecommunications media (Bartolini et al., 2017; Dittmar & Sturm, 2010). The same account can be assumed for the current proliferation of social media. Questions related to this impact and relationship are among the reflective questions that follow.

Regardless of the reason, interest in spirituality has been increasing at both the individual and collective level. Although spirituality must begin at the individual level (Dhiman, 2017), a common spiritual dimension exists in communities and societies that may become more progressively manifest in the future human progression to a more sustainable global society (Dahl, 1996). Spirituality has appeared and been examined at the organizational level, which will be the subject of the following chapter. While Marx described religion as the opiate of the masses (Marx & Engels, 1844), spirituality may become the vitamin of the masses.

An increasing number of individuals have been exploring spirituality as an alternative or supplement to existing religious participation. Spirituality has been demonstrated to be beneficial for individuals in terms of career, health, and relationships. However, it must also be considered that the beneficial outcomes of spirituality are a result of the positive behaviors of the individual, and not necessarily the religious or spiritual motivation behind those behaviors. Regardless of whether the benefits result from spirituality, the behavior resulting from the focus on spirituality, the benefits are nonetheless favorable, and desirable. Spirituality appears to produce a state or condition in which individuals transcend materialist motives, seek a higher purpose in life, and as a direct or indirect result, either achieve a more desirable state of existence, or become satisfied with the current state of existence.

Guillory (1997) proposed the emergence of spiritual organizations, suggesting the Industrial Age was followed by the Information Age, and partially concurrent Knowledge Age, will be followed by the Spiritual Age, and subsequent Age of Oneness. It is highly unlikely that in the early stages of the Industrial Age, academics and practitioners recognized the changing paradigm of their time. Likewise, the term Information Age was not coined until the era was well underway. I propose that regardless of whether we are aware, we currently exist in the Spiritual Age, as evidenced by the increased attention to all forms of spirituality and spiritual endeavors. While newspaper headlines propagate a message of chaos and discord, is an underlying movement of order and harmony concurrently underway? Like previous ages, movements, and philosophies, we will likely determine the answer to the previous question after the events have unfolded considerably. While cynical human nature may only see chaos and discord, the collective consciousness as described by Jung (1934–1954) may recognize and pursue the order and harmony which nature accomplishes, and humankind desires.

Reflection Questions

1. Can religion and spirituality really exist independent of each other?
2. How do you think members of each major religion would respond to, and accept the idea of universal spirituality or Spirituality 2.0?
3. What future trend(s) do you anticipate among technology, social media, religion, and spirituality constructs?
4. Can employment in contemporary, profit-maximization careers ever be considered a calling?

References

Akhtar, S., bin Arshad, M.A., Mahmood, A., & Ahmed, A. (2015). Spiritual quotient and ethical values towards organizational stability. *International Letters of Social and Humanistic Sciences, 58*, 107. https://www.learntechlib.org/p/176798/

Amit, R., MacCrimmon, K. R., Zietsma, C., & Oesch, J. M. (2001). Does money matter? Wealth attainment as the motive for initiating growth-oriented technology ventures. *Journal of Business Venturing, 16*(2), 119–143. https://doi.org/10.1016/S0883-9026(99)00044-0

Ananthram, S., & Chan, C. (2016). Religiosity, spirituality and ethical decision-making: Perspectives from executives in Indian multinational enterprises. *Asia Pacific Journal of Management, 33*(3), 843–880. https://doi.org/10.1007/s10490-016-9460-5

Arnold, J., & Cohen, L. (2008). The psychology of careers in industrial-organizational settings: A critical but appreciative analysis. In G. P. Hodgkinson & J. K. Ford (Eds.), *International Review of Industrial and Organizational Psychology* (pp. 1–44). Wiley.

Arthur, M. B., & Rousseau, D. M. (1996). *The boundaryless career: A new employment principle for a new organizational era.* Oxford University Press.

Ashar, H., & Lane-Maher, M. (2004). Success and spirituality in the new business paradigm. *Journal of Management Inquiry, 13*(3), 249–260. https://doi.org/10.1177/1056493604268218

Baer, R. A., Smith, G. T., Hopkins, J., Krietemeyer, J., & Toney, L. (2006). Using self-report assessment methods to explore facets of mindfulness. *Assessment, 13,* 27–45. https://doi.org/10.1177/1073191105283504

Baer, R. A., Smith, G. T., Lykins, E., Button, D., Krietemeyer, J., Sauer, S., Walsh, E., Duggan, D., & Williams, J. M. G. (2008). Construct validity of the five facet mindfulness questionnaire in meditating and nonmeditating samples. *Assessment, 15,* 329–342. https://doi.org/10.1177/107319110731 3003

Baker, C., Stokes, P., Lichy, J., Atherton, J., & Moss, D. (2011). *Values, beliefs and attitudes in the era of late-capitalism: A consideration of the re-emergence and re-positioning of faith and spirituality as spiritual capital in the workplace.* https://www.academia.edu

Baldacchino, D. (2017). Spirituality in the healthcare workplace. *Religions, 8*(12), 260. https://doi.org/10.3390/rel8120260

Balog, A. M., Baker, L. T., & Walker, A. G. (2014). Religiosity and spirituality in entrepreneurship: A review and research agenda. *Journal of Management, Spirituality & Religion, 11*(2), 159–186. https://doi.org/10.1080/14766086.2013.836127

Bartolini, N., Chris, R., MacKian, S., & Pile, S. (2017). The place of spirit: Modernity and the geographies of spirituality. *Progress in Human Geography, 41*(3), 338–354. https://doi.org/10.1177/0309132516644512

Beddoe, A. E., & Murphy, S. O. (2004). Does mindfulness decrease stress and foster empathy among nursing students? *Journal of Nursing Education, 43,* 305–312. https://doi.org/10.3928/01484834-20040701-07

Berman, M. (1981). *The reenchantment of the world.* Cornell University Press.

Besecke, K. (2013). *You can't put God in a box.* Oxford University Press.

Bloch, D. P., & Richmond, L. J. (1997). *Connections between spirit and work in career development: New approaches and practical perspectives.* Routledge.

Bloch, D. P., & Richmond, L. J. (1998). *SoulWork: Finding the work you love, loving the work you have.* Davies-Black.

Bloch, D. P. (2004). Spirituality, complexity, and career counseling. *Professional School Counseling, 7,* 343–350. http://www.jstor.org/stable/42732603

Bloch, D. P. (2005). Complexity, chaos, and nonlinear dynamics: A new perspective on career development theory. *The Career Development Quarterly, 53*, 194–207. https://doi.org/10.1002/j.2161-0045.2005.tb00990.x

Blustein, D. L., Walbridge, M. M., Friedlander, M. L., & Palladino, D. E. (1991). Contributions of psychological separation and parental attachment to the career development process. *Journal of Counseling Psychology, 38*, 39–50. https://doi.org/10.1037/0022-0167.38.1.39

Boero, M. E., Monteverdi, C. R., Braida, V., Fabello, M., & Zorzella, L. (2005). Spirituality of health workers: A descriptive study. *International Journal of Nursing Studies, 42*, 915–21. https://doi.org/10.1016/j.ijnurstu.2004.11.007

Bourdieu, P. (1986). The forms of capital. In J. Richardson (Ed.), *Handbook of theory and research for the sociology of education* (pp. 241–258). Greenwood.

Brewer, E. W. (2001). Vocational souljourn paradigm: A model of adult development to express spiritual wellness as meaning, being, and doing in work and life. *Counseling and Values, 45*, 83–93. https://doi.org/10.1002/j.2161-007X.2001.tb00187.x

Bright, J. E. H., Pryor, R. G. L., Chan, E. W. M., & Rijanto, J. (2009). Chance events in career development: Influence, control and multiplicity. *Journal of Vocational Behavior, 75*(1), 14–25. https://doi.org/10.1016/j.jvb.2009.02.007

Briscoe, J. P., & Finkelstein, L. M. (2009). The 'new career' and organizational commitment: Do boundaryless and protean attitudes make a difference? *Career Development International, 14*(3), 242–260. https://doi.org/10.1108/13620430910966424

Brown, D. (2002). *Career choice and development*. Jossey-Bass.

Brown, K. W., & Ryan, R. M. (2003). The benefits of being present: Mindfulness and its role in psychological well-being. *Journal of Personality and Social Psychology, 84*(4), 822–848. https://doi.org/10.1037/0022-3514.84.4.822

Buzzanell, P. M., & Goldzwig, S. R. (1991). Linear and nonlinear career models: Metaphors, paradigms, and ideologies. *Management Communication Quarterly, 4*(4), 466–505. https://doi.org/10.1177/0893318991004004004

Carmody, J., & Baer, R. A. (2008). Relationships between mindfulness practice and levels of mindfulness, medical and psychological symptoms and well-being in a mindfulness- based stress reduction program. *Journal of Behavioral Medicine, 31*, 23–33. https://doi.org/10.1007/s10865-007-9130-7

Chairy. (2012). Spirituality, self transcendence, and green purchase intention in college students. *Procedia-Social and Behavioral Sciences, 57*, 243–246. https://doi.org/10.1016/j.sbspro.2012.09.1181

Chang, V. Y., Palesh, O., Caldwell, R., Glasgow, N., Abramson, M., Luskin, F., Gill, M., Burke, A., & Koopman, C. (2004). The effects of a mindfulness based stress reduction program on stress, mindfulness self-efficacy, and positive states of mind. *Stress and Health, 20*(2), 141–147. https://doi.org/10.1002/smi.1011

Chavez, F.I. (2010). Sustainability & spirituality: Common threads. Originally published in the *Green MBA Journal, 6*(1). Dominican University of California. http://feliciachavez.com

Chippendale, P. (2001). On values, ethics, morals & principles. *A Values Inventory. Etik Tanımı, 28*, 1–6. https://www.researchgate.net/profile/Paul-Chippendale/publication/242758616_On_Values_Ethics_Morals_Principles_By/links/5a98d19445851535bce0dbfe/On-Values-Ethics-Morals-Principles-By.pdf

Chu, L. C. (2010). The benefits of meditation vis-à-vis emotional intelligence, perceived stress and negative mental health. *Stress and Health, 26*(2), 169–180. https://doi.org/10.1002/smi.1289

Cigrang, J. A., Hryshko-Mullen, A., & Peterson, A. L. (2003). Spontaneous reports of religious coping by patients with chronic physical illness. *Journal Clinical Psychology in Medical Settings, 10*(3), 133–137. https://doi.org/10.1023/A:1025494309495

Cloke P. & Beaumont, J. (2013). Geographies of postsecular rapprochement in the city. *Progress in Human Geography, 37*(1), 27–51. https://doi.org/10.1177/0309132512440208

Cobb, B.J. (2004). *Nursing students' experiences in personal spiritual formation and in provision of spiritual care to patients* [doctoral dissertation]. Andrews University.

Creighton-Smith, B. A., Cook, M., & Edginton, C. R. (2017). Leisure, ethics, and spirituality. *Annals of Leisure Research, 20*(5), 546–562. https://doi.org/10.1080/11745398.2017.1295873

Dahl, A.L. (1996). *Spiritual dimensions of sustainable development.* Bahai Library Online.

Dany, F. (2003). Free actors' and organizations: Critical remarks about the new career literature, based on French insights. *International Journal of Human Resource Management, 14*(5), 821–838. https://doi.org/10.1080/0958519032000080820

Davidson, J. C., & Caddell, D. P. (1994). Religion and the meaning of work. *Journal of the Scientific Study of Religion, 33*(2), 135–147. https://doi.org/10.2307/1386600

Dent, E. B., Higgins, M. E., & Wharff, D. M. (2005). Spirituality and leadership: An empirical review of definitions, distinctions, and embedded assumptions. *The Leadership Quarterly, 16*(5), 625–653. https://doi.org/10.1016/j.leaqua.2005.07.002

Dhiman, S. K. (2016). Ethics and spirituality of sustainability: What can we all do? *The Journal of Values-Based Leadership, 9(1),* 11. https://scholar.valpo.edu/jvbl/vol9/iss1/

Dhiman, S. (2017). *Holistic leadership: A new paradigm for today's leaders.* Palgrave Macmillan.

Dierendonck, D., & Mohan, K. (2006). Some thoughts on spirituality and eudaimonic well-being. *Mental Health, Religion & Culture, 9*(3), 227–238. https://doi.org/10.1080/13694670600615383

Dittmar, J. & Sturm, T. (2010). *Mapping the end of times: American evangelical geopolitic and apocalyptic visions.* Ashgate.

Dobrow, S. R. (2004). *Extreme subjective career success: A new integrated view of having a calling.* Academy of Management Conference Best Paper Proceedings.

Dries, N. (2011). The meaning of career success: Avoiding reification through a closer inspection of historical, cultural, and ideological contexts. *Career Development International, 16*(4), 364–384. https://doi.org/10.1108/13620431111158788

Dua, J. K., & Swinden, M. L. (1992). Effectiveness of negative-thought-reduction, meditation, and placebo training treatment in reducing anger. *Scandinavian Journal of Psychology, 33*, 135–146. https://doi.org/10.1111/j.1467-9450.1992.tb00893.x

Duchon, D., & Plowman, D. A. (2005). Nurturing the spirit at work: Impact on work unit performance. *The Leadership Quarterly, 16*, 807–833. https://doi.org/10.1016/j.leaqua.2005.07.008

Duffy, R. D. (2006). Spirituality, religion, and career development: Current status and future directions. *The Career Development Quarterly, 55*(1), 52–63. https://doi.org/10.1002/j.2161-0045.2006.tb00004.x

Duffy, R. D., & Blustein, D. L. (2005). The relationship between spirituality, religiousness, and career adaptability. *Journal of Vocational Behavior, 67*, 429–440. https://doi.org/10.1016/j.jvb.2004.09.003

Dunn, E. W., Aknin, L. B., & Norton, M. I. (2008). Spending money on others promotes happiness. *Science, 319*(5870), 1687–1688. https://doi.org/10.1126/science.1150952

Edginton, C. N., & Kangas, K. E. (2014). World heritage sites as sacred places. *International Leisure Review, 3*(1), 53–74. https://doi.org/10.6298/ILR.2014.3.3

Emerich, M. M. (2011). *The gospel of sustainability: Media, market and LOHAS*. University of Illinois Press.

Emmons, R. A. (2000a). Is spirituality an intelligence? Motivation, cognition, and the psychology of ultimate concern. *The International Journal for the Psychology of Religion, 10*, 3–26. https://doi.org/10.1207/S15327582IJPR1001_2

Emmons, R. A. (2000b). Spirituality and intelligence: Problems and prospects. *The International Journal for the Psychology of Religion, 10*, 57–64. https://doi.org/10.1207/S15327582IJPR1001_6

Formosa, A., & Baldacchino, D. (2010). The impact of spiritual care on nurses. In D. Baldacchino (Ed.), *Spiritual care: Being in doing* (pp. 73–88). Preca Library.

Gardner, H. (1983). *Frames of mind: The theory of multiple intelligences*. Basic Books.

Geigle, D. (2012). Workplace spirituality empirical research: A literature review. *Business and Management Review*, *2*(10), 14–27. http://www.businessjournalz.org/bmr

Göçen, A., & Özğan, H. (2018). Spirituality and ethics: A literature review. *Gaziantep University Journal of Social Sciences, 17*, 58–65. https://doi.org/10.21547/jss.452152

Grant, D., O'Neil, K., & Stephens, L. (2004). Spirituality in the workplace: New empirical directions in the study of the sacred. *Sociology of Religion, 65*, 265–283. https://doi.org/10.2307/3712252

Greene, H. F. (2013). The Ethics and Spirituality Initiative in connection with the United Nations sustainable development process. *Tattva-Journal of Philosophy, 5(1)*, 1–35. https://doi.org/10.12726/tjp.9.1

Greenway, K. A. (2006). The role of spirituality in purpose in life and academic engagement. *Journal of College and Character, 7*(6), 1–5. https://doi.org/10.2202/1940-1639.1212

Guillory, WA. (1997). *The living organization – Spirituality in the workplace*. Salt Lake City, UT: Innovations International.

Hanh, T. N. (1976). *Miracle of mindfulness*. Beacon.

Hall, D. T., & Chandler, D. E. (2005). Psychological success: When the career is a calling. *Journal of Organizational Behavior, 26*(2), 155–176. https://doi.org/10.1002/job.301

Harman, W. (1992). 21st century business: A background for dialogue. In J. Renesch (Ed.), *New tradition in business: Spirit and leadership in the 21st century* (pp. 11–24). Berrett- Koehler.

Hayes, S. C. (2004). Acceptance and commitment therapy, relational frame theory, and the third wave of behavioral and cognitive therapies. *Behavior Therapy, 35*, 639–665. https://doi.org/10.1016/j.beth.2016.11.006

Heelas, P. & Woodhead, L. with Seel, B., Szerszynski, B. & Tusting, K. (2005). *The spiritual revolution: Why religion is giving way to spirituality.* Basil Blackwell.

Heintzman, P. (2009). Nature-based recreation and spirituality: A complex relationship. *Leisure Sciences, 32*(1), 72–89. https://doi.org/10.1080/01490400903430897

Helminski, K. (2007). Spiritual perception and the root of the root of religion. *UNESCO International Rumi Symposium.* Istanbul, Turkey.

Hicks, D. A. (2002). Spiritual and religious diversity in the workplace: Implications for leadership. *The Leadership Quarterly, 13*(4), 379–396. https://doi.org/10.1016/S1048-9843(02)00124-8

Hill, A. (2011). *Paranormal media: Audiences, spirits and magic in popular culture*. Routledge.

Hill, P. C., Pargament, K. I., Hood, R. W., McCullough, M. E., Jr., Swyers, J. P., Larson, D. B., & Zinnbauer, B. J. (2000). Conceptualizing religion and spirituality: Points of commonality, points of departure. *Journal for the Theory of Social Behaviour, 30*(1), 51–77. https://doi.org/10.1111/1468-5914.00119

Hill, P. C., & Smith, G. S. (2010). Coming to terms with spirituality and religion in the workplace. In R. A. Giacalone & C. L. Jurkiewicz (Eds.), *Handbook of workplace spirituality and organizational performance* (pp. 171–184). M.E. Sharpe Inc.

Holloway, J. (2003). Make believe: Spiritual practice, embodiment and sacred space. *Environment and Planning A: Economy & Space, 35*(11), 1961–1974. https://doi.org/10.1068/a3586

Holloway, J. (2012). The space that faith makes: Towards a (hopeful) ethos of engagement. In *Religion and place: Landscape, politics and piety.* (pp. 203–218). Dordrecht: Springer Netherlands.

Holthaus, G. (2012). *Learning Native wisdom: What traditional cultures teach us about subsistence, sustainability, and spirituality*. University Press of Kentucky.

Hood, R. W., Spilka, B., Hunsberger, B. & Gorsuch, R. (1996). *The psychology of religion: An empirical approach*. Guilford Press.
Hotchkiss, L., & Borrow, H. (1990). Sociological perspectives on work and career. In D. Brown & L. Brooks (Eds.), *Career choice and development: Applying contemporary theories to practice* (2nd ed., pp. 137–68). Jossey-Bass.
Hülsheger, U. R., Alberts, H. J. E. M., Feinholdt, A., & Lang, J. W. B. (2013). Benefits of mindfulness at work: The role of mindfulness in emotion regulation, emotional exhaustion, and job satisfaction. *Journal of Applied Psychology, 98*(2), 310–325. https://doi.org/10.1037/a0031313
Inglehart, R. F. (2008). Changing values among Western publics from 1970 to 2006. *West European Politics, 31*(1–2), 130–146. https://doi.org/10.1080/01402380701834747
Inoue, S. (1997), *Putting Buddhism to work: A new approach to management and business*. Kodansha International Ltd.
Jantos, M., & Kiat, H. (2007). Prayer as medicine: How much have we learned? *Medical Journal of Australia, 186*(10), S51–S53. https://www.mja.com.au
Jung, C.G. (1934–1954). *The archetypes and the collective unconscious* (in 1981 2nd ed. Collected works Vol.9 Part 1). Bollingen.
Jung, C.G. (1954). The development of personality. In G. Adler & R. F. C. Hull (Ed. & Trans.), *Collected works of C. G. Jung: Vol. 17. Development of personality* (pp. 165–186). Princeton University Press.
Kalafatoğlu, Y. (2022). Workplace spirituality for more sustainable organizations. In *Handbook of research on integrating spirituality in modern workplaces* (pp. 80–95). IGI Global.
Katz, J. A. (1992). A psychological cognitive model of employment status choice. *Entrepreneurship Theory and Practice, 17*(1), 29–37. https://doi.org/10.1177/104225879201700104
Kauanui, S. K., Thomas, K. D., Sherman, C. L., Waters, G. R., & Gilea, M. (2008). Exploring entrepreneurship through the lens of spirituality. *Journal of Management, Spirituality & Religion, 5*(2), 160–189. https://doi.org/10.1080/14766080809518698
King, D.B. (2008). *Rethinking claims of spiritual intelligence: A definition, model, & measure* [Unpublished master's thesis]. Trent University.
King, D. B., & DeCicco, T. L. (2009). A viable model and self-report measure of spiritual intelligence. *International Journal of Transpersonal Studies, 28*(1), 68–85. https://doi.org/10.24972/ijts.2009.28.1.68

King, S., Ashley-Cotleur, C., & Solomon, G. (2003). Parental and gender influence on entrepreneurs intentions, motivation, and attitudes. In *Proceedings for the Unites States Association for Small Business and Entrepreneurship Conference*.

King-Kauanui, S., Thomas, K. D., & Waters, G. R. (2005). Entrepreneurship and spirituality: Integration of spirituality into the workplace. *Journal of Management, Spirituality & Religion, 2*(2), 255–274. https://doi.org/10.1080/14766080509518582

King-Kauanui, S., Thomas, K. D., Sherman, C. L., Ross Waters, G., & Gilea, M. (2010). An exploration of entrepreneurship and play. *Journal of Organizational Change Management, 23*(1), 51–70. https://doi.org/10.1108/09534811011017207

Kinjerski, V., & Skrypnek, B. J. (2004). Defining spirit at work: Finding common ground. *Journal of Organizational Change Management, 17*(1), 26–42. https://doi.org/10.1108/09534810410511288

Konkoly, T. B., Pilling, J., Szekely, A., & Kopp, M. S. (2013). Relationship between religiosity and health: Evidence from a post-communist country. *International Journal of Behavioral Medicine, 20*(4), 477–486. https://doi.org/10.1007/s12529-012-9258-x

Kumari, N. (2014). Spirituality at work place: A macroscopic shift from business to ethics. *Abhinav National Monthly Refereed Journal of Research in Commerce & Management, 3*(12), 1–5. https://doi.org/10.1.1.1011.9217

Leider, R.J. (1997). *The power of purpose: Creating meaning in your life and work.* Berrett-Koehler.

Levin, J. S. (2001). *God, faith, and health: Exploring the spirituality–healing connection.* John Wiley and Sons.

Levin, J. S., Chatters, L. M., Ellison, C. G., & Taylor, R. J. (1996). Religious involvement, health outcomes, and public health practice. *Current Issues in Public Health, 2*, 220–225. https://doi.org/10.1046/j.1525-1497.2003.21031.x

Lips-Wiersma, M. (2002). Analysing the career concerns of spiritually oriented people: Lessons for contemporary organizations. *Career Development International, 7*(7), 385–397. https://doi.org/10.1108/13620430210449911

Lowery, C. M., Duesing, R. J., & Beadles, N. A. (2014). A research note on the relationships among spirituality, contextual variables, and perceptions of ethics in the workplace. *Journal of Managerial Issues, 26*(4), 408–423. https://www.jstor.org/stable/44113662

Lucas, K., Liu, M., & Buzzanell, P. M. (2006). No limits careers: A critical examination of career discourse in the U.S. and China. In M. Orbe, B. J.

Allen & L. A. Flores (Eds.), *International and intercultural communication annual* (Vol. 28, pp. 217–242). Sage.
Lutz, A., Brefczynski-Lewis, J., Johnstone, T., & Davidson, R. J. (2008). Regulation of the neural circuitry of emotion by compassion meditation: Effects of meditative expertise. *PLoS ONE, 3*, 1–10. https://doi.org/10.1371/journal.pone.0001897
MacDonald, R., Kreutz, G., & Mitchell, L. (2012). What is music, health, and wellbeing and why is it important. In R. MacDonald, G. Kreutz, & L. Mitchell (Eds.), *Music, health and wellbeing* (pp. 3–11). Oxford University Press.
MacKian, S. (2012). *Everyday spiritualities: Social and spatial worlds of enchantment*. Palgrave Macmillan.
Marques, J., Dhiman, S., & King, R. (2005). Spirituality in the workplace: Developing an integral model and a comprehensive definition. *The Journal of American Academy of Business, 7*(1), 81–91. https://www.researchgate.net
Marx, K., & Engels, F. (1967 [1844]). *The Communist manifesto*. Penguin.
Mayer, J. D. (2000). Spiritual intelligence or spiritual consciousness? *The International Journal for the Psychology of Religion, 10*, 47–56. https://doi.org/10.1207/S15327582IJPR1001_5
Meraviglia, M. G. (2004). The effects of spirituality on well-being of people with lung cancer. *Oncology Nursing Forum, 31*(1), 89–94. https://doi.org/10.1188/04.ONF.89-94
Miller, W. R., & Thoresen, C. E. (2003). Spirituality, religion, and health: An emerging research field. *American Psychologist, 58*(1), 24. https://doi.org/10.1037/0003-066X.58.1.24
Miller-Tiedeman, A. (1994). The lifecareer process theory: A healthier choice. In D. P. Bloch & L. J. Richmond (Eds.), *Connections between spirit and work in career development* (pp. 87–113). Davies-Black.
Mohan, K. (2001). Spirituality and well-being: Overview. In C. Mattijs (Ed.), *Integral psychology* (pp. 203–226). Sri Aurobindo Asharam Press.
Moore, T. (1992). *Care of the soul: A guide for cultivating depth and sacredness in everyday life*. Harper Collins.
Morris, M., & Schindehutte, M. (2005). Entrepreneurial values and the ethnic enterprise: An examination of six subcultures. *Journal of Small Business Management, 43*(4), 453–479. https://doi.org/10.1111/j.1540-627X.2005.00147.x
Mueller, P. S., Plevak, D. J., & Rummans, T. A. (2001, December). Religious involvement, spirituality, and medicine: Implications for clinical practice.

Mayo Clinic Proceedings, 76(12), 1225–1235. https://doi.org/10.4065/76.12.1225

Myers, D. G. (2000). *The American paradox: Spiritual hunger in an age of plenty.* Yale University Press.

Noble, K. D. (2000). Spiritual intelligence: A new frame of mind. *Spirituality and Giftedness, 9,* 1–29. http://www.gifteddevelopment.com

Nwankwo, S., Gbadamosi, A., & Ojo, S. (2012). Religion, spirituality and entrepreneurship: The church as entrepreneurial space among British Africans. *Society and Business Review, 7*(2), 149–167. https://doi.org/10.1108/17465681211237619

O'Brien, K. M. (1996). The influence of psychological separation and parental attachment of the career development of adolescent women. *Journal of Vocational Behavior, 48,* 257–274. https://doi.org/10.1006/jvbe.1996.0024

Paloutzian, P. F., & Park, C. L. (Eds.). (2013). *Handbook of the psychology of religion and spirituality* (2nd ed., pp. 357–379). Guilford Press.

Pardini, D. A., Plante, T. G., Sherman, A., & Stump, J. E. (2000). Religious faith and spirituality in substance abuse recovery: Determining the mental health benefits. *Journal of Substance Abuse Treatment, 19*(4), 347–354. https://doi.org/10.1016/S0740-5472(00)00125-2

Pargament, K. I., Mahoney, A., & Shafranske, E. (Eds.). (2013). *APA handbook of psychology, religion, and spirituality* (Vol. II). American Psychological Association. https://doi.org/10.1037/14046-000

Peselow E., Pi, S., Lopez E, Besada, A., & Ishak, W. W. (2014). The impact of spirituality before and after treatment of major depressive disorder. *Innovations in Clinical Neuroscience, 11*(3–4): 17–23. https://www.ncbi.nlm.nih.gov

Pettersson, T. (2003). *The relations between religion and politics in the contemporary Western world: The impact of secularization, postmodernization and peoples' basic value orientations.* http://www.worldvaluessurvey.org

Pillai, R. (2016). The complementary role of science, spirituality and ethics for a new world order-The golden age. *Nitte Management Review, 10(1),* 1–19. https://doi.org/10.17493/NMR%2F2016%2F105511

Reuter, T. A. (2015). The green revolution in the world's religions: Indonesian examples in international comparison. *Religions, 6*(4), 1217–1231. https://doi.org/10.3390/rel6041217

Rodriguez-Rad, C. J., & Ramos-Hidalgo, E. (2018). Spirituality, consumer ethics, and sustainability: The mediating role of moral identity. *Journal of Consumer Marketing, 35*(1), 51–63. https://doi.org/10.1108/JCM-12-2016-2035

Roof, W.C. (1993). *A generation of seekers: The spiritual journeys of the baby boom generation.* Harper.

Ross, L., Van Leeuwen, R., Baldacchino, D., Giske, T., McSherry, W., Narayanasamy, A., Downes, C., Jarvis, P., & Schep-Akkerman, A. (2014). Student nurses' perceptions of spirituality and competence in delivering spiritual care: A European pilot study. *Nurse Education Today, 34*, 697–702. https://doi.org/10.1016/j.nedt.2013.09.014

Ross, L., Giske, T., Van Leeuwen, R., Baldacchino, D., McSherry, W., Narayanasamy, A., Jarvis, P., & Schep-Akkerman, A. (2015). Factors contributing to student nurses'/midwives' perceived competency in spiritual care. *Nurse Education Today, 36*, 445–451. https://doi.org/10.1016/j.nedt.2015.10.005

Rowatt, W. C., & Kirkpatrick, L. A. (2002). Two dimensions of attachment to God and their relation to affect, religiosity, and personality constructs. *Journal for the Scientific Study of Religion, 41*, 637–651. https://doi.org/10.1111/1468-5906.00143

Royce-Davis, J., & Stewart, M. (2000). *Addressing the relationship between career development and spirituality when working with college students.* University of the Pacific. Retrieved from ERIC Database (ED452444).

Schultheiss, D. E. P., Palma, T. V., Predragovich, K. S., & Glasscock, J. M. J. (2002). Relational influences on career paths: Siblings in context. *Journal of Counseling Psychology, 49*, 302–310. https://doi.org/10.1037/0022-0167.49.3.302

Schumacher, E. F. (2003). Buddhist economics. *Parabola, 16*(1), 63–69. http://buddhism.lib.ntu.edu.tw/FULLTEXT/JR-ADM/schumaa.htm

Segal, Z. V., Williams, J. M. G., & Teasdale, J. D. (2002). *Mindfulness-based cognitive therapy for depression: A new approach to preventing relapse.* The Guilford Press.

Segal, Z. V., Williams, J. M. G., Teasdale, J. D., & Kabat-Zinn, J. (2007). *The mindful way through depression.* The Guilford Press.

Senge, P.M. (1990). *The fifth discipline: The art and practice of the learning organization.* Doubleday/Currency.

Shapiro, D. H. (1992). Adverse effects of meditation: A preliminary investigation of long-term meditators. *International Journal of Psychosomatics, 39*, 62–67. http://deanehshapirojr.org

Sheldrake, P. (1992). *Spirituality and history: Questions of interpretation and method*. Crossroads.

Sherman, A. C., Plante, T. G., Simonton, S., Latif, U., & Anaissie, E. J. (2009). Prospective study of religious coping among patients undergoing autologous stem cell transplantation. *Journal of Behavioral Medicine, 32*(1), 118–128. https://doi.org/10.1007/s10865-008-9179-y

Sim, T. K., & Loh, B. S. M. (2003). Attachment to God: Measurement and dynamics. *Journal of Social and Personal Relationships, 20*, 373–389. https://doi.org/10.1177/0265407503020003006

Spilka, B. (1993, August). *Spirituality: Problems and directions in operationalizing a fuzzy concept*. Paper presented at the American Psychological Association annual conference, Toronto, Canada.

Spilka, B. & McIntosh, D.N. (1996, August). *Religion and spirituality: The known and the unknown*. Paper presented at the American Psychological Association annual conference, Toronto, Canada.

Spintge, R., & Droh, R. (1992). *Music and medicine*. MMB.

Stead, J. G., & Stead, W. E. (2014). Building spiritual capabilities to sustain sustainability-based competitive advantages. *Journal of Management, Spirituality & Religion, 11*(2), 143–158. https://doi.org/10.1080/14766086.2013.832359

Sulmasy, D. P. (2013). Ethos, mythos, and thanatos: Spirituality and ethics at the end of life. *Journal of Pain and Symptom Management, 46*(3), 447–451. https://doi.org/10.1016/j.jpainsymman.2013.03.016

Tarakeshwar, N., Vanderwerker, L. C., Paulk, E., Pearce, M. J., Kasl, S. V., & Prigerson, H. G. (2006). Religious coping is associated with the quality of life of patients with advanced cancer. *Journal of Palliative Medicine, 9*(3), 646–657. https://doi.org/10.1089/jpm.2006.9.646

Targowski, A. (2012). Spirituality 2.0—A condition for a wise civilization. *Dialogue and Universalism, 22*(2), 133–143. https://www.researchgate.net

Thompson, W. (2001). Spirituality at work: People want to work in a spirited place. *Executive Excellence, 18*(9), 10. https://www.worldcat.org/title/executive-excellence/oclc/67041208

Thrift, N. (1997). The rise of soft capitalism. *Cultural Values, 1*(1), 29–57. https://doi.org/10.1080/14797589709367133

Tietjen, S. (2013). *It's not just a nursing career, It's a calling*. http://www.nursingworldnigeria.com/2013/02/it-rsquo-s-not-just-a-nursing-career-it-rsquo-s-a-calling

Turner, R. P., Lukoff, D., Barnhouse, R. T. & Lu, F. G. (1995). Religious or spiritual problem: A culturally sensitive diagnostic category in the DSM-IV. *Journal of Nervous and Mental Disease, 183*, 435–44. https://www.researchgate.net

Twenge, J. M., Sherman, R. A., Exline, J. J., & Grubbs, J. B. (2016). Declines in American adults' religious participation and beliefs, 1972–2014. *SAGE Open, 6*(1), 2158244016638133.

Van Buren, H. J. (2003). Boundaryless careers and employability obligations. *Business Ethics Quarterly, 13*(2), 131–149. https://doi.org/10.5840/beq20031329

Van Leeuwen, R., Tiesinga, L., Post, D., & Jochemsen, H. (2006). Spiritual care: Implications for nurses' professional responsibility. *Journal of Clinical Nursing, 15*, 875–884. https://doi.org/10.1111/j.1365-2702.2006.01615.x

Vaughan, F. (2002). What is spiritual intelligence? *Journal of Humanistic Psychology, 42*(2), 16–33. https://doi.org/10.1177/0022167802422003

Verter, B. (2003). Spiritual capital: Theorizing religion with Bourdieu against Bourdieu. *Sociological Theory, 21*(2), 150–174. https://doi.org/10.1111/1467-9558.00182

Vitell, S. J., King, R. A., Howie, K., Toti, J. F., Albert, L., Hidalgo, E. R., & Yacout, O. (2016). Spirituality, moral identity, and consumer ethics: A multi-cultural study. *Journal of Business Ethics, 139*(1), 147–160. https://doi.org/10.1007/s10551-015-2626-0

Walker, S. (2013). Design and spirituality: Material culture for a wisdom economy. *Design Issues, 29*(3), 89–107. https://doi.org/10.1162/DESI_a_00223

Watson, J. (1999). *Theory of human caring*. http://watsoncaringscience.org/images/features/library/THEORY%20OF%20HUMAN%20CARING_Website.pdf

Weber, M (1992 [1958]). *The Protestant ethic and the spirit of capitalism*. Routledge.

Weiss, J. W., Skelley, M. F., Haughey, J. C., & Hall, D. T. (2003). Calling, new careers and spirituality: A reflective perspective for organizational leaders and professionals. In Spiritual intelligence at work: Meaning, metaphor, and morals. *Research in Ethical Issues in Organizations, 5*, 175–201. Elsevier.

WHOQOL SRPB Group. (2006). A cross-cultural study of spirituality, religion, and personal beliefs as components of quality of life. *Social Science & Medicine, 62*, 1486–1497. https://doi.org/10.1016/j.socscimed.2005.08.001

Wilber, K. (2000). *Integral psychology: Consciousness, spirit, psychology, therapy*. Shambhala.

Wilford, J. (2010). Sacred archipelagos: Geographies of secularization. *Progress in Human Geography, 43*(3), 328–348. https://doi.org/10.1177/0309132509348558

Witmer, J. M., & Sweeney, T. J. (1992). A holistic model for wellness and prevention over the life span. *Journal of Counseling & Development, 71*, 140–148. https://doi.org/10.1002/j.1556-6676.1992.tb02189.x

Wood, J. L., & Hilton, A. A. (2012). Spirituality and academic success: Perceptions of African American males in the community college. *Religion & Education, 39*(1), 28–47. https://doi.org/10.1080/15507394.2012.648576

Wrzesniewski, A., McCauley, C., Rozin, P., & Schwartz, C. (1997). Jobs, careers and callings: People's relations to their work. *Journal of Research in Personality, 31*(1), 21–33. https://doi.org/10.1006/jrpe.1997.2162

Zinnbauer, B. J., Pargament, K. I., Cole, B., Rye, M. S., Butter, E. M., Belavich, T. G., Hipp, K. M., Scott, A. B., & Kadar, J. L. (1997). Religion and spirituality: Unfuzzying the fuzzy. *Journal for the Scientific Study of Religion, 36*, 549–564. https://doi.org/10.2307/1387689

Zohar, D., & Marshall, I. (2000). *Spiritual intelligence: The ultimate intelligence.* Bloomsbury Publishing.

Zsolnai, L. (2010). Ethics needs spirituality. In S. S. Nandram & M. E. Borden (Eds.), *Spirituality and business* (pp. 87–90). Springer.

3

Workplace and Organizational Spirituality

3.1 Introduction

The exponential growth in interest in workplace spirituality is influenced by many factors including contemporary post-materialist workers seeking meaning and purpose at work as alternatives to, or in addition to wealth accumulation as the primary function of work. The focus of this chapter is to expand upon the spirituality discussion by introducing and examining the concept of workplace spirituality, including the definition, theoretical framework, and literature summary of workplace spirituality. The framework will be broad, interdisciplinary, and non-religious in nature.

In this chapter, the scholarly literature on workplace spirituality is summarized, beginning with the development of definition, measurement methods, theory, and framework, followed by the establishment of a valid construct, and research on the effects and consequences of workplace spirituality. The relationship between workplace spirituality and religion is also examined. The role of ethics in workplace spirituality will be examined. The servant, authentic, spiritual, and values leadership

C. G. Beehner, *Spirituality, Sustainability, and Success*, Palgrave Studies in Workplace Spirituality and Fulfillment, https://doi.org/10.1007/978-3-031-47643-3_3

styles and models will be examined within the context of workplace spirituality. The chapter concludes with examination of spiritual leadership, and spiritual capital within the context of workplace spirituality.

While non-scholarly sources such as Wikipedia suggest workplace spirituality emerged as a grassroots movement in the 1920s, scholarly reference to workplace spirituality does not appear until the 1990s (Soder, 2016), influenced by the introduction of servant leadership (Greenleaf, 1991). Because early workplace spirituality research lacked a universally accepted definition (Gotsis & Kortezi, 2008), the focus of initial research was on the development of definition, measurement methods, theory, and framework (Geigle, 2012). The objective of subsequent research was the establishment of a valid construct, followed by research on the effects and consequences of workplace spirituality (Gotsis & Kortezi, 2008). Workplace spirituality research has grown significantly (Houghton et al., 2016), with the number of scholarly workplace spirituality articles increasing nearly fivefold in the 1999–2008 period compared with the 1989–1998 period (Geigle, 2012; Oswick, 2009). The increased interest in workplace spirituality is apparent with the launch of the *Journal of Management, Spirituality and Religion* in 2004, specifically targeting research in this emerging area of organization and management studies (Case & Gosling, 2010). The premise of much of the earlier workplace spirituality research was that workers are on a spiritual journey and are seeking integration between their work lives and spiritual lives (Fry, 2003).

Robbins and Judge (2010) suggested several reasons for increasd interest in spirituality at work: (a) increasing numbers of people are disappointed with religious institutions, and are seeking spirituality in alternative institutions; (b) contemporary lifestyles have created a desire for community and connection at work; (c) while job demands have transformed the workplace into a dominant institution in many people's lives, many workers question the meaning and purpose of work; (d) an increasing inclination for the integration of personal and spiritual values within career; and (e) an increasing number of people seek an alternative to the pursuit of material rewards. However, despite workplace spirituality having been a research topic for nearly three decades, it is still considered a fad by some management scholars and practitioners (Robbins & Judge, 2010).

3.2 Workplace Spirituality Definition and Framework

The lack of a commonly accepted definition of workplace spirituality made early conceptualization and measurement of the construct difficult (Avolio et al., 2009). While no universally accepted definition of workplace spirituality exists (Gotsis & Kortezi, 2008), similarities exist among the more prominent definitions. Researchers theorized that contemporary post-materialist workers were seeking meaning and purpose at work as alternatives to, or in addition to wealth accumulation as the primary function of work (DeGraaf & Evans, 1996). Mitroff and Denton (1999) defined workplace spirituality as individual effort to find purpose in life, foster strong supervisor and coworker connections, and achieve alignment between individual and organizational values. Giacalone and Jurkiewicz (2010) defined workplace spirituality as a culture in which organizational values encourage sense of purpose through meaningful work taking place within the context of the workplace community, further suggesting workplace spirituality can occur at the individual, group, or organizational level. Bell and Taylor (2001) suggested workplace spirituality would be best founded on the principle of individuals "being" spiritual instead of organizations "having" or possessing spirituality.

Pfeffer (2010) identified the four fundamental dimensions of what employees seek in a spiritual workplace as: (1) interesting and meaningful work that inspires learning and development; (2) meaningful work providing a sense of purpose; (3) a sense of connection and positive relationships with coworkers; and (4) the ability to live an integrated life, in which work and non-work roles are in harmony with who the person is as a human being. This overlaps the three dimensions Ashmos and Duchon (2000) used to conceptualize workplace spirituality: community, meaning at work, and the recognition of an inner life. The following themes (which are related to the topics of this text) emerge from examination of the various definitions and conceptualizations of workplace spirituality: meaningful work that serves a higher purpose, the development of a sense of vocational calling, a focus on global well-being, and an awareness of the need to protect, save, and enhance the planet's resources and inhabitants (Al-Qutop & Harrim, 2014). Three distinct personal aspects of workplace spirituality climate have been identified: intrapersonal, interpersonal, and suprapersonal (Nooralizad et al., 2011). Intrapersonal describes an individual having personal spiritual motivations and seeking involvement in life-enhancing activities. Interpersonal describes individuals collectively seeking connection and community with others. Suprapersonal describes the desire to connect with someone or something superior to oneself.

In the contemporary world of dynamic change, countless perceive a loss of meaning and purpose in their lives, precipitating a feeling of spiritual despair (King & Nicol, 1999). Although the workplace is fundamental to individual survival, the workplace frequently increases despair, inhibits individual growth (King & Nicol, 1999), and neglects the spiritual and emotional dimensions of human need (Barrett, 2009). Laloux (2014) further echoed the notion that the workplace has evolved into an organization without a soul. However, because the workplace spirituality framework suggests a definition of success in terms of non-materialist characteristics (Ashar & Lane-Maher, 2004), several scholars have suggested the application of workplace spirituality might be incompatible with materialistic organizational benefits such as increased productivity or profitability (Gibbons, 2000; Lund Dean et al., 2003).

Because early workplace spirituality research was lacking a solid theoretical base, researchers recommended an interdisciplinary approach, integrating workplace spirituality research with research in psychology, sociology, management, and theology (Giacalone & Jurkiewicz, 2010; Liu & Robertson, 2011; Pawar, 2009). Sheep (2006) supported this proposition by suggesting workplace spirituality research contains a multi-paradigm approach to avoid the preferential treatment of one research interest over another. Workplace spirituality has been theorized to be an element of organizational culture, having a significant impact on team effectiveness, and fostered by creativity, respect, and trust (Daniel, 2010).

Workplace spirituality has been described as a macro-level glimpse of the spiritual climate of an organization, manifest within the organization's culture (Shinde et al., 2010). A spiritual workplace is characterized by an employee-friendly work environment that recognizes, supports, and nurtures the spirit of employees (Chatterjee & Naqvi, 2010), with work units characterized by a high level of workplace spirituality are ones where employees are aligned with the organizational climate (Case & Gosling, 2010). Workplace spirituality has been described as a trait, as a flexible state of being (Liu & Robertson, 2011), and as a state that is subjective in nature (Kinjerski & Skrypnek, 2004). While workplace spirituality occurs at both the individual and organizational levels (Chatterjee & Naqvi, 2010; Garcia-Zamor, 2003), the majority of workplace spirituality research has been performed at the organizational level (Kinjerski & Skrypnek, 2004). At the macro-level, workplace spirituality describes the organizational climate as perceived by individuals within the organizational setting (Kolodinsky et al., 2008). Despite considerable research demonstrating the organizational benefits of workplace spirituality, Barrett (2009) suggests the construct may only provide a partial solution to organizational problems and may not be able to be completely assimilated into organizations in which employees are cohesively aligned with the organizational mission, vision, and values (Barrett, 2009).

To understand the relevance of workplace spirituality, it is necessary to understand the relationship between individual spiritual behavior and organizational spiritual behavior (Lopez et al., 2009). Perhaps Dhiman (2017) best differentiates workplace spirituality from individual spirituality: "Spirituality helps us to discover the deeper transcendental meaning in our work, while workplace spirituality helps us find meaning at work" (p. 182). An individual embracing secular spirituality might have a different perspective of spiritual intervention by the organization than an individual embracing religious or mystical spirituality (Lopez et al., 2009). Although spirituality is considered a personal issue, definitions of *workplace spirituality* expand this issue toward seeking spiritual connections at work, by augmenting deeper values and wholeness (Gibbons, 2015).

Workplace spirituality has been examined in many industries, including information technology, sales, manufacturing, banking, food service, and health care. It would seem intuitive that workplace spirituality might be more readily manifest in a profession such as health care, wherein the primary function of workers is the personal well-being of others. In the healthcare field, workplace spirituality incorporates individual efforts to find meaning and purpose in life; maintenance of healthy relationships with multidisciplinary team members, patients, relatives, and other stakeholders; and, preservation of conformity between inner beliefs and organizational values (Neal, 2013). In the workplace, work provides value when one believes a contribution and difference are being made, and a connection is being made to others and to a greater cause, resulting from the pursuit of a common purpose (Baldacchino, 2017).

Any examination of workplace spirituality must include the viewpoint that employees have spiritual needs, in addition to physical, emotional, and mental needs (Duchon & Plowman, 2005). For some individuals, these spiritual needs are also religious needs (Torskenes et al., 2013). Living in community as spiritual beings demands the need to connect with or belong to a corresponding group, further generating a connectedness to one another through awareness of each other's need, compassion to restore and maintain relationships, and a supportive attitude toward others. Individuals may demonstrate workplace spirituality if they perceive a significant alignment of personal values to the organizational mission and purpose. This alignment triggers acceptance of the importance of work as a contribution to others or society based upon recognition that workplace purpose is greater than individual needs or wants (Baldacchino, 2017).

Earlier in this chapter, community, meaning at work, and the recognition of an inner life were identified as common workplace spirituality dimensions (Ashmos & Duchon, 2000). Sense of community in the workplace necessitates a kinship with others that promotes interactive cooperation among colleagues (Baldacchino, 2017). This connectedness is understood to be a deep relationship whereby employees consider and perceive relationships to be occurring at emotional, mental, and spiritual levels between the inner selves of members of the organization (Baldacchino, 2017). Therefore, the quintessence of community is based on a deeper sense of connection among people, including support, freedom of expression, and authentic caring. This connectedness suggests a state of team spirit in which employees accept membership in a larger organizational community, caring for each other as teammates, and likewise caring for customers, patients, and stakeholders (Arnold et al., 2005; Baldacchino, 2017).

Meaning is the individual sense that life is worth living (Ingersoll, 2003), and meaning at work answers one of the questions new employees ask in an organizational setting: "Why am I here?" (Ashforth, 2001). Meaning at work describes the personal feeling that the hours of life exchanged for wages serve a purpose beyond subsistence and existence (Ingersoll, 2003). Saks (2011) described the importance of workplace spirituality for meaningfulness at work and employee engagement, classifying four psychological conditions of engagement as meaningfulness in work, meaningfulness at work, safety, and availability (Saks, 2011). Moreover, meaningful work has been demonstrated to increase employee satisfaction and organizational commitment, important for conditions for organizational success (Word, 2012).

Workplace spirituality is premised on the recognition that workers have an inner, spiritual life not existing separate from the physical body that participates in the workplace. Workplace spirituality is not about living an isolated, inner spiritual life as a mystic, but rather about acknowledging that individuals have both inner and outer lives, and that nurturing the inner life leads to a more productive outer life (Ashmos & Duchon, 2000). Caring for the whole person begins with organizations recognizing individuals have an inner life accessed through spiritual practices such as meditation, self-reflection, and prayer (Bell & Taylor, 2001).

Workplace spirituality has been demonstrated to be beneficial to organizations and members. Positive relationships have been demonstrated between workplace spirituality and job satisfaction (Altaf & Awan, 2011; Chatterjee & Naqvi, 2010; Chawla & Guda, 2010; Giacalone &

Jurkiewicz, 2010; Gupta et al., 2013; Pawar, 2009; Usman & Danish, 2010), job involvement (Chatterjee & Naqvi, 2010; Kolodinsky et al., 2008; Word, 2012), organizational commitment (Affeldt & MacDonald, 2010; Fry & Slocum, 2008; Marschke et al., 2009; Pawar, 2009; Rego & Pina e Cunha, 2008), productivity (Valasek, 2009), and organizational identification. Negative relationships have been demonstrated between workplace spirituality and organizational frustration (Kolodinsky et al., 2008), employee turnover and turnover intention (Chawla & Guda, 2010; Crawford et al., 2009; Giacalone & Jurkiewicz, 2010; Hong, 2012; Milliman et al., 2003; Riasudeen & Prabavathy, 2011), and absenteeism (Giacalone & Jurkiewicz, 2010; Krahnke et al., 2003). The organizational benefits of workplace spirituality will be examined further in Chapter 10.

There are several limitations to the study of workplace spirituality. First, the lack of a universally endorsed definition of workplace spirituality, which makes scientific measurement of associations and relationship among workplace spirituality and other variables difficult (Gotsis & Kortezi, 2008). Because spirituality is frequently associated with religion (Astin & Astin, 1999), many workplace spirituality research study findings have been dependent upon the definition of spirituality used by the researcher, and the subsequent interpretation of that definition by study participants (Wills, 2009). A second, related limitation is that some researchers have examined workplace spirituality within the context of their respective religious or philosophical beliefs, while others have done so absent any religious mindset (Dent et al., 2005; Fernando & Jackson, 2006; Gotsis & Kortezi, 2008; Hicks, 2003).

The spiritual realm appears to offer superior capacity for meeting contemporary business challenges (Thaker, 2009). Leading corporations recognize this capacity and are transitioning from neo-liberalist to more humane perspectives, and in doing so enhance global quality of life. Initiatives such as corporate social responsibility, sustainability, and workplace spirituality reflect the contemporary trend to overcome the negative side effects of neoliberalism, by synthesizing ethics, values, and global concerns with organizational culture. While this will assist in consciousness raising, and life improvement of organizational members, and those with whom they come in contact, spirituality offers a deeper, more holistic means of improving our deficiencies (Thaker, 2009).

Thaker (2009) proposes Righteous Knowledge Management, as a redefinition of traditional knowledge management, as a means of improving the lives of all stakeholders, by shifting focus from tactical and business knowledge to internal knowledge, in tune with the inner, spiritual voice. Righteous Knowledge Management provides an intrinsic method for business leaders to take responsibility for the organization and the overall ecosystem. Spiritual knowledge leads to superior decision-making, better interpersonal relationships, and organizational culture, resulting in vibrant and sustainable businesses (Thaker, 2009).

While workplace spirituality has been proven beneficial and has been embraced by academia and practitioners alike, three areas of contention have been identified within the literature. First, based upon the ambiguity of existing definitions and frameworks, workplace spirituality may inadvertently abolish any distinction between employee workplace and personal lives (Tourish & Tourish, 2010). The workplace spirituality environment could also encourage employees and management to promote personal spiritual beliefs to proselytize coworkers and supervisors (Lips-Wiersma et al., 2009; Milliman et al., 2003).

The second area of contention concerns the potential for management abuse by utilizing workplace spirituality to maximize productivity through manipulation (Lips-Wiersma et al., 2009; Milliman et al., 2003). Case and Gosling (2010) further argue if spirituality becomes incorporated in the business agenda, it may become so engrained in the organizational structure and dynamics that management comes to expect the alignment of employee personal beliefs and values with those of the organization. Further, employees within a workplace spirituality environment may become so inner-focused that they do not recognize management manipulation and exploitation (Polley et al., 2005), or may even accept management instrumentality as appropriate, or even desirable managerial behavior (Long & Mills, 2010). Accordingly, Hayden and Barbuto (2011) caution any effort to implement workplace spirituality should be non-ideological in nature. Finally, an organization endorsing workplace spirituality may become so close-knit that decisions become biased by groupthink (Polley et al., 2005), a process in which group pressure encourages individuals to conform to the opinions and ideas of the team (Robbins & Coulter, 2012).

Some researchers suggest the recent surge in workplace spirituality research is a result of a paradigm shift from individual neo-liberalist self-interest to the more holistic approach of conscious capitalism, in which all stakeholders' concerns are recognized (Thaker, 2009). However, other researchers challenge the validity of a workplace spirituality paradigm, conceptualizing it as an alternative method of achieving desirable outcomes which cannot qualify as a paradigm, unless those outcome results can be differentiated from those achieved by other means (Grzeda & Assogbavi, 2011), such as transformational, servant, or environmental leadership (Crossman, 2010). Braud (2009) theorized workplace spirituality research should advance beyond qualitative and quantitative research into transpersonal inquiry, whereby the researcher explores the topic experientially.

3.3 Workplace Spirituality and Religion

Workplace spirituality has been examined in both secular (Fry, 2003; Giacalone & Jurkiewicz, 2010; Sheep, 2006), and religious contexts (Fernando & Jackson, 2006; Zafar, 2010), with several studies having explored religion and religiosity concurrent with workplace spirituality (Dent et al., 2005; Fernando & Jackson, 2006). Some researchers suggest the exclusion of religion in most workplace spirituality research is a weakness, noting that the assumption that the workplace is secular may not be correct (Hicks, 2003). Proponents of including religion in workplace spirituality research argue that the study of a topic that encourages bringing the "whole person" to work but excludes the diverse religious customs and perspectives of employees is inconsistent (Hicks, 2003). However, researchers have challenged the applicability of workplace spirituality with non-religious or atheist subjects, especially within the fields of science (Ecklund & Long, 2011). In response, researchers have identified a group within the scientific community capable of spiritual expression without religious orientation (Ecklund & Long, 2011). The unique characteristic of this group is the capacity to find spirituality in science, suggesting the possibility of "spiritual atheism", or a spiritual model without God (Ecklund & Long, 2011). This perspective is persistent with the discussion in Chapter 2 about being spiritual without being religious, and vice versa (Dent et al., 2005).

Although most previous workplace spirituality research avoided the subject of religion (Hicks, 2003), workplace spirituality has been examined within Christian (Lynn et al., 2007) and Buddhist (Petchsawanga & Duchon, 2009) contexts. However, workplace spirituality research still does not adequately address diverse religious traditions (Miller & Ewest, 2013). Researchers including religion in workplace spirituality research did so because prior research examined the function of belief, while ignoring the substance of belief (Lynn et al., 2007). Subsequent research with the Judeo-Christian inspired Faith at Work Scale demonstrated a positive relationship between the integration of faith at work and employee job performance, job satisfaction, and organizational commitment, and a negative relationship with turnover intention (Walker, 2013). However, early workplace spirituality proponents found the introduction of spirituality to the organizational development process to be challenging in organizations predominantly influenced by conservative Christian values (Barrett, 2009).

Liu and Robertson (2011) developed a measurement tool both incorporating and transcending religion, making the tool relevant across multiple religions and denominations (Liu & Robertson, 2011). A theoretical approach to workplace spirituality was proposed in which spirituality was measured by interconnectedness with a higher power, human beings, and nature and all living things (Liu & Robertson, 2011). Other researchers have recommended the necessity for classification of survey respondent spirituality as secular, mystical, or religious (Lopez et al., 2009).

Petchsawanga and Duchon (2009) developed a four-factor workplace spirituality model measuring compassion, meaningful work, mindfulness, and transcendence within a non-Judeo-Christian context. Connection was initially introduced as a fifth factor; however, the researchers eliminated the questions related to the construct due to weak factor loadings and poor fit, due to the lack of familiarity with the term "connection" within the Thai language (Petchsawanga & Duchon, 2009).

An Eastern definition of workplace spirituality was proposed to accommodate non-Judeo-Christian participants: "having compassion toward others, experiencing mindful inner consciousness in the pursuit of meaningful work and that enables transcendence" (Petchsawanga & Duchon, 2009, p. 465).

3.4 The Spiritually-Driven Organization (SDO)

A spirituality-driven organization (SDO) describes one that possesses a culture, processes, and capabilities that develop and facilitate personal and organizational spiritual growth by transcending from being self-centered to we-centered or world-centered (Yin & Mahrous, 2022). While SDOs appear to have much in common with purpose-driven organizations (PDOs), they are significantly different in their organizational goals, business models, organizational structure, and governance (Yin & Mahrous, 2022). Although the primary goal of a PDO is profit maximization, the primary goal of an SDO is maximization of spiritual growth of both the organization and members. PDOs are a compassionate version of the self-centered corporations of the industrial era, while SDOs are an enlightened version of corporations with entirely different purposes (Yin & Mahrous, 2022).

SDOs are members of extended networks of stakeholder organizations sharing similar missions, strategies, and resources. An SDO-based community operates like a symbiotic or cooperative organization in which members are thoroughly interdependent and cultivate the growth of all members based upon common objectives (Yin & Mahrous, 2022). SDOs emphasize the development of one's true nature, or what Wilber (2000) called the "original face" and promote collective exploration of the underlying layers of reality and consciousness (Yin & Mahrous, 2022). Spiritual leadership is demonstrated at both collective and individual levels with decision-making authority and capabilities based upon spiritual intelligence. Leadership is rotational and distributed with a focus on guidance and mentoring instead of self-admiration, chain of command, and control (Yin & Mahrous, 2022). An SDO must maintain a culture, procedures, and capabilities that promote and accelerate individual and organizational spiritual growth by transcending self-centeredness. SDOs that achieve significant individual and organizational transformation possess the following characteristics (six Cs): common mission, compassion, community, connectedness, collaboration, and co-evolution (Yin & Mahrous, 2022).

In the post-digital era (which is discussed further in Chapter 5), SDOs will be a considerable economic driving force, because this new era will be defined by a completely new form of economic culture (Yin & Mahrous, 2022). In this new era, industry structures, operating philosophies, corporate business models, and processes will be unlike those of the previous era. Because the post-digital era will be influenced by the increasingly dominating metaverse, one essential objective of SDOs will be providing meaning and purpose for this deeply engaging and addictive experience. In this new era, industry and society will transform from "a 'closeness and control' model to a 'connection and collaboration' model where the rules and regulations governing individual and corporate behavior will be replaced by spiritual principles that center on shared mission, growth, prosperity, and destiny" (Yin & Mahrous, 2022, p. 86).

Although organizations cannot survive and thrive solely on workplace spirituality (Yin & Mahrous, 2022), organizations lead by spiritual leaders will possess a clear advantage in the future. Several leadership styles and models are supportive of developing workplace spirituality and leading SDOs. These include, but are not limited to servant, authentic, spiritual, and ethical leadership. These leadership styles and models will be explored in the following sections.

3.5 Servant Leadership

Servant leadership was introduced by Greenleaf in 1970, although individuals have been demonstrating servant leadership for millennia. Servant leadership places serving the needs of others first, drawing upon the notion that individuals seek to serve others first, which subsequently inspires a desire for others to lead. The litmus test of successful servant leadership is whether followers grow as individuals, becoming healthier, wiser, more autonomous, and ultimately become servant leaders (Greenleaf, 1977). Servant leaders encourage organizational stewardship and recognize the importance of organizational sustainability (Taylor & Pearse, 2009). Servant leadership can occur anywhere, and impact anyone (Graham, 1998).

Servant leadership emerges from a broad radical vision (McCann & Holt, 2010), with servant leaders transforming organizations, developing new perspectives, inspiring new ideas and innovations, and accomplishing everything through *being* rather than *doing* (Zohar, 1997). Servant leaders understand that no individual in an organization is insignificant (Zohar, 1997). An innate relationship between servant leadership and strategic management seems apparent, with the viewpoints of key organizational leaders significantly influencing organizational values, culture, and ethical practices (Taylor & Pearse, 2009).

Servant leadership may contribute to successful organizational change (van Dierendonck & Sousa, 2016) because leaders play an essential role in creating a purposeful, harmonious work environment, which is essential for meaningful change. This meaningful work environment is created by encouraging self-connection, unification, contribution, and individuation (van Dierendonck & Sousa, 2016). Servant leaders reinforce meaning and purpose by combining personal attention and the ability to suggest that change is a higher purpose that transcends the organization. Servant leadership improves affective trust, organizational citizenship behaviors (OCBs), and task performance of followers (Saleem et al., 2020). Affective trust is the fundamental mechanism to translate servant leadership into positive individual performance (Saleem et al., 2020). A positive and significant relationship exists between servant leadership and subordinate's in-role and extra-role work performance (Gašková, 2020). Servant leadership may enable employers to accommodate the workplace expectations of millennials and Gen Z by "creating value for the community" which aligns with their belief that "business leaders take responsibility for societal needs" (Gašková, 2020, p. 24).

Although Greenleaf did not visualize servant leadership as a means to transform or impact society, one of the logical consequences of servant leadership is societal impact, in which servant leaders create healthier organizations that benefit society through positive social change (Northouse, 2018). Servant leaders understand the importance of stakeholders outside of the organization or community. This is especially significant for business, because "chasing profits is peripheral; the real point of business is to serve as one of the institutions through which society develops and exercises the capacity for constructive action" (Harvey, 2001; pp. 38–39). Servant leadership is relevant for achieving sustainability in organizations (Taylor & Pearse, 2009) and society (Beehner, 2020), because contemporary organizations need servant and sustainable leadership to succeed in a global economy (McCann & Holt, 2010).

3.6 Authentic Leadership

Authentic leadership has emerged as an important area of research in the field of organizational behavior in the past decade (Farid et al., 2020). Authentic leadership does not have a commonly accepted definition (Alomar et al., 2022). However, the concept has received considerable attention in recent academic literature (Northouse, 2018), and several interpretations have been offered by leading scholars, who are becoming interested in this emerging field (Alomar et al., 2022). The concept of authentic leadership was first introduced by George (2003), who predicted the rapid rise of theoretical and practical interest in leadership. George (2003) developed an authentic leadership model consisting of five dimensions: seeking purpose with passion; practicing strong values; leading with the heart; establishing lasting relationships; and, possessing self-discipline. The basis of authentic leadership is the authenticity or genuineness of the leader. Authentic leaders are characterized by a pattern of behavior inspired by their positive psychological qualities and ethics (Walumbwa et al., 2008).

Authentic leadership is frequently set in motion by a critical life event (Northouse, 2018), and includes four dimensions: self-awareness, an internalized moral compass, rational processing, and relational transparency (Ashbihani, 2013; Northouse, 2018). Self-awareness requires the leader to understand their strengths and weaknesses and how they are perceived by others. Others perceive themselves. The internalized moral compass guides the leader's focus toward achieving high moral and ethical standards and actions. Rational or balanced processing describes the ability to analyze information and data objectively and accurately before making decisions. Relational transparency describes the transparent sharing of information and expressing one's genuine feelings to mitigate inappropriate emotions (Ashbihani, 2013).

The authentic leadership is beneficial for organizations because their actions agree with their words, values, and beliefs. This congruence enhances open, honest relationships with followers and promotes work environments conducive to the free exchange of ideas and knowledge (Khan et al., 2019). Authentic leaders reinforce employees' emotional connection with their organizations, resulting in increased creativity and improved on-the-job performance (Duarte et al., 2021). According to Levy (2020), the relationship between authentic leadership and employee performance is a result of employees believing they can act more freely within their job boundaries. Authentic leaders influence employees' emotional attachment to their organization, thereby enhancing feelings of affective commitment in employees (Ribeiro et al., 2020).

Authentic leaders actively create desirable environments and encourage their followers to do the same (Alomar et al., 2022). The objectives of authentic leadership are developing the organization's moral direction, utilizing the employees' potential, creating basic self-awareness skills among employees, accepting responsibility for the mistakes or failures of others, and being genuine (Opatokun et al., 2013). Authenticity is the act of demonstrating character, ideas, deepest desires, emotions, and all-encompassing beliefs (Luthans & Avolio, 2003). When leaders demonstrate quality of character, they become authentic leaders, their followers respond favorably, and the organization and members prosper. Authentic leaders do not seek acceptance from followers or colleagues because they genuinely want what is best for the organization (Alomar et al., 2022). Authentic leaders direct their allegiance to the organization's mission instead of personal gains.

3.7 Spiritual Leadership

Spiritual leadership describes a leadership style consisting of the necessary values, attitudes, and behaviors to intrinsically motivate oneself and others, thereby creating a sense of spiritual survival through calling and membership (Fry, 2003). Spiritual leaders motivate and inspire workers through a transcendent vision and an organizational culture based on genuine care and concern. Spiritual leadership is essential for satisfying the spiritual well-being of leaders and followers through calling and membership, which is achieved through the creation of vision and value congruence across the organizational members, and fostering greater levels of employee well-being, organizational commitment, performance, productivity, and social responsibility (Fry, 2003; Fry & Nisiewicz, 2013; Fry & Slocum, 2008; Fry et al., 2005, 2010). The performative interest in channeling workplace spirituality and leadership is shared by Duchon and Plowman (2005) who view workplace spirituality as a unique psychological climate in which workers view themselves as having an inner life nourished by meaningful work, taking place in the context of a community (Case & Gosling, 2010). While workplace spirituality has been found to be dependent upon several conditions, inspiring leadership was identified as the most important condition for encouraging workplace spirituality (Kinjerski & Skrypnek, 2006). Spiritual leadership begins internally, because it is difficult to lead others unless we first learn to manage ourselves (Dhiman, 2017).

Spiritual Leadership Theory (SLT) was developed as a causal model consisting of a collection of individual and organizational variables which are argued to produce several positive individual and organizational outcomes (Fry, 2003, 2005, 2008; Fry et al., 2005). SLT encourages the adoption of new organizational models emphasizing leadership ethics, sustainability, and social responsibility "without sacrificing profitability, revenue growth, and other indicators of financial performance" (Fry, 2008, p. 110). According to Fry (2003), one SLT objective is to assist managers in facilitation of the triple bottom line of people, planet, and profit (Elkington, 1998). Fry (2008) offered a revised SLT causal model in which "inner life, or spiritual practice" (p. 111) is seen to positively influence, "(1) hope/faith in a transcendent vision of service to key stakeholders and (2) the values of altruistic love" (p. 112). Fry (2008) further suggests leaders who practice spiritual leadership draw on inner life practice and emulate hope, faith, a transcendent vision, and organizational values founded in altruistic love which embolden the manifestation of favorable individual and organizational outcomes (Case & Gosling, 2010). Fry and colleagues assert that practitioners of spiritual leadership will experience greater psychological and physical well-being (Case & Gosling, 2010; Fry, 2003). Managers embracing the spiritual leadership style are more effective managers (Fernando & Jackson 2006). Fry (2003) noted a positive relationship between spiritual leadership and productivity, further observing the integration of spiritual leadership leading to more positive changes in relationships and effectiveness (Case & Gosling, 2010). Spiritual leadership has a significant impact on affective commitment with workplace spirituality mediating the relationship between spiritual leadership and affective commitment (Astuti & Haryani, 2021). Affective commitment describes the perceived emotional attachment of an employee with their organization and occurs when an employee believes their personal values and priorities align with the organizational mission and they feel like they belong to the organization.

Dhiman (2017) developed a framework of holistic leadership based upon the premise that holistic leaders first discover their own divinity and then inspire others through their leadership. There are three types of leadership in holistic leadership: self, authentic, and legacy. Self-leadership is a preparatory phase consisting of self-motivation, self-mastery, and self-creativity. Authentic leadership comprises self-awareness informed by an inner moral perspective expressed as genuine, consistent thought, speech, and action. Legacy leadership involves the quest for meaning and fulfillment which culminates in the creation of a legacy for the leader. Dhiman asserts spiritual leadership is a vital expression of holistic leadership because spiritual leadership addresses all three dimensions of the holistic leadership framework: self, spirit, and service.

Workplace spirituality requires spiritual leadership (Yin & Mahrous, 2022). Workplace spirituality will remain an organizational taboo if leaders do not recognize their need to transcend and inspire members to seek higher meaning and purpose. Effective business leaders should take the opportunity to begin a personal spiritual journey to increase spiritual awareness and reduce excessive ego. This journey should stimulate passion, compassion, and empathy in that leader, which should further inspire everyone in the organization to imitate. For now, any advancement toward workplace spirituality implementation must follow a top-down approach driven by influential and inspiring leaders (Yin & Mahrous, 2022).

Organizational focus is increasingly shifting from a focus primarily on economic and social activities to a focus on spiritual development (Sapta et al., (2021). Contemporary leaders must learn to understand their employees' souls in addition to their physical and mental abilities. Workplace spirituality and spiritual leadership synergize to better align the vision and values of employees with organizational goals (Sapta et al. (2021). Although workplace spirituality can mediate the relationship between spiritual leadership and organizational commitment, a leadership style cannot be effectively applied if the work environment is not supportive (Sapta et al., 2021).

3.8 Ethical Leadership

The challenges of developing and maintaining a sustainable future for humankind are complex, complicated, and interconnected (Beehner, 2020). These challenges will present moral and ethical dilemmas requiring leaders with strong ethical foundations. Because these challenges transcend individuals, organizations, and nations, leading humankind to overcome these challenges requires a focus on all individuals and groups impacted by our decisions and actions. Laub (1999) recommended the need for a leadership style that is not "trendy and transient" (p. 7) but based on significant ethical and moral training, and focused on inspiring, leading, and behaving in a manner acceptable to followers (Beehner, 2020).

The ethical leadership style offers leaders a collection of principles used to inform decision-making (Northouse, 2018). Ethical leaders respect and serve others by placing the well-being of others above their own, make decisions based on equity and justice, are trustworthy, and are dedicated to building community (Northouse, 2018). Because leadership involves influencing others, leaders must demonstrate ethical responsibility for their followers. Ethical leaders use their authority to motivate individuals to overcome obstacles and change and personal growth (Heifetz, 1994).

Leaders are responsible for more than just ensuring that their behavior is ethical. Because leaders influence the decisions of other individuals and groups, they can significantly increase the amount of good that can be achieved by encouraging others to become better individuals and employees (Bazerman, 2020). Individuals often follow the behavior of others, especially when those individuals occupy positions of importance and influence. Employees working for ethical leaders can be expected to demonstrate ethical behavior. By setting the standard and example for ethical behavior, and empowering employees to follow and enforce those standards, ethical leaders can influence hundreds or even thousands of other individuals to behave more ethically (Bazerman, 2020).

3.9 Spiritual Capital

Just as organizations access, control, and manage various forms of capital—human, natural, financial, etc.—organizations also possess spiritual capital. In Chapter 2, we examined the three spiritual capital conditions of embodied, objectified, and institutionalized spiritual capital (Verter, 2003). Within the context of workplace spirituality, it is appropriate that we further consider the institutionalized state of spiritual capital. Spiritual capital is defined as the collection of values, ethical viewpoints, and visions for change held by both individuals and organizations. Spiritual capital is fashioned by traditions, systems, and engagement broadly defined relationships, and the sense of meaning and purpose derived from activities. The characteristics of spiritual capital include: belief in, and commitment to a higher moral order, manifested in commitment to values such as truth, self-knowledge, right action, and purpose in life; connection to extensive relationships in far-reaching communities where the individual feels like he or she "fits in"; and, a sense of meaning and purpose in work or vocation (Baker et al., 2011).

The definition and characteristics of spiritual capital clearly overlap with the construct of workplace spirituality, hence the relevance to the focus of this chapter.

Spiritual capital is frequently the source of motivation for other types of capital, such as social capital, emphasizing the importance of trust and norms as the foundation for participation in any beneficial human activity, as well as how beliefs inform values, where we fit within an organization, and our organizational behavior (Stokes et al., 2016). Spiritual capital may be acquired through the exchange of other forms of capital, including socialization, education, or other investment of temporal or financial capital (Verter, 2003). Likewise, because spiritual capital may be translated into other forms of capital, when strategically invested, spiritual capital may bring social and economic improvement (Verter, 2003). However, spiritual capital that is poorly invested may lead to social and economic failure. The advantage of spiritual capital over religious capital lies in the independent nature of the former. An individual may acquire spiritual capital in whatever form through the exchange of other forms of capital, independent of any religion or religious leader.

Recent research findings suggest businesses that are open to acknowledging expressions of both religious and secular spiritual capital positively influence business productivity (Stokes et al., 2016). The more opportunities for employees to express their innermost values, beliefs, and attitudes for positive change and well-being, the more authentically connected employees will feel to assigned roles. The managerial and organizational implications presented by the research include: managers and employees need to maintain and strengthen awareness of the inherent contribution of spiritual capital in the workplace, resisting the tendency to revert to traditional, human capital management methods which may no longer produce the desired organizational outcome. Recognizing and providing opportunities for spiritual capital development within the workplace may provide an avenue for facilitation of the application of other forms of capital within organizations (Stokes et al., 2016).

3.10 Discussion

There are four primary obstacles to the full support of implementing workplace spirituality: limited consensus on a definition; insufficient measurement tools; limited evidence supporting its practical utility; and, the lack of a theoretical foundation and understanding of relationships with key organizational variables (Yin & Mahrous, 2022). However, these obstacles should not prevent broad acceptance of workplace spirituality as an essential concept in organizational theories and management (Yin & Mahrous, 2022). Workplace spirituality must be established as an important concept to be able to attract the interest of prominent scholars who can resolve these obstacles.

Proponents of workplace spirituality believe it to be the beginning of a new paradigm and will develop into a core competitive advantage (Mitroff & Denton, 1999). This will be especially relevant for organizations in the post-digital era because collaboration, sharing, mutual development, and co-evolution will be the new norms of business operation. Industrial era organizations must evolve from traditional productivity or efficiency-driven models and activities to spirituality-driven ones. However, broad acceptance of this new paradigm by scholars and practitioners will depend on a mutual definition of workplace spirituality (Yin & Mahrous, 2022).

There are risks involved with incorporating spirituality into the workplace. Wadhwa and Pahwa (2018) identified the following three risks: religious conflicts, compatibility issues, and spirituality being used as a manipulative tool. Based upon the overall benefits, many organizations are already encouraging spirituality-focused well-being programs. However, this can occasionally produce religious conflicts among individuals. Individuals may also become discouraged and dissatisfied because they are uncomfortable expressing their personal ideologies or believe that their culture is being disrespected (Brown, 2003; Cavanagh, 1999; Krishnakumar & Neck, 2002; Milliman et al., 2003). Moreover, incorporating religion into spirituality programs may alienate, isolate, or intimidate both individuals and groups (Krishnakumar & Neck, 2002; Mirvis, 2017). There is also a risk that specific groups may command their own agenda (Cavanagh & Bandsuch, 2002). Religious feelings are very sensitive and can become disruptive and damaging without mutual respect for diversity (Krishnakumar & Neck, 2002), and can result in workplace conflict if not properly managed (Wadhwa & Pahwa, 2018).

Corporate culture contains materialist and competitive characteristics which may seem contradictory with spirituality (Wadhwa & Pahwa, 2018). Business success is very dependent on individual growth instead of universal camaraderie. Implementing workplace spirituality may annoy or aggravate professionals who seek to protect their authority and status quo. Some individuals may consider conversations about spiritual beliefs as personal and private. Workplace spirituality may cause some employees to feel intimidated and pressurized (Cavanagh, 1999; Mirvis, 2017), producing compatibility issues in the workplace, causing reduced employee performance and productivity (Wadhwa & Pahwa, 2018).

Workplace spirituality may become a fad or an instrument for management to manipulate employees (Wadhwa & Pahwa, 2018). The risk with this scenario is that spirituality loses its value and legitimacy if it is perceived as a marketing tool (Gibbons, 2000; Mirvis, 2017). Misuse will cause workplace spirituality programs to be short-lived, appear unauthentic (Cavanagh & Bandsuch, 2002; Mirvis, 2017), and adversely impact organizational productivity and performance (Wadhwa & Pahwa, 2018). Workplace spirituality programs and initiatives must be genuine and lead by spiritual leaders to overcome challenges and benefit individuals, organizations, industries, and societies.

3.11 Concluding Thoughts

Workplace spirituality can no longer be considered a passing fad in contemporary organizational behavior. Employees increasingly desire to bring their holistic selves to the workplace, embracing a higher spiritual purpose in their work and personal existence. Further, employers are seeking innovative ways to engage employees in the contemporary work environment. Workplace spirituality, initiated by spiritual leaders, will increase the spiritual capital of organizations, producing an organizational culture necessary to navigate the uncharted course of twenty-first-century business. Research and understanding of workplace spirituality has increased during the last few decades. Workplace spirituality offers a promising avenue for researchers and practitioners to enhance organizational performance in a dynamic, contemporary environment.

Employees are increasingly seeking meaning, purpose, community, and connection within the workplace. Likewise, employers are increasingly creating work environments conducive to holistic employee participation, wherein spiritual expression and attributes are allowed to exist concurrently with physical and mental exertion. Spiritual leadership benefits both leaders and followers and will be necessary to manage future organizations. Spiritual capital may be acquired through the exchange of other forms of capital, may be translated into other forms of capital, and when strategically invested, may bring social and economic improvement (Verter, 2003). The benefits of spirituality for individual success are significant and are further examined in Chapter 5. Likewise, the benefits of workplace spirituality for organizational success are significant and will be further examined in Chapter 10.

Reflection Questions

1. How can spirituality exist within an organization or institution that is not primarily religious or spiritual in nature?
2. How do you think referring to a workplace as being spiritual will affect the importance of the concept of spirituality?
3. Do you agree with some scholars and skeptics that workplace spirituality is a passing fad? Consider why or why not.
4. How prevalent will workplace spirituality become as contemporary societies in developed nations become more secular and less religious?
5. How prevalent will workplace spirituality become as highly religious societies in developing nations become more developed and global?

References

Affeldt, D. L., & MacDonald, D. A. (2010). The relationship of spirituality to work and organizational attitudes and behaviors in a sample of employees from a health care system. *Journal of Transpersonal Psychology, 42*(2), 192–208. https://www.atpweb.org

Alomar, A., Mydin, A., & Alaklabi, S. (2022). A review of authentic leadership and workplace spirituality y campus sustainability in educational institutions. *International Transaction Journal of Engineering, Management, y Applied Sciences y Technologies, 13*(2), 1–13. https://tuengr.com/V13/13A2O.pdf

Al-Qutop, M. A. Y., & Harrim, H. (2014). Spiritual organization: A path to organizational sustainable excellence. *International Business Research, 7*(8), 168. http://www.ccsenet.org

Altaf, A., & Awan, M. A. (2011). Moderating effect of workplace spirituality on the relationship of job overload and job satisfaction. *Journal of Business Ethics, 104*(1), 93–99. https://doi.org/10.1007/s10551-011-0891-0

Arnold, J., Silvester, J., Patterson, F., Robertson, I., Cooper, C., & Burnes, B. (2005). *Work psychology. Understanding human behaviour in the workplace* (4th ed.). Pearson Education.

Ashar, H., & Lane-Maher, M. (2004). Success and spirituality in the new business paradigm. *Journal of Management Inquiry, 13*(3), 249–260. https://doi.org/10.1177/1056493604268218

Ashbihani, M. R. Bin. (2013). *Amalan Kepimpinan Autentik Pengetua Dan Komitmen.* Universiti Teknologi Malaysia.

Ashforth, B. E. (2001). *Role transitions in organizational life: An identity-based perspective.* Erlbaum.

Ashmos, D. P., & Duchon, D. (2000). Spirituality at work: A conceptualization and measure. *Journal of Management Inquiry, 9*(2), 134–145. https://doi.org/10.1177/105649260092008

Astin, A., & Astin, H. (1999). *Meaning and spirituality in the lives of college faculty: A study of values, authenticity and stress.* University of California.

Astuti, R. J., & Haryani, S. P. (2021, January). Workplace spirituality as mediation of spiritual leadership to affective commitment. In *4th International Conference on Sustainable Innovation 2020-Accounting and Management* (ICoSIAMS 2020) (pp. 72–77). Atlantis Press. https://doi.org/10.2991/aer.k.210121.011

Avolio, B., Walumbwa, F., & Weber, T. J. (2009). Leadership: Current theories, research, and future directions. *Annual Review of Psychology, 60*, 421–449. https://doi.org/10.1146/annurev.psych.60.110707.163621

Baker, C., Stokes, P., Lichy, J., Atherton, J., & Moss, D. (2011). *Values, beliefs and attitudes in the era of late-capitalism: A consideration of the re-emergence and re-positioning of faith and spirituality as spiritual capital in the workplace.* https://www.academia.edu

Baldacchino, D. (2017). Spirituality in the Healthcare Workplace. *Religions, 8*(12), 260. https://doi.org/10.3390/rel8120260

Barrett, R. (2009). What's right and wrong with spirituality in the workplace? *Journal of Management, Spirituality & Religion, 6*(3), 261–268. https://doi.org/10.1080/14766080903069372

Bazerman, M. H. (2020). A new model for ethical leadership. Create more value for society. *Harvard Business Review*. https://hbr.org/2020/09/a-new-model-for-ethical-leadership

Beehner, C. G. (2020). Servant leadership as a pathway to a sustainable future. In S. Dhiman & J. Marques (Eds.), *New horizons in positive leadership and change: A practical guide for workplace transformation* (pp. 65–82). Springer Nature.

Bell, E., & Taylor, S. (2001). *A rumor of angels: Researching spirituality in organizations.* Paper presented to the Academy of Management conference, Washington, DC.

Braud, W. (2009). Dragons, spheres, and flashlights: Appropriate research approaches for studying workplace spirituality. *Journal of Management, Spirituality, & Religion, 6*(1), 59–74. https://doi.org/10.1080/14766080802648557

Brown, R. (2003). Organizational spirituality: The Sceptic's version. *Organization, 10*(2), 393–400. https://doi.org/10.1177/1350508403010002013

Case, P., & Gosling, J. (2010). The spiritual organization: Critical reflections on the instrumentality of workplace spirituality. *Journal of Management, Spirituality and Religion, 7*(4), 257–282. https://doi.org/10.1080/14766086.2010.524727

Cavanagh, G. (1999). Spirituality for managers: Context and critique. *Journal of Organizational Change Management, 12*(3), 186–199. https://doi.org/10.1108/09534819910273793

Cavanagh, G. F., & Bandsuch, M. R. (2002). Virtue as a benchmark for spirituality in business. *Journal of Business Ethics, 38*(1–2), 109–117. https://doi.org/10.1023/A:1015721029457

Chatterjee, A., & Naqvi, F. (2010). Spirituality in organizational life: An empirical study of spirituality and job attitudes. *Abhigyan, 28*(3), 18–29. http://www.freepatentsonline.com/article/Abhigyan/249137536.html

Chawla, V., & Guda, S. (2010). Individual spirituality at work and its relationship with job satisfaction, propensity to leave and job commitment: An exploratory study among sales professionals. *Journal of Human Values, 16*(2), 157–167. https://doi.org/10.1177/097168581001600203

Crawford, A., Hubbard, S. S., Lonis-Shumate, S. R., & O'Neill, M. (2009). Workplace spirituality and employee attitudes within the lodging environment. *Journal of Human Resources in Hospitality & Tourism, 8*, 64–81. https://doi.org/10.1080/15332840802274445

Crossman, J. (2010). Conceptualizing spiritual leadership in secular organizational contexts and its relation to transformational, servant and environmental leadership. *Leadership & Organizational Development Journal, 31*(7), 596–608. https://doi.org/10.1108/01437731011079646

Daniel, J. L. (2010). The effect of workplace spirituality on team effectiveness. *Journal of Management Development, 29*(5), 442–456. https://doi.org/10.1108/02621711011039213

De Graaf, N., & Evans, G. (1996). Why are the young more postmaterialist? A crossnational analysis of individual and contextual influences on postmaterial values. *Comparative Political Studies, 28*(4), 608–635. https://doi.org/10.1177/0010414096028004005

Dent, E. B., Higgins, M. E., & Wharff, D. M. (2005). Spirituality and leadership: An empirical review of definitions, distinctions, and embedded assumptions. *The Leadership Quarterly, 16*(5), 625–653. https://doi.org/10.1016/j.leaqua.2005.07.002

Dhiman, S. (2017). *Holistic leadership: A new paradigm for today's leaders*. Palgrave Macmillan.

Duarte, A. P., Ribeiro, N., Semedo, A. S., & Gomes, D. R. (2021). Authentic leadership and improved individual performance: Affective commitment and individual creativity's sequential mediation. *Frontiers in Psychology, 12*, e675749. https://doi.org/10.3389/fpsyg.2021.675749

Duchon, D., & Plowman, D. A. (2005). Nurturing the spirit at work: Impact on work unit performance. *The Leadership Quarterly, 16*, 807–833. https://doi.org/10.1016/j.leaqua.2005.07.008

Ecklund, E. H., & Long, E. (2011). Scientists and spirituality. *Sociology of Religion, 72*(3), 253–276. https://doi.org/10.1093/socrel/srr003

Elkington, J. (1998). *Cannibals with forks: The triple bottom line of 21st Century business*. New Society Publishers.

Farid, T., Iqbal, S., Khan, A., Ma, J., Khattak, A., & Ud Din, M. N. (2020). The impact of authentic leadership on organizational citizenship behaviors: The mediating role of affective-and cognitive-based trust. *Frontiers in Psychology, 11*(1975). https://doi.org/10.3389/fpsyg.2020.01975 https://doi.org/10.3389/fpsyg.2020.01975

Fernando, M., & Jackson, B. (2006). The influence of religion-based workplace spirituality on business leaders' decision-making: An inter-faith study. *Journal of Management & Organization, 12*(1), 23–43. https://doi.org/10.1017/S1833367200004144

Fry, L. W. (2003). Toward a theory of spiritual leadership. *The Leadership Quarterly, 14*(6), 693–729. https://doi.org/10.1016/j.leaqua.2003.09.001

Fry, L. W. (2005). Toward a theory of ethical and spiritual well-being, and corporate social responsibility through spiritual leadership. In R. Giacalone & C. Jurkiewicz (Eds.), *Positive psychology in business ethics and corporate responsibility* (pp. 47–83). Information Age Publishing.

Fry, L. W. (2008). Spiritual leadership: State-of-the-art and future directions for theory, research, and practice. In J. Biberman & L. Tishman, L. (Eds.), *Spirituality in business: Theory, practice, and future directions* (pp. 106–124). Palgrave.

Fry, L. W., Matherly, L. L., & Ouimet, J. R. (2010). The spiritual leadership balanced scorecard business model: The case of the Cordon Bleu-Tomasso Corporation. *Journal of Management, Spirituality, & Religion, 7*(4), 283–314.https://doi.org/10.1080/14766086.2010.524983

Fry, L., & Nisiewicz, N. (2013). *Maximizing the triple bottom line through spiritual leadership.* Stanford University Press.

Fry, L. W., & Slocum, J. W., Jr. (2008). Maximizing the triple bottom line through spiritual leadership. *Organizational Dynamics, 37*(1), 86–96. https://doi.org/10.1016/j.orgdyn.2007.11.004

Fry, L. W., Vitucci, S., & Cedillo, M. (2005). Spiritual leadership and army transformation: Theory, measurement, and establishing a baseline. *The Leadership Quarterly, 16*, 835–862. https://doi.org/10.1016/j.leaqua.2005.07.012

Garcia-Zamor, J. C. (2003). Workplace spirituality and organizational performance. *Public Administration Review, 63*(3), 355–363. https://doi.org/10.1111/1540-6210.00295

Gašková, J. (2020). Servant leadership and its relation to work performance. *Central European Business Review, 9*(3), 24–37. https://www.ceeol.com/search/article-detail?id=881348

Geigle, D. (2012). Workplace spirituality empirical research: A literature review. *Business and Management Review*, *2*(10), 14–27. https://www.se.edu

George, B. (2003). *Authentic leadership: Rediscovering the secrets to creating lasting value.* Wiley.

Giacalone, R. A., & Jurkiewicz, C. J. (2010). The science of workplace spirituality. In R. A. Giacalone & C. J. Jurkiewicz (Eds.), *Handbook of workplace spirituality and organizational performance* (2nd ed., pp. 3–26). M. E. Sharpe.

Gibbons, P. (2000). Spirituality at work: Definitions, measures, assumptions, and validity claims. In J. Biberman & M. Whitty (Eds.), *Work and spirit: A reader of new spiritual paradigms for organizations* (pp. 111–131). University of Scranton Press.

Gibbons, P. (2015). Spirituality at work: Definitions, measures, assumptions, and validity claims. In R. A. Giacalone & C. L. Jurkiewicz (Eds.), *Handbook of workplace spirituality and organizational performance.* Paper presented at the Academy of Management Meeting, Toronto, ON, Canada 6–10 August 2000. Routledge.

Gotsis, G., & Kortezi, Z. (2008). Philosophical foundations of workplace spirituality: A critical approach. *Journal of Business Ethics, 78*(4), 575–600. 10.1007/s10551-007-9369-5

Graham, J. (1998). Servant-leadership and enterprise strategy. In L. Spears (Ed.), *Insights on leadership: Service, stewardship, spirit, and servant-leadership* (pp. 145–156). Wiley.

Greenleaf, R. K. (1970). *The servant as leader.* The Robert K. Greenleaf Center.

Greenleaf, R. K. (1977). *Servant leadership: A journey into the nature of legitimate power and greatness.* Paulist Press.

Greenleaf, R. K. (1991). *The servant as leader*. The Robert K. Greenleaf Center (originally published in 1970 by Robert K. Greenleaf).

Grzeda, M., & Assogbavi, T. (2011). Spirituality in management education and development: Toward an authentic transformation. *Journal of American Academy of Business, Cambridge, 16*(2), 238–244. http://www.jaabc.com/jaabcv16n2preview.html

Gupta, M., Kumar, V., & Singh, M. (2013). Creating satisfied employees through workplace spirituality: A study of the private insurance sector in Punjab (India). *Journal of Business Ethics, 122*(1), 79–88. https://doi.org/10.1007/s10551-013-1756-5

Harvey, M. (2001). The hidden force: A critique of normative approaches to business leadership. *SAM Advanced Management Journal*, *66*(4), 36. http://go.galegroup.com

Hayden, R. W., & Barbuto Jr., J. E. (2011). Expanding a framework for a non-ideological conceptualization of spirituality in the workplace. *Journal of Behavioral & Applied Management, 12*(2), 142–155. https://www.proquest.com

Heifetz, R. (1994). *Leadership without easy answers*. Harvard University Press.

Hicks, D. A. (2003). *Religion and the workplace: Pluralism, spirituality, leadership*. Cambridge University Press.

Hong, Y. J. (2012). Identifying spirituality in workers: A strategy for retention of community health professionals. *Journal of Social Service Research, 38*(20), 175–186. https://doi.org/10.1080/01488376.2011.615275

Houghton, J. D., Neck, C. P., & Krishnakumar, S. (2016). The what, why, and how of spirituality in the workplace revisited: A 14-year update and extension. *Journal of Management, Spirituality & Religion, 13*(3), 177–205. https://doi.org/10.1080/14766086.2016.1185292

Ingersoll, R. E. (2003). Spiritual wellness in the workplace. In R. A. Giacalone & C. L. Jurkeiwicz (Eds.), *Handbook of workplace spirituality and organizational performance* (pp. 289–299). M.E. Sharpe.

Khan, A. M., Jantan, A. H. B., Salleh, L. B. M., Dato'Mansor, Z., Islam, M. A., & Hosen, S. (2019). The impact of transformational leadership effects on innovative work behavior by the moderating role of psychological empowerment. *Journal of Reviews of Global Economics, 8*, 925–938. https://doi.org/10.6000/1929-7092.2019.08.79

King, S., & Nicol, D. M. (1999). Organizational enhancement through recognition of individual spirituality: Reflections of Jaques and Jung. *Journal of Organizational Change Management, 12*(3), 234–243. https://doi.org/10.1108/09534819910274026

Kinjerski, V., & Skrypnek, B. J. (2004). Defining spirit at work: Finding common ground. *Journal of Organizational Change Management, 17*(1), 26–42. https://doi.org/10.1108/09534810410511288

Kinjerski, V., & Skrypnek, B. J. (2006). Creating organizational conditions that foster employee spirit at work. *Leadership & Organizational Development Journal, 27*(4), 280–295. https://doi.org/10.1108/01437730610666037

Kolodinsky, R. W., Giacalone, R. A., & Jurkiewicz, C. L. (2008). Workplace values and outcomes: Exploring personal, organizational, and interactive workplace spirituality. *Journal of Business Ethics, 81*(2), 465–480. https://doi.org/10.1007/s10551-007-9507-0

Krahnke, K., Giacalone, R. A., & Jurkiewicz, C. L. (2003). Point-counterpoint: Measuring workplace spirituality. *Journal of Organizational Change Management, 16*(4), 396–405. https://doi.org/10.1108/09534810310484154

Krishnakumar, S., & Neck, C. P. (2002). The "what", "why" and "how" of spirituality in the workplace. *Journal of Managerial Psychology, 17*(3), 153–164. https://doi.org/10.1108/02683940210423060

Laloux, F. (2014). *Reinventing organizations: A guide to creating organizations inspired by the next stage of human consciousness.* Nelson Parker.

Laub, J. (1999). *Assessing the servant organization: Development of the servant organizational assessment (SOLA) instrument.* (Unpublished doctoral dissertation). Florida Atlantic University, Boca Raton, FL.

Levy, L. (2020). *The relationship between authentic leadership in project managers and project success.* Ph.D. thesis. Minneapolis, MN: Walden University.

Lips-Wiersma, M., Dean, K. L., & Fornaciari, C. J. (2009). Theorizing the dark side of the workplace spirituality movement. *Journal of Management Inquiry, 18*(4), 288–300. https://doi.org/10.1177/1056492609339017

Liu, C. H., & Robertson, P. J. (2011). Spirituality in the workplace: Theory and measurement. *Journal of Management Inquiry, 20*(1), 35–50. https://doi.org/10.1177/1056492610374648

Long, B. S., & Mills, J. H. (2010). Workplace spirituality, contested meaning, and the culture of organization: A critical sense-making account. *Journal of Organizational Change Management, 23*(3), 325–341. https://doi.org/10.1108/09534811011049635

Lopez, L. H., Ramos, R. R., & Ramos, S. R. (2009). Spiritual behavior in the workplace as a topic for research. *Journal of Management, Spirituality & Religion, 6*(4), 273–285. https://doi.org/10.1080/14766080903290119

Lund Dean, K., Fornaciari, C. J., & McGee, J. (2003). Research in spirituality, religion, and work: Walking the line between relevance and legitimacy. *Journal of Organizational Change Management, 16*(4), 378–395. https://doi.org/10.1108/09534810310484145

Luthans, F., & Avolio, B. J. (2003). Authentic leadership development. In K. Cameron & J. Dutton (Eds.), *Positive organizational scholarship: Foundations of a new discipline* (pp. 241–258). Berrett-Koehler.

Lynn, M. L., Naughton, M. J., & VanderVeen, S. (2007). Faith at work scale (FWS): Justification, development, and validation of a measure of Judeo-Christian religion in the workplace. *Journal of Business Ethics, 85*(2), 227–243. https://doi.org/10.1007/s10551-008-9767.3

Marschke, E., Prezioni, R., & Harrington, W. (2009). Professionals and executives support a relationship between organizational commitment and spirituality in the workplace. *Journal of Business and Economics Research, 7*(8), 33–48. https://doi.org/10.19030/jber.v7i8.2320

McCann, J. T., & Holt, R. A. (2010). Servant and sustainable leadership: An analysis in the manufacturing environment. *International Journal of Management Practice, 4*(2), 134–148. https://doi.org/10.1504/IJMP.2010.033691

Miller, D. W., & Ewest, T. (2013). The present state of workplace spirituality: A literature review considering context, theory, and measurement/assessment. *Journal of Religious & Theological Information, 12*(1–2), 29–54. https://doi.org/10.1080/10477845.2013.800776

Milliman, J., Czaplewski, A. J., & Ferguson, J. (2003). Workplace spirituality and employee work attitudes: An exploratory empirical assessment. *Journal of Organizational Change Management, 16*(4), 426–447. https://doi.org/10.1108/09534810310484172

Mirvis, P. H. (2017). "Soul work" in organizations. In A. Hooper (Ed.), *Leadership perspectives* (pp. 477–490). Routledge.

Mitroff, I. I., & Denton, E. A. (1999). A study of spirituality in the workplace. *Sloan Management Review, 40*, 83–92. https://sloanreview.mit.edu

Neal, J. (2013). Faith and spirituality in the workplace: Emerging research and practice. In *Handbook of faith and spirituality in the workplace* (pp. 3–18). Springer.

Nooralizad, R., Ghorchian, N., & Jaafari, P. (2011). A causal model depicting the influence of spiritual leadership and some organizational and individual variables on workplace spirituality. *Advances in Management, 4*(5), 14–20. https://ideas.repec.org/a/mgn/journl/v4y2011i5a3.html

Northouse, P. G. (2018). *Leadership: Theory and practice* (8th ed.). Sage.

Opatokun, K. A., Hasim, C. N., & Hassan, S. S. S. (2013). Authentic leadership in higher learning institution: A case study of International Islamic University Malaysia (IIUM). *International Journal of Leadership Studies, 8*(1), 49–66. https://regentparents.regent.edu/acad/global/publications/ijls/new/vol8iss1/4opatokun.pdf

Oswick, C. (2009). Burgeoning workplace spirituality? A textual analysis of momentum and directions. *Journal of Management, Spirituality & Religion, 6*(1), 15–25. https://doi.org/10.1080/14766080802648615

Pawar, B. S. (2009). Individual spirituality, workplace spirituality and work attitudes: An empirical test of direct and interaction effects. *Leadership & Organization Development Journal, 30*(8), 759–777. https://doi.org/10.1108/01437730911003911

Petchsawanga, P., & Duchon, D. (2009). Measuring workplace spirituality in an Asian context. *Human Resource Development International, 12*(4), 459–468. https://doi.org/10.1080/13678860903135912

Pfeffer, J. (2010). Business and the spirit. In R. A. Giacalone & C. L. Jurkiewicz (Eds.), *Handbook of workplace spirituality and organizational performance* (2nd ed., pp. 27–43). M. E. Sharp.

Polley, D., Vora, J., & SubbaNarasimha, P. N. (2005). Paying the devil his due: Limits and liabilities of workplace spirituality. *International Journal of Organizational Analysis, 13*(1), 50–63. https://doi.org/10.1108/eb028997

Rego, A., & Pina e Cunha, M. (2008). Workplace spirituality and organizational commitment: An empirical study. *Journal of Organizational Change Management, 21*(1), 53-75. https://doi.org/10.1108/09534810810847039

Riasudeen, S., & Prabavathy, R. (2011). Relationship of workplace spirituality and work attitude in manufacturing organization. *Global Management Review, 5*(4), 29–37. http://web.a.ebscohost.com

Ribeiro, N., Duarte, A. P., Filipe, R., & Torres de Oliveira, R. (2020). How authentic leadership promotes individual creativity: The mediating role of affective commitment. *Journal of Leadership & Organizational Studies, 27*, 189–202. https://doi.org/10.1177/1548051819842796

Robbins, S. P., & Coulter, M. (2012). *Management* (12th ed.). Pearson Prentice-Hall.

Robbins, S. P., & Judge, T. A. (2010). *Organizational behavior* (14th ed.). Pearson Prentice-Hall.

Saks, A. M. (2011). Workplace spirituality and employee engagement. *Journal of Management, Spirituality & Religion, 8*(4), 317–340. https://doi.org/10.1080/14766086.2011.630170

Saleem, F., Zhang, Y. Z., Gopinath, C., & Adeel, A. (2020). Impact of servant leadership on performance: The mediating role of affective and cognitive trust. *Sage Open, 10*(1), e2158244019900562. https://doi.org/10.1177/2158244019900562

Sapta, I. K. S., Rustiarini, N. W., Kusuma, I. G. A. E. T., & Astakoni, I. M. P. (2021). Spiritual leadership and organizational commitment: The mediation role of workplace spirituality. *Cogent Business & Management, 8*(1), e1966865. https://doi.org/10.1080/23311975.2021.1966865

Sheep, M. L. (2006). Nurturing the whole person: The ethics of workplace spirituality in a society of organizations. *Journal of Business Ethics, 66*(4), 357–375. https://doi.org/10.1007/s10551-006-0014-5

Shinde, U. S., Shinde, J. S., & Lytle, L. (2010). The impact of organizational spirituality on employee outcomes. *International Journal of the Academic Business World, 4*(2), 123–130. https://s3.amazonaws.com

Soder, P. F. (2016). Workplace spirituality and employee work intentions: Examining the relationship and the mediating role of ethical leadership.

Electronic Theses and Dissertations. Paper 2569. https://doi.org/10.18297/etd/2569

Stokes, P., Baker, C., & Lichy, J. (2016). The role of embedded individual values, belief and attitudes and spiritual capital in shaping everyday post-secular organizational culture. *European Management Review, 13*(1), 37–51. https://doi.org/10.1111/emre.12065

Taylor, S., & Pearse, N. (2009). Creating sustainable organizations through servant leadership. *The International Journal of Interdisciplinary Social Sciences: Annual Review, 4*(4), 223–234. https://doi.org/10.18848/1833-1882/CGP/v04i04/52885.

Thaker, K. B. (2009). Approaches to implement spirituality in business. *Journal of Human Values, 15*(2), 185–198. https://doi.org/10.1177/097168581001500208

Torskenes, K. B., Baldacchino, D., Baldacchino, T., Borg, J., Falzon, M., & Kalfoss, M. (2013). Nurses' and informal caregivers' definition of spirituality from the Christian perspective: A comparative study between Malta and Norway. *Journal of Nursing Management, 23*, 39–53. https://doi.org/10.1111/jonm.12080

Tourish, D., & Tourish, N. (2010). Spirituality at work, and its implications for leadership and followership: A post-structuralist perspective. *Leadership, 6*(2), 207–224. https://doi.org/10.1177/1742715010363210

Usman, A., & Danish, R. Q. (2010). Spiritual consciousness in banking managers and its impact on job satisfaction. *International Business Research, 3*(2), 65–72. https://doi.org/10.5539/ibr.v3n2p65

Valasek, A. J. (2009). *Examining the relationships of spirituality and religiosity to individual productivity in the United States* (Doctoral dissertation, Northcentral University).

van Dierendonck, D., & Sousa, M. (2016). Finding meaning in highly uncertain situations: Servant leadership during change. In *Leadership lessons from compelling contexts* (pp. 403–424). Emerald Group.

Verter, B. (2003). Spiritual capital: Theorizing religion with Bourdieu against Bourdieu. *Sociological Theory, 21*(2), 150–174. https://doi.org/10.1111/1467-9558.00182

Wadhwa, S., & Pahwa, S. (2018). Spirituality at workplace: Is there a dark face too? *IMPACT: International Journal of Research in Humanities, Art s and Literature, 6*(9), 91–100. https://oaji.net/articles/2017/488-1538223616.pdf

Walumbwa, F. O., Avolio, B. J., Gardner, W. L., Wernsing, T. S., & Peterson, S. J. (2008). Authentic leadership: Development and validation of a theory-based measure. *Journal of Management, 34*(1), 89–126. https://doi.org/10.1177/0149206307308913

Walker, A. G. (2013). The relationship between the integration of faith and work with life and job outcomes. *Journal of Business Ethics, 112*(3), 453–461. https://doi.org/10.1007/s10551-012-1271-0

Wilber, K. (2000). *A theory of everything: An integral vision for business, politics, science, and spirituality.* Shambhala Publications.

Wills, E. (2009). Spirituality and subjective well-being: Evidences for a new domain in the personal well-being index. *Journal of Happiness Studies, 10*(1), 49–69. https://doi.org/10.1007/s10902-007-9061-6

Word, J. (2012). Engaging work as a calling: Examining the link between spirituality and job involvement. *Journal of Management, Spirituality & Religion, 9*(2), 147–166. https://doi.org/10.1080/14766086.2012.688622

Yin, E., & Mahrous, A. (2022). Covid-19 global pandemic, workplace spirituality and the rise of spirituality-driven organisations in the post-digital era. *Journal of Humanities and Applied Social Sciences, 4*(2), 79–93. https://doi.org/10.1108/JHASS-11-2021-0177

Zafar, J. (2010). Measuring religiosity and workplace spirituality in Pakistani: A case study of armed forces and university teachers. *Cross Cultural Communication, 6*(4), 93–100. http://cscanada.net

Zohar, D. (1997). *Rewiring the corporate brain: Using the new science to rethink how we structure and lead organizations.* Berrett-Koehler.

4

Indigenous Spirituality

4.1 Introduction

While contemporary society has been established on a foundation of human-made institutions and structures, most Indigenous cultures recognize the interconnectedness of nature and humankind, and that we cannot live and survive outside of nature. Indigenous spirituality is often characterized by a holistic, comprehensive way of living. Although spiritual beliefs vary among the millions of Indigenous cultures, commonalities exist between many of the dominant Indigenous cultures. Common Indigenous cultures and their respective spiritual beliefs and practices will be explored within the context of the role of spirituality in individual and collective success. The similarities and differences of these Indigenous cultures will be examined to develop a better understanding of their role and importance in achieving spirituality. The absence of a spiritual-secular binary in Indigenous cultures will add an important perspective to the discussion about spirituality.

I added this chapter to the second edition with the recognition that as a North American of European descent my ability to present and explain spirituality from any Indigenous perspective is limited. I am not a scholar on the topic of Indigenous spirituality, and as Grimes (1996) has

C. G. Beehner, *Spirituality, Sustainability, and Success*, Palgrave Studies in Workplace Spirituality and Fulfillment, https://doi.org/10.1007/978-3-031-47643-3_4

noted, there is frustration and skepticism that most institutions employ non-Native faculty to teach Indigenous topics. However, the content is relevant to the theme of this text and current discourse on spirituality and sustainability. I have researched this topic from a perspective of respect and humility, acknowledging my position as a colonial descendant and not an original inhabitant.

This chapter is not intended to be a comprehensive discourse on Indigenous spirituality. Entire texts exist on the topic with many texts focusing on one Indigenous society or concept. The intent is to provide a summary of spirituality from the most common Indigenous peoples to provide additional focus and perspective for the topic of this book. Every attempt has been made to be accurate and respectful when describing spirituality from an Indigenous context. While spirituality and sustainability are interrelated and often inseparable within most Indigenous societies, the primary focus of this chapter is with Indigenous spirituality. Indigenous sustainability will be examined separately in Chapter 8, although both topics will appear to some extent in both chapters.

4.2 Who Are Indigenous Peoples?

The term Indigenous is difficult to define (Wijsen & Marcos, 2010) but generally refers to descendants of the original inhabitants of a territory, especially one that was colonized by a now-dominant population of settlers. Although contemporary usage may have originated with the 1970s struggles of Native Americans in the United States and Canada (Moody, 1988; Smith, 1999), the term Indigenous may have originated in Europe where Sir Thomas Browne first used the term in 1646 to differentiate between the Native American inhabitants and the African slaves brought to America by Europeans who were not Indigenous or proper natives of *America* (Mathewson, 2004). According to the International Labour Organisation (1989):

> … Indigenous communities, peoples, and nations are those groups who have a continuous history that originates from earlier stages to the presence of the invasion and colonisation. Groups that develop in their

> territories or part of it and consider themselves different to other sectors of the society that are now dominant. These groups are today subaltern sectors, and they are decided to preserve, develop, and transmit to the future generations their ancestral territories and their ethnic identity. These characteristics are fundamental to their existential continuity as peoples, in relationship with their own cultural, social, institutional, and legal systems.

Estimates of the global Indigenous population range from more than 370 million people in 70 countries (United Nations Permanent Forum on Indigenous Issues, n.d.), to as high as 600 million (Muckle, 2012), representing approximately 5,000 Indigenous nations globally (LaDuke, 2005).

Indigenous peoples practice unique traditions, and retain social, cultural, economic, and political traits that differ from the dominant societies of their territories. Because of the extensive diversity of Indigenous peoples, no United Nations body has adopted an official definition of Indigenous, alternatively choosing to develop a modern interpretation of this term based on the following:

- Self-identification as Indigenous peoples at the individual level and accepted by the community as their member.
- Historical continuity with pre-colonial and/or pre-settler societies.
- Strong link to territories and surrounding natural resources.
- Distinct social, economic, or political systems.
- Distinct language, culture, and beliefs.
- Form non-dominant groups of society.
- Resolve to maintain and reproduce their ancestral environments and systems as distinctive peoples and communities (United Nations Permanent Forum on Indigenous Issues, n.d.).

The United Nations has determined the best approach is identifying instead of defining Indigenous peoples. Various terms are used to identify Indigenous peoples including tribes, first peoples, first nations, aboriginals, ethnic groups, *adivasi*, and *janajati*. In some instances, the idea of being described as "Indigenous" has negative implications and some

Indigenous people may desire to not reveal or define their origin. Those choices must be respected while simultaneously preventing discrimination against Indigenous peoples (United Nations Permanent Forum on Indigenous Issues, n.d.). In 2007, the UN issued the Declaration on the Rights of Indigenous Peoples (UNDRIP) to "guide member-state national policies to the collective rights of Indigenous peoples, including their rights to protect their cultures, identities, languages, ceremonies, and access to employment, health, education, and natural resources" (United Nations, 2007).

Indigenous peoples' lands have historically been appropriated by larger, primarily Western ethnic groups, who justified colonization with attitudes of racial and religious superiority, economic expansion, and natural resource consumption (Miller et al., 2010). In the Americas, Australia, and New Zealand, Indigenous status is often easily applied to peoples whose ancestors occupied the land prior to European settlement. However, in Asia and Africa, Indigenous status has been rejected by certain peoples, or applied to minorities or oppressed peoples, who may not otherwise be considered Indigenous (McIntosh, 2000).

4.3 Indigenous Culture

The term First Nations is often used to describe Indigenous peoples because they were the inhabitants of a region prior to the arrival of Western settlers and colonizers. However, not all Indigenous peoples maintain their traditional cultures, with many having adopted considerable attributes of the colonizing culture, including dress, religion, or language. Indigenous peoples possess unique languages, knowledge, and beliefs, including valuable methods of sustainable natural resource management. The Indigenous philosophical worldview is multigenerational, deep, and spatial and is created and perpetuated through shared narratives (Herman, 2015). Their ancestral land is essential for their collective physical and cultural survival (United Nations Permanent Forum on Indigenous Issues, n.d.).

Indigenous peoples share common challenges with other disadvantaged segments of societies, such as "lack of political representation and participation, economic marginalization and poverty, lack of access to social services and discrimination" (United Nations Permanent Forum on Indigenous Issues, n.d.). Despite cultural differences, all Indigenous peoples experience similar obstacles regarding protection of rights, and recognition of their identities, lifestyles, and right to traditional land and natural resources (United Nations Permanent Forum on Indigenous Issues, n.d.). In this chapter, Indigenous cultures will be explored within the context of Indigenous spirituality.

4.4 Indigenous Spirituality

Indigenous spiritualities are defined by Wijsen and Marcos (2010) as "*the spiritualities of the Indigenous peoples* or *pre-missionary and pre-colonial spiritualities*" (p. 13). The essence of the term Indigenous is often related to "integral", "cosmic" or "holistic" (Wijsen & Marcos, 2010). Indigenous spiritualities can be dissimilar from the world religions but can also exist or coexist within the world religions (Wijsen & Marcos, 2010). Indigenous peoples regard the principles associated with spiritually to not be spiritual but simply the way to live a balanced life. Indigenous spirituality symbolizes the sacred awareness of being significantly interconnected with everything in the universe, both visible and invisible (Jacobs, 2014). This interconnectedness provides for survival, peace, health, and happiness, and has done so for thousands of (Jacobs, 2014). Indigenous knowledge and spiritual traditions are highly interconnected and provide the foundation for Indigenous epistemologies (Neeganagwedgin, 2013). The key themes of Indigenous spirituality identified by Harvey (2012) are:

- The relational nature of personhood and the greater community.
- The equilibrium of dwelling or positioning.
- The requirement for respect among individual members of the greater community.
- The generative power of gifts and gifting, rituals, and etiquette.

Indigenous spirituality differs from Western spirituality in several ways, with the primary difference being an absence of a spiritual-secular binary. While the monotheistic religions of the global West and North operate within a spiritual-secular binary, under an Indigenous approach, there is no spiritual-secular binary. The era of postmodernity initiated the elimination of binary and essentialist explanations of reality. Unlike Western and some Eastern religions, Indigenous traditions are orally transmitted with few written documents or texts.

Western thought often confuses or uses the terms religion and spirituality interchangeably. However, there is no equivalent word for "religion" among Indigenous peoples (Tomaselli & Xanthaki, 2021). Because the term "religion" does not fully coincide with Indigenous belief systems, Indigenous religions are often represented using the term spirituality (Tomaselli & Xanthaki, 2021). Therefore, the term spirituality will be used in this chapter when describing what Westerners would consider the religious or spiritual beliefs of Indigenous peoples.

Although there are many major religions practiced by Indigenous peoples throughout the world, many dating prior to the advancement of Western civilization, there are numerous Indigenous religions and spiritual traditions existing outside the dominant global religions. In fact, if Indigenous religions (which are the oldest religious traditions) were grouped collectively, they would become the world's sixth largest religion (First Peoples Worldwide, 2013).

Indigenous wisdom traditions emphasize the specific and local versus the general and global (Harvey, 2012). This does not suggest a lack of interest in matters of global importance but rather a perspective of rootedness and belonging in their interactions with other communities and peoples (Harvey, 2012).

The Indigenous world does not exist "out there" or separate from them, but rather it exists within them and even "through" them (Marcos, 2010). Indigenous actions and their substance are more interconnected than in Western thought, wherein the "I" can be empirically removed from surroundings. The human body is porous and reflects the fundamental permeability of the universe which is embodied as an order of existence characterized by constant interactions among the tangible and intangible inhabitants (Marcos, 2010).

Weber (1918) used the term enchantment to describe traditional religions and disenchantment to describe the contemporary monotheistic era. He described modernity as being "robbed of gods", having replaced disenchantment and mystery with ritualization and intellectualization. According to Weber (1963/1922), Western society values scientific knowledge more than belief systems, and activities are directed toward logical goals. However, traditional societies view the world as "a great enchanted garden". Enchantment and disenchantment are two of the most elementary means by which individuals mentally organize the world their place within it (Balcomb, 2022). Weber was dissatisfied with the process of disenchantment, noting that while science had filled the void created by the decline of religion, science can clarify questions of values and morals, but cannot answer those questions. Although Weber recognized that a return to traditional religions might not be an appropriate solution, Weber recognized the inadequacy of both science and religion presents a major dilemma for contemporary society (Barrero, 2023).

Although there is no dominant Western worldview, multiple levels of enchantment and disenchantment currently exist, especially in the developing nations, and it is recognized that postmodern society has made space for expressions of enchantment (Balcomb, 2022). Turner (1977) identified six specific characteristics of enchantment: a feeling of affinity with nature in which every living thing has a spiritual existence and place in the universe; a deep feeling that humankind is weak and vulnerable and needs a being that is greater than itself; recognition that humankind is not alone but exists in a spiritual universe consisting of entities greater than itself; acceptance that humankind can develop a relationship with these entities; an acute sense of the afterlife which includes an important place for ancestors; and, belief that the universe is divine with no distinct boundaries between the spiritual and the physical worlds (Balcomb, 2022).

In the enchanted world, meaning exists in the object itself, not in the mind of the observer (Balcomb, 2022), and "can communicate this meaning to us, impose it on us … by bringing us as it were into its field of force" (Taylor, 2007, p. 30). Because objects possess meanings outside the mind, they can have instrumentality, exert influence on other beings, communicate, bring us under their influence, and infiltrate us in some manner. In the disenchanted world, there are no "charged" objects outside the mind, and causal relationships between objects cannot be dependent on meanings which are projected on them from observers (Taylor, 2007). If the source of meanings exists in the mind, their influence can be limited and managed. However, if they exist outside of the observer, control is limited (Balcomb, 2022).

An important element of the enchanted world is "a perplexing absence of certain boundaries which seem to us essential" (Taylor, 2007, p. 33). In the enchanted world, there are no boundaries between individual influence and impersonal force, mind and meaning, individual and group, or knowledge and belief (Balcomb, 2022). In the disenchanted world, there are distinct boundaries "between the material and spiritual worlds, the self and others, individuals, and society, causes and effects, mind and body, subjects and objects, religion, and society" (Balcomb, 2022, p. 128). The buffered self of the disenchanted world can disengage from objects existing beyond established boundaries; however, the porous self of the enchanted world is extremely vulnerable to the outside world (Balcomb, 2022).

Another area in which Indigenous spirituality differs from Western thought is in terms of logic. According to contemporary logic, anything can be inferred from contradictory premises. A logical consequence relationship is considered explosive if according to that relation, any chance conclusion is inviolable by any chance contradiction. Most classical and Western logics are explosive. Although inconsistency cannot be coherently considered in these logic philosophies, paraconsistent logic challenges this accepted perspective (Robison, 2020). A paraconsistent logic is not explosive, meaning that when available information is inconsistent, the consequence relation does not explode into unimportance. Therefore, paraconsistent logic contains inconsistency in a controlled manner by considering inconsistent information as conceivably informative (Priest et al., 2022).

Classical logic is governed by two essential ontological assumptions that reinforce binary understanding of experience and knowledge: the law of exclusion and the law of non-contradiction. According to the law of exclusion, nothing inconclusive can exist, therefore, all beings must be human or non-human, and cannot be both or neither (Robison, 2020). According to the law of non-contradiction, all concepts must be true or false, existent or nonexistent, as determined by empirical and impartial reasoning (Sinclair, 2020). Both laws oppose the paraconsistent logic of Indigenous wisdom that considers a third value system that recognizes the flexibility, relationship, and transformation of categories and identities, instead of their stability and established qualities (Norton-Smith, 2010; Waters, 2004a, 2004b), and acknowledges that contradictions are possible. Paraconsistent logic enables individuals to be described as both individual and communal, natural and cultural, human and non-human, and singular or plural (Sinclair, 2020). Robison (2020) suggested that this logical system could stimulate a more holistic understanding of empirical phenomena, such as climate change, than the binary logic systems of Western societies (Robison, 2020).

4.5 Mesoamerican Indigenous Spirituality

Although in 2014, 425 million Latin Americans were Roman Catholic, representing nearly 40% of the total Catholic population globally, the Catholic population has declined significantly as a percentage of the region's overall population (Pew Research Center, 2014). In 2020, approximately 57% of respondents in 18 Latin American countries claimed to be Catholic with more than 74% of respondents in Mexico identifying as Catholic (Romero, 2022). However, Indigenous social movements increasingly claim the right to develop and define their own spirituality, challenging the most deep-rooted effects of Catholic colonization, and ignoring the contempt and ridicule with which their wisdom, beliefs, and traditions are viewed by the Catholic majority (Marcos, 2010). Spirituality in Latin America bears little resemblance to common conceptual meaning in Christian denominations (Marcos, 2010).

Indigenous peoples no longer accept the images forced upon them by outsiders. Indigenous cultures continue to exist and can only continue to survive if they reinvent themselves and recreate their identity while maintaining their uniqueness (Gil Olmos, 2000). When specific ethnic groups faced cultural annihilation, their leaders developed a collective identity from their inherited oral, mythic, and spiritual traditions (Marcos, 2010). Warren (1999) suggested that the pan-Indigenous collective identity of the Mayan peoples was a result of the need to survive the encroachment of the Guatemalan state. According to Warren, the agents of cultural wisdom began to propose an "assertion of a common past which has been suppressed and fragmented by European colonialism and the emergence of modern liberal states. In this view, cultural revitalization reunites the past with the present as a political force" (Warren & Jackson 2002, p. 11). Regardless of the plausible explanations for the birth of this pan-Indigenous collective identity, it fosters a political universality which may be attributed to a self-defined Indigenous spirituality.

Indigenous women assert this ancestral wisdom, worldview, and spirituality. Traditional concepts that inhibit or limit their space as women are being challenged while concepts that reinforce the role of women in their ancestral spiritual communities are greatly embraced and their continuance is supported and protected by the community (Marcos, 2010). When Indigenous women discuss spirituality, they create a meaning that clearly separates it from the Catholic and Christian denominations of the Western conquistadores and colonizers (Marcos, 2010). Indigenous women are frustrated with the profound dilemma of interacting with a religious institution that has been historically misogynistic and has often demonstrated prejudice against Indigenous cultures. Indigenous women insist on being viewed as adults which contrasts with the assumptions of some Catholic leaders who perceive all Indigenous peoples as minors who require strict admonishment and guidance (Marcos, 2010).

Understanding contemporary Indigenous spirituality requires knowledge of some of the principles of Mesoamerican ancestral "embodied thought" (Marcos, 1998). Duality (which is not to be confused with dualism) is ubiquitous in Indigenous wisdom and spiritualty and provides a foundation for is basic for a spirituality which recognizes a cosmic image of life (Marcos, 2010). The pervasiveness of a viewpoint that has Western equivalent may explain the continuous inability of Westerners to infiltrate and understand Indigenous worlds (Marcos, 2010). According to Mesoamerican worldviews, the dual combination of feminine and masculine is integral to the creation of the universe and its (re)generation and nourishment. Although the gods and goddesses of Mesoamerican cultures have individual genders, the synthesis of feminine and masculine in one dual principle is a common aspect of most contemporary Mesoamerican cultures. The Mesoamerican communities embrace a dual mother-father protector-creator instead of the Judeo-Christian image of a masculine God (Marcos, 2010).

Duality is the primary governing force of the Indigenous universe and is also represented in the arrangement of time. This duality is in contrast with the binary (either or) perspective of contemporary Western thinking. Time is measured with two calendars: a ritual calendar which is linked to the human gestation cycle and an astronomical calendar which guides the seeding, sowing, and planting of corn and other crops (Marcos, 2010). Both human gestation and agricultural cycles are understood within the context of time-duality. In addition, concepts of feminine and masculine, life and death, above and below, light and darkness, and beneficence and malevolence are recognized as dual aspects of the same reality (Marcos, 2010). This concept of fluid duality has bound Indigenous peoples for millennia. Although this principle has been obscured and protected from outsiders, with many Native communities in the Americas considering the sharing of this knowledge with outsiders to be disloyalty to the community, Indigenous women have recently begun revealing it to non-Natives (Marcos, 2010).

In Indigenous Mesoamerica, gender exists within the universal concept of duality (Marcos, 1998, 2006), and is the core personification of the entire cosmos (Marcos, 2010). Every entity, element, and measure of time is identified as either feminine or masculine (Austin, 1988). This gender-based duality is the connecting and guiding force that forms a meaningful context for Indigenous peoples to interconnect despite apparent differences (Marcos, 1993, 2010; Quezada, 1997).

Duality, equilibrium, and harmony are among the basic elements of Mesoamerican Indigenous feminist traditions (Marcos, 2010). Indigenous wisdom holds that equilibrium is not the stillness of two equal weights or masses but a force that continually adjusts the relationship between dual or opposite dyads. Equilibrium penetrates the relationships between men and women but also among gods, between gods and humans, and between the elements of nature. The continuous pursuit of equilibrium is essential for maintaining order in every sphere, from individual life to the activities of the universe (Marcos, 2010).

The South American worldview of buen vivir originated in the Andean Quechua *Sumak Kawsay*, defined as the right way of living or "good living" (Gudynas, 2011a). This Ecuadorian and Bolivian cosmovision is based on living in subjective harmony with the universe, sacred Mother Earth (Pachamama), Nature, other individuals and communities, and the community of life (including the inanimate) while maintaining a balance of spiritual and material wealth (Acosta, 2015; Akchurin, 2015; Government of Ecuador, 2013; Gudynas, 2011b; Hidalgo-Capitán & Cubillo-Guevara, 2014; Van Norren & Beehner, 2021). The wisdom of buen vivir is contained in the four principles of the Andean cross Chakana (Van Norren, 2020):

- Integrality.
- Relationality.
- Complementarity.
- Reciprocity.

The wisdom of buen vivir also exists in the three life rules: do not lie (*ama llulla*), do not steal (*ama suwa*), and do not be lazy (*ama quella*). These life cycles are included in the Bolivian and Ecuadorian constitutions (Van Norren & Beehner, 2021). The three life rules are often complemented by the fourth life rule: loyalty (*ama japa*; Van Norren & Beehner, 2021). Oviedo (2008) suggested that *ama killa* (diligence), *ama llulla* (truth), *ama suwa* (honesty), and *ama yapa* (loyalty) were modified by Catholic priests and must be understood as "being" in the now.

In buen vivir, awareness or maturity is achieved by walking the 12 corners of the Inca cross counterclockwise (which corresponds with the 12 Inca festivals of the year): Love, Trust, Connections, Acknowledgment, Protection, Awareness, Happiness, Passion, Expression, Responsibility, Productivity, and Present (Van Norren & Beehner, 2021). The 12th point suggests achieving the fundamental value of "being" in harmony with the universe and Nature and fully aware of the present. It also requires mastering the four principles of integrality, relationality, in harmony with complementarity and reciprocity which approximately corresponds with the medicine wheels of other Indigenous cultures such as the Native American Hopi and Seneca (Van Norren, 2017).

Sumak Kawsay requires equilibrium between the masculine and feminine values which are qualities that transcend human gender (Oviedo, 2008; Waldmüller, 2014) and are similar to the Buddhist yin-yang (Van Norren & Beehner, 2021). Each leadership role must be fulfilled by male–female complementarity: Qhari Warmi (i.e., collective versus individual, with a minimum of two) (Van Norren & Beehner, 2021). Decisions are made collectively and by consensus with the clan representative bound by the decision made (Clarkson et al., 1992).

4.6 North American Indigenous Spirituality

The North American Indigenous peoples, also known as the First Nations, were forced by the colonial settlers to embrace their religion and culture. Children were removed from their families and sent to residential schools to learn the new ways and forget their traditional cultures and beliefs. Indigenous spirituality has been continually dismissed, rejected, or ridiculed with the governments of the United States and Canada ignoring the legal separation of church and state by imposing the teaching of Christianity on their Indigenous inhabitants (Jacobs, 2014). There are 574 Native American tribes in the United States (World Population Review, 2023), and 600 in Canada (Native Tribe, 2023). Because the Indigenous American peoples live coast-to-coast across the United States and Canada, there is broad variation in Native American spirituality (Gladstone, 2015).

The First Nation Elders have always served as guardians of the First Nations' cultural and spiritual heritage (Stonechild, 2016). Despite Western efforts to influence First Nation belief systems, the Elders have worked diligently and bravely to preserve the surviving remnants of their traditions (Stonechild, 2016). The seven spiritual disciplines of the First Nations are: "fasting, sharing, parenting, learning, teaching, praying, and meditating" (Stonechild, 2016, p. 53). According to Salteaux Elder

Danny Musqua, "The Indian way is not a religion but a way of understanding the spiritual world... It is a close relationship with the Creator in all aspects of our lives" (Stonechild, 2016, p. 63).

Native American spirituality embraces the complex connections between humans, the Earth, all inhabitants, and the broader, more complex universe (Gladstone, 2015). The concept of being interconnected is not understood as being separate and distinct chambers but as a physical and metaphysical attachment to everything temporal, spatial, and physical (Deloria et al., 1999). Native American spirituality stimulates patient observation to comprehend everything (Gladstone, 2015).

Haudenosaunee means "people who build a house" and describes an alliance among six Native American nations in the United States who are more commonly known as the Iroquois Confederacy (National Museum for the American Indian, 2009). The Confederacy originally consisted of five nations, but in 1722, members of the Tuscarora Nation who traveled north from what is now the U.S. state of North Carolina sought refuge among the Haudenosaunee and became the sixth member nation. The members of what is now often called the Six Nations are (National Museum for the American Indian, 2009):

- Mohawk or Kanien'kehaka, which means "People of the Flint".
- Oneida or Onayotekaono, which means "People of the Standing Stone".
- Onondaga or Onundagaono, which means "People of the Hills".
- Cayuga or Guyohkohnyoh, which means "People of the Great Swamp".
- Seneca or Onondowahgah, which means "People of the Great Hill".
- Tuscarora or Skaruhreh, which means "The Shirt Wearing People".

The Haudenosaunee Confederacy has existed since ancient time when the Peacemaker was sent by the Creator to share the *Kariwiio* or "good mind". Aiionwatha, more commonly known as Hiawatha, helped the Peacemaker teach the laws of peace to the Haudenosaunee Peoples. Hiawatha and the Peacemaker traveled from tribe to tribe and succeeded in convincing the Chiefs of each nation to unite in the

Great League of Peace and establish the only government directly linked to the Creator (Haudenosaunee Confederation, n.d.a). Although there are many cultural similarities and family relationships that unite the Six Nations, each nation is unique with its own distinct language and identity.

The Haudenosaunee people call themselves Ongweh'onweh, translated as "real human being" (National Museum for the American Indian, 2009).

The Haudenosaunee nations share a core value called the Seventh Generation which considers the unborn generations who will inherit the Earth (Haudenosaunee Confederation, n.d.b). Chiefs must determine how current decisions will affect their descendants. This principle not only applies to the physical Earth and its resources but more importantly, to their culture. Maintaining their cultural traditions, languages, and rituals is essential to enable future generations to observe Haudenosaunee culture (Haudenosaunee Confederation, n.d.b). Goodman (2015) describes the seventh generation as "choosing our responsibility to the seventh generation over quarterly earnings, regeneration over economic growth, and the pursuit of well-being and harmony over wealth and financial success" (p. 29). The Haudenosaunee Confederacy and the seventh-generation principle will be discussed further in Chapter 8.

4.7 African Indigenous Spirituality

According to Harvard professor Jacob Olupona, "African spirituality simply acknowledges that beliefs and practices touch on and inform every facet of human life, and therefore African religion cannot be separated from the everyday or mundane" (Chiorazzi, 2015). Laubscher (2013) described the essence of being African as constituting four realms: human, spiritual, physical, and external present. Indigenous African religions are multiple, varied, and generally informed by one's ethnic and/or family identity. For example, the Yoruba religion has historically existed in southwestern Nigeria, the Igbo in southeastern Nigeria, and the Zulu primarily in southern Africa. For many Africans, religion is a holistic lifestyle which cannot be separated from the public realm. Indigenous Africans consider sickness to be an imbalance of the body and social life, which may be a result of a breakdown in personal, family, or ancestral relationships (Olupona, as cited by Chiorazzi, 2015).

Unlike many of the dominant Western religions, African spirituality is not a closed belief system with a fixed creed. Africans differ on the role of ancestors in the lives of descendants, with some Africans believing their ancestors are equivalent to deities (Chiorazzi, 2015), and others believing they exist in a higher plane of existence than living humans and are capable of bestowing blessings or illnesses upon their living descendants (Olupona, as cited by Chiorazzi, 2015). Many, but not all African worldviews embrace the concept of a supreme being (Chiorazzi, 2015). For example, the Yoruba religion has a supreme being, named Olorun or Olodumare, who is the creator of the universe, empowered by numerous deities to create and oversee the Earth, and answer the prayers of the Yoruba people. Indigenous

There are approximately 658 million Christians (Gordon-Conwell Theological Seminary, 2023) and 500 million Muslims (Vellturo & Omer, 2020) living in Africa, collectively representing 90% of the population. Christianity dominates the south, and Islam the north, with Indigenous African practices strongest in central Africa. However, there are many Christian and Muslim adherents who participate in Indigenous religious rituals and practices (Olupona, as cited by Chiorazzi, 2015). Moreover, there are indications of a resurgence of African Indigenous practices, influenced by the return of the African diaspora from the Americas and Europe. This returning diaspora are descendants of Africans who were enslaved by Western colonists back as far as the fifteenth century, and seek to reconnect with their ancestral traditions, thereby influencing local African communities to reclaim their heritage (Olupona, as cited by Chiorazzi, 2015).

African spirituality is adaptable to change and capable of incorporating the wisdom and ideas of other belief systems. There is no discord between traditional African spirituality and other beliefs because they are not considered mutually exclusive, with other belief systems complementing and often enhancing African spiritual rituals. This is possible because Indigenous African religions are pragmatic, focusing on obtaining tangible outcomes (Olupona, as cited by Chiorazzi, 2015). The loss of traditional African spirituality would seriously undermine the practice of ceremonial rites of passage, which help enhance feelings of individual self-worth by recognizing important life milestones, such as becoming an adult or an Elder (Olupona, as cited by Chiorazzi, 2015). Olupona suggested that Africans can incorporate multiple religious perspectives without excluding or jeopardizing perspectives. According to an old African proverb: "The sky is large enough for birds to fly around without one having to bump into the other" (Olupona, as cited by Chiorazzi, 2015).

The concept of Ubuntu, approximately translated as "humanness", is an extensive philosophical, anthropological, sociological, and cultural basis for African perspectives of human identity and consciousness and is best expressed by the Zulu maxim "A person is a person through other persons" (Viljoen & Laubscher, 2015). Ubuntu is frequently described as "I am because we are" or "a person is a person through other persons" (Eze, 2010; Gade, 2012; Metz & Gaie, 2010; Ramose, 2005; van Norren, 2017). Ubuntu is a ubiquitous spirit of compassion, community, unity, hospitality, respect, and responsiveness that individuals and groups demonstrate for each other (Mangaliso, 2001). The Ubuntu personality is a representation of the ideal person manifested in living the ancient Ubuntu virtues of kindness; harmonious living; friendliness; modesty; helpfulness; humility; and happiness (Broodryk, 2006).

Ubuntu (or Botho) contains prescriptions on how individuals should relate to each another, nature, and the universe (Van Norren & Beehner, 2021). Ubuntu is characterized as the continuous motion of the *unfoldment* of the universe (abstract Ubu, brought to life by the life force Ntu, see Ramose, 2005), and is a collectivist ontology which emphasizes compassion and relatedness, and "life as mutual aid", restorative justice, and the interdependence of everything (linked by the life force "ntu"; Mbiti, 1990). The "bantu" community includes past, present, and future generations (Van Norren & Beehner, 2021). Ubuntu is generally associated with African Renaissance, brotherhood, and black consciousness, but is also a model of *glocalization* wherein global management and local knowledge are combined (Van den Heuvel, 2007). Ubuntu requires that feminine and masculine assumptions are combined, in a concept known as balancing the "feeling" Mother Mind with the "analytical", Warrior Mind, similar to the concept of *yin* and *yang* in Buddhist cultures (Van Norren & Beehner, 2021).

Balcomb (2015) contended that because Christianity has become so implicit within sub-Saharan African, Christianity may have become "Indigenized". Many Western Christians would find it difficult to recognize some African Christian practices as the same Christianity that they practice. This has deep significance for an African eco-theology because Indigenous religion has become synonymous with environmental stewardship, and Christianity with environmental depletion. Blasu (2020) used the term *theocology* to conceptualize African Christian environmental theology. In contrast to Western eco-theologies that endeavor to diminish the transcendent nature of theism in panentheism, African *theocology* is more traditional in nature, emphasizing theo-centrism and the vice-regency of God, combined with environmentally friendly elements of African culture (Balcomb, 2022).

4.8 Asian and South Pacific Indigenous Spirituality

There are numerous Indigenous spiritual traditions within Asia and the South Pacific. Many of these were introduced in Chapter 1. Hinduism, Buddhism, Judaism, Christianity, Islam, Confucianism, Daoism, Sikhism, Shamanism, and Shintō all originated in and are practiced in Asia and abroad. Lesser practiced religions originating from Asia include Bahá'í, Jainism, and Zoroastrianism. In this section, we will explore some of the common themes and beliefs of Indigenous peoples within the South Pacific.

Indigenous Polynesian religions emphasize animism, a belief that all things, animate and inanimate, are endowed to some degree with sacred supernatural powers (called mana). Polynesians believed that these powers could be invalidated through human activities, with many of the region's tapu or taboos designed to control these behaviors (Biggs, as cited by Greenhill & Clark, 2011). The English word taboo originated from Captain James Cook's visit to the Pacific Island of Tonga in 1777. The taboo/tapu concept exists in many Polynesian cultures, with a similar term kapu used in Hawaii (National Park Service, 2021).

Like most animist cultures, religious concerns permeate all aspects of Polynesian life. Polynesian chiefs possessed considerable mana, and in some cultures, an individual who made contact with the chief's shadow would be executed in compensation for injury to the chief's mana. In portions of Polynesia, it is considered impolite to step over an individual's legs, pass one's hand over someone else's head, or stand taller than someone of high rank, because these actions are believed to reduce a person's mana (Suggs et al., 2024). Women possessed considerable mana, evidenced by their ability to reproduce.

Inanimate objects such as buildings, stones, and tools could possess mana, and some groves, trees, temples, and sections of land were considered to have been infused with the mana of high-status individuals or gods. In addition to mana and tapu, the universe was believed to contain numerous benevolent and malevolent spiritual beings and gods. The gods were worshipped through animal or human sacrifices, chants and orations, feasts, ritual sex to promote fertility, and other ceremonies which were often preceded by long periods of fasting and abstinence (Suggs et al., 2024).

Hawaiian spirituality is based on the belief that natural elements are controlled by gods (akua and kupua), spirits of nature (awaiku), and ancestral spirits (aumakua; Gonzalez, 2020). The spirit world is called pō (the Underworld) and is inhabited by gods, semi-gods, and ancestral spirits. When souls of the deceased do not make it to the Underworld, they continue to exist in the physical realm as spirits. These spirits can be benevolent and protective, or malevolent and harmful and often make their Earthly homes in stones. Stones can be considered sacred or sinister, depending on whether their inhabitants are gods or evil spirits (Gonzalez, 2020). The Hawaiian religion maintain a special place for the kahuna who are mediators between the physical and the spiritual realms, and can be healers, prophets, sorcerers, and magicians.

Spirits are important entities in Hawaiian culture because success or failure in life is attributed to the protective power of guardian spirits or the malevolence of evil spirits (Gonzalez, 2020). Guardian spirits are called the ʻAumakua and may take the form of plants and/or animals.

Ancestral spirits may visit in the form of a large black moth or a strong flower fragrance. They can also appear as sea turtles, sharks, hawks, and crows that suddenly appear in the family yard. Eating an animal that represents one's family 'Aumakua is considered a taboo (Gonzalez, 2020).

Other categories of spirits in the Hawaiian tradition are the Mo'o or water spirits, and the Menehune who are supernatural spirit dwarfs, inhabiting caves and forests (Gonzalez, 2020). All bodies of water in Hawaii are protected by the Mo'o, shapeshifters who can appear as small lizards and geckos, large mythical dragons, or beautiful maidens. The water spirits control the weather and freshwater availability, and when they become guardian spirits, they can provide health and prosperity (Gonzalez, 2020). The Menehune spirit dwarfs are similar to fairies and elves of European folklore, are industrious, and usually benevolent. According to one Hawaiian legend, the Menehune spirits irritated the hero Laka who was making a canoe. Every morning, Laka cut down a tree to make his canoe, and every night the Menehune restored the fallen tree. Laka eventually agreed to allow the Menehune to build the canoe and accompany him on a journey (Gonzalez, 2020).

In early Hawaiian traditions, there were two goddesses and four gods who were considered Sacred Spirits or manifestations of the forces of nature (Gonzalez, 2020). Pele was the Spirit of fire and volcanoes, Hina was the Moon Spirit, Kāne was the Creator Spirit, Kū was the Warrior Spirit, Lono was the Spirit of fertility and peace, and Kanaloa was the Ocean Spirit. Hawaiians considered the abundance of nature to be the presence and gift of the divine (Gonzalez, 2020).

4.9 Shamanism

Shamanism is a religious practice in which a practitioner, known as a shaman or saman, engages with the spirit realm through techniques such as trances (Singh, 2018). The purpose of shamanism is to invite spirits or spiritual energies into the physical realm for the purpose of healing, foretelling the future, changing the weather, or providing various forms of aid to humans (Singh, 2018). Shamans are known by various names including medicine man, witch doctor, holy man, or prophet, but the concept of being a shaman crosses almost all cultural boundaries. This can be explained in part by how humans from traditional hunter-gatherers to urban dwellers are "wired to think about the world and other humans" (Singh, M. as cited in Reuell, 2018). However, many cultures oppose the broad usage of the term *shamanism,* arguing apparent similarities among phenomena in widely dispersed regions does not justify the assertion of a common connection.

In most cultures, shamans are born into their role and possess physical characteristic that differentiates them from the rest of the community such as additional bones, teeth, or fingers. Shamans are believed to be involuntarily chosen by supernatural beings which typically occurs during adolescence. The process of becoming a shaman often includes visions, fainting, hysteria, or other unexplained conditions. Shamans are expected to understand everything, foresee distant and future events, and predict favorable fishing and hunting outcomes. In addition to these abilities, shamans are healers and may accompany the deceased to the otherworldly realm. The shaman's role is important at three significant life passages: birth, marriage, and death.

Singh (as cited by Reuell, 2018) suggested that individuals and groups believe that other individuals have different or special powers when those individuals somehow diverge from humanity. Singh compared this to the contemporary superhero narrative wherein an individual appears to possess superhuman or alien powers because of an accident or incident. (Reuell, 2018). The shaman undergoes some form of biological or physiological transformation in which they become capable of extraordinary actions. This process results in two classes of individuals—"those who have been transformed and those who have not" (Singh, M. as cited by Reuell, 2018).

Shamans believe that they travel between three cosmic zones—the Sky, the Earth, and the Underworld with some cultures believing that multiple levels exist in each zone (Polizzi, 2022). Those worlds include: Upper World (Sky), Middle World (Earth), Lower World (Underworld), and World Tree (also known as the Tree of Life, the Cosmic Tree; Polizzi, 2022). The Upper World is where gods, goddesses, demigods, mystical beings, and spiritual teachers exist, and where shamans receive insights about their being, and achieve deeper perspectives about experiences.

The Middle World is where shamans travel to understand an event that occurred on the physical plane or obtain information about a place. Shamans travel to the Lower World to meet their power animals or guardian/protector spirits, or gain wisdom to assist with the healing and personal transformation of a patient. The World Tree connects the spirit worlds providing a passageway for spirits and shamans to reach the other three worlds. Shamans often include an image of the World Tree on sacred objects to receive power from the other worlds (Polizzi, 2022).

Shamans appear in many continents, with the classic example and most complete expression of shamanism found in the Arctic and Central Asia (Eliade & Diószegi, 2023). In northern Asia, the shaman is not a member of a special profession, with the role typically held by a family member, often an elderly woman. Shamanism also exists in Southeast Asia, Oceania, and North and South America, although shamanism serves a limited primary role in Africa among a small number of groups who have remained hunters and gatherers (Eliade & Diószegi, 2023).

Shamans in the Malay Peninsula use celestial spirits or quartz crystals to heal sick individuals. Shamans in Sumatra, Borneo, and Celebes are believed to be able to communicate with the deceased. Shamans in this region are believed to shapeshift into tigers or induce trances by dancing (Eliade & Diószegi, 2023). Australian Aborigines believe an individual becomes a shaman through a ceremony of initiatory death, followed by resurrection to a new, superhuman state. This initiatory death is similar to that of Siberian shamans wherein several medical procedures are performed on the candidate's body (e.g., opening the abdomen, renewal of the organs, washing and drying of the bones, insertion of magical substances), and an ascent to heaven with possible entranced pilgrimages through the afterlife (Eliade & Diószegi, 2023).

Shamanism prevails in the religious lives of the Inuit and Yupik peoples wherein the primary roles of the shaman (*angakok*; plural *angákut*) are healing and trance-based underwater visits to the Mother of Animals to guarantee abundant hunting, and assist childless women with conception (Eliade & Diószegi, 2023). Among many Native American Peoples, shamanism comprises the most important characteristic of religious life with the shaman possessing supernatural power acquired spontaneously or following a voluntary vision pilgrimage. The shaman's primary role is healing, but other important roles may include magico-religious ceremonies related to communal hunting, secret societies, or esoteric rituals such as the Ghost Dance. South American shamans can serve as sorcerers, being believed to become animals who drink the blood of their enemies (Eliade & Diószegi, 2023).

In the mid-twentieth century, members of Western counter-culture movements such as "hippies" and the New Age coopted many of the Indigenous traditions and practices resulting in the *neoshamanism* or the neoshamanic movement (Gredig, 2009). This resulted in harsh criticism and accusations of cultural appropriation (Kehoe, 2000), exploitation, and misrepresentation when non-Indigenous observers attempted to practice or represent ancient cultures and practices to which they did not belong (Wernitznig, 2007).

4.10 Conclusion

The power offered by local, Indigenous knowledge about nature is unique and cannot be compared with that of science and technology (Narangoa & Cribb, 2003). There is no sense of belonging when an individual works and exists by virtue of externally acquired technology. However, Indigenous knowledge offers more than a means of survival and subsistence because it imposes obligations of environmental management through practices which make life in that environment sustainable over the long term. These obligations, such as the preservation of sacred groves and forests, prohibitions on mining or excavating in certain places, the protection of certain species from hunting, and specific cultivation practices, offer a powerful contribution to a sense of belonging to the land (Narangoa & Cribb, 2003).

Defining and describing Indigenous spirituality is challenging because while Indigenous belief systems share common elements, each is unique to the culture of origin, and the influence of Western settlers. Despite the philosophical and logical differences between Indigenous and Western wisdom and spirituality, cross-cultural cooperation is both possible (Robison, 2020) and imperative. Robison (2020) suggested that instead of ridiculing the Western capitalist worldview, it is better to identify those foundational cracks within contemporary capitalistic society that can be repaired through collaboration with Indigenous peoples. Although Indigenous religions and spirituality provide learning opportunities for the counter modernist trend, however, a return to re-enchantment is unlikely (Balcomb, 2022). Although belief in spirits or demon possession is rare in the postmodern era, this belief exists in various forms in contemporary Christianity, including among many African and Pentecostal Christians. This demonstrates that pre-modern, modern, and postmodern conditions continue to coexist as contemporary realities and should not be categorized in evolutionary or developmental terms (Balcomb, 2022). The Indigenous worldview has survived and ensured the survival of adherents despite centuries of Western colonialization. Protecting and maintaining our ecosystems is essential to the survival of all human and non-human inhabitants. The reemergence and acceptance of Indigenous beliefs and practices are essential for the continued survival of Indigenous and non-Indigenous peoples alike.

Reflection Questions

1. Balcomb (2015) contended that because Christianity has become so implicit within sub-Saharan African, Christianity may have become "Indigenized". How could Christianity become "Indigenized" if it is not an original Indigenous belief system?
2. Members of Western counter-culture movements such as "hippies" and the New Age coopted many of the Indigenous traditions and practices (Gredig, 2009) and were accused of cultural appropriation (Kehoe, 2000), exploitation, and misrepresentation by attempting to practice or represent ancient cultures and practices (Wernitznig, 2007). How could this coopting of Indigenous traditions and practices produce possible unintentional benefits for Indigenous communities by contributing to the acceptance and survival of their traditions and practices?
3. How can Indigenous and Western belief systems and traditions coexist considering their different perspectives? How can the similarities between Indigenous and Western belief systems and traditions be used to develop dialogue between Native and non-Native individuals and groups?

References

Acosta, A. (2015). *Buen Vivir vom Recht auf ein gutes Leben.* Oekom Verlag.

Akchurin, M. (2015). Constructing the rights of nature: Constitutional reform, mobilization, and environmental protection in Ecuador. *Law and Social Inquiry, 40*(4), 937–968. https://doi.org/10.1111/lsi.12141

Austin, A. L. (1988). *The human body and ideology: Concepts of the ancient Nahuas.* University of Utah Press.

Balcomb, A. (2015). Christianity in Africa—Watchdog of imperialism or 'drops of frozen rain melting on the dry palate of the panting earth'. *Alternation—Interdisciplinary Journal for the Study of the Arts and Humanities in Southern Africa, 14*, 8–21.

Balcomb, A. O. (2022). Indigenous religions as antidote to the environmental crisis: Surveying a decade of reflection. In *Ecotheology-sustainability and religions of the world* (pp. 123–142). IntechOpen. https://doi.org/10.5772/intechopen.105209

Barrero, A. F. (2023). *Max Weber on disenchantment: Is religion obsolete?* https://www.thecollector.com/max-weber-disenchantment-world-religion/

Blasu, E. Y. (2020). *African theocology: Studies in African religious creation care.* Wipf and Stock Publishers.

Broodryk, J. (2002). *Ubuntu: Life lessons from Africa.* Ubuntu School of Philosophy.

Broodryk, J. (2006). *Ubuntu African life coping skills: Theory and practice* (Paper Delivered at CCEAM Conference 12–17 October 2006). Lefkosia, Cyprus.

Chiorazzi, A. (2015). *The spirituality of Africa.* The Harvard Gazette. https://news.harvard.edu/gazette/story/2015/10/the-spirituality-of-africa/

Chunhabunyatip, P., Sasaki, N., Grünbühel, C., Kuwornu, J. K., & Tsusaka, T. W. (2018). Influence of Indigenous spiritual beliefs on natural resource management and ecological conservation in Thailand. *Sustainability, 10*(8), 2842. https://doi.org/10.3390/su10082842

Clarkson, L., Morisette, V., & G. Régallet. (1992). *Our responsibility to the seventh generation, Indigenous peoples and sustainable development*. Institute for Sustainable Development.

Cumbre de Mujeres Indígenas de América (C.D.M.I.). (2003). *Memoria de la primera cumbre de mujeres indígenas de América.* Fundación Rigoberta Menchú Tum.

Deloria, V., Jr., Deloria, B., Foehner, K., & Scinta, S. (Eds.). (1999). *Spirit & reason: The Vine Deloria, Jr. Reader*. Fulcrum.

Eliade, M., & Diószegi, V. (2023). *Shamanism*. Encyclopædia Britannica. https://www.britannica.com/topic/shamanism

Eze, M. O. (2010). *Intellectual history of contemporary South Africa*. Palgrave McMillan, St Martin's Press.

First Peoples Worldwide. (2013). *Indigenous religions face persecution in Asia and around the world*. https://www.culturalsurvival.org/news/indigenous-religions-face-persecution-asia-and-around-world

Gade, C. B. N. (2012). What is Ubuntu? Different interpretations among South Africans of African descent. *South African Journal of Philosophy, 31*(3), 484–503. https://hdl.handle.net/10520/EJC125037

Gil Olmos, J. (2000, March 26). Interview with Yvon Le Bot, "Moderno y creativo el movimiento de indígenas en América Latina". La Jornada.

Gladstone, J. S. (2015). Native American transplanar wisdom. In C. Spiller & R. Wofgramm (Eds.), *Indigenous spiritualities at work: Transforming the spirit of enterprise* (pp. 21–32). Information Age Publishing.

Gonzalez, J. (2020). *What do spirits mean in Hawaiian culture?* Spirit Restoration. https://www.spiritrestoration.org/signs-symbols/spirit-in-hawaiian-culture/

Goodman, D. (2015). Deep in the Amazon, a tiny tribe is beating big oil. *Yes Magazine, 2015*(Spring), 28–32.

Gordon-Conwell Theological Seminary. (2023). *Status of global Christianity 2023*. https://www.gordonconwell.edu/center-for-global-christianity/resources/status-of-global-christianity/

Government of Ecuador (GoE). (2013). *National development plan, National plan for good living 2013–2017, A better world for everyone* (Summarized Version). Republic of Ecuador, Quito, Ecuador.

Gredig, F. (2009). *Finding new cosmologies: Shamans in contemporary Europe* (Vol. 40). LIT Verlag Münster.

Greenhill, S. J., & Clark, R. (2011). POLLEX-Online: The Polynesian Lexicon Project Online. *Oceanic Linguistics, 50*(2), 551–559. https://pollex.eva.mpg.de/

Grimes, R. L. (1996). This may be a feud, but it is not a war: An electronic, interdisciplinary dialogue on teaching Native Religions. *American Indian Quarterly, 20*(3/4), 433–450. https://doi.org/10.2307/1185786

Gudynas, E. (2011a). Buen vivir: Today's tomorrow. *Development, 54*, 441–447. https://doi.org/10.1057/dev.2011.86

Gudynas, E. (2011b). Good life: Germinating alternatives to development. *Latin America in movement*. Latin American Information Agency (ALAI).
Harvey, G. (2012). Indigenous spiritualities. In *Oxford textbook of spirituality in healthcare* (pp. 49–54). Oxford Academic.
Haudenosaunee Confederation. (n.d.a). *Confederacy's creation*. https://www.haudenosauneeconfederacy.com/confederacys-creation/
Haudenosaunee Confederation. (n.d.b). *Values*. https://www.haudenosauneeconfederacy.com/values/
Herman, R. D. K. (2015). Traditional knowledge in a time of crisis: Climate change, culture and communication. *Sustainable Science, 11*, 163–176. https://doi.org/10.1007/s11625-015-0305-9
Hidalgo-Capitán, A. L., & Cubillo-Guevara, A. P. (2014). Six open debates on Sumak Kawsay. *ICONOS Revista de Ciencias Sociales, 48*, 25–40. https://doi.org/10.17141/iconos.48.2014.1204
International Labor Organisation. (1989). Doc. UN, ICN 41, Sub 2/1989/33 Add 3 paragraph 4. Convention n.169 of the ILO of the United Nations.
Jacobs, D. T. (2014). Seven Indigenous spiritual principles for guiding all students toward survival, peace, health, and happiness. In S. Gill & G. Thomson (Eds.), *Redefining religious education: Spirituality for human flourishing* (pp. 91–101). Palgrave Macmillan.
Jaggar, A. M., Bordo, S. R., & Bordo, S. (Eds.). (1989). *Gender/body/knowledge: Feminist reconstructions of being and knowing*. Rutgers University Press.
Kehoe, A. B. (2000). *Shamans and religion: An anthropological exploration in critical thinking*. Waveland Press.
LaDuke, W. (2005). *Voices from White Earth: Gaa-waabaabiganikaag*. Schumacher Society.
Laubscher, L. (2013). *Human niches—Spiral dynamics for Africa* (Unpublished Doctoral thesis). The Da Vinci.
Mangaliso, M. P. (2001). Building competitive advantage from *Ubuntu*: Management lessons from South Africa. *Academy of Management Executive, 15*(3), 23–32. https://doi.org/10.5465/ame.2001.5229453
Marcos, S. (1993). La construcción del género en Mesoamerica: Un reto Epistemológico. Paper read at 13th *CICAES*, Mexico, August 4.
Marcos, S. (1998). Embodied religious thought: Gender categories in Mesoamerica. *Religion, 26*(4), 371–382. https://doi.org/10.1006/reli.1998.0146
Marcos, S. (2006). *Taken from the lips: Gender and eros in Mesoamerica*. Brill.
Marcos, S. (2010). Spirituality; Perspectives from the first Indigenous Women's Summit of the Americas. In F. Wijsen & S. Marcos (Eds.), *Indigenous voices*

in the sustainability discourse: Spirituality and the struggle for a better quality of life (pp. 49–70). LIT Verlag.
Mathewson, K. (2004). Drugs, moral geographies, and Indigenous peoples: Some initial mappings and central issues. In M. K. Steinberg, J. J. Hobbs, & K. Mathewson (Eds.), *Dangerous harvest: Drug plants and the transformation of Indigenous landscapes* (pp. 11–23). Oxford University Press.
Mbiti, J. S. (1990). *African religions and philosophy* (2nd ed.). Heinemann Educational Publishers.
McIntosh, I. (2000). Are there Indigenous peoples in Asia. *Cultural Survival Quarterly, 24*(3), 4–7.
Metz, T., & Gaie, J. B. R. (2010). The African ethic of Ubuntu/Botho: Implications for research on morality. *Journal of Moral Education, 39*(3), 273–290. https://doi.org/10.1080/03057240.2010.497609
Miller, R. J., Ruru, J., Behrendt, L., & Lindberg, T. (2010). *Discovering Indigenous lands: The doctrine of discovery in the English colonies*. Oxford University Press.
Moody, R. (1988). *The Indigenous voice*. Zed.
Muckle, R. J. (2012). *Indigenous peoples of North America: A concise anthropological overview*. University of Toronto Press.
Narangoa, L., & Cribb, R. (2003). Dynamics of land and identity in Pacific Asia. *International Journal of the Humanities, 1*. https://doi.org/10.18848/1447-9508/CGP/v01/58158
National Museum for the American Indian. (2009). Haudenosaunee guide for educators. https://americanindian.si.edu/sites/1/files/pdf/education/HaudenosauneeGuide.pdf
National Park Service. (2021). *Hawai'i Volcanoes.* https://nps.gov/havo/learn/management/world_heritage_site.htm
Native Tribe. (2023). *Discovering Canada's rich cultural heritage: Exploring the diversity of Native American tribes in Canada—A comprehensive guide to know how many Native American tribes are in Canada.* https://nativetribe.info/discovering-canadas-rich-cultural-heritage-exploring-the-diversity-of-native-american-tribes-in-canada-a-comprehensive-guide-to-know-how-many-native-american-tribes-are-in-canada/
Neeganagwedgin, E. (2013). Ancestral knowledges, spirituality and Indigenous narratives as self-determination. *AlterNative: An International Journal of Indigenous Peoples, 9*(4), 322–334. https://doi.org/10.1177/117718011300900404
Norton-Smith, T. (2010). *The dance of person and place: One interpretation of American Indian philosophy*. SUNY Press.

Oviedo, A. M. (2008). *Les Marcheurs de l'Arc en Ciel et les Mythes du Développement*. Ambre éditions.

Pew Research Center. (2014). *Religion in Latin America: Widespread change in a historically Catholic region*. https://www.pewresearch.org/religion/2014/11/13/religion-in-latin-america/

Polizzi, N. (2022). *What is shamanism? Ultimate beginner's guide*. The Sacred Science. https://www.thesacredscience.com/what-is-shamanism-ultimate-beginners-guide/

Priest, G., Tanaka, K., & Weber, Z. (2022). Paraconsistent logic. In E. N. Zalta (Ed.), *The Stanford encyclopedia of philosophy* (Spring 2022 ed.). https://plato.stanford.edu/archives/spr2022/entries/logic-paraconsistent/

Quezada, N. (1997). *Sexualidad amor y erotismo: México prêhispanico y México colonial*. IIA-Universidad Nacional Autónoma de México y Plaza Valdez.

Ramose, M. B. (1999/2005 revision). *African philosophy through Ubuntu*. Mond Books.

Robison, C. (2020). *Decolonizing climate discourse and legitimating Indigenous wisdom: Toward an ecosystemic episteme* (Master's theses). Rollins College. https://scholarship.rollins.edu/honors/112

Romero, T. (2022). *Latin America: Religion affiliation share 2020, by type*. https://www.statista.com/statistics/996386/latin-america-religion-affiliation-share-type/

Reuell, P. (2018). The mystery of the medicine man. *The Harvard Gazette*. https://news.harvard.edu/gazette/story/2018/12/study-suggests-shamans-acted-as-the-first-professional-class-in-human-society/

Sinclair, R. (2020). Exploding individuals: Engaging Indigenous logic and decolonizing science. *Hypatia, 35*(1), 58–74. https://doi.org/10.1017/hyp.2019.18

Singh, M. (2018). The cultural evolution of shamanism. *Behavioral and Brain Sciences, 41*(e66), 1–17. https://doi.org/10.1017/S0140525X17001893

Smith, L. (1999). *Decolonizing methodologies: Research and Indigenous people*. Zed.

Stonechild, B. (2016). *The knowledge seeker: Embracing Indigenous spirituality*. University of Regina Press.

Suggs, R. C., Kiste, R. C., & Kahn, M. (2024). *Religion of Polynesian culture*. https://www.britannica.com/place/Polynesia/Religion

Taylor, C. (2007). *A secular age*. Harvard University Press.

Tomaselli, A., & Xanthaki, A. (2021). The struggle of Indigenous peoples to maintain their spirituality in Latin America: Freedom of and from religion(s), and other threats. *Religions, 12*(10), 869. https://doi.org/10.3390/rel12100869

Turner, H. W. (1977). Primal religions and their study. In V. C. Hayes (Ed.), *Australian essays in world religions* (pp. 27–37). Australian Association for the Study of Religions.

United Nations. (2007). *United Nations declaration on the rights of Indigenous peoples.* https://social.desa.un.org/issues/Indigenous-peoples/united-nations-declaration-on-the-rights-of-Indigenous-peoples

United Nations Permanent Forum on Indigenous Issues. (n.d.). *Who are Indigenous peoples?* United Nations. https://www.un.org/esa/socdev/unpfii/documents/5session_factsheet1.pdf

Van den Heuvel, H. (2007). *Between optimism and opportunism, deconstructing 'African management' discourse in South Africa* (PhD dissertation). Free University, Amsterdam, the Netherlands.

van Norren, D. (2017). *Development as service: A happiness, ubuntu and buen vivir interdisciplinary view of the sustainable development goals* (Doctoral dissertation). Tilburg University, Tilburg, the Netherlands.

van Norren, D. (2020). The sustainable development goals viewed through gross national happiness, Ubuntu, and Buen Vivir. *International Environmental Agreements (INEA), 20,* 431–458. https://doi.org/10.1007/s10784-020-09487-3

van Norren, D., & Beehner, C. (2021). Sustainability leadership, UNESCO competencies for SDGs, and diverse leadership models. *International Journal of Development & Sustainability, 10*(1), 24–49. https://isdsnet.com/ijds-v10n1-03.pdf

Vellturo, M., & Omer, M. (2020). *Factsheet on Muslims in Africa.* Unites States Commission on International Religious Freedom. https://www.uscirf.gov/sites/default/files/2021-10/2021%20Muslims%20in%20Africa%20Factsheet.pdf

Viljoen, R., & Laubscher, L. I. (2015). African spirituality: Insights from the cradle of mankind. In C. Spiller & R. Wofgramm (Eds.), *Indigenous spiritualities at work: Transforming the spirit of enterprise* (pp. 137–158). Information Age Publishing.

Waldmüller, J. M. (2014). Buen Vivir, Sumak Kawsay, good living: An introduction and overview. *Alternautas, 1*(1), 17–28.

Warren, K. B., & Jackson, J. E. (2002). *Indigenous movements, self-representation and the state in Latin America.* University of Texas Press.

Warren, K. (1999). *Indigenous movements and their critics.* Princeton University Press.

Waters, A. (2004a). Language matters: Nondiscrete, nonbinary dualism. In A. Waters (Ed.), *American Indian thought: Philosophical essays.* Blackwell Publishing.

Waters, A. (2004b). That alchemical Bering Strait theory. In A. Waters (Ed.), *American Indian thought: Philosophical essays.* Blackwell Publishing.

Weber, M. (1918). *Science as a vocation* (pp. 129–158). H. Gerth and C. Wright.

Weber, M. (1963/1922). *The sociology of religion.* Beacon.

Wernitznig, D. (2007). *Europe's Indians, Indians in Europe: European perceptions and appropriations of Native American cultures from Pocahontas to the present.* University Press of America.

Wijsen, F., & Marcos, S. (2010). Indigeneity and sustainability: An introduction. In F. Wijsen & S. Marcos (Eds.), *Indigenous voices in the sustainability discourse: Spirituality and the struggle for a better quality of life* (pp. 9–30). LIT Verlag.

World Population Review. (2023). *Native American tribes by state 2023.* https://worldpopulationreview.com/state-rankings/native-american-tribes-by-state

5

Spirituality in the Post-Pandemic Era

5.1 Introduction

While religious affiliation and participation began declining decades before the COVID-19 pandemic, the pandemic stimulated inward reflection in many individuals and cultures. Many individuals were reminded of their mortality and used time working at home and loss of friends and loved ones as opportunities to find meaning and spirituality in their lives. The concept that spirituality exists both within and absent religious institutions became more evident as churches were closed or provided services virtually. The role of spirituality in the post-pandemic era will be examined within the context of individual and organizational success. The content and reflection topic will provide perspective on the role of spirituality during and after unexpected global crises.

The first cases of COVID-19 were reported in December 2019, and the World Health Organization (WHO) declared the COVID-19 outbreak a Public Health Emergency of International Concern on January 30, 2020, and a pandemic on March 11, 2020. As of May 17, 2023, there have been 766,440,796 cumulative cases and 6,932,591 deaths globally (WHO, 2023a). The WHO declared an end to the COVID-19 emergency on May 5, 2023 (WHO, 2023b).

C. G. Beehner, *Spirituality, Sustainability, and Success*, Palgrave Studies in Workplace Spirituality and Fulfillment, https://doi.org/10.1007/978-3-031-47643-3_5

5.2 Spirituality During the Pandemic

The COVID-19 pandemic impacted individual religiosity and spirituality, although the level varied by nation. A 2020 Pew Research Center survey conducted in countries affected by social distancing, lockdown mandates, or both indicated individuals in the United States were more likely than individuals in other developed nations to report increased religious faith. Of the 14,276 participants in 14 nations, early 28 percent of Americans reported stronger personal faith because of the pandemic, and the same percentage believe the religious faith of Americans overall has increased (Pew Research Center, 2021). The percentages of respondents in other nations indicating religious faith was affected by the coronavirus were much lower, with 10% of British adults and 5% of Japanese adults reporting stronger faith because of the pandemic (Pew Research Center, 2021). Majorities or pluralities in all nations surveyed *do not* feel their religious faith increased by the pandemic, with 68% of U.S. adults reporting no significant change in their faith, and 47% of U.S. adults indicating the faith of their fellow citizens has not changed (Pew Research Center, 2021).

Although church attendance declined during the pandemic (Nortey, 2022), individual faith was not affected, with most adults surveyed indicating their religious affiliation during the pandemic was the same as pre-pandemic. Moreover, one study indicated the pandemic may have enhanced many Americans' religious faith (Sahgal & Connaughton, 2021). A study by the Survey Center on American Life at AEI and researchers at NORC at the University of Chicago indicated that religious identity remained steady through the pandemic (Witt-Swanson et al., 2023). The decline in religious attendance combined with the stability of religious identification during the pandemic suggests a divergence of religious identification and experience (Witt-Swanson et al., 2023). Religious affiliation appears to be less of an indicator of the extent of religious and spiritual experiences and the extent of their religious commitments. Almost every major religion has experienced a decline in regular attendance, possibly signaling an increase in cultural religiosity in which identity is associated with the ethnic or cultural elements of a religion instead of the beliefs or rituals (Witt-Swanson et al., 2023).

COVID-19 was initially called the "rich man's disease" because the virus infected well-off individuals who traveled by plane, but quickly spread globally infecting both wealthy and the poor. Danielle Widmann Abraham, professor of Islamic studies and comparative religion at Ursinus College, described the coronavirus as "a profound equalizer", reminding humankind of the universal understanding that we are all more similar than different (Lubrano, 2020). In the Islamic world, COVID-19 was perceived as either a punishment or a test from God causing religious people to seek meaning in the pandemic (Lubrano, 2020). According to Adnan Zulfiqar, an expert on Islamic law at Rutgers Law School, when communities are decimated by diseases, "you can see the potential for the already religious to become even more religious" (Lubrano, 2020). Judeo-Christian religions contain a belief of a day of judgment linked to an ultimate cataclysm signaling the final days of Earth. For the profoundly religious, COVID-19 may have signaled doomsday (Lubrano, 2020).

During the pandemic, spiritual skills may have been an important resource to manage mental health issues, especially among the most vulnerable, who are at a higher risk of mental health disorders (Chirico, 2021). During the pandemic, increased spiritual distress was associated with reduced mental health in the general population. This demonstrates the importance of ensuring that spiritual and religious activities continue during major crises and catastrophes and of training healthcare professionals to address the spiritual and religious needs of patients and families. Globally, spiritual resources and values may be significant mechanisms for moderating the negative consequences of crises in the short and long terms, such as the socioeconomic inequalities created by the COVID-19 pandemic. However, they may also be essential for addressing climate change and other emerging issues including global health security and achieving the UN SDGs (Chirico, 2021).

Religiosity and spirituality contribute positively to individual mental and physical health and increase levels of well-being, life satisfaction, and meaning and purpose in life, and decrease instances of anxiety, depression, and substance abuse (Luccheti et al., 2021). Prior to the pandemic, pathological religiosity was considered a major factor in regional and global conflicts and terrorism (Koenig, 2012). Although radicalism, pathological religiosity, violent extremism, and terrorism can create and expand broad mental health crises nationally and globally, healthy spirituality and religiosity may significantly improve public and global mental health and creation of a more compassionate civilization (Fox & Sandler, 2005). In this era of globalization and technological proliferation, many governments have ignored global public health issues and disasters which have subsequently resulted in ongoing conflicts and wars between and within nations (Chirico, 2021).

The pandemic will have both short- and long-term mental health implications, with increased instances of anxiety, depression, fatigue, sleep disorders, and stress (Rogers et al., 2020). The lockdown measures which were necessary weapons to combat the pandemic resulted in increased mental health problems (Pfefferbaum & North, 2020). Millions of emergency and healthcare workers were disproportionately affected by the pandemic, due to higher instances of coronavirus exposure, increased workloads, and watching patients die without the support of loved ones (Chirico, 2021). Disrupted funeral rituals and practices caused by the lockdown and social distancing measures exasperated grief processes because of the inability to connect with loved ones and the deceased (Mayland et al., 2020), further undermining mental health of the bereaved (Coppola et al., 2021). Feelings of social isolation, the fear of death, socioeconomic challenges, and uncertainty about the future intensified and complicated the grief experience (Santos et al., 2021).

Although consistent religious participation, which contributes to improved mental and emotional health, was prohibited during the pandemic lockdown, faith and spirituality have remained the primary method for emotional endurance during life-threatening circumstances (Chirico, 2021). During the pandemic, religious and spiritual beliefs were associated with increased levels of hopefulness and decreased levels of fear, anxiety, and sadness (Chirico, 2021). This suggests that spirituality and religion can be applied by individuals in a positive manner to find meaning, spiritual connections, and beneficial religious perspectives (Pargament et al., 1998).

5.3 Post-Pandemic Era

The post-pandemic era refers to the period after the COVID-19 pandemic which occurred between 2019 and 2023. This period is also referred to by some scholars and practitioners as the post-digital era, defined by *PC Magazine* (n.d.) as being beyond the digital age, or as a humanistic approach to problem-solving which places less emphasis on numerical analysis and computerized solutions. The post-digital era is currently in the embryonic stage, and discussion of this era is currently conjectural (Yin & Mahrous, 2022). According to leading management consulting firms, the focus of the post-digital era has shifted from the digital transformation of the digital era to applying digital technologies in significant ways to enhance competitive advantage (Accenture, 2019). Moreover, while the industrial era prioritized self-interest, control, hierarchy, productivity, and linearity, the post-digital is characterized by several unique characteristics: fully connected, meaning-based, and trust-centered (Yin & Mahrous, 2022).

In the post-digital era, advanced technologies such as distributed ledger technology (DLT), blockchain, artificial intelligence (AI), extended reality, quantum computing (DARQ), and the internet of things (IoT) will enable customers to acquire deeply engaging, highly personalized, interactive, AI-driven intelligent digital experiences (i.e., the 4I experience; Yin & Mahrous, 2022). Customers will be spontaneously served by highly customized products, services, and surroundings whenever needed (Accenture, 2019).

To adapt in the post-digital era and be instantly responsive to consumer demands, companies must develop thoroughly integrated, deeply interconnected, and highly coordinated ecosystems (Yin & Mahrous, 2022). In this intensely agile, flexible, and rapid ecosystem, each interdependent company functions as a node of equal status within the broader network. Resources and information are shared to maximize the collective success of the complete network, with power, authority, and capabilities decentralized and allocated using rotating leadership. The powerful bonding force and resulting development among nodes cannot be generated solely by the profit motive. Because these companies must be united by a higher purpose that creates a community of common mission, development, and future, workplace spirituality may become the foundation for such a network of completely connected organizations (Yin & Mahrous, 2022).

Creating value and wealth in the post-digital era will be primarily achieved through AI-enabled automation and robotics (McKinsey, 2020). However, the development of advanced technologies will mitigate the resource scarcity that has historically dominated humankind. Material abundance will eliminate competition for resources or goods for both consumers and organizations (Yin & Mahrous, 2022). Therefore, consumers will measure value by the content and meaning provided by the goods and services in the physical and continuously expanding metaverse (Yin & Mahrous, 2022). In this content-intensive era, organizations will transition from producing goods to creating meaning with their effectiveness determined by their ability to engage millions of individuals in co-creation and co-consumption within their unique realities. In the quest for quality of content and meaning, workplace spirituality will transform from an organizational principle to a powerful means of value creation (Yin & Mahrous, 2022).

The vast amounts of information created in an ultra-connected society will require organizations to develop trust-centered relationships with all stakeholders to ensure success and survival (Yin & Mahrous, 2022). Although a "trust architecture" based on distributed ledger technologies such as blockchain can substantially limit the risk of data breaches (McKinsey, 2020), an organization governed by sound moral and spiritual principles will receive genuine trust from stakeholders. These principles include selflessness, accepting responsibility for the betterment of humankind, complete equality and inclusiveness, transparency, and higher purpose. Spirituality, morality, and ethics will become the foundation for legitimacy in the post-digital era (Yin & Mahrous, 2022).

5.4 Individual Spirituality in the Post-Pandemic Era

Despite the devastation of recent pandemic, COVID-19 has exposed the pain of seclusion and social isolation, revealed the deepest desires of most individuals to focus on what is most important, and stimulated astonishing innovation and resilience (Philips, 2023). Individuals who were liberated from the restrictions of physical meetings learned that meaningful community could occur at home. The Fetzer Institute identified five significant COVID-influenced shifts in our religious and spiritual horizon (Philips, 2023):

1. Meaning takes the center stage.
2. Traditional delivery pathways for religious life are breaking down.
3. Community can be home-based.
4. Spiritual leadership is de-professionalizing.
5. Virtual connection can be surprisingly meaningful.

During the pandemic lockdown, millions of individuals globally stayed home to protect the most vulnerable members of the population. Humankind intentionally participated in the greatest event of collective solidarity in the history of humankind (Philips, 2023). People gathered on street corners and stood on their balconies to show their appreciation for healthcare workers. Forty six percent of young people reported attempting new spiritual practices during the pandemic (Philips, 2023). However, the devastation of economic inequality and unequal access to health care was apparent globally.

Priests and ministers held services which no one physically attended. Without church attendance and the liturgical rhythm of time, space, word, and music, important elements of meaning were lost (Philips, 2023). Decreased satisfaction with and membership in religious organizations began pressuring traditional religious institutions decades before the pandemic. Decades of financial decline impacted the ability of traditional congregations to deliver spiritual care virtually. The pandemic did not create these pressures, but the subsequent social disruption and adverse economic impact will accelerate deterioration of the foundations of religious and spiritual institutions (Philips, 2023). Despite the increasing trend toward religious disaffiliation, Millennials and GenZers have found new ways to create community connections, occasionally filling the gap created by the decline of religious and social institutions (Philips, 2023).

Spiritual resources are an important method for becoming resilient and managing the consequences of stressful events like pandemics (Clark & Hunter, 2019; Coppola et al., 2021), especially in elderly individuals (Koenig, 2020), who are typically the most active in religious and spiritual activities (Zimmer et al., 2016), but also among the most vulnerable (Chirico, 2021). Both believers and atheists need spiritual care and assistance during a crisis to avoid the distress that can impact mental well-being (Chirico, 2021). The pandemic empowered new leaders who performed community and spiritual tasks, such as meditation on Instagram, informal daily chapel services, and family members officiating funerals. Although the pandemic will expedite the decline of traditional religious institutions and traditions that supported earlier generations, it has also revealed new ways to find meaning and connection in contemporary society (Philips, 2023).

The COVID-19 pandemic has provided an opportunity to create new ways of living. Chirico (2021) proposed the need for a new spirituality in the post-pandemic era to confront new global challenges. Spirituality includes both philosophical and cultural elements that may contribute to solving emerging challenges such as climate change, unsustainable growth, migrant emergencies, conflicts, and global health insecurity (Chirico, 2021; Sinclair, 2019). Public health stakeholders should help maintain the continuity of spiritual and religious activities during crises and properly train healthcare professionals about this topic (Luccheti et al., 2021). The most vulnerable members of society (the elderly, sick, and marginalized) require special attention to cope with sudden major stressor events concurrent with pre-existing major life stressors (Del Castillo, 2021).

5.5 Workplace and Organizational Spirituality in the Post-Pandemic Era

The contemporary business environment has been described as "VUCA" (volatile, uncertain, complex, and ambiguous; White, 2013). The increased degree of improbability in business has generated significant interest of individuals, groups, organizations, industries, communities, and societies in resilience, to guarantee organizational continuity, sustainability, survival, and success (Kantur and Iseri-Say, 2015). Success in the VUCA environment can only be achieved with the flexibility, adaptability, and agility of resilient businesses (Esievo et al., 2019). Research findings demonstrated a significant influence of workplace spirituality on organizational resilience (Esievo et al., 2019). Using organizational culture to create an environment conducive to adopting workplace spirituality promotes robustness and adaptability which contributes to overall resilience. Esievo et al. (2019) recommended businesses continue to focus on meaningful work; develop policies to improve employees' work-life balance; align to common organizational tenets to enhance collective wisdom, determination, and excellence; and, embrace the interconnectedness as a means to enhance spirituality at work.

Technological advances continue to occur at an exponential rate, impacting how work is organized and performed. The organization of work at the collective and individual levels is dependent upon access to technologies that reinforce production and service along with the relationships between actors (Neal et al., 2022). Three important issues will impact the future of workplace spirituality: the decoupling of space and performance; increased real-time monitoring; and, optimizing oneself and others (Neal et al., 2022).

Technological advancements will increase the number of jobs that do not require employees to occupy a specific spatial setting. The COVID-19 pandemic clearly demonstrated the vast potential for work to be performed outside a traditional location provided by the employer (Neal et al., 2022). The proliferation of technology enables continuous surveillance of multiple aspects of individual, group, and organizational activities. Our lives have become entrenched in a capitalist system in which efficiency, effectiveness, and excellence are the individual and collective tenets that govern our lives, requiring vast amounts of personal information (Neal et al., 2022).

The following workplace developments should, and in some instances, already are occur in workplace spirituality implementation (Neal et al., 2022): increasing emphasis on the physical body; supporting the present beyond functionalization; and establishing, defending, and increasing sacred spaces. Many spiritual worldviews recognize the significance of the body as an essential component of the configuration of human beings. Workplace spirituality is affected when the area in which work is performed is disconnected from the group in which performance is accomplished, increasing concern about issues such as accountability, integrity, and meaningfulness (Neal et al., 2022). Offering areas in which employees and groups can intentionally explore and experience spirituality is essential in an environment in which high performance and productivity are expected (Neal et al., 2022). The element of a sacred space is present in most spiritual traditions and practices, and a common characteristic is the seclusion from everything that permeates daily life (Neal et al., 2022).

A positive relationship has been demonstrated between workplace spirituality and well-being, with workforce agility and organizational identification concurrent mediators of this relationship (Srivastava & Gupta, 2022). Supportive organizational procedures and systems are necessary to ensure flexibility, adaptability, and preparedness for reacting to disruptive events (Srivastava & Gupta, 2022). Employee negative emotions may adversely impact organizational outcomes, especially during crises (Quy et al., 2023). Moreover, the positive connection between workplace spirituality and creative adaptability has been found to be negatively related to the negative emotions of employees (Quy et al., 2023).

5.6 Risks and Dangers of Post-Pandemic Workplace Spirituality

In Chapter 3, several concerns were raised about the risks associated with workplace spirituality. First, workplace spirituality may inadvertently eliminate any differentiation between employee workplace and personal lives (Tourish & Tourish, 2010). Employees and managers could coopt workplace spirituality to promote personal spiritual beliefs to proselytize colleagues (Lips-Wiersma et al., 2009; Milliman et al., 2003), or one interest group could dominate the organization (Karakas, 2010). Second, management could utilize workplace spirituality to maximize productivity through instrumentality and manipulation (Lips-Wiersma et al., 2009; Milliman et al., 2003). This darker side to workplace spirituality has been described by some researchers as the "symbolic violence" of organizational spirituality through the cultural intolerance of managerial power and the effects of indoctrination (Kamoche & Pinnington, 2012). Case and Gosling (2010) were concerned that if spirituality becomes incorporated in the business agenda, it may become so intrinsic in the organizational structure and dynamics that management expects complete alignment of employee beliefs and values with those of the organization. Finally, an organization endorsing workplace spirituality may become so homogenous that decisions become biased by groupthink (Polley et al., 2005), a process in which peer pressure encourages individuals to conform to the opinions and ideas of the group (Robbins & Coulter, 2012).

The marketing of the mindfulness practice as workplace commodity has been labeled McMindfulness (Kristensen, 2018). Despite the individual and societal benefits of mindfulness, the introduction of mindfulness activities in the workplace poses risks. Kristensen suggested workplace mindfulness practices risk reinforcing the problems they were intended to solve. Mindfulness practices have been commodified to become a ubiquitous and superficial McMindfulness experience (Hyland, 2016) that is disregarding and replacing the ethical basis of the meditative practices and traditions from which mindfulness originated (Purser & Loy, 2013). Bazzano (2014) suggested that corporate mindfulness programs have become "a quick fix for the anxieties of late-capitalist society" (p. 164). These mindfulness programs have become acceptable to the business community because they enhance the exclusive quest for corporate objectives and profitability masquerading as means of caring for employees (Kristensen, 2018). McMindfulness programs completely satisfy Ritzer's (1993) model of McDonaldization characterized by the commodification of every aspect of life through standardization, calculability, and control for the uncompromising achievement of profit (Hyland, 2016).

The term *workism* was introduced prior to the pandemic, defined as "the belief that work is not only necessary to economic production but also the centerpiece of one's identity and life's purpose" (Thompson, 2019, 2023). Thompson suggested that American priorities can be determined by how they spend their time. In 2022, while only just 30% of Americans attended a religious service during a given week (Gallup, 2022), 76% of Americans worked during a given week (Montgomery, 2022 as cited in Hess, 2023). According to Thompson, everyone worships something—beauty, political identities, or children (Hess, 2023). *Workism* is one of the most powerful of the new religions competing for adherents (Thompson, 2023). Thompson was raised Jewish, but "followed the classic path from Reform Judaism to atheism to agnosticism to a kind of bastardized-westernized-godless-Buddhism". This pseudo-Buddhist perspective is evident in his work, for example, his definition of happiness being a balance between "busyness" and leisure (Thompson, 2023).

Thompson (2023) suggested that *workism* has three pillars and multiple potential negative side effects. The pillars are: employees use work to replace the meaning previously provided by religion; employees demand more from employers (e.g., sense of community); and, work can offer meaning and increase productivity but can also overextend and exhaust employees. Thompson (2023) stated that on an individual level, *workism* increases academic anxiety in children and economic anxiety in adults, creates a "leaky" workday in which employees feel obligated to work all hours of the day, and intensifies feelings of isolation in retirees. Thompson warned that *workism* negatively influences public policy, noting that in the United States, work is so centered in policy that it is the only OECD (Organisation for Economic Co-operation and

Development) nation without national policies on medical or parental leave (Thompson, 2023).

Thompson's greatest concern is that *workism* places greater emphasis on work relationships than personal relationships (Thompson, 2023). Thomson further suggested that *workism* increases vulnerability to artificial intelligence, and job elimination by automation. Thompson admitted that his critique of *workism* can appear excessive because religious institutions can also harm individuals, noting that many major established religions have excluded LGBTQ individuals, abused Indigenous Peoples, and engaged in wars and acts of violence (Hess, 2023). Thompson concluded that when compared to all the current problems in the world, people loving their jobs a little too much is not a significant problem.

5.7 Discussion

During the COVID-19 pandemic, policymakers faced unprecedented challenges concerning public health because social and economic turmoil resulting from lockdown measures proved detrimental to the physical and psychological well-being of the global population (ILO, FAO, IFAD, WHO, 2020). Health inequity and socioeconomic inequality between developed and developing countries will remain the primary challenges to be addressed by global health stakeholders. In a broader sense, individual spiritual well-being is dependent upon planetary well-being. However, as noted by the One Health Initiative (2023), a global strategy to expand interdisciplinary collaborations and communications in all areas of health care for humans, animals, and the environment, it is critical that we acknowledge that humankind and our health are "one" with the Earth, and this interconnection incorporates the physical, psychological, social, economic, and spiritual elements of our well-being (Chirico, 2016; Chirico et al., 2019).

Businesses and organizations that survived the pandemic experienced significant impacts to how they operate. Three long-lasting impacts include: placing organizational resilience at the top of the corporate agenda, changing how employees work (remote and hybrid), and employees reassessing the role of work and the overall meaning of life based on feelings of uncertainty, insecurity, and anxiety (Yin & Mahrous, 2022). More than half of the global workforce worked remotely in 2021, replacing decades of 9-to-5, office-centric practice with a remote home office work model. Employers responded by rapidly transitioning to a hybrid-workforce model and developing expansive virtual work platforms (Yin & Mahrous, 2022).

Remote work from home (WFH) in a digital organization appears to be the new normal (Yin & Mahrous, 2022). However, the absence of in-person engagement has contributed to feelings of isolation, resulting in reduced motivation, focus, and organizational commitment (Pew Research Center, 2021). Therefore, employers and researchers must determine how to maintain feelings of connection and belonging among employees in highly virtual environments where physical contact has been replaced by digital communication. This feeling of connection and belonging is essential for defining organizational culture and identity to foster employee loyalty, motivation, and organizational commitment to work, which are the key ingredients for organizational resilience (Yin & Mahrous, 2022).

The movement toward more purpose-driven work began before the pandemic because of the increased social conscience of millennials and has since accelerated. Therefore, creating deeper meaning for employees' work and lives has become a critical issue for organizations (Yin & Mahrous, 2022). Developing deeper connections between employees and organizations and creating meaning and purpose in the workplace will become more essential for organizations to become resilient and achieve sustainable growth in the post-pandemic VUCA business environment (Yin & Mahrous, 2022).

There are three ways workplace spirituality can serve an important role in accomplishing this (Yin & Mahrous, 2022). First, workplace spirituality provides employees an original, effective means to connect with peers and employers (Yin & Mahrous, 2022). An employee who is spiritually connected to an organization is more likely to view work as a vocation or a calling, thereby becoming more committed to the organization. Second, because spirituality is a profoundly private and individual experience that requires minimal interaction with other individuals, a spiritual connection with an organization enables employees to experience a sense of belonging and connectedness with colleagues and employers in a virtual organization. Third, because the substance of workplace spirituality is meaning and higher purpose, organizational support for workplace spirituality inevitably introduces meaning and purpose into employees' work and the organization. This sense of meaning and purpose empowers employees to achieve excellence, resulting in unprecedented organizational performance (Yin & Mahrous, 2022).

5.8 Conclusion

Major events and catastrophes often trigger religious and spiritual participation and movements. However, those events and behaviors are often temporary and acquiesce to the overarching trend of secular modernism and postmodernity. The human quest for spirituality is influenced by the forces of secularism, technology, institutions, culture, and current events. The enchantment of traditional and Indigenous belief systems is continually suppressed and replaced with the disenchantment of science and enlightenment. Events that occurred concurrently with the pandemic such as the economic recession, police brutality, and racial inequality may have influenced the willingness of individuals and groups to embrace change influencing their sense of spirituality. Spirituality has influenced and been influenced by the pandemic and its effect on humankind. Spirituality is more than a belief, philosophy, or theme, but is also a method for dealing with unexpected and uncertain events in an equanimous manner. Perhaps the pandemic has sufficiently reminded humankind of our mortality that we will embrace and retain our spiritual compass, with all individuals doing so either present or absent any formal religious dogma.

The pandemic reminded individuals of the frailty of human life, and while church attendance had been declining pre-pandemic, humans are by nature spiritual, and may find an increased need to connect with their god after the pandemic (Sterling, as cited by Lubrano, 2020).

Being forced to contemplate death on a substantial scale forces individuals to contemplate their purpose in living (Lubrano, 2020). During the Black Death in the fourteenth century, between 25 and 30 million people died, and, according to historians, the medieval mind blamed the disease on God's inability to hear the prayers of the infected, and not on a disease spread by rodents carrying infected fleas. The resulting catastrophe diminished the faith of religious believers (Lubrano, 2020). Fortunately, scholars predict less turmoil in the aftermath of the current pandemic, suggesting we may witness a post-pandemic resurgence in faith (Lubrano, 2020).

Reflection Topic

Watts and Houtman (2023) suggested a deep divide exists in the discussion of workplace spirituality. Advocates of workplace spirituality consider it the ultimate solution to the problems faced by contemporary work organizations while critics consider it another method of capitalist expropriation. Proponents advocate a *schema of purification* suggesting that after the moral abuses of bureaucracy and justification are removed from the workplace, the realms of spirituality and work will become integrated, leading to the sanctification of work by spirituality. This releases the authentic inner self of workers (the *spiritual/sacred*) from being subject to alienating compartmentalization which enables employees to achieve higher ethical values and increased existential meaning at work (Watts & Houtman, 2023).

Critics of workplace spirituality advocate a *schema of pollution* suggesting that any attempt to integrate spirituality and work under capitalist conditions will fail because the infection or pollution from the evils of capitalism ultimately desacralizes spirituality and removes any meaning from work. The outcome will be increased discomfort from alienation, instrumentality, and the commodification of spirituality, and work becoming more manipulative and overwhelming. Among advocates of the *schema of purification*, the integration of spirituality and work may appear to be a win–win scenario, in which individual integration and self-fulfillment result in increased productivity and profitability. However, advocates of the *schema of pollution* believe that any integration of spirituality and work within capitalist organizations can only produce moral and political disaster (Watts & Houtman, 2023).

Reflection Questions

1. Workplace spirituality research and programs have existed for decades. How will workplace spirituality programs and success change in the post-pandemic era?
2. What are the strengths and weaknesses of the *schema of purification* perspective of workplace spirituality in the post-pandemic era? What are the risks for corporate abuse if this perspective is applied in the workforce?
3. What are the strengths and weaknesses of the *schema of pollution* perspective of workplace spirituality in the post-pandemic era? What actions can researchers and practitioners take to mitigate the suggested risks of corporate abuse if this perspective is applied in the workforce?
4. What changes may occur in the workforce and among workers in the post-pandemic era that may support or refute the *schema of purification* and *schema of pollution* perspectives?

References

Accenture. (2019). *Accenture technology vision 2019.* https://www.accenture.com/_acnmedia/pdf-94/accenture-techvision-2019-tech-trends-report.pdf

Bazzano, A. (2014). *After mindfulness.* Palgrave Macmillan.

Case, P., & Gosling, J. (2010). The spiritual organization: Critical reflections on the instrumentality of workplace spirituality. *Journal of Management, Spirituality and Religion, 7*(4), 257–282. https://doi.org/10.1080/14766086.2010.524727

Chirico, F. (2016). Spiritual well-being in the 21st century: It is time to review the current WHO's health definition. *Journal of Health Social Sciences, 1*(1), 11–16. https://doi.org/10.19204/2016/sprt2.

Chirico, F. (2021). Spirituality to cope with COVID-19 pandemic, climate change and future global challenges. *Journal of Health Social Sciences,*

6(2), 151–158. https://journalhss.com/wp-content/uploads/jhhs_62_151-158.pdf
Chirico, F., Heponiemi, T., Pavlova, M., Zaffina, S., & Magnavita, N. (2019). Psychosocial risk prevention in a global occupational health perspective. A descriptive analysis. *International Journal of Environmental Research on Public Health, 16*(14), 2470. https://doi.org/10.3390/ijerph16142470
Clark, C. C., & Hunter, J. (2019). Spirituality, spiritual well-being, and spiritual coping in advanced heart failure. *Journal of Holistic Nursing, 37*, 56–73. https://doi.org/10.1177/0898010118761401
Coppola, I., Rania, N., Parisi, R., & Lagomarsino, F. (2021). Spiritual well-being and mental health during the CO- VID-19 pandemic in Italy. *Front Psychiatry, 12*, 626944. https://doi.org/10.3389/fpsyt.2021.626944
Del Castillo, F. A. (2021). Health, spirituality and Covid-19: Themes and insights. *Journal of Public Health, 43*(2), e254–e255. https://doi.org/10.1093/pubmed/fdaa185
Esievo, F. K., Oshi, J. E. O., Hettey, H. D., & Tende, F. B. (2019). Workplace spirituality and organizational resilience of shipping companies in rivers state. *Scholarly Journal of Business Administration, 8*(3), 45–51. http://www.scholarly-journals.com/SJBA
Fox, J., & Sandler, S. (2005). Separation of religion and state in the twenty-first century: Comparing the Middle East and Western Democracies. Comparative Politics, 37(3), 317–335. https://doi.org/10.2307/20072892
Gallup. (2022). *Religion*. https://news.gallup.com/poll/1690/religion.aspx
Hess, A.J. (2023). *How 'workism' replaced religion*. https://www.fastcompany.com/90875705/how-workism-replaced-religion
Hyland, T. (2016). *McMindfulness: Is Buddhism contaminated by capitalism?—Interview with Terry Hyland*. Accessed February 12, 2017. https://www.researchgate.net/publication/293170265_McMindfulness_Is_Buddhism_contaminated_by_capitalism
ILO, FAO, IFAD, WHO. (October 13, 2020). *Impact of Covid-19 on people's livelihoods, their health and our food systems*. https://www.who.int/news/item/13-10-2020-impact-of-covid-19-on-people's-livelihoods-their-health-and-our-food-systems
Kalafatoğlu, Y. (2022). Workplace spirituality for more sustainable organizations. In *Handbook of research on integrating spirituality in modern workplaces* (pp. 80–95). IGI Global.
Kamoche, K., & Pinnington, A. H. (2012). Managing people 'spiritually': A bourdieusian critique. *Work, Employment and Society, 26*(3), 497–513. https://doi.org/10.1177/0950017012438573

Kantur, D., and Iseri-Say, A. (2015). Measuring organizational resilience: A scale development. *Journal of Business, Economics and Finance, 4*(3), 456–472. https://doi.org/10.17261/PRESSACADEMIA.2015313066

Karakas, F. (2010). Spirituality and performance in organizations: A literature review. *Journal of Business Ethics, 94*(1), 89–106. https://doi.org/10.1007/s10551-009-0251-5

Koenig, H. G. (2012). Religion, spirituality, and health: The research and clinical implications. *International Scholarly Research Notices, 2012*, 278730. https://doi.org/10.5402/2012/278730

Koenig, H. G. (2020). Maintaining health and well-being by putting faith into action during the COVID-19 pandemic. *Journal of Religion & Health, 59*(5), 2205–2214. https://doi.org/10.1007/s10943-020-01035-2

Kristensen, M. L. (2018). Mindfulness and resonance in an era of acceleration: A critical inquiry. *Journal of Management, Spirituality & Religion, 15*(2), 178–195. https://doi.org/10.1080/14766086.2017.1418413

Lips-Wiersma, M., Dean, K. L., & Fornaciari, C. J. (2009). Theorizing the dark side of the workplace spirituality movement. *Journal of Management Inquiry, 18*(4), 288–300. https://doi.org/10.1177/1056492609339017

Lubrano, A. (August 1, 2020). Could COVID-19 inspire the faithful? Scholars predict spirituality surge in our future. *Philadelphia Inquirer*. https://www.inquirer.com/news/religion-coronavirus-god-pandemic-mortality-islam-judaism-christianity-20200801.html

Lucchetti, G., Góes, L. G., Amaral, S. G., Ganadjian, G. T., Andrade, I., Almeida, P. O. D. A., & Mendes do Carmo, V., & Manso, M. E. G. (2021). Spirituality, religiosity and the mental health consequences of social isolation during Covid-19 pandemic. *International Journal of Social Psychiatry, 67*(6), 672–679. https://doi.org/10.1177/0020764020970996

Mayland, C. R., Harding, A. J. E., Preston, N., & Payne, S. (2020). Supporting adults bereaved through COVID-19: A rapid review of the impact of previous pandemics on grief and bereavement. *Journal of Pain Symptom Management, 60*(2), 33–39. https://doi.org/10.1016/j.jpainsymman.2020.05.012

McKinsey, (2020). *The top trends in tech.* McKinsey Report.

Milliman, J., Czaplewski, A. J., & Ferguson, J. (2003). Workplace spirituality and employee work attitudes: An exploratory empirical assessment. *Journal of Organizational Change Management, 16*(4), 426–447. https://doi.org/10.1108/09534810310484172

Montgomery, D. H. (2022). *Who's not working in the U.S.? Learn the basics.* Federal Reserve Bank of Minneapolis. https://www.minneapolisfed.org/article/2022/whos-not-working-in-the-us-learn-the-basics

Neal, J., Altman, Y., & Mayrhofer, W. (2022). The past, present and future of workplace spirituality. In Y. Altman, J. Neal, & W. Mayrhofer (Eds.), *Workplace spirituality—Making a difference* (pp. 3–20). De Gruyter.

Nortey, J. (2022). *More houses of worship are returning to normal operations, but in-person attendance is unchanged since fall.* Pew Research Center. https://www.pewresearch.org/fact-tank/2022/03/22/more-houses-of-worship-are-returning-to-normal-operations-but-in-person-attendance-is-unchanged-since-fall.

One Health Initiative. (2023). *About*. https://onehealthinitiative.com/about/

Pargament, K. I., Smith, B. W., Koenig, H. G., & Perez, L. (1998). Patterns of positive and negative religious coping with major life stressors. *Journal for the Scientific Study of Religion,* 710–724. https://doi.org/10.2307/1388152

PC Magazine. (n.d.). Post-digital era. https://www.pcmag.com/encyclopedia/term/post-digital-era

Pew Research Center. (2021). *More Americans than people in other advanced economies say COVID-19 has strengthened religious faith.* https://www.pewresearch.org/religion/2021/01/27/more-americans-than-people-in-other-advanced-economies-say-covid-19-has-strengthened-religious-faith/

Pfefferbaum, B., & North, C. S. (2020). Mental health and the Covid-19 pandemic. *New England Journal of Medicine, 383*(6), 510–512. https://doi.org/10.1056/NEJMp2008017

Philips, S. (2023). *Five COVID-fueled shifts in our religious and spiritual landscape.* Fetzer Institute. https://fetzer.org/blog/five-covid-fueled-shifts-our-religious-and-spiritual-landscape

Polley, D., Vora, J., & SubbaNarasimha, P. N. (2005). Paying the devil his due: Limits and liabilities of workplace spirituality. *International Journal of Organizational Analysis, 13*(1), 50–63. https://doi.org/10.1108/eb028997

Purser, R., & Loy, D. (2013). Beyond McMindfulness. *Huffington Post, 7*, 13.

Quy, H. T. K., Tran, M. D., & Dinh, T. M. (2023). Mitigating the negative emotions of employees in times of crisis: The role of workplace spirituality and employees' creative adaptability. *Global Business and Organizational Excellence.* https://doi.org/10.1002/joe.22232

Ritzer, G. (1993). *The McDonaldization of society: An investigation into the changing character of contemporary social life.* Pine Forge Press.

Robbins, S.P., & Coulter, M. (2012). *Management* (12th ed.). Pearson Prentice-Hall.

Rogers, J. P., Chesney, E., Oliver, D., Pollak, T. A., McGuire, P., Fusar-Poli, P., Zandi, M. S., Lewis, G., & David, A. S. (2020). Psychiatric and neuropsychiatric presentations associated with severe coronavirus infections: A systematic review and meta-analysis with comparison to the COVID-19 pandemic. *The Lancet Psychiatry, 7*(7), 611–627. https://doi.org/10.1016/S2215-0366(20)30203-0

Sahgal, N., & Connaughton, A. (2021). *More Americans than people in other advanced economies say COVID-19 has strengthened religious faith.* Pew Research Center. https://www.pewresearch.org/religion/2021/01/27/more-americans-than-people-in-other-advanced-economies-say-covid-19-has-strengthened-religious-faith

Santos, S., Sá, T., Aguiar, I., Cardoso, I., Correia, Z., & Correia, T. (2021). Case report: Parental loss and childhood grief during COVID-19 pandemic. *Frontiers in Psychiatry, 12*, 626940. https://doi.org/10.3389/fpsyt.2021.626940

Sinclair, J. R. (2019). Importance of a One Health approach in advancing global health security and the Sustainable Development Goals. *Revue scientifique et technique (International Office of Epizootics), 38*(1), 145–154. https://doi.org/10.20506/rst.38.1.2949.

Srivastava, S., & Gupta, P. (2022). Workplace spirituality as panacea for waning well-being during the pandemic crisis: A SDT perspective. *Journal of Hospitality and Tourism Management, 50*, 375–388. https://doi.org/10.1016/2Fj.jhtm.2021.11.014

Thompson, D. (2019). Workism is making Americans miserable. *The Atlantic,* February 24.

Thompson, D. (2023). *On work: Money, meaning, identity.* Atlantic Editions.

Tourish, D., & Tourish, N. (2010). Spirituality at work, and its implications for leadership and followership: A post-structuralist perspective. *Leadership, 6*(2), 207–224. https://doi.org/10.1177/1742715010363210

Watts, G., & Houtman, D. (2023). Purification or pollution? The debate over 'workplace spirituality.' *Cultural Sociology, 17*(4), 439–456. https://doi.org/10.1177/17499755221108607

White, M. (2013). *Building a resilient organizational culture.* UNC Kenan-Flagler Business School.

Witt-Swanson, L., Benz, J., & Cox, D. A. (2023). *Faith after the pandemic: How COVID-19 changed American religion: Findings from the 2022 American Religious Benchmark Survey*. American Survey Center. https://www.americansurveycenter.org/research/faith-after-the-pandemic-how-covid-19-changed-american-religion/

World Health Organization (2023a). *WHO coronavirus (COVID-19) dashboard*. https://covid19.who.int/

World Health Organization. (2023b). *WHO Director-General's opening remarks at the media briefing—5 May 2023.* https://www.who.int/news-room/speeches/item/who-director-general-s-opening-remarks-at-the-media-briefing---5-may-2023

Yin, E., & Mahrous, A. (2022). Covid-19 global pandemic, workplace spirituality and the rise of spirituality-driven organisations in the post-digital era. *Journal of Humanities and Applied Social Sciences, 4*(2), 79–93. https://doi.org/10.1108/JHASS-11-2021-0177

Zimmer, Z., Jagger, C., Chiu, C. T., Ofstedal, M. B., Rojo, F., & Saito, Y. (2016). Spirituality, religiosity, aging and health in global perspective: A review. *SSM-Population Health, 2*, 373–381. https://doi.org/10.1016/j.ssmph.2016.04.009

6
Sustainability and Success

6.1 Introduction

The following chapter includes an examination of the benefits of sustainability in terms of individual and career success. We begin with the definition(s), theoretical framework, and a synthesized literature summary of sustainability. The benefits of applying sustainability at the individual level, and the methods by which individuals have successfully applied sustainability to achieve success are explored. While individual sustainability is an important consideration, research examining individual sustainability, and how sustainability initiatives provide individual meaning or fulfillment at the individual level is limited. The focus of this chapter is the examination of how sustainability contributes to individual and career success. Success is explored in terms of finance and career, as well as quality of life and well-being. Contemporary movements influencing individual sustainability, including simple living or voluntary simplicity, and the tiny house movement will be explored. Career theory will be examined as a lens through which to examine the relationship between sustainability and individual success. Responsible careers, boundaryless careers, and the differentiation between job, career, and calling will be discussed. Various sustainable careers opportunities

C. G. Beehner, *Spirituality, Sustainability, and Success*, Palgrave Studies in Workplace Spirituality and Fulfillment, https://doi.org/10.1007/978-3-031-47643-3_6

will be explored, and the chapter concludes with a personal interview of someone who has been successful in a sustainability career.

While studies have examined leaders who engage in sustainability (Rimanoczy, 2014), limited academic research has addressed how sustainability initiatives provide personal meaning or fulfillment at the individual level (Visser & Crane, 2010). Researchers have paid little attention to corporate sustainability at the individual level, resulting in limited knowledge about the profound psychological motivations of sustainability leaders, and how these motivations influence behavior and effectiveness as facilitators of organizational change (Schein, 2014; Visser & Crane, 2010). Moreover, few theoretical studies have examined the integration of ecological worldviews and action within the sustainability leadership context (Boiralet al., 2009; Esbjorn-Hargens & Zimmerman, 2011).

The focus of existing literature examining corporate sustainability at the individual level has occurred in four categories: values alignment between individual and organizational values; the instrumental relationship between individual consideration, engagement, and knowledge and corporate social and environmental responsiveness; narrative accounts of business 'greening' by sustainability managers; and, the role of sustainable managers as organizational champions or change agents (Visser & Crane, 2010). The literature enhances our understanding of individual sustainability within an organizational context by emphasizing: the importance of values, attitudes, and beliefs in advancing corporate sustainability; the essential role of education and awareness in achieving behavioral change; the importance of managerial discretion in implementing change; the power of corporate culture in assembling a common sustainability narrative; and, the essential role of leadership in supporting sustainability (Visser & Crane, 2010).

While individual sustainability is an important consideration, it is frequently missing from most sustainability conversations (Pappas & Pappas, 2014). The issue of individual sustainability is controversial because individuals often seem incapable of aligning demonstrated behaviors with desired values within the context of sustainability. According to Pappas and Pappas, sustainable individuals are described as individuals who create harmony, interconnection, and possess relatively high levels of self-awareness of their values, thoughts, behaviors, and actions. These individuals possess a well-developed and determined value system recognizing the importance and interconnectedness of all planetary biological and social systems, and our suitable place within them. Pappas and Pappas suggest sustainable individuals possess awareness, motivation, and the ability to undertake intentional self-development.

Personality, and the manifestations thereof comprise a complex, interdependent system related to multiple factors, the alteration of any of which would likely produce unpredictable changes in one or more of the remaining factors (Pappas & Pappas, 2014). One of the major impediments of this systems approach to personality is that the five individual sustainability contexts (emotional, social, physical, economic, and intellectual) have a complex influence on each other, an interaction requiring increased awareness to fully understand. The measurement of individual sustainability appears dependent upon thorough assessment and evaluation of multiple human factors (Pappas & Pappas, 2014). Further understanding of the reciprocal influences of complex personality systems is necessary to understand how personality influences sustainability behavior. However, existing research indicates student desire for integrity and individual value consistency, tends to produce value and behavior alignment, because successful behaviors usually emerge as personality characteristics (Pappas & Pappas, 2014).

6.2 Sustainability Defined

Over the past 20 years, sustainability has become more than a passing fad or a buzzword (Rogers, 2016). While there are countless definitions of sustainability, most related to specific fields of study, the focus of the chapters in this book is sustainability as related to business and development. While academia strives for consistent terminology usage, the terms green and sustainable (or sustainability) are sometimes used interchangeably (Collins et al., 2016). However, in business, the term green is increasingly applied to products and processes, while sustainability is applied to systems and enterprises (Yanarella et al., 2009). The word sustainability is an unintentional *portmanteau* suggesting an *ability* to *sustain* the planet for future generations' enjoyment and use.

A commonly accepted definition of sustainability is from the field of sustainable development, drawn from the World Commission on Environment and Development (WCED), commonly known as the Brundtland Report. "Sustainable development is the development that meets the needs of the present without compromising the ability of future generations to meet their own needs" (WCED, 1987). Hence, because the focus of several chapters of this book is examining sustainability within the context of individual and organizational success, we will consider sustainability as referring to actions taken by individuals and organizations to ensure that their present needs are met without compromising the ability of future individuals and organizations to meet their needs in similar fashion.

The term 'sustainability' is used interchangeably with sustainable development (Seghezzo, 2009), although there are some recognizable distinctions between the two concepts (Dresner, 2002). Because the term sustainability originated in the environmental movement, the focus is frequently with environmental issues and challenges (Soyka, 2012). The WCED concept of sustainability is often characterized by the 'triple bottom line' of economy, environment, and society (Elkington et al., 2007), referred to colloquially as the three Ps—profits, planet, and people (Seghezzo, 2009). According to Down and McKeown (2017), the characteristics of sustainable development include: interconnectedness, a whole system approach, and working for the common good. Contemporary sustainability principles and themes include: change; environmental protection; balance and integration of environment, society, and economy (triple bottom line); human-centered development; the right of nations to development with respect for boundaries; intergenerational equity; equity for all people; partnership; decentralization; transparency and accountability; family; livable communities; and, education (Cooper & Vargas, 2004).

6.3 Historical Background of Sustainability

Concern for environmental sustainability can be traced back to Malthus in the eighteenth century, and as far back as Greece in the period of antiquities. Many attribute the current sustainability movement to the Brundtland Commission, formerly known as the World Commission on Environment and Development, established by the United Nations in 1983. The WECD produced a document entitled *Our common future*, which among other things, coined the term sustainable development (WECD, 1987). The conceptual definition of the Brundtland Commission report contains two key concepts: the concept of "needs", with predominant priority given to meeting the essential needs of the poor; and, the concept of restrictions imposed by the state of technology and social organization on the ability of the planet to meet the present and future needs of all inhabitants (Mebratu, 1998).

The Rio Declaration on Environment and Development was a document prepared by the United Nations at the Earth Summit in Rio de Janeiro, Brazil in 1992. The Rio Declaration consists of 27 principles, many of which have a strong sustainability focus. Although the declaration signed by 170 countries raised environmental awareness globally, critics argue little progress has been made in environmental areas (Palmer & Nursey-Bray, 2007). However, one initiative successfully originating from the Earth Summit was the Earth Charter which was formally inaugurated in 2002 at the Hague. "The Earth Charter is a document with sixteen principles that drive a global movement toward a more just, sustainable and peaceful world" (Earth Charter International, n.d.).

While the genesis of sustainability is often associated with the Brundtland Commission and the subsequent WECD report, nearly two centuries earlier, prominent economist Thomas Robert Malthus (1766–1834) recognized the impact of natural resource scarcity on economic growth (Mebratu, 1998). Prior to the beginning of the nineteenth century, Malthus and other economists recognized the adverse effects of the Industrial Revolution in terms of disease, poverty, and unemployment (Mebratu, 1998). While other economists blamed the problems of society on evil institutions, Malthus attributed the adverse effects on the expanding productivity of humans (Mebratu, 1998). The premise of Malthusian economics is that overpopulation of the human species would result in catastrophic depletion of natural resources. If humankind did not keep their numbers in check, war, environmental crises, or natural resource scarcity would accomplish the task (Malthus, 1798). Potential planetary catastrophe would be a result of the intersection of unchecked geometrical population increases and arithmetical increases in subsistence (Oser & Blanchfield, 1975).

The prognostications of Malthus would be echoed 150 years later by Ernest F. Schumacher in his 1959 lectures at London University entitled *The Crucial Problems of Modern Living*. Schumacher proposed a post-industrial society, in which humankind has left behind its lethal obsession with the megasystems of production and distribution that John Maynard Keynes endeavored to manage tried so hard to make manageable (Roszak, 1989). Schumacher is best known for *Small Is Beautiful*, published in 1979 wherein he proposed a transition from the emergent technocratic world system to a renaissance of organic husbandry, communal households, and do-it-yourself proficiency (Roszak, 1989). The key themes addressed in *Small Is Beautiful* included (McClaughry, 1989): criticism of large, over-organized systems as destructive to people and planet; concern about resource and environmental degradation; the concept of "appropriate technology" and the significance of human scale; failure of traditional economics to influence policy concerning non-economic factors; and, the need for humankind to nurture the planet. With the environmental movement already underway, Schumacher's book became a rallying cry against pollution, natural resource overconsumption, and corporate excesses (McClaughry, 1989; Mebratu, 1998). Schumacher's reiteration of Malthusian planetary concerns provided a contemporary voice for the emerging environmental movement, while adding a new dimension of organizational scale to the triple bottom line characterization of sustainability (Mebratu, 1998).

While environmental degradation and deterioration have become a prevalent topic during the previous few centuries, concern for the adverse effect of humankind on the environment dates to ancient Greece. The Athenians became concerned with deforestation and agricultural excesses as early as the sixth century BCE (Wright, 2004). Examples of societies and empires late to recognize their adverse effects on nature include Easter Island and Sumeria, while the Mayan and Roman empires survived adverse environmental actions though losing empire status in the process (Wright, 2004).

On September 25, 2015, the United Nations adopted 17 goals to end poverty, protect the planet, and ensure prosperity for all inhabitants as part of a new sustainable development agenda (United Nations, 2015). Each goal has specific targets to be achieved over the next 15 years. The 17 sustainable development goals (SDGs) superseded the Millenium Development Goals (MDGs) and are summarized below:

1. End poverty in all its forms everywhere.
2. End hunger, achieve food security and improved nutrition, and promote sustainable agriculture.
3. Ensure healthy lives and promote well-being for all at all ages.
4. Ensure inclusive and equitable quality education and promote life-long learning opportunities for all.
5. Achieve gender equality and empower all women and girls.
6. Ensure availability and sustainable management of water and sanitation for all.
7. Ensure access to affordable, reliable, sustainable, and modern energy for all.
8. Promote sustained, inclusive, and sustainable economic growth, full and productive employment, and decent work for all.
9. Build resilient infrastructure, promote inclusive, and sustainable industrialization and foster innovation.
10. Reduce inequality within and among countries.
11. Make cities and human settlements inclusive, safe, resilient, and sustainable.
12. Ensure sustainable consumption and production patterns.
13. Take urgent action to combat climate change and its impacts.
14. Conserve and sustainably use the oceans, seas, and marine resources for sustainable development.
15. Protect, restore, and promote sustainable use of terrestrial ecosystems, sustainably manage forests, combat desertification, and halt and reverse land degradation and halt biodiversity loss.

16. Promote peaceful and inclusive societies for sustainable development, provide access to justice for all and build effective, accountable, and inclusive institutions at all levels.
17. Strengthen the means of implementation and revitalize the global partnership for sustainable development (United Nations, 2015).

The goals clearly extend beyond environmental aspects, suggesting sustainability is not only about preservation of the planet, but also of the inhabitants.

6.4 Current State of and Necessity for Sustainability

The present ecological disaster is a result of human exploitation of natural resources in a capitalist, consumerist global economy dominated by a mechanistic worldview (van Schalkwyk, 2011). The root of our primary environmental problem is human arrogance which places immediate personal welfare above the long-term needs of present and future generations, and the planet (Berry, 1999). The term Anthropocene is being used by geologists to identify the current geological era in which humankind are now radically altered terrestrial systems (Heaton, 2016). These changes are resulting in climate change, biodiversity loss, and interruption of the nitrogen cycle (Rockström et al., 2009), potentially creating catastrophic crises of geopolitical, natural resource, and economic order (Sörlin, 2014).The number and magnitude of crises necessitate scholars from multiple disciplines, including management to address the rapid and significant movement toward the Anthropocene era (Hoffman & Jennings, 2015).

The planet has an estimated 1.9 hectares of biologically productive land per capita to satisfy human resource and waste absorption needs. However, current human usage is 2.3 hectares, with "ecological footprints" ranging from 9.7 hectares for the average American, to 0.47 hectares for the average Mozambican (Worldwatch Institute, 2011). While the United States contains less than 5% of the global population, the U.S. consumes approximately 25% of the Earth's fossil fuels.

The United States currently has more private cars than licensed drivers, with gas-guzzling sport utility vehicles (SUVs) among the best-selling automobiles. Despite the declining average size of U.S. households, the average size of new houses in the United States increased 38% from 1975 to 2001 (Worldwatch, 2011).

We currently live in the sixth millennium of civilization. While the expansion of civilization, commerce, and population was slow and methodical for the first 57 centuries, the last three centuries have witnessed population increase 22-fold, per capita income increase 855%, and global income increase 300-fold (Targowski, 2012). Indeed, during the 1820–1998 time, the population increased 500%, and per capita income increased 800% (as compared with a 53% increase in per capita income from 1000 to 1820 (Maddison, 2001)). At present rates of consumption, it will take the resources of three Earths to allow the Chinese and Indian population to achieve American consumption levels, and another six Earths to allow the remaining population to achieve those levels (Targowski, 2012).

Human business activity utilizes a considerable volume of natural resources, producing the largest cumulative environmental impact on the planet. Because of the volume and structure of work and employment, business prescribes the architecture of most social contracts and social organizational in developed nations (Jones & Upward, 2014). However, contemporary business is frequently characterized by profit-driven enterprises providing a narrow range of social benefits, while frequently permitting considerable environmental exploitation. Corporations have categorized environmental and social impacts as a cost of doing business, with environmental responsibility frequently consisting of cursory actions to become "less unsustainable", continuing to promote business growth strategies without considering the impact of continual growth on a limited ecosystem (Jones & Upward, 2014). Holthaus (2012) paints a more dismal picture of capitalism as a system that is not based on innovation, entrepreneurship, brains, or the free market, but on the exploitation of resources, racism, child abuse, sexism, and war, with weapons being the United States' biggest commercial export. However, others optimistically advocate for a circular economy as "an alternative to a traditional linear economy (make, use, dispose) in which we keep

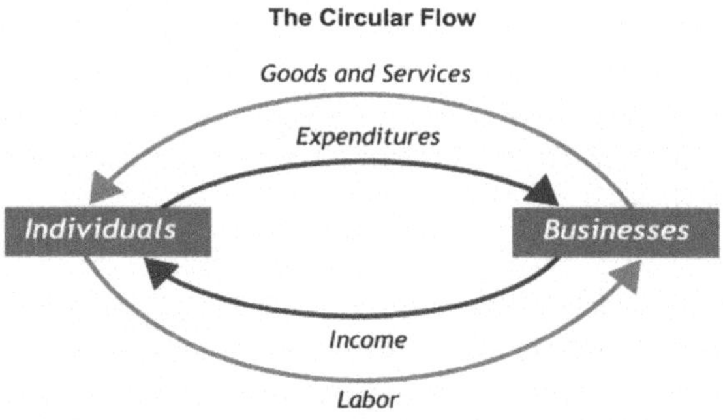

Fig. 6.1 The circular economy (*Source* https://upload.wikimedia.org/wikipedia/commons/8/8f/Circular_flow_of_income_and_expenditure.jpg)

resources in use for as long as possible, extract the maximum value from them whilst in use, then recover and regenerate products and materials at the end of each service life" (Waste & Resources Action Programme, 2018). The circular economy is graphically represented in Fig. 6.1.

Likewise, Jones and Upward (2014) introduce a more optimistic sustainable business model of flourishing, which will be discussed in greater detail in Chapter 11.

6.5 Contemporary Sustainability Movements

There are several movements influencing sustainability at the individual level, including simple living or voluntary simplicity, and the tiny house movement. The voluntary simplicity movement, also known as simple living, describes several movements or practices in which individuals, and often groups seek to simplify their lives, become self-sufficient, and minimize their impact on the planet in the process. Some adherents practice minimalism, in which the number of possessions is reduced, learning to practice the line by Sheryl Crow in *Soak up the Sun*, "It's not having what you want, it's wanting what you have!" (Trott & Crow, 2002). While some adherents practice ascetism in which all forms of luxury and vice are shunned, many adherents simply want to live more deliberate lifestyles as described in the writings of Henry David Thoreau. The term voluntary simplicity originated with social philosopher Richard Gregg (1936) who promoted ideas such as nonviolent resistance which later influenced Dr. Martin Luther King Jr. (Ansbro, 1982). Voluntary simplicity is related to sustainability since many adherents practice reduced consumption. The suggested benefits include reduced work hours, reduced dependence on career and money, improved health, and better quality of life.

The tiny house movement is a social movement where people choose to downsize their living space (Tiny Life, 2018). While typical American home is approximately 2,600 square feet, the typical tiny house measure less than 400 square feet, and is frequently built on wheels, facilitating ease of relocation. Tiny houses have become the focal point in a broader system to address current issues, concerns, and problems, providing benefits that include increased environmental consciousness, life simplification, sound fiscal plans, self-sufficiency, and life adventures (due to mobility). Compared with the lifetime cost of home ownership estimated to exceed $1,000,000 for a typical single-family home with an initial purchase price of $290,000, a tiny home offers an affordable alternative (Tiny Life, 2018). The increased interest in tiny houses has caught the attention of colleges, several of which offer courses in tiny house construction, including Seminole State College of Florida, in Sanford, Florida, Central Oregon Community College in Bend, Oregon, and Sydney Community College in Australia. In addition, tiny houses have been built as construction curriculum projects at Laney College in Oakland, CA, Frontier Community College (FCC) in Fairfield, Illinois, and St. Cloud Technical & Community College in Minnesota. While the voluntary simplicity and tiny house lifestyle may not appeal to all demographic segments, these lifestyles provide a method to live a more sustainable lifestyle.

Opportunities exist for individuals interested in living a more sustainable lifestyle, without sacrificing residential square footage, and other contemporary amenities. In support of the Sustainable Development Goals (SDG), the United Nations (UN) published *The lazy person's guide to saving the world*, a collection of simple tasks to promote sustainability (United Nations, 2018). The SDGs are summarized in Fig. 6.2.

Fig. 6.2 United Nations Sustainable Development Goals (*Source* https://upload.wikimedia.org/wikipedia/commons/4/46/Sustainable_Development_Goals.jpg)

Many of the suggestions in *The lazy person's guide to saving the world* not only benefit the planet, but also the participant. Examples of suggestions with a personal financial benefit include: saving electricity by plugging appliances into a power strip and turning them off completely when not in use, including your computer; no unnecessary printing; replacing old appliances with newer, energy-efficient appliances; plugging window and door leaks; not purchasing more food than will be consumed (restaurant and supermarket); and, properly maintain automobiles for greater fuel efficiency. Examples of suggestions with both personal financial and health benefits include: reducing meat consumption; and, transportation via bicycle, walking, or public transportation. Health benefits derived from a sustainable lifestyle include increased happiness and reduced depression, and increased vitamin D from natural light (Rippon, 2014). In his book, *Last Child in the Woods* Richard Louv (2008) coined the term nature deficit disorder to describe the lack of contact with nature in our contemporary, wired society, suggesting the trend is a contributor to health conditions such as *obesity, attention disorders, and depression. Last Child in the Woods* is the first book to synthesize a new and growing body of research indicating direct exposure to nature is essential for healthy childhood development, and physical and emotional health of both children and adults.

Saving money is one of the primary benefits for homeowners embracing the sustainable lifestyle (Rippon, 2014). Financial savings are derived from reduced energy costs from heating and air conditioning, and lighting, and from reduced water consumption. Purchasing environmentally friendly building materials and appliances during renovation may cost more, however, the long-term savings will outweigh the initial expense. Moreover, the cost of purchasing energy-efficient materials and appliances may be partially offset by tax rebates and incentives offered by many state, local, and national government agencies, and rebates and incentives offered by utility companies. Further financial savings can be realized through minor lifestyle changes such as turning off lights and appliances when not in use (Rippon, 2014).

However, homes and offices are filled with appliances and electronic devices that continue to consume electricity when not in use. Often referred to as electrical or electronic 'vampires', these devices continue to consume a reduced amount of electricity while in off or standby mode (Treacy, 2015). A report from the National Resource Defense Council (NRDC) indicated Americans spend US$19 billion annually in electricity costs from vampire appliances and electronics (National Resources Defense Council, 2015). According to the report, the average U.S. household spends $165 annually powering devices that are turned off or are in standby mode, equal to the output of 50 large power plants.

Because contemporary society frequently measures individual success in financial terms, it is important to consider the financial benefits attributed to sustainability. Previously examined lifestyle modifications clearly produce cost savings in terms of reduced energy, health, gastronomic, and housing expenditures. Thriftiness is beneficial in providing funds for retirement, travel, and pursuit of hobbies and recreational activities. However, arguments for thrift may not be sufficiently compelling to motivate all individuals to reflect upon a more sustainable lifestyle. Therefore, the focus of the remainder of this chapter will be with career and entrepreneurial opportunities for individuals seeking financial reward while still desiring to make a sustainable planetary and societal contribution.

6.6 Career Theory

One lens through which responsible and sustainability-focused careers have been examined is career theory. Arthur and Rousseau (1996) identified four themes relevant to responsible careers: concerns about responsibility need not be related to personal experience or employment situation or position; careers are not static but unfold over time; career examination must be conducted from an interdisciplinary approach; and, subjective and objective career aspects are interdependent psychologically and sociologically.

Tams and Marshall (2011) identified six career practices of people seeking responsible careers: expressing self, connecting to others, constructing contribution, institutionalizing, field shaping, and engaging systematically. Expressing self refers to work being seen as making a statement, articulating work as being consistent with personal values about topics such as social justice and sustainability. Connecting to others [a concept found in workplace spirituality definitions] refers to the desire to associate with like-minded people, thereby supporting one's values and vision. Constructing contribution refers to endeavoring to define how expertise can be applied in a responsible manner. Institutionalizing refers to activities wherein responsible practices are validated and established within organizations and fields. Field shaping practices assist in defining a developing field by modifying established operating patterns and promote new standards of responsibility. Engaging systematically refers to philosophically different method of influencing social change, operating from field awareness with a profound appreciation of the interdependence, complexity, and uncertainty of 'shifting landscapes' (Tams & Marshall, 2011).

The development of the previous six career practices is influenced by four learning movements: shifting landscapes, because careers occur within context that is emerging, experimental, and often contested; through exploratory learning such as returning to college or performing volunteer work in order to acquire additional, necessary career skills; biographical reflexivity which describes understanding from where the person's career desire originated; and, systemic reflexivity, described as articulating contribution to change and associated career practices based on reflective approach to shifting landscapes (Tams & Marshall, 2011).

In Chapter 2, we reviewed how careers have been previously characterized by income and promotion. With the emergence of the post-industrial economy, a shift to postmaterialism has been observed (Inglehart, 2008), with the transition from an industrial to a knowledge society characterized by an emphasis on self-expression, suggesting an increased focus on subjective well-being, self-expression, and individual spirituality (Pettersson, 2003). Job, career, and calling were differentiated, with that a job is associated with the material benefits of work, with interests and ambitions expressed primarily during leisure activities, a career is associated with a deeper personal investment in work intended to achieve advancement, and a calling is associated with morally and socially significant work resulting in personal fulfillment (Dries, 2011; Wrzesniewski et al., 1997).

In Chapter 2, we also considered the contemporary concept of a boundaryless career (Dries, 2011), which challenges traditional employment concepts of continuous single-employer service, upward mobility focus, separation of work and personal life (Arthur & Rousseau, 1996), and weakened employee-employer connection (Arnold & Cohen, 2008). However, despite the boundaryless career having become a mainstream topic career literature, some researchers suggest the theoretical career approach is not entirely accommodative to actual individual career experiences (e.g., Briscoe & Finkelstein, 2009), and critics note boundaryless career literature disregards the contributions and requirements of unskilled workers (Dries, 2011). Unfortunately, boundaryless career literature generally ignores the needs and contributions of unskilled people, and primarily focuses on agency determinants of career (Dries, 2011). According to Dany (2003), individual career definitions are continuously shaped throughout life, changing whenever personal life changes influence priorities.

6.7 Sustainability Careers

The corporate scandals at the turn of the twentieth century, combined with increasing concern about the impact of business on the environment, have positively influenced the literature on responsibility within management careers (Khurana & Nohria, 2008; Waddock, 2007; Walck, 2009). The notion of responsible careers was introduced to address the literature gap of careers responding to the societal debate concerning responsible business practices (Tams & Marshall, 2011). Responsible careers are defined as those in which workers seek to have positive impact on social justice and environmental sustainability through their employment (Tams & Marshall, 2011). While such noble career ambitions were previously dismissed as counterculture (Meyerson & Scully, 1995; Turner, 2006), they now echo a broader shift in public attitudes (Inglehart, 2008; Ray & Anderson, 2000). Responsible careers demand the ability to recognize the interconnectedness of business, environmental, and social systems, coupled with the ability to interface multiple stakeholder groups (Alvord et al., 2004; Ospina & Foldy, 2008; Waddock, 2008).

The field of sustainability has expanded significantly since first appearing in literature in the 1980s. Businesses, nonprofit organizations, and governmental agencies are hiring sustainability managers and directors to develop, implement, and manage sustainability initiatives. Careers in the field of sustainability are diverse and evolving, with students challenged to prepare for jobs that do not yet exist (Kross, 2012). Leadership and talent are critical ingredients for the development of a low-carbon economy (Nidumoluet al., 2009).

While sustainability offers opportunities for careers and new business ventures, the field may be found by some to be rewarding due to the altruistic aspect of sustaining existing resources for future generations. Further, employees and business owners who incorporate sustainability components and attitudes into their work role may receive both intrinsic and extrinsic benefits. In addition to careers in the fields of environmental science and engineering, sustainability-related careers exist in the fields of accounting and auditing, cost estimating, occupational health and safety, human resources, regulatory compliance, logistics, and business operations (Hamilton, 2012). Likewise, career opportunities are expanding in the skilled and semi-skilled disciplines, with workers in the new constellation of opportunities identified as the green-collar workforce (Gregson, 2010).

Despite the significant role fossil fuels have played in the Industrial Revolution, the renewable energy field is creating more jobs than the fossil fuel industry. In 2016, the U.S. solar industry employed 260,077 workers, a nearly 25% increase from the previous year, driven by an unprecedented increase in solar panel installations (Korosec, 2017). Andrea Luecke, president and executive director of The Solar Foundation, attributes the increase in installations to the combination of rapid deflation in solar panel costs, and increasing consumer demand (Korosec, 2017). Based upon 2016 solar capacity growth doubling previous year growth, The Solar Foundation predicts solar will likely exceed all other sources of new electric generating capacity for the year (Korosec, 2017). New solar photovoltaic (PV) capacity increased by 50% in 2017, with China leading the provider of solar energy (International Energy Agency, 2018).

The solar jobs census followed a U.S. Department of Energy study finding more Americans work in solar installations (187,117) than at natural gas or coal power plants (374,000; Korosec, 2017). However, the optimistic growth in solar employment and installations may be adversely impacted by President Trump's solar panel tariff, announced prior to publication of this book (Eckhouse et al., 2018). Moreover, policy changes related to the U.S. Clean Power Plan, the North American Free Trade Agreement (NAFTA), and trade with China under Trump Administration may temporarily introduce setbacks for the renewable energy industry (Korosec, 2017).

Rooftop solar panel installers make up the largest employee group in the solar industry, followed by manufacturing, product development, and sales and distribution (Korosec, 2017). Solar industry employment highlights include: creating one out of 50 new U.S. jobs; employment growth outpacing the overall U.S. economy by 17 times; job growth in 44 of the 50 states; women representing an increasing proportion of the workforce than in previous years, rising from 18.7% in 2013 to 28% in

2016; and, California, Massachusetts, Texas, Nevada, and Florida being the states employing the most workers (Korosec, 2017).

U.S. Energy Information Administration (2017) statistics indicate wind power has grown dramatically in recent years, currently providing 6.6% of U.S. total electric power generation. Wind energy has created both manufacturing and installation jobs, as companies such as Vestas (Denmark), Siemens Gamesa (Germany and Spain, General Electric (United States), and Goldwind (China) leading global manufacturing efforts (Wind Power Monthly, 2017). The U.S. Energy Independence and Security Act (U.S. Department of Energy, 2007) mandated increases in renewable motor fuel from 9 billion gallons (34 billion liters) in 2008 to 36 billion gallons (136 billion liters) by 2022. The policy will likely encourage rapid biofuel job growth, including ethanol manufacturing facility construction and operation, feedstock production, and delivery infrastructure development (Handwerk, 2018). The wave power and tidal power industries are small but growing, with the potential of wave power enormous for coastal regions. Using separate technologies, both systems use water movement to generate electricity which is transmitted ashore using undersea cables.

The U.S. Green Building Council (USGBC) is a U.S. nonprofit organization that promotes sustainable building design, construction, maintenance, and operation. In conjunction with Natural Resources Defense Council (NRDC) senior scientist Robert K. Watson, USGBC launched the Leadership in Energy and Environmental Design (LEED) third-party green building rating systems. LEED certification covers all types of residential and commercial buildings and neighborhoods, with four levels of LEED certification: certified, silver, gold, and platinum. Green building certification provides employment opportunities in various fields including construction, architecture, engineering, environmental consulting, and building inspection.

In addition to LEED certification, existing buildings may benefit from energy management services. Determining the energy management needs of a facility requires an energy audit, in which sources of energy loss such as air leaks are identified. Energy auditors, also known as energy consultants, help reduce energy loss and waste by buildings to locate areas of air leakage and advise customers on how to repair and prevent leaks.

Reducing energy loss not only benefits the environment but also provides cost savings to building owners and tenants. Energy auditors work for utility providers, maintenance companies, and engineering, architecture, electrical, and heating ventilating and cooling (HVAC) firms. However, some energy auditors perform work on a part-time, consulting basis, often while employed full-time in related industries (Lime, 2012).

According to the most recent Green Technologies and Practices (GTP) survey by the U.S. Department of Labor, approximately 75% of businesses reported using at least one green technology or practice during August 2011 (Bureau of Labor Statistics, 2012b). The Department of Labor defines green technologies and practices as those that lessen the environmental impact of business operations. At the time of the survey, approximately 854,700 jobs were held by workers who spent more than one-half of their working hours involved in green technologies and practices.

In addition to employment information, survey respondents provided examples of GTP in place within their organizations. Examples of renewable energy usage by survey respondents included: electricity generation, heat, or fuel use from wind, geothermal, ocean, hydropower, biomass, solar, landfill gas (LFG), and municipal solid waste (MSW). Energy efficiency practices and technologies reported included: cogeneration or combined heat and power (CHP); motor system optimization; oxy-fuel firing; isothermal melting process; server virtualization; energy-efficient fume hoods; LEED-certified buildings; weatherization measures for existing construction; and, energy-efficient devices such as Energy Star rated appliances, compact fluorescent lights (CFLs), motion detection lighting, or programmable thermostats. Examples of reported greenhouse gas (GHG) emission reduction (excluding renewable energy or energy efficiency) included: carbon capture and storage (CCS) technologies, purchase and use of carbon offsets; promotion and/or subsidy of alternative forms of employee transportation, such as carpools, fuel efficient vehicles, cycling, or mass transit; implementation of employee telecommuting programs; and, methane emissions reduction and/or reuse (Bureau of Labor Statistics, 2012a). Reported recycling and reuse technologies and practices included: collecting and reusing or recycling waste materials created as a result of business operations; managing and/

or recycling wastewater effluent; composting solid waste; and, remanufacturing. Reported natural resource conservation methods included: managing land resources; managing stormwater; conserving soil, water, or wildlife; practice of sustainable agriculture tilling processes; organic agriculture; agroforestry; and, implementing paper reduction or elimination programs (Bureau of Labor Statistics, 2012a). These green practices are mentioned in this chapter because all represent areas from which green or sustainable jobs and careers are emerging, some of which are discussed in this section.

Green jobs benefit both the economy and the environment and include everything from alternative fuels to tasty foods. The National Geographic recently identified the 11 fastest growing green jobs: urban growers; water quality technicians; clean car engineers; recyclers; natural scientists; green builders; solar cell technicians; green design professionals; wave energy producers; wind energy workers; and, biofuels jobs (Handwerk, 2018). Urban residents have turned to green roof gardens to produce locally grown foods to protect the environment by minimizing pesticide and fossil fuel use. Green roofs provide an indirect benefit by insulating buildings to mitigate energy loss, managing stormwater, improving air quality, and providing recreational space (Handwerk, 2018). A green roof does not trap heat, resulting in building interior temperatures as much as 10 °F (5.6 °C) cooler than with traditional asphalt roof construction. Sustainable architecture and landscaping, and sustainable urban planners are examples of career options related to the growing sustainability worldview (Handwerk, 2018).

Transportation is another important green jobs category because the auto industry is presently retooling to respond to increased demand for individual and fleet vehicles that consume less fossil fuel and produce less pollution (Handwerk, 2018). Transportation currently consumes approximately two-thirds of U.S. oil and produces approximately one-third of greenhouse gas emissions (GHG). Electric cars are a promising alternative to the existing internal combustion engine technology but are only as sustainable as the method of recharging power. Electric charging stations are becoming more prevalent; however, the majority are connected to the fossil fuel electrical grid. A promising trend is the appearance of solar-powered electric vehicle charging stations across the country.

The United States recycles more paper than all other recyclable materials combined, excluding steel (Handwerk, 2018). According to the American Forest & Paper Association, in 2011 two-thirds of all paper consumed in the United States was diverted from landfills and recycled. Recycling creates green jobs along with a favorable environmental impact. The U.S. Environmental Protection Agency (EPA, 2016) reports recycling one ton of paper saves enough energy to power an American home for six months, saves 7,000 gallons (26,500 liters) of water, and reduces GHG emissions by one metric ton. Recycling and waste reduction apply equally well to the building construction industry, where green, sustainable buildings reduce waste during construction, and often use recycled materials. The global movement toward sustainable lifestyles and greener economies will require trained professionals to monitor, analyze, and mitigate the environmental impact of human activity (Handwerk, 2018).

The goal of the development of a green-collar workforce is creation of living wages, equal opportunities, pathways to success, and job creation (Gregson, 2010). Sustainable jobs are not just about mitigation of pollution, but also mitigation of poverty, suggesting a correlation between economic and social injustice, and environmental degradation (Hawkin, 2007; Jones, 2008). The green-collar workforce will require sustainability literacy, not necessarily in the areas of environmental science and engineering, but in more traditional areas such as manufacturing, materials, agriculture, and construction (Gregson, 2010). Traditional career opportunities are emerging within companies devoted to sustainable technologies such as manufacturers of lighting fixtures and lamps, energy management equipment, and energy-efficient appliances and products.

Career-based higher education programs containing a component in which students reflect on sustainability values have received positive feedback (Murray & Murray, 2007). An increasing number of community colleges and universities are offering courses, certificates, and degrees in the field of sustainability (Beehner, 2018). While sustainability was initially a topic of study within environmental degree programs, and later business schools, community colleges have introduced an increased number of offerings in sustainability and sustainable business. Many of the programs are designed to prepare students for entry-level supervisory, technical, and professional positions in sustainable industries, such as renewable energy, as well as sustainability-related positions within traditional industries.

Zimring, professor of sustainability studies at the Pratt Institute, identified an indirect career-related benefit of sustainability—sanitation industry worker deaths. According to Zimring, 50 years after the Memphis Strike, and Martin Luther King Jr.'s final speech before his assassination (in which he offered support for the striking sanitation workers), 31 sanitation workers died in the United States in 2016 (2018a, 2018b). When all waste-related occupational categories are included (non-residential janitorial services, laundry work, salvage yards, hazardous waste remediation, landscape maintenance, and pest extermination), the number amounts to more than one worker daily in the 2013–2016 period. While this may seem to only impact the sanitation industry and workers employed therein, the costs related to these deaths are passed on to customers and taxpayers in one form or another. Therefore, reduced waste through sustainability benefits individual and organizational customers in terms of reduced costs, as well as industry workers through reduced risk of death, and reduced workload.

Sustainable jobs are not just about mitigation of pollution, but also mitigation of poverty, suggesting a correlation between economic and social injustice, and environmental degradation (Hawkin, 2007; Jones, 2008). While sustainability offers opportunities for careers and new business ventures, the field may be found by some to be rewarding due to the altruistic aspect of sustaining existing resources for future generations. Further, employees and business owners who incorporate sustainability components and attitudes into their work role may receive both intrinsic and extrinsic benefits.

On August 16, 2022, President Biden signed the Inflation Reduction Act (IRA) of 2022 which was the largest U.S. government investment in clean energy and climate change action. One of the goals of the congressional act was the creation of green and clean energy jobs. As of July

2023, the Inflation Reduction Act has created more than 170,000 clean energy jobs (Climate Power, 2023). The act and the identified benefits are discussed further in Chapter 9.

6.8 Sustainability Leaders and Managers

The topics of sustainability leadership and management have received increased attention in both practical and academic literature. Moreover, numerous higher education institutions globally have introduced undergraduate and graduate courses, certificates, and degrees in sustainable management, with Arizona State University now offering a fully online Master of Sustainable Leadership (MSL). The increased interest in sustainability and sustainable business calls for leaders who understand the concept and possess the necessary skills to incorporate sustainability into organizations, public policy, and communities.

In a study of 65 sustainability leaders, primarily occupying senior executive positions in multinational companies, Schein (2014) identified 10 common sustainable leadership characteristics. Sustainable leaders have definitive ecological worldviews; connect beliefs about the natural world with motivation for sustainability efforts; ecological beliefs formed over a significant time frame; possess considerable ecological intelligence, and have a philosophical stance on their relationship with nature; are highly educated in global environmental science complexity, possessing awareness of the greater philosophical questions facing humanity regarding our relationship to nature; have an enhanced capacity to comprehend a growing range of viewpoints alongside their global sustainability practices; are able to consistently think in long-term horizons, while operating within short-term horizons of public companies. Sustainability leaders operate with a long-term horizon, have highly developed systems of consciousness, and can identify with, and care about an expanded sphere of identity and influence (Schein, 2014). Three sustainability leadership themes emerged during Schein's (2014) study: experiences that alter ecological worldviews, interpretations of eco-centric worldviews, and interpretations of post-conventional action philosophies by sustainability leaders.

Sustainability has become a business mega-trend significantly altering business leadership requirements, necessitating a new form of leadership—sustainable leadership, which incorporates many of the attributes of transformational leadership (Tideman et al., 2013). Six categories of sustainable leadership characteristics have been identified, conveniently labeled the 6C-model. The leadership characteristics categories are summarized as follows:

- Context—awareness of interdependence; complexity; ambiguity; interconnectedness; resource constraint; mega-trends.
- Consciousness—mind-sets; viewpoints; beliefs; mental models; attitudes.
- Continuity—long-term vision; courage; strength; common purpose; centeredness; change management.
- Connectedness—serving broad stakeholder needs; long-term and short-term influencing; collaboration; trust; fairness; altruism; relatedness; needs versus wants.
- Creativity—sustainable, creative innovation; sustainable business models; new value measurement frameworks.
- Collectiveness—scope for collective impact; sustainability engrained in business structures; sustainable consumption (Tideman et al., 2013).

In addition to the six categories of leadership attributes, the following six sustainable leadership competencies have been identified: collaborating, influencing, delivering results, commercial awareness, anticipating long-term trends, and evaluating long-term trends (Tideman et al., 2013).

Visser and Crane (2010) identified four types of sustainability managers have been identified: expert, facilitator, catalyst, and activist (Visser & Crane, 2010). While the sustainability management role has previously been portrayed one-dimensionally (Vick, 2001), research shows not all sustainability managers extract satisfaction in the same manner, and individuals demonstrate an innate predisposition for certain role types (Visser & Crane, 2010). Individuals who match sustainability manager roles with meaning type may be more likely to experience improvements in job satisfaction, commitment, motivation, and productivity (Brown, 2002). Moreover, insight into meaning types of sustainability managers may also improve team performance (Visser & Crane, 2010).

Sustainability management concentrates on economic practices at the micro-level, realizing that on this level one can, through the discovery and exploration of human self-consciousness, combine freedom and order (Zsolnai, 2014). Consciousness of the self allows man to generate compassion, justice, and temperance. Such an outcome is possible only if man's inner or spiritual faculties are not neglected. The emergence of specific sustainable economic alternatives is associated to development of practical sustainable experiments to stimulate others to embrace more sustainable practices (Opdebeeck, 2014). However, further research is needed to determine how to develop a sustainability mindset (Rimanoczy, 2014), because understanding how to develop a sustainability mindset would further the creation of a much-needed generation of leaders with such a focus (Vinkhuyzena & Karlsson-Vinkhuyzena, 2014).

6.9 Role of Ethics in Sustainability and Success

Ethics is an important component of any meaningful effort to achieve success. This becomes even more important when incorporating sustainability into an endeavor. An ethical foundation contextualized by sustainability provides a moral framework for appropriate decision-making when choosing techniques or strategies (Biedenweg et al., 2013). Ethics assists individuals with lifestyle and purchasing decisions (Irving et al., 2002). Ethical or moral rules assist with determining how much information is necessary when sufficient information is not available (Tversky & Kahneman, 1986). An ethical foundation helps students assess future decisions as engineers, researchers, managers, designers, and consumers of products that are designed to enhance sustainability (Kibert et al., 2011).

Despite ethical career planning and established safeguards, overcoming ethical challenges can be difficult in practice. Individuals may overlook the ramifications of their decisions on others, the environment, and the future. Unethical behavior may be justified to achieve an important goal, and sometimes, the ethical dilemma is not easily apparent until the consequences are eventually experienced (Kouchaki & Smith, 2020). Kouchaki and Smith (2020) recommend three tests to prevent self-deceptive rationalizations:

- *The publicity test:* Would you be comfortable having your decision and supportive reasoning published on the front page of the local newspaper?
- *The generalizability test:* Would you be comfortable having your decision serve as a model for everyone making a similar decision?
- *The mirror test:* Would you like the individual you see in the mirror after making this decision?

Research demonstrates that individuals are more likely to behave unethically under pressure (Kouchaki & Smith, 2020). Individuals facing difficult decisions should take ownership of their actions and remember that similar ethical challenges have likely already been confronted by others (Kouchaki & Smith, 2020). Ethical people make mistakes, but they review and learn from their mistakes so that they do not repeat them in the future. Significant research in multiple fields has demonstrated that reflection is an important first step in learning from past experiences. However, self-reflection has limitations because not all ethical lapses are obvious, and sometimes potential options may appear ambiguous. Because it is natural to be restricted by personal histories and biases, it is important to seek counsel from trusted colleagues and mentors (Kouchaki & Smith, 2020).

Ethical decision-making in career and business requires thinking beyond traditional financial formulas such as cost–benefit analysis and return on investment (ROI). Individuals must develop the habit of seeking the moral issues and ethical implications involved in each decision and analyze them from multiple philosophical viewpoints. The three common philosophical perspectives include deontology (the ethics of rules and obligations), utilitarianism (consequence-based), and the Aristotelian perspective (virtue ethics; Kouchaki & Smith, 2020). Although each perspective has advantages and disadvantages including the key decision criteria of all three perspectives will reduce the likelihood of overlooking important ethical considerations (Kouchaki & Smith, 2020).

The Earth Charter was introduced in an earlier section and provides an ethical framework for achieving sustainability. The document contains four pillars and sixteen principles for establishing a "a sustainable global society founded on respect for nature, universal human rights, economic justice, and a culture of peace" (Earth Charter International, n.d.):

I. Respect and Care for the Community of Life

1. Respect Earth and life in all its diversity.
2. Care for the community of life with understanding, compassion, and love.
3. Build democratic societies that are just, participatory, sustainable, and peaceful.
4. Secure Earth's bounty and beauty for present and future generations.

II. Ecological Integrity

5. Protect and restore the integrity of Earth's ecological systems, with special concern for biological diversity and the natural processes that sustain life.
6. Prevent harm as the best method of environmental protection and, when knowledge is limited, apply a precautionary approach.
7. Adopt patterns of production, consumption, and reproduction that safeguard Earth's regenerative capacities, human rights, and community well-being.
8. Advance the study of ecological sustainability and promote the open exchange and wide application of the knowledge acquired.

III. Social and Economic Justice

9. Eradicate poverty as an ethical, social, and environmental imperative.

10. Ensure that economic activities and institutions at all levels promote human development in an equitable and sustainable manner.
11. Affirm gender equality and equity as prerequisites to sustainable development and ensure universal access to education, health care, and economic opportunity.
12. Uphold the right of all, without discrimination, to a natural and social environment supportive of human dignity, bodily health, and spiritual well-being, with special attention to the rights of indigenous peoples and minorities.

IV. Democracy, Nonviolence, and Peace

13. Strengthen democratic institutions at all levels, and provide transparency and accountability in governance, inclusive participation in decision-making, and access to justice.
14. Integrate into formal education and lifelong learning the knowledge, values, and skills needed for a sustainable way of life.
15. Treat all living beings with respect and consideration.
16. Promote a culture of tolerance, nonviolence and peace.

The Earth Charter document neatly overlaps and complements the UNS SDGs. The Earth Charter International provides online and onsite training about the Earth Charter Principles and how to apply them in business, leadership, and academic settings at their Education Centre located at the UN-mandated University for Peace in San Jose, Costa Rica.

Although short-term unethical behavior can result in material success, most instances of unethical behavior end poorly. Wealthy and famous individuals have seen their careers ruined by inappropriate behavior and actions. It is essential to have an ethical foundation to achieve any meaningful and lasting success. Combining ethics and sustainability provides a framework for achieving success that also contributes to the success of all humankind.

6.10 Career Customization Through Job Crafting

Job crafting expands job design by empowering employees to create their jobs by making physical and cognitive changes to the tasks and relational boundaries of their jobs (Wrzesniewski & Dutton, 2001). Employees alter the social and task components of their jobs by changing the task and relational boundaries to experience renewed meaning of work and self. Regardless of complexity or hierarchical position (Berg et al., 2010a), all employees have some degree of latitude in crafting their jobs. Therefore, job crafting allows employees to change the meaning of work and their work identities across a broad range of job scenarios (Wrzesniewski et al., 2013). Job crafting has been found to positively influence employee well-being (Berg et al., 2010b), and employee engagement and performance (Tims et al., 2012).

Considerable research indicates that job crafting can be a robust method for workers seeking to reenergize and reimagine their work lives (Wrzesniewski et al., 2010). Job crafting involves employees redefining their job to integrate motives, strengths, and passions into their work. The process of job crafting prompts individuals to envision the job, map the essential components, and restructure them to best accommodate their purpose. Employees develop a stronger feeling of control through personalizing how they see and perform their jobs. This feeling of control becomes especially important as workers remain at work longer and postpone retirement (Wrzesniewski et al., 2010).

6.11 Concluding Thoughts

In this chapter, sustainability has been examined as a worldview for individual success, presenting opportunities for sustainable lifestyles and careers as well as enhancement of existing careers. Sustainable lifestyles and careers contribute to improved quality of life for all humankind through more efficient and effective use of planetary resources. Moreover, sustainability presents opportunities for minor or major lifestyle modifications and enhancements, resulting in peace of mind, reduced work hours, reduced dependence on career and money, improved health, increased life satisfaction, and better quality of life. Harman (1992) suggested twenty-first-century business is reflecting a "change of mind" in competitive, exploitive materialism, and consumerism will be replaced by a new business paradigm with alternative values of relationship quality, the oneness of humanity, cooperation, caring, nurturing, and spiritual values. Worthwhile societal change begins at the individual level because an individual cannot accomplish for society what cannot be accomplished individually (Pappas & Pappas, 2014).

Navigation of the ecological and economic "new normal" of the twenty-first century will require sustainability leaders and managers, capable of conceptualizing existing relationships and organizations in creative new ways. The thinking that has created our existing problems cannot be relied upon to provide the solutions. Individuals capable of and willing to become sustainability leaders within their fields will lead a global paradigm shift in social, political, and economic thought. Sustainable individuals possess awareness, motivation, and the ability to undertake intentional self-development (Pappas & Pappas, 2014), all traits appropriate for individual success. The new generation of sustainability leaders will find success in career and personal life, and the planet and inhabitants will flourish.

Personal Interview Summary

In support of the argument that sustainability is beneficial for individual success, I conclude this chapter with a personal interview of an industry professional who has applied sustainability in their career. I had the pleasure of interviewing former co-worker and long-time friend Alexa Stone, founder, and president of ecoPreserve LLC. In less than ten years, Alexa has developed an organization of experienced, credentialed environmental services professionals who consistently bring sustainability and resiliency to client operations and facilities (ecoPreserve, 2018a). In addition to managing ecoPreserve, Alexa is a founding member of the Central Florida Energy Efficiency Alliance, she has chaired the Green Committee for the Building Owners and Managers Association (BOMA) served on the boards of the U.S. Green Building Council (USGBC), and the International Facilities Management Association (IFMA), and she currently serves on the Board of Directors for the Florida Green Chamber and judges for the Orange County Florida Public Schools Green Schools Recognition Program. As the president of ecoPreserve, and "through her ongoing community service, she has championed and enabled building efficiency, materials management, human factors, and team engagement" (ecoPreserve, 2018a).

Alexa worked in the lighting industry for several years and increasingly began to recognize the vast amount of energy consumed by electrical lighting. Since leaving the lighting industry to start ecoPreserve in 2009, Alexa has witnessed the public, commercial, and governmental realization, and recognition of the importance of sustainability morph and grow through a brilliant thought process evolution. Two factors have driven this evolution: independence and health. Beginning with the advent of ENERGY STAR and the U.S. Green Building Council (USGBC) in the late 1980s, government has had the foresight to see that efficiency, which in many cases equals sustainability, produces independence. Independence from oil is a matter of national security. The second major factor was health because we have witnessed China's crippling air problems for decades.

Alexa acknowledges that sustainability is not that readily accepted by some stakeholders. Her key to successfully communicating sustainability is to learn to look at it from a business perspective—and that learning the language of the client is even more than the language of the environment. She has learned to articulate the business value of sustainability, and to not assume that a client with a potential opportunity will be as passionate about the environment as she is, but that they may still have a particular need for the efficiency that sustainability provides. Her approach is to meet the client where they are, and not get lost in enthusiasm.

Regarding her success, Alexa notes ecoPreserve has impacted more than 11 million square feet of buildings to date. She is proud of her team's efforts with the Orlando International Airport, because millions of people pass through major airports each year, and while airports have not always demonstrated sustainable leadership, they are becoming government leaders in sustainability. She is equally proud of the largest project on which her team has participated to date, the Orange County Convention Center in Orlando, Florida, which is the world's largest Leadership in Energy and Environmental Design (LEED) EBOM Gold convention center, totaling 3.1 million square feet (ecoPreserve, 2018b).

Regarding the future of sustainability, Alexa suggests businesses, governments, and individuals are recognizing the interconnectedness of all entities, spaces, and devices that we share. Watching the sustainability ripple turn into a wave, moving into commercial business and later to the public domain has been encouraging for her. Regarding the resistance of some to sustainability, Alexa believes that "if you feel something is logical, be patient". She believes sustainability will become a mutual responsibility as well as potential benefit. Our awareness and care help us to keep the water and air around us cleaner and more abundant for today and the future. More people recognize that they can have healthier and better buildings when they have addressed sustainability, even if ecoPreserve does not use those words with them. Alexa suggests people and organizations are increasingly relying on technology, which is becoming incorporated into a wider range of activities. Devices, which were once thought to be modern because they were mechanical, are not digital but are rapidly becoming digitized. Digital technology, when carefully designed, acquired, and managed, becomes a powerful component of tools that improve the quality of organizational and individual lives by saving time, avoiding waste, and increasing security. Sustainability becomes a win–win for organizations, their members, and the greater society.

References

Alvord, S. H., Brown, L. D., & Letts, C. W. (2004). Social entrepreneurship and societal transformation. *Journal of Applied Behavioral Science, 30*, 260–282. https://doi.org/10.1177/0021886304266847

Ansbro, J. J. (1982). *Martin Luther King, Jr: The making of a mind*. Orbis Books.

Arnold, J., & Cohen, L. (2008). The psychology of careers in industrial-organizational settings: A critical but appreciative analysis. In G. P. Hodgkinson & J. K. Ford (Eds.), *International review of industrial and organizational psychology* (Vol. 23, pp. 1–44). Wiley.

Arthur, M. B., & Rousseau, D. M. (1996). *The boundaryless career: A new employment principle for a new organizational era*. Oxford University Press.

Beehner, C. G. (2018). Expanding sustainable business education beyond business schools. In S. Dhiman & J. Marques (Eds.), *Handbook of engaged sustainability*. Springer Nature. https://doi.org/10.1007/978-3-319-53121-2_51-1

Berg, J. M., Grant, A. M., & Johnson, V. (2010a). When callings are calling: Crafting work and leisure in pursuit of unanswered occupational callings. *Organization Science, 21*(5), 973–994. https://doi.org/10.1287/orsc.1090.0497

Berg, J. M., Wrzesniewski, A., & Dutton, J. E. (2010b). Perceiving and responding to challenges in job crafting at different ranks: When proactivity requires adaptivity. *Journal of Organizational Behavior, 31*, 158–186. https://doi.org/10.1002/job.645

Berry, T. M. (1999). *The great work: Our way into the future*. Belltower.

Biedenweg, K., Monroe, M. C., & Oxarart, A. (2013). The importance of teaching ethics of sustainability. *International Journal of Sustainability in Higher Education, 14*(1), 6–14. https://doi.org/10.1108/14676371311288912

Boiral, O., Cayer, M., & Baron, C. M. (2009). The action logics of environmental leadership: A developmental perspective. *Journal of Business Ethics, 85*, 479–499. https://doi.org/10.1007/s10551-008-9784-2

Briscoe, J. P., & Finkelstein, L. M. (2009). The 'new career' and organizational commitment: Do boundaryless and protean attitudes make a difference? *Career Development International, 14*(3), 242–260. https://doi.org/10.1108/13620430910966424

Brown, D. (2002). *Career choice and development*. Jossey-Bass.

Bureau of Labor Statistics. (2012a). Solar and wind generation occupations: a look at the next decade. U.S. Department of Labor. https://www.bls.gov/opub/btn/volume-10/solar-and-wind-generation-occupations-a-look-at-the-next-decade.html

Bureau of Labor Statistics. (2012b). *Green technologies and practices*. U.S. Department of Labor. https://www.bls.gov/news.release/pdf/gtp.pdf

Climate Power. (2023). *One year of our clean energy boom*. https://climatepower.us/wp-content/uploads/sites/23/2023/07/Clean-Energy-Boom-Anniversary-Report-1.pdf

Collins, D., Junghans, A., & Haugen, T. (2016). *Green and sustainable—How are these terms reflected in the context of facilities management?* CFM Second Nordic Conference 29–30 August 2016 Technical University of Denmark.

Cooper, P. J., & Vargas, C. M. (2004). *Implementing sustainable development: From global policy to local action*. Rowman & Littlefield.

Dany, F. (2003). Free actors' and organizations: Critical remarks about the new career literature, based on French insights. *International Journal of Human Resource Management, 14*(5), 821–838. https://doi.org/10.1080/0958519032000080820

Down, L., & McKeown, R. (2017). *What is sustainable development?* Earth Charter Institute.

Dresner, S. (2002). *The principles of sustainability*. Earthscan Publications Ltd.

Dries, N. (2011). The meaning of career success: Avoiding reification through a closer inspection of historical, cultural, and ideological contexts. *Career Development International, 16*(4), 364–384. https://doi.org/10.1108/13620431111158788

Earth Charter International. (n.d.). *Turning conscience into action*. https://earthcharter.org/

Eckhouse, B., Natter, A., & Martin, C. (2018, January 22). President Trump slaps tariffs on solar panels in major blow to renewable energy. *Time*. http://time.com/5113472/donald-trump-solar-panel-tariff/

ecoPreserve. (2018a). *Meet the team*. Author. http://ecopreserve.net/about-us/meet-the-team/

ecoPreserve. (2018b). *Project experience*. Author. http://ecopreserve.net/wp-content/uploads/2018/01/ecoPreserve-Projects-Experience-January-2018.pdf

Elkington, J., Tickell, S., & Lee, M. (2007). *SustainAbility. 20 Years of global leadership* [online]. SustainAbility. http://www.sustainability.com

Energy Information Administration. (2017). *Electric power monthly*. U.S. Department of Energy. https://www.eia.gov/electricity/monthly/

Environmental Protection Agency. (2016). *Benefits of paper recycling*. Author. https://archive.epa.gov/wastes/conserve/materials/paper/web/html/index-2.html

Esbjorn-Hargens, S., & Zimmerman, M. E. (2011). *Integral ecology: Uniting multiple perspectives on the natural world*. Shambhala Publications.

Gregg, R. (1936). *The value of voluntary simplicity*. Pendle Hill.

Gregson, J. A. (2010). A conceptual framework for green career and technical education: Sustainability and the development of a green-collar workforce. *Journal of Technical Education and Training, 2*(1), 123–137. http://penerbit.uthm.edu.my

Hamilton, J. (2012). *Is a sustainability career on your green horizon*? U.S. Department of Labor, Bureau of Labor Statistics. http://www.bls.gov/green/sustainability/sustainability.htm

Handwerk, B. (2018). *11 of the fastest growing green jobs.* National Geographic. https://www.nationalgeographic.com/environment/sustainable-earth/11-of-the-fastest-growing-green-jobs/

Harman, W. (1992). 21st century business: A background for dialogue. In J. Renesch (Ed.), *New tradition in business: Spirit and leadership in the 21st century* (pp. 11–24). Berrett- Koehler.

Hawkin, P. (2007). *Blessed unrest: How the largest social movement in history is restoring grace, justice, and beauty to the world*. Penguin Books.

Heaton, D. (2016). Higher consciousness for sustainability-as-flourishing. In S. Dhiman & J. Marques (Eds.), *Spirituality and sustainability: New horizons and exemplary approaches* (pp. 121–137). Springer International.

Hoffman, A. J., & Jennings, P. D. (2015). Institutional theory and the natural environment: Research in (and on) the Anthropocene. *Organization & Environment, 28*(1), 8–31. https://doi.org/10.1177/1086026615575331

Holthaus, G. (2012). *Learning native wisdom: What traditional cultures teach us about subsistence, sustainability, and spirituality*. University Press of Kentucky.

Inglehart, R. F. (2008). Changing values among Western publics from 1970 to 2006. *West European Politics, 31*(1–2), 130–146. https://doi.org/10.1080/01402380701834747

International Energy Agency. (2018). *Renewables 2017*. Author. https://www.iea.org/publications/renewables2017/

Irving, S., Harrison, R, & Rayner, M. (2002). Ethical consumerism-democracy through the wallet. *Journal of Research for Consumers, 3*, 1–20. https://www.jrconsumers.com/academic_articles/issue_3/irvingharrisonrayner.pdf

Jones, J. V. (2008). *The green collar economy: How one solution can fix our two biggest problems*. HarperCollins.

Jones, P. H., & Upward, A. (2014). *Caring for the future: The systemic design of flourishing enterprises.* The Third Symposium of Relating Systems Thinking and Design (RSD3), Oslo, Norway. 1–8. Slides and other materials from conference presentation: http://systemic-design.net/rsd3-proceedings/business-enterprise-design/

Khurana, R., & Nohria, N. (2008). It's time to make management a true profession. *Harvard Business Review, 86*, 70–77. http://www.hbr.org

Kibert, C., Thiele, L., Peterson, A., Monroe, M. & Plate, R. (2011). *Working toward sustainability: Ethical decision-making in a technological world*. Wiley.

Korosec, K. (2017, February 7). U.S. solar jobs jumped almost 25% in the past year. *Forbes*. http://fortune.com/2017/02/07/us-solar-jobs-2016/

Kouchaki, M., & Smith, I. H. (2020). *Building an ethical career*. Harvard Business Review. https://hbr.org/2020/01/building-an-ethical-career

Kross, K. (2012). *Sustainability offers variety of career opportunities*. Worcester Polytechnic Institute. https://web.wpi.edu/Images/CMS/Business/SustainabilityCareerOpp.pdf

Lime, D. (2012). *Energy auditors*. Washington, DC: U.S. Department of Labor, Bureau of Labor Statistics. https://www.bls.gov/green/greencareers.htm

Louv, R. (2008). *Last child in the woods: Saving our children from nature deficit disorder*. Algonquin Books.

Maddison, A. (2001). *The world economy, a millennial perspective* (pp. 17–31). OECD.

Malthus, T. R. (1798). *An essay on the principle of population as it affects the future improvement of society, with remarks on the speculations of Mr. Goodwin, M. Condorcet and other writers* (1st ed.). J. Johnson in St Paul's Church-yard.

McClaughry, J. (1989). Preface. In E. F. Schumacher (Eds.), *Small is beautiful*. Harper Perennial.

Mebratu, D. (1998). Sustainability and sustainable development: Historical and conceptual review. *Environmental Impact Assessment Review, 18*(6), 493–520. https://doi.org/10.1016/S0195-9255(98)00019-5

Meyerson, D., & Scully, M. (1995). Tempered radicalism and the politics of ambivalence and change. *Organization Science, 6*, 585–600. https://doi.org/10.1287/orsc.6.5.585

Murray, P. E., & Murray, S. A. (2007). Promoting sustainability values within career-oriented degree programmes: A case study analysis. *International Journal of Sustainability in Higher Education, 8*(3), 285–300. https://doi.org/10.1108/14676370710817156

National Resources Defense Council. (2015, May 7). *Always-on inactive devices may devour $19 billion worth of electricity annually*. Author. https://www.nrdc.org/media/2015/150506-0

Nidumolu, R., Prahalad, C. K., & Rangaswami, M. R. (2009). Why sustainability is now the key driver of innovation. *Harvard Business Review, 87*(9), 56–64. http://www.hbr.org

Opdebeeck, H. (2014). Spiritual sustainability management. In L. Zsolnai (Ed.), *The spiritual dimension of business ethics and sustainability management* (pp. 15–26). Springer. https://doi.org/10.1007/978-3-319-11677-8_20

Oser, J., & Blanchfield, W. C. (1975). *The evolution of economic thought*. Harcourt Brace Jovanovich.

Ospina, S., & Foldy, E. (2008). Building bridges from the margins: The work of leadership in social change organizations. *Integrative Leadership Conference*, University of Minnesota, October 5–7.

Palmer, R., & Nursey-Bray, M. (2007). Rio declaration on environment and development. In P. Robbins (Ed.), *Encyclopedia of environment and society* (pp. 1512–1514). Sage.

Pappas, J. B., & Pappas, E. C. (2014). The sustainable personality: Values and behaviors in individual sustainability. *International Journal of Higher Education, 4*(1), 12. https://doi.org/10.5430/ijhe.v4n1p12

Pettersson, T. (2003). *The relations between religion and politics in the contemporary Western world: The impact of secularization, postmodernization and peoples' basic value orientations.* http://www.worldvaluessurvey.org

Ray, P. H., & Anderson, S. R. (2000). *The cultural creatives.* Three Rivers Press.

Rimanoczy, I. (2014). A matter of being: Developing sustainability-minded leaders. *Journal of Management for Global Sustainability, 2*(1), 95–122. https://doi.org/10.13185/1902

Rippon, J. (2014, November 13). *Benefits of sustainable living*. Homify Online. https://www.homify.co.uk/ideabooks/10681/benefits-of-sustainable-living

Rockström, J., Steffen, W., Noone, K., Persson, A., Chapin, F. S., Lambin, E. F., et al. (2009, September 24). A safe operating space for humanity. *Nature, 461*, 472–475. https://doi.org/10.1038/461472a

Rogers, M. (2016, March 29). *6 benefits of becoming a sustainable business.* Business Sector Media. https://www.environmentalleader.com/2016/03/6-benefits-of-becoming-a-sustainable-business/

Roszak, T. (1989). Introduction. In E. F. Schumacher (Ed.), *Small is beautiful*. Harper Perennial.

Schein, S. (2014). *The ecological world views and post-conventional action logics of global sustainability leaders* (Doctoral dissertation). Fielding Graduate University.

Seghezzo, L. (2009). The five dimensions of sustainability. *Environmental Politics, 18*(4), 539–556. https://doi.org/10.1080/09644010903063669

Sörlin, S. (2014). Environmental turn in the human sciences: Will it become divisive enough? *The Institute Letter (Summer).* Institute for Advance Study.

Soyka, P. A. (2012). *Creating a sustainable organization: Approaches for enhancing corporate value through sustainability*. Pearson Education.

Tams, S., & Marshall, J. (2011). Responsible careers: Systemic reflexivity in shifting landscapes. *Human Relations, 64*(1), 109–131. https://doi.org/10.1177/0018726710384292

Targowski, A. (2012). Spirituality 2.0—A condition for a wise civilization. *Dialogue and Universalism, 22*(2), 133–143. www.researchgate.net

Tideman, S. G., Arts, M. C., & Zandee, D. P. (2013). Sustainable leadership: Towards a workable definition. *Journal of Corporate Citizenship, 49*(6), 17–33. http://www.jstor.org/stable/jcorpciti.49.17
Tims, M., Bakker, A. B., & Derks, D. (2012). Development and validation of the job crafting scale. *Journal of Vocational Behavior, 80*, 173–186. https://doi.org/10.1016/j.jvb.2011.05.009
Tiny Life. (2018). What is the tiny house movement? https://thetinylife.com/what-is-the-tiny-house-movement/
Treacy, M. (2015, May 12). *Vampire power costs Americans $19 billion in electricity every year*. Narrative Content Group. https://www.treehugger.com/energy-efficiency/vampire-power-costs-americans-19-billion-electricity-every-year.html
Trott, J., & Crow, S. (2002). *Soak up the Sun* [music recording]. Ole Media Management & Reservoir Media Management.
Turner, F. (2006). *From counterculture to cyberculture*. University of Chicago Press.
Tversky, A., & Kahneman, D. (1986). Rational choice and the framing of decisions. *Journal of Business, 59*(4), 251–278.
United Nations. (2015). *Sustainable development goals*. Author. http://www.un.org/sustainabledevelopment/sustainable-development-goals/
United Nations. (2018). *The lazy person's guide to saving the world*. Author. http://www.un.org/sustainabledevelopment/takeaction/
U.S. Department of Energy. (2007). Energy Independence and Security Act of 2007. https://afdc.energy.gov/laws/eisa.html
Van Schalkwyk, A. (2011). Sacredness and sustainability: Searching for a practical eco-spirituality. *Religion and Theology, 18*(1–2), 77–92. https://doi.org/10.1163/157430111X613674
Vick, R. C. (2001). The evolving role of the corporate environmental professional. *Pollution Engineering, 33*(4), 38–39. https://www.highbeam.com
Vinkhuyzena, O. M., & Karlsson-Vinkhuyzena, S. I. (2014). The role of moral leadership for sustainable production and consumption. *Journal of Cleaner Production, 63*, 102–113. https://doi.org/10.1016/j.jclepro.2013.06.045
Visser, W. & Crane, A. (2010). Corporate sustainability and the individual: Understanding what drives sustainability professionals as change agents. *SSRN Paper Series*, No. 1. https://doi.org/10.2139/ssrn.1559087
Waddock, S. (2007). Leadership integrity in a fractured knowledge world. *Academy of Management Learning & Education, 6*, 543–557. https://doi.org/10.5465/AMLE.2007.27694954

Waddock, S. (2008). *The difference makers.* Greenwood.
Walck, C. (2009). Integrating sustainability into management education: A dean's perspective. *Journal of World Business, 33*, 384–390. https://doi.org/10.1177/1052562908323091
Waste and Resources Action Programme. (2018). *WRAP and the circular economy.* Author. http://www.wrap.org.uk/about-us/about/wrap-and-circular-economy.
Wind Power Monthly. (2017, October 2). *Top ten turbine makers of 2017*. https://www.windpowermonthly.com/article/1445638/top-ten-turbine-makers-2017
World Commission on Environment and Development. (1987). *Our common future*. Oxford University Press.
Worldwatch Institute. (2011). *The state of consumption today*. Author. http://www.worldwatch.org/node/810
Wright, R. (2004). *A short history of progress.* Da Capo Press.
Wrzesniewski, A., Berg, J. M., & Dutton, J. E. (2010). Managing yourself: Turn the job you have into the job you want. *Harvard Business Review.* https://hbr.org/2010/06/managing-yourself-turn-the-job-you-have-into-the-job-you-want
Wrzesniewski, A., & Dutton, J. E. (2001). Crafting a job: Revisioning employees as active crafters of their work. *Academy of Management Review, 26*, 179–201.
Wrzesniewski, A., LoBuglio, N., Dutton, J. E., & Berg, J. M. (2013). Job crafting and cultivating positive meaning and identity in work. In *Advances in positive organizational psychology* (Vol. 1, pp. 281–302). Emerald Group Publishing Limited. https://doi.org/10.1108/S2046-410X(2013)0000001015
Wrzesniewski, A., McCauley, C., Rozin, P., & Schwartz, C. (1997). Jobs, careers and callings: People's relations to their work. *Journal of Research in Personality, 31*(1), 21–33. https://doi.org/10.1006/jrpe.1997.2162
Yanarella, E. J., Levine, R. S., & Lancaster, R. W. (2009). Research and solutions: "Green" vs. sustainability: From semantics to enlightenment. *Sustainability: The Journal of Record, 2*(5), 296–302. https://doi.org/10.1089/SUS.2009.9838
Zimring, C. A. (2018a, February 9). A waste worker dies every day. *New York Times.* https://www.nytimes.com/2018/02/09/opinion/sanitation-workers-deaths-unions.html

Zimring, C. A. (2018b, February 12). *On an error in my New York Times essay: Where the "death every day" mistake originated*. https://carlzimring.com/2018/02/12/on-an-error-in-my-new-york-times-essay-where-the-death-every-day-mistake-originated/

Zsolnai, L. (Ed.). (2014). Spirituality for business ethics and sustainability management. In L. Zsolnai (Ed.), *The spiritual dimension of business ethics and sustainability management*. Springer. https://doi.org/10.1007/978-3-319-11677-8_20

7

Sustainable Business

7.1 Introduction

Because of the career and business focus of this text, in this chapter sustainability will be examined from a business perspective. The emerging sustainable business model is compared with the traditional business models. While many have argued that capitalism may be the cause of our current environmental state, others argue capitalism is a powerful means to create value while solving our environmental problems. The systems perspective and the stakeholder approach will be discussed to support the necessity for achieving and the interconnectedness of the UN SDGs. The transition from capitalism solely as a means for profit maximization to newer models of conscious capitalism, the circular economy, environmental social and governance (ESG) investing, and social entrepreneurship will be explored. The role, benefits, and challenges of business achieving sustainability will be explored in this chapter. Other topics include environmental, social, and governance (ESG), diversity, equity, and inclusion (DEI), and microfinance. The chapter's case study will illustrate the dark side of integrating spirituality and performative attempts at greening.

C. G. Beehner, *Spirituality, Sustainability, and Success*, Palgrave Studies in Workplace Spirituality and Fulfillment, https://doi.org/10.1007/978-3-031-47643-3_7

7.2 Sustainable Business

While the traditional business model described a company providing shareholder return on investment (Balestrero & Udo, 2014), the emerging sustainable business model incorporates the environmental definition, suggesting a sustainable business provides goods and services of value to the current generation while ensuring goods and services can also be provided to future generations (Beehner, 2017). One objection to the triple bottom line approach is whether the incorporation of environmental sustainability into the business model will be perceived as a legitimate function within the context of capitalist organizations (Springett & Kearins, 2001; Thomas, 2005). However, progressive businesses are responding to the noticeable disconnect between financial and environmental performance, strengthening the belief that businesses can "do well by doing good" (Molnar & Mulvihill, 2003).

According to the value proposition, the primary purpose of business is creation and maximization of value (Rainey, 2006), necessitating any sustainable business strategy be approached from a value-creation perspective (Soyka, 2012). While the traditional model measures value in terms of increased performance, decreased costs, or both, the sustainable business model measures value in terms of increasing enhanced benefits and decreasing environmental impacts. The sustainable business value proposition encourages value creation and maximization for all current and future stakeholders. A successful sustainable business strategy increases performance and decreases costs for the business, simultaneously creating and maximizing sustainable value for all stakeholders (Beehner, 2017).

While the primary goal of capitalism is profit maximization, Dean (2014) reminds us that the overarching goal of an economic system is providing value to society, not capital accumulation. Within the field of economics, environmental economics is concerned with the efficient and effective allocation of resources, approaching environmental problems as economic problems. While traditional capitalism does not consider the market value of environmental resources, neoliberalism encourages a sustainability-focused market approach, culminating in the valuation of nature for its comprehensive economic worth (Kopnina, 2014). Market failures occur when a system fails to incentivize a desirable activity, or fails to prevent undesirable activities (Bator, 1958). Dean (2014) argues against rejecting capitalism due to the apparent adverse effects of the current capitalist approach, but rather requiring markets and capital to work for, and not against the environment.

While many have argued that capitalism is the cause of our current environmental state, others argue capitalism is a powerful means to create value while solving our environmental problems (Dean, 2014). Global sustainable development depends on wealth-producing enterprises delivering financial performance with integrity (Tichy & McGill, 2003). Sustainable entrepreneurship is a subset of the larger field of entrepreneurship; however, as society adjusts to the environmental realities of the present and the future, the two fields will become more aligned (Dean, 2014). Sustainable venturing is one method of creating socially and ecologically sustainable value through blending a unique resource combination to pursue an economic opportunity (Dean, 2014). Ecologically sustainable value describes value created for society that simultaneously sustains and improves the social and environmental resources of the planet (Dean, 2014). The drivers of ecological value opportunity are:

- Costs (declining costs of clean technology and increasing costs of natural resources).
- Capital (increased investor and government funding of sustainable businesses).
- Consumers (increased desire of consumers to purchase green).
- Climate (global climate change).
- Consciousness (increased awareness about environmental issues).
- Convergence (increased alignment between economic incentives and sustainable outcomes (Dean, 2014).

Beginning in the latter decade of the twentieth century, an increasing number of consumers and organizations began demanding the business community take steps to preserve our planet and resources for future generations. If customers are demanding sustainable products and services, the financial sustainability of the business is dependent upon responding to the voice of the customer (VoC) as voiced in the market (Beehner, 2017). Sustainable marketing describes the marketing of sustainable practices and services. Green marketing is a marketing approach defined as developing and marketing products with a sustainability focus being the core of the marketing and business process (Gordon et al., 2011). Sustainable marketing is not only a method for business differentiation, but also as a means of value maximization. Capitalist businesses should not only market the sustainable aspects of their products or services, but may enjoy a price premium for those products, as the market allows.

Preparing business students for the contemporary business environment necessitates higher education demonstrating how businesses can be successful while simultaneously considering environmental effects of managerial decision-making and activities (Hoffman, 1999). Higher education plays a crucial role in training and development of sustainable business leaders at all levels (Beehner, 2018). One challenge with sustainable business education is justification of a business necessity for and relevance of sustainability. One method of explaining sustainability to business students is to use the language of business. An example for the finance and accounting field is by comparison of sustainability with the retirement planning principle of living off the interest and not the principle of an investment (Down & McKeown, 2017).

One area in which businesses are capitalizing on profits through sustainable business practices is in the clean energy industry. Clean energy refers to devices that capture and distribute energy with minimal adverse environmental effects than traditional counterparts (Wengrovitz & Banerjee, 2010). Solar, wind, biomass, geothermal, and certain types of hydropower are examples of clean technology (Wengrovitz & Banerjee, 2010). On a national level, clean energy increases employment in areas such as construction and information technology (Wengrovitz & Banerjee, 2010). Duke Energy is an example of an energy company that has moved toward sustainability through clean technology, which has become more profitable, reduced risk, and become more socially responsible through acquisitions of wind energy companies such as Catamount Energy and Tierra Energy (Wengrovitz & Banerjee, 2010). The increasing global demand for energy, combined with the decreasing supply of fossil fuels and increased awareness of the adverse effects of climate change and pollution, has made clean energy a viable sustainable business model (Wengrovitz & Banerjee, 2010).

A significant area in which businesses and organizations can take steps to become sustainable is with buildings. Existing buildings account for the largest percentage of energy consumption and environmental impact, with buildings accounting for 40% of global emissions (Soni, 2010). Sustainable building practices provide at least three organizational benefits: extended building life, cost savings (energy and maintenance), and enhanced employee productivity (increased health leading to reduced absenteeism and improved morale; Soni, 2010). The U.S. Green Building Council (USGBC) launched the Leadership in Energy and Environmental Design (LEED) program in 1993, establishing levels of sustainable building standards for new, existing, and remodeled buildings. Five areas of green assessment are applied: energy efficiency, water conservation, indoor air and environmental quality, materials and construction, and site sustainability. The U.S. Department of Energy estimates that homes and buildings could reduce heating, air conditioning, and lighting energy consumption by up to 80% simply by implementing currently available energy-efficiency technologies (Soni, 2010).

Environmental sustainability is the hope for humankind to maintain planetary life-reinforcing capabilities so all planetary life, and natural resources can be sustained (Shastri & Banerjee, 2010). The segregation of environmentally beneficial processes is a complex and complicated task. Conscious capitalism is a new business transformation movement gaining ground in the United States and other countries (Shastri & Banerjee, 2010). Business scholars and practitioners have combined efforts to reinvent a system of capitalism with a conscience and a feeling of interconnectedness. Natural capitalism recognizes the dependence of the global economy on natural resources and systems, suggesting the long-term existence of humankind requires the recognition and proper valuation of natural capital. Four strategies are suggested as a means to enable all stakeholders to behave as if all resources are valued (Hawken et al., 2008): Radical Resource Productivity (efficient resource use slows resource depletion, reduces pollution, and creates jobs); Biomimicry (resource waste can be reduced through mimicking natural systems);

Service and Flow Economy (shift from goods and purchases economy to one of service and flow in which quality, utility, and performance contribute to well-being); and, Investing in Natural Capital (investments in sustaining, restoring, and expanding natural resource inventories).

Hart (2008) refers to the existence of three separate, overlapping economies within the global economy: the market economy, the survival economy, and the natural economy. The market economy consists of the commerce developed and emerging countries, with the developed countries consuming most resources, but feeling limited adverse effects of that consumption. The survival economy contains most traditional, rural, village-based communities who are subsistence focused, and frequently feel the adverse effects of the market economy. The nature's economy consists of the natural resources and systems supporting the other two economies. Ehrlich and Holdren (1971) and Commoner (1972) argued the environmental burden on the planet is a function of three factors: population, affluence, and technology. Hart (2008) argues because population reduction and affluence reduction are not viable options for reducing our economic burden, technology is the solution through pollution prevention, product stewardship, and clean technologies. While individual and regulatory efforts are important, the responsibility for ensuring a sustainable world rest on businesses which are the economic engines of the future (Hart, 2008).

7.3 Contemporary Sustainability Models and Systems

While some have sought to modify the capitalist business model to embrace sustainability, others have suggested the need for new models (Blowfield & Murray, 2014). Birkin (2000) referred to the interconnectedness of business decisions, advocating an extension or alternative of systems thinking to recognize the relationships within business processes and their components. In contrast to the conventional technocentric worldview and the alternative ecocentric worldview, Gladwin and colleagues (1995) proposed the potential emergence of an integrated "sustaincentric" worldview. These researchers argue neither technocentrism nor ecocentrism present a foundation upon which sustainable development can be established. Because both existing paradigms are in competition, they remain in a state of mutual contempt and negation (Myers & Simon, 1994), thereby failing to promote development or conserve the environment (Gladwin et al., 1995). The notion of a sustainable development-focused paradigm can be accepted as a dialectical consequence of this competitive struggle.

The proposed sustaincentric paradigm represents an evolving synthesis for deeper integration. While many scholars are attempting to "green" technocentrism, the amalgamation of ecocentrism and technocentrism seems unlikely, given the radically differentiated and pathologically disassociated state in which matter, life, and mind are observed in modernity (Wilber, 1995). The sustaincentric worldview offers an alternative lens through which to explore the reconciliation of the two existing worldviews. Sustaincentrism is grounded in the affirmation of the universalism of life, the stewardship directives common to major religions, the field of ecological economics (Costanza et al., 1991), traditions of conservation and natural resource management (Norton, 1991), and developing scientific theories based on the complexity and self-organizing properties of nature (Botkin, 1990; Prigogine & Stengers, 1984; Wheatley, 1992). Proponents of sustaincentrism include numerous environmental and social action groups, think tanks, the U.S. National Academy of Sciences, and the United Nations (Gladwin et al., 1995). Promising efforts to evaluate the emergent dimensions and principles of sustaincentrism can be identified in many studies (Brown, 1994; Daly & Cobb, 1994; Gladwin, 1992; Gladwin & Krause, 1992; Gore, 1992; Jansson et al., 1994; Korten, 1990; Porrit, 1991; Stead & Stead, 1992). Sustaincentric ethics rejects the moral monism of technocentrism and ecocentrism, instead actively embracing the pluralist conceptualization of political, civil, social, economic, and cultural human rights (Gladwin et al., 1995).

Nunez (2011) advocates using the transdisciplinary perspective as a means of going beyond rationalism, dualism, and fragmentation of knowledge as a response to the challenge of the future sustainability of our planet. Transdisciplinarity argues complexity is descendant from the ancient principle of interconnectedness, providing a multidimensional, systemic view of knowledge and reality. Spirituality and sustainability are linked by a common characteristic of connectedness among people with each other and the planet, a theme echoed by countless scholars. This perspective allows for the recognition of a spiritual level of reality, with that spirituality or sacredness located in the intersection where the object and subject interact and interconnect.

While traditional definitions of sustainability have been environmental in nature, Orr emphasizes sustainability should not only be concerned with ecological integrity, but also social and economic justice, nonviolence, democracy, and peace (McDaniel, 2002). Orr makes the distinction between the two by noting the focus of environmentalism is with ecological integrity, while the focus of sustainability is more holistic and inclusive. Coates (2012) concurs by arguing our environmental problem is a social problem. Orr (2002) describes the barriers to sustainability as not simply technological, but also social, political, and psychological. Orr further expresses concern not with whether society makes the transition to sustainability, but with how gracefully society makes the transition. Orr (2002) described the four challenges of sustainability as: the need for accurate models, metaphors, and measures to describe humankinds' relationship with the biosphere; the necessity for creativity and improvement in the areas of citizenship and governance; the necessity of informing the public through improved education; and, learning how to identify and solve multiple, disparate problems, which will require a higher level of spiritual awareness. This level of spiritual awareness recognizes that religious fundamentalism is part of the problem, not the solution, and the alternative models of scientism and consumerism are likewise part of the sustainability problem (McDaniel, 2002).

Many scholars suggest the current religious and political systems are no longer functioning. Three socio-political systems (or combinations thereof) have dominated civilization: capitalism, communism, and socialism (Targowski, 2012). While capitalism has been promoted for centuries as a democratic, free-market system, the current state of capitalism is subservient to global business managers, controlled by lobbyists, bearing little resemblance to the invisible hand of the market envisioned by Adam Smith (1778). The main objective of capitalism has been profit maximization, some suggesting for the benefit of the wealthy elite, with corporate executives and board members frequently receiving bonuses and stock options totaling millions of dollars, at the expense of line level employees, who bear the brunt of the financial sacrifice when corporations face financial downturns. Socialism, even in more democratic forms, is too costly to be applied to the overall population, regardless of whether inhabitants are 7 or 9 billion in number. Communism, however noble the aspirations, proved to be a destructive, authoritarian system, in terms of both the adherents and the environment (Targowski, 2012).

Close (2014) believes history books will report the beginning of the twenty-first century as a brief but profoundly significant period in history when humankind finally became conscious of its spiritual self. This evolutionary human era will result in a new, conscious global human society, replacing "having" (possession) and "taking" (greed) "being" (talent) and "giving" (creation), resulting in genuine sustainable progress. Close defined sustainable progress as collective, continuous human efforts based in a healthy, safe, and dynamically progressive, self-sufficient human society within the context of the dynamic natural environment in which we exist (Close, 2014). Sustainable progress requires complex responses from four levels of authority: the local population; the local government; business enterprises; and, science and academia. Traditionally, these authorities do not purposefully associate, or take responsibility for complex co-creative problems, rather playing fragmented roles in a consequence-driven, opportunistic socioeconomic system.

Close (2014) suggests the emergence of sustainocracy, an evolutionary democratic movement, characterized by the acceptance that certain issues, such as health, security, wellness, environmental sustainability, and human self-sufficiency are not political or economic options. The afore-mentioned issues are common, discerning responsibilities of all persons, organizations, and communities (Nieuwsbank, 2013). The suffering of significant portions of the human population can be mitigated through voluntary testing of the emerging society using the stress points of human complexity to convert fear into proactive passion and beneficence (Close, 2014).

In active demonstration of sustainocracy, these four constituencies recently collaborated to solve the related air quality and health problem in the Dutch city of Eindhoven. Through a collaborative civic system called AiREAS, everyone in the community partnered to improve air quality and health. The Eindhoven AiREAS experience demonstrates that a new form of society can be swiftly developed and deployed to cultivate genuine sustainable progress in complex societies using the dominant instruments of the previous paradigm. This sustainocratic process epitomizes an act of responsibility challenging traditional bureaucratic dependencies and structures in a powerful, proactive way.

In response to the inequality and unsustainable trajectory of existing socio-political systems, Targowski (2012) proposed the development of a new system: ecologism. The primary tenets of ecologism would be: the primary importance of nature; people are more important than markets; health is more important than money; sufficiency being more important than efficiency; and, business should be subservient to and regulated by society (Targowski, 2012). Ecologism includes seven subsystems: eco-education; wise society; eco-democracy; eco-justice; eco-infrastructure; deep economics; and, deep media (Targowski, 2012).

Eco-education is described as education based on ecological knowledge and wisdom. A wise society is trained and educated with ecological intelligence and is therefore qualified to make wise decisions. In an eco-democracy all citizens are equal, but the environment is predominant to humankind. Eco-justice requires environmental harm to be legally remedied by the transgressor. An eco-infrastructure operates harmoniously with the environment and prevents environmental destruction. Deep economics combines traditional business and administrative calculations with environmental and social costs. Deep media requires dissemination of comprehensive and impartial information concerning the development and status of the sustainable civilization (Targowski, 2012).

Targowski has written significantly about Spirituality 2.0, which alongside the Wise Society and Eco-education performs a critical function in the Wise Civilization architecture, and greatly determines the success of the remaining ecologism subsystems. Spirituality 2.0 introduces a shared platform to overlay existing religion with a common spiritual foundation based upon the common values of the primary global religions. Spirituality 2.0 was discussed in greater length in Chapter 2. Smith (2009) echoes this proposal suggesting ecospirituality as a missing element in spirituality and sustainability education. Targowski (2012) summarizes the current crisis of Contemporary Civilization:

1. Mass food production threatens human and environmental health.
2. Inexpensive industrial production promotes ultra-consumerism, leading to inevitable strategic resource exhaustion.
3. Advanced technology and information access increase unemployment at a time when population and available worker growth remains unchecked.
4. Representative democracy being replaced by more radical, extreme forms of direct democracy.
5. Market economy has been transformed into the market society, where everything is for sale, and individual advantage has supplanted the common good.
6. Business no longer serves society but demands service by society.
7. Politicians oriented to short-term election cycles do not encourage long-term action.
8. Societies lack confidence in politicians who do not address common issues or promote the common good.
9. Political crisis abdicates societal development and management to business and bureaucrats, who frequently replace the common good with a commercial, profit-driven approach.
10. Academia appears reluctant to jeopardize benefits of research and consultation cooperation by challenging the status quo (Targowski, 2012).

Global problems exist and persist because political and economic leadership utilizes invalid, outdated business and economic systems, dependent upon limited assumptions about human behavior drivers and the nature of economic, social, and environmental phenomenon (Tideman et al., 2013). A new worldview is emerging in which commerce, economics, environment, and society are no longer independent, separate realms, but a single, interconnected, and interdependent entity (Tideman et al., 2013). Humankind's immeasurable, collective sustainability efforts include sustainable agriculture, communities, energy, economies, ecosystems, bioregions, timber, and fisheries (Holthaus, 2012). However, it often seems these efforts occur independently, with no concerted effort to organize activities, and consider ways we might create a sustainable culture, acknowledging humans, all other creatures, plants, soil, and landforms (Holthaus, 2012).

Eco-socialism is an emerging alternative to current failing socio-political systems, based on the belief that sustainable, environmentally sound capitalism is an unattainable contradiction in terms, suggesting the current ecological crisis is an expression of the implicit crisis within the capitalist system that can only be overcome through environmentally oriented socialism (Mebratu, 1998). The major principles of eco-socialism are:

- Eco-socialism is anthropocentric and humanist, rejecting the bewilderment of nature and anti-humanism, and adding emphasis to human spirituality, satisfied partially through non-material interchange with nature.
- Humans are not a pollutant, and any expression of hubris, greed, aggression, or over-competitiveness results from the predominant socioeconomic system, and not inherited or inherent behavior.
- While humans are unlike other species, humans are natural, existing in a socially perceived natural system.
- Disconnecting ourselves from nature is disconnecting from a part of ourselves, a process that can be overcome by reasserting control over our relationship with nature, through collective ownership of production systems, because production is at the heart of our relationship with nature.
- Humans should not dominate nature through attempts to transcend natural limits and laws. Instead, we should collectively dominate our relationship with nature for collective good (Pepper, 1999).

The eco-socialist response to natural resource questions is not merely distribution-focused, recognizing no historical limits of significance to human growth as socialist development. However, there are absolute natural limits forming the boundaries of human transformational power. Moreover, each type of socioeconomic organization has a distinct avenue and dynamic for comprehending historical conditions and the non-human environment. Changing the production method requires changing multiple needs, the related necessary resources, and the corresponding environmental problems to be solved (Mebratu, 1998).

Ims (2014) investigated the deep ecology approach developed by Norwegian philosopher Arne Næss and inspired by both Eastern and Western philosophies. Næss (1989) distinguished deep and shallow environmental approaches to environmental problems as follows: *Shallow ecology* represents a technocratic attitude to environmental problems by supporting rules, regulations, and technological fixes, valuing human affluence over production and consumption reduction. *Deep ecology* represents a relational, comprehensive approach by changing the basic ideological structure, valuing production and consumption reduction over human affluence, subsequently changing how we regard ourselves as humans. Deep ecology redefines and transforms the perspective of self as an eco-self, achieved through self-realization that humans are part of a larger ecological entity. Næss advocates quality of life over standard of living, embodied in his motto: "*Simple in means and rich in ends*" (Ims, 2014).

The deep ecology movement unites individuals and groups based on eight points, some of which may be controversial, and perhaps misunderstood:

1. The well-being and flourishing of all life on Earth have value independent of their human utility.
2. Abundance and diversity of life on Earth have inherent value.
3. Humans have no right to reduce the abundance and diversity of life except when necessary to satisfy essential human needs.
4. The necessity for a substantial decrease in human population.
5. The current interference with the environment is excessive.
6. Existing policies governing basic economic, technological, and ideological systems must be revised.
7. The required ideological change concerns appreciating life rather than insisting on continued increases in the standard of living.

8. Those who support these points have an obligation to implement required changes, in a non-violent way (Ims, 2014).

Indigenomics is an economic design that introduces an Indigenous perspective to economic and social development. Indigenomics provided a collective response to the coercive suppression of the Indigenous economic perspective and the systemic exclusion of Indigenous Peoples from contemporary economies (Hilton, 2020). This system reminds us that the purpose of Indigenous economies is to improve well-being, live in ecological balance and prosperity, and share the Indigenous principles of balance, wealth, and generosity across generations (Hilton, 2020). Indigenomics honors the robust Indigenous wisdom of local economy, relationships, and human values and increases the role and perspective of Indigenous peoples in the new economy. Indigenomics employs ancient principles that have sustained Indigenous economies for millennia and takes action to execute them as modern practices (Indigenomics Institute, 2023). Indigenomics is explored further in Chapter 8.

7.4 Sustainability Trends

Young and Dhanda (2013) suggest the current sustainability movement has occurred because of a perfect storm of increased energy costs, numerous natural and human-made environmental calamities, increased attention being paid to the green movement, and the Great Recession of 2007–2008. Much of humankind currently lives as isolated, self-focused individuals, in a perpetual struggle to survive, and obtain comfort, money, and power (Nunez, 2011). Our continued existence on Earth requires imagining another way of life on our planet, accomplished through the creation of new relationships with life and ourselves (Nunez, 2011). Influenced by the environmental movement in the 1970s, and environmental mishaps in subsequent decades, alternative systems, models, and methodologies have been proposed as responses, and even replacements to the existing unsustainable systems. A selection of the most prevalent will be examined in the following section.

Seghezzo (2009) suggested the WCED sustainability framework, and the corresponding triple bottom line may no longer be a valid paradigm for the explanation and solution of contemporary environmental, social, and economic problems. Segghezo proposed a more inclusive, plural, and useful model in which the existing three Ps (people, planet, and profits) would be replaced with place, permanence, and persons. Place refers to the three-dimensional physical and geographic (space), and the culturally constructed space where we live and interact. Permanence, largely neglected in the sustainability debate, requires further consideration of the potential long-term effects of our actions. Persons describes people as individual human beings, and not as indistinguishable members of society, an approach all but excluded in the WCED sustainability framework (Seghezzo, 2009). Sustainability is viewed as a guide for economic and social policymaking in equilibrium with environmental conditions. However, three decades after the WCED defined sustainable development, placing the sustainability concept on the global agenda, the absolute meaning and suitability of these terms remains a subject of debate. The WCED definition limitations could be mitigated if sustainability is accepted as the conceptual framework for the open discussion of the territorial, temporal, and personal aspects of sustainable development (Seghezzo, 2009).

Holthaus (2012) questioned the triple bottom line image, as represented in some workshops as a three-legged stool. Holthaus believes the three-component image is detrimental to the sustainability cause, because when the environment, society, and the economy are partitioned into three categories, we are separating humans from nature, and the economy from both humans and nature as if it were equal to and independent of the natural and social environments. However, the economy is not only dependent upon and interconnected with both the natural and social environments, and the complex relationship among the three cannot be simplified. As an alternative to the three-legged stool metaphor, Holthaus proposes the reintegration of the three categories into a one-legged stool representation. "Perhaps sustainability is always more complicated than it seems" (Holthaus, 2012, p. 38).

While much of the consideration of this chapter has been with what sustainability *is*, consideration is necessary of what sustainability *is not*.

Although not entirely comprehensive, the following are ten sustainability myths:

- Nobody knows what sustainability really means.
- Sustainability is all about the environment.
- Sustainable is a synonym for green.
- It's all about recycling.
- Sustainability is too expensive.
- Sustainability means lowering our standard of living.
- Consumer choices and grassroots activism, not government intervention, offer the fastest, most efficient routes to sustainability.
- New technology is always the answer.
- Sustainability is ultimately a population problem.
- Once you understand the concept, sustainability is a breeze to figure out (Lemonick, 2009).

Sustainability success is dependent on complex interactions between both governments and stakeholders, and industries and stakeholders (Deshpande, 2010). These interactions require the development of strategies for integration of economic, environmental, and social causes to deliver sustainable equity, affordability, and profitability. Everything on Earth is intertwined, with nothing existing in isolation, including sustainable economic and environmental systems. Therefore, sustained economic growth is limited without sustainable environmental initiatives.

Daly (1996) identified three characteristics of a sustainable society: renewable resource usage rates do not exceed regeneration rates; nonrenewable resource usage rates do not exceed the sustainable, renewable substitute development rate; and, pollution emission rates do not exceed the environmental pollution assimilation capacity. Five components of sustainability have been identified as inclusiveness, connectivity, equity, prudence, and security (Gladwin et al., 1995). Inclusiveness suggests a duality of sustainability, consisting of both environmental and social systems, local and global, present and the future. Connectivity necessitates an understanding of global problems as systemically interconnected and interdependent. Equity necessitates the fair distribution of resources, both within and between generations, and is a central element of most interpretations of sustainable development. Prudence demands environmental systems, and interrelated socioeconomic systems remain buoyant to avoid irrevocable consequences, and for maintaining the scale and impact of human existence within the functional limits of those systems. Finally, security acknowledges the human-centered facet of sustainability, focused on ensuring a secure, healthy, quality of life for current and future populations (Gladwin et al., 1995).

7.5 Circular Economy

The dominant economic model of modern civilization is linear, characterized by the extraction, processing, consumption, and disposal of resources. The circular economy (CE) or circularity is a model of resource production and consumption characterized by sharing, leasing, reusing, repairing, refurbishing, and recycling existing resources and products for as long as possible. The circular economy presents an intentionally restorative and regenerative framework (Ellen MacArthur Foundation, 2021). The 9R framework of circularity provides strategies on a scale from circularity to linearity: refuse, reduce, reuse, repair, refurbish, remanufacture, repurpose, recycle, and recover (Potting et al., 2017). The highest level of circularity describes obtaining product redundancy through the elimination of product function or achieving similar functionality with another product (Potting et al., 2017).

The concept of a CE can be attributed to several intellectual traditions, including industrial ecology, biomimicry, and cradle-to-cradle (C2C) design (Kutschke et al., 2016). Industrial ecology is the study of material and energy flows through industrial systems (Kutschke et al., 2016), to restructure the industrial ecosystem to manage and design closed-loop industrial production and consumption systems (Awan, 2022). The goal of industrial ecology is to create harmonized relationships between ecological and human systems thereby producing sustainable benefits in all areas of sustainability. IE tools and practices are useful for mitigating global challenges to sustainable consumption and production through the UN SDGs (Awan, 2022).

Biomimicry is the process of designing human systems that mimic nature's time-tested processes and strategies. The goal of biomimicry is creating products, processes, and procedures that are appropriate for long-term life on Earth. Proponents of biomimicry realize that nature has already solved most of the problems humans currently experience (Biomimicry Institute, 2019). Contemporary business structures already imitate natural systems on several levels: on an organizational level as social units and entities, on a broader level as actors in trade systems, and trade systems operating as components of both social and environmental systems (Kassel, 2014). Current examples of biomimicry include photovoltaic solar panel cells that are structured like plant leaves, steel fibers that are woven similar to spider webs, and a closed-loop economy that mimics coral reefs and forests (Benyus, 1997).

Cradle-to-cradle describes a holistic approach to designing products and systems that considers their entire life cycle, from raw material extraction to end-of-life disposal with an end goal of waste minimization and resource efficiency maximization (Kutschke et al., 2016). The phrase C2C was conceived in 1976 by Walter R. Stahel, a Swiss architect and industrial analyst as an alternative to the existing linear economic system (Reday-Mulvey, 1977). C2C is a registered trademark that is owned and licensed by McDonough Braungart Design Chemistry, LLC (MBDC, 2016). The current model of C2C was popularized in the 1990s by American architect William Andrews McDonough and German chemist Michael Braungart who formalized the model in their 2002 book "*Cradle to cradle: Remaking the way we make things*" (McDonough & Braungart, 2002). The C2C policy improves safety for humans and the environment and provides optimization strategies for social improvement, and the C2C process is becoming increasingly popular with businesses seeking to differentiate more environment-friendly products (Mohajan, 2021). The interrelated concepts of IE, biomimicry, and C2C collectively contribute to development and implementation of the circular economy (Kutschke et al., 2016).

Velenturf and Purnell (2021) developed a framework of principles based on essential circularity characteristics. The framework proposes establishment of a sustainable circular society, defined as an equitable society that cultivates individual and collective well-being, environmental quality, and economic prosperity for current and future generations (Velenturf & Purnell, 2021). The ten principles of a sustainable circular economy are (Velenturf & Purnell, 2021):

1. Beneficial reciprocal flows of resources between nature and society.
2. Reduce and decouple resource use.
3. Design for circularity.
4. Circular business models to integrate multidimensional value.
5. Transform consumption.
6. Citizen participation in sustainable transitions.
7. Coordinated participatory and multi-level change.
8. Mobilize diversity to develop a plurality of circular economy solutions.
9. Political economy for multidimensional prosperity.
10. Whole system assessment.

Circularity offers an admirable solution to the wicked problems created by prolonged unsustainable human behavior (Beehner, 2023). Although the CE concept offers a solution to better utilize resources and reduce environmental impact, the CE definition is weak and inconsistent, and lacks reliable performance measurements (Semertzidis, 2023). Regardless of potential weaknesses, the circular economy model is an improvement over the inefficient linear economic model.

7.6 Environmental, Social, and Governance (ESG)

The term environmental, social, and governance (ESG) describes a broad range of issues that may directly or indirectly impact company performance and profitability. Environmental criteria measure company performance as a custodian of the environment through energy use, waste generation, pollution, natural resource management, and treatment of animals. Social criteria measure how a company deals with employees, suppliers, customers, and communities. Governance criteria measure how a company operates and includes leadership, executive compensation, audits, internal controls, and shareholder rights (ESG.org, n.d.). Some of the issues in the domain of ESG reporting include resource management, supply-chain management, organizational health, safety policies, and transparency (ESG.org, n.d.).

ESG provides a snapshot of a business and its long-term value potential and importance to stakeholders. An ESG assessment determines the environmental and social impacts of the business and the efficacy of corporate governance in managing them. Organizations develop ESG strategies to enable them to pursue and measure activities that are mutually beneficial for the triple bottom line of profits, people, and the planet (ESG.org, n.d.). ESG investing is a socially responsible investment management approach that considers companies' overall ESG performance in addition to traditional financial metrics. While nearly 25% of all U.S. professional investments today qualify as ESG investments, very few ESG investments are in company-sponsored retirement plans (ESG.org, n.d.).

Although skepticism exists about the impact of ESG on profitability and company value (Dowell et al., 2000; Hart and Ahuja, 1996; Konar & Cohen, 2001; Lee et al., 2018), companies with higher ESG performance also have higher value and lower risk (Chen et al., 2009; El Ghoul et al., 2011, 2018), and a reduced cost of equity (Dhaliwal et al., 2014; Gupta, 2018; Matthiesen & Salzmann, 2017). Specifically, Pellegrini et al. (2019) found that firms with higher ESG scores exhibit cheaper equity financing, noting that a 10 percent increase in the ESG score reduced cost of equity by 134 basis points. Aydoğmuş et al. (2022) found that ESG had a positive and highly significant relationship with company value. Although the social and governance scores had a positive and significant relationship, the environment score did not have a significant relationship with company value.

The focus of organizational change efforts is often with developing newer, improved policies (Sandhu et al., 2022). However, without a comprehensive approach that considers all internal and external stakeholders, even the best developed policies will not produce optimal outcomes (Sandhu et al., 2022). The *Three Spaces Framework for Sustainable Change* framework was developed by Sandhu et al. to better ensure that organizational ESG change efforts succeed. The framework identifies three spaces across which organizations operate: physical, mental, and social. The physical space describes the formal organizational structures including roles, policies, and programs related to strategic issues. Mental space describes the shared understanding of employees and managers concerning these issues. Social space refers to shared perception of external stakeholders about organizational action on these issues. Although organizations can initiate efforts in any space, because the three spaces are interconnected, success will only be maintained when their actions are supported across all three spaces concurrently (Sandhu et al., 2022).

7.7 Diversity, Equity, and Inclusion (DEI)

Diversity, equity, and inclusion (DEI) describes organizational frameworks that promote equitable treatment and full participation of all individuals, especially members of groups who have historically been underrepresented or faced discrimination based on identity or disability. Diversity describes the employment of a variety of individuals by an organization, based on factors of identity (e.g., gender, culture, ethnicity, religion, disability), age, or opinion (McKinsey & Company, 2022). Equity describes the concepts of fairness and justice, such as equal compensation. The focus of equity is usually with societal disparities and allocation of resources and "decision making authority to groups that have historically been disadvantaged" (University of Washington, n.d.), and consideration of "a person's unique circumstances, adjusting treatment accordingly so that the end result is equal" (McKinsey & Company, 2022). Inclusion describes developing an organizational culture that creates an experience where all employees believe they have a voice (McKinsey & Company, 2022), and a sense of community and connection.

While the topic of DEI is relatively new in the business literature, a growing body of evidence suggests DEI is beneficial to businesses, either directly through increased profitability and employee productivity, or indirectly through employee satisfaction and retention. A study by

Deloitte Insights determined that inclusive cultures create value. "Organizations with inclusive cultures are twice as likely to meet or exceed financial targets, three times more likely to be high performing, six times more likely to be innovative and agile, and eight times more likely to achieve better business outcomes" (Bourke & Dillon, 2018, p. 85).

Researchers at McKinsey and Company found that the top 25% of companies in terms of executive gender diversity were 25% more likely to experience above-average profitability than companies in the bottom 25% (Dixon-Fyle et al., 2020). This increased from 21% in 2017 and 15% in 2014. They also found that the higher the gender representation, the higher the likelihood of outperformance. They concluded that there was a substantial performance divergence of 48% from the most to least gender-diverse companies (Dixon-Fyle et al., 2020).

Goldman and Zhang (2021) examined corporate DEI objective and measurement disclosures of diversity, equity, and inclusion (DEI) and found that company's DEI commitment is positively related to employee productivity. The relationship slightly weakened during the COVID-19 pandemic but remained significant. The relationship between DEI commitment and employee productivity decreased with financial constraints, and was not attributed to increased profitability, a focus on general human capital management, or board composition. Goldman and Zhang concluded that the positive effects of DEI commitment on employee productivity are likely a result of increased employee satisfaction and improved corporate innovation.

The principles of DEI complement and support the UN SDGs and the Earth Charter principles. Specifically, UN SDG 5 (gender equity) and SDG 10 (reduced inequalities) are achieved through DEI efforts. Three of the Earth Charter principles are supported by DEI efforts:

> 10. Ensure that economic activities and institutions at all levels promote human development in an equitable and sustainable manner.
> 11. Affirm gender equality and equity as prerequisites to sustainable development and ensure universal access to education, health care, and economic opportunity.
> 15. Treat all living beings with respect and consideration (Earth Charter, n.d.).

Business owners and managers who apply DEI principles in their operations contribute to a more sustainable world and likely increase profitability.

7.8 Microfinance

Microfinance describes the process of offering loans and savings services to the poor. Some microfinance institutions also offer additional financial services such as savings accounts, checking accounts, insurance, and financial training. Microfinance encourages financial inclusion in the economy and assists countries with economic and social improvement (AngelOne, n.d.). The primary recipients of microfinance loans are women, individuals with disabilities, unemployed workers, and anyone who need funds to cover basic necessities (AngelOne, n.d.). Microfinance has become an increasingly popular method for helping small business owners in developing nations obtain short-term assistance to manage gaps in their cash flow. Although most microfinance practitioners recognize that their purpose is to improve the welfare of the poor, there is little agreement about how best to accomplish this (Schreiner, 2002).

Microfinance has assisted the financially poor to limit susceptibility to external shocks, improve their income, and create small, practical businesses. Because women in many developing nations have limited interactions with formal financial institutions, microfinance enables them to become more self-sufficient and empowered change agents (AngelOne, n.d.). Interest rates on loans vary between 17 and 80 percent with the global average rate approximately 35 percent (Kneiding & Rosenberg, 2008). The higher interest rates are a result of the small loan sizes and high transaction and management costs.

While the concept of microcredit and microfinance has origins in the 1800s, contemporary use of the term began in the 1976 when Muhammad Yunus founded Grameen Bank of Bangladesh. The previous methods for providing financial services were relationship-based banking for individual entrepreneurs and small businesses; and, group-based models, where multiple entrepreneurs collectively applied for loans as a group. The current global microfinance market is estimated to be

US$188.8 billion and to reach US$640 billion by 2033 (Fact.MR, 2023).

In developing economies, especially in rural areas, many common financial activities are not monetized. Frequently, individuals and families lack dispensable funds to acquire needed services and must revert to other methods of acquiring funds. Lack of monetary assets requires creating and exchanging alternative forms of non-cash assets such as livestock, grains, jewelry, and precious metals. Rutherford and Arora (2009) identified four types of needs:

- *Life Cycle Needs* (weddings, funerals, childbirth, education, home construction, holidays, festivals, widowhood, and retirement).
- *Personal Emergencies* (illness, injury, unemployment, theft, harassment, or death).
- *Disasters* (natural disasters and human-made events such as war or bulldozing of houses).
- *Investment Opportunities* (business expansion, purchasing land or equipment, improving housing, employment).

According to Schreiner (2002), most microfinance methods exist on a continuum between two extremes—the poverty approach and the self-sustainability approach. The *poverty approach* targets the poorest clients who are the costliest to serve, measuring success by how well the short-term needs of poorest recipients are met. The *self-sustainability approach* targets clients who are less poor but operate on the periphery of the established financial system, measuring success by how well it expands the boundary of the mainstream economy (Von Pischke, 1991). Both approaches are logical based on their assumptions (Morduch, 1998; Rhyne, 1998; Woller et al., 1999).

Schreiner (2002) proposed an outreach framework based on six characteristics: worth to clients, cost to clients, depth, breadth, length, and scope. According to the poverty approach, great depth can counteract narrow breadth, short length, and limited scope. By contrast, the self-sustainability approach assumes that great breadth, long length, and broad scope can counteract shallow depth (Schreiner, 2002). Because the social costs and benefits of microfinance cannot be thoroughly measured, most public policy choices will be based on judgments that cannot be proven, and must be argued (Schreiner, 2002). Each of the six characteristics of outreach is dependent on the other five and the change in social benefits resulting from a change in one outreach characteristic is dependent upon how all six characteristics interact. The six characteristics of outreach are briefly described in the following paragraphs.

Worth of outreach to clients describes willingness to pay and depends on the terms of the agreement, and the interests, constraints, and opportunities of clients. For loans, worth increases when contract terms align with borrower demand. For deposits, worth increases with increased interest rates and less restrictive terms such as low minimum balances and unlimited, convenient withdrawals (Schreiner, 2002). Cost of outreach to clients is the total amount of price costs and transaction costs. Price costs are direct cash payments for interest and fees, and transaction costs consist of non-price costs such as the time to apply for a loan and indirect cash expenses such as the transportation, documents, and taxes necessary to obtain a financial agreement. Cost to clients does not include cost of supply, which is incurred by the microfinance organization, and cost to society, which includes any costs incurred by non-clients such as when clients with loans prevent others from obtaining loans (Schreiner, 2002). Net gain to clients is the total worth minus costs and represents the increased benefit resulting from microfinance.

Depth of outreach describes the value attributed by society to the net gain of a specific client. Continuous measurement of depth in terms of income or wealth is challenging but is generally determined by gender, location, education, ethnicity, housing type, and access to public services (Schreiner, 2002). Breadth of outreach is measured by the total number of clients. Self-sustainable organizations with significant breadth may reach the same number of the very poor as poverty-oriented organizations with limited breadth (Rosenberg, 1996). Length of outreach describes the timespan of the supply of microfinance which is difficult to measure because it will occur later. Scope of outreach describes the variety of types of financial activities supplied. Scope between products may include offering both loans and savings accounts, and scope within a product may include contracts with several options for terms (Schreiner, 2002).

Microfinance offers multiple benefits, including (AngelOne, n.d.):

- Providing an additional level of resilient behavior in the overall economy.
- Alleviating poverty by assisting households in working more efficiently and effectively.
- Enabling small businesses to simultaneously operate and expand.
- Providing an opportunity for small businesses to obtain immediate resources to remain solvent.
- Improves capital accumulation which leads to increased access to funds when needed (AngelOne, n.d.).
- Providing loans that are too small for traditional financial institutions to consider.
- Providing loans to women who may not possess the necessary documents for identification or proof of ownership that are required by traditional institutions.

Microfinance institutions usually target women because they are statistically less likely to default on loan repayment of loans with an average repayment rate of 98% (AngelOne, n.d.). Women are not only a safer investment opportunity, but they also empower women by holding significant business leadership positions and assisting other women in becoming entrepreneurs. Children of poorer families either do not enroll in school or do not attend regularly because these families are typically from agricultural backgrounds and need their children to work to contribute to the family financially. Microfinance assists these children by providing funding to fulfill the financial needs of the family, thereby enabling the children to complete their education (AngelOne, n.d.). In assisting women and families, microfinance directly supports UN SDG 1 (no poverty), 4 (quality education), and 5 (gender equality).

When entrepreneurs obtain microfinance funding to start businesses, they create employment opportunities for others in their families and communities. Increased employment improves the local economy because more money circulates between local individuals and businesses.

Several key microfinance principles were encapsulated by the Consultative Group to Assist the Poor (CGAP) and endorsed by the Group of Eight leaders at the G8 Summit on 10 June 2004 (Helms, 2006, p. xi):

1. Poor people need not just loans but also savings, insurance, and money transfer services.
2. Microfinance must be useful to poor households: helping them raise income, build up assets, and/or cushion themselves against external shocks.
3. Subsidies from donors and government are scarce and uncertain and so, to reach large numbers of poor people, microfinance must pay for itself.
4. Microfinance means building permanent local institutions.
5. Microfinance also means integrating the financial needs of poor people into a country's mainstream financial system.
6. "The job of government is to enable financial services, not to provide them".
7. "Donor funds should complement private capital, not compete with it".
8. Donors should focus on capacity building.
9. Interest rate ceilings hurt poor people by preventing microfinance institutions from covering their costs, which chokes off the supply of credit.
10. Microfinance institutions should measure and disclose their performance—both financially and socially.

The gains from participating in microfinance programs include access to better nutrition, and increased and consistent consumption, gains which are not monetary but represent stability (AngelOne, n.d.). The satisfaction gained from microfinance is evident because loan repayment rates are high. Therefore, microfinance has several advantages and is an important tool for breaking the cycle of poverty (AngelOne, n.d.).

7.9 Concluding Thoughts

Sustainability has been defined and examined in many ways. Sustainable development is both a model for understanding the world and a method for solving global problems (Sachs, 2015). Sustainability is "socially inclusive and environmentally sustainable economic growth" (Sachs, 2015, p. 3), and is not a disciplinary perspective, but a worldview (Nolet, 2016), or lens through which all disciplines may examine human behavior and events. Sustainability is a paradigm for contemplating a future state in which environmental, social, and economic considerations are balanced in the pursuit of human progress and quality of life (Down & McKeown, 2017). Genuine sustainability cannot occur without "a deep change in values and lifestyle at both the individual and organizational level" (Dhiman, 2016).

Sustainability is an ever-changing goal or endpoint, one that changes as we learn and progress (Down & McKeown, 2017). The sustainability paradigm reflects a desirable alternative to the previous paradigm in which environmental and social catastrophe resulting from economic development is accepted as inevitable (McKeown, 2002). The sustainability paradigm demands for collaborative solutions to multiple seemingly unmanageable problems, (e.g., poverty, affordable housing, potable water, and sewage disposal) rather than simple solutions to individual problems (Down & McKeown, 2017).

Contemporary management theory is constricted by a fragmented body of knowledge, separating humankind from nature and truth from morality. Reintegration of humanity into nature is essential for organizational science to support environmentally, socially sustainable development (Gladwin et al., 1995). Sustainability scholars must tolerate the permeation of observable phenomenon and human entrusted value, the opaque boundary between description and prescription, and the dual filters of scientific feasibility and policy usefulness inherent in sustainability (Gladwin et al., 1995). For the moment, it is necessary to deal with sustainability at a rather high level of detachment, because the technical characteristics, operational indicators, and moral mandates of sustainable development do not presently experience universal consensus (Gladwin et al., 1995).

Because human business activity utilizes a considerable volume of natural resources and produces the largest cumulative environmental impact on the planet, likewise, business offers the greatest opportunity for sustainable action. Rather than proposing that business and commerce cease or dramatically reduce activity, business can and should lead action toward a more sustainable planet, and improved inhabitant quality of life. Suriyankietkaew et al. (2022) suggested sustainable leaders and entrepreneurs should cultivate and integrate value-based practices and competencies in their businesses. These competencies are categorized as strategic, systems thinking, interpersonal, anticipatory, and ethical. Essential sustainability practices include enhancing human capital by caring for stakeholders, cultivating ethical values and norms using altruism, developing social capital through social innovation, and encouraging pro-environmental behavior (PEB) and social responsibility to accomplish inclusive growth, sustainability, and resilience (Suriyankietkaew et al., 2022). PEB is discussed further in Chapter 13.

The rewards will not only be intrinsic, but extrinsic to those first movers who exercise leadership within the sustainable business movement that has already begun. While the opinions and conclusions of some of the scholars cited within this chapter are pessimistic, others have an optimistic message and vision for humankind. The human species has achieved tremendous accomplishments, leaving their mark upon nearly every corner of the planet and solar system. Imagine the impact that can be made when the passengers on spaceship Earth unite to sustain our vessel, and all inhabitants and operating systems for a long-term cosmic journey!

7.10 Case Study

Greenwashing refers to the process of providing misleading information about the favorable environmental or sustainability characteristics of a product or service. Greenwashing consists of making an unsubstantiated claim that misleads consumers into thinking that a company's products or services are sustainable or green. The chapter's case study illustrates one unfortunate attempt at greenwashing. The Competition

Bureau fined Keurig Canada $3 million for making false or misleading statements concerning the recyclability of single-use K-Cup pods. Keurig Canada voluntarily agreed to pay the fine, donate $800,000 to an environmental charity, and reimburse the bureau for $85,000 in expenses incurred during the case (The Canadian Press, 2022). Keurig agreed to a similar settlement in a class-action lawsuit in the United States.

Keurig had claimed that its single-use plastic beverage pods could be recycled if consumers removed the metallic lid and emptied out the contents. However, the bureau determined that the K-Cups were only accepted for recycling in two Canadian provinces, and the recycling instructions are insufficient for many cities to accept them in their recycling programs (The Canadian Press, 2022). In addition to the financial penalties, Keurig Canada agreed to change the product packaging, publish notices about the changes on their websites, social media, and on local and national media, include information in packaging for new Keurig brewing machines, and notify subscribers via email (The Canadian Press, 2022).

Keurig's actions were a violation of the Competition Act which is a Canadian federal law governing competition. The purpose of the Constitution Act is "to maintain and encourage competition in Canada in order to promote the efficiency and adaptability of the Canadian economy, in order to expand opportunities for Canadian participation in world markets while at the same time recognizing the role of foreign competition in Canada, in order to ensure that small and medium-sized enterprises have an equitable opportunity to participate in the Canadian economy and in order to provide consumers with competitive prices and product choices" (Competition Act, 1985). The Act prohibits companies from making false or misleading statements about products, including environmental claims that are ambiguous, trivial, or incomplete and cannot be substantiated through verifiable testing (The Canadian Press, 2022). According to Commissioner of Competition Matthew Boswell: "False or misleading claims by businesses to promote 'greener' products harm consumers who are unable to make informed purchasing decisions, as well as competition and businesses who actually offer products with a lower environmental impact" (The Canadian Press, 2022).

Keurig Canada responded that they had previously modified their pods to contain the type of plastic accepted by most Canadian recycling programs. However, they recognized that many recycling programs did not accept K-Cups. According to Cynthia Shanks, senior director for communications and sustainability at Keurig Canada, "As we continue working with municipalities and the recycling industry to increase K-Cup pod recycling acceptance, we've been evolving our communications with consumers to share that the pods are recyclable in select communities and remind them of the appropriate steps to recycle" (The Canadian Press, 2022).

Case Study Questions:

1. How common do you think greenwashing incidents like the one in this case are?
2. Are incidents like this ethical breaches or honest mistakes or oversights?
3. Keurig's penalty included direct financial costs (fines, donations) and indirect costs (communicating updated recycling information with stakeholders). Are these simply costs of business that corporate executives anticipate and willingly incur to maintain profitability and status quo while overcoming negative publicity?
4. What steps could Keurig Canada take to achieve genuine and significant sustainability?

Reflection Questions:

1. Eco-socialism was introduced as an alternative to existing socio-political systems which seem to struggle in addressing current environmental problems. How could such a system be implemented in nations which embrace or are beginning to embrace capitalism?
2. Malthus warned of the impact of overpopulation on planetary resources at a time when the human population was a mere fraction of what it is today. According to Malthus, if humankind did not keep their numbers in check, war, environmental crises, or natural resource scarcity would accomplish the task (Malthus, 1798).

Which of Malthus' population control mechanisms is most likely to accomplish the task, and why?

3. Many have argued that technology is both the cause and cure for humankind's problems. Are current and future technologies likely to move society to a more sustainable lifestyle?
4. While many have argued that the contemporary capitalist business model has contributed to our current, unsustainable global system, the notion that business can contribute to sustainability while making a profit was discussed in a previous section of this chapter. Can capitalist business models truly coexist with sustainability? Can business innovation continue to occur in a model redirecting focus from profit maximization to human and planetary well-being maximization?

References

AngelOne. (n.d.). *Microfinancing and its benefits.* https://www.angelone.in/knowledge-center/income-tax/microfinance-and-its-benefits

Awan, U. (2022). Industrial ecology in support of sustainable development goals. In *Responsible consumption and production* (pp. 370–380). Springer International Publishing.

Aydoğmuş, M., Gülay, G., & Ergun, K. (2022). Impact of ESG performance on firm value and profitability. *Borsa Istanbul Review, 22*(S2), S119–S127. https://doi.org/10.1016/j.bir.2022.11.006

Balestrero, G., & Udo, N. (2014). *Organizational survival: Profitable strategies for a sustainable future*. McGraw-Hill Education.

Bator, F. M. (1958). The anatomy of market failure. *Quarterly Journal of Economics, 72*, 351–359. https://doi.org/10.2307/1882231

Beehner, C. G. (2017, January). Teaching sustainability to a traditional business audience. In *Conference Proceedings of the International Academy of Business and Public Administration Discipline, 14(1).* Paper presented at IABPAD 2017 Conference, Orlando, FL (pp. 298–308).

Beehner, C. G. (2018). Expanding sustainable business education beyond business schools. In S. Dhiman & J. Marques (Eds.), *Handbook of Engaged*

Sustainability. Springer Nature. https://doi.org/10.1007/978-3-319-53121-2_51-1

Beehner, C. (2023). System leadership for overcoming the impossibilities of a circular economy. In H. Lehmann, C. Hinske, V. de Margerie, & A. S. Nikolova (Eds.), *The impossibilities of the circular economy: Separating aspirations from reality* (pp. 156–166). The fifth Factor X publication from the Federal Environment Agency (Umweltbundesamt, UBA). Routledge/ Taylor & Francis.

Benyus, J. M. (1997). *Biomimicry: Innovation inspired by nature*. William Morrow.

Biomimicry Institute. (2019). *What is biomimicry?* https://biomimicry.org/what-is-biomimicry/

Birkin, F. (2000). The art of accounting for science: A prerequisite for sustainable development? *Clinical Perspectives on Accounting, 11*, 289–309. https://doi.org/10.1006/cpac.1999.0367

Blowfield, M., & Murray, A. (2014). *Corporate responsibility*. Oxford University Press.

Botkin, D. B. (1990). *Discordant harmonies: A new ecology for the twenty-first century*. Oxford University Press.

Bourke, J., & Dillon, B. (2018). The diversity and inclusion revolution. Eight powerful truths. *Deloitte Insights, 22*. https://www2.deloitte.com/content/dam/insights/us/articles/4209_Diversity-and-inclusion-revolution/DI_Diversity-and-inclusion-revolution.pdf

Brown, L. R. (1994). *State of the world: 1994*. Norton.

Chen, K., Chen, Z., & Wei, K. (2009). Legal protection of investors, corporate governance, and the cost of equity capital. *Journal of Corporate Finance, 15*, 273–389. https://doi.org/10.1016/j.jcorpfin.2009.01.001

Close, J-P. (2014). Sustainocracy: Spirituality and sustainable progress. In L. Zsolnai (Ed.) *The spiritual dimension of business ethics and sustainability management* (pp. 83–98). Springer. https://doi.org/10.1007/978-3-319-11677-8_20

Coates, J. (2012). Prisoners of the story: A role for spirituality in thinking and living our way to sustainability. In J. Groen, D. Coholic, & J. R. Graham (Eds.), *Spirituality in social work and education: Theory, practice, and pedagogies* (pp. 57–76). Wilfrid Laurier University Press.

Collins, D., Junghans, A., & Haugen, T. (2016). Green and sustainable—How are these terms reflected in the context of facilities management? *CFM Second Nordic Conference 29–30 August 2016 Technical University of Denmark.*

Commoner, B. (1972). The environmental cost of economic growth. In *Population, Resources and the Environment* (pp. 339–363). Government Printing Office.

Competition Act R.S.C., 1985, c. C-34. (1985). https://laws.justice.gc.ca/eng/acts/C-34/FullText.html

Cooper, P. J., & Vargas, C. M. (2004). *Implementing sustainable development: From global policy to local action.* Rowman & Littlefield Publishers.

Costanza, R., Daly, H. E., & Bartholomew, J. A. (1991). Goals, agenda and policy recommendations for ecological economics. In R. Costanza (Ed.), *Ecological economics: The science and management of sustainability* (pp. 1–20). Columbia University Press.

Daly, H. E. (1996). *Beyond growth: the economics of sustainable development.* Beacon Press.

Daly, H. E., & Cobb, J. (1994). *For the common good: Redirecting the economy toward community, the environment, and a sustainable future.* Beacon Press.

Dean, T. J. (2014). *Sustainable venturing: Entrepreneurial opportunity in the transition to a sustainable economy.* Pearson.

Deshpande, V. V. (2010). Environmental sustainability—Managing stakeholders through education. In P. M. Banerjee & V. Shastri (Eds.), *Social responsibility and environmental sustainability in business: How organizations handle profits and social duties* (pp. 99–110). Sage Publications.

Dhaliwal, D., Li, O. Z., Tsang, A., & Yang, Y. G. (2014). Corporate social responsibility disclosure and the cost of equity capital: The roles of stakeholder orientation and financial transparency. *Journal of Accounting Public Policy, 33*, 328–355. https://doi.org/10.1016/j.jaccpubpol.2014.04.006

Dhiman, S. K. (2016). Ethics and spirituality of sustainability: What can we all do? *The Journal of Values-Based Leadership, 9*(1), 11. https://scholar.valpo.edu/jvbl/vol9/iss1/11

Dixon-Fyle, S., Dolan, K., Hunt, D. V., & Prince, S. (2020). *Diversity wins. How inclusion matters.* McKinsey & Company. https://www.mckinsey.com/featured-insights/diversity-and-inclusion/diversity-wins-how-inclusion-matters

Dowell, G., Hart, S., & Yeung, B. (2000). Do corporate global environmental standards create or destroy market value? *Management Science, 46*(8), 1013–1169. https://doi.org/10.1287/mnsc.46.8.1059.12030

Down, L., & McKeown, R. (2017). *What is sustainable development?* Earth Charter Institute.

Earth Charter. (n.d.). *The Earth Charter.* https://earthcharter.org/read-the-earth-charter/

EDG.org. (n.d.). *What is ESG?* https://www.esg.org/what-is-esg

Ehrlich, P. R., & Holdren, J. P. (1971). Impact of population growth. *Science, 171*, 1212–1217. http://www.jstor.org/stable/1731166

El Ghoul, S., Guedhami, O., Kim, H., & Park, K. (2018). Corporate environmental responsibility and the cost of capital: International Evidence. *Journal of Business Ethics, 149*, 335–36126. https://doi.org/10.1007/s10551-015-3005-6

El Ghoul, S., Guedhami, O., Kwok, C. C. Y., & Mishra, D. R. (2011). Does corporate social responsibility affect the cost of capital? *Journal of Banking & Finance, 35*, 2388–2406. https://doi.org/10.1016/j.jbankfin.2011.02.007

Ellen MacArthur Foundation. (2021). *Concept.* https://www.ellenmacarthurfoundation.org/circular-economy/concept

Fact.MR. (2023). Microfinance market outlook (2023 to 2033). https://www.factmr.com/report/microfinance-market

Gladwin, T. N. (1992). *Building the sustainable corporation: Creating environmental sustain-ability and competitive advantage.* National Wildlife Federation.

Gladwin, T. N., Kennelly, J. J., & Krause, T.-S. (1995). Shifting paradigms for sustainable development: Implications for management theory and research. *The Academy of Management Review, 20*(4), 874–907. https://doi.org/10.5465/AMR.1995.9512280024

Gladwin, T.N., & Krause, T. (1992). *Business, nature and society: Toward sustainable enterprise.* Irwin.

Goldman, N. C., & Zhang, Y. (2021). *Corporate commitment to diversity and employee productivity* (November 2, 2021). https://ssrn.com/abstract=3955017

Gordon, R., Carrigan, M., & Hastings, G. (2011). A framework for sustainable marketing. *Marketing Theory, 11*(2), 143–163. https://doi.org/10.1177/1470593111403218

Gore, A. (1992). *Earth in balance: Ecology and the human spirit*. Houghton Mifflin.

Gupta, K. (2018). Environmental sustainability and implied cost of equity: International evidence. *Journal of Business Ethics, 147*, 343–365. https://doi.org/10.1007/s10551-015-2971-z

Hart, S. L. (2008). Beyond greening: Strategies for a sustainable world. In M. V. Russo (Ed.), *Environmental management: Readings and cases* (pp. 191–204). Sage Publications.

Hart, S. L., & Ahuja, G. (1996). Does it pay to be green? An empirical examination of the relationship between emission reduction and firm performance. *Business Strategy and the Environment, 5*(1), 30–37. https://doi.org/10.1002/(SICI)1099-0836(199603)5:13.0.CO;2-Q
Hawken, P., Lovins, A., & Lovins, L. H. (2008). The next industrial revolution. In M. V. Russo (Ed.), *Environmental management: Readings and cases* (pp. 3–14). Sage Publications.
Helms, B. (2006). *Access for all: Building inclusive financial systems.* The World Bank.
Hilton, C. A. (2020). An introduction to Indigenomics. In Indigenomics: Harnessing the power of our communities. *Cultural Survival.* https://www.culturalsurvival.org/publications/cultural-survival-quarterly/indigenomics-harnessing-power-our-communities
Hoffman, A. J. (1999). Environmental education in business school. *Environment, 4*, 41. https://www.proquest.com
Holthaus, G. (2012). *Learning Native wisdom: What traditional cultures teach us about subsistence, sustainability, and spirituality.* University Press of Kentucky.
Ims, K. J. (2014). Deep ecology and personal responsibility. In L. Zsolnai (Ed.), *The spiritual dimension of business ethics and sustainability management* (pp. 47–56). https://doi.org/10.1007/978-3-319-11677-8_20
Indigenomics Institute. (2023). *About.* https://indigenomicsinstitute.com/about-us/
Inter-American Investment Corporation. (1991). *Report to the board of directors on a proposed equity investment in COBANCO, La Paz.* Inter-American Investment Corporation.
Jansson, A., Hammer, M., Folke, C., & Costanza, R. (Eds.). (1994). *Investing in natural capital: The ecological economics approach to sustainability.* Island Press.
Kassel, K. (2014). *The thinking executive's guide to sustainability.* Business Expert Press.
Kneiding, C., & Rosenberg, R. (2008). *Variations in microcredit interest rates.* CGAP brief. World Bank. http://hdl.handle.net/10986/9510
Konar, S., & Cohen, M. A. (2001). Does the market value environmental performance? *Review of Economics and Statistics, 83*(2), 281–289. https://doi.org/10.1162/00346530151143815
Kopnina, H. (2014). Metaphors of nature and economic development: Critical education for sustainable business. *Sustainability, 6*(11), 7496–7513. https://doi.org/10.3390/su6117496

Korten, D. C. (1990). *Getting to the 21st century: Voluntary action and the global agenda*. Kumarian Press.

Kutschke, A., Rese, A., & Baier, D. (2016). The effects of locational factors on the performance of innovation networks in the German energy sector. *Sustainability, 8*(12), 1281. https://doi.org/10.3390/su8121281

Lee, J., Graves, S. B., & Waddock, S. (2018). Doing good does not preclude doing well: Corporate responsibility and financial performance. *Social Responsibility Journal, 14*(4), 768–781. https://doi.org/10.1108/SRJ-03-2017-0044

Lemonick, M. (2009, March 9). Top 10 myths about sustainability. *Scientific American*. https://www.scientificamerican.com/article/top-10-myths-about-sustainability/

Malthus, T. R. (1798). *An essay on the principle of population as it affects the future improvement of society, with remarks on the speculations of Mr. Goodwin, M. Condorcet and other writers* (1st ed.). J. Johnson in St Paul's Church-yard.

Matthiesen, M.-L., & Salzmann, A. J. (2017). Corporate social responsibility and firms' cost of equity: How does culture matter? *Cross Cultural & Strategic Management, 24*(1), 105–124. https://doi.org/10.1108/CCSM-11-2015-0169

McDaniel, J. (2002). Spirituality and sustainability. *Conservation Biology, 16*(6), 1461–1464. http://www.jstor.org/stable/3095400

McDonough, W., & Braungart, M. (2002). *Cradle to Cradle: Remaking the Way We Make Things*. North Point Press.

McKeown. R. (with Hopkins, C., Rizzi, R. & Chrystalbridge, M.) (2002). *Education for sustainable development toolkit*. Waste Management Research and Education Institute. http://www.esdtoolkit.org

McKinsey & Company. (2022). What is diversity, equity, and inclusion? https://www.mckinsey.com/featured-insights/mckinsey-explainers/what-is-diversity-equity-and-inclusion

MBDC. (2016). *Cradle to Cradle Certified (TM) Product Standard v3.1*. MBDC.

Mebratu, D. (1998). Sustainability and sustainable development: Historical and conceptual review. *Environmental Impact Assessment Review, 18*(6), 493–520. https://doi.org/10.1016/S0195-9255(98)00019-5

Mohajan, H. K. (2021). Cradle to cradle is a sustainable economic policy for the better future. *Annals of Spiru Haret University. Economic Series, 21*(4), 569–582. https://mpra.ub.uni-muenchen.de/111334/1/MPRA_paper_111334.pdf

Molnar, E., & Mulvihill, P. R. (2003). Sustainability-focused organizational learning: Recent experiences and new challenges. *Journal of Environmental Planning and Management, 46*(2), 167–176. https://doi.org/10.1080/0964056032000070990\

Morduch, J. (1998). *The microfinance schism.* Princeton.

Myers, N., & Simon, J. L. (1994). *Scarcity or abundance: A debate on the environment*. Norton.

Næss, A. (1989). *Ecology, community and lifestyle. Outline of an ecosophy*. (trans. and revised by D. Rothenberg). Cambridge University Press.

Nieuwsbank, B. V. (2013). *Eindhoven's unique way to address air pollution and human health*. Author. http://www.nieuwsbank.nl/en/2013/08/14/J001.htm

Nolet, V. (2016). *Educating for sustainability: Principles and practices for teachers.* Routledge.

Norton, B. G. (1991). *Toward unity among environmentalists*. Oxford University Press.

Nunez, M. C. (2011). Sustainability and spirituality: A transdisciplinary perspective. *Transdisciplinary Journal of Engineering & Science, 7*, 74–80. https://www.atlas-journal.com

Orr, D. W. (2002). Four challenges of sustainability. *Conservation Biology, 16*(6), 1457–1460. https://doi.org/10.1046/j.1523-1739.2002.01668.x

Pellegrini, C. B., Caruso, R., & Mehmeti, N. (2019). The impact of ESG scores on cost of equity and firm's profitability. *New Challenges in Corporate Governance, Theory and Practice, 3*, 38–40. https://doi.org/10.22495/ncpr_9

Pepper, D. (1999). *Eco-socialism*. Routledge.

Porrit, J. (1991). *Save the earth*. Turner Publishing.

Potting, J., Hekkert, M. P., Worrell, E., & Hanemaaijer, A. (2017). *Circular economy: Measuring innovation in the product chain* (No. 2544). PBL Publishers

Prigogine, I., & Stengers, I. (1984). *Order out of chaos*. Bantam Books.

Rainey, D. L. (2006). *Sustainable business development: Inventing the future through strategy, innovation, and leadership*. Cambridge University Press.

Reday-Mulvey, G. (1977). *The potential for substituting manpower for energy: Final report 30 July 1977 for the Commission of the European Communities.* Battelle, Geneva Research Centre.

Rhyne, E. (1998). The yin and yang of microfinance: Reaching the poor and sustainability. *Microbanking Bulletin*, 2, 6–8. https://www.marketlinks.org/sites/default/files/media/file/2020-09/Rhyne_yingyang.pdf

Rosenberg, R. (1996). *Microcredit interest rates.* Occasional Paper No. 1. The World Bank. www.worldbank.org/html/cgap/occ1.htm.

Rutherford, S., & Arora, S. (2009). *The poor and their money: Micro finance from a twenty-first century consumer's perspective.* Practical Action.

Sachs, J. (2015). *The age of sustainable development*. Columbia University Press.

Sandhu, S., Kulik, C. T., Perera, S., & Jarvis, S. A. (2022). How to ensure success in environmental, social, and governance efforts. *USApp–American Politics and Policy Blog*. https://blogs.lse.ac.uk/usappblog/2022/08/06/how-to-ensure-success-in-environmental-social-and-governance-efforts/

Schreiner, M. (2002). Aspects of outreach: A framework for discussion of the social benefits of microfinance. *Journal of International Development, 14*(5), 591–603. https://doi.org/10.1002/jid.908

Seghezzo, L. (2009). The five dimensions of sustainability. *Environmental Politics, 18*(4), 539–556. https://doi.org/10.1080/09644010903063669

Semertzidis, T. (2023). From panacea for sustainability to conceptual and resource realities. In H. Lehmann, C. Hinske, V. de Margerie, & A. S. Nikolova (Ed.), *The impossibilities of the circular economy: Separating aspirations from reality* (pp. 81–89). The fifth Factor X publication from the Federal Environment Agency (Umweltbundesamt, UBA). Routledge/ Taylor & Francis.

Shastri, V., & Banerjee, P. M. (2010). From corporate social responsibility to global social entrepreneurship. In P. M. Banerjee & V. Shastri (Eds.), *Social responsibility and environmental sustainability in business: How organizations handle profits and social duties* (pp. 1–14). Sage Publications.

Smith, A. (1778). *An inquiry into the nature and causes of the wealth of nations* (1st ed.). W. Strahan & T. Cadell.

Smith, C. (2009). Reconnecting with Earth: Ecospirituality as the missing dimension in spirituality and sustainability education. *International Handbook of Education for Spirituality, Care and Wellbeing, 653–675*,. https://doi.org/10.1007/978-1-4020-9018-9_35

Soni, A. (2010). Greening the built environment. In P. M. Banerjee & V. Shastri (Eds.), *Social responsibility and environmental sustainability in business: How organizations handle profits and social duties* (pp. 133–146). Sage Publications.

Soyka, P. A. (2012). *Creating a sustainable organization: Approaches for enhancing corporate value through sustainability.* Pearson Education.

Springett, D., & Kearins, K. (2001). Gaining legitimacy? Sustainable development in business school curriculum. *Sustainable Development, 9*, 213–221. https://doi.org/10.1002/sd.164

Stead, W. E., & Stead, J. G. (1992). *Management for a small planet: Strategic decision making and the environment.* Sage Publications.

Suriyankietkaew, S., Krittayaruangroj, K., & Iamsawan, N. (2022). Sustainable Leadership practices and competencies of SMEs for sustainability and resilience: A community-based social enterprise study. *Sustainability, 14*(10), 5762. https://doi.org/10.3390/su14105762

Targowski, A. (2012). Spirituality 2.0—A condition for a wise civilization. *Dialogue and Universalism, 22*(2), 133–143. www.researchgate.net

The Canadian Press. (2022). *Keurig Canada fined $3 million for misleading claims over coffee pod recycling.* Canadian Broadcasting Corporation. https://www.cbc.ca/news/business/keurig-fined-3-million-fine-1.6307150

Thomas, T. E. (2005). Are business students buying it? A theoretical framework for measuring attitudes toward the legitimacy of environmental sustainability. *Business Strategy and the Environment, 14*(3), 186–197. https://doi.org/10.1002/bse.446

Tichy, N. M., & McGill, A. R. (2003). *The ethical challenge: How to lead with unyielding integrity.* Jossey-Bass.

Tideman, S. G., Arts, M. C., & Zandee, D. P. (2013). Sustainable leadership: Towards a workable definition. *Journal of Corporate Citizenship, 49*(6), 17–33. http://www.jstor.org/stable/jcorpciti.49.17

University of Washington. (n.d.). *Diversity, equity, and inclusion definitions.* https://www.washington.edu/research/or/office-of-research-diversity-equity-and-inclusion/dei-definitions/

Velenturf, A. P., & Purnell, P. (2021). Principles for a sustainable circular economy. *Sustainable Production and Consumption, 27*, 1437–1457. https://doi.org/10.1016/j.spc.2021.02.018

Von Pischke, J. D. (1991) *Finance at the frontier: Debt capacity and the role of credit in the private economy.* World Bank.

Wengrovitz, D., & Banerjee, P. M. (2010). The clean technology industry: Social entrepreneurship and sustainability. In P. M. Banerjee & V. Shastri (Eds.), *Social responsibility and environmental sustainability in business: How organizations handle profits and social duties* (pp. 111–132). Sage Publications.

Wheatley, M. J. (1992). *Leadership and the new science: Learning about organizations from an orderly universe.* Berrett-Koehler.
Wilber, K. (1995). *Sex, ecology, spirituality: The spirit of evolution.* Shambhala.
Woller, G. M., Dunford, C., & Woodworth, W. (1999). Where to microfinance? *International Journal of Economic Development*, *1*(1), 29–64. www.spaef.com/IJED_PUB/index.html
Young, S. T., & Dhanda, K. K. (2013). *Sustainability: Essentials for business.* Sage Publications.

8
Indigenous Sustainability

8.1 Introduction

While contemporary society is established on a foundation of human-made institutions and structures, Indigenous cultures recognize the interconnectedness of nature and humankind, and that we cannot live and survive outside of nature. Creation is conceived as a living process wherein all inhabitants are members of a living universe. Most Indigenous traditions and belief systems regard nature with deep respect. They have a strong sense of place and belonging which sustains knowledge and ways of life that promote nature conservation and sustainable natural resource use. Common Indigenous cultures and their respective spiritual beliefs and practices will be explored within the context of the role of sustainability in individual and collective success. The absence of a spiritual-secular binary in Indigenous cultures will add an important perspective to the discussion about sustainability.

I added this chapter to the second edition with the recognition that as a North American of European descent, my ability to present and explain sustainability from any Indigenous perspective is limited. However, the content is relevant to the theme of this text and current discourse on spirituality and sustainability. I have researched this topic from a perspective

C. G. Beehner, *Spirituality, Sustainability, and Success*, Palgrave Studies in Workplace Spirituality and Fulfillment, https://doi.org/10.1007/978-3-031-47643-3_8

of respect and humility, acknowledging my position as a colonial descendant and not an original inhabitant. The greatest challenge in developing Chapters 4 and 8 was that spirituality and the environment are so interwoven in Indigenous wisdom that it was often difficult to choose in which of the two chapters (or both) should contain some of the content. I want to be careful in my discussion to not suggest that Indigenous peoples should adopt Western frameworks and concepts of sustainable development, or that they should assimilate into our way of thinking. The Indigenous peoples have always lived sustainably. Western society became unsustainable and are the ones who must assimilate and change.

The concept of sustainable development originated in the Global North in the late 1980s. The need for a sustainable approach to human development is the result of the assumption that humankind defines nature within the context of the benefit of nature to society (Knippenberg, 2010). Civilization implies separation from natural restrictions with the natural environment primarily functioning as a platform and resource to support humanity and its development (Knippenberg, 2010). Under his assumption, nature exists to be consumed and controlled in an instrumental manner (Dijksterhuis, 1998) or for enjoyment. The Global North worldview of nature and the environment is grounded in historical Western beliefs and philosophies, including the Bible, especially the book of Genesis (Kay, 1988; White, 1967) ancient Greek and Roman philosophy including [neo]-Platonism and Stoicism (Boersema, 1991), and to a lesser extent, the Middle Ages (Knippenberg, 2010).

Wijsen and Marcos (2010) suggested that there is a conflict between the developmental views of contemporary science and traditional Indigenous knowledge, with each claiming to be most appropriate for achieving sustainability. Proponents of either worldview (or a hybrid of both) propose that scientific research can demonstrate which cognitive description of reality (knowledge) is preferable, while recognizing that this may be easier in one context or field than others. Although a value or habit that is developed in one culture through cooperation and collaboration, may be embraced and eventually attain universality, this may be difficult to accomplish in practice (Tarimo, 2004, pp. 28–29).

8.2 Indigenous Business and Economics Perspectives

An Indigenous cosmology is relational and understands that relationships require time to develop and includes reciprocal responsibilities. From an Indigenous perspective, commerce occurs inside, not outside of the natural environment and the community (Bansal, 2021). Earth is more than a planet, she is "Mother Earth", who provides for and receives from everything that exists (Bansal, 2021). Therefore, when business activities harm the community or the environment, those activities harm themselves (Bansal, 2021). This relational worldview is also temporal because past, present, and future are connected, therefore, the interests of ancestors and descendants are as important as the interests of people today (Bansal, 2021). Meanwhile, a Western business perspective considers people, objects, activities, and communities as detached with transactions administered by markets and contracts.

Indigenous entrepreneurship is defined as "the creation, management, and development of new ventures by Indigenous people for the primary benefit of their own community" (Hindle & Lansdowne, 2005, p. 132). Indigenous entrepreneurial activities are inclined to be community-based because of the nature of operating with the engagement of community members (Khumukcham, 2021). Indigenous commerce is owned and performed by Indigenous people themselves who share a common perspective for achieving social and cultural self-determination and economic success (Anderson et al., 2007a, 2007b). Stakeholders include the entrepreneur and employees, the entrepreneur's family, extended family, and the community who are all involved in business creation and development (Lindsay, 2005). This collective approach includes a combination of social, cultural, and economic objectives (Anderson et al., 2007a, 2007b) that benefit the entrepreneur, their families, and the entire Indigenous community (Lindsay, 2005). The concept of a market is quite familiar to Indigenous peoples (Nathan et al., 2004) whose transactions frequently occur in the bazaar and the informal sector (Dana, 2007a, 2007b; Khumukcham, 2021). Research indicates that Indigenous entrepreneurship is concerned with the target customer (Dana & Anderson, 2007; Osinubi, 2007) and their preferences (Lituchy et al.,

2007), and developing customer attraction strategies (Anderson et al., 2007a, 2007b; Winsa, 2007). However, there is limited research about Indigenous entrepreneurial business models in the study of Indigenous entrepreneurship, with few authors attempting to include an innovative perspective within Indigenous entrepreneurship (Khumukcham, 2021).

Indigenous knowledge is unique to a specific community (Onwuegbuzie, 2017), and culture (Capel, 2014), and is orally disseminated through stories, knowledgeable experiences, useful examples, and idioms (Sen, 2005 as in Onwuegbuzie, 2017). This knowledge is accumulated through generations of traditional experiences through trial and error that is relevant to the mode of production (Ashok, 2013), and has been demonstrated to be useful in solving community problems (Onwuegbuzie, 2017). Because of this flexibility, Indigenous knowledge can be used to modify products and services to add value resulting in increased market acceptance (Capel, 2014). Indigenous entrepreneurs have fundamental knowledge that increases awareness about the local market and customer needs (see: Capel, 2014; Dana, 2007a, 2007b), enhances use of available resources and modified production methods (Agwu & Me, 2018), and creates innovative solutions (Ganguli, 2000).

The number of individuals engaged in Indigenous business activities exceeds the number of individuals performing conventional business or entrepreneurial activities (Khumukcham, 2021). However, the difference between these activities is that Indigenous entrepreneurship typically occurs within their geographic region while mainstream business activities normally target a larger population. To fully appreciate the Indigenous business model, it is necessary to examine that model within their cultural context (Khumukcham, 2021).

Indigenomics is an economic design that introduces an Indigenous perspective to economic and social development. Indigenomics provides a collective response to the destructive eradication of the Indigenous economic cosmology and the systemic omission of Indigenous Peoples from contemporary economies. This system reminds us that the purpose of Indigenous economies is to promote Indigenous well-being, exist and flourish in ecological balance, and pass on Indigenous concepts of balance, abundance, and generosity across generations (Hilton, 2020). Indigenomics recognizes the powerful understanding and wisdom of local economy, relationships, and human values, is based on ancient knowledge that has maintained Indigenous economies for millennia and seeks to implement them as modern practices (Indigenomics Institute, 2023).

Carol Anne Hilton founded the Indigenomics Institute in 2018 to operate as an Indigenous economic advisory organization to public governments, Indigenous communities, and industry. Hilton is the author of *Indigenomics: Taking a seat at the economic table* and is *Nuu-chah-nulth* of the Hesquiaht nation on Vancouver Island in Canada. She graduated in 2004 from Hertfordshire University in the United Kingdom with a Master of Business Administration. The mission of the Institute is "to facilitate positive leadership and relationships to support the growth and development of Indigenous economies, with a focus on four core areas in overcoming Indigenous economic barriers and addressing challenges: dialogue platform for Indigenous economic solutions; economic policy, research, analysis, and planning; education and training; and partnership development" (Indigenomics Institute, 2023). The Indigenomics Institute developed a Canadian Indigenous economic agenda to increase the Indigenous economy from $32 billion to $100 billion CAD by 2025 (Hilton, 2020).

The traditional Indigenous economic knowledge systems have become nearly invisible by more than five centuries of colonization and systemic racism. Because of the major disruptions in Indigenous economies and lifestyles, Indigenous Peoples have experienced four economic stages (Hilton, 2020):

1. Disruption, characterized by the systemic interruption of traditional Indigenous economic systems, lifestyles, and separation from their land which eradicated inherent authority and responsibility to place.
2. Entanglement, characterized by the complexity of the Indigenous relationship locally, nationally, and globally.
3. Emergence, characterized by the emergence of the Indigenous legal environment which reinforced a new contemporary economic space for Indigenous Nations, businesses, and representation.

4. Empowerment, characterized by the ascent of Indigenous economic empowerment resulting from increased Indigenous rights and title legal status, economic equality, and inclusion.

The fourth and current stage represents an increase in Indigenous business development and economic activity recognized as a feasible and competitive business model (Hilton, 2020). Through increased legal influence, Indigenous Peoples possess considerable land and entitlements, and operate in all areas of business and industry, increasingly reintroducing their economic footprint on the contemporary national and global economies (Hilton, 2020).

8.3 Indigenous Peoples and Sustainable Development

Indigenous peoples have existed for millennia as independent and unique nations within difficult and demanding environments because their cultural values are compatible with sustainability (Tsosie, 2014). Indigenous Peoples are unique because they have inhabited their lands for millennia, and their intergenerational presence and relationship with their lands is deeply engrained within their cultures and societies (Tsosie, 2014). For most Indigenous peoples, sustainability is the result of conscious and deliberate activities intended to maintain harmony between humankind and nature for the benefit of future generations (Tsosie, 2014).

Indigenous communities recognize themselves, members of their communities, and the natural environments as interconnected through an attached spirit or energy (Robison, 2020). The principle of everyone and everything being interconnected is common among many Indigenous Peoples, including the Maori of New Zealand who recite the *whakapapa* or the genealogy of all things, which connects individuals to the past, present, future, and the non-human world (Haley, 2021). The concept of considering future generations is common in most Indigenous cultures, with one common representation being the seventh-generation principle. The seventh-generation principle involves considering the seventh generation of descendants, and remembering the seventh generation of ancestors in decision-making, speech, and action (Haley, 2021). "The seventh-generation principle is based on an ancient philosophy of the Haudenosaunee Confederacy (Iroquois), which is recognized as the oldest democracy in the world and believed to be the model of the American Constitution" (Haley, 2021). Goodman (2015) describes the principle as "choosing our responsibility to the seventh generation over quarterly earnings, regeneration over economic growth, and the pursuit of well-being and harmony over wealth and financial success" (p. 29). Everyone must respect the relationality and interdependence of, and reciprocity with every entity (including deceased ancestors and inanimate subjects; Van Norren & Beehner, 2021). Maintaining cultural traditions, language, and ceremonies is essential so that unborn generations can continue to practice Haudenosaunee culture (Haudenosaunee Confederation, n.d.).

The word Haudenosaunee means "people who build a house" (National Museum for the American Indian, 2009). The name describes an alliance among six Native American nations who are also known as the Iroquois Confederacy with each nation maintaining their unique identity. These nations are known as (National Museum for the American Indian, 2009):

- Mohawk or Kanien'kehaka, which means "People of the Flint".
- Oneida or Onayotekaono, which means "People of the Standing Stone".
- Onondaga or Onundagaono, which means "People of the Hills".
- Cayuga or Guyohkohnyoh, which means "People of the Great Swamp".
- Seneca or Onondowahgah, which means "People of the Great Hill".
- Tuscarora or Skaruhreh, which means "The Shirt Wearing People".

In 1722, the Tuscarora Nation became the sixth nation to join the confederation, and the Confederacy has also been called the Six Nations (National Museum for the American Indian, 2009). The Haudenosaunee describe themselves as Ongweh'onweh (ongk-way-HON-way), which means "real human beings". Although there are many cultural similarities and family relationships between the six nations, each nation is unique with its own distinct language (National Museum for the American Indian, 2009).

There are numerous ways in which Indigenous peoples respond sustainably to climate change. The Kichwa Sarayaku people of Ecuador developed the Kawsay Sacha (Living Forest) program as an Indigenous-led strategy to maintain the forests and stop extracting fossil fuels based on guidelines developed within their own community (Eisenstadt & West, 2017). Kawsay Sacha is a proposal for coexisting with the natural environment that originates with the traditional knowledge of the Indigenous inhabitants of the Amazonian rainforest. *Sumak kawsay* (translated to Spanish as *buen vivir*, and to English as good living) reinforces acceptance of the instrumentality of nature, and augments Western science (Eisenstadt & West, 2017). Buen vivir is a flowing and relational notion, establishing a continuously adapting connection between humankind, nature, spirituality, and a responsibility for preserving this connection for future generations (Seiwald, 2012). Similar concepts describing the flow between humans and nature absent manmade boundaries has been observed in Asia, the Pacific, North America, and South America (Allison, 2015; Becken et al., 2013; Haluza-DeLay, 2014). Sumak kawsay is juxtaposed with developmentalism which emphasizes the duality of wealth and poverty, and the hierarchical situation of individuals and their work in relation to global centers of commerce (Eisenstadt & West, 2017).

The public dialogue about the conflict between science and Indigenous wisdom for solving environmental problems includes four positions: primordialist, utilitarian, developmentalist, and positivist (Eisenstadt & West, 2017). The primordialist view advocates that the Indigenous peoples are best suited to protect the environment, their needs precede the needs of others, and governments should fund development of Native technologies and reconciling the lost connection between people and the land. At the other extreme, Western positivists insist that modern science overrides Indigenous wisdom (Eisenstadt & West, 2017). The utilitarian and developmentalist positions lie in the middle between the primordialist and positivist views (Eisenstadt & West, 2017). The Indigenous Knowledge (IK) movement challenges the idea that IK should be understood independent of, or contradictory to scientific or Western knowledge (Turnbull, 2009).

Buddhist Gross National Happiness (GNH) is an innovative sustainability philosophy introduced by the fourth King of Bhutan, Jigme Singye Wangchuck in 1972, that is based on four pillars (Gross National Happiness Commission, 2009):

1. sustainable and equitable socioeconomic development;
2. environmental conservation;
3. preservation and promotion of culture; and
4. good governance.

The objective of GNH is balancing material and spiritual development resulting in moderation and living a simple life (Van Norren & Beehner, 2021). GNH values respect for nature, compassion, and the interdependence of all things (Phuntsho, 2013; Tideman, 2004; Ura et al., 2012). The Bhutanese government policies of GNH and broader well-being offer an alternative to conventional economic thinking based on Gross National Product (GNP; Ura & Galay, 2004; Ura et al., 2012). GNH is measured by an index consisting of nine dimensions: psychological well-being, use of time, cultural diversity and resilience, community vitality, education, health, good governance, ecological diversity, and resilience, and living standards (Ura et al., 2012).

8.4 Challenges and Opportunities

Climate change poses significant threats to Indigenous Peoples' livelihoods and traditional knowledge because most Indigenous Peoples live in areas heavily impacted by climate change and modern development that damage the natural environment (Tsosie, 2014), and are dependent upon, and closely connected with the environment and natural resources (Jerez, 2021). The homes of Indigenous Peoples, such as the Inuit in Alaska, Canada, and Greenland, are being destroyed by flooding and they are having trouble maintaining their traditional, subsistence lifestyles because of the loss of sea ice and the impacts on their food sources (Tsosie, 2014). Other negative impacts include diseases, drought and desertification, excessive rainfall, increased flooding, melting snow, glaciers and sea ice, increased insect infestations, and erosion (Jerez, 2021). The increased frequency and intensity of climate disasters is destroying their land and homes causing many Indigenous peoples to become environmental refugees (Jerez, 2021). Fossil fuel-driven economic growth and climate change have increased flooding and sea level rise in some regions destroys crops, communities, and occasionally sacred burial grounds (Jerez, 2021). Increased demand for biofuels in developed nations has resulted in the development of expansive monocrop palm plantations that decimate tropical rain forests in Asia, Latin America, and West Africa, requiring the forced relocation of Indigenous Peoples from their lands (Jerez, 2021).

Indigenous Peoples are stewards of the world's biodiversity and cultural diversity and essential stakeholders for natural resource and biodiversity protection (Jerez, 2021). Although Indigenous Peoples only represent approximately five percent of the global population, they effectively manage approximately 20–25% of the Earth's land surface. Their traditional lands possess 80% of the planet's biodiversity and approximately 40% of all protected and ecologically intact areas (Jerez, 2021).

Although the resilience and survival of Indigenous Peoples resilience is threatened by vulnerability to the negative effects of humankind-induced climate change, these Peoples have thus far adapted to these changes through the continued practice of the traditional ways passed down from previous generations (Jerez, 2021). Therefore, Indigenous Peoples have a proven and essential contribution to climate change and biodiversity loss mitigation and resilience strategies. These contributions are evidenced by their successful resistance against deforestation and natural resource extraction in their ancestral lands; efforts to prevent further expansion of single crop plantations; advocacy for sustainable production and consumption methods through traditional knowledge and reciprocity with nature; and, the successful stewardship of Indigenous lands and territories (Jerez, 2021).

While consensus exists concerning the adverse effects of climate change on Indigenous peoples, there is uncertainty about how governments should respond. International agreements have acknowledged the value and importance of traditional knowledge, with the Intergovernmental Panel on Climate Change (IPCC) acknowledging the importance of traditional knowledge in mitigating the negative effects of climate change. However, despite the contributions and solutions of Indigenous Peoples, climate action initiatives often neglect individual and collective Indigenous rights or exclude the genuine inclusion of Indigenous Peoples in all levels of decision-making (Jerez, 2021). Because of the increased global demand, the exploitation of natural resources has accelerated the biodiversity loss and ecosystem destruction. This has resulted in displacement, loss of land, water, and livelihood, and increased militarization, violence, and oppression to acquire natural resources located in Indigenous lands. Indigenous Peoples have increasingly resisted these environmental transgressions resulting in the deaths of 287 Indigenous environmental and human rights defenders in 2020 (Jerez, 2021).

There is a significant gap between the rights of Indigenous women that exists in the law and exercise of those rights in real life (Jerez, 2021). Indigenous men are increasingly migrating to urban areas seeking work which has resulted in an increasing proportion of Indigenous women assuming additional responsibility for management and governance of traditional lands. Jerez (2021) suggested it is essential to ensure the inclusion, legal recognition, and meaningful engagement of Indigenous women in matters of land ownership and governance (Jerez, 2021). The perspectives, roles, and knowledge of both Indigenous women and men complementary, and essential for climate change action. However, despite the unique contributions of Indigenous women to the environment, food security, and enhanced spiritual well-being, their traditional knowledge is often not appreciated and is often eradicated (Jerez, 2021).

8.5 Agriculture and Forests

Agriculture has served an important role in Indigenous society for millennia. Crop yield is often explained by Indigenous peoples in ancestral terms (Robison, 2020). Many Indigenous cultures believe that ancestral creator beings are physically incarnate in natural elements such as rocks, mountains, and bodies of water. Many Indigenous African Peoples respond to the environmental destruction of Western agricultural technology by reverting to traditional agricultural and environmental stewardship wisdom (Wangiri, 1999). However, although the African attitude toward nature is relational (Daneel, 1998), there are peoples who do not embrace this tradition (Wijsen & Marcos, 2010), whose relationship with nature may be described as exploitive (Brandström, 1991). Moreover, traditional Indigenous agriculture will not be able to feed the growing population in Africa (Getui, 1999), suggesting that Indigenous knowledge may not be able to fully solve global environmental problems (Ndungu, 2005; Taringa, 2006, p. 212; Wijsen & Marcos, 2010).

In much of Latin America, controversy about the sustainability of traditional agriculture is undermined by multiple factors: misunderstanding the relationship between productivity and quality; conflict between professional agronomists' perspectives and the territorial practices of peasant farmers; the belief that urban areas are dependent on surpluses from rural areas and imports, and confusion between extensive rural agriculture and intensive urban gardening; and, the loss of historical perspective of colonization (Wijsen & Marcos, 2010). The Mexican agronomists' perspective assumes that arable land must be cultivated using modern methods, guaranteeing a minimum level of productivity. However, this contradicts actual experience (Wijsen & Marcos, 2010):

- Non-tillage agriculture can be equally or more productive than tillage agriculture (Fukuoka, 1975).
- There is a significant difference between northern and tropical soils in which the effects of wind erosion after cultivation are much greater (Derpesch et al., 2006).
- With some crops, such as maize which is the primary crop of Mexico, quality is inversely proportionate to productivity.

- The peasants' map of farmland is much more elaborate than professional agronomists, who frequently convert *milpas* (traditional rain irrigated maize fields) into shallow lands. The peasants' perspective of usefulness is based on a moral economy instead of quantitative measures of productivity (Kaller-Dietrich, 2002; Thompson, 1971), prioritizing subsistence over profitability.
- The urban populations in most of the world obtain some of their food from urban gardening with productivity levels of productivity that often surpass tillage agriculture on northern soils (Jacobs, 1969; Robert, 1994).
- Development projects gradually destroy the bases of *self-sufficiency* in communities, making land a *fictitious commodity* (Polanyi, 1957, pp. 68–76) that is sold to the highest bidder.

The Indigenous Amazigh people of Morocco are experiencing major climate change impacts of drought and disruption of hydrologic cycles, which is further exacerbated by their living outside the circle of favor under authoritarian rule by the Kingdom and the *makhzen* (Jacques, 2023). The makhzen are a group of elites in the military, government, and industry who are close to the King and distribute or deny opportunities, government resources, and services. Jacques (2023) found that water insecurity was the most frequent climate change concern of the Amazigh people. They also experience challenges in adapting to water insecurity, such as difficulty accessing education (especially for girls), health issues, poverty, and inconsistent work availability. Study findings also indicated the concerns of the Amazigh are associated with basic subsistence, an end to socio-political marginalization, and the receipt of governmental support (Jacques, 2023). Each of these essential concerns demonstrate that the role of the Amazigh civil society under authoritarian rule is to provide funding and programs to relieve discomfort and hardships (Jacques, 2023).

Most natural ecosystems have disappeared or are threatened because of human activities (Camino et al., 2023). Globally, 40% of remaining forest cover are in Indigenous Peoples Lands (IPL). These lands can be classified as IPL with land-tenure security (IPL-S) and IPL with land-tenure insecurity (IPL-I). In a study of the role of IPL in forest conservation and loss in the South American Dry Chaco region, Camino et al. found that while 44% of the remaining forests are in IPL, 67% of them are in IPL-I. The study results indicated that IPL-S work as deforestation barriers, with Camino et al. concluding that land-tenure security is essential for IPL to reduce deforestation, demonstrating the importance of guaranteeing land-tenure rights of Indigenous communities for conservation purposes. On a regional level, most remaining forests are Indigenous and conservation efforts should occur collaboratively with locals, respecting their rights, needs, and worldviews (Camino et al., 2023).

Traditional practices such as crop rotation increase the overall health of forests and jungles and are essential strategies for mitigation of climate change (Jerez, 2021). These practices which have been improved over time and through traditional knowledge are still practiced by many Indigenous cultures including the Igorot of the Philippines; the Karen of China, Myanmar, and Thailand; and the Achiks of India. The resilience of Indigenous agricultural practices is further demonstrated by the Agroforestry Research Project established by the International Council for Research in Agroforestry (ICRAF) in Kenya in 1981. Knowledge gaps in areas such as soil management and drought and famine were identified when the project was expanded in 1983. These knowledge gaps were a direct result of the exclusion of Indigenous women from the preliminary stages of the research project (Jerez, 2021). Once the Indigenous women and their traditional, gender-specific environmental knowledge were included, program improvements were noted which enabled distribution of sustainable and effective agroforestry knowledge for the entire district (Jerez, 2021).

8.6 Water and Wetlands

The amount of freshwater available on the planet is estimated to be approximately three percent of the total amount of water with only 0.4% accessible to humans (Zac, 2023). Many developing countries do not have the resources to provide safe and clean drinking water to their citizens. In 2022, 2.2 billion people still lacked safely managed drinking water, with 115 million people drinking surface water (Joint Monitoring Programme for Water Supply, Sanitation and Hygiene, JMP, 2022). Approximately 3.6 million people die annually from diseases acquired from unsafe drinking water (World Atlas, n.d.). Increasing global freshwater scarcity supports the need to manage the vast potential of groundwater, and Indigenous knowledge offers practical methods of sustainable water management.

López-Maldonado (2021) suggested that integrating the traditional knowledge of the Indigenous Maya People may provide a more collective approach to managing this scarce resource. The Maya emerged in Yucatán, Mexico over 4,000 years ago, prospering for several millennia until their civilization's collapse which may have been the result of a drought (Lopez-Maldonado, 2021). Surviving for millennia in a region without surface water required collective and collaborative water management. The hydraulic system developed by the Maya was adaptable to the rapidly changing requirements of a population which increased from about 3 million to 13 million over several hundred years. To manage seasonal rainfall fluctuations, the Maya developed methods for water management and storage by constructing dams on hilltops, using canals built into the slopes to distribute water in a complex irrigation system (Lopez-Maldonado, 2021).

The Mayan landscape contained countless circular reservoirs known as *cenotes*, which was the primary source of freshwater (Lopez-Maldonado, 2021). Cenotes (from the Mayan word for sinkhole: d'zonot) form when a significant rainfall penetrates the soil, flows through the porous rock, and slowly creates a water-filled cavity which expands until the sinkhole width and height may exceed ten meters (Lopez-Maldonado, 2021). "The Maya believed in the concept of a holy world beneath the ground and considered cenotes to be portals for entering this holy world" (Lopez-Maldonado, 2021). Water management in a region without natural surface water required communal institutions. Community members received water extraction rights which were monitored and managed by the Mayan elite and supernatural beings (Lopez-Maldonado, 2021).

Cenotes remain the primary source of freshwater in Yucatán which contains one of the largest aquifers in the world (Lopez-Maldonado,

2021). Yucatán's groundwater infrastructure is shared by three Mexican states: Yucatán, Campeche, and Quintana Roo. Water ownership and management performed by the local governments who do not acknowledge traditional environmental knowledge as integral to monitoring efforts. All socioeconomic sectors rely extensively on groundwater which is currently being overexploited and polluted by agriculture, construction, industry, and tourism. Moreover, increasing temperatures and unpredictable rainfall adversely impact water storage efforts (Lopez-Maldonado, 2021). Local inhabitants do not necessarily recognize that water is a scarce resource, and the younger generation appears indifferent about preserving traditional water collection and storage practices (Lopez-Maldonado, 2021).

Ancestral spiritual beliefs are still important in how Indigenous communities manage natural resources because they provide a connection between people and nature. In the Lower Songkhram River Basin of Thailand, the elderly members of Indigenous communities continue to embrace the spiritual beliefs and rituals which formed based on the traditional function of wetlands to regulate behaviors and actions (Chunhabunyatip et al., 2018). However, the younger members of the Indigenous community consider the wetland a source of employment and economic benefits, which could result in the permanent loss of traditional beliefs and the continued destruction of natural resources. Echoing the previously cited findings of Camino et al. (2023) who concluded that land-tenure security is essential for IPL to reduce deforestation, Chunhabunyatip et al. (2018) found that granting property rights to Indigenous people contributed to natural resource conservation.

Traditional Indigenous natural resource management systems have evolved over time and have been proven more effective and sustainable than contemporary forms of management (Abu & Millar, 2006; Tupper, 2002; Utkarsh et al., 1999). Collective management of natural resources is established by traditions, beliefs, morality, norms, and cultural practices because some plants and animals within the wetlands are protected by Indigenous practices which encouraged natural resource management and conservation (Chunhabunyatip et al., 2018). Adherence to these beliefs and practices has influenced natural resource management by using taboos, respect for sacred areas, and rules and institutions

(Abu & Millar, 2006). This demonstrates the ability of existing community institutions to manage natural resources provided that within the surroundings of the wetlands, the code of conduct of the Indigenous belief system must be fulfilled (Chunhabunyatip et al., 2018).

8.7 Sustainability Policy

Understanding how Indigenous Peoples manage natural resources offers a foundation for developing resource management policies that benefit Indigenous Peoples and perpetuate their cultural beliefs (Chunhabunyatip et al., 2018). The relationship between Indigenous Peoples and sustainability policy is generally approached in one of two ways: placing them inside sustainability, or at the perimeter. The latter approach was the subject of controversy when a draft of the Sustainable Development Goals (SDGs) substituted all references of "Indigenous peoples", with the term "Indigenous and local communities" (Tsosie, 2014). Although the change might have appeared harmless to the non-Indigenous, the omission undermined the achievements of Indigenous Peoples in claiming their rightful identity as "peoples" with a right to "self-determination" (Tsosie, 2014). The term "peoples" within international law describes autonomous political groups possessing the right of self-governance in domestic matters and who must receive respect and dignity from national governments in their collective capacity (Tsosie, 2014). According to U.N. experts, the decision to omit "Indigenous peoples" from the SDGs represented a "step backwards for Indigenous peoples", especially because "Indigenous peoples face distinct development challenges and fare worse in terms of social and economic development than non-Indigenous sectors of the population in nearly all of the countries that they live in" (Tsosie, 2014). Fortunately, the final draft of the 2030 Agenda for Sustainable Development included multiple references to Indigenous Peoples.

The United States maintains trust relationships with more than 560 federally recognized Native American and Alaska Native Nations and acknowledges that these Indigenous Nations are autonomous sovereigns with governance authority over their territories, resources, and members

(Tsosie, 2014). Therefore, federal and state agencies should respect tribal governments when developing sustainability policies. However, despite executive orders and other mandates in the United States requiring such consultations, frequently, tribal consultation protocols have become procedural requirements that ignore the significant value of including tribal governments in policy development (Tsosie, 2014).

The sustainability dialogue must occur within Indigenous and Western thought systems, in a platform of mutual respect engagement. This knowledge sharing between and among diverse peoples will provide new opportunities to unlock our potential as human beings in a dynamic natural world (Tsosie, 2014). Indigenous practices and knowledge, which coexist harmoniously with the natural environment, can teach humankind how to achieve UN SDGs which is critical for the survival of the estimated 370 million Indigenous People globally, because their traditional lifestyles and livelihoods are increasingly at risk (Acciona, n.d.).

International frameworks to protect Indigenous knowledge are urgently needed. However, despite national and regional regulations that protect traditional knowledge and encourage cooperation in treatment of traditional knowledge, communication, and collaboration among Indigenous peoples and policymakers, these laws have limited impact (Jerez, 2021). Jerez (2021) offered the following recommendations for governments, representative bodies, United Nations organizations, industry, and other stakeholders (Jerez, 2021):

- Ensure that the UN Declaration on the Rights of Indigenous Peoples is the primary framework for planning and implementing climate change mitigation, adaptation, and finance programs, and include full participation of Indigenous.
- Develop policies that conform with the UN Declaration on the Rights of Indigenous Peoples to prevent misappropriation of Indigenous traditional knowledge and acknowledge Indigenous Peoples as equal participants, and legitimate custodians of their knowledge.
- Provide technical support to improve the adaptive capacity and mitigation ability of Indigenous Peoples, including inclusive sector-specific

programs based upon gender, values, and economic conditions of the communities.

- Conduct genuine gender analyses to understand which aspects of Indigenous natural resource stewardship are performed by men and women respectively, or the extent that Indigenous environmental knowledge is gender-specific (Jerez, 2021).

Most development programs in the Pacific region have overwhelmingly benefited "outsider" perspectives that emphasize scientific and technocratic solutions, which contradict the spirituality-based perspectives and knowledge of local communities (Luetz & Nunn, 2023). Many development and climate change mitigation strategies have subsequently not been sustainable having been contextualized, sponsored, and funded by outside agendas (Luetz & Nunn, 2020, 2021). Although spirituality is fundamental to cultural beliefs and practices in Pacific Island nations (Fair, 2018; Nunn et al., 2016), many development and mitigation strategies are based on "a scientific and technocratic worldview perspective, in which climate change is seen as a science-informed issue, rather than a faith-informed issue" (Luetz & Nunn, 2020, p. 293). Therefore, these programs and strategies fail because they do not sufficiently resonate with the beneficiaries spiritual and sustainability perspectives (Atkinson-Nolte et al., 2021; Bertana, 2020). This problem is relevant globally and involves a multitude of spiritual beliefs and traditions that may infringe on sustainability and territorial ethics (Dawson et al., 2021; De Silva, 2023; Gupta & Agrawal, 2017; Mamani-Bernabé, 2015; Sponsel, 2020; Yangka et al., 2018).

Because of the complexity of spirituality and sustainability, contemporary adaptation and development policy and practice should engage both concepts concurrently, to utilize their symbiotic abilities to significantly enhance sustainability and climate change mitigation (Fair, 2018; Nunn et al., 2016). Policymakers should enlist traditional beliefs to achieve sustainable resource management, and these practices should be acknowledged and included in resource management policies in locations inhabited by Indigenous Peoples (Chunhabunyatip et al., 2018).

Assimilating spirituality and sustainability will create understandings that are favorable to enduring and sympathetic sustainable development (Luetz & Nunn, 2020, 2021; Yunkaporta, 2019).

8.8 Conclusion

Research demonstrates that the eco-centric and nature-focused lifestyles of many Indigenous Peoples are more sustainable than the anthropocentric and nature-consumptive practices of the contemporary global economic system (Dawson et al., 2021; Ellis et al., 2021; Fernández-Llamazares et al., 2021; Fischer et al., 2022; Salmón, 2000; Yunkaporta, 2019). Many of the most biodiversity-rich areas remain unadulterated because of stewardship of the Indigenous cultures coexisting through "time-tested land-care practices of reverential reciprocity" (Nelson, 2020, p. 10). However, Indigenous wisdom has been historically colonized and delegitimated, evidenced by the global climate crisis and environmental destruction resulting from implicitly colonial assumptions and natural resource consumption patterns of capitalism (Robison, 2020). The term "Capitalocene" has been used to describe the overwhelming environmental and cultural impacts of capitalism that began with the European colonization in the fifteenth through the seventeenth centuries (Moore, 2016), and continues exponentially and unabated today. Capitalism has infiltrated social relationships, self-conceptions, and environmental perspectives, increasingly demonstrating that expectations of exponential growth and human dominance of nature are unsustainable (Robison, 2020).

Indigenous Peoples must participate in the development of natural resource management policies to retain the right to manage and conserve their land through incorporation of traditional knowledge and rights in the policies to preserve their cultural and spiritual traditions (Devereux, 2000; Swamy et al., 2003). Because Indigenous wisdom intimately connects humans and nature, some suggest that "the human mind is not separate from the natural world but an aspect of the larger psyche of nature" (Kapfhammer, 2012, p. 147). Indigenous wisdom would likely suggest that the climate crisis be conceptualized as an intimately personal crisis connected with emotional well-being (Robison, 2020). The climate change dialogue must validate Indigenous knowledge by including the voices of those Peoples for whom environmental sustainability is a measure of individual and community well-being (Robison, 2020).

Research continues to demonstrate and support the effectiveness of Indigenous approaches to sustainable environmental rehabilitation (Jerez, 2021). Traditional knowledge serves an important role in preserving biodiversity and maintaining entire ecosystems. Indigenous knowledge of plants, animals, microorganisms, and ecosystems is indispensable for conservation and use of biodiversity to meet their sustenance and ceremonial needs. However, abuse and exploitation of Indigenous knowledge can cause irreparable harm to custodians of the knowledge and entire communities or Peoples (Jerez, 2021). The U.N. Declaration on the Rights of Indigenous Peoples advises governments to acknowledge that Indigenous Peoples are the owners and custodians of their traditional knowledge, and they should control the circumstances in which that knowledge is shared (Tsosie, 2014).

Traditional knowledge and modern resources can provide a synergistic response to the current climate crisis. The Aboriginal People of Australia have ingeniously utilized controlled fire burns to increase food resources, maintain open vegetation, and create habitats for game species through land regeneration. However, since colonialism, the practice of fire burning has been mostly eliminated. Although climate change is amplifying wild bushfire problems, the combination of Indigenous knowledge and modern technology could offer a strategy to improve fire management and biodiversity effects throughout Australia (Jerez, 2021). Market-based responses to climate change cannot mitigate our shared global climate crisis (Robison, 2020). However, Indigenous voices can provide non-Native thinkers with an alternate understanding of the impacts of industrial systems on the environment through deforestation, pollution, and fossil fuel dependency, and assess the underlying thinking that preserves those systems (Robison, 2020).

Reflection Questions

1. What obligation do Indigenous Peoples have to help solve the climate crisis which they did not help create?
2. How can the greater society adopt Indigenous environmental knowledge to solve our climate and environmental problems without exploiting or destroying the Indigenous knowledge and culture?
3. How can adopting Indigenous wisdom and knowledge achieve sustainability in a capitalist system? Under what circumstances can the two concepts coexist?
4. What fundamental changes are necessary to achieve just and equitable sustainability for all eight billion inhabitants of the planet?

References

Abu, A., & Millar, D. (2006). *Land natural resources and spirituality: Policy implications on rural livelihoods in the Northern Regions of Ghana*. Centre for Cosmovision and Indigenous Knowledge Conference, pp. 24–29.

Acciona. (n.d.). *How do Indigenous peoples contribute to sustainable development?* Sustainability for all. https://www.activesustainability.com/sustainable-development/Indigenous-peoples-sustainable-development/?_adin=02021864894

Agwu, E., & Me, A. (2018). Changing the present and creating the future through Indigenous knowledge and entrepreneurship. *Academy of Entrepreneurship Journal, 24*(1), 1–15. https://ssrn.com/abstract=3153290

Allison, Elizabeth A. (2015). The spiritual significance of glaciers in an age of climate change. *Wiley Interdisciplinary Reviews (WIREs): Climate Change, 6*(5), 493–508. https://doi.org/10.1002/wcc.354

Anderson, R. B., Honig, B., & Peredo, A. M. (2007b). Communities in the global economy: Where social and Indigenous entrepreneurship meet. In C. Steyaert & D. Hjorth (Eds.), *Entrepreneurship as social change: A third new movements in entrepreneurship book* (pp. 56–78). Edward Elgar.

Anderson, R. B., McGillivray, S., & Giberson, R. J. (2007a). The Nk'Mip cellars: Wine and tourism with an aboriginal flavour. In L.-P. Dana & R. B. Anderson (Eds.), *International handbook of research on Indigenous entrepreneurship* (pp. 336–351). Edward Elgar.

Ashok, D. G. (2013). Indigenous knowledge and women entrepreneurs among Rajbanshis: A case study. *International Research Journal of Social Sciences, 2*(2), 12–20.

Atkinson-Nolte, J., Nunn, P. D., & Millear, P. (2021). Influence of spiritual beliefs on autonomous climate-change adaptation: A case study from Ono Island, southern Fiji. In J. M. Luetz & P. D. Nunn (Eds.), *Beyond belief—Opportunities for faith-engaged approaches to climate-change adaptation in the Pacific Islands* (pp. 345–375). Springer Nature.

Bansal, T. (2021). What business leaders can learn from an Indigenous worldview. *Forbes*. https://www.forbes.com/sites/timabansal/2021/06/15/what-business-leaders-can-learn-from-an-indigenous-worldview/?sh=5780d1eb5c2f

Becken, S., Lama, A. K., & Espiner, S. (2013). The cultural context of climate change impacts: Perceptions among community members in the annapurna conservation area. *Nepal. Environmental Development, 8*, 22–37. https://doi.org/10.1016/j.envdev.2013.05.007

Bertana, A. (2020). The impact of faith-based narratives on climate change adaptation in Narikoso. *Fiji Anthropological Forum, 30*(3), 254–273. https://doi.org/10.1080/00664677.2020.1812050

Boersema, J. J. (1991). Eerst de jood, maar ook de Griek. In *Op zoek naar een ecologische cultuur. Milieufilosofie in de jaren negentig* (pp. 27–56). Ambo.

Brandström, P. (1991). *Boundless universe. The culture of expansion among the Sukuma-Nymanwezi people* (Doctoral dissertation). Uppsala University.

Camino, M., Aceves, P. A. V., Alvarez, A., Chianetta, P., de la Cruz, L. M., Alonzo, K., Vallejos, M., Zamora, L., Neme, A., Altrichter, M., & Cortez, S. (2023). Indigenous lands with secure land-tenure can reduce forest-loss in deforestation hotspots. *Global Environmental Change, 81*, 102678. https://doi.org/10.1016/j.gloenvcha.2023.102678

Capel, C. (2014). Mindfulness, Indigenous knowledge, Indigenous innovations and entrepreneurship. *Journal of Research in Marketing and Entrepreneurship, 16*(1), 63–83. https://doi.org/10.1108/JRME-10-2013-0031

Chunhabunyatip, P., Sasaki, N., Grünbühel, C., Kuwornu, J. K., & Tsusaka, T. W. (2018). Influence of Indigenous spiritual beliefs on natural resource management and ecological conservation in Thailand. *Sustainability, 10*(8), 2842. https://doi.org/10.3390/su10082842

Dana, L.-P. (2007a). Towards a multidisciplinary definition of Indigenous entrepreneurship. In L.-P. Dana & R. B. Anderson (Eds.), *International handbook of research on Indigenous entrepreneurship* (pp. 3–7). Edward Elgar.

Dana, L.-P. (2007b). Basuto culture and entrepreneurship in Lesotho. In L.-P. Dana & R. B. Anderson (Eds.), *International handbook of research on Indigenous entrepreneurship* (pp. 100–114). Edward Elgar.

Dana, L.-P., & Anderson, R. B. (2007). *International handbook of research on indigenous entrepreneurship*. Edward Elgar.

Daneel, M. (1998). *African earthkeepers*, vol. 1. *Interfaith mission in earth care.* University of South Africa.

Dawson, N. M., Coolsaet, B., Sterling, E. J., Loveridge, R., Gross-Camp, N. D., Wongbusarakum, S., Sangha, K. K., Scherl, L. M., Phuong Phan, H., Zafra-Calvo, N., Lavey, W. G., Byakagaba, P., Idrobo, C. J., Chenet, A., Bennett, N. J., Mansourian, S., & Rosado-May, F. J. (2021). The role of Indigenous peoples and local communities in effective and equitable conservation. *Ecology & Society, 26*(3), 19–58. https://doi.org/10.5751/ES-12625-260319

Derpesch, R., Florentin, M., Moriya, K. (2006). The law of diminishing yields in the tropics. In Kiel, *Proceedings of the 17th ISTRO conference.* Rodale Press.

De Silva, W. (2023). Comprehending genius loci, towards spiritual sustainability: Lessons from Buddhist heritage city Anuradhapura. *International Journal of Heritage Studies, 29*(1–2), 1–20. https://doi.org/10.1080/13527258.2023.2169333

Devereux, P. (2000). *The sacred place: The ancient origins of holy and mystical sites.* Cassell.

Dijksterhuis, E. J. (1998). *De Mechanisering van ons Wereldbeeld*. Codex.

Eisenstadt, T., & West, K. (2017). Indigenous belief systems, science, and resource extraction: Climate change attitudes in Ecuador. *Global Environmental Politics, 17*(1), 40–58. https://doi.org/10.1162/GLEP_a_00389

Ellis, E. C., Gauthier, N., Klein Goldewijk, K., Bliege Bird, R., Boivin, N., Díaz, S., Fuller, D. Q., Gill, J. L., Kaplan, J. O., Kingston, N., & Locke, H. (2021). People have shaped most of terrestrial nature for at least 12,000 years. *Proceedings of the National Academy of Sciences, 118*(17), e2023483118. https://doi.org/10.1073/pnas.2023483118

Fair, H. (2018). Three stories of Noah: Navigating religious climate change narratives in the Pacific Island region. *Geo: Geography and Environmant, 5*(2). https://doi.org/10.1002/geo2.68

Fernández-Llamazares, Á., Lepofsky, D., Lertzman, K., Armstrong, C. G., Brondizio, E. S., Gavin, M. C., Lyver, P. O., Nicholas, G. P., Pascua, P., Reo, N. J., Reyes-García, V., Turner, N. J., Yletyinen, J., Anderson, E. N., Balée, W., Cariño, J., David-Chavez, D. M., Dunn, C. P., Garnett, S. C., & Vaughan, M. B. (2021). Scientists' warning to humanity on threats to Indigenous and local knowledge systems. *Journal of Ethnobiology, 41*(2), 144–169. https://doi.org/10.2993/0278-0771-41.2.144

Fischer, M., Maxwell, K., Nuunoq, P. H., Greeno, D., Jingwas, N., Blair, J. G., Hugo, S., Mustonen, T., Murtomäki, E., & Mustonen, K. (2022). Empowering her guardians to nurture our ocean's future. *Reviews in Fish Biology & Fisheries, 32*(1), 271–296. https://doi.org/10.1007/s11160-021-09679-3

Fukuoka, M. (1975). The one straw revolution: An introduction to natural farming. *New York Review of Books.*

Ganguli, P. (2000). Intellectual property rights: Mothering innovations to markets. *World Patent Information, 22*(1–2), 43–52. https://doi.org/10.1016/S0172-2190(00)00029-6

Getui, M. (1999). At variance but in harmony. In A. de Jong (Ed.), *Ethnicity: Blessing or curse* (pp. 9–19). Paulines Publications Africa.

Goodman, D. (2015, Spring,). Deep in the Amazon, a tiny tribe is beating big oil. *Yes Magazine*, 28–32.

Gross National Happiness Commission. (2009). *Tenth five-year plan: 2008–2013.* Royal Government of Bhutan.

Gupta, K., & Agrawal, R. (2017). Sustainable development and spirituality: A critical analysis of GNH index. *International Journal of Social Economics, 44*(12), 1919–1939. https://doi.org/10.1108/IJSE-10-2015-0283

Haley, M. (2021). *Introducing the seventh generation principle—To promote true sustainability*. The Seventh Generation Tours. https://theseventhgeneration.org/blog-the-seventh-generation-principle/

Haluza-DeLay, R. (2014). Religion and climate change: Varieties in viewpoints and practices. *Wiley Interdisciplinary Reviews (WIREs): Climate Change, 5*(2), 261–279. https://doi.org/10.1002/wcc.268

Haudenosaunee Confederation. (n.d.). *Values.* https://www.haudenosauneeconfederacy.com/values/

Hilton, C. A. (2020). An introduction to indigenomics. In *Indigenomics: Harnessing the power of our communities.* Cultural Survival. https://www.culturalsurvival.org/publications/cultural-survival-quarterly/indigenomics-harnessing-power-our-communities

Hindle, K., & Lansdowne, M. (2005). Brave spirits on new paths: Towards a globally relevant paradigm of Indigenous entrepreneurship research. *Journal of Small and Business & Entrepreneurship, 18*(2), 131–141. https://doi.org/10.1080/08276331.2005.10593335

Indigenomics Institute. (2023). *About*. https://indigenomicsinstitute.com/about-us/

Jacobs, J. (1969). *The economy of cities*. Random House.

Jacques, P. J. (2023). Civil society and survival: Indigenous Amazigh climate adaptation in Morocco. *Global Environmental Change, 81*, e102682. https://doi.org/10.1016/j.gloenvcha.2023.102682

Jerez, M. M. (2021). *Challenges and opportunities for Indigenous peoples' sustainability* (UN/DESA Policy Brief No. 101). https://www.un.org/development/desa/dspd/2021/04/Indigenous-peoples-sustainability/

Joint Monitoring Programme for Water Supply, Sanitation and Hygiene (JMP). 2022. *Progress on WASH in health care facilities 2000–2021: Special focus on WASH and infection prevention and control (IPC)*. World Health Organization (WHO) & UNICEF. https://washdata.org/reports/jmp-2022-wash-hcf

Kaller-Dietrich, M. (2002). *Mach tuber Mägen. Essen statt Knappheit verwalten. Haushalten in einem südmexikanischen Dorf*. Vienna: Promedia.

Kapfhammer, W. (2012). Amazonian pain. *Indiana, 29*, 145–169.

Kay, J. (1988). Concepts of nature in the Hebrew Bible. *Environmental Ethics, 10*(4), 309–327. https://doi.org/10.5840/enviroethics198810438

Khumukcham, J. (2021). Community-based business model of Indigenous people: Indigenous entrepreneurship, innovation and value proposition. In S. Guha & S. Majumdar (Eds.), *In search of business models in social entrepreneurship* (pp. 209–231). Springer.

Knippenberg, L. (2010). Chasing God: The idea of sustainable development and its implications. In F. Wijsen & S. Marcos (Eds.), *Indigenous voices in the sustainability discourse. Spirituality and the struggle for a better quality of life* (pp. 31–48). LIT Verlag.

Lindsay, N. J. (2005). Toward a cultural model of Indigenous entrepreneurial attitude. *Academy of Marketing Science Review, 5*, 1–17. http://www.amsreview.org/articles/lindsay05-2005.pdf

Lituchy, T. R., Oppenheimer, R., O'Connell, T., & Abraira, R. J. (2007). Mohawk first nations: Successes and challenges of small business owners. In L.-P. Dana & R. B. Anderson (Eds.), *International handbook of research on Indigenous entrepreneurship* (pp. 378–403). Edward Elgar.

Lopez-Maldonado, Y. (2021). Understanding groundwater common-pool resources: Commonisation and decommonisation of cenotes in Yucatan, Mexico. In *Making Commons Dynamic* (pp. 138–163). Routledge.

Luetz, J. M., & Nunn, P. D. (2020). Climate change adaptation in the Pacific Islands: A review of faith-engaged approaches and opportunities. In F. W. Leal (Ed.), *Managing climate change adaptation in the Pacific region* (pp. 293–311). Springer. https://doi.org/10.1007/978-3-030-40552-6_15

Luetz, J. M., & Nunn, P. D. (2021). *Beyond belief: Opportunities for faith-engaged approaches to climate-change adaptation in the Pacific Islands.* Springer. https://doi.org/10.1007/978-3-030-67602-5

Luetz, J. M., & Nunn, P. D. (2023). Spirituality and sustainable development: An entangled and neglected relationship. *Sustainability Science, 18*, 2035–2042. https://doi.org/10.1007/s11625-023-01347-8

Mamani-Bernabé, V. (2015). Spirituality and the pachamama in the Andean aymara worldview. In J. J. Armesto, J. B. Callicott, F. S. Chapin III, R. H. May Jr., S. T. A. Pickett, M. E. Power, & R. Rozzi (Eds.), *Earth stewardship: Linking ecology and ethics in theory and practice* (pp. 65–76). Springer. https://doi.org/10.1007/978-3-319-12133-8_6

Moore, J. (2016). *Anthropocene or Capitalocene? Nature, history, and the crisis of capitalism.* PM Press.

Nathan, D., Kelkar, G., & Walter, P. (2004). *Globalization and Indigenous peoples in Asia: Changing the local-global interface.* Sage.

National Museum of the American Indian. (2009). *Haudenosaunee guide for educators.* https://americanindian.si.edu/sites/1/files/pdf/education/HaudenosauneeGuide.pdf

Ndungu, N. (2005). Environmental management constraints and prospects in Africa in the 21st century. In N. Ndungu & Ph. Mwaura (Eds.), *Challenges and prospects of the church in Africa* (pp. 55–70). Paulines Publications.

Nelson, M. K. (2020). *Decolonizing conquest consciousness.* https://www.humansandnature.org/decolonizing-conquest-consciousness

Nunn, P. D., Mulgrew, K., Scott-Parker, B., Hine, D. W., Marks, A. D. G., Mahar, D., & Maebuta, J. (2016). Spirituality and attitudes towards nature in the Pacific Islands: Insights for enabling climate-change adaptation. *Climate Change, 136*(3–4), 477–493. https://doi.org/10.1007/s10584-016-1646-9

Onwuegbuzie, H. (2017). The role of diaspora in disseminating Indigenous knowledge entrepreneurship. *Journal of International Business Research and Marketing, 2*(4), 20–24. https://doi.org/ https://doi.org/10.18775/jibrm.1849-8558.2015.24.3003

Osinubi, T. S. (2007). Women in development: The case of Bodija marketing Ibadan, South Western Nigeria. In L.-P. Dana & R. B. Anderson (Eds.), *International handbook of research on Indigenous entrepreneurship* (pp. 46–59). Edward Elgar.

Phuntsho, K. (2013). *The history of Bhutan*. Haus Publishing.

Polanyi, K. (1957 [1944]). *The great transformation. The political and economic origins of our time*. Beacon Press.

Robert, J. (1994). *Special sources, bibliography of water is a commons*. Habitat International Coalition.

Robison, C. (2020). *Decolonizing climate discourse and legitimating Indigenous wisdom: Toward an ecosystemic episteme* (Master's theses). Rollins College. https://scholarship.rollins.edu/honors/112

Salmón, E. (2000). Kincentric ecology: Indigenous perceptions of the human–nature relationship. *Ecological Applications, 10*(5), 1327–1332. https://doi.org/10.1890/1051-0761(2000)010[1327:KEIPOT]2.0.CO;2

Seiwald, M. (2012). *REDD and Indigenous peoples: The socio bosque Programme in Ecuador*. AV Akademikerverlag.

Sen, B. (2005). Indigenous knowledge for development: Bringing research and practice together. *The International Information & Library Review, 37*(4), 375–382. https://doi.org/10.1016/j.iilr.2005.10.004

Sponsel, L. E. (2020). *Religious environmental activism in Asia: Case studies in spiritual ecology*. MDPI. https://doi.org/10.3390/books978-3-03928-647-8

Swamy, P. S., Kumar, M., & Sundarapandian, S. M. (2003). *Spirituality and ecology of sacred groves in Tamil Nadu, India* (pp. 53–55). UNASYLVA-FAO. http://www.fao.org/tempref/docrep/fao/005/y9882e/y9882e10.pdf

Tarimo, A. (2004). *Human rights, cultural differences and the church in Africa*. Salvatorian Institute of Philosophy and Theology.

Taringa, N. (2006). How environmental is African traditional religion? *Exchange, 35*(2), 191–214. https://doi.org/10.1163/157254306776525672

Thompson, E. (1971). The moral economy of the english crowd in the eighteenth century. *Past and Present, 50*, 76–136. https://www.jstor.org/stable/650244

Tideman, S. G. (2004). Gross national happiness: Towards a new paradigm in economics. In K. Ura & K. Galay (Eds.), *First international conference on operationalization of gross national happiness* (pp. 222–246). The Centre of Bhutan Studies. https://doi.org/ https://doi.org/10.11588/xarep.00000378

Tsosie, R. (2014). *Indigenous peoples and sustainability policy: Exploring the politics and practice of "Indigenous sustainability"*. Sustainability News.

Arizona State University. https://sustainability-innovation.asu.edu/news/archive/Indigenous-peoples-sustainability-policy-exploring-politics-practice-Indigenous-sustainability/

Tupper, M. H. (2002). Marine reserves and fisheries management. *Science, 295*(5558), 1233–1235. https://doi.org/10.1126/science.295.5558.1233b

Turnbull, D. (2009). Futures for Indigenous knowledge. *Futures, 41*(1), 1–5. https://doi.org/10.1016/j.futures.2008.07.002

Ura, K., Alkire, S., Zangmo, T., & Wangdi, K. (2012). *A short guide to gross national happiness index*. The Centre for Bhutan Studies.

Ura, K., & Galay, K. (2004). Gross national happiness and development. In *Proceedings of the first international seminar on operationalization of gross national happiness*. The Centre for Bhutan Studies.

Utkarsh, G., Gadgil, M., & Rao, P. S. (1999). Intellectual property rights on biological resources: Benefiting from biodiversity and people's knowledge. *Current Science, 77*(11), 1418–1425. https://www.jstor.org/stable/24105227

van Norren, D., & Beehner, C. (2021). Sustainability leadership, UNESCO competencies for SDGs, and diverse leadership models. *International Journal of Development & Sustainability, 10*(1), 24–49. https://isdsnet.com/ijds-v10n1-03.pdf

Wangiri, E. (1999). *Urumwe* spirituality and the environment. In M. Getui & E. Obeng (Eds.), *Theology of reconstruction. Exploratory essays* (pp. 71–89). Acton Publishers.

White, L. J. (1967). The historical roots of our ecologic crisis. *Science, 155*(3767), 1203–1207.

Wijsen, F., & Marcos, S. (2010). Indigeneity and sustainability: An introduction. In F. Wijsen & S. Marcos (Eds.), *Indigenous voices in the sustainability discourse. Spirituality and the struggle for a better quality of life* (pp. 9–30). LIT Verlag.

Winsa, B. (2007). Social capital of Indigenous and autochthonous ethnicities. In L.-P. Dana & R. B. Anderson (Eds.), *International handbook of research on Indigenous entrepreneurship* (pp. 257–286). Edward Elgar.

World Atlas. (n.d.). *What percentage of the Earth's water is drinkable?* https://www.worldatlas.com/articles/what-percentage-of-the-earth-s-water-is-drinkable.html

Yangka, D., Newman, P., Rauland, V., & Devereux, P. (2018). Sustainability in an emerging nation: The Bhutan case study. *Sustainability, 10*(5), 1622. https://doi.org/10.3390/su10051622

Yunkaporta, T. (2019). *Sand talk: How Indigenous thinking can save the world*. Text Publishing.

Zac, J. (2023). *What is the percentage of drinkable water on Earth?* World Water Reserve. https://worldwaterreserve.com/percentage-of-drinkable-water-on-earth/

9

Sustainability in the Post-pandemic Era

9.1 Introduction

The increase in work from home (WFH) employment during and following the COVID-19 pandemic demonstrated that many business and organizational activities can be performed remotely, in a more sustainable manner. The brief pause in atmospheric CO2 rise gave hope that meaningful climate change mitigation was possible. This chapter will explore sustainability research, initiatives, and topics in the aftermath of the COVID-19 pandemic to provide perspective on achieving sustainability during, or despite unexpected global crises. The COVID-19 pandemic and the actions taken to mitigate the virus have created disruptions to nearly every aspect of individual and societal life (Lehmann et al., 2021). The side effects of these disruptions include favorable environmental impacts such as short-term reduced greenhouse gas (GHG) emissions and improved air quality during lockdowns (He et al., 2020; Ju et al., 2021; Zhang et al., 2021), and unfavorable impacts such as increased waste production (Aldaco et al., 2020; You et al., 2020).

The current environmental crises introduce significant normative questions related to the challenges to economic prosperity, justice and rights concerns, and conflicts concerning economic development (Stern,

C. G. Beehner, *Spirituality, Sustainability, and Success*, Palgrave Studies in Workplace Spirituality and Fulfillment, https://doi.org/10.1007/978-3-031-47643-3_9

2016). Although sustainable development was originally regarded as a social directive, the social aspect of sustainable development has been historically overlooked with sustainability primary focused on the economic and development aspects (Morrissey & Heidkamp, 2022; Vallance et al., 2011).

An equitable transition to sustainability requires a transition to a low-to-no-carbon economy, while equitably distributing the costs, risks, and benefits of the societal shift (Sareen & Haarstad, 2018). Although the social dimension is essential to achieving sustainability, knowledge of how to achieve a just transition to a low-to-no carbon society is currently limited (Morrissey & Heidkamp, 2022). The COVID-19 pandemic demonstrated that society could make significant progress toward sustainability while maintaining adequate social and economic standards. What is yet to be determined is whether society will collectively take the necessary actions to achieve and maintain a sustainable future.

9.2 The COVID-19 Crisis and the Climate Change Crisis

The COVID-19 pandemic demonstrated how society is unable to quickly respond to global health threats with most governments delaying action and missing an important opportunity to minimize transmission (Guerriero et al., 2020). Likewise, most governments are slow to respond with climate change mitigation action despite climate change being described by the World Health Organization (WHO, 2021) as the greatest global health threat in the twenty-first century. In addition to contributing to climate change, GHG emissions produce air pollution which increases the risk of heart disease, chronic respiratory disease, stroke, and medical conditions which increase the risk of death from COVID-19 (Guerriero et al., 2020; Williamson et al., 2020). In 2018, more than 8 million people died from air pollution, representing more than 20% of all deaths globally (Vohra et al., 2021). Climate change mitigation would improve health standards and reduce healthcare costs globally.

During the pandemic, air quality improved significantly, GHG emissions, water pollution, and air pollution declined, and the reduction in tourism benefited numerous ecological systems. However, there were also negative environmental impacts, such as increased medical and biohazardous waste, proliferation of disposable protective devices, and increases in untreated waste (Rume & Islam, 2020). Although plastic use declined in 2020 by 2.2%, driven by reduced demand in most industries, plastic use increased in the healthcare industry, while plastic recycling was disrupted in many communities (OECD, 2022).

The COVID-19 pandemic offered a representative comparison for climate change and sustainability challenges because the COVID-19 pandemic and climate change pose similar problem characteristics and response dynamics (Lehmann et al., 2021). Moreover, the large-scale societal strategies implemented in response to the COVID-19 pandemic may serve as a prototype for responding to environmental crises (Lehmann et al., 2021). The pandemic may have reinforced the case for transition toward environmental sustainability because of the co-benefits that may help manage and prevent pandemics (Lehmann et al., 2021). Environmental regulations and green stimulus packages must be strengthened and enforced to better manage future pandemics (Cawthorn et al., 2021; Ventura et al., 2020). The socio-techno-ecological resilience that is needed to mitigate and manage environmental crises may also help respond to future pandemics (Srivastava et al., 2021).

Applying the lessons learned from the pandemic response requires a thorough understanding of the dynamics of individual, organizational, and societal decisions are made, and how societies have responded to external threats such as pandemics and disasters (Lehmann et al., 2021). Although similarities exist between the pandemic and environmental crises, policy makers may not be able to apply the lessons learned from the pandemic response to better address environmental crises. COVID-19 policy strategies did not provide an example of an aggressive, united global effort. Moreover, structural differences such as time scale make responses to environmental crises more challenging than pandemic responses. COVID-19 policy strategies best demonstrate how ***not*** to respond to environmental crises (Lehmann et al., 2021).

Achieving environmental sustainability by reducing environmental destruction and developing socio-techno-ecological resilience may create co-benefits, depending upon what type of governance model is needed (Lehmann et al., 2021). Three conditions exist for determining the type of governance model needed to achieve these co-benefits (Lehmann et al., 2021):

- The interaction of political systems and individual behavior for confronting pandemics must be better understood including the distinctiveness of pandemics versus economic and environmental crises.
- The possible connection between sustainability transitions and managing pandemic risks must be examined more completely, and the possible co-benefits from sustainability strategies must be accurately determined.
- Improved and more interdisciplinary modeling methods are needed to answer these questions.

The COVID-19 pandemic provided solid proof of the increasingly harmful relationship between humankind and the ecosystem. The emergence and spread of the COVID-19 virus were a direct result of multiple factors including wildlife habitat destruction, urbanization, live animal trade, and excessive livestock farming (Barouki et al., 2021). Global overconsumption is placing unprecedented stress on the planet's natural life-support systems (Morrissey & Heidkamp, 2022). The twenty-first century has been shaped by outbreaks, epidemics, and a global pandemic, all of which likely resulted from the destructive behavior of humans toward nature (Chirico, 2021). Contemporary infectious diseases include anthroponoses which can be transmitted between humans, zoonoses which can be transmitted from living animals to humans, and sapronoses which can be transmitted from abiotic environments to humans (Russo-Netzer, 2017). These diseases are damaging natural ecosystems at unparalleled rates because of increased human mobility, climate change, and the alteration of habitat conditions (Hubálek, 2003).

The World Wildlife Federation (WWF, 2018) reported a 60% decline in overall species populations from 1970 to 2010. According to the

United Nations Development Programme, "17% of children born in 2000 in so-called low human development countries will have died before age 20, compared with a figure of 1% in very high human development countries" (UNDP, 2019, p. 1). Although economic growth is vital for poverty mitigation, the current economic growth model is based on consumption of significant amounts of natural resources and fossil fuels (Morrissey & Heidkamp, 2022). The current development model poses a societal dilemma: how can society simultaneously achieve climate change mitigation, sufficient economic development, and poverty alleviation (Morrissey & Heidkamp, 2022). This dilemma becomes polarized by unequitable resource use, development consequences, and overconsumption in wealthier nations, versus energy poverty, inadequate infrastructure, and poor health and economic standards in poorer nations (Morrissey & Heidkamp, 2022).

9.3 Post-Pandemic Sustainability

There is a high likelihood that society will return to the pre-pandemic behaviors that contributed to our current unsustainable trajectory. The recession that occurred during the pandemic was minimized in many nations through government fiscal stimulus. Many industries suffered during the pandemic (e.g., travel and hospitality, while others were overwhelmed by demand (e.g., healthcare, home entertainment products, food, and grocery suppliers). The post-pandemic economic environment has been characterized by higher-than-normal inflation, increased demand for travel and leisure products and services, and increased economic activity.

The environmental impact of the economic rebound is evident. Although carbon dioxide (CO2) and other GHG emissions declined 4.6% in 2020, because of restricted global mobility and reduced economic activity, GHG emissions increased 6.4% in 2021, surpassing the pre-pandemic level and reaching a new record (Bhanumati et al., 2022). According to a recent study by the Alliance of Bioversity International and the International Center for Tropical Agriculture (CIAT; Alliance of Bioversity International & International Center for Tropical Agriculture, 2022), global deforestation continued at the existing rate during the pandemic.

On August 16, 2022, U.S. President Biden signed the Inflation Reduction Act (IRA) of 2022 constituting the largest U.S. government investment in clean energy and climate change action. The IRA will help the United States meet its climate targets, improve energy security, create good-paying jobs, and reduce energy and healthcare costs. One of the goals of the law was increasing investment in domestic energy production while promoting clean energy and included US$783 billion in energy and climate change mitigation funding. As of July 2023, the IRA's clean energy and climate change provisions have created more than 170,000 clean energy jobs (Climate Power, 2023), and private sector businesses have announced more than US$110 billion in clean energy manufacturing investments. These investments include more than US$70 billion in the electric vehicle (EV) industry, and more than US$10 billion in the solar industry. The IRA is projected to produce more than 1.5 million additional jobs by 2033 (The White House, 2023).

The combined public and private sector investments resulting from the IRA and the Bipartisan Infrastructure Law should reduce GHG emissions by approximately 1 billion tons in 2030 (The White House, 2023), which constitutes up to a 41% reduction from 2005 levels (Department of Energy, 2023). The law provides billions of dollars in funding to protect communities from climate change impacts (The White House, 2023). American families should save $27–38 billion on their electric utility bills by 2030 (U.S. Department of Energy, 2023). Nonenvironmental benefits stemming from healthcare provisions in the IRA include nearly 15 million people saving an average of $800 per year on their health insurance premiums, and millions of senior citizens enrolled in the Medicare program paying lower prices for prescription drugs, including insulin, which is now capped at $35 per month (The White House, 2023).

The global economy quickly rebounded from the pandemic maintaining considerable momentum despite frictional undertones in supply chains, workforce availability, and inflation (Schwab & Sternfels, 2022). The pandemic response occurred within the context of a menacing climate crisis and increasing economic inequality. These collective challenges demonstrate that crises can create policy and strategy opportunities. The foundations of future growth are often built when societies react to the vulnerabilities revealed by crises. History demonstrates that during times of disruption, resilience depends on versatility and determination. Resilience will be necessary to ensure the long-term prosperity of humankind (Schwab & Sternfels, 2022).

9.4 The Sharing Economy

Although the sharing economy (SE) is a business-related concept, its discussion seemed more appropriate in this chapter because of the dramatic increase in SE activity during and after the pandemic. The SE offers a radical transition in resource consumption and ownership that would deliver a more circular and sustainable future (Rathnayake et al., 2023). The SE concept has gained momentum by enabling shared consumption of assets, services, and skills to balance supply and demand and maximize the utilization of natural resources (Allen & Berg, 2014; Huang et al., 2023). Although the concept of sharing has existed for millennia, these practices were rarely scaled and occurred mostly in personal networks (Belk, 2014). However, the SE has expanded significantly because of technological advancements that allow strangers to connect and share resources outside of their usual networks (Huynh & Gurtner, 2023).

The characteristics of the SE include increased utilization rates (Schor, 2016), economic interaction between multiple agents (Lehto et al., 2018), the ability to reimburse (Teubner, 2014), no transfer of ownership (Fraiberger & Sundararajan, 2017), ICT-based transactions (Hamari et al., 2016), temporary access to resources (Belk, 2014; Fraiberger & Sundararajan, 2017), and a platform that connects resource providers and consumers to facilitate appropriate processes (Business Model Toolbox, 2022). Curtis and Mont (2020) proposed a SE business modeling tool that identified SE characteristics across three dimensions: value facilitation, value delivery, and value capture. Although social interactions are key elements for SE business transactions, the types of interactions remain unclear (Altrock & Suh, 2017).

There are multiple factors that influence SE implementation, and numerous types of sharable resources. Rathnayake et al. (2023) identified eight groups of factors that significantly influence successful SE implementation: regulatory and organizational, technological and research, social, cultural, and behavioral, demographical, health, safety and security, environmental, product and service, as well as financial and economic factors. Rathnayake et al. (2023) further discovered 14 types of potential sharable resources: people; animals; robots; goods; space and storage; mobility and logistics; capital; food and ingredients; drugs; materials, equipment, tools, machines, and devices; data and information; energy; Wi-Fi; and, fashion elements. To better facilitate the SE, Rathnayake et al. (2023) introduced a 7-step SE process consisting of: identification of idle resources to be shared; registration of idle resources on a digital platform; exploration and identification of suitable resources; negotiation and decision-making on terms and conditions; transaction; use and return; and, review and feedback.

Rapid development of information and communication technology (ICT) facilitated simplified and scalable sharing practices and the transformation of SE into a modern economic model that enables maximum utilization of idle resources (Panniello et al., 2022). The SE was selected as a model for the new economy and one of the ten concepts that changed the world by Time Magazine in 2011 (Su et al., 2022). The SE was estimated to be valued at $150US billion (Statistica, 2024), and increase to $335US billion by 2025 (Bloomberg, 2020), and $794US billion by 2031 (Statistica, 2024).

9.5 Discussion

The unsustainable and inequitable effects of present carbon-intensive lifestyles and behavior are apparent (Morrissey & Heidkamp, 2022). The contributing factors to climate change have a direct relationship with economic inequality, resulting in the GHG emissions of the 'haves' creating a crisis which will harm the 'have-nots' the most (Gore, 2015).

For example, the sub-Saharan African nations contribute the least CO_2 per capita, yet they are the most vulnerable to the effects of climate change (Eckstein et al., 2019). Although G20 nations contribute 78% of all emissions (UNEP, 2019), the G20 members are collectively behind schedule in meeting 2030 emissions reduction commitments (UNEP, 2021). By 2030, poverty may claim an additional 100 million individuals absent immediate action (Eckstein et al., 2019). Countries experiencing the highest levels of temperature volatility are least able to afford to economically manage the impacts (Bassetti, 2019).

Although the COVID-19 pandemic created significant global suffering, it presented one beneficial side-effect—significant declines in air pollution and GHG emissions. However, any environmental benefits were temporary and quickly disappeared. Previous global financial crises have demonstrated that any reductions in GHG emissions are temporary and eventually rebound, supported by fiscal stimulus packages and low oil prices (Tienhaara, 2010). For example, after the Great Recession of 2007–2009, subsequent increases in CO_2 emissions exceeded the overall decline observed, and approximately 40% of the rebound effect was from a handful of emerging economies, including China and India (Tienhaara, 2010).

The long-term consequences of the pandemic on the attitudes about sustainability among government leaders and their constituents are uncertain (Dalsace, 2021). The long-term impact of the pandemic on sustainability efforts will depend on the common narrative that is currently being developed. This narrative may be country-specific and influenced by two important criteria: the extent to which humankind collectively believes the pandemic was either an isolated or recurring event; and, our collective post-pandemic attitude toward institutions and governments (Dalsace, 2021). The combination of these two variables leads to four very different potential scenarios: little or no change, bigger government, a shift in mindset, and authoritarian changes (Dalsace, 2021).

There will be little or no change if the pandemic is considered an isolated crisis that was properly managed by institutions. The focus will return to economic growth and sound government fiscal policies at the expense of sustainability initiatives (Dalsace, 2021). Institutions with distressed constituencies will be more motivated to implement reforms even if the pandemic is considered an isolated event. This scenario would empower governing bodies to increase their sphere of influence, become more powerful, and expand their intervention in the governance of individuals and industries (Dalsace, 2021).

If citizens decide that the pandemic was not an isolated incident but the first of many crises and view the performance of governments during the pandemic favorably, the collective mindset may change significantly (Dalsace, 2021). This is the optimal scenario for sustainability because citizens and NGOs will become change agents, collectively questioning the existing development model and demanding change. With sufficient pressure, businesses and governments will have no choice but to listen and respond (Dalsace, 2021).

If citizens believe the pandemic signifies the beginning of a series of crises for which established institutions are ill-prepared, the opportunity for change might be the greatest (Dalsace, 2021). In this scenario, extensive changes would be required, with citizens possibly willing to exchange some individual freedoms for improvements in health and safety. However, these trade-offs could present serious privacy concerns because some governments might consider this an opportunity for authoritarian action (Dalsace, 2021). While this scenario might offer the most significant opportunity to achieve sustainability, any success would be dependent on the commitment of governments and constituents.

Religion has been demonstrated to positively influence individual attitudes and behavior about climate change (Meentemeyer et al., 2012), and is beneficial for institutions to create in meaning regarding climate change (Morrison et al., 2015). Although climate change is primarily a cultural issue (Jenkins et al., 2018), research about the impact of spirituality on climate change is limited. This supports the paradox that declining spirituality has likely contributed to acceleration of climate change. Regardless, climate change is harming the natural resources and biodiversity which will in turn harm our collective way of life and spiritual needs (Chirico, 2021). The relationship between spirituality and sustainability was discussed in Chapter 1, and spirituality in the post-pandemic era was explored in Chapter 5.

The sharing economy offers promise for a post-pandemic direction of sustainability. According to Alharthi et al. (2021), the COVID-19 pandemic served as both an enabler and a barrier for the SE. During economic recessions, most consumers reduce expenses by meeting needs at prices below the market level, and suppliers sell excess inventory or pause production to reduce costs and maintain profits (Su et al., 2022). Mondal and Samaddar (2020) noted uncertain economic conditions influence consumers to increase focus on savings and monetary value, which have further benefited the advancement of the SE. However, Veith et al. (2022) suggested that high economic growth is also an advantage for advancement of the SE. Although Mondal and Samaddar (2020) found that consumers may question the quality of the products and services they receive, Chang et al. (2022) identified quality as the success factor for the SE within the food and beverage (F&B) industry. The environmental benefit of the SE is waste reduction (Chuah et al., 2021), but the environmental consequences include the haphazard placement of shared bicycles and improper handling of abandoned bicycles (Cui et al., 2022).

9.6 Recommendations

It is possible to guide the significant amount of public funding that will be necessary for the post-pandemic recovery to realize large-scale employment, health, environmental, and socioeconomic benefits (Guerriero et al., 2020). This approach was taken by U.S. Congress and the Biden administration with passage of the Inflation Reduction Act which was discussed in an earlier section of this chapter. However, it may take several years to measure and understand the effects of the post-pandemic economic stimulus. Although the policy actions of the 2008–2009 and 2011–2012 financial crises were primarily focused on economic objectives such as employment and growth (Tienhaara, 2010), post-pandemic policies should prioritize health and sustainability to achieve an equitable socioeconomic recovery (Guerriero et al., 2020). The post-pandemic economic response should seek integrated actions to improve health and reduce GHG emissions by removing subsidies that are detrimental to health and the environment and assisting renewable energy in remaining competitive regardless of the price of oil (Guerriero et al., 2020).

Guerriero et al. (2020) recommended that post-pandemic economic stimulus be redirected away from fossil fuel subsidies and other harmful products and services to more productive and beneficial goods and sustainable energy. Fossil fuel subsidies are currently high in many countries and exceed renewable energy subsidies (Belesova et al., 2020). Establishing energy prices at fully efficient levels absent subsidies would have reduced global CO_2 emissions by approximately 28% and deaths from air pollution by 46% (Coady et al., 2019). Investments in renewable energy projects were significantly reduced during the Great Recession, even though investment returns from renewable energy projects are comparable to those of fossil fuel investments (Alers, 2020). Eliminating environmental exemptions and transferring subsidies from unsustainable and inefficient industries to accelerate decarbonization is an urgent priority and would be beneficial for global health, the environment, and the economy (Guerriero et al., 2020).

Genuine sustainable and inclusive growth initiatives must transcend improving business and economic performance. They must promote reparation and improvement of the natural environment, enrich underdeveloped and developing countries, and legitimately improve the lives and livelihoods of historically marginalized groups (Schwab & Sternfels, 2022). This realization can be fully adopted in the mission statements and actions of both private and public institutions. Businesses can contribute to positive social impact by adopting environmental, social, and governance (ESG) principles and metrics (Schwab & Sternfels, 2022).

Morrissey and Heidkamp (2022) proposed five 'pillars' from which to rebuild the global economy, based on principles of a shared sustainable prosperity: an ecological prosperity; a decarbonized economy; a shared cost burden; a governance new deal; and, a just resilience. The premise of the five-pillar model is that sustainability must extend beyond being an environmental concern by including social and economic dimensions which are essential for a stable and prosperous society. The five-pillar model is briefly justified in the following paragraphs.

The 'Doughnut for the Anthropocene' model introduced by Raworth (2017) provides a resourceful and useful response to both planetary boundaries and the SDGs (Morrissey & Heidkamp, 2022). The doughnut concept offers a concise integration of two groups of boundaries: an environmental 'ceiling' guided by the planetary boundaries' efforts of Rockström et al. (2009) and Steffen et al. (2015), and a social 'floor' or foundation, guided by the SDGs. The purported doughnut represents a form of compass which may be applied by policy makers to outline the conversation about just transitions and navigate society to "an ecologically safe and socially just space" (Raworth, 2017, p. e48).

Contemporary economic thinking demonstrates limited application of ecological economics concepts such as the *polluter pays* and the *precautionary principle* to the carbon pollution problem (Morrissey & Heidkamp, 2022). According to Titon (2016), the "polluter pays principle contends that firms and in turn countries should be charged for the full costs to society of their current pollution" (p 117). Mainstream economics has mostly ignored global environmental externalities, and the spatial and temporal shifting of fossil fuel extraction and consumption costs to global and intergenerational communities (Morrissey & Heidkamp, 2022). There is increasing acceptance that the extraction of finite natural resources cannot maintain infinite economic growth, while simultaneously increasing societal risk, biodiversity loss, climate change (Özdemir, 2019).

Over time, more radical options such as steady-state economies, or degrowth economics must be considered (Morrissey & Heidkamp, 2022). However, because these alternatives will not occur in the near future without unprecedented socio-political unrest, the immediate priority is decarbonization of the global economy. The Project Drawdown report, published in 2017, identified the 100 most significant solutions to the climate crisis problem, all using existing technology. Examples include improved refrigerant management (potential reduction of 57.75 gigatons of CO_2-e over 30 years) and better healthcare and education for women and girls (potential reduction of 85.42 gigatons of CO_2-e over 30 years) (Hawken, 2017).

Efforts to reduce wealth inequality are urgently needed, including reforms to guarantee that taxes, prices, and subsidies consider the real ecological and social costs of present consumption behavior (Ripple et al., 2017). Meeting necessary emission reductions will require extensive infusions of public sector funding. Green New Deal (GND) proposals would enact an ecological restructuring of the economy through continuous investment (Bauhardt, 2014), including radical commitment to major economic restructuring and public (Galvin & Healy, 2020). Major investments will be needed to build the extensive and systemwide infrastructure necessary for a zero-carbon economy (Morrissey & Heidkamp, 2022). These investments will be less expensive than the longer-term consequences of inaction.

Governance for sustainable development is significantly lacking, evidenced by inconsistent policy implementation and inadequate stakeholder collaboration and engagement (Leal Filho et al., 2016). Cooperation is essential for addressing issues of sustainable development, specifically related to achieving the SDGs (Glass & Newig, 2019). Because governance decisions reached through participatory processes are more likely to succeed, a diversity of societal actors must actively participate in governance of the complex, long-term challenges of the climate crisis (Gerhardinger et al., 2020). Academia must also thoroughly reconsider how scientific data and knowledge are communicated to the public (Morrissey & Heidkamp, 2022).

Previous and present sustainable development policies assume that the political-economic structure is sound and target socio-technical change instead of major systemic transformation (Morrissey & Heidkamp, 2022). However, Gleeson (2018) warned that "the tsunami of human and global change will overtake well-intentioned action" (p.39). It is imperative that public funding for mitigation, adaptation, loss, and damage be increased dramatically (Eckstein et al., 2019). Moreover, responses to climate change disruptions will likely be space and location specific with much of the financial burden of the present unsustainable growth unfairly paid by developing countries (Morrissey & Heidkamp, 2022). Investment in climate change reduction, mitigation, and adaptation will be less costly than managing social unrest and immeasurable climate refugee migration.

The impact of 2 °C warming to combined global economic growth by 2100 may reach USD 69 trillion by 2100 compared to the 1961–1990 period (Hoegh-Guldberg et al., 2018). In addition, if commitments in the Paris agreement continue unmet, global GDP could be reduced by an additional 10% by 2050, with economies in south and southeast Asia more significantly impacted (Swiss Re Institute, 2021). However, many developed economies are less vulnerable, benefiting from lower exposure levels and higher response capacities (Swiss Re Institute, 2021). The principle of fair burden sharing suggests that countries with higher climate stability should pay a larger portion of the costs of climate change mitigation and adaptation (Puaschunder, 2020).

Short-term thinking and planning must be replaced with long-term strategies to achieve global sustainability. Rume and Islam (2020) identified eight strategies to achieve lasting benefits and sustainable environmental management: sustainable industrialization; use of green and public transport; use of renewable energy; wastewater treatment and reuse; waste recycling and reuse; ecological restoration and ecotourism; behavioral change in daily life; and, international cooperation.

Sustainable industrialization requires shifting to less energy dependent industries, using cleaner fuels and technologies, and strengthening energy efficiency policies (Pan, 2016). Industries should be located within specific zones to take advantage of waste from one industry becoming the raw materials of another (Hysa et al., 2020). Industries employing large numbers of workers should implement appropriate distance and hygienic procedures to mitigate the spread of infectious communicable diseases (Rume & Islam, 2020). Public transportation availability and use must be increased, and personal vehicle use decreased to significantly reduce GHG emissions. Walking and bicycling offer healthy alternatives for short trips (Rume & Islam, 2020). Transitioning to renewable energy can reduce demand for fossil fuels which is essential for reducing GHG emissions (CCAC & UNEP, 2019; Ellabban et al., 2014).

To decrease the financial burden of waste management and environmental pollution, industrial and household wastes should be recycled and reused, and the circular economy should be promoted to limit raw material consumption and waste generation (Hysa et al., 2020). Public awareness of proper waste segregation, handling, and disposal methods must be increased dramatically, especially regarding hazardous and medical waste (Rume & Islam, 2020). Tourist destinations could periodically close to improve ecological restoration, and ecotourism encouraged to encourage sustainable occupations, cultural preservation, and biodiversity protection (Islam & Bhuiyan, 2018).

Large-scale behavioral change is needed to meaningfully reduce GHG emissions. These changes include reduced processed food consumption, increased composting, and local food consumption, turning off electronic devices when not in use, and increased use of bicycles and walking for short trips (Rume & Islam, 2020). Coordinated global effort is essential to achieve sustainable development goals, protection of global natural resources, climate change mitigation, and reverse biodiversity loss (ICIMOD, 2020). Therefore, a responsible international authority such as United Nations Environment Programme (UNEP) should take the initiative to develop timely policies, convene global conventions, and guide global leaders in appropriate implementation (Rume & Islam, 2020).

Achieving just and sustainable growth will depend on effectively and holistically addressing the conditions and interdependency of our economies and societies. Schwab and Sternfels (2022) offer three suggestions for moving forward:

1. The public and private sectors must have a broad view of the resilience agenda.
2. Strategies and structures must be designed for agility and speed.
3. The public and private sectors must supplement business and economic resilience with social resilience.

Economic and social issues such as labor shortages, transitioning to a digital economy, supply-chain disruptions, inflation, and inequality are currently managed in isolation with discipline-specific responses. This method does not sufficiently address the interdependencies among these issues, and the major, longer-term trends influenced by climate change, social developments, and geopolitical events (Schwab & Sternfels, 2022). We must prepare for disruption and uncertainty and approach these issues with internal adaptability and flexibility. The pandemic demonstrated the need for timely information, timely strategic agendas, and faster decision cycles (Schwab & Sternfels, 2022). Leaders must focus on anticipating and predicting disruptions and trends instead of preparing detailed budgets and plans (Schwab & Sternfels, 2022).

Humankind can develop a shared resilience agenda, but the dialogue between the public and private sectors must accelerate (Schwab & Sternfels, 2022). The important decisions and financial commitments that are made now will determine our long-term trajectory after the pandemic. We must share a consolidated view of resilience themes to better understand the opportunities for sustainable and inclusive growth for everyone. We must develop resilience now to ensure a prosperous future for every living being on our planet (Schwab & Sternfels, 2022).

9.7 Conclusion

The COVID-19 pandemic has and will continue to have a lasting impact on society and the planet. The pandemic demonstrated that many business and organizational activities can be performed remotely, in a more sustainable manner, and the brief pause in carbon emissions proved that climate change mitigation was possible. However, the pause in CO2 emissions quickly ended and the lessons learned from the pandemic may be short-lived. Maintaining the social change necessary to support a transition to environmental sustainability requires a precise, straightforward political structure that includes private investments and behavioral change (Lehmann et al., 2021). Progress toward environmental sustainability by reducing environmental degradation and achieving socio-techno-ecological resilience may create strategies beneficial for preventing and managing future pandemics (Lehmann et al., 2021). Swilling (2020) recommended transformational change comparable to the Neolithic agricultural revolution or the Industrial Revolution (Morrissey & Heidkamp, 2022).

To create a more promising future, our focus must change from short-term and reactive measures and goals to a more just and sustainable growth agenda (Schwab & Sternfels, 2022). Such an agenda would focus on growth that strengthens the health and rehabilitation of the natural environment while enhancing the livelihood of the overall population. We must find avenues to a genuinely improved society so that our actions create a more resilient and secure planet and economy (Schwab & Sternfels, 2022).

It is uncertain whether humankind will learn from and apply the lessons learned (and not learned) from the pandemic to make useful progress forward. It is likewise uncertain how much time we have until additional and reversible damage occurs to the environment and society. However, humankind has demonstrated resilience and survived numerous local, regional, and global crises, and possesses the tools and skills to accomplish the necessary changes. Environmental progress occurred during the pandemic and can continue into the post-pandemic era. It is our choice as to whether and how much we react and respond. Morrissey and Heidkamp (2022) suggested the post-pandemic response offers a once-in-a lifetime opportunity to dramatically shift current trajectories to more sustainable pathways, rebalance the realm of sustainability, and respond to related longer-term crises. According to Professor Klaus Schwab Founder and Executive Chairman of the World Economic Forum, "The pandemic represents a rare but narrow window of opportunity to reflect, reimagine, and reset our world".

Case Study

The New Zealand Government introduced the Living Standards Framework (LSF) in 2021 to document more of what is important for New Zealanders' present and future well-being. The LSF is an adaptable framework that informs how the government thinks about policy impacts across various aspects of well-being, and long-term policy issues and implications. It provides Treasury analysts with a method for understanding the origins of well-being and the broader impacts of their policy guidance in a systematic and unambiguous manner (The Treasury, 2021). The framework solicits stakeholder feedback to better represent culture and children's well-being, including increased compatibility with te ao Māori and Pacific cultures. The LSF includes three levels (The Treasury, 2021):

1. Our Individual and Collective Well-being: This level captures the resources and aspects of our lives that have been identified by research

or public engagement as important for our well-being as individuals, families, whānau, and communities.

2. Our Institutions and Governance: This level captures the role our institutions and organizations play in facilitating the well-being of individuals and collectives, as well as safeguarding and building our national wealth.
3. The Wealth of Aotearoa New Zealand: This captures how wealthy we are overall, including aspects of wealth not fully captured in the system of national accounts such as human capability and the natural environment.

The framework enables the government to analyze well-being across several dimensions: distribution, resilience, productivity, and sustainability. The LSF does not comprehensively include everything that is important for children or from te ao Māori and Pacific perspectives. They have attempted to include the most important concepts at a high level, complementing the LSF with these in-depth frameworks (The Treasury, 2021):

- He Ara Waiora for a mātauranga Māori perspective on well-being
- Fonofale for a Pacific perspective on well-being, and
- The Children's Commissioner's Wellbeing Wheel for a perspective on children's well-being.

Taking this approach prevents making the LSF too complex and maintains the integrity of those interdependent perspectives (The Treasury, 2021).

The government considers using a range of data and evidence to understand the interdependencies and accommodations across the different dimensions of well-being to be compatible with comprehensive economics and policy analysis. Economics provides powerful instruments for examining a broad range of policy obstacles and opportunities for improving living standards of New Zealanders. The LSF Dashboard is a measurement tool that supports the LSF by presenting multiple indicators of well-being outcomes to assist with advising ministers about priorities for well-being improvement (The Treasury, 2021).

Case Study Questions

1. How successful would a progressive framework like the LSF be in a more conservative political environment?
2. How successful would a progressive framework like the LSF be in a politically and/or culturally diverse nation?
3. The New Zealand government chose to focus on the most important high-level concepts and not comprehensively include everything that is important for children or from te ao Māori and Pacific perspectives. How inclusive is this approach?
4. What economic, social, and political risks does a government face when focusing on well-being?

References

Aldaco, R., Hoehn, D., Laso, J., Margallo, M., Ruiz-Salmón, J., Cristobal, J., Kahhat, R., Villanueva-Rey, P., Bala, A., & Batlle-Bayer, L. (2020). Food waste management during the COVID-19 outbreak: A holistic climate, economic and nutritional approach. *Science of the Total Environment, 742*, 140524. https://doi.org/10.1016/j.scitotenv.2020.140524

Alers, M. (2020). *How clean energy can power a COVID-19 recovery.* United Nations Development Program. https://www.undp.org/blog/how-clean-energy-can-power-covid-19-recovery

Alharthi, M., Alamoudi, H., Shaikh, A. A., & Bhutto, M. H. (2021). "Your ride has arrived"–Exploring the nexus between subjective well-being, socio-cultural beliefs, COVID-19, and the sharing economy. *Telematics and Informatics, 63*, e101663. https://doi.org/10.1016/j.tele.2021.101663

Allen, D., & Berg, C. (2014). *The sharing economy—how over-regulation could destroy an economic revolution.* https://ipa.org.au/publications-ipa/research-papers/the-sharing-economy-how-over-regulation-could-destroy-an-economic-revolution

Alliance of Bioversity International & International Center for Tropical Agriculture. (2022). *New analysis finds pandemic didn't dampen deforestation.* https://phys.org/news/2022-11-analysis-pandemic-didnt-dampen-deforestation.html

Altrock, S., & Suh, A. (2017). Sharing economy versus access economy: A critical reflection on social interaction between peers. In *HCI in business, government and organizations. Supporting business: 4th International Conference, HCIBGO 2017, Held as Part of HCI International 2017, Vancouver, BC, Canada, July 9–14, 2017, Proceedings, Part II 4* (pp. 3–15). Springer International Publishing.

Barouki, R., Kogevinas, M., Audouze, K., Belesova, K., Bergman, A., Birnbaum, L., Boekhold, S., Denys, S., Desseille, C., Drakvik, E., & Frumkin, H. (2021). The COVID-19 pandemic and global environmental change: Emerging research needs. *Environment International, 146*, 106272. https://doi.org/10.1016/j.envint.2020.106272

Bassetti, F. (2019). The cruel irony of climate debt. In *Migrations and inequalities, Foresight: The CMCC observatory on climate policies and futures*. https://www.climateforesight.eu/migrations-inequalities/the-cruel-irony-of-climate-debt/.

Bauhardt, C. (2014). Solutions to the crisis? The Green New Deal, Degrowth, and the Solidarity Economy: Alternatives to the capitalist growth economy from an ecofeminist economics perspective. *Ecological Economics, 102*, 60–68. https://doi.org/10.1016/j.ecolecon.2014.03.015

Belesova, K., Haines, A., Ranganathan, J., Seddon, J., & Wilkinson, P. (2020). Monitoring environmental change and human health: Planetary Health Watch. *The Lancet, 395*(10218), 96–98. https://doi.org/10.1016/S0140-6736(19)33042-9

Belk, R. (2014). You are what you can access: Sharing and collaborative consumption online. *Journal of Business Research, 67*(8), 1595–1600. https://doi.org/10.1016/j.jbusres.2013.10.001

Bhanumati, P., de Haan, M., & Tebrake, J. W. (2022). *Greenhouse emissions rise to record, erasing drop during pandemic.* International Monetary Fund. https://www.imf.org/en/Blogs/Articles/2022/06/30/greenhouse-emissions-rise-to-record-erasing-drop-during-pandemic

Bloomberg. (2020). *Global sharing economy could reach $335 Billion by 2025* [online].

Business Model Toolbox. (2022). *Sharing economy.* https://bmtoolbox.net/patterns/sharing-economy/.

Cawthorn, D.-M., Kennaugh, A., & Ferreira, S. M. (2021). The future of sustainability in the context of COVID-19. *Ambio, 50*, 812–821. https://doi.org/10.1007/s13280-020-01430-9

Chang, Y. Y., Wu, H. C., Cheng, C. C., & Chen, C. T. (2022). Identifying the key success factors of F&B sharing services: New insights from a multiple-phase decision-making model. *British Food Journal, 124*(12), 4161–4187. https://doi.org/10.1108/BFJ-04-2021-0444

Chirico, F. (2021). Spirituality to cope with COVID-19 pandemic, climate change and future global challenges. *Journal of Health Social Sciences, 6*(2), 151–158. https://journalhss.com/wp-content/uploads/jhhs_62_151-158.pdf

Chuah, S. H. W., Tseng, M. L., Wu, K. J., & Cheng, C. F. (2021). Factors influencing the adoption of sharing economy in B2B context in China: Findings from PLS-SEM and fsQCA. *Resources Conservation & Recycling, 175*, e105892. https://doi.org/10.1016/j.resconrec.2021.105892

Climate and Clean Air Coalition (CCAC) & United Nations Environment Programme (UNEP; 2019). *25 clean air measures for Asia and the Pacific.* https://ccacoalition.org/en/resources/25-clean-air-measures-asia-and-pacific

Climate Power. (2023). *One year of our clean energy boom.* https://climatepower.us/wp-content/uploads/sites/23/2023/07/Clean-Energy-Boom-Anniversary-Report-1.pdf

Coady, M. D., Parry, I., Le, N. P., & Shang, B. (2019). *Global fossil fuel subsidies remain large: An update based on country-level estimates.* International Monetary Fund.

Cui, L., Yang, K., Lei, Z., Lim, M. K., & Hou, Y. (2022). Exploring stakeholder collaboration based on the sustainability factors affecting the sharing economy. *Sustainable Production & Consumption, 30*, 218–232. https://doi.org/10.1016/j.spc.2021.12.009

Curtis, S. K., & Lehner, M. (2019). Defining the sharing economy for sustainability. *Sustainability, 11*(3), 567. https://doi.org/10.3390/su11030567

Curtis, S. K., & Mont, O. (2020). Sharing economy business models for sustainability. *Journal of Cleaner Production, 266*, e121519. https://doi.org/10.1016/j.jclepro.2020.121519

Dalsace, F. (2021). *Sustainability post pandemic: The four scenarios for change.* Institute for Management Development. https://www.imd.org/ibyimd/sustainability/sustainability-post-pandemic-the-four-scenarios-for-change/

Eckstein, D., Hutfils, M., & Winges, M. (2019). *Global climate risk index 2019 who suffers most from extreme weather events? Weather-related loss events in 2017 and 1998 to 2017.* Germanwatch. https://germanwatch.org/sites/default/files/Global%20Climate%20Risk%20Index%202019_2.pdf

Ellabban, O., Abu-Rub, H., & Blaabjerg, F. (2014). Renewable energy resources: Current status, future prospects and their enabling technology. *Renewable & Sustainable Energy Reviews, 39*, 748–764. https://doi.org/10.1016/j.rser.2014.07.113

Fraiberger, S.P., Sundararajan, A. (2017). Peer-to-peer rental markets in the sharing economy. *NYU Stern School of Business.* Research Paper First version March 2015. https://doi.org/10.2139/ssrn.2574337

Galvin, R., & Healy, N. (2020). The Green New Deal in the United States: What it is and how to pay for it. *Energy Research & Social Science, 67*, 101529. https://doi.org/10.1016/j.erss.2020.101529

Gerhardinger, L. C., de Andrade, M. M., Corrêa, M. R., & Turra, A. (2020). Crafting a sustainability transition experiment for the Brazilian blue economy. *Marine Policy, 120*, 104157. https://doi.org/10.1016/j.marpol.2020.104157

Glass, L. M., & Newig, J. (2019). Governance for achieving the Sustainable Development Goals: How important are participation, policy coherence, reflexivity, adaptation and democratic institutions? *Earth System Governance, 2*, 100031. https://doi.org/10.1016/j.esg.2019.100031

Gleeson, B. J. (2018). A dangerous transition to hope. In T. Moore, F. de Haan, R. Horne & B. J. Gleeson (Eds.) *Urban sustainability transitions. Australian cases-international perspectives* (pp. 35–49). Springer.

Gore, T. (2015). *Extreme carbon inequality: Why the Paris climate deal must put the poorest, lowest emitting and most vulnerable people first.* Oxfam.

Guerriero, C., Haines, A., & Pagano, M. (2020). Health and sustainability in post-pandemic economic policies. *Nature Sustainability, 3*, 494–496. https://doi.org/10.1038/s41893-020-0563-0

Hamari, J., & Sj¨oklint, M., &. (2016). The sharing economy: Why people participate in collaborative consumption. *Journal of the Association for Information Science and Technology, 67*(9), 2047–2059. https://doi.org/10.1002/asi.23552

Hawken, P. (2017). *Drawdown: The most comprehensive plan ever proposed to reverse global warming.* Penguin.

He, G., Pan, Y., & Tanaka, T. (2020). The short-term impacts of COVID-19 lockdown on urban air pollution in China. *Nature Sustainability, 3*, 1005–1011. https://doi.org/10.1038/s41893-020-0581-y

Hoegh-Guldberg, O., Jacob, D., Taylor, M., Bindi, M., Brown, S., & Camilloni, I. (2018). *Impacts of 1.5 c of global warming on natural and human* *systems. In global warming of 1.5: An IPCC special report on the impacts of global warming of 1.5\C above pre-industrial levels and related global greenhouse gas emission pathways, in the context of strengthening the global response to the threat of climate change, sustainable development, and efforts to eradicate poverty* (p. 138). Intergovernmental Panel on Climate Change.

Huang, L., Yuan, H., Dong, X., Chen, Z., & Zhou, L. (2023). Social norms and socially responsible consumption behavior in the sharing economy: The mediation role of reciprocity motivation. *Journal of Cleaner Production*, e137750. https://doi.org/10.1016/j.jclepro.2023.137750

Hubálek, Z. (2003). Emerging human infectious diseases: Anthroponoses, zoonoses, and sapronoses. *Emerging Infectious Diseases, 9*(3), 403–404. https://doi.org/10.3201/eid0903.020208

Huynh, T., &Gurtner, S. (2023). Resistance to the sharing economy: Why some consumers and providers do not participate in P2P sharing. *Journal of Cleaner Production*, e138628. https://doi.org/10.1016/j.jclepro.2023.138628

Hysa, E., Kruja, A., Rehman, N. U., & Laurenti, R. (2020). Circular economy innovation and environmental sustainability impact on economic growth: An integrated model for sustainable development. *Sustainability, 12*, 4831. https://doi.org/10.3390/su12124831

International Centre for Integrated Mountain Development. (ICIMOD; 2020). COVID-19 impact and policy responses in the Hindu Kush Himalaya. https://lib.icimod.org/record/34863

Islam, S. D. U., & Bhuiyan, M. A. H. (2018). Sundarbans mangrove forest of Bangladesh: Causes of degradation and sustainable management options. *Environmental Sustainability, 1*(2), 113–131. https://doi.org/10.1007/s42398-018-0018-y

Jenkins, W., Berry, E., & Kreider, L. B. (2018). Religion and climate change. *Annual Review of Environmental Research, 43*, 85–108. https://doi.org/10.1146/annurev-environ-102017-025855

Ju, M. J., Oh, J., & Choi Y. -H. (2021). Changes in air pollution levels after COVID-19 outbreak in Korea. *Science of the Total Environment, 750*, 141521. https://doi.org/10.1016/j.scitotenv.2020.141521

Leal Filho, W., Platje, J., Gerstlberger, W., Ciegis, R., Kääriä, J., Klavins, M., & Kliucininkas, L. (2016). The role of governance in realising the transition towards sustainable societies. *Journal of Cleaner Production, 113*, 755–766. https://doi.org/10.1016/j.jclepro.2015.11.060

Lehmann, P., Beck, S., de Brito, M. M., Gawel, E., Groß, M., Haase, A., Lepenies, R., Otto, D., Schiller, J., Strunz, S., & Thrän, D. (2021). Environmental sustainability post-covid-19: Scrutinizing popular hypotheses from a social science perspective. *Sustainability, 13*(16), 8679. https://doi.org/10.3390/su13168679

Lehto, X., Luo, W., Miao, L., & Ghiselli, R. F. (2018). Shared tourism experience of individuals with disabilities and their caregivers. *Journal of Destination Marketing & Management, 8*, 185–193. https://doi.org/10.1016/j.jdmm.2017.04.001

Meentemeyer, R. K., Haas, S. E., & Václavík, T. (2012). Landscape epidemiology of emerging infectious diseases in natural and human-altered ecosystems. *Annual Review of Phytopathology, 50*, 379–402. https://doi.org/10.1146/annu-rev-phyto-081211-172938

Mondal, S., & Samaddar, K. (2020). Issues and challenges in implementing sharing economy in tourism: A triangulation study. *Management of Environmental Quality: An International Journal, 32*(1), 64–81. https://doi.org/10.1108/MEQ-03-2020-0054

Morrison, M., Duncan, R., & Parton, K. (2015). Religion does matter for climate change attitudes and behavior. *PLoS ONE, 10*(8), e0134868. https://doi.org/10.1371/journal.pone.0134868

Morrissey, J., & Heidkamp, P. (2022). Sustainability after COVID-19: Pillars for a just transition. *Environmental Sustainability, 5*, 261–269. https://doi.org/10.1007/s42398-022-00231-y

OECD. (2022). Global plastics outlook: Economic drivers, environmental impacts and policy options. *OECD Publishing*. https://doi.org/10.1787/de747aef-en

Özdemir, V. (2019). Innovating governance for planetary health with three critically informed frames. *OMICS: A Journal of Integrative Biology, 23*(12), 623–630. https://doi.org/10.1089/omi.2019.0175

Pan, J. (2016). *China's environmental governing and ecological civilization.* Springer.

Panniello, U., Ardito, L., & Petruzzelli, A. M. (2022). Scoping the state of the sharing economy and its antecedents at the country level: Cross-country differences in Europe. *Geoforum, 133*, 140–152. https://doi.org/10.1016/j.geoforum.2022.05.013

Puaschunder, J. (2020) Mapping climate justice. In: *Governance and climate justice.* Palgrave Macmillan.

Rathnayake, I., Paniagua, J. O., Gu, N., Rameezdeen, R., Statsenko, L., & Sandhu, S. (2023). A critical review of the key aspects of sharing economy:

A systematic literature review and research framework. *Journal of Cleaner Production, 434*, e140378. https://doi.org/10.1016/j.jclepro.2023.140378

Raworth, K. (2017). A doughnut for the anthropocene: Humanity's compass in the 21st century. *Lancet Planet Health, 1*, e48–e49. https://doi.org/10.1016/S2542-5196(17)30028-1

Ripple, W. J., Wolf, C., Newsome, T. M., Galetti, M., Alamgir, M., Crist, E., Mahmoud M. I., Laurance W. F., & 15,364 Scientist Signatories from 184 Countries. (2017). World scientists' warning to humanity: A second notice. *BioScience, 67*(12), 1026–1028. https://doi.org/10.1093/biosci/bix125

Rockström, J., Steffen, W., Noone, K., Persson, Å., Chapin III, F. S., Lambin, E., Lenton, T. M., Scheffer, M., Folke, C., Schellnhuber, H. J., & Nykvist, B. (2009). Planetary boundaries: exploring the safe operating space for humanity. *Ecology and Society, 14*(2). https://www.jstor.org/stable/26268316

Rume, T., & Islam, S. M. D. (2020). Environmental effects of COVID-19 pandemic and potential strategies of sustainability. *Heliyon, 6*(9), e04965. https://doi.org/10.1016/j.heliyon.2020.e04965

Russo-Netzer P. (2017). Spiritual development. In M. E. Arterberry, K. L. Fingerman, & J. E. Lansford (Eds.) *SAGE encyclopedia of lifespan human development.* Sage.

Sareen, S., & Haarstad, H. (2018). Bridging socio-technical and justice aspects of sustainable energy transitions. *Applied Energy, 228*, 624–632. https://doi.org/10.1016/j.apenergy.2018.06.104

Schor, J. (2016). Debating the sharing economy. *Journal of Self-Governance & Management Economics, 4*(3), 7–22. https://www.ceeol.com/search/article-detail?id=430188

Schwab, K., & Sternfels, B. (2022). *3 keys to a resilient post-pandemic recovery.* World Economic Forum. https://www.weforum.org/agenda/2022/02/3-keys-to-a-resilient-post-pandemic-recovery/

Srivastava, L., Gomez Echeverri, L.G., Schlegel, F., Denis, M., Deubelli, T.M., Havlik, P., Kaplan, D., Mechler, R., Paulavets, K., Rovenskaya, E., & Sizov, S. (2021). *Transformations within Reach: Pathways to a sustainable and resilient world-Synthesis Report.* IIASA Report; IIASA-ISC: Laxenburg, Austria, 2021. https://pure.iiasa.ac.at/id/eprint/16818/1/Synthesis-NEW.pdfets

Statistica. (2024). *Value of the global sharing economy 2021 and 2023, with 2027 and 2031 forecast.* https://www.statista.com/statistics/830986/value-of-the-global-sharing-economy/

Steffen, W., Richardson, K., Rockström, J., Cornell, S. E., Fetzer, I., Bennett, E. M., Biggs, R., Carpenter, S. R., De Vries, W., De Wit, C. A., & Folke, C.

(2015). Planetary boundaries: Guiding human development on a changing planet. *Science, 347*(6223), 1259855. https://doi.org/10.1126/science.1259855
Stern, N. (2016). Growth and sustainability: 10 years on from the Stern Review. In *Grantham Research Institute on Climate Change and the Environment Public Lecture.* Grantham Research Institute on Climate Change and the Environment.
Su, B. C., Lin, H., & Wang, Y. M. (2022). The business model of digital platforms for the sharing economy: Intensive case study methodology for rover.com pet boarding platform. *Sustainability, 14*(23), e16256. https://doi.org/10.3390/su142316256
Swilling, M. (2020). *The age of sustainability*. Routledge.
Swiss Re Institute. (2021). *The economics of climate change: No action not an option.* Swiss Re Institute.
Teubner, T. (2014, May). Thoughts on the sharing economy. In *Proceedings of the International Conference on e-Commerce* (Vol. 11, pp. 322–326).
The Treasury. (2021). *Our living standards framework.* New Zealand Government. https://www.treasury.govt.nz/information-and-services/nz-economy/higher-living-standards/our-living-standards-framework
The White House. (2023). *Fact sheet: One year in, President Biden's Inflation Reduction Act is driving historic climate action and investing in America to create good paying jobs and reduce costs.* https://www.whitehouse.gov/briefing-room/statements-releases/2023/08/16/fact-sheet-one-year-in-president-bidens-inflation-reduction-act-is-driving-historic-climate-action-and-investing-in-america-to-create-good-paying-jobs-and-reduce-costs/
Tienhaara, K. (2010). A tale of two crises: What the global financial crisis means for the global environmental crisis. *Environmental Policy and Governance, 20*(3), 197–208. https://doi.org/10.1002/eet.537
Tilton, J. E. (2016). Global climate policy and the polluter pays principle: A different perspective. *Resource Policy, 50*, 117–118. https://doi.org/10.1016/j.resourpol.2016.08.010
UNDP. (2019). *Beyond income, beyond averages, beyond today: inequalities in human development in the 21st century.* Human Development Report 2019. United Nations Development Programme (UNDP).
UNEP. (2019). *Emissions Gap Report 2019.* United Nations Environmental Programme.
UNEP. (2021). *Emissions Gap Report 2021: The heat is on-A world of climate promises not yet delivered-Executive Summary*. United Nations Environmental Programme.

U.S. Department of Energy. (2023). *Investing in American energy: Significant impacts of the inflation reduction act and bipartisan infrastructure law on the U.S. energy economy and emissions reductions.* https://www.energy.gov/policy/articles/investing-american-energy-significant-impacts-inflation-reduction-act-and

Vallance, S., Perkins, H. C., & Dixon, J. E. (2011). What is social sustainability? *A Clarification of Concepts. Geoforum, 42*(3), 342–348. https://doi.org/10.1016/j.geoforum.2011.01.002

Veith, C., Vasilache, S. N., Ciocoiu, C. N., Chiţimiea, A., Minciu, M., Manta, A. M., & Isbaita, I. (2022). An empirical analysis of the common factors influencing the sharing and green economies. *Sustainability, 14*(2), 771. https://doi.org/10.3390/su14020771

Ventura, D. D. F. L., Giulio, G. M. D., & Rached, D. H. (2020). Lessons from the Covid-19 pandemic: Sustainability is an indispensable condition of Global Health Security. *Ambiente & Sociedade, 23.* https://doi.org/10.1590/1809-4422asoc20200108vu2020L3ID

Vohra, K., Vodonos, A., Schwartz, J., Marais, E. A., Sulprizio, M. P., & Mickley, L. J. (2021). Global mortality from outdoor fine particle pollution generated by fossil fuel combustion: Results from GEOS-Chem. *Environmental Research, 195*, 110754. https://doi.org/10.1016/j.envres.2021.110754

Williamson, E. J., Walker, A. J., Bhaskaran, K., Bacon, S., Bates, C., Morton, C. E., Curtis, H. J., Meherkar, A., Evans, D., Inglesby, P., Cockburn, J., McDonald, H. I., MacKenna, B., Tomlinson, L., Douglas, I. J., Rentsch, C. T., Mathur, R., Wong, A., Grieve, R., Harrison, D., Forbes, H., Schultze, A., Croker, R., Parry, J., & Goldacre, B. (2020). Factors associated with COVID-19-related death using OpenSAFELY. *Nature, 584*, 430–436. https://doi.org/10.1038/s41586-020-2521-4

World Health Organization. (2021). *Climate change and health.* https://www.who.int/news-room/fact-sheets/detail/climate-change-and-health

World Wildlife Federation. (2018). *Living planet report: 2018: Aiming higher.* WWF. https://www.worldwildlife.org/publications/living-planet-report-2018

Yin, E., & Mahrous, A. (2022). Covid-19 global pandemic, workplace spirituality and the rise of spirituality-driven organisations in the post-digital era. *Journal of Humanities and Applied Social Sciences, 4*(2), 79–93. https://doi.org/10.1108/JHASS-11-2021-0177

You, S., Sonne, C., & Ok, Y. S. (2020). COVID-19's unsustainable waste management. *Science, 368*, 1438. https://doi.org/10.1126/science.abc7778

Zhang, Q., Pan, Y., He, Y., Walters, W. W., Ni, Q., Liu, X., Xu, G., Shao, J., & Jiang, C. (2021). Substantial nitrogen oxides emission reduction from China due to COVID-19 and its impact on surface ozone and aerosol pollution. *Science of the Total Environmental, 753*, 142238. https://doi.org/10.1016/j.scitotenv.2020.142238

10

Workplace and Organizational Spirituality for Organizational Success

10.1 Introduction

In line with the broad, interdisciplinary, and non-religious framework of the text, the business and organizational benefits of workplace spirituality from a secular perspective will be examined in this chapter. However, this chapter would be incomplete if the focus was solely with the benefits of applying workplace spirituality at the organizational level, without discourse concerning the methods by which organizational leaders have applied spirituality to achieve success. The characteristics and development of spiritual organizations, workplace spirituality programs, demonstrated benefits, and methods of implementation will also be explored. Moreover, the potential risks, challenges, and controversies surrounding both spiritual organizations and workplace spirituality will be discussed. Spiritual intelligence is briefly examined because the development of organizational spiritual capabilities is an antecedent to the development of successful triple bottom line strategies. Finally, the Spiritual Incorporated Argument (SIA) is introduced as a method of providing intrinsic justification for the incorporation of spirituality into

C. G. Beehner, *Spirituality, Sustainability, and Success*, Palgrave Studies in Workplace Spirituality and Fulfillment, https://doi.org/10.1007/978-3-031-47643-3_10

business management. Existing literature will be synthesized to demonstrate the benefits, and a case study to assist with practical application of workplace spirituality on a business/organizational level concludes the chapter.

10.2 Organizational Benefits of Workplace Spirituality

Organizations must recognize the spiritual need for employees to bring their "entire self" to work because doing so produces direct and indirect organizational benefits. Abundant literature exists examining the relationship between workplace spirituality and various dimensions of organizational behavior (Giacalone & Jurkiewicz, 2010). Based upon a literature review of 140 articles, Karakas (2010) identified three different perspectives on how spirituality benefits employees and supports organizational performance. According to the literature, spirituality contributes to employee well-being and quality of life, provides employees with meaning and purpose at work, along with a sense of community interconnectedness.

There are numerous organizational benefits from workplace spirituality. Pawar (2016) found workplace spirituality to have a positive relationship with emotional, psychological, social, and spiritual well-being. Iqbal and Khan (2020) reaffirmed previous findings that spirituality has a positive and significant effect on psychological well-being. A positive and meaningful relationship exists between organizational spirituality and happiness (Amanollahi Baharvand et al., 2023). Positive relationships have been demonstrated between workplace spirituality and job satisfaction in multiple industries (Altaf & Awan, 2011; Chatterjee & Naqvi, 2010; Chawla & Guda, 2010; Giacalone & Jurkiewicz, 2010; Gupta et al., 2013; Pawar, 2009; Usman & Danish, 2010). However, other studies have found workplace spirituality predicted intrinsic job satisfaction but not extrinsic satisfaction (Marschke et al., 2011).

Saadatyar et al. (2020) found that workplace spirituality indirectly encourages development of competitive advantages by improving all three measures of organizational commitment (affective, continuance, and normative). Therefore, organizational leaders should develop long-term strategies to align employee emotions and values with organizational values to enhance the competitive position of the organization (Saadatyar et al., 2020). The level of workplace spirituality affects commitment to change resulting in change-oriented organizational citizenship behavior (C-OCB; Sulastini et al., 2023). Workplace spirituality also increases employee loyalty and commitment to the organization (Sapta et al., 2021) which can be a radical solution for overcoming contemporary human resource problems (Garg et al., 2019). However, spirituality is not a universal antidote for all workplace problems (Saks, 2011), and spiritual intention must be demonstrated in the form of a vision, mission, and practices that encourage a more cooperative and accountable workforce (Sapta et al., 2021).

Positive relationships have also been demonstrated between workplace spirituality and job involvement (Chatterjee & Naqvi, 2010; Kolodinsky et al., 2008; Rathee & Rajain, 2020; Word, 2012), organizational commitment (Affeldt & MacDonald, 2010; Fry & Slocum, 2008; Marschke et al., 2009; Pawar, 2009; Rego & Pina e Cunha, 2008), and organizational identification, while a negative relationship was found between workplace spirituality and organizational frustration (Kolodinsky et al., 2008). Workplace spirituality negatively influenced both employee cynicism and employee turnover (Shrestha & Jena, 2021). Gull and Doh (2004) suggest spirituality can provide the foundation for ethical business conduct. Workplace spirituality is positively related with employee engagement, with the relationship modeled by the workplace spirituality dimensions of transcendence, community, and spiritual values being related to the four psychological employee engagement conditions of meaningfulness in work, meaningfulness at work, safety, and availability (Saks, 2011). Workplace spirituality enhances spiritual leadership styles in the workplace by strengthening employees to enhance self-fulfillment and cultivate a variety of career pathways (Ali et al., 2023).

Employee turnover and turnover intention were found to be lower among organizations with higher levels of workplace spirituality (Chawla & Guda, 2010; Crawford et al., 2009; Giacalone & Jurkiewicz, 2010; Hong, 2012; Milliman et al., 2003; Riasudeen & Prabavathy,

2011). A positive relationship has been demonstrated between workplace spirituality and employee retention (Kaur & Dhilion, 2021). Further, individual spirituality was found to be negatively correlated with turnover intention (Chawla & Guda, 2010; Hussain et al., 2020). However, recent research found no significant change in turnover intention after a workplace spirituality program was implemented within a multi-location organization in the food services industry (Beehner & Blackwell, 2016). Workplace spirituality results in lower employee absenteeism (Giacalone & Jurkiewicz, 2010; Krahnke et al., 2003), further reducing organizational employment costs.

Workplace spirituality has been found to have a positive relationship with the three vital components of employee well-being: employee commitment, job satisfaction, and work-life balance, establishing workplace spirituality as essential for employee well-being (Garg, 2017). Garg examined five dimensions of workplace spirituality from the Indian context of *Swadharma* (meaningful and meditative work), authenticity, *Lokasangraha* (planetary maintenance and welfare), sense of community, and *Karma*, four of which overlap with previous workplace spirituality dimensions. Karma capital, defined as the combination of individual actions in current and previous states of existence which are believed to determine fate in future existences, was added because the study of spirituality in India would be incomplete if that dimension were excluded.

10.3 Spiritual Organizations

While considerable literature supports the worldview of workers as social entities, contemporary organizations are frequently characterized as machines, structured and managed using traditional command and control techniques (Geh & Tan, 2009). However, an increasing number of scholars and practitioners are embracing the social and spiritual nature of organizations, encouraging the development of spiritual organizations. Guillory (1997) describes a spiritual organization as a living organization, arguing organizational spirituality is inevitable, occurring through a personal and collective transformational process. The living organization is characterized as adaptable to change through continual re-creation and possessing the Darwinian principles of a living organism: uniqueness, endurance, acclimation, and heritage (Guillory, 1997). Guillory suggests the amalgamation of spiritual principles and sound business practices creates a highly effective organization, characterized by diversity, empowerment, environmentalism, teamwork, and a customer focus. His definition of environmentalism mirrors the current definition of sustainability in caring for the environment to provide for the well-being of all inhabitants, while managing the impact of the organization on both people and planet.

Guillory (1997) theorized the Industrial Age, which was followed by the Information Age and partially concurrent Knowledge Age, will be followed by the Spiritual Age and subsequent Age of Oneness. Organizations surviving and thriving in the coming ages will be organizations cognizant of the potential of the human spirit (Guillory, 1997). Successful organizations in the latter two stages will utilize quantum thinking to anticipate the next paradigm, developing products and services that will meet the spiritual needs of the subsequent age.

Case and Gosling (2010) introduce a theoretical framework to explain recent, and potential future organizational developments, suggesting we consider a spectrum of organizational technologies ranging from those seeking to control the workforce, through those evoking moral and ideological commitment, to those that would commandeer employees' spirits and souls. Case and Gosling (2010) proposed a new category in Etzioni's model of complex organizations to be designated the spiritual organization. The proposed category of spiritual organization is characterized by member involvement encompassing hope for revelation or enlightenment, and power executed pastorally through conscience, willing obedience, self-reflection, and internal discipline (Bell & Taylor, 2003; Foucault, 1978; Mitchell, 2009). While organizations such as monasteries are clearly spiritual organizations, it is unclear whether we can anticipate a pattern of behaviors associated with the proposed spiritual organization beginning to percolate while secular, normative organizations have been intruding relentlessly upon Etzioni's utilitarian organizations (Case & Gosling, 2010).

Etzioni (1961) developed a classification system for complex organizations consisting of three classes: coercive, utilitarian, and normative systems. Complex organizations are classified according to the 'forms of relationship', 'member involvement', and 'types of power' that predominate in them (1961). Coercive organizations, which include prisons, mental hospitals, and other organizations with involuntary membership, ensure member compliance through actual or threatened violence. Utilitarian organizations, which include most business workplaces, as well as peacetime military organizations obtain calculative member involvement, utilizing resource sanctions to induce compliance. Normative organizations, such as religious, healthcare, and political organizations, and educational institutions, are characterized by the moral commitment of members, seeking to influence them through the administration of values, attitudes, and beliefs (Case & Gosling, 2010).

While critical of the spiritual organizational construct, Case and Gosling (2010) proposed three alternative methods of reconsidering the relationship between spirituality and the workplace (Case & Gosling, 2010). First, employee spirituality is subject to the organized manipulation of beliefs and practices, thereby producing behaviors beneficial to corporate objectives. While Case and Gosling concur with positivist authors that spirituality is a model of constructed consciousness, they are skeptical of their manipulations. Second, despite the headaches and heartaches of the material world, individuals often view work, organizational life, and employment as instruments in their spiritual lives. Third, despite incidental connections between spirituality and workplace, both are more appropriately considered separately, with disproportionate goals, and no substantial relationship with each other. The workplace may simply be another location in which subjective spiritual journeys may or may not be undertaken Hadot (1995) supports the notion of incidental connections between spirituality and workplace which might be strengthened through association and friendship, noting the discipline of spiritual exercises, might be good in themselves, without regard to the workplace.

Case and Gosling (2010) further suggest spiritual organizations form part of an historical movement of social technologies (Total Quality Management, Business Process Engineering), designed to incrementally colonize and control the bodies, minds, emotions, and souls of workers. However, spiritual organizations may also be perceived as a possible liberating notion acknowledging the renaissance of multiple grassroots spiritualities currently finding expression in the workplace. The workplace spirituality movement may be representative of a more ambitious effort to access employee subjectivity, possibly positioning employee identity as the most prominent expression of selfhood. The workplace would transform from a scene of discovery and expression of socially sanctioned values and norms, to a location providing material and metaphysical conditions for selfhood. In this new organizational paradigm, employees become compelled to find self and fulfillment through willing acquiescence to the whole (Case & Gosling, 2010).

10.4 Workplace Spirituality Programs and Benefits

Workplace spirituality programs have been implemented in organizations in multiple industries, with most programs producing positive organizational results (Dhiman & Marques, 2011; Han et al., 2010; Kinjerski & Skrypnek, 2008; Pawar, 2008; Yong et al., 2011). Although numerous organizations have successfully implemented workplace spirituality programs, the existence of a workplace spirituality program is not necessary for workplace spirituality to exist within an organization (Pawar, 2008). Two categories of workplace spirituality implementation have been identified: accommodating, when an employer permits spiritual expression and a spiritual environment in the workplace; and, encouraging when an employer encourages spiritual expression and a spiritual environment within the workplace (Polley et al., 2005).

Empirical evidence indicates workplace spirituality programs influence beneficial individual outcomes such as increased joy, peace, serenity, job satisfaction, and commitment, along with beneficial organizational outcomes such as improved productivity and reduced absenteeism and employee turnover (Case & Gosling, 2010). Increased job satisfaction and commitment was reported in employees participating in workplace spirituality programs (Burack, 1999; Fry, 2003; Giacalone & Jurkiewicz,

2010; Krishnakumar & Neck, 2002; Paloutzian et al., 2003; Reave, 2005). De Diego-Cordero et al. (2021) found that workplace spirituality interventions improved employee health and that yoga was an effective intervention which also reduced employee stress. Workplace spirituality has been described as a crucial integrative mechanism for achieving employee commitment, and organizational mission, vision and values alignment (Wong & Hu, 2011). Creating an improved spiritual work climate promotes organizational commitment, resulting in enhanced organizational performance (Dehaghi et al., 2012).

There are two opposing viewpoints regarding inquiries on the relationship between workplace spirituality and organizational performance (Karakas, 2010). One viewpoint considers spirituality as anti-materialist (Gibbons, 2000; Lips-Wiersma, 2003) and anti-positivist (Lund-Dean et al., 2003), questioning positivist workplace spirituality research methods (Fornaciari & Lund Dean, 2001; Gibbons, 2000; Lips-Wiersma, 2003; Lund-Dean et al., 2003; Mitroff & Denton, 1999). These researchers argue the anti-materialist characteristic of spirituality may present significant challenges in the empirical investigation of links between spirituality and financial performance (Dent et al., 2005; Fornaciari & Lund Dean, 2001; Lund-Dean et al., 2003). Moreover, some researchers supporting this viewpoint cite ethical and moral concerns regarding research examining profitability and performance improvements resulting from workplace spirituality initiatives (Dent et al., 2005; Fernando, 2005). Further, several researchers supporting this view express concern about workplace spirituality implementation as an administrative tool to for employee manipulation (Brown, 2003; Cavanagh & Bandsuch, 2002; Fernando, 2005; Mirvis, 1997), arguing spirituality should be viewed as an end in itself, not as a managerial tool for financial performance improvement (Case & Gosling, 2010; Cavanagh & Bandsuch, 2002; Fernando, 2005).

Clearly there has been considerable confusion and controversy regarding the role and legitimacy of workplace spirituality, and its relationship with organizational performance (Giacalone & Jurkiewicz, 2010). However, numerous scholars still argue spirituality can be used to improve employee and organizational performance (Ashmos & Duchon, 2000; Fry, 2005; Garcia-Zamor, 2003; Giacalone & Jurkiewicz, 2010;

Jena, 2022; Mousa, 2020), and spirituality research should demonstrate the links existing among spirituality, productivity, and profitability (Ashmos & Duchon, 2000; Fry, 2005; Garcia-Zamor, 2003; Giacalone & Jurkiewicz, 2010). Through the empirical demonstration of positive effects and outcomes of spirituality in organizations, workplace spirituality research will achieve greater legitimacy in mainstream organizational studies (Karakas, 2010).

Researchers have suggested organizations encouraging workplace spirituality might improve their organizational performance and profitability (Biberman & Whitty, 1997; Biberman et al., 1999; Burack, 1999; Korac-Kakabadse et al., 2002; Kriger & Hanson, 1999; Neck & Milliman, 1994; Thompson, 2000). Earlier workplace spirituality research findings showed positive relationships between workplace spirituality and organizational productivity and performance (Bierly et al., 2000; Delbecq, 1999; Korac-Kakabadse & Korac-Kakabadse, 1997; Mitroff & Denton, 1999). Research findings also indicated organizations with voluntary spirituality programs reported higher profits (Dehler & Welsh, 1994; Konz & Ryan, 1999; Mitroff & Denton, 1999), and higher levels of productivity and performance (Mehta & Joshi, 2010; Reave, 2005). Increased productivity has been associated with both employee religiosity and spirituality (Valasek, 2009), beneficial to both the individual and the business or organization.

Researchers suggest workplace spirituality may indirectly influence customer satisfaction and loyalty through increased employee job satisfaction and organizational commitment (Lee et al., 2013). Workplace spirituality improves team effectiveness because it promotes the organizational attributes of creativity, respect, and trust (Daniel, 2010), and most managers agree the integration of spirituality into the workplace increases organizational effectiveness (Neal, 2001). While a positive relationship has been demonstrated between workplace spirituality and employee workplace success, such a relationship with other dimensions of individual employee success has not been substantiated (Tischler et al., 2002).

Literature is replete with practical and theoretical research examining the various methods of harnessing the 'inner lives' of employees to extract maximum productivity and performance (Case & Gosling, 2010). Motivation theorists (Alderfer, 1972; Maslow, 1970; McClelland, 1971) emphasized the importance of satisfying employee desire for belonging and self-actualization in productivity maximization (Case & Gosling, 2010). However, Whyte (1965) was critical of corporatist attempts to not only demand the 'sweat', but also the 'soul' of workers (Case & Gosling, 2010).

We may pause to question whether the goal of workplace spirituality research is conducted simply for the sake of humanizing the workplace. In these situations, the argument suggests the promotion of workplace spirituality results in some humanitarian value (Fry, 2005; Giacolone, 2004; Giacalone & Jurkiewicz, 2003; Giacalone & Thompson, 2006). Consideration about performance and profit gives permission to discuss spirituality, providing a safe space in which to consider an association between spirituality and materiality. Obviously, this is necessary when performance and profit are the only criteria of legitimacy, and possibly in academia, there would be no interest in workplace spirituality, absent consideration of organizational benefits (Case & Gosling, 2010).

The implementation of a workplace spirituality program at a South Korean hospital resulted in reduced burnout levels, and increased spiritual integrity, spiritual well-being, psychosocial well-being, and improved leadership practice (Yong et al., 2011). The significant improvement in spiritual well-being and spiritual integrity resonates with similar results in other healthcare settings (Bormann et al., 2006; Richards et al., 2006; Shapiro et al., 2005). The improved leadership practice finding is supported by the findings of Strack and colleagues (2008), indicating more spiritually oriented groups demonstrated excellent leadership performance, suggesting workplace spirituality programs may play an important role in effective leadership development.

The findings that workplace spirituality programs resulted in decreased nurse burnout were similar to workplace meditation study findings (Cohen-Katz et al., 2005). Because healthcare employee burnout has a negative influence on patient care, burnout reduction enables nurses to serve patients with optimal quality care and spiritual care (Shanafelt et al., 2002). Workplace meditation programs are cost-effective and easily applied in any work environment, resulting in a beneficial program for promoting the spiritual and psychosocial well-being of healthcare professionals who experience stress resulting from working in complicated, rapidly changing healthcare systems (Yong et al., 2011). It should be easily recognized that personal spirituality readily fits within the healthcare context since many of the workplace spirituality concepts are intrinsic components of caring for others (Baldacchino, 2017). Research has consistently demonstrated that enhancing spirituality in the healthcare workplace is beneficial for both staff and patients (Daniel, 2012; McKee et al., 2011; Sadeghifar et al., 2013).

An important outcome of the South Korean hospital study (Yong et al., 2011) is the correlation of results between Eastern and Western spirituality, suggesting spiritual issues appear to cross cultural boundaries, an important finding for improved healthcare outcomes as societies become more increasingly multicultural. However, despite the empirical evidence, many South Korean hospitals still do not recognize spirituality as a key high-quality healthcare component, with spirituality-based interventions and training programs limited. While South Korean healthcare is primarily disease/cure-oriented, the favorable results provided by the workplace spirituality program may encourage hospital leaders to consider the value of development and implementation of similar training programs (Yong et al., 2011).

When members of a sports team demonstrate camaraderie and work well together, the members are said to be demonstrating "team spirit". Likewise, a spiritual organization may demonstrate organizational or team "spirit" through the workplace spirituality attributes of connection and community among organizational members. Recent workplace spirituality research findings have shown a spiritual workplace climate to be positively correlated with teamwork, suggesting spiritual climate may be responsive to intervention, and may be a target for teamwork improvement initiatives (Doram et al., 2017).

10.5 Workplace Spirituality Implementation

Thaker (2009) proposes a two-step workplace spirituality program implementation approach: envision and define spirituality for the organization; and, define the highest purpose of the organization. This approach assumes acceptance of a business case for adoption of a spiritual view, primarily focusing on operationalization and implementation of spirituality in the organizational context. Practical compassion is an accepted approach for introduction of spirituality into business, with Thaker (2009) suggesting four pathways of a practical compassion approach to organizational spirituality: character, human development, oneness, and response. The four practical compassion pathways can be implemented with several performance measurement frameworks and models, integrated and modeled in the form of a spirituality scorecard. Traditionally, when a business intends to pursue organizational spirituality integration, the starting point is with one of the practical compassion pathways, while over time, all pathways may be implemented, with the performance measurement framework a useful tool for accomplishment (Thaker, 2009).

Al-Qutop and Harrim (2014) proposed a framework for building spirituality-based organization consisting of five interacting "Core Pillars":

1. A clear, compelling organization mission and vision that are understood and accepted by organizational members.
2. An organizational culture that is ethical, innovative, customer-responsive, and promotes workplace spirituality.
3. Spiritual leadership, which is the key to maintaining an organizational culture, also influences the selection and socialization of employees.
4. Human development, because workplace spirituality is a learnable behavior, therefore human resource management (HRM) should incorporate into their training programs.
5. An organizational design that is decentralized, organic, adaptive, and flexible distinguished by low formalism, low specialization, cross-functional and hierarchical teams, free communication, closely connected with stakeholders at all levels (Al-Qutop & Harrim, 2014).

The five key elements for integrating organizational spirituality are people, service, organizational self-awareness, wisdom, and the new leadership (Guillory, 1997). The new leadership is an integrated combination of transformational (learning-driven), visionary (vision-driven), traditional (business-driven), and spiritual (values-driven) leadership (Guillory, 1997). Lund-Dean and Safranski (2008) suggest employer-sponsored workplace spirituality programs follow a non-interventionist approach to accommodate legal and cultural considerations. A non-interventionist approach would allow voluntary employee participation, absent conditions of supervisory sanction, or pressure concerning program participation (Lund Dean & Safranski, 2008).

The work environment is so central to employee existence, yet often contributes to the sense of desperation occasionally experienced during life events, thwarting individual growth. However, if management recognizes the potential mutual benefits of coordination of individual spiritual excursion and organizational structure, the organizational contribution can be positive. King and Nicol (1999) propose integration of the theoretical frameworks of Carl Jung and Elliot Jaques as a determinant of managerial insight into the individual spiritual growth process within the organizational context. This perspective not only enhances management possibilities for precluding the dysfunctional behavior of the spiritually bankrupt, but also enhances organizational capacity to foster increased employee initiative and productivity (King & Nicol, 1999).

The concept of spiritual intelligence was introduced in Chapter 2 but deserves mention in this chapter. Spiritual intelligence is defined as a collection of mental capacities contributing to the awareness, integration, and adaptive application of the intangible and transcendent characteristics of one's existence, resulting in deep existential reflection, meaning enhancement, recognition of a transcendent self, and spiritual environment mastery (King, 2008). Zohar and Marshall (2000) introduced the concept of a spiritual quotient (SQ) as a measurement of the spiritual intelligence (SI) of a person. Spiritual Intelligence was suggested as a means of unethical behavior reduction within organizations, which in the first decade of the twenty-first century caused multiple high-profile business failures (Akhtar et al., 2015). Senge (1990) suggested the creation of a shared vision to be essential to the formation of spiritual intelligence, which then becomes the cultural foundation that binds organizational members together (Stead & Stead, 2014). The development of organizational spiritual capabilities is antecedent to the development of successful triple bottom line strategies, which reinforce sustainability-based core competencies, thereby creating a difficult to imitate competitive advantage (Stead & Stead, 2014).

The corporate world recognizes that spiritual values are essential to both personal well-being and organizational success (Dhiman, 2017). While businesses often exclude spirituality from the business model, researchers suggest that doing so threatens to separate employees from moral integrity (Brophy, 2015). Spirituality should not be viewed as external interference, but rather as internal embodiment, and should be included in a business to the extent these values are shared by leadership (Brophy, 2015).

Brophy (2015) developed the Spiritual Incorporated Argument (SIA) to provide intrinsic justification for the incorporation of spirituality into business management. Brophy (2015) posits the moral incumbency of business to incorporate the spiritual values of its leadership to fully respect their freedom and liberty. If commonality of organizational member spiritual values can be determined, this provides an intersection at which spiritual values may be incorporated into a business in an unobjectionable manner, enabling exercise of individual freedom. With that goal in mind, SIA offers the idea of convergent consensus: the shared values common among individual religious, spiritual, and ideological views. The convergent consensus should be presumed to consist of spiritual values, not beliefs, as common spiritual values can be identified, while beliefs vary widely (Brophy, 2015).

Brophy (2015) has identified five convergent spiritual values transcending belief systems to be compassion, interconnection, human dignity, transcendence, and profundity. Compassion is common to most belief systems, as is interconnection which suggests humans are connected to each other in some ethically compelling way. Human dignity likewise seems to be a universal value (Hicks, 2003), recognizing humans as possessing intrinsic worth, and deserving of respect. Transcendence suggests humankind should expand their consciousness to attain an unbiased frame of reference while simultaneously capable of perceiving situations from multiple perspectives, much like putting oneself into another's shoes. Convergent consensus need not represent all existing spiritual value sets, only those representing the shared spiritual values of organizational members, which may differ from company to company. Therefore, if a stakeholder corporate governance model is assumed, there may be broad stakeholder convergent consensus, while if a stockholder corporate governance model is assumed, the convergent consensus may be narrow (Brophy, 2015).

One limitation with SIA is that the existence of shared values will not always be possible. Recognizing the limitations of convergent consensus, it is necessary to consider those who may deny spirituality, such as a self-identifying atheist. However, many atheists identify as being spiritual, possessing a secular version of spirituality, wherein spiritual values are not considered supernatural in nature. While considerable research advocating inclusion of spirituality in business is based on instrumental benefits, Brophy provides intrinsic reasons to include spirituality in business management, specifically that incorporation enhances organizational member freedom, and avoids alienating individuals from deeply held values. This scenario allows all stakeholders to be engaged in a manner conducive to optimal performance and flourishing (Brophy, 2015).

10.6 Workplace Spirituality Risks, Challenges, & Controversies

Dehler and Welsh (2010) described how the workplace has transformed during the transition from the industrial era, followed by the service economy, and into the current experience-based economy. The experience economy is characterized by a transition from a focus on the producer or the consumer to the relationship created between the producer and the consumer. In the experience economy, the producer's ability to align its services with the consumer's needs creates an experience that becomes an added value. In addition to product or service customization, producers must be able to collaborate with consumers to create an opportunity to personalize their experience (Dehler & Welsh, 2010).

Three dimensions of the New Economy are the most significant: environmental instability, information technology, and the democratization of organizations (Dehler & Welsh, 2010). The environmental consequences of climate change, pollution, biodiversity loss, and natural resource overconsumption will have both predictable and unpredictable global consequences. The present pace of technological advances is unprecedented in human history with the half-life of products, new product development cycle times, and advantages to first movers rapidly decreasing. Technology rapidly increases information flow within and across organizations, and organizations are becoming flatter to respond with greater speed, flexibility, and agility in this rapidly changing environment (Dehler & Welsh, 2010).

As employees develop new careers based on their abilities and expertise instead of organizational membership, work will become a more important emotional element. Work is transitioning from being the means to the end to becoming the end goal: a source of pleasure, satisfaction, and achievement. Purpose and meaning become more emotionally connected with and entrenched within work activities. This transition from why we do what we do to how we do it (Richards, 1995) spills over into the domain of spirituality (Dehler & Welsh, 2010).

There is a darker side to this spillover that deserves attention. The greatest danger may come from managerial attempts to exploit employees through instrumentality, by taking advantage of their spiritual beliefs to enhance the bottom line. Tension in the relationship between employees and their organizations will increase, partially because of business cycles. Business managers will make decisions about layoffs and facility closures during economic downturns (Hammonds, 1996) which will test the spirits of employees. There are also reasonable concerns about the appropriation of the bodies, minds, and hearts of employees by employers (Dehler & Welsh, 2010). Welch (1998) cautions about legitimate concerns that the boundary between the personal and professional lives of employees is being penetrated without considering the consequences. Welch further warns that business has already become cultlike with employees expected to believe in and trust management.

The new workplace presents a noteworthy paradox. As work dominates more of our lives and becomes fundamental to how we define ourselves, the workplace becomes an inspiring place of meaning and purpose, but also a potentially treacherous place (Kruger, 1999). Because the greatest determinants of workplace satisfaction are intrinsic and emotional (Schwartz, 2000, 400), workers risk creating opportunities for disappointment and emotional injury (Dehler & Welsh, 2010). Pink (2001) suggested that the era of the "benevolent corporation" and workplace loyalty has ended. In the new work environment, employee loyalty should be to profession which reduces vulnerability to toxic work environments, abusive supervisors and coworkers, and economic uncertainty. Loyalty to employer is replaced by loyalty to profession, colleagues, family, friends, and clients (Dehler & Welsh, 2010).

The future workplace becomes a place where employees not only perform work but create a participatory experience within the context of their work (Dehler & Welsh, 2010). The workplace transforms into a place for personal expression and fulfillment which provides meaning and purpose through the experience. Dehler and Welsh (2010) describe this opportunity to transcend the physical and mental demands of work into an emotional connection through performing *inspirited* work.

This new workplace requires that employees to be allowed to align their purpose with organizational mission and purpose (Dehler & Welsh, 2010). This organization may be a spiritually driven organization (SDO; see Chapter 3), whose goal is maximization of spiritual growth of both the organization and members (Yin & Mahrous, 2022). SDOs promote and enhance this spiritual growth by encouraging a culture, processes, and capabilities to transcend from being self-centered to we-centered or world-centered (Yin & Mahrous, 2022). Profitability is important. However, if spirituality is introduced solely to enhance profitability it will lose its currency for achieving meaning and employees will leave the organization. Workplace spirituality will only be effective if introduced to create a healthy workplace where individual and organizational purpose are united (Dehler & Welsh, 2010).

The key concerns of this new spiritual workplace are recognizing that employees bring their whole selves (body, mind, and soul) to work, and jobs must be designed to energize (*inspirit*) employees to relate to their work (Dehler & Welsh, 2010). This job design may occur at the organizational level, or at the individual level through job crafting (see Chapter 6). Job crafting expands job design by empowering employees to create their jobs by making physical and cognitive changes to the tasks and relational boundaries of their jobs (Wrzesniewski & Dutton, 2001). Employees alter the social and task components of their jobs by changing the task and relational boundaries to experience renewed meaning of work and self.

Contemporary workers must manage the traditional trade-offs of work-life balance and the new paradigm of intermittent project-based employment as free agents (Dehler & Welsh, 2010). Fluctuating economic cycles will require the most employee-focused organizations to adjust staff levels to remain profitable and competitive. Workers in this new paradigm must find passion and purpose by treating employment as a tool for personal growth. In the new workplace, organizations must create a thriving workplace where employees are not only productive, but can engage on a mental, emotional, and spiritual level with their tasks (Dehler & Welsh, 2010).

10.7 Concluding Thoughts

Workplace spirituality is beneficial for organizational success, and with the growing interest in both spirituality and workplace spirituality, it may provide an opportunity for contemporary organizations to be reinvented. While the organizational benefits of workplace spirituality are apparent, Marques (2006) found workplace spirituality to follow an inside-out approach with workers at different levels able to contribute toward the establishment of workplace spirituality. This may have been a turning point in workplace spirituality literature with most previous research focusing on the role of management in establishing a spiritual workplace. We are now beginning to understand the key role played by both individuals and management in workplace spirituality implementation, and benefit recognition.

While there are many theorized and actual organizational benefits of workplace spirituality, there are likewise concerns about management and organizational abuse of workplace spirituality (Brown, 2003; Case & Gosling, 2010; Cavanagh & Bandsuch, 2002; Jackson, 2000; Mitroff & Denton, 1999). Management may use workplace spirituality as a manipulative tool for the achievement of increased performance and productivity and total employee control, cloaked in a seemingly altruistic motive (Case & Gosling, 2010). Moreover, the goal of workplace spirituality research may simply be the extension of previous research to determine how more productivity can be exacted from employees by aligning their motivations, beliefs, and values with those of the corporation (Case & Gosling, 2010).

Clearly future research is necessary to understand how workplace spirituality may be implemented in a manner mutually beneficial for both employer and employee. However, the current workplace model has become less relevant, as employees challenge systems requiring that they leave a part of themselves at the door and embrace values they can no longer internalize. The changing global economy, environmental degradation, and growing wealth inequity require a new workplace model. The existing model need not be replaced or rejected, but rather recycled and remodeled into a model better representing the needs of present and future generations.

Case Study

Ascension Health is the nation's largest nonprofit health system, and the world's largest Catholic health system, operating in 19 states, and the District of Columbia (Ascension Health, n.d.a). Ascension employs 134,000 associates, has a network of 35,000 providers, and operates 140 hospitals and 40 senior living facilities. Ascension has implemented workplace spirituality programs at many facilities, guided by the *Framework for Fostering a Spirituality of Work* (Ascension Health, 2014). Spirituality is defined in the framework as distinguishable from "religion", and a universal reality possessed by every person, regardless of conscious awareness. The framework is inclusive of all religions, noting "spiritual development in the workplace can benefit from the personal gifts that all associates bring, and from the gifts of their various religious and spiritual traditions" (Ascension Health, 2004). The workplace spirituality mission at Ascension Health is described as:

> **Diverse**: At Ascension, we share universal experiences, but each is unique and personal to us as individuals. This diversity of experience strengthens our work toward our Mission.
> **Inclusive**: We benefit from the personal gifts all associates bring from their various religious beliefs, spiritual traditions, and backgrounds.
> **Relational**: We discover our wholeness in community. The community calls us to serve. We answer this call by listening with openness to our own experiences and those of others.
> **Life-giving and soul-satisfying**: We see our work as life-giving. It allows us to use our unique abilities to serve others, giving us purpose, personal meaning, and satisfaction.
> **Rooted in reality and truth**: Spirituality does not imply "out of the ordinary", but rather it leads us to be whole in the ordinary. Ordinary experiences and events are where we encounter the Sacred.
> **Discoverable in awareness**: Our spirit is where we are right now—where action and contemplation meet in the present moment.
> **Effective in service**: As we find meaning, satisfaction, and a sense of calling in our work, we give more fully of ourselves and are led toward excellence—faithful, passionate, and generous service (Ascension Health, n.d.b).

Reported program benefits include decreased costs, higher quality, patient safety, patient satisfaction, return on care, and return on investment. While Ascension noted the difficulty in quantifying direct cost reductions resulting from the program, the program has resulted in increased employee retention (Ascension Health, 2004), which is shown to reduce employee-rated recruitment and selection costs (Jacobs, 2011), and costs resulting from reduced productivity (Hausknecht & Trevor, 2011; Shaw, 2011), and service disruption (Hausknecht & Trevor, 2011). According to Eileen Jaskolski, Executive Vice President, Mission Integration at St. Mary's Hospital of Milwaukee, program participants are more effective and efficient, more mindful, and possess better active listening skills when working with patients and coworkers (Ascension Health, 2004). In 2004, Ascension Health received the International Spirit at Work Award, an award presented to secular and faith-based companies with explicit spiritual practices, policies, or programs (Gallagher, 2010).

Case Study Questions

1. How effective would Ascension Health's workplace spirituality program be if implemented in a non-faith-based healthcare organization?
2. How effective would Ascension Health's workplace spirituality program be if implemented in a for-profit healthcare organization?
3. How effective would Ascension Health's workplace spirituality program be if implemented in a non-healthcare organization?

References

Affeldt, D. L., & MacDonald, D. A. (2010). The relationship of spirituality to work and organizational attitudes and behaviors in a sample of employees from a health care system. *Journal of Transpersonal Psychology, 42*(2), 192–208. https://www.atpweb.org

Alderfer, C. P. (1972). *Existence, relatedness, and growth*. Free Press.

Ali, H., Shahid, T., Timsal, A., & Naseer, S. (2023). Sustainable careers under spiritual leadership and workplace spirituality: A subordinates' perspective during Covid 19. *Review of Applied Management and Social Sciences, 6*(1), 89–103. https://doi.org/10.47067/ramss.v6i1.286

Al-Qutop, M. A. Y., & Harrim, H. (2014). Spiritual organization: A path to organizational sustainable excellence. *International Business Research, 7*(8), 168. http://www.ccsenet.org

Altaf, A., & Awan, M. A. (2011). Moderating effect of workplace spirituality on the relationship of job overload and job satisfaction. *Journal of Business Ethics, 104*(1), 93–99. https://doi.org/10.1007/s10551-011-0891-0

Amanollahi Baharvand, Y., Piraysh, R., & Jafari, M. (2023). Investigating the role of organizational spirituality in happiness with the mediation of organizational belonging among human resources working in Eshtehard Industrial Tow. *Journal of Psychology New Ideas, 16*(20), 1–16. http://jnip.ir/article-1-891-en.html

Ashmos, D. P., & Duchon, D. (2000). Spirituality at work: A conceptualization and measure. *Journal of Management Inquiry, 9*(2), 134–145. https://doi.org/10.1177/105649260092008

Akhtar, S., bin Arshad, M. A., Mahmood, A., & Ahmed, A. (2015). Spiritual quotient and ethical values towards organizational stability. *International letters of Social and Humanistic Sciences, 58*, 107. https://www.learntechlib.org/p/176798/

Ascension Health. (2004). *Application for 2004 International spirit at work award*. https://tfsw.uark.edu/_resources/files/AscensionHealthAppl.pdf

Ascension Health. (2014). *Framework for fostering a spirituality of work*. Author. https://ascension.org/our-mission/workplace-spirituality

Ascension Health. (n.d.a). *About us*. https://about.ascension.org/about-us

Ascension Health. (n.d.b). *Workplace spirituality*. Author. https://ascension.org/our-mission/workplace-spirituality

Baldacchino, D. (2017). Spirituality in the healthcare workplace. *Religions, 8*(12), 260. https://doi.org/10.3390/rel8120260

Beehner, C. G., & Blackwell, M. J. (2016). The impact of workplace spirituality on food service worker turnover intention. *Journal of Management, Spirituality & Religion, 13*(4), 304–323. https://doi.org/10.1080/14766086.2016.1172251

Bell, E., & Taylor, S. (2003). The elevation of work: Pastoral power and the New Age work ethic. *Organization, 10*(2), 329–349. https://doi.org/10.1177/1350508403010002009

Biberman, J., & Whitty, M. (1997). A postmodern spiritual future for work. *Journal of Organizational Change Management, 10*(2), 130–138. https://doi.org/10.1108/09534819710160790

Biberman, J., Whitty, M., & Robbins, L. (1999). Lessons from Oz: Balance and wholeness in organizations. *Journal of Organizational Change Management, 12*(3), 243–252. https://doi.org/10.1108/09534819910274035

Bierly, P., Kessler, E., & Christensen, E. (2000). Organizational learning, knowledge and wisdom. *Journal of Organizational Change Management, 13*(6), 595–618. https://doi.org/10.1108/09534810010378605

Bormann, J. E., Becker, S., Gershwin, M., Kelly, A., Pada, L., Smith, T. L., & Gifford, A. L. (2006). Relationship of frequent mantram repetition to emotional and spiritual well-being in healthcare workers. *Journal of Continuing Education in Nursing, 37*(5), 218–224. https://doi.org/10.3928/00220124-20060901-02

Brophy, M. (2015). Spirituality incorporated: Including convergent spiritual values in business. *Journal of Business Ethics, 132*(4), 779–794. https://doi.org/10.1007/s10551-014-2337-y

Brown, R. B. (2003). Organizational spirituality: The sceptic's version. *Organization, 10*, 393–400. https://doi.org/10.1177/1350508403010002013

Burack, E. H. (1999). Spirituality in the workplace. *Journal of Organizational Change Management, 12*(4), 280–292. https://doi.org/10.1108/09534819910282126

Case, P., & Gosling, J. (2010). The spiritual organization: Critical reflections on the instrumentality of workplace spirituality. *Journal of Management, Spirituality and Religion, 7*(4), 257–282. https://doi.org/10.1080/14766086.2010.524727

Cavanagh, G. F., & Bandsuch, M. R. (2002). Virtue as a benchmark for spirituality in business. *Journal of Business Ethics, 38*(1–2), 109–117. https://doi.org/10.1023/A:1015721029457

Chatterjee, A., & Naqvi, F. (2010). Spirituality in organizational life: An empirical study of spirituality and job attitudes. *Abhigyan, 28*(3), 18–29. http://www.freepatentsonline.com/article/Abhigyan/249137536.html

Chawla, V., & Guda, S. (2010). Individual spirituality at work and its relationship with job satisfaction, propensity to leave and job commitment: An exploratory study among sales professionals. *Journal of Human Values, 16* (2), 157–167. https://doi.org/10.1177/097168581001600203

Cohen-Katz, J., Wiley, S. D., Capuano, T., Baker, D. M., & Shapiro, S. (2005). The effects of mindfulness-based stress reduction on nurse stress and burnout: Part II. *Holistic Nursing Practice, 19*(1), 26–35. https://journals.lww.com

Crawford, A., Hubbard, S. S., Lonis-Shumate, S. R., & O'Neill, M. (2009). Workplace spirituality and employee attitudes within the lodging environment. *Journal of Human Resources in Hospitality & Tourism, 8*, 64–81. https://doi.org/10.1080/15332840802274445

Daniel, J. L. (2010). The effect of workplace spirituality on team effectiveness. *Journal of Management Development, 29*(5), 442–456. https://doi.org/10.1108/02621711011039213

Daniel, J.L. (2012). *A study of the impact of workplace spirituality on employee outcomes: A comparison between US and Mexican employees* [Ph.D. dissertation]. Texas A&M International University, Laredo, TX, USA. https://repositories.tdl.org/tamiu-ir/bitstream/handle/2152.4/18/DANIEL-DISSERTATION-2012.pdf?sequence=1

Dehaghi, M. R., Goodarzi, M., & Arazi, Z. K. (2012). *The effect of spiritual values on employees' organizational commitment and its models*. World Conference on Business, Economics and Management (BEM-2012), May 4–6, 2012, Antalya, Turkey, 62(24), 159–166. https://doi.org/10.1016/j.sbspro.2012.09.025

De Diego-Cordero, C. R., Zurrón Pérez, M. P., Vargas-Martínez, A. M., Lucchetti, G., & Vega-Escaño, J. (2021). The effectiveness of spiritual interventions in the workplace for work-related health outcomes: A systematic review and meta-analysis. *Journal of Nursing Management, 29*(6), 1703–1712. https://doi.org/10.1111/jonm.13315

Dehler, G., & Welsh, M. (1994). Spirituality and organizational transformation: Implications for the new management paradigm. *Journal of Managerial Psychology, 19*(6), 17–26. https://doi.org/10.1108/02683949410070179

Dehler, G. E., & Welsh, M. A. (2010). The experience of work: Spirituality and the new workplace. In *Handbook of workplace spirituality and organizational performance* (pp. 75–88). Routledge.

Delbecq, A. (1999). Christian spirituality and contemporary business leadership. *Journal of Organizational Change Management, 12*(4), 345–349. https://doi.org/10.1108/09534819910282180

Dent, E. B., Higgins, M. E., & Wharff, D. M. (2005). Spirituality and leadership: An empirical review of definitions, distinctions, and embedded assumptions. *The Leadership Quarterly, 16*(5), 625–653. https://doi.org/10.1016/j.leaqua.2005.07.002

Dhiman, S. (2017). *Holistic leadership: A new paradigm for today's leaders.* Palgrave Macmillan.

Dhiman, S., & Marques, J. (2011). The role and need of offering workshops and courses on workplace spirituality. *Journal of Management Development, 30*(9), 816–835. https://doi.org/10.1108/02621711111164312

Doram, K., Chadwick, W., Bokovoy, J., Profit, J., Sexton, J. D., & Sexton, J. B. (2017). Got spirit? The spiritual climate scale, psychometric properties, benchmarking data and future directions. *BMC Health Services Research, 17*(1), 132–138. https://doi.org/10.1186/s12913-017-2050-5

Etzioni, A. (1961). *A comparative analysis of complex organizations.* Free Press.

Fernando, M. (2005). Workplace spirituality: Another management fad? In M. Adams & A. Alkhafaji (Eds.), *Business research yearbook: Global business perspectives, XII*(2). International Academy of Business Disciplines.
Fornaciari, C., & Lund Dean, K. (2001). Making the quantum leap: Lessons from physics on studying spirituality and religion in organizations. *Journal of Organizational Change Management, 14*(4), 335–351. https://doi.org/10.1108/EUM0000000005547
Foucault, M. (1978). Governmentality. In G. Burchell, C. Gordon, & P. Miller (Eds.), *The Foucault effect: Studies in governmentality*. Harvester.
Fry, L. W. (2003). Toward a theory of spiritual leadership. *The Leadership Quarterly, 14*(6), 693–729. https://doi.org/10.1016/j.leaqua.2003.09.001
Fry, L. W. (2005). Toward a theory of ethical and spiritual well-being, and corporate social responsibility through spiritual leadership. In C. Dunne, R. A. Giacolone & C. L. Jurkiewicz (Eds.), *Positive psychology and corporate responsibility*. Information Age Publishing.
Fry, L. W., & Slocum, J. (2008). Maximizing the triple bottom line through a strategic scorecard business model of spiritual leadership. *Organizational Dynamics, 31*(1), 86–96. https://doi.org/10.1016/j.orgdyn.2007.11.004
Gallagher, T. (2010, April 29). *Connecting with God while at work*. National Catholic Reporter. https://www.ncronline.org/news/spirituality/connecting-god-while-work
Garcia-Zamor, J. C. (2003). Workplace spirituality and organizational performance. *Public Administration Review, 63*(3), 355–363. https://doi.org/10.1111/1540-6210.00295
Garg, N. (2017). Workplace spirituality and employee well-being: An empirical exploration. *Journal of Human Values, 23*(2), 129–147. https://doi.org/10.1177/0971685816689741
Garg, N., Punia, B. K., & Jain, A. (2019). Workplace spirituality and job satisfaction: Exploring mediating effect of organization citizenship behaviour. *Vision: The Journal of Business Perspective, 23*(3), 287–296. https://doi.org/10.1177/0972262919850928
Geh, E., & Tan, G. (2009). Spirituality at work in a changing world: Managerial and research implications. *Journal of Management, Spirituality & Religion, 6*(4), 287–300. https://doi.org/10.1080/14766080903290093
Giacolone, R. A. (2004). A transcendent business education for the 21st century. *Academy of Management Learning and Education, 3*(4), 415–420. https://doi.org/10.5465/AMLE.2004.15112547

Giacalone, R. A., & Jurkiewicz, C. L. (2003). Toward a science of workplace spirituality. In R. A. Giacalone & C. L. Jurkeiwicz (Eds.), *Handbook of workplace spirituality and organizational performance*. M.E. Sharpe.

Giacalone, R. A., & Jurkiewicz, C. J. (2010). The science of workplace spirituality. In R. A. Giacalone & C. J. Jurkiewicz (Eds.), *Handbook of workplace spirituality and organizational performance* (2nd ed., pp. 3–26). M.E. Sharpe.

Giacalone, R. A., & Thompson, K. R. (2006). Business ethics and social responsibility education: Shifting the worldview. *Academy of Management Learning and Education, 5*(3), 266–277. https://doi.org/10.5465/AMLE.2006.22697016

Gibbons, P. (2000). Spirituality at work: Definitions, measures, assumptions, and validity claims. In J. Biberman & M. Whitty (Eds.), *Work and spirit: A reader of new spiritual paradigms for organizations* (pp. 111–131). University of Scranton Press.

Guillory, W. A. (1997). *The living organization—Spirituality in the workplace*. Innovations International.

Gull, G. A., & Doh, J. (2004). The "transmutation" of the organization: Towards a more spiritual workplace. *Journal of Management Inquiry, 13*(2), 128–139. https://doi.org/10.1177/1056492604265218

Gupta, M., Kumar, V., & Singh, M. (2013). Creating satisfied employees through workplace spirituality: A study of the private insurance sector in Punjab (India). *Journal of Business Ethics, 122*(1), 79–88. https://doi.org/10.1007/s10551-013-1756-5

Hadot, P. (1995). *Philosophy as a Way of Life*. Blackwell.

Hammonds, K. H. (1996, May 13). Soul-searching in the corner office. *Business Week*, 42–43.

Han, Y., Lu, X., & Li, Z. (2010). In search of excellence: Spiritual training program and junior managers counterproductive work behavior in China. *Human Resource Management International Digest, 18*(2), 10–12. https://doi.org/10.1108/09670731011028401

Hausknecht, J. P., & Trevor, C. O. (2011). Collective turnover at the group, unit, and organizational levels: Evidence, issues, and implications. *Journal of Management, 37*(1), 352–388. https://doi.org/10.1177/0149206310383910

Hicks, D. A. (2003). *Religion and the workplace: Pluralism, spirituality, leadership*. Cambridge University Press.

Hong, Y. J. (2012). Identifying spirituality in workers: A strategy for retention of community health professionals. *Journal of Social Service Research, 38*(20), 175–186. https://doi.org/10.1080/01488376.2011.615275

Hussain, S., Hussain, Z., & Hussain, S. (2020). Workplace spirituality and turnover intentions among the doctors working in private hospitals in Karachi, Pakistan: a cross sectional study. *British Journal of Medical & Health Sciences (BJMHS), 2*(8), 402–407. http://www.jmhsci.org/wp-content/uploads/2020/08/BJMHS450137.pdf

Iqbal, S., & Khan, M. I. (2020). Spirituality as a predictor of psychological well-being: An explanatory mechanism of religiosity and sustainable consumption. *Religions, 11*(12), 634. https://doi.org/10.3390/rel11120634

Jackson, J. (2000). Some practical implications of Mitroff and Denton's 'Spirituality in the Workplace' study. *Spirituality Leadership and Management Conference Proceedings*, SLAM, Sydney, Australia, pp. 20–25.

Jena, L. K. (2022). Does workplace spirituality lead to raising employee performance? The role of citizenship behavior and emotional intelligence. *International Journal of Organizational Analysis, 30*(6), 1309–1334. https://doi.org/10.1108/IJOA-06-2020-2279

Karakas, F. (2010). Spirituality and performance in organizations: A literature review. *Journal of Business Ethics, 94*(1), 89–106. https://doi.org/10.1007/s10551-009-0251-5

Kaur, J., & Dhilion, P. S. (2021). The impact of workplace spirituality on talent retention: Evidence from insurance sector in Punjab. *Turkish Online Journal of Qualitative Inquiry, 12*(10), 5642–5656.

King, D.B. (2008). *Rethinking claims of spiritual intelligence: A definition, model, & measure* [Unpublished master's thesis]. Trent University.

King, S., & Nicol, D. M. (1999). Organizational enhancement through recognition of individual spirituality: Reflections of Jaques and Jung. *Journal of Organizational Change Management, 12*(3), 234–243. https://doi.org/10.1108/09534819910274026

Kinjerski, V., & Skrypnek, B. J. (2008). The promise of spirit at work: Increasing job satisfaction and organizational commitment and reducing turnover and absenteeism in long-term care. *Journal of Gerontological Nursing, 34*(10), 17–25. https://doi.org/10.3928/00989134-20081001-03

Kolodinsky, R. W., Giacalone, R. A., & Jurkiewicz, C. L. (2008). Workplace values and outcomes: Exploring personal, organizational, and interactive workplace spirituality. *Journal of Business Ethics, 81*(2), 465–480. https://doi.org/10.1007/s10551-007-9507-0

Konz, G., & Ryan, F. (1999). Maintaining an organizational spirituality: No easy task. *Journal of Organizational Change Management, 12*(3), 200–210. https://doi.org/10.1108/09534819910273865

Korac-Kakabadse, A., & Korac-Kakabadse, N. (1997). Best practice in the Australian Public Service (APS): An examination of discretionary leadership. *Journal of Managerial Psychology, 12*(7), 187–193. https://doi.org/10.1108/02683949710181209

Korac-Kakabadse, N., Kouzmin, A., & Kakabadse, A. (2002). Spirituality and leadership praxis. *Journal of Managerial Psychology, 17*(3), 165–182. https://doi.org/10.1108/02683940210423079

Krahnke, K., Giacalone, R. A., & Jurkiewicz, C. L. (2003). Point-counterpoint: Measuring workplace spirituality. *Journal of Organizational Change Management, 16*(4), 396–405. https://doi.org/10.1108/09534810310484154

Kriger, M., & Hanson, B. (1999). A value-based paradigm for creating truly healthy organizations. *Journal of Organizational Change Management, 12*(4), 302–317. https://doi.org/10.1108/09534819910282144

Krishnakumar, S., & Neck, C. P. (2002). The "what", "why" and "how" of spirituality in the workplace. *Journal of Managerial Psychology, 17*(3), 153–164. https://doi.org/10.1108/02683940210423060

Kruger, P. (1999). Betrayed by work. *Fast Company, 29*, 182–196.

Lee, S., Lovelace, K. J., & Manz, C. C. (2013). Serving with spirit: An integrative model of workplace spirituality within service organizations. *Journal of Management, Spirituality & Religion, 11*(1), 45–64. https://doi.org/10.1080/14766086.2013.801023

Lips-Wiersma, M. (2003). Making conscious choices in doing research on workplace spirituality. *Journal of Organisational Change Management, 16*(4), 406–425. https://doi.org/10.1108/09534810310484163

Lund-Dean, K., Fornaciari, C. J., & McGee, J. (2003). Research in spirituality, religion, and work: Walking the line between relevance and legitimacy. *Journal of Organizational Change Management, 16*(4), 378–395. https://doi.org/10.1108/09534810310484145

Lund-Dean, K., & Safranski, S. R. (2008). No harm, no foul? Organizational intervention in workplace spirituality. *International Journal of Public Administration, 31*(4), 359–371. https://doi.org/10.1080/01900690701590751

McClelland, D. C. (1971). *Motivational trends in society*. General Learning Press.

Marques, J. F. (2006). The spiritual worker: An examination of the ripple effect that enhances quality of life in-and outside the work environment. *Journal of Management Development, 25*(9), 884–895. https://doi.org/10.1108/02621710610692089

Marschke, E., Prezioni, R., & Harrington, W. (2009). Professionals and executives support a relationship between organizational commitment and spirituality in the workplace. *Journal of Business and Economics Research, 7*(8), 33–48. https://doi.org/10.19030/jber.v7i8.2320

Marschke, E., Preziosi, R., & Harrington, W. J. (2011). How sales personnel view the relationship between job satisfaction and spirituality in the workplace. *Journal of Organizational Culture, Communications and Conflict, 15*(2), 71–110. https://www.researchgate.net

Maslow, A. (1970 [1954]). *Motivation and personality* (2nd ed.). Harper & Row.

McKee, M. C., Driscoll, C., Kelloway, E. K., & Kelley, E. (2011). Exploring linkages among transformational leadership, workplace spirituality and well-being in health care workers. *Journal of Management, Spirituality and Religion, 8*, 233–255. https://doi.org/10.1080/14766086.2011.599147

Mehta, Y., & Joshi, S. (2010, August 22). Impact of workplace spirituality on organization culture through improved employee productivity. In *AIMS International Conference on Value-based Management*. Presented at the meeting of Association of Indian Management Scholars, Houston, TX. http://www.aims-international.org

Milliman, J., Czaplewski, A. J., & Ferguson, J. (2003). Workplace spirituality and employee work attitudes: An exploratory empirical assessment. *Journal of Organizational Change Management, 16*(4), 426–447. https://doi.org/10.1108/09534810310484172

Mitchell, L. (2009). *Cyrus the Great and the obedience of the willing*. University of Exeter.

Mitroff, I. I., & Denton, E. A. (1999). A study of spirituality in the workplace. *Sloan Management Review, 40*, 83–92. https://sloanreview.mit.edu

Mirvis, P. H. (1997). "Soul work" in organizations. *Organization Science, 8*(2), 193–206. http://www.jstor.org/stable/2635311

Mousa, A. E. (2020). The impact of workplace spirituality on employee performance: Evidence from Abu Dhabi University. *International Business Research, 13*(5), 1–79. https://doi.org/10.5539/ibr.v13n5p79

Neal, J. A. (2001). Leadership and spirituality in the workplace. In R. N. Lussie & C. F. Achua (Eds.), *Leadership theory, application, skill development* (pp. 464–473). South-Western Cengage.

Neck, C. P., & Milliman, J. F. (1994). Thought self-leadership: Finding spiritual fulfillment in organizational life. *Journal of Managerial Psychology, 9*(6), 9–16. https://doi.org/10.1108/02683949410070151

Paloutzian, R. F., Emmons, R. A., & Keortge, S. G. (2003). Spiritual well-being, spiritual intelligence, and healthy workplace policy. In R. A. Giacolone & C. L. Jurkiewicz (Eds.), *Handbook of workplace spirituality and organizational performance* (pp. 123–137). M.E. Sharpe.

Pawar, B. S. (2008). Two approaches to workplace spirituality facilitation: A comparison and implications. *Leadership & Organization Development Journal, 29*(6), 544–567. https://doi.org/10.1108/01437730810894195

Pawar, B. S. (2009). Individual spirituality, workplace spirituality and work attitudes: An empirical test of direct and interaction effects. *Leadership & Organization Development Journal, 30*(8), 759–777. https://doi.org/10.1108/01437730911003911

Pawar, B. S. (2016). Workplace spirituality and employee well-being: An empirical examination. *Employee Relations, 38*(6), 975–994. https://doi.org/10.1108/ER-11-2015-0215

Pink, D. H. (2001). *Free agent nation: How America's new independent workers are transforming the way we live*. Warner Books.

Polley, D., Vora, J., & SubbaNarasimha, P. N. (2005). Paying the devil his due: Limits and liabilities of workplace spirituality. *International Journal of Organizational Analysis, 13*(1), 50–63. https://doi.org/10.1108/eb028997

Rathee, R., & Rajain, P. (2020). Workplace spirituality: A comparative study of various models. *Jindal Journal of Business Research, 9*(1), 27–40. https://doi.org/10.1177/2278682120908554

Reave, L. (2005). Spiritual values and practices related to leadership effectiveness. *Leadership Quarterly, 16*(5), 655–687. https://doi.org/10.1016/j.leaqua.2005.07.003

Rego, A., & Pina e Cunha, M. (2008). Workplace spirituality and organizational commitment: An empirical study. *Journal of Organizational Change Management, 21*(1), 53–75. https://doi.org/10.1108/09534810810847039

Riasudeen, S., & Prabavathy, R. (2011). Relationship of workplace spirituality and work attitude in manufacturing organization. *Global Management Review, 5*(4), 29–37. http://web.a.ebscohost.com

Richards, D. (1995). *Artful work: Awakening joy, meaning, and commitment in the workplace.* Berrett-Koehler.

Richards, T. A., Oman, D., Hedberg, J., Thoresen, C. E., & Bowden, J. (2006). A qualitative examination of a spiritually-based intervention and self-management in the workplace. *Nursing Science Quarterly, 9*(3), 231–239. https://doi.org/10.1177/0894318406289490

Saadatyar, F. S., Poursalimi, M., Al-Tabbaa, O., & Iannotta, M. (2020). Workplace spirituality as a source for competitive advantage: An empirical study. *International Journal of Organizational Analysis, 28*(3), 655–676. https://doi.org/10.1108/IJOA-10-2019-1915

Sadeghifar, J., Bahadori, M., Baldacchino, D., Radaabadi, M., & Jafari, M. (2013). Relationship between career motivation and perceived spiritual leadership in health professional educators: A correlational study in Iran. *Global Journal of Health Science, 6*, 1–10. https://doi.org/10.5539/gjhs.v6n2p145

Saks, A. M. (2011). Workplace spirituality and employee engagement. *Journal of Management, Spirituality & Religion, 8*(4), 317–340. https://doi.org/10.1080/14766086.2011.630170

Sapta, I. K. S., Rustiarini, N. W., Kusuma, I. G. A. E. T., & Astakoni, I. M. P. (2021). Spiritual leadership and organizational commitment: The mediation role of workplace spirituality. *Cogent Business & Management, 8*(1), e1966865. https://doi.org/10.1080/23311975.2021.1966865

Schwartz, T. (2000). The greatest sources of satisfaction in the workplace are internal and emotional. *Fast Company, 40*, 398–402.

Senge, P.M. (1990). *The fifth discipline: The art and practice of the learning organization.* Doubleday/Currency.

Shanafelt, T. D., Bradley, K. A., Wipf, J. E., & Back, A. L. (2002). Burnout and self-reported patient care in an internal medicine residency program. *Annals of Internal Medicine, 136*, 358–367. https://doi.org/10.7326/0003-4819-136-5-200203050-00008

Shapiro, S. L., Astin, J. A., Bishop, S. R., & Cordova, M. (2005). Mindfulness-based stress reduction for health care professionals: Results from a randomized trial. *International Journal of Stress Management, 12*(2), 164–176. https://doi.org/10.1037/1072-5245.12.2.164

Shaw, J. D. (2011). Turnover rates and organizational performance: Review, critique, and research agenda. *Organizational Psychology Review, 1*(3), 187–213. https://doi.org/10.1177/2041386610382152

Shrestha, A. K., & Jena, L. K. (2021). Interactive effects of workplace spirituality and psychological capital on employee negativity. *Management and Labour Studies, 46*(1), 59–77. https://doi.org/10.1177/0258042X20962994

Stead, J. G., & Stead, W. E. (2014). Building spiritual capabilities to sustain sustainability-based competitive advantages. *Journal of Management, Spirituality & Religion, 11*(2), 143–158. https://doi.org/10.1080/14766086.2013.832359

Strack, J. G., Fottler, M. D., & Kilpatrick, A. O. (2008). The relationship of health-care managers' spirituality to their self-perceived leadership practices. *Health Services Management Research, 21*, 236–247. https://doi.org/10.1258/hsmr.2008.008004

Sulastini, W. T. C., & Rajiani, I. (2023). Workplace spirituality as an alternative model for promoting commitment to change and change-oriented organisational citizenship behaviour. *Administrative Sciences, 13*(3), 86. https://doi.org/10.3390/admsci13030086

Thaker, K. B. (2009). Approaches to implement spirituality in business. *Journal of Human Values, 15*(2), 185–198. https://doi.org/10.1177/097168581001500208

Thompson, W.D. (2000). "Can you train people to be spiritual?" *Training and Development, 54*(12), 18–19. https://www.questia.com

Tischler, L., Biberman, J., & McKeage, R. (2002). Linking emotional intelligence, spirituality and workplace performance: Definitions, models and ideas for research. *Journal of Managerial Psychology, 17*(3), 203–218. https://doi.org/10.1108/02683940210423114

Usman, A., & Danish, R. Q. (2010). Spiritual consciousness in banking managers and its impact on job satisfaction. *International Business Research, 3*(2), 65–72. https://doi.org/10.5539/ibr.v3n2p65

Valasek, A. J. (2009). *Examining the relationships of spirituality and religiosity to individual productivity in the United States* [Doctoral dissertation]. Northcentral University.

Welch, J. (1998). Creed is good. *People Management, 24*, 28–33.

Whyte, W. H. (1965). *The organization man.* Penguin.

Wong, H. R., & Hu, J. S. (2011). Why do people hesitate? Perceived risk in workplace spirituality. *International Journal of Business and Management, 6*(11), 57–66. https://doi.org/10.5539/ijbm.v6n11p57

Word, J. (2012). Engaging work as a calling: Examining the link between spirituality and job involvement. *Journal of Management, Spirituality & Religion, 9*(2), 147–166. https://doi.org/10.1080/14766086.2012.688622

Wrzesniewski, A., & Dutton, J. E. (2001). Crafting a job: Revisioning employees as active crafters of their work. *Academy of Management Review, 26*, 179–201.

Yin, E., & Mahrous, A. (2022). Covid-19 global pandemic, workplace spirituality and the rise of spirituality-driven organisations in the post-digital era. *Journal of Humanities and Applied Social Sciences, 4*(2), 79–93. https://doi.org/10.1108/JHASS-11-2021-0177

Yong, J., Kim, J., Park, J., Seo, I., & Swinton, J. (2011). Effects of a spirituality training program on the spiritual and psychosocial well-being of hospital middle manager nurses in Korea. *Journal of Continuing Education in Nursing, 42*(6), 280–288. https://doi.org/10.3928/00220124-20101201-04

Zohar, D. & Marshall, I. (2000). *Spiritual intelligence: The ultimate intelligence.* Bloomsbury Publishing.

11 Sustainability for Organizational Success

11.1 Introduction

In this chapter, the business and organizational benefits of sustainability will be examined. However, this chapter would be incomplete if the focus was solely with the benefits of sustainability at the organizational level, without discourse concerning the methods by which organizational leaders have applied sustainability to achieve success. Existing literature will be synthesized in order to demonstrate the benefits, and the chapter concludes with a case study to stimulate critical thinking and provide instructional tools for academic use and practical application.

While the goal of traditional capitalism is with making money, there is growing concern within and without industry about how that money is made. In this chapter, the business and organizational benefits of sustainability will be examined, along with the risks and costs of sustainability inaction. Methods and models of sustainable business implementation will be examined, along with examples of companies that have implemented and benefited from sustainable business strategies. Sustainability is presented from a practical business perspective, transcending environmental and political agendas. Rather than adding cost and additional work, sustainability reduces costs, increases profitability, and introduces

C. G. Beehner, *Spirituality, Sustainability, and Success*, Palgrave Studies in Workplace Spirituality and Fulfillment, https://doi.org/10.1007/978-3-031-47643-3_11

innovative opportunities for marketplace differentiation. The contributions and roles of sustainability NGOs and IGOs will be examined.

The current economic system has placed colossal pressure on the planetary environment while only gratifying the needs of about one-quarter of the inhabitants. As both the number of inhabitants, and the proportion becoming consumers and producers expands, traditional business models will become less successful, forcing companies to develop innovative, sustainable solutions. The key to long-term business survival is the recognition that Sustainability = Innovation (Nidumolu et al., 2009). Sustainability and social factors are rarely considered business model components (Jones & Upward, 2014). However, while the goal of traditional capitalism is with making money, there is growing concern within and without industry about how that money is made (Soyka, 2012). Sustainability management challenges the fundamental assumptions of the dominant economic worldview, such as the need for consumer satisfaction maximization and utility optimization, both of which are grounded on a belief in reasonable, calculable growth (Opdebeeck, 2014).

11.2 The Sustainable Business Case and Benefits

Contemporary business leaders are increasingly recognizing the role business plays in sustainability, and the role that sustainability should play in business success. Business sustainability is increasingly understood to be both the right thing and the smart thing to do (Soyka, 2012). Regardless of whether the motive is altruistic and genuine, many corporate managers recognize the increased consumer demand for sustainable products and services, and the increasing number of competitors incorporating sustainability into their business models (Beehner, 2017). Numerous multinational corporations (MNCs) have incorporated sustainability into their mission and vision, with 93% of global CEOs stating sustainable development is important to future company success (Accenture, 2010).

The results of a 2011 MIT Sloan Management Review survey of nearly 3,000 global business leaders indicated two-thirds of respondents believed sustainability was essential to compete in today's market, an increase from 55% in the previous year (Haanaes et al., 2012). According to respondents, 70% of companies surveyed have permanently included sustainability in their management agendas, with most having done so since 2005 (Haanaes et al., 2012). Corporate Knights founder Toby Heaps has identified several areas in which Global 100 companies outperform companies in the MSCI All Country World Index (ACWI), an index of stocks designed to represent a wide range of global companies. While 80% of Global 100 firms pay top executives receive higher bonuses for meeting sustainability targets, only 23% of ACWI companies offer such bonuses. Global 100 companies are 25% more energy efficient than ACWI companies. While companies investing heavily in sustainability might be expected to incur greater costs and reduced profitability, the cumulative return of Global 100 companies is 24 percentage points higher than the ACWI benchmark. With 19 members, the United States had the greatest number of Global 100 companies, followed by France with 12, the UK with 11, Canada and Germany each with six, and the Netherlands with five. Industries represented in the Global 100 include industrials, financials, information technology, healthcare, materials, utilities, real estate, consumer staples, consumer discretionary, energy, and telecommunication services (Kauflin, 2017).

Recognizing sustainability to be more than just an environmental gesture, numerous companies are realizing sustainability makes long-term economic sense (Spector, 2012). Spector identified 10 reasons companies should be concerned with sustainability: cost savings; consumer demand; risk mitigation; leadership; tax incentives; employee retention; brand reputation and publicity; resource limitation; keeping up with the competition; and, new revenue opportunities (Spector, 2012). The previously mentioned justifications for business sustainability are echoed by many scholars and practitioners and will be discussed throughout this chapter. The following are some of the benefits identified with having a sustainable business strategy:

- Gaining competitive advantage from goodwill.

- Preference of green brands by consumers.
- Recruiting and retaining good employees.
- Saving money from efficiency and waste reduction.
- Making money from creative forms of waste re-generation.
- Sustainability as a point of differentiation.
- Shaping future of industry.
- Becoming preferred supplier.
- Providing competitive edge to customers.
- Changing image and brand (Senge, 2008).

Sustainable business models have been organized into eight archetypes: maximize material productivity and energy efficiency; create value from waste; substitute existing processes with renewables and natural processes; deliver functionality, not ownership; adoption of a stewardship role; encouraging sufficiency; re-purpose the business for society and environment; and, developing scale-up solutions (Bocken et al., 2014). The purpose of these archetypes is development of a common vernacular for acceleration of sustainable business models development in theory and practice.

Maximizing material productivity and energy efficiency requires producing more with fewer resources, while generating less waste, emissions, and pollution. Creating value from waste requires conversion of waste into practical, useful inputs for production and more efficient capacity usage. Substituting existing technologies with renewables and natural processes involves mitigating environmental influences, while increasing business resilience by addressing the limitations presented by non-renewable resources and existing production systems. Delivering functionality rather than ownership necessitates that the production of services enables meeting user needs absent product ownership (e.g., car sharing). Adopting a stewardship role describes the proactive involvement of all stakeholders in their long-term health and well-being considerations. Encouraging sufficiency involves seeking to actively reduce consumption and production. Re-purposing the business for society/environment requires the prioritization of social and environmental benefit delivery in parallel with profit maximization, through collaborative integration among businesses, communities, and related stakeholders. Developing scale-up solutions requires the scalable delivery of sustainable solutions that maximize environmental and societal benefits (Bocken et al., 2014). Although each of the previous solutions can be applied in isolation, different archetypes may be combined because lasting sustainability will require innovative combinations of archetypes (e.g., deliver functionality rather than ownership, while maximizing energy and material efficiency; Bocken et al., 2014).

Sustainability requires dedication, commitment, and follow-through from upper management if rank-and-file employees are expected to sail the sustainability ship into uncharted territory. However, Rogers (2016) suggests businesses embracing sustainability experience increased morale and productivity, regardless of increasing or decreasing sales. Rogers identified six major advantages for practicing sustainability: improved brand image and competitive advantage; increased productivity and reduced costs; increased regulatory compliance capability; employee and investor attraction and retention; waste reduction; and, happy shareholders.

Support for improved brand image comes from Natural Marketing Institute survey results indicating 58% of more than 53,000 U.S. consumers surveyed consider company environmental impact when making purchasing decisions. Respondents indicated being more likely to purchase from sustainability-practicing companies that demonstrate positive track records in individual, social, and environmental values. Resource conservation encouragement and practice not only improves brand awareness, but also reaches a deeper level with employees, their families, and external stakeholders (Rogers, 2016).

Sustainability skeptics suggest sustainable business practices, reduce corporate profit (Rogers, 2016), and erode competitiveness (Nidumolu et al., 2009). Dissenting executives behave as if faced with the choice between the social benefits of sustainable product development, and the related processes and the financial costs (Nidumolu et al., 2009). However, sustainable business practice development produces efficient operations that streamline work and conserve resources, further enhancing employee productivity and cost reductions. Cost reduction also encompasses energy conservation strategies ranging from turning off unnecessary lights (or installing occupancy sensors), and insulating walls to more sophisticated strategies such as geothermal heating and cooling system installation. Strategies offering greater overall impact will be more costly, however, long-term results justify the investment (Rogers, 2016).

Waste reduction is likely the simplest and most obvious method of engagement in sustainable practices. Waste reduction began in the 1990s with offices providing collection containers for recycling aluminum cans. The effort has increased to encompass paper reduction and recycling, value engineering of products, reworking or developing new processes for raw material reduction, and replacement of incandescent lights with fluorescent, and more recently LED lights (Rogers, 2016).

Sustainable business practices not only reduce operating costs but often result in increased profitability. Findings of a Deutsche Bank study (2012) analyzing more than 100 academic studies indicated companies with high environmental, social, and governance factor ratings outperformed the market in medium and long-range terms. Moreover, all the study findings demonstrated companies with high corporate social responsibility (CSR) and high environmental, social, and governance (ESG) incurred lower capital costs. Further, 89% of studies showed high ESG companies displayed market-based outperformance, while 85% displayed accounting-based outperformance (Deutsche Bank, 2012). Moreover, high sustainability businesses have outperformed low sustainability businesses in terms of both stock market performance and profitability, demonstrating stock market performance 4.8% higher than low sustainability businesses over one 18-month period (Eccles et al., 2012a). Over longer periods, high-sustainable business share prices outperform low-sustainable business prices, with an investment of $1 at the beginning of 1993 in a high-sustainable value-weighted portfolio having increased in value to $22.60 by the end of 2010, compared with $15.40 for a low-sustainable value-weighted portfolio (Rogers, 2016).

McKinsey & Company reported similar findings in their research of 40 companies, seeking to understand sustainability challenges, and identify practical recommendations for adding value through sustainability (Bonini & Swartz, 2014). According to an earlier McKinsey & Company survey (2011), an increasing number of companies are managing sustainability for process improvement, growth, and adding value to their companies rather than simply focusing on reputation.

Companies are also integrating sustainability across multiple processes with 57% of survey respondents reporting the integration of sustainability into strategic planning, including mission and values, external communications, supply-chain management, and budget. Growth, risk management, and return on capital are three ways identified by the researchers in which industry leaders indicate sustainability creates value. More than half of respondents in the leaders category reported sustainability is aligned with their goals, mission, and values, and nearly one-half indicated sustainability strengthens competitive position (McKinsey, 2011).

Respondents to the McKinsey survey (2011) cited multiple value creation levers for the next five years: managing corporate reputation, capturing sustainability trends in the business portfolio, and committing research and development (R&D) capital to sustainable products. Identified barriers to value creation include: lack of capabilities and lack of sustainability performance incentives. More than one-half of respondents agreed company sustainability performance to be somewhat important in attracting and retaining employees, with companies implementing sustainability more likely to succeed in employee retention (McKinsey, 2011). The survey results provided insight into the specific practices of businesses that treat sustainability holistically, with sustainability embedded in business practices and actively managed (Bonini & Görner, 2011). Sustainability-oriented companies first determine baseline performance on sustainability issues, and then develop a portfolio of initiatives to create value in those areas. While many business leaders understand the impact of carbon emissions or human rights on operations, few comprehend the impact of these factors on the entire value chain (Bonini & Görner, 2011).

A new group of stakeholders has emerged within the sustainability movement: financial services and insurance companies (Esty & Winston, 2016), with an increasing number of insurance and reinsurance giants recognizing the costs of managing risks from environmental catastrophes. The combined costs of hurricanes Harvey, Irma, and Maria, along with other natural disasters in 2017, amount to a record US$135 billion for the insurance industry (MunichRe, 2018). When combined with uninsured losses, 2017 natural disasters cost a staggering US$330 billion, an amount only surpassed in 2011 which included the Tohoku earthquake in Japan, and amounted to US$354 billion in 2017 dollars (MunichRe, 2018). The U.S. share of losses in 2017 totaled 50% as compared to the long-term average of 32%, while the combined North American share totaled 83% (MunichRe, 2018).

While a small percentage of the global population still denies that climate change is occurring, or that humans are contributing to climate change, most major business leaders and entire industries are actively engaged in the conversation. In response to climate change, insurance companies are citing the need for resilience investment as an antecedent to the effects of climate change and natural disasters. According to Samantha Medlock (2018), Senior Vice President Capital, Science & Policy for Willis Towers Watson, every $1US of resilience investment produces a $4US return on investment.

Moody's Investor Services has placed US coastal states and municipalities on notice that they must prepare for climate change or risk increased borrowing costs (Flavelle, 2017). Moody's announced they will begin incorporating risks from sea level rise and increased storm intensity into credit rating calculations, a decision driven by investor pressure for business transparency concerning how climate change is incorporated into the ratings process. While no climate change-related credit rating downgrades have been reported to date, and no specific municipalities have been identified as having the greatest exposure, Moody's identified six climate change risk indicators as the share of economic activity derived from coastal areas, hurricane and extreme-weather damage in proportion to the overall economy, and the proportion of homes in a flood plain, suggesting Texas, Florida, Georgia, and Mississippi are among the highest climate change risk states (Flavelle, 2017).

Moody's is a bond rating agency that assigns ratings based upon the risk of default of public and private organizations that raise funds through issuing bonds. The interest rate paid by the bond issuer becomes higher as the risk of default increases. Coastal municipalities are at risk from declining property values (and their corresponding decline in tax revenue), and increased spending on sea walls, storm drains, and flood-resistant buildings (Flavelle, 2017). Rob Moore, senior policy analyst at the Natural Resources Defense Council, argued increased attention from rating agencies could push cities to reconsider allowable building locations (Flavelle, 2017). Some investors worry Moody's outlook about the desire of cities to adapt to climate change risks is too optimistic. Shalini Vajjhala, a former Obama administration official who is now a municipal climate change preparation consultant, argues nothing will happen on a large scale until cities face consequences for failure to act, such as a ratings downgrade (Flavelle, 2017).

In stark contrast to the colossal financial risk posed by human-induced climate change, an equally substantial financial risk is presented by efforts to reduce carbon emissions generated by fossil fuels. Citibank recently reported in an examination of the issue of unburnable carbon and stranded assets, in which countries, industries, and companies they are located, and found that at current prices, around \$100 trillion of assets could be 'carbon stranded', if not already economically so. These assets include untapped fossil fuel reserves, and the potential obsolescence of fossil fuel infrastructure. The clear loser stands to be the coal industry, although researchers also considered an upside to fossil fuel reduction and carbon emission mitigation to be the economics and potential offered by carbon capture and storage (Channell et al., 2015).

Inspired by philosopher and economist Rudolf Steiner, Soppe (2014) developed two propositions to support sustainable finance. Steiner proposed all material objects such as consumer goods, capital goods, and services are subject to depreciation, and therefore diminish in quality and value over time. However, money does not intrinsically depreciate because money represents a right to future purchasing power which is fundamentally timeless in nature, further implying that over time, money becomes 'overvalued' relative to goods and services. Moreover, interest payments lead to social injustice through wealth because the quality of purchased goods and services can only be maintained through labor inputs, while the interest mechanism causes capital to increase in value (Soppe, 2014).

Soppe's (2014) first proposition is the average interest rate should fluctuate with the real economic growth rate of growth of the real economy, which is representative of organic growth in economic processes. While lower interest rates are undesirable due to economic opportunity impacts, higher interest rates are equally undesirable due to the required implicit additional positive time preference. His second proposition concerns the imbalanced accumulation of wealth. Assuming the existence of a positive interest rate, the absence of financial taxes and bankruptcies, financial capital increases exponentially. A structural imbalance between the monetary sector and the real economy creates the illusion of purchasing power. The exponential financial capital growth needs to be institutionally managed for achievement of economic sustainability (Soppe, 2014).

While near the end of the previous century, business managers viewed sustainability as adding nothing but cost to their organization, contemporary business managers recognize sustainability to be beneficial to maintaining a long-term competitive advantage (Hind et al., 2013). According to C. R. Herro (2018), Vice President of Innovation and Sustainability at Meritage Homes, "sustainability is not a compromise, it is a solution". Former Maryland Governor and 2016 U.S. Presidential candidate Martin O'Malley (2018) describes climate change to be the biggest business opportunity in 100 years. Environmental challenges create sustainable business opportunities (Bonini & Görner, 2011), with the clean technology market expected to reach $1.6 trillion by 2020 (McKinsey, 2011).

11.3 Methods and Models for Sustainable Business Implementation

Sustainability is a new development in holistic management that includes the entire business system from beginning to end, incorporating concepts such as enterprise thinking and life cycle thinking (Rainey, 2008). Successful sustainable business requires transparency, openness, and accountability. While accountability is usually mandated or pressured by outside sources, openness and transparency are voluntary, and as such may stimulate trust (Rainey, 2008). The changing business context of the twenty-first century is driving demand for openness and transparency, necessitating businesses desiring value creation for sustained business success must embrace openness and transparency within their business models (Rainey, 2008).

Four organizational configurations were identified as successful sustainable business structures: interdependent cost leader, bottom-up organic differentiator, timeless differentiator, and indifferent differentiator (Walker et al., 2015). These structures vary in terms of stakeholder focus, mechanistic versus organic structure, and top management participation, suggesting there is not one recipe for achieving successful sustainability, but multiple depending on organizational structure. Four main points have been suggested for implementing and maintaining a sustainable business or organization: educate and communicate with supply-chain partners about sustainability; develop a comprehensive global policy; measure environmental impacts; and, foster a culture of creativity and innovation (Banerjee & Shastri, 2010). Townsend (2006) identified five segments of a company to be addressed in becoming environmentally responsible or sustainable: mission, employees, operations, facilities and sites, and products and/or services.

A report from British Telecommunications (BT) and Cisco suggests sustainability can increase business innovation and profitability, providing the following ten steps taken by businesses to become sustainability-driven:

1. Make innovating for sustainability part of overall corporate vision.
2. Formulate a strategy with sustainability at its heart.
3. Embed sustainability in every part of your business.
4. Emphasize actions, not words.
5. Set up effective board-level governance to make sustainability matter.
6. Set firm rules.
7. Bring stakeholders on board by engaging them.
8. Use people power through recruitment, staffing, training, and rewards.
9. Join networks focused on sustainability.
10. Think beyond reporting—align all business systems with the company's sustainability vision (GreenBiz Staff, 2008).

On the surface, sustainability might seem to be a "feel good" notion for successful businesses who want to give something back to society, or perhaps look better in the eyes of one or more stakeholder groups. A deeper look reveals sustainability to be a business process for increased revenue and profitability, and reduced costs, in addition to the favorable view customers and stakeholders might have of a business that has "gone green". Often, a business establishes a sustainability program or strategy because a competitor has done so, or worse yet, in response to an environmental mishap. Environmental accidents can create public relations nightmares, destroy companies and careers, and reduce shareholder value by billions of dollars (Esty & Winston, 2006).

Companies that do not have a sustainable approach within their strategy risk missing opportunities influenced by the increasingly "green" consumer (Esty & Winston, 2006). However, rather than join a movement that is well underway, many businesses have pioneered the shift toward sustainable business practices, creating a competitive advantage. These smart companies move ahead of the curve, taking sustainable actions to lower both financial and operational risk by providing added degrees of freedom to operate, profit, and expand (Esty & Winston, 2006). The following "green-to-gold plays" have been identified as methods of increasing profit and competitive edge through sustainability:

1. Eco-efficiency—improve resource efficiency.
2. Eco-expense reduction—cut environmental costs and regulatory burden.
3. Value chain eco-efficiency—lower costs upstream and downstream.
4. Eco-risk control—manage environmentally driven business risk.
5. Eco-design—meet customer environmental needs.
6. Eco-sales and marketing—build product position and customer loyalty on green attributes.
7. Eco-defined new market space—promote value innovation and develop breakthrough products.
8. Intangible value—build corporate reputation and trusted brands (Esty & Winston, 2016).

In almost any sector one can now find leading companies labeled high sustainability organizations (HSOs) by Eccles and colleagues (2012b), engaged in transformational sustainability initiatives with multiple stakeholders in their value chains (Tideman et al., 2013). These HSO sustainability initiatives involve a praxis of redefining and restructuring their production processes and supply chains to meet existing and future needs (Tideman et al., 2013). Goleman and Lueneberger (2010) have identified three phases for driving sustainable change initiatives within a business. The first phase involves making the case for change wherein the sustainable leader must be adept at collaborating and influencing others to become consciously reactive in responding to sustainability challenges. A clear and compelling case must be made for change so that sustainability becomes a strong directive that is ubiquitous throughout the organization. The second phase requires translating vision into action wherein the organization excels at results delivery with strong commercial sense for sustainability to become commercially oriented within the business. The third phase requires expanding boundaries wherein organizational leaders proficient at anticipating and evaluating long-term sustainability trends to make sustainability a strategic orientation.

Entrepreneurship and innovation are essential skills for incorporating sustainability into organizational and business models. The combination of entrepreneurship, innovation, and sustainability is of relevance from a European perspective based upon the European Commission (EC) focus on corporate social responsibility (CSR) and sustainability, alongside the prominent role of sustainability in the European Union (EU) Framework Programme (Wagner, 2012). Moreover, the Lisbon Agenda, with a focus on European quality of life, requires firms reconcile sustainability and profitability, with innovation and entrepreneurship identified as essential for alleviating sustainability demands. While a firm may altruistically pursue sustainability-oriented or socially responsible activities, products, or services, the resulting product or corporate image improvement may result in increased sales volumes or prices which may cause some stakeholder groups to question whether the motives were ever truly altruistic. However, altruistically motivated sustainability-oriented or socially responsible activities should result in reputation gains and economic benefits, whereas similar activities motivated by self-interest will likely reduce economic benefits or even cause disbenefits (Wagner, 2012).

There are multiple methods through which to implement sustainability at the business or organizational level. Systems thinking is a management discipline based upon understanding an organization or industry as a system, by examining linkages and interactions between components constituting the entirety of the defined system (Tate, 2009). Enterprise thinking recognizes the business as a connected system, not merely individual, disconnected components (Rainey, 2006). The premise of enterprise thinking is that sustainability should pervade the entire organization, influencing all functions, rather than exist as an independent function. The benefits of approaching sustainability through enterprise thinking are: improved understanding of the organization and relationship with other organizations; flexibility in responding to customer and stakeholder needs and demands; increased organizational effectiveness culminating from an integrated approach; comprehensive reduced organizational waste; and, improved communication and relationships across organizational functions (Rainey, 2006).

Another method through which to implement sustainability at the business or organizational level is life cycle thinking (LCT), and the related life cycle assessment (LCA) tool. Life cycle thinking (LCT) is an innovative methodology for examination, assessment, and improvement of products, processes, and technologies (Rainey, 2006). While the focus of enterprise thinking is strategic management, LCT is operationally focused, substituting the current state of a program, process, or technology with a more ideal state. LCA describes the cradle-to-grave analysis of a product's environmental impacts throughout the entire life cycle: raw materials; manufacturing; delivery; consumption; and, disposal (Rainey, 2006). LCA is a business tool useful for protection and improvement of the business environment, natural environment, and the participants of both. Rainey (2006) identifies seven adverse business process/product impacts as: destruction; degradation; damage; depletion; disruption; disturbance; and, defects.

Hofstra (2014) examined nature-inspired entrepreneurship models, defining *eco-innovation* as the use of ecological knowledge to produce ecological progress. While numerous companies have been developing ecological innovations primarily designed to reduce environment-related costs, eco-efficiency does not guarantee environmental effectiveness.

Innovation with a regenerative character creates new opportunities for eco-innovation, producing products and services based upon an understanding of the interconnectedness and unity of all physical and spiritual life. Eco-innovators acknowledge nature as both mentor and teacher based upon an understanding of the synergistic relationship humankind has with nature (Hofstra, 2014). The 'cradle-to-cradle' concept of eco-innovation promotes the use of waste as a manufacturing resource. The 'bioneers' (biological pioneer) movement is based on a neologism coined by social entrepreneur Kenny Ausubel (Utne Reader, 1999), suggesting innovative methods to confront and mimic design and innovation in a life-conducive way. This viewpoint introduces a completely innovative domain for entrepreneurs, simultaneously awakening humankind to the magnitude of opportunities, instruction, and wonder our planet can provide (Hofstra, 2014).

The pathway to a sustainable economy might include the following features: a system encouraging consumption minimization, or imposing personal and institutional limits on resource consumption; a system structured for societal and environmental benefit maximization, instead of economic growth maximization; a closed-loop system where waste is no longer discarded into the environment, reusing and repairing instead of recycling; a system emphasizing delivery of functionality and experience, rather than product ownership; a system designed to provide fulfilling, rewarding work for all individuals, enhancing human creativity and skills; and, a system where collaboration and sharing replace aggressive competition (Bocken et al., 2014, developed from Jackson, 2009).

Individuals at all organizational levels are essential for successful sustainable business implementation. Tariq and colleagues (2016) found empowered employees were more motivated to perform environmental tasks which promote sustainability, adding that an empowered, motivated green workforce have a significant impact on organization profitability and productivity. Two enterprise-wide initiatives enable companies to become sustainable: top management focuses on sustainability which facilitates rapid change; and, recruiting and retaining the right employees (Nidumolu et al., 2009). Three-fourths of current U.S. workforce entrants consider social responsibility and environmental commitment to be important criteria in employer selection. Because employees who are satisfied with their employers' positions on those issues enjoy working for them, companies embracing sustainability may experience more effortless talent recruiting and retention.

Sustainability strategy implementation can be difficult because it requires large-scale change, something few companies desire or do well (Eccles et al., 2012b). Implementation of a sustainability strategy has been described as a two-stage process. The first stage includes restructuring organizational identity through leadership commitment and stakeholder engagement. The second stage involves arranging the new identity through employee engagement and strategy execution. During stage two, the two stages strengthen and support each other. Businesses with an established organizational culture and strong capacity for change, a commitment to innovation, and high levels of trust will have a competitive advantage. Sustainable business leaders develop a competitive advantage by accepting a long-term decision-making horizon, accepting greater risk when pursuing sustainability, and demonstrating a contagious personal commitment to sustainability (Eccles et al., 2012b).

A sustainable business strategy would be incomplete without an effective marketing plan. Dean (2014) presents five opportunities for sustainable or environmental marketing. The Pure-Green Play markets the environmental attributes of products and services to environmentally concerned consumers. Green Status involves marketing the status attributes of a product or service in which customers identify or affiliate with a brand or image, making a personal statement. Functional Value Propositions market the functional value of green products, as high quality, efficient, and safe. Commercial or Industrial Markets involves marketing sustainable attributes to commercial buyers who understand efficiency and performance improvement, possibly desiring to be identified as sustainable. Finally, the Holistic Brand involves companies creating a brand that is affiliated with sustainability, creating consumer identification with the feel or image of the company. Success through environmental product differentiation requires three conditions be met: willingness to pay (customers must be willing to pay more for sustainable products through perceiving an overall long-term savings through reduced long-term ownership costs); credible information (customers want to believe the company claims as not being "green washing");

and, barriers to imitation (innovation should not be easily replicated by competition; Reinhardt, 2008).

In Chapter 6, I briefly introduced flourishing as a strongly sustainable business model conceived by Jones and Upward (2014), based upon a holistic view of organizational operation consistent with a planet containing finite, shared resources, and a collective societal future. Limited research is available regarding strongly sustainable or flourishing business models, which Jones and Upward propose are characterized by stakeholder design of strongly sustainable enterprises for the objective of whole system flourishing across ecosystems and social systems. A flourishing organization is a purpose-oriented organization. The flourishing or strongly sustainable framework provides a conceptual framework of an anticipatory system of business governance, theoretically maintainable, and methodologically evaluated by several applications with small, medium, and large enterprises. The flourishing framework provides a formal foundation for business model description, regardless of current level of sustainability performance, and is similar to the triple bottom line in that the flourishing model contains a "tri-profit" incorporating ecological and societal components with economic profitability. Within the three "tri-profit" boundaries reside four perspectives on the definition of an enterprise, which are a strongly sustainable adaptation of Kaplan and Norton's (1996) Balanced Scorecard: stakeholder; product, learning and development; process; and, measurement (Jones & Upward, 2014).

The Jones and Upward business model is consistent with Rosen's (1991) system model, also represented as an anticipatory system, represented as a natural system containing an internal predictive model of both system and environment, enabling dynamic changes of state based upon forecasts of potential future events (Jones & Upward, 2014). The anticipatory system model is a proactive, rather than reactive system, and is an appropriate lens for the examination of business models. While traditional system models are feedback-based, an anticipatory system consists of feed-forward loops which enable participants to anticipate preferred future outcomes. The anticipatory model assumes a continual adaptation of the living system (e.g., a business and employees) with its environment (Jones & Upward, 2014).

Recent business model innovation research (Chesbrough, 2010; Kiron et al., 2013) has led to definitive inquiry into the development of preferred operating and strategic assumptions from which to guide business model design and decision-making. However, these approaches are frequently "too little, too late" because when assimilated into business model assumptions, they maintain the status quo, resulting in limited ecosystemic improvement (Jones & Upward, 2014). A systemic design process based on solid sustainable business models can enable a diversity of organizational stakeholders to adopt business strategies that measure success in terms of environmental, social, and monetary benefits. To achieve such a radically redefined business model, the business model definition must transit from monetary value generation toward a holistically shared value (Porter & Kramer, 2011).

11.4 Examples of Successful Sustainable Businesses

Research findings demonstrate sustainability to be an abundant source of organizational and technological innovations yielding both bottom-line and top-line results (Nidumolu et al., 2009). Becoming environment-friendly lowers business costs because companies reduce input consumption, along with generating additional revenue from improved products. The business sustainability initiative is beginning to transform the competitive landscape, forcing companies to reconsider how they develop products, technologies, processes, and business models. By considering sustainability to be a prevailing goal, early movers will develop competencies that rivals may be unable to duplicate. Sustainable business enterprises undergo five distinct stages, facing different challenges at each stage, necessitating development of new capabilities to overcome those challenges. The five stages of developing a sustainable business are: viewing compliance as opportunity; making value chains sustainable; designing sustainable products and services; developing new business models; and, creating next-practice platforms (Nidumolu et al., 2009). These five stages will be examined throughout this section with examples of businesses that have successfully implemented sustainable business strategies and programs.

The first steps companies take to become sustainable involve conformance with legal standards, and voluntary codes, such as the Greenhouse Gas Protocol, and the Forest Stewardship Council code (Nidumolu et al., 2009). While many businesses are tempted to achieve minimal environmental compliance, sustainable business leaders recognize and view compliance as an opportunity. Enterprises focusing on meeting or exceeding emerging norms become first movers, gaining additional time to experiment with materials, technologies, and processes. Aspiring for the gold standard globally saves money, because compliance with minimum standards requires sourcing, production, and logistics to be managed separately for each market, due to regional regulatory variations. Once companies have exceeded standards and regulations, they become more environmentally proactive, focusing increased effort on developing more sustainable value chains. While the focus is frequently on improved brand image, most corporations achieve cost reductions or create new businesses, a beneficial process for difficult economic times, when corporations desperately seek profits (Nidumolu et al., 2009). Dow Chemical is an example of a company exceeding standards and regulations, having invested almost $2 billion from 1994 to 201 to improve resource efficiency, realizing more than $9.8 billion in savings from reduced energy consumption and manufacturing process water waste. Dow also achieved a 20% reduction in absolute GHG emissions, exceeding Kyoto Protocol targets (Bonini & Görner, 2011).

Several organizations have incorporated sustainability into their business models. Levi Strauss spent ten years identifying water use reduction methods and sharing their best practices with other businesses and competitors (Winston, 2016). More than 25 companies in Minnesota, including 3M and Target, launched a project to share circular economy expertise (Winston, 2016). IKEA expanded its circular offerings including reselling used furniture and creating new products from leftover textiles (Winston, 2016). The Real Junk Food Project (TRJFP) is an organization in the UK that is revolutionizing food waste through their food banks and "pay-as-you-feel" cafés. This company has now expanded their offering to include a supermarket that sells food that would otherwise be destined for landfills. The goal of the project is to address two global problems: reducing the 10 million tons of food waste generated in the UK each year and helping individuals and families struggling financially by selling necessities at affordable prices (Moss, 2016).

In 2002, Hewlett-Packard (HP) management determined Europe's pending Waste Electrical and Electronic Equipment (WEEE) regulations would require computer hardware manufacturers to pay for recycling costs in proportion to hardware sales (Nidumolu et al., 2009). Recognizing government-sponsored recycling arrangements would likely be expensive, HP partnered with three electronics manufacturers—Sony, Braun, and Electrolux—to create the private European Recycling Platform. In 2007, the platform expanded to more than 1,000 companies in 30 countries, recycling approximately 20% of equipment required by the WEEE directive. Moreover, based upon operation scale, the platform's charges are approximately 55% lower than competitor charges. In addition to realizing more than $100 million in savings from 2003 to 2007, HP enhanced its reputation with consumers, policymakers, and the electronics industry because of the initiative (Nidumolu et al., 2009).

The Global 100 is an annual list of the world's most sustainable companies compiled by Toronto-based magazine and research firm Corporate Knights (Kauflin, 2017). Using publicly available data, Corporate Knights rates companies with market values of at least $2 billion on 14 key measures, evaluating their management of resources, finances, and employees. In 2016, German industrial Siemens giant ranked first on the Global 100, producing more revenue per kilowatt used than any other industrial corporation, and scoring high on nearly every metric, including low carbon footprint, and low employee turnover (Kauflin, 2017).

Examples abound of large multinational corporations (MNCs) persuading suppliers to become environmentally conscious by offering incentives. Cargill and Unilever have invested in technology development, working with farmers to develop sustainable practices in palm oil, soybeans, and cacao cultivation (Nidumolu et al., 2009). Analytical tools such as enterprise carbon management, carbon and energy footprint analysis, and life cycle assessment assist companies with identification of supply-chain waste sources (Nidumolu et al., 2009). Operational innovations leading to increased energy efficiency and reduced dependence on fossil fuels are an essential aspect of a sustainable supply chain. FedEx maintains a fleet of 700 aircraft and 44,000 motorized vehicles consuming more than 4 million gallons of fuel daily. Despite the 2007–2008 global recession, FedEx replaced older aircraft with Boeing 757 s as part of its Fuel Sense program, reducing overall fuel consumption 36% while increasing capacity 20% (Nidumolu et al., 2009).

In the United States, merchandise returns reduce corporate profitability by approximately 4% annually. Many companies attempt to recapture some of the lost value of returned merchandise instead of scrapping or recycling the items. Not only does this practice allow for a cost center to be converted into a profitable business, change in attitude signals to the market that the company is more concerned about environmental responsibility and waste reduction cannibalizing sales (Nidumolu et al., 2009). For example, network hardware manufacturer Cisco Systems traditionally regarded returned equipment as scrap, recycling it at a cost of about US$8 million annually. In 2005, Cisco sought alternative uses for the equipment, based on the discovery that 80% of the returns were in good, working condition. Cisco designated the recycling group as a separate business unit, established clear performance objectives, and created a profit and loss (P&L) account for the department. Returned equipment reuse increased from 5% in 2004 to 45% in 2008, and company recycling costs decreased by 40%. The recycling unit is now a profit center contributing US$100 million to Cisco's 2008 bottom line (Nidumolu et al., 2009).

Business executives are increasingly recognizing that a growing segment of consumers prefer eco-friendly products and services, and their businesses can outperform rivals by being first to redesign existing products or develop new sustainable products. The discovery of which products are environmentally unfriendly is frequently a surprise to business executives. For example, Procter & Gamble (P&G) performed life cycle assessments to determine product energy consumption requirements, with detergents identified as requiring significant amounts of household energy. Recognizing 3% of annual U.S. household electricity usage is devoted to heating water for washing clothes, P&G determined switching to cold-water washing, would reduce annual energy consumption by 80 billion kilowatt-hours of electricity, and reduce carbon dioxide emissions by 34 million tons. In 2005, P&G launched Tide Coldwater in the United States, and Ariel Cool Clean in Europe, resulting in British household cold-water washing increasing from 2% in 2002 to 21% in 2008, and from 5 to 52% in Holland during the same period (Nidumolu et al., 2009).

Businesses frequently develop novel new business models to capture additional revenue, often delivering services in collaboration with other companies or subsidiaries. In 2008, FedEx began integrating the Kinko's chain of print stores acquired in 2004 with its document-delivery business. FedEx customers could now electronically transfer files to Kinko's locations for printing and delivery on location, using FedEx vehicles for local delivery of the finished product. FedEx increased sales, reduced costs, and became more environmentally friendly as a result (Nidumolu et al., 2009). Development of new business models requires exploring alternative methods of conducting business, and understanding how to meet customer demands in creative new ways.

Developing innovations resulting in new business practices requires executives to question the implicit assumptions behind existing practices, challenge the status quo, and create alternative platforms. The smart grid is one such next best practice platform, emerging at the nexus of the internet and energy management. The smart grid uses digital technology to manage power generation, transmission, and distribution from multiple sources with consumer demand, leading to reduced costs and increased energy efficiency. The smart grid enables development of cross-industry platforms for energy management of households, buildings, and entire cities. Companies currently investing in the smart grid include technology manufacturers Cisco, HP, Dell, and IBM, and utility providers Duke Energy, SoCal Edison, and Florida Power & Light (Nidumolu et al., 2009).

Regarding the smart grid, Rifkin (2017) has promoted the nexus of the internet and energy as the Third Industrial Revolution (TIR), driven by evidence the current fossil fuel-driven industrial revolution has been peaking for several decades. According to Rifkin, fossil fuel industries are 'sunsetting', and the supporting infrastructure is antiquated and needing repair. In the TIR, hundreds of millions of people and organizations will produce their own energy, sharing excess power in an "energy Internet" much like the current information-sharing Internet. The democratization of energy will change how we conduct business, govern society, educate children, and engage in civic life. Although some Americans are reluctant to accept peak oil forecasts, climate change, or challenges to the validity of the capitalist economic system, many Europeans have already embraced the Third Revolution.

According to Rifkin, the TIR will create hundreds of thousands of new businesses and hundreds of millions of new jobs. The five pillars of TIR are: shifting to renewable energy; transforming buildings globally into miniature power plants collecting renewable energy on site; installing energy storage technologies in every building and throughout the energy infrastructure; using Internet-type technologies to transform the power grid into multiple energy-sharing grids; and, shifting transportation into electric and fuel-cell vehicles capable of exchanging energy on smart interactive grids. Just as the democratization of communication and information disrupted commerce and social relations in the Second Industrial Revolution, the TIR will disrupt energy access, improving the lives of the poorest planetary inhabitants (Rifkin, 2017).

An increasing number of businesses encourage employees to telecommute, resulting in reduced travel time, travel costs, and energy consumption. One-fourth of IBM's 320,000 employees telecommute, resulting in an annual savings of US$700 million in real estate costs, and AT&T estimates annual saving from telecommuting of US$550 million. Studies demonstrate productivity increases 10–20%, and job satisfaction increases when employees telecommute up to three days per week. Healthcare services provider McKesson reported the highest job satisfaction level in 2007 among 1,000 telecommuting nurses (Nidumolu et al., 2009).

11.5 Contributions of NGOs and IGOs

Countless NGOs and IGOs are engaged in sustainability activities. Many of these organizations are successful because of their sustainability focus but also contribute to the success of individuals and organizations by improving their environmental, social, and economic conditions. The NGOs and IGOs which contribute to and attribute their success to sustainability are too numerous to mention. The United Nations is likely the most recognized IGO in terms of sustainability, having established the millennium development goals (MDGs) in 2000 and the sustainable development goals (SDGs) in 2015. A few of the UN agencies that are involved and successful in the areas of sustainability include the UN Environmental Programme (UNEP), the UN Development Programme, the UN Global Compact, United Nations Educational, Scientific and Cultural Organization (UNESCO), and UNICEF, originally known as the United Nations International Children's Emergency Fund.

The Earth Charter provides a framework for achieving sustainability. The document, which was formally launched in 2000 at the Hague in the Netherlands, contains four pillars and sixteen principles for establishing a "a sustainable global society founded on respect for nature, universal human rights, economic justice, and a culture of peace" (Earth Charter, n.d.). The pillars and principles were described in Chapter 6. The Earth Charter provides online and onsite training about the Earth Charter Principles and how to apply them in business, leadership, and academic settings at their Education Centre located at the UN-mandated University for Peace in San Jose, Costa Rica.

The goal of the Earth Charter is "to inspire in all people a new sense of global interdependence and shared responsibility for the well-being of the whole human family, the greater community of life, and future generations" (Earth Charter International, n.d.). The Earth Charter influences a global movement of individuals and organizations from 90 nations who have embraced the vision of the Earth Charter and promote it in numerous ways. To date, the Earth Charter has received 50,000 endorsements, and their education center has over 2,000 alumni (Earth Charter International, n.d.).

The International Red Cross and Red Crescent (ICRC) Movement is a humanitarian effort consisting of more than 16 million volunteers, members, and staff globally. The ICRC was organized to protect human life and health, promote respect for all human beings, and prevent and limit human suffering. The ICRC consists of three separate organizations that are legally independent but united through fundamental principles, objectives, symbols, statutes, and governing bodies. The seven fundamental principles of the International Red Cross and Red Crescent movement (humanity, impartiality, neutrality, independence, voluntary service, unity, and universality) provide an ethical and operational framework for combined organizations (International Committee of the Red Cross, 2021). The Red Cross has recognized climate change as a humanitarian crisis, with the American Red Cross noting that they regularly witness the heartbreak of families and communities who cope with increasingly powerful storms, increased rainfall, higher temperatures, more intense hurricanes, and more destructive wildfires (American Red Cross, 2021).

There are too many nonprofit organizations and NGOs to mention in one chapter or even one book. Prominent sustainability global NGOs include CERES, Conservation International (CI), Doctors Without Borders, Food and Water Watch, Greenpeace, Heifer International, Natural Resources Defense Council (NRDC), The Nature Conservancy (TNC), Ocean Conservancy, Oxfam, Sierra Club, Slow Food International, World Resources Institute, and World Wildlife Fund (WWF; Sustainability Degrees, 2014). These NGOs work with businesses, academics, policymakers, individuals, and communities in protecting communities, land, water, biodiversity, and ecosystems. Their approaches are diverse and impact billions of individuals, millions of hectares of land, and trillions of dollars of investments and government budgets. Their efforts contribute to the betterment and success of individuals and organizations globally.

11.6 Concluding Thoughts

Sustainability clearly provides opportunities for organizational success, in terms of decreased costs, and increased profitability and performance. Indirect benefits identified include increased employee retention, improved brand image, decreased costs, and increased profitability and performance to name a few. The sustainable business model differs from traditional and historic business models in that the purpose is not only profit maximization but focusing on a larger purpose measured by concepts such as the triple bottom line, is beneficial to the ecosystem and society, and can be internalized and shared among all stakeholders (Jones & Upward, 2014). With growing discussion regarding climate change, dwindling energy resources, and environmental impact, it's no surprise that state and national government agencies are enacting regulations to protect the environment. Integrating sustainability into the business model will position the business to meet changing regulations in a timely manner (Rogers, 2016), regardless of whether management agrees with the regulations, or the environmental concerns driving them.

Building a holistic corporate sustainability foundation requires systemic corporate changes (Hui, 2008). These organizational changes require new perspectives in how we describe and understand organizations, and the world in which these organizations operate. When we attempt to conceptualize the world as a machine, we feel alienated because we cannot locate ourselves in the machine. However, the world is not a machine, but rather a living system, filled with life and history (Wheatley & Kellner-Rogers, 1999). Moreover, while the planet seeks organization, it does not need humankind to organize it (Wheatley & Kellner-Rogers, 1999). Rather than seeking to manage and organize the world and all the interrelated systems, humankind must seek to manage and organize themselves in a more holistic and harmonious manner.

Case Study

General Electric (GE) CEO Jeff Immelt introduced Ecomagination as GE's sustainable growth strategy in 2005. The goal of ecomagination was to enhance resource productivity and reduce environmental impact on a global scale through commercial customer solutions and internal operations (General Electric, 2018). Through the ecomagination initiative, GE invested in cleaner technology and business innovation, developed solutions to enhance economic growth, while reducing emissions and water consumption, committed to reduce the environmental impact of operations, and developed strategic partnerships to solve environmental problems, creating a cleaner, faster, smarter tomorrow. Ecomagination successes include US$270 billion in revenue, 18% reduction in GHG emissions, and 29% reduction in freshwater usage over the 12-year history (General Electric, 2018).

The economic horizon at GE began to change in November 2017, when incoming CEO John Flannery reduced the dividend, and announced restructuring plans to divest multiple business lines (Chesto, 2017), including businesses operating more than one century, and linked to founder Thomas Edison. A series of negative news reports followed, including the January 2018 announcement that the company would take a US$6.2 billion charge in the fourth quarter because of insurance subsidiary, North American Life & Health underestimating costs of providing long-term care of policyholders living longer than projected (CBS News, 2018). This announcement, which included a long-term charge of approximately US$15 billion, prompted a Securities Exchange Commission (SEC) investigation into the insurance unit miscalculations (CBS News, 2018). In February 2018, GE announced in a regulatory filing that the U.S. Justice Department was investigating GE Capital, and its' now defunct WMC Mortgage business, concerning possible violation of financial regulatory law, regarding sale of subprime mortgage loans in 2006 and 2007 (Sheetz, 2018). GE has lost one-half of market value since the 2007–2008 financial crisis and will likely continue to become a smaller, less conglomerated corporation with CEO Flannery pledging an additional US$20 billion asset reduction over the next two years (CBS News, 2018). Scott Davis of Melius Research suggested several holdings are performing well, with the power-related holdings of gas, wind, and grid the only remaining concerns (CBS News, 2018). GE appears to be financially viable, and will likely weather the financial storm, emerging as a smaller, leaner, and more focused business.

Case Study Questions

1. How do you think restructuring efforts at GE will impact the ecomagination initiative?
2. Do you think ecomagination may have in any way contributed to the current financial concerns at GE, or rather, may ecomagniation have mitigated some of the impacts of the recent events?
3. How does the negative news being reported at GE relate to non-environmental aspects of sustainability (e.g., corporate social responsibility)?

References

Accenture. (2010). *A new era of sustainability: UN Global Compact-Accenture CEO study*. http://www.unglobalcompact.org

American Red Cross. (2021). *Red Cross statement on climate change*. https://www.redcross.org/about-us/news-and-events/press-release/2019/red-cross-statement-on-climate-change.html

Banerjee, P. M., & Shastri, V. (2010). New beginnings in age-old philosophies. In P. M. Banerjee & V. Shastri (Eds.), *Social responsibility and environmental sustainability in business: How organizations handle profits and social duties* (pp. 163–169). Sage.

Beehner, C. G. (2017, January). Teaching sustainability to a traditional business audience. In *Conference proceedings of the International Academy of Business and Public Administration Discipline (IABPAD), 14(1)*. Paper presented at IABPAD 2017 Conference: Orlando, FL, pp. 298–308.

Bocken, N. M., Short, S. W., Rana, P., & Evans, S. (2014). A literature and practice review to develop sustainable business model archetypes. *Journal of Cleaner Production, 65*, 42–56. https://doi.org/10.1016/j.jclepro.2013.11.039

Bonini, S., & Görner, S. (2011, October). *Putting it into practice*. McKinsey & Company. https://www.mckinsey.com

Bonini, S., & Swartz, S. (2014). *Profits with purpose: How organizing for sustainability can benefit the bottom line.* McKinsey & Company. http://www.highmeadowsinstitute.org

CBS News. (2018, January 24). *SEC investigating GE over $15 billion charge.* https://www.cbsnews.com/news/sec-investigating-ge-over-15-billion-charge/

Channell, J., Curmi, E., Nguyen, P., Prior, E., Syme, A. R., Jansen, H. R., & Kruger, T. (2015). *Energy Darwinism II: Why a low carbon future doesn't have to cost the Earth.* Citibank. https://ir.citi.com

Chesbrough, H. (2010). Business model innovation: Opportunities and barriers. *Long Range Planning, 43*(2–3), 354–363. https://doi.org/10.1016/j.lrp.2009.07.010

Chesto, J. (2017, November 17). *General electric plans job cuts, slash in quarterly dividend.* Boston Globe. https://www.bostonglobe.com/business/2017/11/13/general-electric-plans-slice-quarterly-dividend-half/AZqYqgb6iL7sZ64VvBPmFO/story.html

Dean, T. J. (2014). *Sustainable venturing: Entrepreneurial opportunity in the transition to a sustainable economy.* Pearson.

Deutsche Bank Group. (2012). *Sustainable investing 2012.* Author. https://www.db.com/cr/en/docs/Sustainable_Investing_2012.pdf

Eccles, R. G., Ioannou, I., & Serafeim, G. (2012a). *The impact of a corporate culture of sustainability on corporate behavior and performance* (No. W17950). National Bureau of Economic Research.

Eccles, R. G., Miller Perkins, K., & Serafeim, J. (2012b). How to become a sustainable company. *MIT Sloan Management Review, 53*(4), 43–50. https://sloanreview.mit.edu

Esty, D. C., & Winston, A. S. (2006). *Green to gold: How smart companies use environmental strategy to innovate, create value, and build competitive advantage.* Yale University Press.

Flavelle, C. (2017, November 27). *Moody's warns cities to address climate risks or face downgrades.* Bloomberg. https://www.bloomberg.com/news/articles/2017-11-29/moody-s-warns-cities-to-address-climate-risks-or-face-downgrades

General Electric. (2018). *Ecomagination.* Author. https://www.ge.com/about-us/ecomagination

Goleman, D., & Lueneburger, C. (2010). The change leadership sustainability demands. *MIT Sloan Management Review, 51*(4), 49. https://sloanreview.mit.edu

GreenBiz Staff. (2008, October 22). *BT-and Cisco-sponsored paper says sustainability breeds innovation and profitability*. http://www.greenbiz.com/print/1601

Haanaes, K., Reeves, M., von Streng, I., Audretsch, M., Kiron, D., & Kruschwitz, N. (2012). Sustainability nears a tipping point. *MIT Sloan Management Review*. https://sloanreview.mit.edu/projects/sustainability-nears-a-tipping-point/

Herro, C. R. (2018, January 8). *Disruptive strategies for the evolving housing market*. Presented at Sustainability Symposium 2018, Orlando, FL.

Hind, P., Smit, A., & Page, N. (2013). Enabling sustainability through an action research process of organizational development. *Journal of Corporate Citizenship, 49*, 137–161. http://www.jstor.org/stable/jcorpciti.49.137

Hofstra, N. (2014). Entrepreneurship inspired by nature. In L. Zsolnai (Ed.), *The spiritual dimension of business ethics and sustainability management* (pp. 159–168). Springer. https://doi.org/10.1007/978-3-319-11677-8_20

Hui, L. T. (2008). Combining faith and CSR: A paradigm of corporate sustainability. *International Journal of Social Economics, 35*(6), 449–465. https://doi.org/10.1108/03068290810873429

International Committee of the Red Cross. (2021). *The fundamental principles of the International Red Cross and Red Crescent movement*. https://blogs.icrc.org/cross-files/the-fundamental-principles-of-the-international-red-cross-and-red-crescent-movement/

Jackson, T. (2009). *Prosperity without growth: Economics for a finite planet*. Earthscan.

Jones, P. H., & Upward, A. (2014). *Caring for the future: The systemic design of flourishing enterprises*. The Third Symposium of Relating Systems Thinking and Design (RSD3), Oslo, Norway, pp. 1–8. http://systemic-design.net/rsd3-proceedings/business-enterprise-design/

Kaplan, R. S., & Norton, D. P. (1996). *The balanced scorecard: Translating strategy into action*. Harvard Business Press.

Kauflin, J. (2017, January 17). The world's most sustainable companies 2017. *Forbes*. https://www.forbes.com

Kiron, D., Kruschwitz, N., Reeves, M., & Goh, E. (2013). The benefits of sustainability-driven (business model) innovation. *MIT Sloan Management Review, 54*(2), 69–73. https://sloanreview.mit.edu

McKinsey & Company. (2011, October). *The business of sustainability: McKinsey Global Survey results*. https://www.mckinsey.com

Medlock, S. (2018, January 8). *Innovative financing solutions for resilience building*. Presented at Sustainability Symposium, Orlando, FL.

Moss, R. (2016, October 9). *The real junk food project opens UK's first food waste supermarket*. Huffington Post UK. http://www.huffingtonpost.co.uk

MunichRe. (2018). *Natural catastrophe review: Series of hurricanes makes 2017 year of highest insured losses ever*. Munich. https://www.munichre.com

Nidumolu, R., Prahalad, C. K., & Rangaswami, M. R. (2009). Why sustainability is now the key driver of innovation. *Harvard Business Review, 87*(9), 56–64. http://www.hbr.org

O'Malley, M. (2018, January 8). *Seizing America's renewable energy future*. Presented at Sustainability Symposium 2018, Orlando, FL.

Opdebeeck, H. (2014). Spiritual sustainability management. In L Zsolnai (Ed.), *The spiritual dimension of business ethics and sustainability management* (pp. 15–26). Springer. https://doi.org/10.1007/978-3-319-11677-8_20

Porter, M. E., & Kramer, M. R. (2011). Creating shared value. *Harvard Business Review, 89*(1/2), 62–77. http://www.hbr.org

Rainey, D. L. (2006). *Sustainable business development: Inventing the future through strategy, innovation, and leadership*. Cambridge University Press.

Rainey, D. L. (2008). Transparency, openness, and accountability: A new imperative. In M. V. Russo (Ed.), *Environmental management: Readings and cases* (pp. 228–242). Sage.

Reinhardt, F. L. (2008). Environmental product differentiation: Implications for corporate strategy. In M. V. Russo (Ed.), *Environmental management: Readings and cases* (pp. 205–227). Sage.

Rifkin, J. (2017, November/December). *Sustainability's third act*. Green Builder.

Rogers, M. (2016, March 29). *6 benefits of becoming a sustainable business*. Business Sector Media. https://www.environmentalleader.com/2016/03/6-benefits-of-becoming-a-sustainable-business/

Rosen, R. (1991). *Life itself: A comprehensive inquiry into the nature, origin, and fabrication of life* (1st ed.). Columbia University Press.

Senge, P. (with Smith, B., Kruschwitz, N., Laut, J., & Schley, S.). (2008). *The necessary revolution: How individuals and organizations are working together to create a sustainable world*. Penguin Random House.

Sheetz, M. (2018, February 26). *General electric shares fall below $14 after justice probe revealed; taps accounting, turnaround experts for board*. CNBC. https://www.cnbc.com/2018/02/26/general-electric-shares-fall-below-14-after-naming-three-new-board-members.html

Soppe, L. (2014). Sustainability and long-term growth in the financial market system. In L. Zsolnai (Ed.), *The spiritual dimension of business ethics and sustainability management* (pp. 109–124). Springer. https://doi.org/10.1007/978-3-319-11677-8_20

Soyka, P. A. (2012). *Creating a sustainable organization: Approaches for enhancing corporate value through sustainability*. Pearson Education.

Spector, D. (2012, March 1). *10 more reasons companies should care about sustainability*. Business Insider. http://www.businessinsider.com

Sustainability Degrees. (2014). *The 14 most influential sustainability NGOs*. https://www.sustainabilitydegrees.com/blog/most-influential-sustainability-ngos/

Tariq, S., Jan, F. A., & Ahmad, M. S. (2016). Green employee empowerment: A systematic literature review of state-of-art in green human resource management. *Quality & Quantity, 50*(1), 237–269. https://doi.org/10.1007/s11135-014-0146-0

Tate, W. (2009). *The search for leadership: An organisational perspective*. Triarchy Press.

Tideman, S. G., Arts, M. C., & Zandee, D. P. (2013). Sustainable leadership: Towards a workable definition. *Journal of Corporate Citizenship, 45*(6), 17–33. http://www.jstor.org/stable/jcorpciti.49.17

Townsend, A. K. (2006). *Green business: A five-part model for creating an environmentally responsible company*. Schiffer Publishing.

Utne Reader. (1999, March–April). *Fifteen ideas that could shake the world*. https://www.utne.com/politics/15ideasthatcouldshaketheworld

Wagner, M. (Ed.). (2012). *Entrepreneurship, innovation and sustainability*. Greenleaf Publishing.

Walker, K., Ni, N., & Dyck, B. (2015). Recipes for successful sustainability: Empirical organizational configurations for strong corporate environmental performance. *Business Strategy and the Environment, 24*, 40–57. https://doi.org/10.1002/bse.1805

Wheatley, M. J., & Kellner-Rogers, M. (1999). *A simpler way*. Berrett-Koehler Publishers.

Winston, A. (2016, December 30). 9 sustainable business stories that shaped 2016. *Harvard Business Review*. https://hbr.org

12

Integrating Spirituality and Sustainability for Individual Success

12.1 Introduction

In this chapter I will argue that the combination of spirituality and sustainability is beneficial for individual success. Existing literature will be synthesized to demonstrate the benefits, along with a personal interview to assist with practical application of spirituality on an individual level. Recognizing that limited research exists concerning the relationships among sustainability, spirituality, and success at the individual level, much of the focus of this chapter will be with the development of an argument for, and a conceptual framework from which to examine the proposed relationship of these constructs at the individual level. The premise of this book is that spirituality (individual and workplace), and sustainability are beneficial for individual (and organizational) success.

The central theme of this chapter is that the combination of spirituality and sustainability are beneficial for individual success. Because limited research exists concerning the relationships among sustainability, spirituality, and individual success, much of the focus of this chapter will be with the development of an argument for, and a conceptual framework from which to examine the proposed relationship of these constructs. Spiritual and sustainable lifestyles such as voluntary

C. G. Beehner, *Spirituality, Sustainability, and Success*, Palgrave Studies in Workplace Spirituality and Fulfillment, https://doi.org/10.1007/978-3-031-47643-3_12

simplicity and flourishing, and corresponding benefits will be examined. Systems thinking, Holistic Model of Wellness, Vocational Souljourn, and complexity theory are introduced as frameworks through which to understand the individual-level benefits of combined spirituality and sustainability. Spiritual intelligence, sustainable leadership, eco-spirituality, and ecologism are discussed within the context of individual spirituality, sustainability, and success.

In an earlier chapter, spirituality was defined as "the desire to find ultimate purpose in life, and to live accordingly" (Cavanagh, 1999, p. 186), and "the feeling individuals have about the fundamental meaning of who they are, what they are doing, [and] the contributions they are making" (p. 218). Pfeffer (2010) identified the four fundamental dimensions of what employees seek in a spiritual workplace as: (1) interesting and meaningful work that inspires learning and development; (2) meaningful work providing a sense of purpose; (3) a sense of connection and positive relationships with coworkers; and (4) the ability to live an integrated life, in which work and non-work roles are in harmony with who the person is as a human being. Sustainability was defined as meeting the needs of present generations without compromising future generational needs (WCED, 1987). Moreover, both spirituality and sustainability are characterized by a holistic perspective of self, others, and the universe.

The commonalities of, and interconnection between spirituality (both individual and workplace), and sustainability support the hypothesis: ***A combination of spirituality and sustainability positively impacts both individual and organizational success***. Sustainability meets the workplace spirituality dimensions of (1) meaningful work, and (2) sense of purpose through preservation of planetary resources for future generations, (3) connection and positive relationship, by the collective need for sustainable action, and (4) a harmonious, integrated life, through the integration of spirituality, sustainability, life, and career. Likewise, sustainability meets the spiritual dimensions of finding ultimate purpose in life and making a meaningful contribution through the preservation of planetary resources for future generations, clearly a meaningful purpose to seek. Because both religion and secularism played a major part in the development of civilization, the contemporary spirituality (individual and workplace) discussed in previous chapters will play a major role in

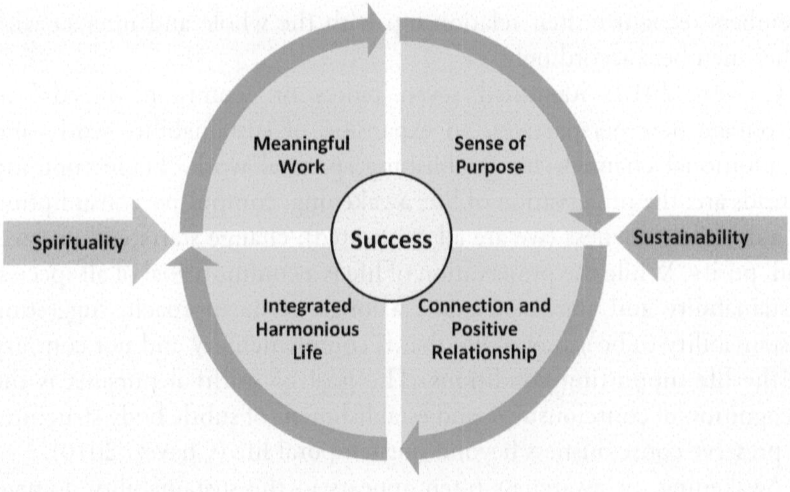

Fig. 12.1 Spirituality, sustainability and individual success

the development of sustainable civilization. Figure 12.1 provides a visual representation of the spirituality, sustainability, and individual success proposition.

12.2 The Nexus of Individual Spirituality, Sustainability, and Success

It can be argued that one's inner and outer world are not only interconnected, but reflections of each other. As such, individuals embody the whole universe in some sense and must demonstrate the order of the cosmos in their lives (Carroll, 2004). This interconnectedness is so powerful that the human community is meaningless without the entire planetary community, suggesting the appropriate role of human intelligence is natural world enhancement, not exploitation (Carroll, 2004). Albert Einstein's colleague David Bohm believed quantum theory described the wholeness of the universe—*separate without separateness* (Dhiman, 2017). Therefore, an interconnected system necessitates all members recognize their relationship with the whole and interact with other members accordingly.

Chavez (2010) identified seven tenets or "common threads" to encourage new perspectives, an expansion of sustainability work, and as additional channels for establishing spiritual work. These common threads are: the preservation of life; awakening; compulsive consumption as a disorder; oneness (we are all connected); change starts within; awe; and, purity. While the preservation of life is a common goal of all species, sustainability and spirituality take a longer-term approach, suggesting sustainability to be a way of life that is complementary and not contrary to the life-supporting conditions. The goal of spiritual pursuits is the recognition of consciousness, and establishment of subtle body structures to preserve consciousness beyond our temporal life (Chavez, 2010).

Awakening, or awareness often appears in the sustainability domain in reference to "waking up" to critical ecological realities, or to "awaken" to the fact humans are consuming natural resources at an *unsustainable* rate. The term awakening is commonplace in spiritual traditions referring to the conscious awareness of, for example breathing or the presence of surroundings. Awakening also signifies becoming aware of a greater, overarching level of consciousness. While the specifics of awakening or enlightenment vary between traditions, common characteristics include cognitive functioning becoming subordinate to pure consciousness, in contrast with the more common human condition in which pure consciousness is subordinate to cognitive thinking except extraordinary moments (Chavez, 2010).

Compulsive consumption is a disorder describing the current materialistic state in which individuals consistently assume more is needed, requiring a shift to a more sustainable system of consumption. While some spiritual traditions are fundamentally based on denial of physical desires as a major method of spiritual attainment, other traditions simply require the summoning of as much consciousness as capable to live life in the moment when the desired object is obtained. Regardless of differences between traditions, a key tenant of most major wisdom traditions is that true fulfillment cannot be found solely in material existence (Chavez, 2010).

The tenet of oneness may be the most obvious common ground between sustainability and spirituality. Humanity senses that the interdependency of life may remain beyond the realms of human comprehension. From a spiritual perspective, the interconnectedness of life is a tangible demonstration of "oneness", with sacred scriptures abundant with examples of legendary experiences of oneness or "universal consciousness". Members of both sustainability and spiritual circles cite quantum physics and the realization that seemingly separate, solid objects are not atomically separate or solid at all as evidence of universal oneness (Chavez, 2010).

The tenet that changes begins within as a cornerstone tenant of many sustainability campaigns, imploring individuals to take responsibility for recycling, diet modification, transportation habits, and purchasing decisions. "You must be the change you want to see in the world" is a familiar quote from Mahatma Gandhi, who was exemplary of an individual who was a deeply effective social activist, and whose life was modeled by deep spirituality. Tolle (1999) suggests spirituality is the process of an individual cleaning up their inner space after which the external world is then renewed. Without this inner element, we may not have national parks or wildlife refuges, and would have lacked action in the face of so many human tragedies. It is the sheer significance of wonder in the face of life's miracles that has driven humanity to take action to protect it (Chavez, 2010).

Awe refers to the spiritual practice of seeking communion with the sacred or unknown that is a basis of most spiritual traditions. As one begins to experience the sacred within the context of personal spiritual beliefs, it is difficult to not detect the sacred in all of nature. When an individual begins to recognize all of creation as sacred, an immense shift occurs in how that individual occupies and relates to creation (Chavez, 2010). Finally, purity is best understood by the antonym of impure. Today, countless natural areas have been adversely impacted by human activities to the level that "impure" seems an inadequate description. While religious attempts throughout history to "purify" people and places have seen horrific outcomes, purity remains a powerful principle. For many people, fasting for a period of time is a spiritual, or health practice intended to "purify" the mind, body, or senses, much as washing of feet has been a tradition in several wisdom traditions. Fasting and washing can be either practical, symbolic, or both, invoked in reference to one's state of consciousness, referring to a mind free from distractions or impurities (Chavez, 2010).

While many of the seven tenets are intrinsic to one another, their examination illuminates important facets common to both sustainability and spirituality. Sustainability implies infinity—the preservation of our life-sustaining systems for an infinite amount of time. While infinity may seem beyond comprehension, each being possesses a part of this infinity. It is at this level that we may find the necessary resources to undertake a seemingly impossible task—the urgent need for global recovery and restoration of our planetary life system (Chavez, 2010).

While it may seem intuitive that spirituality and sustainability would contribute to individual success, science, while perhaps originating with intuition, requires a theoretical foundation or framework which can be researched and proven. "A spirituality that encourages ecological practice must be compatible with the best available science of the day" (Carroll, 2004, p. 129). The inclusion of spirituality in the understanding of sustainability, creates a sense of personal meaning, which may have a more substantive effect, because this profound meaning-seeking human state is often cited as the source of inner peace and genuine happiness (Walker, 2013).

Holthaus (2012) noted Native American and Inuit cultures present models of sustainability, further recognizing a link between subsistence, sustainability, and spirituality. While Westerners interpret subsistence as living with the basics, Native participants routinely consider subsistence as a way of life. Some Indigenous cultures consider subsistence to be more than a way of life, but to be "their life". Native cultures view subsistence as a foundation upon which an entire culture establishes identity through beliefs, practice, art, ritual, law, ethics, and education. If subsistence is a way of life, or life in and of itself, it is dependent upon how people live, not on the availability of certain foods or resources (Holthaus, 2012).

Although our inner intellectual, emotional, or spiritual lives may be incapable of measurement, we witness measurable manifestations of our lives. The health, harmony, balance, beauty, and intelligence, or lack thereof in contemporary society are a direct manifestation of our spiritual health. For Indigenous peoples, subsistence required direct, personal engagement with nature, and the recognition of human dependence on nature for energy, nutrition, tools, clothing, and shelter. The culture of the developed world no longer requires such personal engagement, but ultimately all subsistence depends on resolution in maintaining a healthy worldview, not on technology, agriculture, or the fossil fuel industry (Holthaus, 2012). Leal Filho et al. (2022) found widespread recognition for making connections between spirituality and sustainability and consensus about the usefulness of including spiritual elements in sustainability education and research. However, progress is hindered by the lack of a common definition of spirituality and inadequate training on handling matters related to spirituality within teaching and research.

12.3 Spiritual and Sustainable Lifestyles

In our contemporary culture of technology, entertainment, and climate-controlled dwellings, we seem to exist outside of nature. It is logical that this disconnect from nature has weakened awareness of our relationship with, and impact on our environment. This deteriorating relationship with nature may coincide with or be a result of humankind's strained relationship with religion and spirituality. This argument receives support, and perhaps optimistic confidence in the recent surge in interest in both spirituality and sustainability, establishing a nuance that perhaps both are in fact related. It seems no wonder that as individuals seek a spiritual component in their lives, they have been seeking comfort in nature. Moreover, our existence outside nature may adversely impact health, as noted by *Richard Louv's (2008) in Last child in the woods, wherein Louv* synthesized a growing body of research indicating direct exposure to nature is essential for healthy childhood development, and physical and emotional health of both children and adults.

Nature-based recreation has been demonstrated to be promotive of spiritual well-being (Heintzman, 2000), provide spiritual value (Rule & Udd, 2002; Trainor & Norgaard, 1999), and provide opportunity to reflect on spiritual values (Brayley & Fox, 1998). Research studies indicate participants engaged in more nature-related activities, such as hiking, canoeing, or observing nature, rated higher on the degree to which spiritual introspection increased satisfaction when compared to participants engaged in activities such as biking, motor boating, and playground usage (Heintzman, 1998, 2002). These findings were supported by Behan and colleagues (2001), who discovered spiritual benefits were more valued by foot travelers than mountain bikers. Research studies repeatedly identify *being in nature*, either in the backyard or in a remote setting, to be an important component influencing nature-based spiritual outcomes (Heintzman, 2009). Nature is beneficial to spirituality because nature creates a sense of wonder, awe, and amazement (Fox, 1997; Grafanaki et al., 2005; Heintzman, 2000; Loeffler, 2004; Schmidt & Little, 2007); assists some individuals to connect with God or a higher power (Livengood, 2009; Loeffler, 2004); provides a feeling of serenity, calm, stillness, and tranquility (Fox, 1997; Grafanaki et al., 2005; Loeffler, 2004; Stringer & McAvoy, 1992); provides a place to explore spirituality through reflection (Bobilya et al., 2009); and is powerful and therapeutic (Fox, 1997).

The voluntary simplicity movement, also known as simple living, describes a number of movements or practices in which individuals, and often groups seek to simplify their lives, become self-sufficient, and often minimize their impact on the planet in the process. Some adherents practice minimalism, in which the number of possessions is reduced, learning to practice the line by Sheryl Crow in *Soak up the Sun*, "It's not having what you want, it's wanting what you have! (Trott & Crow, 2002)". While some adherents practice ascetism in which all forms of luxury and vice are shunned, many adherents simply want to live more deliberate lifestyles as described in the writings of Henry David Thoreau. The term voluntary simplicity originated with social philosopher Richard Gregg (1936) who promoted ideas such as nonviolent resistance which later influenced Dr. Martin Luther King Jr. (Ansbro, 1982). Voluntary simplicity is related to sustainability since many adherents practice reduced consumption. The suggested benefits include reduced work hours, reduced dependence on career and money, improved health, and better quality of life.

Voluntary simplicity involves embracing a lifestyle less focused on consumption and material acquisition, and more focused on the "inward riches" of personal growth, family, community, spirituality, and communion with nature (Kasser, 2009). Iqbal and Khan (2020) determined that reusing items such as clothing as a sustainable consumption behavior (SCB) was beneficial by significantly mediated spirituality and psychological well-being. Anecdotal voluntary simplicity research suggests despite certain individual struggles, the majority of voluntary simplicity practitioners report improved well-being, are living in more ecologically sustainable ways (Elgin, 1993; Pierce, 2000). Brown and Kasser (2005) surveyed 200 North American voluntary simplicity participants, and 200 mainstream individuals matched on age, gender, and geographical location. Survey findings indicated voluntary simplicity participants were significantly happier than the mainstream group, participated in substantially more ecologically sustainable behaviors, and had lower ecological footprints, concluding that living a simple life enables individuals reduce environmental impact while remaining happy (Kasser, 2009).

Various religious, spiritual, and cultural traditions continue to promote simple living as a beneficial lifestyle. The intent of this text is not to promote a particular lifestyle or philosophy, especially if such a notion is unappealing and uncomfortable to the reader. Rather, it is appropriate in such a text to consider lifestyles in which adherents incorporate the concepts of spirituality and sustainability into their lives and report beneficial outcomes as a result. According to Pope Francis, integral ecology requires "an attitude of the heart, one which approaches life with serene attentiveness" (Vatican Insider, 2015). Sufism is the spiritual path of Islam leading followers to divine knowledge, followed in a selfless, tolerant, and peaceful spiritual journey of transformation (Akman, 2008). Capitalism encourages consumption as a lifestyle, yet many contemporary individuals question whether receiving and spending money are solutions to inner problems (Akman, 2008). According to Sufism, God created the universe in harmony, and we should recognize that harmony individually and in the collective groups and organizations in which we participate (Akman, 2008).

A monograph representing an Eastern spiritual opinion (ANGOC, IRED Asia, & PCDF Forum, 1993) proposed: "A balanced and harmonious relationship between human communities and their natural environment is strongly associated with a reverence for the spiritual unity of life and a strong bonding to community and place. It is a symbiotic relationship in which the individual exists and functions as integral to the whole. The related sense of social and spiritual union is likely to be most fully developed within communities that share a strong link to the regenerative gifts of their natural habitat. Such communities almost universally develop cultural values that maintain a sense of continuity linking both past and future generations to physical place (p. 14)".

The concept of flourishing was discussed in Chapters 1 and 6 as alternatives to the unsustainable contemporary lifestyle. The flourishing model is one in which Laszlo et al. (2014) introduced the concept of a transition in perspective of sustainability from the reduction of negative consequences to the creation of positive human well-being, further described as a transition from sustainable enterprise to flourishing enterprise (Heaton, 2016). This transition requires a change in consciousness, reflecting higher states of awareness of and interconnectedness with the holistic model of nature. These higher states of consciousness create conditions of holistic awareness, concern, and action through which life on Earth not only survives, but thrives (Ehrenfeld & Heaton, 2016; Hoffman, 2013). This higher state, described as flourishing invokes a positive image of a planet working and operating for the health and benefit of all inhabitants (Ehrenfeld & Heaton, 2016; Hoffman, 2013), enabling humankind to both overcome the sustainability challenge, and progress to a more favorable model of individual and collective quality of life (Heaton, 2016). Flourishing is not about living a life of basic sustenance, but rather a life of inner abundance and appreciation, absent attachment to unnecessary materialist artifacts.

12.4 Individual Spirituality and Sustainability Framework

Because limited research exists concerning the relationships among sustainability, spirituality, and success, at either the individual or organizational level exists, much of the focus of this chapter will be with the development of a conceptual framework from which to examine the interrelationship of these constructs at the individual level. The interdependence of spirituality and sustainability was discussed in the first chapter of this text, with scholars suggesting spirituality enhances efforts to act in a sustainably responsible manner, and sustainability reinforces the connectedness of all life (Marques et al., 2010). Hopefully, the content in this chapter will stimulate thought and further research leading to a reification of the position that spirituality and sustainability, when combined contribute to individual success.

Several frameworks exist for examination of the relationship among and benefits of spirituality, sustainability, and success. Systems thinking may provide a valid framework for the interaction of the three variables, because workplace spirituality recognizes and embraces the whole person as a system consisting of multiple interacting components, and sustainability recognizes and embraces the planet and inhabitants as a system consisting of multiple interacting components. Systems thinking was discussed in Chapters 1 and 7, defined as based upon understanding an organization or industry as a system, by examining linkages and interactions between components constituting the entirety of the defined system (Tate, 2009). Because systems thinking views whole systems as being composed of systems, entities, and subsystems, it provides a useful framework to consider the interconnectedness of spirituality, sustainability, and success. The relevance of systems theory to our framework is with the focus on the individual components together in a system, rather than with considering spirituality, sustainability, and success as independent concepts. Because a system may be more than the sum of its parts, modifying one component or subsystem usually impacts other components, subsystems, and the whole system.

Support for spirituality and sustainability within the context of career success can be found in the Holistic Model of Wellness (Witmer &

Sweeney, 1992), discussed in Chapter 2. The Holistic Model of Wellness consists of five basic individual life tasks: spirituality, self-regulation, work, friendship, and love, each of which builds upon and guides the others. The focal point of Witmer and Sweeney's model is spirituality, which serves as the primary instrument of value development, in turn guiding work behavior. While the Holistic Model of Wellness is not empirically supported, the proposition that spirituality influences values and purpose, thereby influencing work, supports the premise of sustainable values, and spiritual purpose providing an outlet for career success.

Further support for the spirituality, sustainability, success triad comes from Brewer's Vocational Souljourn (2001) model, wherein an individual's life is prescribed by three fundamental principles: meaning, being, and doing. Meaning describes the "what" of life and defines individual values, being describes who the individual is, and doing describes the action or "how" of life (Brewer, 2001). The Souljourn model depicts work as a spectrum, with a job at one end of the spectrum, characterized as temporary, financially driven activity, and a vocation at the other end, characterized as a personally significant path serving as the highest expression of work. Brewer (2001) suggested that for stability to occur in an individual's life, the three principles of meaning, being, and doing must be in equilibrium. Both spirituality and sustainability offer an outlet for meaning, being, and doing as higher expressions of work.

Finally, support for the triad comes from Bloch (2004, 2005), whose theory concerning the spiritually and career development connection was founded in complexity theory, suggesting any system component is directly or indirectly affected by the other components. In complexity theory, each system contains a specific amount of energy to be shared among all components in a constant state of flux. Within this system, spirituality and work are connected through principles originally developed by Bloch and Richmond (1998), including: viewing work as a calling; recognizing work has a purpose beyond financial reward; working in an environment consistent with personal values; and, experiencing community and connection at work. Bloch (2004) suggested people who consider work to be spiritual also consider their contribution to the world, avoid self-centeredness, and integrate their work and personal lives.

Rimanoczy (2014) found two categories identified by sustainability leaders to be: creating the intentionality for sustainability personal mission, and the development of social sensitivity. The study confirmed previous research observations suggesting a connection between spiritual leadership and corporate social responsibility (CSR; Fry & Wigglesworth, 2010), and the role of spiritual intelligence in the twenty-first-century world of sustainability (Stead & Stead, 2014). Rimanoczy (2014) offered several recommendations for the facilitation of a sustainability mindset: development of a personal mission (secular, not religious); development of self-awareness (values, beliefs, ambiguities, relationship with consumption and material world); development of awareness of relationship between self and world (and personal contribution); development of awareness of relationship between self and nature (domination of nature as resource versus humankind as part of nature); recognition of whole self (body, mind, and soul); development of meditative practice; development of reflective practice (use of personal journal); and, development of a spiritual organization (secular, aware of global citizenship responsibilities). Schein (2014) identified common sustainable leadership characteristics, many of which are beneficial for individual career success: operate with a long-term horizon, have highly developed systems of consciousness, and can identify with, and care about an expanded sphere of identity and influence (Schein, 2014).

The title of this text contains three terms that this author, and others believe to be interrelated: spirituality, sustainability, and success. These terms also share ingredients of the three Ps of the triple bottom line (Elkington, 1998). One of the Merriam-Webster definitions of spirituality that was introduced in the second chapter was "an animating or vital principle held to give life to physical organisms". Hence, *spirituality* may be considered the principle that gives life to *people*. Because *sustainability* refers to the preservation of natural resources for future generations, sustainability may be considered the principle that gives life to the *planet*. Finally, the success of a business organization is measured in terms of *profit*, while it can certainly be argued that an individual may profit from achieving success in terms of material rewards as well as personal and professional recognition. In the development of this framework, I do not aver that the three Ss are either supplemental or superior to the three Ps. Rather, they are a methodology for or perhaps a measurement of achievement and advancement of the triple bottom line. Moreover, this author suggests the framework of spirituality, sustainability, and success is a means of extending the conversation about the triple bottom line. The three Ss may be the alchemy for achievement of the three Ps.

In Chapter 2, I mentioned a study in which two groups of participants were given money to spend, one group on themselves, and the other group on other people. The participants who spent money on other people reported greater satisfaction than those who spent money on themselves (Dunn et al., 2008). All wisdom traditions include a component of giving or service to others, and of receiving according to what has been given. A few of the labels applied to this attribute include the Golden Rule, *karma*, the Law of Attraction, to name a few. The universality of this attribute suggests an innate understanding of the benefits of helping others. Likewise, in Chapter 1 I summarized the case for sustainability being a component of all major religious and spiritual traditions. Perhaps, at the intersection of both concepts one finds reward for serving others, with that service including an aspect of service to the planet as well. The resulting rewards and favorable outcomes may be bestowed from the Divine in gratitude for commission of honorable actions. However, the rewards may be received because of a subconscious (or conscious) recognition by others that an honorable act requires reward. Swiss psychoanalyst Carl Jung coined the term collective unconscious to describe structures of the unconscious mind shared among members of the same species (Jung 1934–1954). According to Jung, the human collective unconscious is populated by universal instincts and by archetypes. Perhaps this desire to reward others for desirable actions is an innate unconscious instinct within the human species.

Eco-spirituality is defined as "the direct consciousness and experience of the Sacred in the ecology which may serve as a sustained source for communities' and individuals' practical search to live sustainably from the Earth's resources" (van Schalkwyk, 2011, p. 77). The ecological crisis, combined with the inability of established religions to deal with the crisis necessitates a new paradigm which encourages an awareness of the sacredness of the ecosystem and humankind's participation in the whole system, not merely a separate observer (van Schalkwyk, 2011). If we are consciously aware of our connection with nature, and the impact of our actions on the well-being of the planet, we can begin to modify our lifestyles and actions in a manner than produce a sustainable relationship with nature (van Schalkwyk, 2011). The Earth must be understood as a total community or system, one in which we participate, not dominate (van Schalkwyk, 2011). James Lovelock (1972) developed the Gaia hypothesis wherein he suggested that the entire Earth is one living organism or system, with Russell (2008) adding that in the Information Age, Gaia is developing a nervous system, or global brain (van Schalkwyk, 2011).

In Chapter 7 we considered ecologism as an alternative to the capitalist and socialist systems which have contributed to the current non-sustainable trajectory of civilization (Targowski, 2012). An outcome of ecologism is the creation of a wise society, trained and educated with ecological intelligence, and is therefore qualified to make wise decisions. Three elements play a vital role in the creation of a wise civilization: eco-education, Spirituality 2.0, and wise society, which determine the success of the remaining elements. The main policies of ecologism would be: nature being the most important; people are more important than markets; health is more important than money; sufficiency is more important than efficiency; and, business is subservient to and controlled by society (Targowski, 2012). Smith (2009) echoes this proposal suggesting that eco-spirituality is a missing element in spirituality and sustainability education.

The most important contemporary task is not environmental protection, or the creation of social justice, but rather the creation of a sustainable culture (Holthaus, 2012). The path to a better planetary future is not found in continual economic growth, but through subsistence and spirituality, working toward sustainability. The issues faced by contemporary society are human made issues requiring self-discipline, perseverance, and humility to address them. Holthaus suggests we will not succeed in the creation of a sustainable culture consisting of a just and justifiable economy and society, completely respectful of the environment, until we develop spiritual lives nurturing greater respect for each other.

Carroll (2004) refers to spiritually based sustainable living as "an endless dance of reason and faith". Reason without faith acquiesces to pride and arrogance, while faith without reason contradicts the very essence of humanity. Beginning in the 1990s an influential new dialogue was established at the intersection of ecology and religion. This dialogue heralds a renewed public interest in ecological or environmental ethics, religion, religious values, spirituality, and spiritual values in the new century (Carroll, 2004). The essential foundation of this new spiritually based sustainable living is the concept idea of maximum independence and self-sufficiency (Carroll, 2004).

As mentioned in Chapter 2, Harman (1992) suggested twenty-first-century business is reflecting a "change of mind" in competitive, exploitive materialism and consumerism will be replaced by a new business paradigm with alternative values of relationship quality, the oneness of humanity, cooperation, caring, nurturing, and spiritual values. Worthwhile societal change begins at the individual level because an individual cannot accomplish for society what cannot be accomplished individually (Pappas & Pappas, 2014).

12.5 Systems Thinking and System Leadership

Integrating spirituality and sustainability requires the ability to think systemically because both concepts are systemic in nature. Systems thinking offers a perspective for understanding complex economic, social, and environmental systems (Holling, 2001). The advantage of applying this perspective to sustainability lies in understanding the dynamic interplay among multiple actors and broad social, economic, and ecological systems (Lozano, 2008; Valente, 2012; Williams et al., 2017), which is beneficial to scholars and practitioners when addressing major social problems (Whiteman et al., 2013). Systems thinking is beneficial for developing a better understanding of comprehensive structures, patterns, and cycles in systems (McNamara, 2006). Because sustainability involves a complex economic, social, and environmental system, systems thinking provides an important method for solving sustainability problems (Beehner, 2019).

Siebert suggested that systems thinking is the best approach for solving sustainability problems (Siebert, 2018), while Tarrant and Thiele (2016) add that systems thinking enables complex conditions to be appreciated as adaptive processes. While systems thinking is important in operationalizing sustainability, it has not been fully applied in sustainable development (Davidson & Venning, 2011). However, according to Confino (2012), systems thinking may represent the next stage in evolution of sustainability.

Sustainability has been defined within the context of systems thinking as "the ability of systems to persist, adapt, transform or transition in the face of constantly changing conditions" (Williams et al., 2017, p. 13). The complexity of sustainability, and the need for a systems thinking approach to achieve sustainability are becoming more acknowledged, and recognized as indispensable for overcoming existing reductionist approaches (Barile et al., 2018). We cannot understand sustainability without a systemic approach because understanding sustainability requires general knowledge of the nature of systems, and specific knowledge about human and ecological systems (Clayton & Radcliffe, 1996).

System leadership is defined as leadership that attempts to achieve transformation across multiple organizations in which the individual leading does not have direct control or responsibility (Timmins, 2015). The term first appeared in literature at the beginning of the twenty-first century within the discipline of education but has since expanded to multiple fields. System leadership is an emerging process constituting a broad range of responsibilities that are developed locally or within individual systems or programs, and when combined, promote systemic change (Hopkins & Higham, 2007). Senge et al. (2015) suggested that the broad changes required to expedite progress against society's most unmanageable problems necessitate "a unique type of leader—the system leader, a person who catalyzes collective leadership" (p. 27).

The notion of system leadership expanded upon Senge's (1990) previous work in systems thinking. System leaders are described as possessing three characteristics:

1. They are not unique, extraordinary individuals, but are facilitators of the conditions necessary for successful social change.
2. Anyone (leader or follower) can be a system leader.
3. Core capabilities include being able to see the larger system, encourage contemplation and more innovative discourse, and transform collective attention from reactive problem solving to proactive co-creation of the future (Senge et al.).

System leadership has been proposed as appropriate for achieving sustainability, because system leadership embraces systems theory and systems thinking foundations (Beehner, 2019). The system leadership for sustainability model was developed based on a natural environmental structure, the ability to transcend boundaries and barriers, and willingness to embrace a holistic perspective (Beehner, 2019). Because both sustainability and spirituality are systemic in nature, system leadership would likely be appropriate for combining the two concepts to achieve meaningful results.

12.6 Discussion

Research has demonstrated links between spirituality and sustainable behavior. The resulting behavior is beneficial to the individual, organization, community, and society in terms of reduced financial costs and environmental impacts. These benefits support the proposition that spirituality and sustainability contribute to individual success. In one study, spirituality served as a moderator affecting customers making green choices in automobile purchase decisions (Saleem et al., 2018). In a study of ecological practices in Benedictine monasteries, researchers found that ecological practices existed in agriculture, forestry, energy, and food consumption (Freyer et al., 2018). However, the ecological behavior occurred on an individual level with few organization-wide strategies implemented (Freyer et al., 2018). In a study of undergraduate students in Pacific Island countries, most participants were concerned about climate change and believed that the world is in bad condition in terms of the natural environment (Nunn et al., 2016). The authors concluded that participant spirituality was positively related to a close relationship with nature which explained their pro-environmental behavior. This indicates that it would be more effective to present pro-environmental messages in a religious framework when individuals report strong spiritual beliefs (Kalafatoğlu, 2022).

Garfield et al. (2014) proposed a spiritual oneness approach that measures spiritual beliefs within any religious inclination. Spiritual oneness describes "a belief in the spiritual interconnectedness and essential oneness of all phenomena, both living and nonliving; and a belief that happiness depends on living in accord with this understanding" (p. 357). Their study examined the role of spiritual oneness on spirituality, religiosity, and pro-environmental behavior among adherents of various religions, finding spiritual oneness to be distinct from religiosity, and a better predictor of pro-environmental behavior. Spiritual oneness was determined to be positively related to pro-environmental attitudes and actual pro-environmental behavior (Kalafatoğlu, 2022).

Spirituality and sustainable development are interwoven concepts that can only be meaningfully discussed together (Gupta & Agrawal, 2017). Yet, literature about the advantages of spirituality in enabling climate change adaptation is almost nonexistent (Luetz et al., 2023). Luetz and Nunn (2023) recommended a reexamination and rediscovery of the sustainability-spirituality relationship from the viewpoint of Pacific Island communities who have lived sustainably for millennia (Ellis et al., 2021; Fischer et al., 2022; Leal Filho et al., 2020; Nunn, 2007; Walshe & Nunn, 2012).

Luetz and Nunn (2023) offered several examples of spirituality-sustainability virtues including frugality, modesty, humility, happiness, peace, and contentment (e.g., Gupta & Agrawal, 2017; Yangka et al., 2018), the deep ecology movement (e.g., Fellows, 2019; Lovelock, 2009; Næss, 1973, 1995), Eastern practices of place-based spiritual sustainability (e.g. De Silva, 2023), and meditation practices such as mindfulness (Wamsler, 2018). In the Judeo-Christian traditions, Pope

Francis' (2015) encyclical Laudato Si' offers a model of how Christians can harmonize with sustainability to restrain capitalism and extractivism (Nelson & Luetz, 2019). These examples demonstrate that spirituality and sustainability can be applied together to achieve major change by non-Indigenous communities, and possibly exist within urban communities and "city-zens" (Berejnoi et al., 2019; Cloutier, 2015; UN-Habitat, 2006). Luetz and Nunn (2023) suggested that adaptation and development policies and practices should employ both concepts simultaneously to utilize their cooperative capacity to employ more effective sustainability and climate change transformation (Fair, 2018; Nunn et al., 2016).

12.7 Concluding Thoughts

In this chapter a framework for the integration of spirituality and sustainability for individual success was developed. It is likely some within academia, and the general population will reject the proposition introduced in this chapter, and which forms the theme of this book. Many do not understand the difference between religion and spirituality, a misunderstanding likely to produce apprehension of any effort to introduce a form of non-religious spirituality into individual or organizational life. This would especially be the case within cultures whose religion(s) espouse being the "only way" (e.g., Christianity, Islam), or in cultures perceiving Earth-based religious viewpoints as being pagan or primitive. The recipe provided in this book may take time to prepare, consume, and digest. However, it is hoped to provide a starting point for further dialogue on how spirituality and sustainability may be harnessed for improvement of the individual, and subsequently societal condition.

The proposed success resulting from the combination of individual spirituality and sustainability would contribute to the advancement of the United Nations Sustainable Development Goals (SDGs). While many of the SDGs would benefit, specific examples include:

Goal 1: No poverty.
Goal 3: Good health and well-being.

Goal 8: Decent work and economic growth.
Goal 12: Responsible consumption and production.

Because the SDGs are interconnected, achieving one SDG often contributes to the achievement of one or more others.

Misery exists because of our attachment to specific states of impermanent feelings and uncontrolled greed for transitory possessions (Kovacs, 2014). The recognition of response to this condition results in the mitigation of greed and dependence, and the development of a more temperate lifestyle resulting in a more enhanced effect on the quality of nature (Kovacs, 2014). Several secular philosophers extolled the side effects of living an extravagant lifestyle, with Epicurus suggesting a happy life was an untroubled life resulting from careful life choices. To Epicurus, troubles were the result of the maintenance of a luxurious lifestyle exceeding the benefits of such a lifestyle. In 1922, Albert Einstein did not have money to tip a hotel bellboy, so he scribbled a quick note explaining the theory of happiness, a note which sold at an auction for US$1.3 million (Inskeep, 2017). According to Einstein, "*A calm and modest life* brings more happiness than the pursuit of success combined with constant restlessness".

Combining spirituality and sustainability to achieve success must be performed from and within an ethical foundation. The topic of ethics has been discussed in several chapters. However, it is important to reemphasize that success without ethics is short-term and selfish in nature. Lasting success should be sought while respecting others and the environment. As our global neighborhood becomes more crowded it is becoming increasingly more difficult to exist without impacting others. Humankind's activities should be ethical, responsible, and guided by the universal golden rule: treat others the way you wish to be treated. This rule applies to other humans, living organisms, and the environment.

Personal Interview Summary

In support of the argument that spirituality and sustainability are beneficial for individual success, I conclude this chapter with a personal interview of an industry professional who has applied spirituality and sustainability in his career. I had the pleasure of interviewing Mark

Tercek, when he was CEO of The Nature Conservancy, and an organizational leader who has applied both spirituality and sustainability in his personal career. The Nature Conservancy is the largest nonprofit environmental organization in the world (Jaret, 2017). Prior to becoming CEO of TNC, Mark was a managing director and partner at Goldman Sachs for 24 years, and a faculty member at the New York University Stern School of Business. While at Goldman Sachs, Mark developed the Goldman Sachs Environmental Markets Group (Jaret, 2017) which focused on investment opportunities beneficial for both clients and the environment. Mark Tercek is not an individual who embraces spirituality and sustainability with token participation. Rather, he has incorporated both concepts into the code of his operating system. Mark joined TNC after the 2007–2008 financial crisis. The shift to leading a nonprofit—especially during difficult economic times—was stressful. He began to sense on the inner front that he wasn't doing his job the way he should. He felt this stress affected him both at work and at home with his wife and four kids.

Mark is good friends with CEO Coach, Marshal Goldsmith who agreed to coach Mark for free since he was working for a nonprofit. After meeting with staff, Goldsmith suggested Mark was being too negative, cutting people off in mid-sentence, and was worrying too much about small details. All of this was getting in the way of organizational effectiveness. Based on the suggestions of Goldsmith and his staff, Mark identified three things that he could do better: (1) be a better listener, (2) be more positive, and (3) not sweat the little stuff. However, just having a game plan does not make it easy. He had an interest in meditation for a long time but had never done it before. While he by no means claims to be an expert, Mark commented minor meditation helped the other things click, and helped him to be more thoughtful. The combination of the coaching process and meditation resulted in him becoming a more thoughtful person at work and home. Mark believes he has always been at the right place right time in his career, having enjoyed a satisfying 24-year career on Wall Street. When he came to TNC, even when times were difficult at one point, he "pinched himself" to realize how important what he was doing was. He learned a lot through the process, and his children have benefited by watching what their father did. They learned as a family. The personal benefits of his work have been enormous. He encourages others in the business sector to consider how they can make a difference, too, whether that means making a big career shift like him or serving on a nonprofit board.

Mark came to TNC as a businessperson who was chosen by the board because they desired someone to lead the organization with business strategies, aligning market forces to develop environmental progress. While those strategies are important, he realized that they are not sufficient to achieve TNC's mission. He believes in the need to lead with both the head and the heart, and not just with sheer determination. People at TNC might be able to make more money in the private sector, but many of them choose work at TNC because they want psychic income, not just material income. They desire to give back, and not just think of themselves. Nonprofit leaders must mobilize people for a higher cause, and in essence are doing a form of spiritual work. He is a better CEO because he understands strategy better (that it is not just about business). He would not have said something like that prior to his arrival at TNC. Mark believes TNC employees and volunteers are interested in sustainability because they are interested in vulnerable people and species. They have compassion. Mark believes that through their work, TNC employees are expressing a spiritual commitment.

Mark believes meditation is a good preparation for negotiation in our polarized world. To make environmental progress stakeholders need more time to find common ground. This culture (similar to workplace spirituality) helps to facilitate negotiation. His previous habits of interrupting and worrying about the small details are not a good formula for progress. When he first started at TNC, employees wanted to get to know him and were interested in him but observed that he seemed remote when employees needed to get to know him. As a result of meditation and spirituality he tried to be candid about who he was. Meditation reinforces the behaviors that are important to people like Mark, and while he wants his colleagues to have opportunities to develop mindful practices, he won't impose those practices on others. TNC has always been a collaborative organization, and while this quality is associated with spiritual practices, the organization doesn't talk about this characteristic in that way.

References

Akman, K. (2008). Sufism, spirituality and sustainability: Rethinking Islamic mysticism through contemporary sociology. *Comparative Islamic Studies, 4*(1/2), 1–15. https://doi.org/10.1558/cis.v4i4.1-4.2.1

ANGOC, IRED Asia, & PCDF Forum. (1993). *Economy, ecology & spirituality: Toward a theory and practice of sustainability*. Quezon City, Philippines: Asian NGO Coalition for Agrarian Reform and Rural Development, IRED Asia, and People-Centered Development Forum. http://angoc.org/portal/economy-ecology-and-spirituality-toward-a-theory-and-practices-of-sustainability/

Ansbro, J. J. (1982). *Martin Luther King, Jr: The making of a mind*. Orbis Books.

Barile, S., Orecchini, F., Saviano, M., & Farioli, F. (2018). People, technology, and governance for sustainability: The contribution of systems and cyber-systemic thinking. *Sustainability Science, 13*(5), 1197–1208. https://doi.org/10.1007/s11625-018-0621-y

Beehner, C. G. (2019). *System leadership for sustainability*. Routledge.

Behan, J. R., Richards, M. T., & Lee, M. E. (2001). Effects of tour jeeps in a wildland setting on non-motorized recreationist benefits. *Journal of Park and Recreation Administration, 19*(2), 1–19. https://www.cabdirect.org/cabdirect/abstract/20013130719

Berejnoi, E., Ulluwishewa, R., Cloutier, S., Gibbons, L., Puga, S., & Uthumange, A. (2019). Spirituality: The missing link of sustainability and happiness as a framework for holistic development. In Y. Kee, S. Lee, & R. Phillips (Eds.), *Perspectives on community well-being. Community quality-of-life and well-being*. Springer. https://doi.org/10.1007/978-3-030-15115-7_11

Bloch, D. P., & Richmond, L. J. (1998). *SoulWork: Finding the work you love, loving the work you have*. Davies-Black.

Bloch, D. P. (2004). Spirituality, complexity, and career counseling. *Professional School Counseling, 7*, 343–350. http://www.jstor.org/stable/42732603

Bloch, D. P. (2005). Complexity, chaos, and nonlinear dynamics: A new perspective on career development theory. *The Career Development Quarterly, 53*, 194–207. https://doi.org/10.1002/j.2161-0045.2005.tb00990.x

Bobilya, A. J., Akey, L., & Mitchell, D., Jr. (2009). Outcomes of a spiritually focused wilderness orientation program. *Journal of Experiential Education, 31*(3), 440–443. https://doi.org/10.1177/105382591003300403

Brayley, R. E., & Fox, K. M. (1998). Introspection and spirituality in the backcountry recreation experience. In M. D. Bialeschki, & W. P. Stewart (Eds.), *Abstracts from the 1998 symposium on leisure research* (p. 24). National Recreation and Parks Association.

Brewer, E. W. (2001). Vocational Souljourn paradigm: A model of adult development to express spiritual wellness as meaning, being, and doing in work and life. *Counseling and Values, 45*, 83–93. https://doi.org/10.1002/j.2161-007X.2001.tb00187.x

Brown, K. W., & Kasser, T. (2005). Are psychological and ecological well-being compatible? The role of values, mindfulness, and lifestyle. *Social Indicators Research, 74*, 349–368. https://doi.org/10.1007/s11205-004-8207-8

Carroll, J.E. (2004). *Sustainability and spirituality.* State University of New York Press.

Cavanagh, G. (1999). Spirituality for managers: Context and critique. *Journal of Organizational Change Management, 12*(3), 186–195. https://doi.org/10.1108/09534819910273793

Chavez, F. I. (2010). Sustainability & spirituality: Common threads. Originally published in the *Green MBA Journal, 6*(1). Dominican University of California. http://feliciachavez.com

Clayton, A. M., & Radcliffe, N. J. (1996). *Sustainability. A systems approach.* Earthscan.

Cloutier, S. A. (2015). In pursuit of happiness: Moving our communities toward a sustainable and happy future. *International Journal of Social Sustainability in Economic, Social & Cultural Context, 11*(3), 29–40. https://doi.org/10.18848/2325-1115/CGP/v11i03/55162

Confino, J. (2012, October 15). *The art of systems thinking in driving sustainable transformation.* Retrieved from https://www.theguardian.com/sustainable-business/systems-thinking-sustainable-transformation

Davidson, K. M., & Venning, J. (2011). Sustainability decision-making frameworks and the application of systems thinking: An urban context. *Local Environment, 16*(3), 213–228. https://doi.org/10.1080/13549839.2011.565464

De Silva, W. (2023). Comprehending genius loci, towards spiritual sustainability: Lessons from Buddhist heritage city Anuradhapura. *International Journal of Heritage Studies, 29*(1–2), 1–20. https://doi.org/10.1080/13527258.2023.2169333

Dhiman, S. (2017). *Holistic leadership: A new paradigm for today's leaders.* Palgrave Macmillan.

Dunn, E. W., Aknin, L. B., & Norton, M. I. (2008). Spending money on others promotes happiness. *Science, 319*(5870), 1687–1688. https://doi.org/10.1126/science.1150952

Ehrenfeld, J., & Hoffman, A. J. (2013). *Flourishing: A frank conversation about sustainability.* Stanford University Press.

Elgin, D. (1993). *Voluntary simplicity* (Rev. ed.). William Morrow.

Elkington, J. (1998) *Cannibals with forks: The triple bottom line of 21st Century business.* New Society Publishers.

Ellis, E. C., Gauthier, N., Klein Goldewijk, K., Bliege Bird, R., Boivin, N., Díaz, S., Fuller, D. Q., Gill, J. L., Kaplan, J. O., Kingston, N., & Locke, H. (2021). People have shaped most of terrestrial nature for at least 12,000 years. *Proceedings of the National Academy of Sciences, 118*(17), e2023483118. https://doi.org/10.1073/pnas.2023483118

Fair, H. (2018). Three stories of Noah: Navigating religious climate change narratives in the Pacific Island region. *Geo: Geography & Environment, 5*(2), e00068. https://doi.org/10.1002/geo2.68

Fellows, A. (2019). *Gaia, psyche and deep ecology: Navigating climate change in the Anthropocene.* Routledge.

Fischer, M., Maxwell, K., Nuunoq, P. H., Greeno, D., Jingwas, N., Blair, J. G., Hugo, S., Mustonen, T., Murtomäki, E., & Mustonen, K. (2022). Empowering her guardians to nurture our Ocean's future. *Reviews in Fish Biology & Fisheries, 32*, 271–296. https://doi.org/10.1007/s11160-021-09679-3

Fox, R. J. (1997). Women, nature and spirituality: A qualitative study exploring women's wilderness experience. In D. Rowe & P. Brown (Eds.), *Proceedings, ANZALS conference 1997* (pp. 59–64). Australian and New Zealand Association for Leisure Studies, and Department of Leisure and Tourism Studies, The University of Newcastle.

Freyer, B., Aversano-Dearborn, V., Winkler, G., Leipold, S., Haidl, H., Brand, K. W., Rosenberger, M., & Wallnig, T. (2018). Is there a relation between ecological practices and spirituality? The case of Benedictine monasteries. *Journal of Agricultural & Environmental Ethics, 31*(5), 559–582. https://doi.org/10.1007/s10806-018-9745-4

Fry, L. W., & Wigglesworth, C. G. (2010). Towards a theory of spiritual intelligence and spiritual leader development. Management, Spirituality & Religion Conference Paper Abstracts. *Academy of Management Annual Meeting Proceedings*, August 1–17.

Garfield, A. M., Drwecki, B. B., Moore, C. F., Kortenkamp, K. V., & Gracz, M. D. (2014). The Oneness Beliefs Scale: Connecting spirituality with pro-environmental behavior. *Journal for the Scientific Study of Religion, 53*(2), 356–372. https://doi.org/10.1111/jssr.12108

Grafanaki, S., Pearson, D., Cini, F., Godula, B., McKenzie, B., Nason, S., & Anderegg, M. (2005). Sources of renewal: A qualitative study of the experience and role of leisure in the life of counselors and psychologists. *Counselling Psychology Quarterly, 18*(1), 31–40. https://doi.org/10.1080/09515070500099660

Gregg, R. (1936). *The value of voluntary simplicity.* Pendle Hill.

Gupta, K., & Agrawal, R. (2017). Sustainable development and spirituality: A critical analysis of GNH index. *International Journal of Social Economics, 44*(12), 1919–1939. https://doi.org/10.1108/IJSE-10-2015-0283

Harman, W. (1992). 21st century business: A background for dialogue. In J. Renesch (Ed.), *New tradition in business: Spirit and leadership in the 21st century* (pp. 11–24). Berrett- Koehler.

Heaton, D. (2016). Higher consciousness for sustainability-as-flourishing. In S. Dhiman & J. Marques (Eds.), *Spirituality and Sustainability: New horizons and exemplary approaches* (pp. 121–137). Springer International Publishing.

Heintzman, P. (1998). The role of introspection/spiritual in the park experience of campers at Ontario Provincial Parks. In *Culture, environment, and society. Book of abstracts from the seventh international symposium on society and resource management* (pp. 169–170). University of Missouri-Columbia.

Heintzman, P. (2000). Leisure and spiritual well-being relationships: A qualitative study. *Society and Leisure, 23*(1), 41–69. https://doi.org/10.1080/07053436.2000.10715603

Heintzman, P. (2002). The role of introspection and spirituality in the park experience of day visitors to Ontario Provincial Parks. In S. Bondrup-Nielsen, N. Munro, G. Nelson, M. Willison, T. Herman, & P. Eagles (Eds.), *Managing protected areas in a changing world* (pp. 992–1004). Science and Management of Protected Areas Association.

Heintzman, P. (2009). Nature-based recreation and spirituality: A complex relationship. *Leisure Sciences, 32*(1), 72–89. https://doi.org/10.1080/01490400903430897

Holling, C. S. (2001). Understanding the complexity of economic, ecological, and social systems. *Ecosystems, 4*(5), 390–405. https://doi.org/10.1007/s10021-001-0101-5

Holthaus, G. (2012). *Learning Native wisdom: What traditional cultures teach us about subsistence, sustainability, and spirituality*. University Press of Kentucky.

Hopkins, D., & Higham, R. (2007). System leadership: Mapping the landscape. *School Leadership and Management, 27*(2), 147–166. https://doi.org/10.1080/13632430701237289

Inskeep, S. (2017, October 25). *Albert Einstein's quote about living a modest life sells for $1.3 million*. National Public Radio (NPR). https://www.npr.org/2017/10/25/559963919/albert-einsteins-quote-about-living-a-modest-life-sells-for-1-3-million

Iqbal, S., & Khan, M. I. (2020). Spirituality as a predictor of psychological well-being: An explanatory mechanism of religiosity and sustainable consumption. *Religions, 11*(12), 634. https://doi.org/10.3390/rel11120634

Jaret, P. (2017, December). *Common ground. Mindful, 64–70.*

Jung, C. G. (1934–1954). *The archetypes and the collective unconscious* (In 1981 2nd ed. Collected works Vol. 9 Part 1). Bollingen.

Kalafatoğlu, Y. (2022). Workplace spirituality for more sustainable organizations. In *Handbook of research on integrating spirituality in modern workplaces* (pp. 80–95). IGI Global.

Kasser, T. (2009). Psychological need satisfaction, personal well-being, and ecological sustainability. *Ecopsychology, 1*(4), 175–180. https://doi.org/10.1089/eco.2009.0025

Kovacs, G. (Ed.). (2014). Buddhist spiritual orientation to nature and sustainability. In L. Zsolnai (Ed.), *The spiritual dimension of business ethics and sustainability management* (pp. 57–68). Springer. https://doi.org/10.1007/978-3-319-11677-8_20

Laszlo, C., Saillant, R., Pose, I. B., & Brown, J. S. (2014). *Flourishing enterprise: The new spirit of business*. Stanford University Press.

Leal Filho, W., Ha'apio, M. O., Luetz, J. M., & Li, C. (2020). Climate change adaptation as a development challenge to small Island states: A case study from the Solomon Islands. *Environmental Science Policy, 107*, 179–187. https://doi.org/10.1016/j.envsci.2020.03.008

Leal Filho, W., Salvia, A. L., Ulluwishewa, R., Abubakar, I. R., Mifsud, M., LeVasseur, T. J., Correia, V., Consorte-McCrea, A., Paço, A., Fritzen, B., Ray, S., Gordon, N., Luetz, J. M., Borsari, B., Venkatesan, M., Mukul, S. A., Carp, R. M., Begum, H., Nunoo, E. K., ... Farrugia, E. (2022). Linking sustainability and spirituality: A preliminary assessment in pursuit of a sustainable and ethically correct world. *Journal of Cleaner Production, 380*, 135091. https://doi.org/10.1016/j.jclepro.2022.135091

Livengood, J. (2009). The role of leisure in the spirituality of new paradigm Christians. *Leisure/loisir, 33*(1), 389–417. https://doi.org/10.1080/14927713.2009.9651444

Loeffler, T. A. (2004). A photo elicitation study of the meanings of outdoor adventure experiences. *Journal of Leisure Research, 36*(4), 536–556. https://doi.org/10.1080/00222216.2004.11950035

Lovelock, J. E. (1972). Gaia as seen through the atmosphere. *Atmospheric Environment, 6*(8), 579–580. https://doi.org/10.1007/978-94-009-7944-4_2

Lovelock, J. (2009). *The vanishing face of Gaia.* Basic Books.

Lozano, R. (2008). Envisioning sustainability three-dimensionally. *Journal of Cleaner Production, 16*, 1838–1846. https://doi.org/10.1016/j.jclepro.2008.02.008

Luetz, J. M., Nichols, N., Du Plessis, K., & Nunn, P. D. (2023). Spirituality and sustainable development: A systematic word frequency analysis and an agenda for research in Pacific Island Countries. *Sustainability, 15*(3), 2201. https://doi.org/10.3390/su15032201

Luetz, J. M., & Nunn, P. D. (2023). Spirituality and sustainable development: An entangled and neglected relationship. *Sustainability Science, 18*, 2035–2042. https://doi.org/10.1007/s11625-023-01347-8

Marques, J., Dhiman, S., & King, R. (2010). Exploring the link between spirituality and sustainability. *Business Renaissance Quarterly*, 5(1), 19. https://www.proquest.com

McNamara, C. (2006). *Field guide to consulting and organizational development: A collaborative and systems approach to performance, change and learning.* Authenticity Consulting.

Næss, A. (1973). The shallow and the deep, long-range ecology movement: A summary. *Inquiry, 16*(1–4), 95–100. https://doi.org/10.1080/00201747308601682

Næss, A. (1995). Self-realization: An ecological approach to being in the world. In G. Sessions (Ed.), *Deep ecology for the twenty-first century* (pp. 225–239). Shambhala.

Nelson, W., & Luetz, J.M. (2019). What can we learn from Pope Francis about change management for environmental sustainability? A case study on success factors for leading change in change-resistant institutional environments. In W. Leal Filho, & A. Consorte McCrea (Eds.), *Sustainability and the Humanities* (pp. 503–524). Springer. https://doi.org/10.1007/978-3-319-95336-6_29

Nunn, P. D. (2007). *Climate, environment and society in the Pacific during the Last Millennium*. Elsevier.

Nunn, P. D., Mulgrew, K., Scott-Parker, B., Hine, D. W., Marks, A. D., Mahar, D., & Maebuta, J. (2016). Spirituality and attitudes towards nature in the Pacific Islands: Insights for enabling climate-change adaptation. *Climatic Change, 136*(3–4), 477–493. https://doi.org/10.1007/s10584-016-1646-9

Pappas, J. B., & Pappas, E. C. (2014). The sustainable personality: Values and behaviors in individual sustainability. *International Journal of Higher Education, 4*(1), 12. https://doi.org/10.5430/ijhe.v4n1p12

Pfeffer, J. (2010). Business and the spirit. In R. A. Giacalone, & C. L. Jurkiewicz (Eds.), *Handbook of workplace spirituality and organizational performance* (2nd ed., pp. 27–43). M. E. Sharp.

Pierce, L. B. (2000). *Choosing simplicity: Real people finding peace and fulfillment in a complex world*. Gallagher Press.

Pope Francis. (2015). Laudato Si' [On Care for Our Common Home] encyclical letter. Vatican Press. https://www.vatican.va/content/dam/francesco/pdf/encyclicals/documents/papa-francesco_20150524_enciclica-laudato-si_en.pdf

Rimanoczy, I. (2014). A matter of being: Developing sustainability-minded leaders. *Journal of Management for Global Sustainability*, *2*(1), 95–122. https://doi.org/10.13185/1902

Rule, M., & Udd, E. (2002). Resident camp directors, spirituality, and wilderness. In S. Todd (Ed.), *Proceedings of the 2001 Northeastern Recreation Research Symposium* (Gen. Tech. Rep. NE- 289) (pp. 418–420). U.S. Department of Agriculture, Forest Service, Northeastern Research Station.

Russell, P. (2008). *The global brain: The awakening Earth in a new century* (3rd ed.). Floris Books.

Saleem, M. A., Eagle, L., Yaseen, A., & Low, D. (2018). The power of spirituality: Exploring the effects of environmental values on eco-socially conscious consumer behaviour. *Asia Pacific Journal of Marketing and Logistics, 30*(4), 867–888. https://doi.org/10.1108/APJML-10-2017-0259

Schein, S. (2014). *The ecological world views and post-conventional action logics of global sustainability leaders* (Doctoral dissertation, Fielding Graduate University).

Schmidt, C., & Little, D. E. (2007). Qualitative insights into leisure as a spiritual experience. *Journal of Leisure Research, 39*(2), 222–247. https://doi.org/10.1080/00222216.2007.11950106

Senge, P. M. (1990). *The fifth discipline: The art & practice of the learning organization.* New Doubleday/Currency.

Senge, P., Hamilton, H., & Kania, J. (2015). The dawn of system leadership. *Stanford Social Innovation Review, 13*(1), 27–33. https://ssir.org/articles/entry/the_dawn_of_system_leadership

Siebert, M. (2018). *Systems thinking and how it can help build a sustainable world.* Post Carbon Institute. Retrieved from: https://www.resilience.org/stories/2018-07-11/systems-thinking-and-how-it-can-help-build-a-sustainable-world/

Smith, C. (2009). Reconnecting with Earth: Ecospirituality as the missing dimension in spirituality and sustainability education. *International Handbook of Education for Spirituality, Care and Wellbeing, 653–675*,. https://doi.org/10.1007/978-1-4020-9018-9_35

Stead, J. G., & Stead, W. E. (2014). Building spiritual capabilities to sustain sustainability-based competitive advantages. *Journal of Management, Spirituality & Religion, 11*(2), 143–158. https://doi.org/10.1080/14766086.2013.832359

Stringer, L. A., & McAvoy, L. H. (1992). The need for something different: Spirituality and wilderness adventure. *The Journal of Experiential Education, 15*(1), 13–21. https://doi.org/10.1177/105382599201500103

Targowski, A. (2012). Spirituality 2.0—A condition for a wise civilization. *Dialogue and Universalism, 22*(2), 133–143. https://www.researchgate.net

Tarrant, S. P., & Thiele, L. P. (2016). Practice makes pedagogy–John Dewey and skills-based sustainability education. *International Journal of Sustainability in Higher Education, 17*(1), 54–67. https://doi.org/10.1108/IJSHE-09-2014-0127

Tate, W. (2009). *The search for leadership: An organisational perspective.* Triarchy Press.

Timmins, N. (2015). *The practice of system leadership: Being comfortable with chaos.* The King's Fund. https://www.kingsfund.org.uk/sites/default/files/field/field_publication_file/System-leadership-Kings-Fund-May-2015.pdf

Tolle, E. (1999). *The power of now: A guide to spiritual enlightenment.* New World Library.

Trainor, S. F., & Norgaard, R. B. (1999). Recreation fees in the context of wilderness values. *Journal of Park and Recreation Administration, 17*(3), 100–115. http://js.sagamorepub.com/jpra/article/view/1634

Trott, J., & Crow, S. (2002). *Soak up the Sun* [music recording]. Ole Media Management & Reservoir Media Management.
UN-Habitat. (2006). *State of the world's cities 2006/7.* https://sustainabledevelopment.un.org/content/documents/11292101_alt.pdf
Valente, M. (2012). Theorizing firm adoption of sustaincentrism. *Organization Studies, 33*(4), 563–591. https://doi.org/10.1177/0170840612443455
Van Schalkwyk, A. (2011). Sacredness and sustainability: Searching for a practical eco-spirituality. *Religion and Theology, 18*(1–2), 77–92. https://doi.org/10.1163/157430111X613674
Vatican Insider. (2015). *Pope Francis' encyclical: This "wounded world" needs "an ecological conversion"*. The Vatican. http://www.lastampa.it/2015/06/17/vaticaninsider/eng/the-vatican/pope-francis-encyclical-this-wounded-world-needs-an-ecological-conversion-VIDiWxrhCcCwmSDen1R9yI/pagina.html
Walker, A. G. (2013). The relationship between the integration of faith and work with life and job outcomes. *Journal of Business Ethics, 112*(3), 453–461. https://doi.org/10.1007/s10551-012-1271-0
Walshe, R. A., & Nunn, P. D. (2012). Integration of indigenous knowledge and disaster risk reduction: A case study from Baie Martelli, Pentecost Island, Vanuatu. *International Journal of Disaster Risk Science, 3*, 185–194. https://doi.org/10.1007/s13753-012-0019-x
Wamsler, C. (2018). Mind the gap: The role of mindfulness in adapting to increasing risk and climate change. *Sustainability Science, 13*, 1121–1135. https://doi.org/10.1007/s11625-017-0524-3
Whiteman, G., Walker, B., & Perego, P. (2013). Planetary boundaries: Ecological foundations for corporate sustainability. *Journal of Management Studies, 50*(2), 307–336. https://doi.org/10.1111/j.1467-6486.2012.01073.x
Williams, A., Kennedy, S., Philipp, F., & Whiteman, G. (2017). Systems thinking: A review of sustainability management research. *Journal of Cleaner Production, 148*, 866–881. https://doi.org/10.1016/j.jclepro.2017.02.002
Witmer, J. M., & Sweeney, T. J. (1992). A holistic model for wellness and prevention over the life span. *Journal of Counseling & Development, 71*, 140–148. https://doi.org/10.1002/j.1556-6676.1992.tb02189.x
World Commission on Environment and Development. (1987). *Our common future*. Oxford University Press.
Yangka, D., Newman, P., Rauland, V., & Devereux, P. (2018). Sustainability in an emerging nation: The Bhutan case study. *Sustainability, 10*(5), 1622. https://doi.org/10.3390/su10051622

13

Integrating Workplace and Organizational Spirituality with Sustainability for Organizational Success

13.1 Introduction

In this chapter I propose that the combination of workplace spirituality and sustainability are beneficial for business and organizational success. Existing literature will be synthesized to demonstrate the benefits, along with interviews to assist with practical application of workplace spirituality and sustainability on a business/organizational level. I included a comment in Chapter 12 concerning the intuitive sense that spirituality and sustainability would contribute to the success of an individual, which nonetheless would require a theoretical foundation or framework which can be researched and proven to be considered scientifically valid. Recognizing that limited research exists concerning the relationships among sustainability, spirituality, and success, at the organizational level, much of the focus of this chapter will be with the development of an argument for, and a conceptual framework from which to examine the proposed relationship of these constructs at the organizational level. The mutual dependence of spirituality and sustainability was discussed in Chapter 1 of this text, with scholars suggesting that spirituality enhances efforts to act in a sustainably responsible manner, and sustainability reinforces the connectedness of all life (Marques et al., 2010). Hopefully, the content in

C. G. Beehner, *Spirituality, Sustainability, and Success*, Palgrave Studies in Workplace Spirituality and Fulfillment, https://doi.org/10.1007/978-3-031-47643-3_13

this chapter will stimulate thought and further research leading to a reification of the position that spirituality and sustainability, when combined contribute to individual success.

The central theme of this chapter is that the combination of spirituality and sustainability is beneficial for organizational success. Systems thinking, the Quadruple Bottom Line for Sustainability, and Man-Environment-Organism (M-E-O) are introduced as frameworks through which to understand the proposed relationship. Flourishing, conscious capitalism, and spiritual entrepreneurship are introduced within the context of the chapter theme. The chapter concludes with an examination of Laloux's proposed model of organizational evolution, and the emerging evolutionary "teal" organization.

The premise of this book is that spirituality (individual and workplace), and sustainability are beneficial for individual (and organizational) success. In an earlier chapter, spirituality was defined as "the desire to find ultimate purpose in life, and to live accordingly" (Cavanagh, 1999, p. 186), and "the feeling individuals have about the fundamental meaning of who they are, what they are doing, [and] the contributions they are making" (p. 218). Pfeffer (2010) identified the four fundamental dimensions of what employees seek in a spiritual workplace as: (1) interesting and meaningful work that inspires learning and development; (2) meaningful work providing a sense of purpose; (3) a sense of connection and positive relationships with coworkers; and (4) the ability to live an integrated life, in which work and non-work roles are in harmony with who the person is as a human being. Sustainability was defined as meeting the needs of present generations without compromising future generational needs (WCED, 1987). Moreover, both spirituality and sustainability are characterized by a holistic perspective of self, others, and the universe.

The commonalities of, and interconnection between spirituality (both individual and workplace), and sustainability support the hypothesis: ***A combination of spirituality and sustainability positively impacts both individual and organizational success***. Sustainability meets the workplace spirituality dimensions of (1) meaningful work, and (2) sense of purpose through preservation of planetary resources for future generations, (3) connection and positive relationship, by the collective need

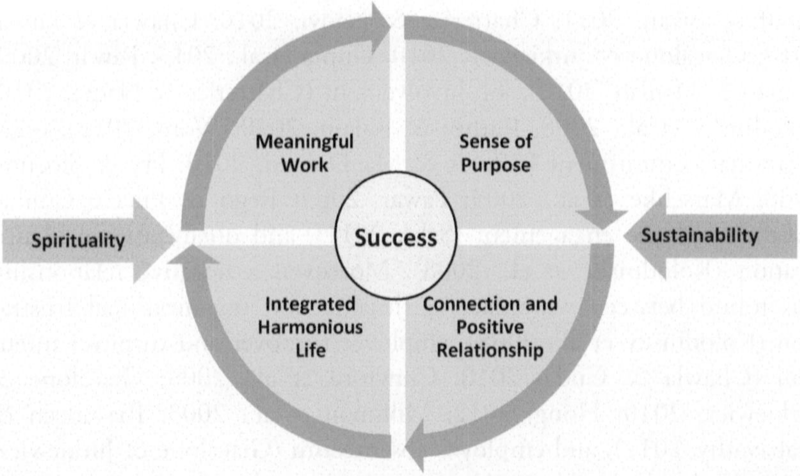

Fig. 13.1 Spirituality, sustainability, and organizational success, Christopher Beehner (2018)

for sustainable action, and (4) a harmonious, integrated life, through the integration of spirituality, sustainability, life, and career. Likewise, sustainability meets the spiritual dimensions of finding ultimate purpose in life and making a meaningful contribution through the preservation of planetary resources for future generations, clearly a meaningful purpose to seek. Because both religion and secularism played a major part in the development of civilization, the contemporary spirituality (individual and workplace) discussed in previous chapters will play a major role in the development of sustainable civilization. Figure 13.1 provides a visual representation of the spirituality, sustainability, and organizational success proposition.

13.2 The Nexus of Organizational Spirituality, Sustainability, and Success

Chapter 10 is replete with the examples of beneficial effects of workplace spirituality and spiritual organizations. Positive relationships have been demonstrated between workplace spirituality and job satisfaction

(Altaf & Awan, 2011; Chatterjee & Naqvi, 2010; Chawla & Guda, 2010; Giacalone & Jurkiewicz, 2010; Gupta et al., 2013; Pawar, 2009; Usman & Danish, 2010), job involvement (Chatterjee & Naqvi, 2010; Kolodinsky et al., 2008; Rathee & Rajain, 2020; Word, 2012), organizational commitment (Affeldt & MacDonald, 2010; Fry & Slocum, 2008; Marschke et al., 2009; Pawar, 2009; Rego & Pina e Cunha, 2008), employee engagement (Saks, 2011), and organizational identification (Kolodinsky et al., 2008). Moreover, a negative relationship was found between workplace spirituality and organizational frustration (Kolodinsky et al., 2008), employee turnover and turnover intention (Chawla & Guda, 2010; Crawford et al., 2009; Giacalone & Jurkiewicz, 2010; Hong, 2012; Milliman et al., 2003; Riasudeen & Prabavathy, 2011), and employee absenteeism (Giacalone & Jurkiewicz, 2010; Krahnke et al., 2003). Organizations that have implemented workplace spirituality programs have experienced beneficial organizational outcomes (Burack, 1999; Case & Gosling, 2010; De Diego-Cordero et al., 2021; Dhiman & Marques, 2011; Fry, 2003; Giacalone & Jurkiewicz, 2010; Han et al., 2010; Kinjerski & Skrypnek, 2008; Krishnakumar & Neck, 2002; Paloutzian et al., 2003; Pawar, 2008; Reave, 2005; Yong et al., 2011).

Chapter 11 provided substantial evidence of the organizational benefits of sustainability, including specific examples of businesses benefiting from incorporating sustainability into their business models. Specific reasons companies should be concerned with sustainability included: cost savings; consumer demand; risk mitigation; leadership; tax incentives; employee retention; brand reputation and publicity; resource limitation; keeping up with the competition; and, new revenue opportunities (Spector, 2012). Some of the benefits of a sustainable business strategy include: gaining competitive advantage from goodwill; preference of green brands by consumers; recruiting and retaining good employees; saving money from efficiency and waste reduction; making money from creative forms of waste re-generation; sustainability as a point of differentiation; shaping future of industry; becoming preferred supplier; providing competitive edge to customers; and, changing image and brand (Senge, 2008). Companies not having a sustainable approach within their strategy risk missing opportunities influenced by the increasingly "green" consumer (Esty & Winston, 2006). Businesses that have pioneered the shift toward sustainable business practices, create a competitive advantage by getting ahead of the curve, and taking sustainable actions to lower both financial and operational risk by providing added degrees of freedom to operate, profit, and expand (Esty & Winston, 2006).

Pro-environmental behavior (PEB) is environmentally responsible behavior or "green behavior" that protects the environment (Choong et al., 2019). Environmental passion is characterized by positive emotions resulting in an individual's desire to engage in PEB and practices (Akhshik et al., 2021). Workplace spirituality can increase PEB among workers in the hospitality sector in three ways (Rezapouraghdam et al., 2019). First, workplace spirituality may influence employees to connect with nature, other individuals, the planet, and the employer. Second, workplace spirituality may help develop self-transcendent values which may influence employees to feel benevolent toward other individuals. Third, workplace spirituality may encourage feelings of empathy and compassion for others (Rezapouraghdam et al., 2019). In an earlier study, Rezapouraghdam et al. (2018) found that connectedness to nature moderates the relationship between workplace spirituality and organizational citizenship behavior toward the environment. The study findings revealed that when employees' spiritual needs are met, they feel more connected with nature resulting in increased sustainability behavior in the workplace (Kalafatoğlu, 2022). Workplace spirituality may increase sustainability behavior because it permeates employees' higher needs and strengthens intrinsic motivation (Chalofsky & Krishna, 2009). Iqbal et al. (2018) found that perceived job characteristics, mediated by workplace spirituality indirectly affected environmental sustainability. When employees feel motivated, they become more connected, experience meaningfulness, and embrace organizational values resulting in increased sustainability behavior (Kalafatoğlu, 2022).

Environmental passion can have a significant positive impact on organizations through actions that contribute to environmental preservation (Sankar & Suresh, 2018). Sembiring et al. (2020) found that workplace spirituality had a significant influence on employee environmental passion, which had a significant influence on employee PEB. Workplace spirituality also has a significant influence on PEB through environmental passion (Sembiring et al., 2020). According to Peng et al. (2021), the increasing frequency of environmental crises will force organizations to increase implementation of PEB initiatives to achieve environmental sustainability.

Both workplace spirituality and organizational sustainability are holistic organizational worldviews, with workplace spirituality considering the whole employee (Hicks, 2003), and organizational sustainability encompassing the entire business or organizational system from beginning to end (Rainey, 2008). Both concepts require consideration for all stakeholders, not just shareholders and customers. Both concepts suggest a purpose for collective action, a connection and connectedness with each other and nature, and instill a sense of community among organizational members. The similarities among spirituality and sustainability encourage a holistic worldview, through which spiritual, sustainable organizations may provide purpose, sense of connection with nature and other individuals, and a sense of community, both within the organization, and with society. This purposeful, connected community of individuals should provide exceptional organizational success.

13.3 Spiritual Organizations

One of the topics of Chapters 3 and 10 was spiritual organizations. Guillory (1997) describes a spiritual organization as a living organization, arguing organizational spirituality is inevitable, occurring through a personal and collective transformational process. The living organization is characterized as adaptable to change through continual re-creation and possessing the Darwinian principles of a living organism: uniqueness, endurance, acclimation, and heritage (Guillory, 1997). Guillory suggests the amalgamation of spiritual principles and sound business practices creates a highly effective organization, characterized by diversity, empowerment, environmentalism, teamwork, and a customer focus. His definition of environmentalism mirrors the current definition of sustainability in caring for the environment to provide for the well-being of all inhabitants, while managing the impact of the organization on both people and planet.

The spiritual organization may replace the contemporary organizations which are frequently characterized as machines, structured, and managed using traditional command and control techniques (Geh & Tan, 2009). Guillory (1997) theorized the Industrial Age which was followed by the Information Age and partially concurrent Knowledge Age, will be followed by the Spiritual Age, and subsequent Age of Oneness. Organizations surviving and thriving in the coming ages will be organizations cognizant of the potential of the human spirit (Guillory, 1997). Successful organizations in the latter two stages will utilize quantum thinking to anticipate the next paradigm, developing products and services that will meet the spiritual needs of the subsequent age.

Spiritual organizations must be managed and motivated by authentic spirituality. Driscoll and Wiebe suggested authentic workplace spirituality must have human welfare as the primary goal, transforming management instead of simply using spirituality as a tool for productivity improvement (Driscoll & Wiebe, 2007). Authentic workplace spirituality involves improving the world and not just improving the workplace or appeasing employee psyches (Driscoll & Wiebe, 2007). Leaders of spiritual organizations achieve authentic spirituality by applying the servant, authentic, ethical, and spiritual leadership styles that were described in Chapter 3.

Lázár (2004) suggested economy and ecology are related categories, having the same etymological root, "*oikos*": *oikos-nomos* and *oikos-logos*. Based upon their similarities, ecology and economy must be integrated as an ecological economy if we are to achieve sustainability. At the semantic root there is no contradiction, but there may be antagonism between economic success and ecological balance. According to Lazar, spirituality challenges economics by seeking humanity in the inner wealth, and the creative and responsible being, not in material wealth. Leaders of spiritual organizations recognize the interconnectedness of economy and ecology.

13.4 Spirituality, Sustainability, and Success Frameworks

Several frameworks exist for understanding the relationship among, and benefits of spirituality, sustainability, and success. Systems thinking may provide a valid framework for the interaction of the three variables, because workplace spirituality recognizes and embraces the whole person as a system consisting of multiple interacting components, and sustainability recognizes and embraces the planet and inhabitants as a system consisting of multiple interacting components. Systems thinking was discussed in several chapters, defined as based upon understanding an organization or industry as a system, by examining linkages and interactions between components constituting the entirety of the defined system (Tate, 2009). Because systems thinking views whole systems as being composed of systems, entities, and subsystems, it provides a useful framework to consider the interconnectedness of spirituality, sustainability, and success. The relevance of systems thinking to our framework is the focus on individual components together in a system, rather than with spirituality, sustainability, and success as independent concepts. Because a system may be more than the sum of its parts, modifying one component or subsystem usually impacts other components, subsystems, and the whole system.

Supporting the argument for the integration of spirituality and sustainability for organizational success, Walker (2013) proposed a *Quadruple Bottom Line for Sustainability*. Similar to the existing triple bottom line (Elkington et al., 2007), Walker's model consists of social responsibility, environmental care, and economic issues, with the latter relegated to a lower-order factor, not considered to be an end goal, but a means to an end. Walker's fourth component, personal meaning is characterized as spirituality, combined with the personal ethic and values that emerge from attention to inner growth. The quadruple bottom line model emphasizes a deeper concept of human meaning initiates a movement from a *knowledge* economy toward a *wisdom* economy, in which the value of knowledge acquisition is recognized, but greater emphasis is placed on the priorities and practices of wisdom attainment.

Walker (2013) argues the inclusion of spirituality within the sustainability paradigm may reposition individual motivation from an external encumbrance of rules and regulations to an internal voluntary repositioning of priorities. This internal avidity would temper our current obsession with consumerism, growth, and technological advancements, leading to a more comprehensive attitude toward organizational design. This paradigm shift would redirect efforts away from the present self-destructive, essentially unsustainable path to a more positive and constructive path.

Eco-spirituality is a contemporary movement combining spirituality and sustainability and defined as "the direct consciousness and experience of the Sacred in the ecology which may serve as a sustained source for communities' and individuals' practical search to live sustainably from the Earth's resources" (van Schalkwyk, 2011, p. 77). The ecological crisis, combined with the inability of established religions to deal with the crisis necessitates a new paradigm which encourages an awareness of the sacredness of the ecosystem and humankind's participation in the whole system, not merely a separate observer. If we are consciously aware of our connection with nature, and the impact of our actions on the well-being of the planet, we can begin to modify our lifestyles and actions in a manner that produces a sustainable relationship with nature. The Earth must be understood as a total community or system, one in which we participate, not dominate. Lovelock (1972) developed the Gaia hypothesis wherein he suggested that the entire Earth is one living organism or system, with Russell (2008) adding that in the Information Age, Gaia is developing a nervous system, or global brain (van Schalkwyk, 2011).

Similarly, Targowski (2012) proposed ecologism as an alternative to the capitalist and socialist systems which have contributed to the current non-sustainable trajectory of civilization. An outcome of ecologism is the creation of a wise society, trained and educated with ecological intelligence, and is therefore qualified to make wise decisions. Three elements play a vital role in the creation of a wise civilization: eco-education, Spirituality 2.0, and wise society, which determine the success of the remaining elements. The main policies of ecologism are: nature being the most important; people are more important than markets; health is more important than money; sufficiency is more important than efficiency;

and, business is subservient to and controlled by society (Targowski, 2012). Smith (2009) echoes this proposal suggesting eco-spirituality is a missing element in spirituality and sustainability education. Lestar and Böhm (2020) suggested eco-spirituality offers a significant lens to understanding contemporary efforts to transition from infinite economic growth and resource dependency mantras toward more revolutionary worldviews of degrowth and alternative pathways to achieve happiness and fulfillment.

Lázár (2004) suggests the need for an integrative, holistic representation of the interrelatedness of economy, spirituality, and the environment. Lázár (2000) offered the metaphor of man-environment-organism (M-E-O) as a representation of humankind's interaction with the environment. The nature-dominated M-E-O model demonstrated reliability for hundreds of thousands of years. However, the technocratic M-E-O resulting from the Industrial Revolution, transformed the local, cyclically integrated ecological production systems to global scale, throughput systems resulting in biodiversity and ecological integrity destruction. Because culture, technology, ideas, and value systems may not be reduced to psychological, biological, and other non-cultural phenomena, the concept of culture accumulates super-organic character and complexity. This holistic, integrated view of socio-cultural phenomena should include the economy, nature, and spirituality. This super-organism may be represented as a network of mutual interrelationships among nature, society, technology, and the ideo-sphere, having dominant, symbiotic, competitive-exclusive relationships with each other. This human environment concept connects technological, social, and info-spherical environments as supra-individual human ecosystems, possibly generating adaptive (or maladaptive) networks of interrelations (Lázár, 2000).

In Chapter 1, I briefly introduced flourishing as a strongly sustainable business model conceived by Jones and Upward (2014), based upon a holistic view of organizational operation that is consistent with a planet containing finite, shared resources, and a collective societal future. A flourishing organization is a purpose-oriented organization. The flourishing or strongly sustainable framework provides a conceptual framework of an anticipatory system of business governance, theoretically maintainable, and methodologically evaluated by several applications with small, medium, and large enterprises. The anticipatory system model is a proactive, rather than reactive system, assumes a continual adaptation of the living system (e.g., a business and employees) with its environment, and is an appropriate lens for the examination of business models. The flourishing model finds support among spirituality scholars suggesting the cultivation of spirituality is essential for business to succeed in the development of a sustainable and flourishing world (Laszlo et al., 2014). Bouckaert (2014) supported a spiritual approach to business ethics and responsibility, suggesting sustainability characterized by "caring for future generations" exhibits a spiritual commitment that prepares for, and makes possible every declaration of rights, transforming the economy according to those rights.

Conscious capitalism is a new business transformation movement gaining ground in the United States and other countries (Shastri & Banerjee, 2010). Business scholars and practitioners have combined efforts to reinvent a system of capitalism with a conscience and a feeling of interconnectedness. Natural capitalism recognizes the dependence of the global economy on natural resources and systems, suggesting the long-term existence of humankind requires the recognition and proper valuation of natural capital.

As previously mentioned in Chapter 12, the most important contemporary task is not environmental protection, or the creation of social justice, but rather the creation of a sustainable culture (Holthaus, 2012). The path to a better planetary future is not found in continual economic growth, but through subsistence and spirituality, working toward sustainability. The issues faced by contemporary society are humanmade issues requiring self-discipline, perseverance, and humility to address. Holthaus suggested we will not succeed in the creation of a sustainable culture consisting of a just and justifiable economy and society, completely respectful of the environment, until we develop spiritual lives nurturing greater respect for each other.

Virmani and Lépineux (2014) examined *Navdanya* as a spirituality-based entrepreneurship for promotion of an alternative food culture in India. The *Navdanya* movement demonstrates how spiritual values and traditions can be deployed to create a sustainable agriculture vision, defending individuals against more powerful corporate rights. The multi-level transformational power of *Navdanya* has the potential of being a catalyst for an economic model based on fairness, social change, defense of the common good (Virmani & Lépineux, 2014). The focus of the *Navdanya* philosophy is peace with nature through sustainable agriculture, organic farming, and celebrating biodiversity, creating a holistic view of humankind's relation with the planet. It affirms fundamental human right to food, increases awareness of the hazards of chemical fertilizers, pesticides, and genetically modified seeds. The goal of *Navdanya* is the organization and promotion of farmers, preservation of biological and cultural diversity, and defense of seed sovereignty, food sovereignty, and water democracy, all of which are themes covered by the slogan "Earth Democracy" (Virmani & Lépineux, 2014).

Navdanya is a form of *transformational entrepreneurship*, one which prepares for, and allows the realization of a "great transition" of the earth system, based upon the three perspectives of foresight, global civil society, and the common good. Transformational entrepreneurship encourages economic, social, and cultural change toward a sustainable, global civilization, relying on the combination of three mechanisms: foresight, a global civil society, and the promotion of living systems benefiting the common good (Virmani & Lépineux, 2014). Foresight requires possession of a vision of the unfolding of the great transition ahead, of a desirable future state for the world, and being able to link this vision to the present. A global civil society requires raising public awareness of the stakes of the great transition at all levels, from local to global. Promotion of the living systems benefiting the common good requires emphasis on the importance of nature conservation and restoration, promotion of global justice, and placement of human needs at the heart of economic relations.

13.5 Spiritual and Sustainable Organizational Management

Laloux (2014) suggests our organizational management methods have become increasingly outdated. Employees desire soulful workplaces, authenticity, community, passion, and purpose. According to Laloux, every time humanity has shifted to a new stage of consciousness, it has achieved amazing breakthroughs in collaboration. Such a consciousness shift is currently taking place, one that may enable humankind to create more purposeful and soulful methods of organizational management. Laloux described the evolution of organizations within the context of human consciousness development, describing each stage with an adjective and a color. Beginning with the reactive (infrared) through impulsive (red), conformist (amber), achievement (orange), and pluralistic (green), Laloux prepares the stage for the emergence of the evolutionary (teal) stage, characterized as a living organism, unlike the machine or family metaphors of previous stages. While a detailed discussion of the evolutionary stages of organizations is beyond the scope of this chapter, Laloux suggests most contemporary organizations operate at the conformist (amber), achievement (orange), and occasionally the pluralist (green) level. However, an increasing number of evolutionary (teal) organizations are beginning to emerge in response to a shift in individual and organizational consciousness (Laloux, 2014).

Sustainability requires change, which is intuitive in Laloux's teal organizations. While traditional change management approaches often require change to occur from the outside in, spirituality enables change management to occur from the inside out (Geh & Tan, 2009). Organizations structured like self-managing, living systems do not need to impose change from the outside (Laloux, 2014). Living systems have an innate capacity to sense the environment and adapt internally. In a forest, there is no master tree that coordinates and manages change in response to environmental circumstances. Organizations have moods such as frustration, resignation, and ambition, which predispose members to a course of action and discourage them from others. Individual and organizational purposes go together, with one needing the other for both to flourish. When individual and organizational purposes resonate with and reinforce one another, exceptional events take place.

The teal perspective of an organization is that it is no longer property that can be owned, but rather, an energy field, or a lifeform transcending stakeholders and pursuing its own evolutionary purpose. The components of a teal organization are: organizational structures, systems, processes, practices, and cultures, with the three breakthroughs characteristic of teal organizations self-management, wholeness, and listening to purpose. Every previous shift to a new organizational model has triggered a quantum leap in organizational performance. People in teal organizations are more intrinsically motivated, doing what feels right in relation to inner values and assumptions. Laloux identified the two categories of drivers of breakthrough performance. The first group of drivers liberates previously unavailable energies through purpose, distribution of power, learning, better use of talent, and wasting less energy propping up the ego, with compliance, and in meetings. The second group of drivers harnesses and directs energy with more clarity and wisdom through better sensing, better decision-making, more decision-making, timely decision-making, and alignment with evolutionary purpose (Laloux, 2014).

According to Laloux, we have mistaken prosperity for growth. While the contemporary assumption is that growth must be financially measurable, in Laloux's teal organization we may observe the emergence of growth in spiritual, physical, and emotional well-being areas. One of the important aspects of the teal organization is that the organization has a soul and purpose of its own. The evolutionary, teal organization is characterized by: zero-growth, closed loop economies; alternative forms of consumerism; revival of existing industries; alternative monetary systems; stewardship; global communities; end of work as we know it; evolutionary democracy; and, spiritual re-enchantment (Laloux, 2014). Similar to the propositions of workplace spirituality scholars that workers no longer want to leave their spiritual lives at the door when arriving at work, Laloux posits teal organizations create a space where employees can be whole, bringing their entire selves to work.

In Chapter 12, I summarized study findings in which participants who spent money on other people reported greater satisfaction than those who spent money on themselves (Dunn et al., 2008). All wisdom traditions include a component of giving or service to others, and of receiving according to what has been given. Moreover, I referred to previous Chapter 1 content summarizing the case for sustainability being a component of all major religious and spiritual traditions. I further proposed at the intersection of both concepts one finds reward for serving others, with that service including an aspect of service to the planet as well. I called upon the work of Swiss psychoanalyst Carl Jung theorizing existence of a collective unconscious to describe structures of the unconscious mind shared among members of the same species (Jung, 1934–1954). According to Jung, the human collective unconscious is populated by universal instincts and by archetypes. Perhaps this desire to reward others for favorable actions is an innate, Jungian unconscious instinct within the human species.

While Jung applied collective unconsciousness in individual psychotherapy, the concept is appropriate in group behavioral settings, based upon the collective aspect of the theory. Collective unconsciousness helps explain why collections of unrelated individuals join efforts in a common cause, formally in nonprofit and nongovernmental organizations, and informally in less organized grassroots campaigns. Perhaps individuals advocating spirituality and sustainability in the workplace possess instinctive awareness of the relevance of their proposed actions. Perhaps individuals who associate and conduct business with individuals and organizations who are "doing the right thing" do so out of an instinctual response to the collective unconsciousness.

13.6 Servant and Sustainability Leadership in Organizational Success

Servant leadership was introduced by Greenleaf in 1970 as a leadership style in which leaders place serving the needs of others first (Greenleaf, 1970, 1977). Sustainable, or sustainability leadership describes leaders who accept responsibility for understanding and responding to sustainability challenges, regardless of whether the individual possesses a formal leadership role (Ferdig, 2007). The Sustainability Leadership Institute defined sustainability leaders as "individuals who are compelled to make a difference by deepening their awareness of themselves in relation to the world around them. In doing so, they adopt new ways of seeing, thinking, and interacting that result in innovative, sustainable solutions (n.d.)".

Leaders who demonstrate both servant and sustainability leadership are more likely to make strategic decisions that acknowledge the economic, social, and environmental dimensions of those decisions, and the interests of diverse stakeholders (Peterlin et al., 2015). Servant and sustainability leadership offer three unique contributions to strategic decision-making (Peterlin et al., 2015). First, both leadership styles require placing the interests and well-being of others and nature above self-interest. Second, leaders who demonstrate both styles consider the long-term interests of multiple stakeholders. Finally, servant and sustainability leaders accept the responsibility to behave as stewards of organizational and natural resources to achieve the greatest benefit for everyone (Peterlin et al., 2015). Although both servant and sustainability leadership consider the needs of followers more than the needs of leaders (Avery & Bergsteiner, 2011a), the focus of sustainability leadership is with balancing the future needs of numerous stakeholders with the present needs of followers (Avery & Bergsteiner, 2011b).

Many contemporary sustainability leaders also (often unknowingly) practice servant leadership. Senge suggested, "In an era of massive institutional failure, the ideas in servant leadership point toward a possible path forward and will continue to do so" (Senge, 2002, p. 345). Servant leadership has been suggested to provide a path forward to a sustainable future (Beehner, 2020). The servant leadership style was explored in more detail in Chapter 3.

13.7 Spirituality and Workplace Behavior

Spirituality has been found to improve workplace behavior, including the sustainability behavior of employees (Kalafatoğlu, 2022). Afsar et al. (2016) found that intrinsic motivation and environmental sentiments moderated the relationship between workplace spirituality and environmentally favorable behavior. Workplace spirituality also moderated the relationship between spiritual leadership and sustainability behavior. Afsar et al. suggested that spiritual leadership increases workplace spirituality which has a buffering effect on employees' positive attitudes resulting in increased sustainability behavior.

Rocha and D'Angelo (2021) examined the 2015 Mariana dam disaster, also known as Samarco's Scandal. A dam located at the Mariana Mining Complex operated by Samarco in Brazil suffered a catastrophic failure, destroying villages, killing 19 people, and spreading across 668 km of waterways. They analyzed and compared information shared with the public before and after the accident, noting that there were some spiritual and benevolent components in their public documents which did not seem to transform into practice. The authors suggested that spirituality was not intrinsic to the organization, with any spiritual or benevolent statements likely made to fulfill legal requirements. Organizational behavior should be analyzed to determine whether an organization is genuinely spiritual (Kalafatoğlu, 2022).

Organizations should place concern for the benefits of all stakeholders above competitive advantage and survival (Barron & Chou, 2017). Spirituality may be integrated into the triple bottom line (TB), which Zawawi and Wahab (2019) suggested should be relabeled the quadruple bottom line (QBL) by including corporate spirituality in addition to environmental, social, and economic components. In the QBL, spirituality becomes the "glue" that binds the other three factors and increases their positive effects (Zawawi & Wahab, 2019). QBL can benefit organizations by increasing the level of positive emotions and virtues of leaders, resulting in more ethical and better decisions. QBL can also contribute to a positive stakeholder image and improve organizational culture.

Leadership and ethics have a symbiotic relationship with spirituality (Meng, 2016). The actions of leaders determine the ethical character of organizations regardless of whether employees agree with those decisions. The spiritual foundation of leaders determines how ethical their decisions are (Göçen & Özğan, 2018). The level of spirituality or spiritual life shared by members of an organization may be a strong predictor of ethical behavior and decisions in the workplace (Göçen & Özğan,

2018). Spirituality affects decision-making in a business or organizational context as well as larger-scale contexts such as environmental problems (Göçen & Özğan, 2018).

Spirituality can serve an important role in enhancing workplace behavior and culture. However, despite the benefits of workplace spirituality, there are dangers and risks in the infiltration and apparent authority of the technical imperative that currently exists in much of the workplace spirituality movement (Driscoll & Wiebe, 2007). Workplace spirituality cannot be used as an instrument to exploit employees for increased productivity and profitability (Driscoll & Wiebe, 2007). Moreover, Ali et al. (2023) determined that employees were generally satisfied with spiritual workplaces and leadership, but their health, happiness, and productivity were affected differently when elements of time, individual, and organizational context were modified. Spirituality is not a skill or an ability that managers must learn but instead involves a radically different approach to management and achieving organizational purpose (Driscoll & Wiebe, 2007). Scholars advocate for the integration of spirituality, work, and learning, but only when spiritual development becomes an end in and of itself, and not an instrument for obtaining organizational outcomes and results (Zhuravleva & Jones, 2006). Workplaces should become spiritual for benevolent and not greedy or unethical purposes.

13.8 Barriers to and Implementation of Spirituality and Sustainability Framework

The concepts of spirituality and sustainability are often considered to exist outside of a traditional workplace environment. Although most individuals embrace some form of religiosity or spirituality, and many recognize the importance of sustainability, any organized, collective effort to combine the concepts to achieve a benefit may be viewed with suspicion or resistance. Therefore, barriers exist to the successful implementation of the sustainability and spiritualty worldview paradigm.

Some of these barriers have been discussed in previous chapters and will be summarized in this section. The barriers and challenges can be categorized as being related to spirituality, sustainability, and both. In addition, potential solutions will be presented for overcoming those barriers.

Some researchers have challenged the applicability of workplace spirituality with non-religious or atheist subjects (Ecklund & Long, 2011). Moreover, the anti-materialist characteristic of spirituality may present significant challenges in the empirical investigation of links between spirituality and financial performance (Dent et al., 2005; Fornaciari & Lund Dean, 2001; Lund-Dean et al., 2003). The greatest danger of workplace spirituality may come from managerial attempts to exploit employees through instrumentality, by taking advantage of their spiritual beliefs to enhance the bottom line. Tension in the relationship between employees and their organizations will increase, partially because of business cycles. Business managers will make decisions about layoffs and facility closures during economic downturns (Hammonds, 1996) which will test the spirits of employees. There are also reasonable concerns about the appropriation of the bodies, minds, and hearts of employees by employers (Dehler & Welsh, 2010). Welch (1998) cautions about legitimate concerns that the boundary between the personal and professional lives of employees is being penetrated without considering the consequences. Welch further warns that business has already become cultlike with employees expected to believe in and trust management.

There are four primary obstacles to the full support of implementing workplace spirituality: limited consensus on a definition; insufficient measurement tools; limited evidence supporting its practical utility; and, the lack of a theoretical foundation and understanding of relationships with key organizational variables (Yin & Mahrous, 2022). However, these obstacles should not prevent broad acceptance of workplace spirituality as an essential concept in organizational theories and management (Yin & Mahrous, 2022). Workplace spirituality must be established as an important concept to be able to attract the interest of prominent scholars who can resolve these obstacles.

Sustainability management challenges the fundamental assumptions of the dominant economic worldview, such as the need for consumer satisfaction maximization and utility optimization, both of which are grounded on a belief in reasonable, calculable growth (Opdebeeck, 2014). One challenge with sustainable business education is justification of a business necessity for and relevance of sustainability. Orr (2002) described the barriers to sustainability as not simply technological, but also social, political, and psychological. Orr further expressed concern not with whether society makes the transition to sustainability, but with how gracefully society makes the transition. Orr (2002) described the four challenges of sustainability as: the need for accurate models, metaphors, and measures to describe humankinds' relationship with the biosphere; the necessity for creativity and improvement in the areas of citizenship and governance; the necessity of informing the public through improved education; and, learning how to identify and solve multiple, disparate problems, which will require a higher level of spiritual awareness.

Bocken and Geradts (2020) identified three groups of barriers to implementing sustainability: institutional, strategic, and operational. Institutional barriers to implementing sustainability included focus on profit maximization, uncertainty avoidance and focus on short term. Strategic barriers include functional strategy, dominant focus on exploitation, and prioritizing on short-term profits. Operational barriers included functional excellence, standard innovation process and procedures, fixed resource planning and allocation, short-term focus of incentive systems, and financial performance metrics (Bocken & Geradts, 2020). Leal Filho et al. (2022) found considerable awareness about connecting spirituality and sustainability and a general agreement about the benefits of incorporating spirituality in sustainability teaching and research practices. However, progress in this area is hindered by the lack of a common definition of spirituality and limited training in handling spirituality within the context of teaching and research. Leal Filho et al. suggested actions to encourage integration of sustainability and spirituality, including greater emphasis on including matters related to sustainability, human well-being, and ethics in initiatives on spirituality, and the involvement of key stakeholders (Leal Filho et al., 2022).

The barriers to implementing the spirituality and sustainability for success model can and must be overcome to ensure the planet and all inhabitants continue to survive and thrive. Potential solutions for overcoming these barriers include:

- Demonstrating and disseminating the benefits of this model through education.
- Appealing to the desires of individuals to both succeed and feel good about how they achieved their success.
- Embedding the spirituality, sustainability, and success model within organizational strategies, missions, visions, and cultures.

In the previous chapters we have explored how spirituality and sustainability contribute to individual and organizational success through both academic literature, and case studies and examples. These benefits should be demonstrated and disseminated through education and training programs directed at individuals, organizations, industries, and sectors. Indrajaya (2018) noted that students who have been interacting with a spiritual development program, have transformed their toward a sustainability mindset in which they recognize the new perspective of developing flourishing businesses that consider social and environmental impacts. Demonstrating the practical and pragmatic benefits of this model would provide the first step in implementation.

Appealing to the desires of individuals to both succeed and feel good about how they achieved their success may be easier in the post-pandemic era. In Chapters 5 and 9 we discussed how the pandemic caused individuals to reconsider what is important in their lives. According to Suganthi (2020), concern about the environment and the need for better stewardship of our ecosystem is increasing. The desire and interest to make changes is present and growing and would provide further support for desiring the benefits offered by this model.

Embedding the spirituality, sustainability, and success model within organizational strategies, missions, visions, and cultures may offer the greatest method for overcoming barriers to implementation. This would build upon the first two solutions by formally operationalizing the model for collective application. According to Suganthi (2020), eco-spirituality attitudes among employees significantly improved corporate social responsibility (CSR), performance, and PEB (Suganthi, 2020).

Shah et al. (2023) found that workplace spirituality and responsible leadership (RL) have a positive and significant impact on PEB which enhances implementation of workplace spirituality and RL practices at the individual level. Shah et al. suggested human resource managers and strategists should incorporate workplace spirituality and RL initiatives to modify employee behavior instead of forcing compliance through penalties. Organizations could develop practices to encourage employees to develop an emotional attachment to the organization, which can increase recognition of the importance of pro-environmental values and their ability to implement them in their daily lives. Li et al. (2023) determined that green HRM practices have a positive effect on employees' in-role green behavior and that these sustainability-focused initiatives are more likely to produce green behavior among employees (Li et al., 2023).

Embedding this model in the DNA of organizations requires the development of a sustainability mindset. A sustainability mindset is a way of thinking and being which results from a comprehensive understanding of the ecosystem, social sensitivity, and contemplative concentration on individual values and the higher self (Sustainability Mindset Indicator, 2020). The Sustainability Mindset Indicator (SMI) is the first instrument to identify and outline where an individual is on the transition to a sustainability mindset (Sustainability Mindset Indicator, 2020). The SMI is a 36-question survey that explores three dimensions of the sustainability mindset (cognitive, behavioral, and affective), and provides participants with individualized reports identifying their unique skills and opportunities for creating a better world (Sustainability Mindset Indicator, 2020). Fry and Egel (2021) developed a model of global leadership for sustainability (GLfS) that integrates and extends the concept beyond current approaches to sustainability leadership. Fry and Egel suggested that spirituality, through the qualities of self-transcendence and interconnectedness, is essential for sustainability and is foundational for the GLfS model. It is essential to develop a global mindset for sustainability, which combines an ethic of remote moral responsibility with an ethic of care and compassion (Fry & Egel, 2021).

13.9 Concluding Thoughts

In this chapter a framework for the integration of spirituality and sustainability for individual success was developed. Early in the chapter, I hypothesized the commonalities of, and interconnection between spirituality (both individual and workplace), and sustainability support the statement: ***A combination of spirituality and sustainability positively impacts both individual and organizational success***. Further on, I argued similarities among spirituality and sustainability encourage a holistic worldview, through which spiritual, sustainable organizations may provide purpose, sense of connection with nature and other individuals, and a sense of community, both within the organization, and with society. This purposeful, connected community of individuals should provide exceptional organizational success.

The proposed success resulting from the combination of organizational spirituality and sustainability would contribute to the advancement of the United Nations Sustainable Development Goals (SDGs). While many of the SDGs would benefit, direct examples include:

Goal 1: No poverty.
Goal 3: Good health and well-being.
Goal 8: Decent work and economic growth.
Goal 9: Industry, innovation, and infrastructure.
Goal 10: Reduced inequality.
Goal 12: Responsible consumption and production.

Today the proposition is theoretical, requiring further research to challenge, build upon, or refute the suggestion spirituality and spirituality collectively produce greater success than individually. Skepticism exists and is justified about the premise of using spirituality as a tool for organizational benefit, especially when the organization is a for-profit business. Driscoll and Wiebe (2007) noted that no significant business transformation occurred after the increased interest in workplace spirituality. The disparity between rich and poor, and developed and developing nations continues and corporate ethical scandals and ecological degradation occur continuously (Driscoll & Wiebe, 2007). Authentic workplace spirituality may require achieving reduced profits from incorporating spiritual values into the workplace because "morality must guide the means of economic activity, not the other way around" (Driscoll & Wiebe, 2007, p. 342). Driscoll and Wiebe echo the sentiments of Ellul (1954/1964): "I am somehow unable to believe in the revolutionary value of an act which makes the cash register jingle so merrily" (p. 417).

The chapter concludes with two personal interview summaries, wherein two C-level organizational leaders support the premise of this chapter. Spiritual, sustainable organizations exist, and are thriving. Future research is necessary to quantify and qualify how, to what extent, and in what manner the phenomena occur. Laloux (2014) proposed the emergence of the evolutionary (teal) organization characterized as a living organism, unlike the machine or family metaphors of previous stages. The concept of a spiritual, sustainable organization is clearly evolutionary, exceptional, and essential for the challenging era in which humankind currently exists. This new organization is capable of endogenous transformation that will likely externally influence the future transformation of humankind.

Personal Interview Summaries

In support of the argument that spirituality and sustainability are beneficial for organizational success, I conclude this chapter with two personal interviews of industry professionals who have applied spirituality and sustainability in their organizations. Portions of one of these interviews was discussed in Chapter 12 as an example of an industry professional who applied spirituality and sustainability for individual career success. In the following paragraphs I will include content from the interviews related to the application of spirituality and sustainability for organizational success.

I had the pleasure of interviewing Mark Tercek, CEO of The Nature Conservancy (TNC), and an organizational leader who has applied both spirituality and sustainability in his personal career. The Nature Conservancy is the largest nonprofit environmental organization in the world (Jaret, 2017). Prior to becoming CEO of TNC, Mark was a managing director and partner at Goldman Sachs for 24 years, and a faculty member at the New York University Stern School of Business. While at Goldman Sachs, Mark developed the Goldman Sachs Environmental Markets Group (Jaret, 2017) which focused on investment opportunities beneficial for both clients and the environment. Mark Tercek is not an individual who embraces spirituality and sustainability with token participation. Rather, he has incorporated both concepts into the code of his operating system.

Mark came to TNC as a businessperson who was chosen by the board because they desired someone to lead the organization with business strategies, aligning market forces to develop environmental progress. While those strategies are important, he realized that they are not sufficient to achieve TNC's mission. He believes in the need to lead with both the head and the heart, and not just with sheer determination. People at TNC might be able to make more money in the private sector, but many of them choose to work at TNC because they want psychic income, not just material income. They desire to give back, and not just think of themselves. Nonprofit leaders must mobilize people for a higher cause, and in essence are doing a form of spiritual work. He is a better CEO because he understands strategy better (that it is not just about business). He would not have said something like that prior to his arrival at TNC. Mark believes TNC employees and volunteers are interested in sustainability because they are interested in vulnerable people and species. They have compassion. Mark believes that through their work, TNC employees are expressing a spiritual commitment.

Because most of the culture and success at TNC occurred prior to Mark's arrival, he believes it would be wrong for him to take much credit. He is proud of the organization and of what has happened since his arrival. While he has used language related to meditation to encourage collaboration at TNC, other TNC champions could do and have done what he has done with different (non-meditation) language. He believes that despite the partisan divide we hear about in the news, people are less divided than one might think. By listening to those with different perspectives, agreeing to learn from one another, respecting your critics, and recognizing that we don't need to see eye to eye on every detail, Mark believes we can bring together diverse groups to achieve progress. TNC bases its work on this type of inclusive, collaborative approach.

As a centrist, nonpartisan organization, TNC brings together diverse groups of people to help nature. "They are walking the talk", and "they bring people together by finding common ground". They do not label bad actors as evil but approach all parties with optimism and kindness, hoping to find common ground and encourage bad actors to support the environment. TNC also shows humility by giving its many partners credit for their role in the organization's successes.

Mark encouraged (but did not push) the practice of meditation at TNC, including establishing a meditation room at headquarters. An anonymous donor paid for meditation training (he confessed to being this donor). He felt meditation training was an inexpensive method for achieving positive impact at TNC. Mark believes meditation is a good preparation for negotiation in our polarized world. TNC has always maintained a culture of bringing people together to find ways to get along and compromise. To make environmental progress stakeholders need more time to find common ground. This culture [similar to workplace spirituality] helps to facilitate negotiation. Employees who participated in the meditation training said it was helpful. Meditation reinforces the behaviors that are important to people like him (who are spiritual), but he won't impose his practice on others. TNC wants to develop collaborative qualities, and these qualities are associated with spiritual practices.

TerraCycle was founded in 2001 by Tom Szaky, a Princeton University student with a mission of Eliminating the Idea of Waste® (TerraCycle, 2018a). TerraCycle is the global leader in collecting and repurposing hard-to-recycle waste, engaging over 80 million people in 21 countries, and has recycled billions of pieces of waste. TerraCycle profitably recycles items traditionally considered "unrecyclable" and posits everything considered non-recyclable waste is capable of being collected and transformed into raw materials for the creation of new products (TerraCycle, 2018b). The company combines strategy, logistics, science and technology, promotion and custom business models to create profitable and scalable platforms for clients, customers, and shareholders, while simultaneously eliminating the idea of waste. Recycling partners include Clorox, Coca-Cola, Kraft, Office Depot, Pepsico, Waste Management, Procter &

Gamble (P&G), ESPN, Lowe's, and The Home Depot (TerraCycle, 2018b).

I had the pleasure of interviewing Tom Szaky, CEO of TerraCycle, about how he has incorporated both spirituality and sustainability in his business model. Tom explained that he does not subscribe to a specific religion but believes in the balance and energy that many religions teach. He believes that since most of our waking time is spent working, what he does should not be just a "side show" that he does once per month. At TerraCycle, every single minute, every action, everything they do is about improving the planet, improving society, or a combination of the two. What he loves about this is it allows the business to "ooze" purpose in everything they do. Literally, there is not a project they take, not a single step they take that does not fulfill that purpose. Tom believes the business receives a "huge push of purpose", that cannot be placed on the balance sheet, but is a very, very powerful thing to drive key motivation, and happiness.

Sustainability has greatly impacted TerraCycle, because it is deeply embedded in the organization, and is the one reason for existence. In the interview, Tom highlighted the reason for existence of most corporations is shareholder profit, which is not surprising since that is what is taught in business schools and drilled into employees. However, Tom considers profit to be more of a function of health, which he equated to fat on the body. Humans need to have some fat on their bodies, or they will become unhealthy, but if the body has too much fat, the person becomes obese, and unhealthy. Therefore, profit should not be viewed as the reason for showing up to work, but more of an indication of the health of the workplace. As such, the reason for existence at TerraCycle is very specific—the elimination of waste, and everything that employees do echoes into that reason of being and drives this idea of purpose full force. Tom suggested the purpose of an organization becomes manifest through transparency, wherein all employees have access to all information and are therefore aligned for the same purpose. Tom also added TerraCycle is a diverse organization with 75% of the 200 global employees who are women. This culture translates into an innovative environment, absent a rigid hierarchy, and with whom many interesting stakeholders desire to conduct business. While Terra-Cycle is currently a US$30 million company, the company has access to stakeholders beyond what a company of that scale would normally attract.

Tom believes the combination of workplace spirituality and sustainability has greatly impacted TerraCycle, because this combination makes people feel happy, fulfilled, and a sense of community and family in the workplace. The spiritual, sustainable culture influences a greater pool of applicants, and improves employee retention. Employees do not say that something is not in their job description, and they are not just focused on their own key performance indicators (KPIs). Tom agrees there is an overlap between spirituality and sustainability, although the word spirituality makes some people feel uncomfortable, and may be considered taboo depending on where the individual rests in terms of religion. Moreover, many of the terms describing both spirituality and sustainability are synonymous and convey the same general idea.

Regarding the future of spirituality and sustainability, Tom suggests the world faces more challenge—environmental, such as climate change, deforestation, or the global garbage crisis, and political, with the United States, and many other countries more divided. Our environmental and political challenges are not just driven by internationalism, nationalism, or tribalism, but all are driven by selfish or self-focused decision-making. Decisions are being made without consideration of the true costs. Tom finds it interesting that any sort of spiritual doctrine, whether formal or informal, really pushes this idea of focusing on others versus self, and getting back either directly or indirectly, in terms of *karma* or the Golden Rule.

Tom believes the challenges we face will get worse before they get better. He used the analogy of an alcoholic who is functioning well, and therefore it is hard to convince that person that he or she is an alcoholic because things are going well. However, when things start falling apart it becomes obvious there is a problem, and that something needs to be done. Moreover, Tom argues if we continue to make businesses' primary purpose making money for a few shareholders, it will compound the problem, because that is what got us here in the first place. He cited examples of the massive inequality that has come about, and all of the anger and hatred from rural areas of the world to the United States, France, and other major countries.

Concerning the future role spirituality and sustainability will play in businesses and organizations, Tom believes this combination is another tool that will make organizations more successful. In other words, it is not going to be mandatory for organizations to adopt these concepts, and there will be organizations that do not adopt them. He believes people will wake up and see the value of spirituality and sustainability, and they become more of a standard that they weave into the culture of work, much like the equality movement has been breaking down the glass ceiling.

References

Affeldt, D. L., & MacDonald, D. A. (2010). The relationship of spirituality to work and organizational attitudes and behaviors in a sample of employees from a health care system. *Journal of Transpersonal Psychology, 42*(2), 192–208. https://www.atpweb.org

Afsar, B., Badir, Y., & Kiani, U. S. (2016). Linking spiritual leadership and employee pro-environmental behavior: The influence of workplace spirituality, intrinsic motivation, and environmental passion. *Journal of Environmental Psychology, 45*, 79–88. https://doi.org/10.1016/j.jenvp.2015.11.011

Akhshik, A., Ozturen, A., & Rezapouraghdam, H. (2021). A passionate travel to mind green turtles—Unpacking the complexity of visitors' green behaviour. *International Journal of Tourism Research, 23*(3), 301–318. https://doi.org/10.1002/jtr.2407

Ali, H., Shahid, T., Timsal, A., & Naseer, S. (2023). Sustainable careers under spiritual leadership and workplace spirituality: A subordinates' perspective during Covid 19. *Review of Applied Management and Social Sciences, 6*(1), 89–103. https://doi.org/10.47067/ramss.v6i1.286

Altaf, A., & Awan, M. A. (2011). Moderating effect of workplace spirituality on the relationship of job overload and job satisfaction. *Journal of Business Ethics, 104*(1), 93–99. https://doi.org/10.1007/s10551-011-0891-0

Avery, G. C., & Bergsteiner, H. (2011a). *Sustainable leadership: Honeybee and locust approaches*. Routledge.

Avery, G. C., & Bergsteiner, H. (2011b). How BMW successfully practices sustainable leadership principles. *Strategy & Leadership, 39*(6), 11–18. https://doi.org/10.1108/10878571111176583

Barron, K., & Chou, S. Y. (2017). Toward a spirituality mode of firm sustainability strategic planning processes. *Society and Business Review, 12*(1), 46–62. https://doi.org/10.1108/SBR-01-2016-0008

Beehner, C. G. (2018). Expanding sustainable business education beyond business schools. In S. Dhiman & J. Marques (Eds.), *Handbook of engaged sustainability*. Springer Nature. https://doi.org/10.1007/978-3-319-53121-2_51-1

Beehner, C. G. (2020). Servant leadership as a pathway to a sustainable future. In S. Dhiman & J. Marques (Eds.), *New horizons in positive leadership and change: A practical guide for workplace transformation* (pp. 65–82). Springer Nature.

Bocken, N. M., & Geradts, T. H. (2020). Barriers and drivers to sustainable business model innovation: Organization design and dynamic capabilities. *Long Range Planning, 53*(4), 101950. https://doi.org/10.1016/j.lrp.2019.101950

Bouckaert, L. (2014). Spirituality: The missing link in business ethics. In L. Zsolnai (Ed.), *The spiritual dimension of business ethics and sustainability management* (pp. 15–26). Springer. https://doi.org/10.1007/978-3-319-11677-8_20

Burack, E. H. (1999). Spirituality in the workplace. *Journal of Organizational Change Management, 12*(4), 280–292. https://doi.org/10.1108/09534819910282126

Case, P., & Gosling, J. (2010). The spiritual organization: Critical reflections on the instrumentality of workplace spirituality. *Journal of Management, Spirituality and Religion, 7*(4), 257–282. https://doi.org/10.1080/14766086.2010.524727

Cavanagh, G. (1999). Spirituality for managers: Context and critique. *Journal of Organizational Change Management, 12*(3), 186–195. https://doi.org/10.1108/09534819910273793

Chalofsky, N., & Krishna, V. (2009). Meaningfulness, commitment, and engagement: The intersection of a deeper level of intrinsic motivation. *Advances in Developing Human Resources, 11*, 189–203. https://doi.org/10.1177/1523422309333147

Chatterjee, A., & Naqvi, F. (2010). Spirituality in organizational life: An empirical study of spirituality and job attitudes. *Abhigyan, 28*(3), 18–29. http://www.freepatentsonline.com/article/Abhigyan/249137536.html

Chawla, V., & Guda, S. (2010). Individual spirituality at work and its relationship with job satisfaction, propensity to leave and job commitment: An exploratory study among sales professionals. *Journal of Human Values, 16*(2), 157–167. https://doi.org/10.1177/097168581001600203

Choong, Y. O., Ng, L. P., Tee, C. W., Kuar, L. S., Teoh, S. Y., & Chen, I. C. (2019). Green work climate and pro-environmental behaviour among academics: The mediating role of harmonious environmental passion. *International Journal of Management Studies, 26*(2), 77–97. https://www.scienceopen.com/document_file/9ddca49a-fdd1-4b49-b737-341e6079feee/API/77-97.pdf

Crawford, A., Hubbard, S. S., Lonis-Shumate, S. R., & O'Neill, M. (2009). Workplace spirituality and employee attitudes within the lodging environment. *Journal of Human Resources in Hospitality & Tourism, 8*, 64–81. https://doi.org/10.1080/15332840802274445

De Diego-Cordero, C. R., Zurrón Pérez, M. P., Vargas-Martínez, A. M., Lucchetti, G., & Vega-Escaño, J. (2021). The effectiveness of spiritual interventions in the workplace for work-related health outcomes: A systematic review and meta-analysis. *Journal of Nursing Management, 29*(6), 1703–1712. https://doi.org/10.1111/jonm.13315

Dehler, G. E., & Welsh, M. A. (2010). The experience of work: Spirituality and the new workplace. In *Handbook of workplace spirituality and organizational performance* (pp. 75–88). Routledge.

Dent, E. B., Higgins, M. E., & Wharff, D. M. (2005). Spirituality and leadership: An empirical review of definitions, distinctions, and embedded assumptions. *The Leadership Quarterly, 16*(5), 625–653. https://doi.org/10.1016/j.leaqua.2005.07.002

Dhiman, S., & Marques, J. (2011). The role and need of offering workshops and courses on workplace spirituality. *Journal of Management Development, 30*(9), 816–835. https://doi.org/10.1108/02621711111164312

Driscoll, C., & Wiebe, E. (2007). Technical spirituality at work: Jacques Ellul on workplace spirituality. *Journal of Management Inquiry, 16*(4), 333–348. https://doi.org/10.1177/1056492607305899

Dunn, E. W., Aknin, L. B., & Norton, M. I. (2008). Spending money on others promotes happiness. *Science, 319*(5870), 1687–1688. https://doi.org/10.1126/science.1150952

Ecklund, E. H., & Long, E. (2011). Scientists and spirituality. *Sociology of Religion, 72*(3), 253–276. https://doi.org/10.1093/socrel/srr003

Elkington, J., Tickell, S., & Lee, M. (2007). *SustainAbility. 20 Years of global leadership [online]*. SustainAbility. http://www.sustainability.com

Ellul, J. (1964). *The technological society*. Knopf (Original work published 1954).

Esty, D. C., & Winston, A. S. (2006). *Green to gold: How smart companies use environmental strategy to innovate, create value, and build competitive advantage*. Yale University Press.

Ferdig, M. A. (2007). Sustainability leadership: Co-creating a sustainable future. *Journal of Change Management, 7*(1), 25–35. https://doi.org/10.1080/14697010701233809

Fornaciari, C., & Lund Dean, K. (2001). Making the quantum leap: Lessons from physics on studying spirituality and religion in organizations. *Journal of Organizational Change Management, 14*(4), 335–351. https://doi.org/10.1108/EUM0000000005547

Fry, L. W. (2003). Toward a theory of spiritual leadership. *The Leadership Quarterly, 14*(6), 693–729. https://doi.org/10.1016/j.leaqua.2003.09.001

Fry, L. W., & Egel, E. (2021). Global leadership for sustainability. *Sustainability, 13*(11), 6360. https://doi.org/10.3390/su13116360

Fry, L. W., & Slocum, J. (2008). Maximizing the triple bottom line through a strategic scorecard business model of spiritual leadership. *Organizational Dynamics, 31*(1), 86–96. https://doi.org/10.1016/j.orgdyn.2007.11.004

Geh, E., & Tan, G. (2009). Spirituality at work in a changing world: Managerial and research implications. *Journal of Management, Spirituality & Religion, 6*(4), 287–300. https://doi.org/10.1080/14766080903290093

Giacalone, R. A., & Jurkiewicz, C. J. (2010). The science of workplace spirituality. In R. A. Giacalone & C. J. Jurkiewicz (Eds.) *Handbook of workplace spirituality and organizational performance* (2nd ed., pp. 3–26). M. E. Sharpe.

Göçen, A., & Özğan, H. (2018). Spirituality and ethics: A literature review. *Gaziantep University Journal of Social Sciences, 17*, 58–65. https://doi.org/10.21547/jss.452152

Greenleaf, R. K. (1970). *The servant as leader.* The Robert K. Greenleaf Center.

Greenleaf, R. K. (1977). *Servant leadership: A journey into the nature of legitimate power and greatness*. Paulist Press.

Guillory, W. A. (1997). *The living organization—Spirituality in the workplace*. Innovations International.

Gupta, M., Kumar, V., & Singh, M. (2013). Creating satisfied employees through workplace spirituality: A study of the private insurance sector in Punjab (India). *Journal of Business Ethics, 122*(1), 79–88. https://doi.org/10.1007/s10551-013-1756-5

Hammonds, K. H. (1996, May 13). Soul-searching in the corner office. *Business Week*, 42–43.

Han, Y., Lu, X., & Li, Z. (2010). In search of excellence: Spiritual training program and junior managers counterproductive work behavior in China. *Human Resource Management International Digest, 18*(2), 10–12. https://doi.org/10.1108/09670731011028401

Hicks, D. A. (2003). *Religion and the workplace: Pluralism, spirituality, leadership*. Cambridge University Press.

Holthaus, G. (2012). *Learning native wisdom: What traditional cultures teach us about subsistence, sustainability, and spirituality*. University Press of Kentucky.

Hong, Y. J. (2012). Identifying spirituality in workers: A strategy for retention of community health professionals. *Journal of Social Service Research, 38*(20), 175–186. https://doi.org/10.1080/01488376.2011.615275

Indrajaya, A. N. (2018). Spiritual development programs, individual spirituality and sustainability mindset toward higher commitment to social and environmental impact. *International Journal of Business Studies, 2*(3), 150–163. http://ijbs.ipmi.ac.id/index.php/ijbs/article/download/82/51

Iqbal, Q., Ahmad, N. H., & Ahmad, B. (2018). Enhancing sustainable performance through job characteristics via workplace spirituality: A study on SMEs. *Journal of Science and Technology Policy Management, 12*(3), 463–490. https://doi.org/10.1108/JSTPM-02-2018-0022

Jaret, P. (2017, December). Common ground. *Mindful*, 64–70.

Jones, P. H., & Upward, A. (2014). *Caring for the future: The systemic design of flourishing enterprises.* The Third Symposium of Relating Systems Thinking and Design (RSD3), Oslo, Norway, pp. 1–8. Slides and other materials from conference presentation: http://systemic-design.net/rsd3-proceedings/business-enterprise-design/

Jung, C. G. (1934–1954). *The archetypes and the collective unconscious* (In 1981 2nd ed. Collected works Vol. 9 Part 1). Bollingen.

Kalafatoğlu, Y. (2022). Workplace spirituality for more sustainable organizations. In *Handbook of Research on Integrating Spirituality in Modern Workplaces* (pp. 80–95). IGI Global.

Kinjerski, V., & Skrypnek, B. J. (2008). The promise of spirit at work: Increasing job satisfaction and organizational commitment and reducing turnover and absenteeism in long-term care. *Journal of Gerontological Nursing, 34*(10), 17–25. https://doi.org/10.3928/00989134-20081001-03

Kolodinsky, R. W., Giacalone, R. A., & Jurkiewicz, C. L. (2008). Workplace values and outcomes: Exploring personal, organizational, and interactive

workplace spirituality. *Journal of Business Ethics, 81*(2), 465–480. https://doi.org/10.1007/s10551-007-9507-0
Krahnke, K., Giacalone, R. A., & Jurkiewicz, C. L. (2003). Point-counterpoint: Measuring workplace spirituality. *Journal of Organizational Change Management, 16*(4), 396–405. https://doi.org/10.1108/09534810310484154
Krishnakumar, S., & Neck, C. P. (2002). The "what", "why" and "how" of spirituality in the workplace. *Journal of Managerial Psychology, 17*(3), 153–164. https://doi.org/10.1108/02683940210423060
Laloux, F. (2014). *Reinventing organizations: A guide to creating organizations inspired by the next stage of human consciousness.* Nelson Parker.
Laszlo, C., Saillant, R., Pose, I. B., & Brown, J. S. (2014). *Flourishing enterprise: The new spirit of business.* Stanford University Press.
Lázár, I. (2000). Mothers and Mother Nature: Attachment, detachment and human ecological integrity. In P. J. Crabbe et al. (Eds.), *Implementing ecological integrity restoring regional and global environmental and human health.* NATO Science Series: IV Earth and Environment Sciences. Kluwer.
Lázár, I. (2004). Spirituality and human ecosystems. In *Spirituality and ethics in management* (pp. 87–96). Springer. https://doi.org/10.1007/1-4020-2365-0_7
Leal Filho, W., Salvia, A. L., Ulluwishewa, R., Abubakar, I. R., Mifsud, M., LeVasseur, T. J., Correia, V., Consorte-McCrea, A., Paço, A., Fritzen, B., Ray, S., Gordon, N., Luetz, J. M., Borsari, B., Venkatesan, M., Mukul, S. A., Carp, R. M., Begum, H., Nunoo, E. K., … Farrugia, E. (2022). Linking sustainability and spirituality: A preliminary assessment in pursuit of a sustainable and ethically correct world. *Journal of Cleaner Production, 380*, e135091. https://doi.org/10.1016/j.jclepro.2022.135091
Lestar, T., & Böhm, S. (2020). Ecospirituality and sustainability transitions: Agency towards degrowth. *Religion, State & Society, 48*(1), 56–73. https://doi.org/10.1080/09637494.2019.1702410
Li, W., Abdalla, A. A., Mohammad, T., Khassawneh, O., & Parveen, M. (2023). Towards examining the link between green HRM practices and employee green in-role behavior: Spiritual leadership as a moderator. *Psychology Research and Behavior Management, 2023*, 383–396. https://doi.org/10.2147/PRBM.S396114
Lovelock, J. E. (1972). Gaia as seen through the atmosphere. *Atmospheric Environment, 6*(8), 579–580. https://doi.org/10.1007/978-94-009-7944-4_2
Lund-Dean, K., Fornaciari, C. J., & McGee, J. (2003). Research in spirituality, religion, and work: Walking the line between relevance and legitimacy.

Journal of Organizational Change Management, 16(4), 378–395. https://doi.org/10.1108/09534810310484145

Marques, J., Dhiman, S., & King, R. (2010). Exploring the link between spirituality and sustainability. *Business Renaissance Quarterly, 5*(1), 19. https://www.proquest.com

Marschke, E., Prezioni, R., & Harrington, W. (2009). Professionals and executives support a relationship between organizational commitment and spirituality in the workplace. *Journal of Business and Economics Research, 7*(8), 33–48. https://doi.org/10.19030/jber.v7i8.2320

Meng, Y. (2016). Spiritual leadership at the workplace: Perspectives and theories. *Biomedical Reports, 5*(4), 408–412. https://doi.org/10.3892/br.2016.748

Milliman, J., Czaplewski, A. J., & Ferguson, J. (2003). Workplace spirituality and employee work attitudes: An exploratory empirical assessment. *Journal of Organizational Change Management, 16*(4), 426–447. https://doi.org/10.1108/09534810310484172

Mohd Zawawi, N. F., & Abd Wahab, S. (2019). Organizational sustainability: A redefinition? *Journal of Strategy and Management, 12*(3), 397–408. https://doi.org/10.1108/JSMA-08-2018-0077

Opdebeeck, H. (2014). Spiritual sustainability management. In L Zsolnai (Ed.) *The spiritual dimension of business ethics and sustainability management* (pp. 15–26). Springer. https://doi.org/10.1007/978-3-319-11677-8_20

Orr, D. W. (2002). Four challenges of sustainability. *Conservation Biology, 16*(6), 1457–1460. https://doi.org/10.1046/j.1523-1739.2002.01668.x

Paloutzian, R. F., Emmons, R. A., & Keortge, S. G. (2003). Spiritual well-being, spiritual intelligence, and healthy workplace policy. In R. A. Giacolone & C. L. Jurkiewicz (Eds.), *Handbook of workplace spirituality and organizational performance* (pp. 123–137). M. E. Sharpe.

Pawar, B. S. (2008). Two approaches to workplace spirituality facilitation: A comparison and implications. *Leadership & Organization Development Journal, 29*(6), 544–567. https://doi.org/10.1108/01437730810894195

Pawar, B. S. (2009). Individual spirituality, workplace spirituality and work attitudes: An empirical test of direct and interaction effects. *Leadership & Organization Development Journal, 30*(8), 759–777. https://doi.org/10.1108/01437730911003911

Peng, J., Chen, X., Zou, Y., & Nie, Q. (2021). Environmentally specific transformational leadership and team pro-environmental behaviors: The roles of pro-environmental goal clarity, pro-environmental harmonious passion, and power distance. *Human Relations, 74*(11), 1864–1888.

Peterlin, J., Pearse, N. J., & Dimovski, V. (2015). Strategic decision making for organizational sustainability: The implications of servant leadership and sustainable leadership approaches. *Economic & Business Review, 17*(3), 273–290. https://doi.org/10.15458/85451.4

Pfeffer, J. (2010). Business and the spirit. In R. A. Giacalone, & C. L. Jurkiewicz (Eds.), *Handbook of workplace spirituality and organizational performance* (2nd ed., pp. 27–43). M. E. Sharp.

Rainey, D. L. (2008). Transparency, openness, and accountability: A new imperative. In M. V. Russo (Ed.), *Environmental management: Readings and cases* (pp. 228–242). Sage Publications.

Rathee, R., & Rajain, P. (2020). Workplace spirituality: A comparative study of various models. *Jindal Journal of Business Research, 9*(1), 27–40. https://doi.org/10.1177/2278682120908554

Reave, L. (2005). Spiritual values and practices related to leadership effectiveness. *Leadership Quarterly, 16*(5), 655–687. https://doi.org/10.1016/j.leaqua.2005.07.003

Rego, A., & Pina e Cunha, M. (2008). Workplace spirituality and organizational commitment: An empirical study. *Journal of Organizational Change Management, 21*(1), 53–75. https://doi.org/10.1108/09534810810847039

Rezapouraghdam, H., Alipour, H., & Arasli, H. (2019). Workplace spirituality and organization sustainability: A theoretical perspective on hospitality employees' sustainable behavior. *Environment, Development and Sustainability, 21*(4), 1583–1601. https://doi.org/10.1007/s10668-018-0120-4

Rezapouraghdam, H., Alipour, H., & Darvishmotevali, M. (2018). Employee workplace spirituality and pro-environmental behavior in the hotel industry. *Journal of Sustainable Tourism, 26*(5), 740–758. https://doi.org/10.1080/09669582.2017.1409229

Riasudeen, S., & Prabavathy, R. (2011). Relationship of workplace spirituality and work attitude in manufacturing organization. *Global Management Review, 5*(4), 29–37. http://web.a.ebscohost.com

Rocha, R. G., & d'Angelo, M. J. (2021). Samarco's scandal: A perspective of organizational spirituality and corporate social responsibility. *The International Journal of Organizational Analysis, 31*(2), 387–411. https://doi.org/10.1108/IJOA-05-2020-2220

Russell, P. (2008). *The global brain: The awakening Earth in a new century* (3rd ed.). Floris Books.

Saks, A. M. (2011). Workplace spirituality and employee engagement. *Journal of Management, Spirituality & Religion, 8*(4), 317–340. https://doi.org/10.1080/14766086.2011.630170

Sankar, H., & Suresh, M. (2018). Modelling the factors of workplace spirituality in healthcare organization. *International Journal of Engineering & Technology (UAE), 7*(2.33), 786–790. https://www.sciencepubco.com/index.php/IJET

Sembiring, M. J., Eliyana, A., & Wibawa Ningrum, L. S. (2020). Effect of workplace spirituality on pro-environmental behaviour mediated by environmental passion. *Systematic Reviews in Pharmacy, 11*(11), 1282–1290.

Senge, P. (2002). Afterword. In R. Greenleaf (Ed.), *Servant leadership: A journey into the nature of legitimate power and greatness,* 25th anniversary ed., (pp. 343–359). Paulist Press.

Senge, P. (with Smith, B., Kruschwitz, N., Laut, J., & Schley, S.). (2008). *The necessary revolution: How individuals and organizations are working together to create a sustainable world*. Random House Digital.

Shah, S. H. A., Fahlevi, M., Jamshed, K., Aman, N., Rafiq, N., Jermsittiparsert, K., & Aljuaid, M. (2023). Sustaining the earth: Unraveling the synergy of workplace spirituality, responsible leadership, and pro-environmental behavior in Pakistan's SMEs. *Psychology Research and Behavior Management, 16*, 3075–3093. https://doi.org/10.2147/PRBM.S413606

Shastri, V., & Banerjee, P. M. (2010). From corporate social responsibility to global social entrepreneurship. In P. M. Banerjee & V. Shastri (Eds.), *Social responsibility and environmental sustainability in business: How organizations handle profits and social duties* (pp. 1–14). Sage Publications.

Smith, C. (2009). Reconnecting with Earth: Ecospirituality as the missing dimension in spirituality and sustainability education. *International Handbook of Education for Spirituality, Care and Wellbeing*, 653–675. https://doi.org/10.1007/978-1-4020-9018-9_35

Spector, D. (2012, March 1). *10 more reasons companies should care about sustainability*. Business Insider. http://www.businessinsider.com

Suganthi, L. (2020). Ecospirituality for organizational sustainability: An empirical study. *Journal of Cleaner Production, 266*, e121849. https://doi.org/10.1016/j.jclepro.2020.121849

Sustainability Leadership Institute. (n.d). *Leadership.* http://www.sustainabilityleadershipinstitute.org/leadership.php

Sustainability Mindset Indicator. (2020). *Become a 'change accelerator'*. https://smindicator.com/

Targowski, A. (2012). Spirituality 2.0—A condition for a wise civilization. *Dialogue and Universalism, 22*(2), 133–143. www.researchgate.net

Tate, W. (2009). *The search for leadership: An organisational perspective*. Triarchy Press.

TerraCycle. (2018a). *About TerraCycle*. https://www.terracycle.com/en-US/about-terracycle

TerraCycle. (2018b). *The TerraCycle breakthrough*. https://www.ownterracycle.com

Usman, A., & Danish, R. Q. (2010). Spiritual consciousness in banking managers and its impact on job satisfaction. *International Business Research, 3*(2), 65–72. https://doi.org/10.5539/ibr.v3n2p65

Van Schalkwyk, A. (2011). Sacredness and sustainability: Searching for a practical eco-spirituality. *Religion and Theology, 18*(1–2), 77–92. https://doi.org/10.1163/157430111X613674

Virmani, A., & Lépineux, F. (2014). Spiritual-based entrepreneurship for an alternative food culture: The transformational power of *Navdanya*. In L. Zsolnai (Ed.), *The spiritual dimension of business ethics and sustainability management* (pp. 125–142). Springer. https://doi.org/10.1007/978-3-319-11677-8_20

Walker, S. (2011). *The spirit of design: Objects, environment and meaning*. Earthscan.

Walker, S. (2013). Design and spirituality: Material culture for a wisdom economy. *Design Issues, 29*(3), 89–107. https://doi.org/10.1162/DESI_a_00223

Welch, J. (1998). Creed is good. *People Management, 24*, 28–33.

Word, J. (2012). Engaging work as a calling: Examining the link between spirituality and job involvement. *Journal of Management, Spirituality & Religion, 9*(2), 147–166. https://doi.org/10.1080/14766086.2012.688622

World Commission on Environment and Development. (1987). *Our common future*. Oxford University Press.

Yin, E., & Mahrous, A. (2022). Covid-19 global pandemic, workplace spirituality and the rise of spirituality-driven organisations in the post-digital era. *Journal of Humanities and Applied Social Sciences, 4*(2), 79–93. https://doi.org/10.1108/JHASS-11-2021-0177

Yong, J., Kim, J., Park, J., Seo, I., & Swinton, J. (2011). Effects of a spirituality training program on the spiritual and psychosocial well-being of hospital middle manager nurses in Korea. *Journal of Continuing Education in Nursing, 42*(6), 280–288. https://doi.org/10.3928/00220124-20101201-04

Zhuravleva, E., & Jones, G. (2006). *Keep walking the road: Outgrowing our instrumental approach to workplace spirituality*. Paper presented at the annual meeting of the Academy of Management, Atlanta, GA.

14

Epilogue: The Synthesis of Spirituality and Sustainability for Success

14.1 Introduction

In this text, the author has examined two seemingly unrelated, yet mutually intertwined topics, presenting the case for both to be characteristics of, and tools for both individual and organizational success. The underlying framework of both topics is the interconnectedness and oneness of everyone and everything on the planet. In this concluding chapter, I will summarize the key principles of the preceding chapters, as well as identify future recommendations, trends, and applications relevant to the application of spirituality and/or sustainability for success at both the individual and organizational level. As the writing of this text progressed, the author continually recognized the commonalities between the interconnectedness of spirituality and sustainability.

In this concluding chapter, I summarize the key principles of the preceding chapters, as well as identify future recommendations, trends, and applications relevant to the application of spirituality and sustainability for success at both the individual and organizational levels. The social, political, economic, and environmental challenges faced by humankind may benefit from contemporary alternatives to existing systems and models such as the circular economy and Spirituality 2.0.

C. G. Beehner, *Spirituality, Sustainability, and Success*, Palgrave Studies in Workplace Spirituality and Fulfillment, https://doi.org/10.1007/978-3-031-47643-3_14

Future research suggestions are included to reinforce (or refute) the propositions that spirituality and sustainability, when combined, produce both individual success and organizational success.

Several assumptions were made while writing this book. First, because considerable research and evidence exists supporting the occurrence of human-induced climate change, this author assumes that the reader recognizes climate is occurring and that human action is necessary to mitigate further environmental harm. Second, while most of the planetary inhabitants believe in God and adhere to some form of religious or spiritual doctrine, this author did not assume that the reader possesses a particular religious or spiritual condition. Therefore, spirituality was addressed from a secular perspective—the desire for meaning and purpose in life, and for connection and community with other like-minded individuals.

14.2 Chapter Summaries

The intent of this text was to provide: an understanding of the benefits of incorporating spirituality and sustainability in both personal/career success, and in business/organizational success; and, examples and resources to assist the reader in practical application of these principles, and in educating others about benefits and practical application. Chapter 1 provided a foundation of the definition, characteristics, and framework of spirituality and sustainability, and the suggested commonalities existing between spirituality and sustainability. Spirituality was defined as "the desire to find ultimate purpose in life, and to live accordingly" (Mitroff as cited in Cavanagh, 1999, p. 186), and further described as "the feeling individuals have about the fundamental meaning of who they are, what they are doing, [and] the contributions they are making" (Vaill, 1996, p. 218). Numerous secular definitions of spirituality have emanated in recent organizational science literature (Dent et al., 2005), ranging from the process of seeking a relationship with a higher power believed to influence the order of things, and is broader than any one religion (Zellars et al., 2003), to the process of placing value on the non-material characteristics of life (Krishnan, 2008).

A commonly accepted definition of sustainability comes from the field of sustainable development, drawn from the World Commission on Environment and Development (WCED), commonly known as the Brundtland Report. "Sustainable development is the development that meets the needs of the present without compromising the ability of future generations to meet their own needs" (WCED, 1987). Therefore, because the focus of several chapters of this book was an examination of sustainability within the context of individual and organizational success, we considered sustainability as referring to actions taken by individuals and organizations to ensure present needs are met without compromising the ability of future individuals and organizations to meet their needs in similar fashion. The chapter concluded with detailed examination of the nexus of spirituality and sustainability.

Chapter 2 expanded the individual spirituality discussion in greater detail, including the theoretical framework, and literature summary of spirituality. The framework was broad, interdisciplinary, and non-religious, with spirituality defined as a mental phenomenon taking place in the mind and spirit, and as such, transcendent of religion or culture. Spirituality was described as existing independent of institutionalized religion. While the focus of religion is external, characterized by rites and rituals, the focus of spirituality is internal (Hicks, 2002; Marques et al., 2005), characterized by self-reflection about "the kingdom within" (Marques et al., 2005). Hicks (2002) attributed the internalization of spirituality as a means of making spirituality accessible to everyone, regardless and irrespective of religion. Further, Dent et al. (2005) maintain that a person can be religious without ever experiencing spirituality, and likewise, a person can be spiritual without ever participating in a religion. Spiritual capital and spiritual intelligence were explored as sources of spirituality. In Chapter 2, the argument was made for individual spirituality as a factor in success. In their study of spirituality and success, Ashar and Lane-Maher (2004) found three definitions of success reported by study participants: sense of accomplishment, work-family balance, and contributions to the community. Moore (1992) suggests when work becomes a vocation and a calling, it provides an individual with increased meaning and identity. Moreover, when individuals find meaning and purpose through their life's work, it becomes a calling (Thompson, 2001). Work transits from being a job or vocation to a calling when unique individual talents become aligned with organizational and societal needs (Leider, 1997).

Researchers suggest a necessity of including the recognition, validation, and discussion of spirituality in career planning, because individuals desiring career success also require resources and support that respond to their holistic needs (Royce-Davis & Stewart, 2000). Spirituality and individual success may be examined through the lens of career theory, proponents of which suggest individuals express spirituality within the context of personal life meaning as well as the organizational context in which they are achieved (Lips-Wiersma, 2002). While the premise of psychological career theory is with a personally constructed reality, assuming individuals have a degree of career direction control, the premise of sociological career theory is that institutions influence career direction within a socially constructed reality (Hotchkiss & Borrow, 1990). Lips-Wiersma (2002) found the achievement of spirituality to be the result of a positive relationship between individual spirituality and the organizational environment in which it is achieved. Individuals often change careers when they determine they are no longer authentically achieving their life purposes, supporting the argument that spirituality influences work behavior.

The focus of much of the early management literature on workplace spirituality was with the individual spiritual journey as a process of inner focus as a means of development of self-awareness and self-expression (King & Nicol, 1999). Organizational members who fully express their spirituality not only find personal enrichment but benefit the organization through increased creativity and intuition (Biberman & Whittey, 1997; Neck & Milliman, 1994), heightened teamwork and sense of community (Hawley, 1993; Henson, 1991), improved and increased leadership (Conger, 1994), and a stronger vision and purpose (Kahnweiler & Otte, 1997). Workplace spirituality also impacts work performance, with Javanmard (2012) noting faith in work improves communication which in turn improves sense of community, inner life, and work meaning. Increased productivity has been associated with both employee religiosity and spirituality (Valasek, 2009), beneficial to both the individual and the business or organization.

This edition included content about entrepreneurship and spirituality. While most traditional entrepreneurship literature has ignored spirituality when examining motivation, one study identified two groups of entrepreneurs: those who combine mind, body, and soul with their work and those who do not (Kauanui et al., 2008). These two groups were further broken down into five modalities. The "make me whole" group are internally motivated, are engaged in work that they love and in which they find meaning and purpose, and who fully engage spirituality at work. The soul seekers do not fully integrate spirituality or religion in their work, struggle with a definition of spirituality, and consider work to be rewarding, with financial security as the primary motivation. The "conflicting goals" perceive a relationship between spirituality and entrepreneurship, but struggle to integrate the two, considering work to be a means of achieving success and goal or dream gratification. The "mostly business" group may perceive a connection between spirituality and work, but do not apply that connection in practice, considering work as "a means to an end". The "strictly business" group are not spiritual, separate business from personal life, and consider work to acquire wealth which is the measure of success (Kauanui et al., 2008).

Ethics and spirituality are new topics for this edition. Ethics prescribes behaviors that are considered appropriate and what is considered right in living one's life (Chippendale, 2001). An individual with spiritual principles and values may have a better understanding of the ethical problems which exist in business (Kumari, 2014). Spirituality serves a vital role in guiding ethical behaviors of both leaders and followers. According to s (2013), every system of ethics requires stories and narratives to address fundamental questions and inspirations such as the nature of the universe, and the meaning of life. Creighton-Smith et al. (2017) suggested the forces in the realm of spirituality or religiosity may be one of the most effective determinants of ethical behavior. Edginton and Kangas (2014) claimed spirituality is one of the most significant influences impacting humankind and guides most societal beliefs, cultures, practices, and decisions.

Chapter 3 expanded the spirituality discussion to the organizational level by examining the concept of workplace spirituality, including the definition, theoretical framework, and literature summary. Several common themes emerged regarding the definitions and conceptualizations of workplace spirituality: meaningful work that serves a higher purpose, the development of a sense of vocational calling, a focus on global well-being, and an awareness of the need to protect, save, and enhance the planet's resources and inhabitants (Al-Qutop & Harrim, 2014). Workplace spirituality has been described as a macro-level glimpse of the spiritual climate of an organization, manifest within the organizational culture (Shinde et al., 2010), and as a trait, a flexible state of being (Liu & Robertson, 2011), and a state that is subjective in nature (Kinjerski & Skrypnek, 2004). Perhaps Dhiman (2017) best differentiated individual spirituality from workplace spirituality with the following statement: "Spirituality helps us to discover the deeper transcendental meaning in our work, while workplace spirituality helps us find meaning at work" (p. 182).

Several reasons were identified for increased interest in workplace spirituality, including: increased disappointment with religious institutions; increased desire for community and connection at work; workers questioning the meaning and purpose of work; increased inclination for integration of personal and spiritual values within career; and, increased desire for an alternative to the pursuit of material rewards (Robbins & Judge, 2010). In the contemporary world of dynamic change, countless individuals perceive a loss of meaning and purpose in their lives, precipitating a feeling of spiritual despair (King & Nicol, 1999). Although the workplace is fundamental to individual survival, the workplace frequently increases despair, inhibits individual growth (King & Nicol, 1999), and neglects the spiritual and emotional dimensions of human need (Barrett, 2009).

While workplace spirituality has been proven beneficial, and been embraced by academia and practitioners alike, three areas of dissension have been identified within the literature. First, based upon the ambiguity of existing definitions and frameworks, workplace spirituality may inadvertently abolish any distinction between employee workplace and personal lives (Tourish & Tourish, 2010), as well as encourage employees and management to promote personal spiritual beliefs to proselytize coworkers and supervisors (Lips-Wiersma et al., 2009; Milliman et al., 2003). The second area of contention concerns the potential for management abuse by utilizing workplace spirituality to maximize productivity through manipulation (Case & Gosling, 2010; Lips-Wiersma et al., 2009; Milliman et al., 2003). Employees within a workplace spirituality environment may become so inner-focused that they do not recognize management manipulation and exploitation (Polley et al., 2005), or may even accept management instrumentality as appropriate, or even desirable managerial behavior (Long & Mills, 2010). Finally, an organization endorsing workplace spirituality may become so close-knit that decisions become biased by groupthink (Polley et al., 2005), a process in which group pressure encourages individuals to conform to the opinions and ideas of the team (Robbins & Coulter, 2012).

The servant, authentic, spiritual, and ethical leadership styles were added to this edition. Servant leadership was introduced by Greenleaf in 1970, although individuals have been demonstrating servant leadership for millennia. Servant leadership places serving the needs of others first, drawing upon the notion that individuals seek to serve others first, which subsequently inspires a desire for others to lead. The litmus test of successful servant leadership is whether followers grow as individuals, becoming healthier, wiser, more autonomous, and ultimately become servant leaders (Greenleaf, 1977). Servant leaders encourage organizational stewardship and recognize the importance of organizational sustainability (Taylor & Pearse, 2009). Servant leadership can occur anywhere, and impact anyone (Graham, 1998).

Authentic leadership does not have a commonly accepted definition (Alomar et al., 2022). However, the concept has received considerable attention in recent academic literature (Northouse, 2018), and several interpretations have been offered by leading scholars, who are becoming interested in this emerging field (Alomar et al., 2022). The concept of authentic leadership was first introduced by George (2003), who predicted the rapid rise of theoretical and practical interest in leadership. Spiritual leadership describes a leadership style consisting of the necessary values, attitudes, and behaviors to intrinsically motivate oneself and others, thereby creating a sense of spiritual survival through calling and membership (Fry, 2003). Spiritual leaders motivate and inspire workers through a transcendent vision and an organizational culture based on genuine care and concern. Spiritual leadership is essential for satisfying the spiritual well-being of leaders and followers through calling and membership, which is achieved through the creation of vision and value congruence across the organizational members, and fostering greater levels of employee well-being, organizational commitment, performance, productivity, and social responsibility (Fry, 2003; Fry & Nisiewicz, 2013; Fry & Slocum, 2008; Fry et al., 2005, 2010). The ethical leadership style offers leaders a collection of principles used to inform decision-making (Northouse, 2018). Ethical leaders respect and serve others by placing the well-being of others above their own, make decisions based on equity and justice, are trustworthy, and are dedicated to building community (Northouse, 2018). Because leadership involves influencing others, leaders must demonstrate ethical responsibility for their followers. Ethical leaders use their authority to motivate individuals to overcome obstacles and change and personal growth (Heifetz, 1994).

Chapter 4 is new to this edition and explored Indigenous spirituality. While contemporary society has been established on a foundation of human-made institutions and structures, most Indigenous cultures recognize the interconnectedness of nature and humankind, and that humankind cannot exist and survive outside of nature. Indigenous spirituality is often characterized by a holistic, comprehensive way of living. Although spiritual beliefs vary among the millions of indigenous cultures, commonalities exist between many of the dominant indigenous cultures. Common Indigenous cultures and their respective spiritual beliefs and practices were explored. The similarities and differences of these Indigenous cultures were examined to develop a better understanding of their role and importance in achieving spirituality. The absence of a spiritual-secular binary in Indigenous cultures added an important perspective to the discussion about Indigenous spirituality.

Indigenous knowledge and spiritual traditions are highly interconnected and provide the foundation for Indigenous epistemologies (Neeganagwedgin, 2013). The key themes of Indigenous spirituality identified by Harvey (2012) are:

- The relational nature of personhood and the greater community.
- The equilibrium of dwelling or positioning.

- The requirement for respect among individual members of the greater community.
- The generative power of gifts and gifting, rituals, and etiquette.

The Indigenous world does not exist "out there" or separate from them, but rather it exists within them and even "through" them (Marcos, 2010). Weber (1918) used the term enchantment to describe traditional religions and disenchantment to describe the contemporary monotheistic era. He described modernity as being "robbed of gods", having replaced disenchantment and mystery with ritualization and intellectualization. Enchantment and disenchantment are two of the most elementary means by which individuals mentally organize the world their place within it (Balcomb, 2022). Weber was dissatisfied with the process of disenchantment, noting that while science had filled the void created by the decline of religion, science can clarify questions of values and morals, but cannot answer those questions. Although Weber recognized that a return to traditional religions might not be an appropriate solution, Weber recognized the inadequacy of both science and religion presents a major dilemma for contemporary society (Barrero, 2023).

Shamanism was discussed as a religious practice in which a practitioner, known as a shaman or saman engages with the spirit realm through techniques such as trances (Singh, 2018). The purpose of shamanism is to invite spirits or spiritual energies into the physical realm for the purpose of healing, foretelling the future, changing the weather, or providing various forms of aid to humans (Singh, 2018). Shamans are known by various names including medicine man, witch doctor, holy man, or prophet, but the concept of being a shaman crosses almost all cultural boundaries. However, many cultures oppose the broad usage of the term *shamanism,* arguing apparent similarities among phenomena in widely dispersed regions do not justify the assertion of a common connection.

Defining and describing Indigenous spirituality is challenging because while Indigenous beliefs systems share common elements, each is unique to the culture of origin, and the influence of Western settlers. Despite the philosophical and logical differences between Indigenous and Western wisdom and spirituality, cross-cultural cooperation is both possible

(Robison, 2020) and imperative. The Indigenous worldview has survived and ensured the survival of adherents despite centuries of Western colonialization. Protecting and maintaining our ecosystems is essential to the survival of all human and non-human inhabitants. The reemergence and acceptance of Indigenous beliefs and practices are essential for the continued survival of Indigenous and non-Indigenous Peoples alike.

Chapter 5 is also new to this edition and includes research and perspectives on spirituality in the post-pandemic era. While religious affiliation and participation began declining decades before the COVID-19 pandemic, the pandemic stimulated inward reflection in many individuals and cultures. Many individuals were reminded of their mortality and used time working at home and loss of friends and loved ones as opportunities to find meaning and spirituality in their lives. The concept that spirituality exists both within and absent religious institutions became more evident as churches were closed or provided services virtually. The role of spirituality in the post-pandemic era was examined within the context of individual and organizational success. The reflection topic and questions provided perspective on the role of spirituality during and after unexpected global crises.

The post-pandemic era refers to the period after the COVID-19 pandemic which occurred between 2019 and 2023. This period is also referred to by some scholars and practitioners as the post-digital era, defined by *PC Magazine* (n.d.) as being beyond the digital age, or as a humanistic approach to problem-solving which places less emphasis on numerical analysis and computerized solutions. The post-digital era is currently in the embryonic stage, and discussion of this era is currently conjectural (Yin & Mahrous, 2022). According to leading management consulting firms, the focus of the post-digital era has shifted from the digital transformation of the digital era to applying digital technologies in significant ways to enhance competitive advantage (Accenture, 2019). Moreover, while the industrial era prioritized self-interest, control, hierarchy, productivity, and linearity, the post-digital is characterized by several unique characteristics: fully connected, meaning-based, and trust-centered (Yin & Mahrous, 2022).

Despite the devastation of recent pandemic, COVID-19 has exposed the pain of seclusion and social isolation, revealed the deepest desires of most individuals to focus on what is important, and stimulated astonishing innovation and resilience (Philips, 2023). Individuals who were liberated from the restrictions of physical meetings learned that meaningful community could occur at home. The Fetzer Institute identified five significant COVID-19-influenced shifts in our religious and spiritual horizon (Philips, 2023):

1. Meaning takes the center stage.
2. Traditional delivery pathways for religious life are breaking down.
3. Community can be home-based.
4. Spiritual leadership is de-professionalizing.
5. Virtual connection can be surprisingly meaningful.

The contemporary business environment has been described as "VUCA" (volatile, uncertain, complex, and ambiguous; White, 2013). Success in the VUCA environment can only be achieved with the flexibility, adaptability, and agility of resilient businesses (Esievo et al., 2019). Research findings demonstrated a significant influence of workplace spirituality on organizational resilience (Esievo et al., 2019). Using organizational culture to create an environment conducive to adopting workplace spirituality promotes robustness and adaptability which contributes to overall resilience. Esievo et al. (2019) recommended businesses continue to focus on meaningful work; develop policies to improve employees' work-life balance; align to common organizational tenets to enhance collective wisdom, determination, and excellence; and, embrace the interconnectedness as a means to enhance spirituality at work.

Several risks related to workplace spirituality in the post-pandemic era were discussed. The marketing of the mindfulness practice as workplace commodity has been labeled McMindfulness (Kristensen, 2018). Despite the individual and societal benefits of mindfulness, the introduction of mindfulness activities in the workplace poses risks. Kristensen suggested workplace mindfulness practices risk reinforcing the problems they were intended to solve. Bazzano (2014) suggested that corporate mindfulness programs have become "a quick fix for the anxieties of late-capitalist society" (p. 164). These mindfulness programs have become acceptable to the business community because they enhance the exclusive quest for corporate objectives and profitability masquerading as means of caring for employees (Kristensen, 2018).

The term *workism* was introduced prior to the pandemic, defined as "the belief that work is not only necessary to economic production but also the centerpiece of one's identity and life's purpose" (Thompson, 2019, 2023). *Workism* is one of the most powerful of the new religions competing for adherents (Thompson, 2023). Thompson (2023) suggested that *workism* has three pillars and multiple potential negative side effects. The pillars are: employees use work to replace the meaning previously provided by religion; employees demand more from employers (e.g., sense of community); and, work can offer meaning and increase productivity but can also overextend and exhaust employees. Thompson warned that *workism* negatively influences public policy, noting that in the United States, work is so centered in policy that it is the only OECD (Organisation for Economic Co-operation and Development) nation without national policies on medical or parental leave (Thompson, 2023).

The movement toward more purpose-driven work began before the pandemic because of the increased social conscience of millennials and has since accelerated. Therefore, creating deeper meaning for employees' work and lives has become a critical issue for organizations (Yin & Mahrous, 2022). Developing deeper connections between employees and organizations and creating meaning and purpose in the workplace will become more essential for organizations to become resilient and achieve sustainable growth in the post-pandemic VUCA business environment (Yin & Mahrous, 2022).

Chapter 6 introduced the definition, theoretical framework, and literature summary of sustainability. While concepts such as climate change often appear in sustainability conversations, sustainability was examined in a broader context of individual and organizational responsibility and citizenship toward the environment. Because this text has a career and business focus, sustainability was examined from a pragmatic business perspective. While traditional definitions of sustainability have been environmental in nature, Orr emphasized sustainability should not only be concerned with ecological integrity, but also social and economic justice, nonviolence, democracy, and peace (McDaniel, 2002). Orr made the distinction between the two by noting the focus of environmentalism is ecological integrity, while the focus of sustainability is more holistic and inclusive.

While the genesis of sustainability is often associated with the Brundtland Commission and the subsequent WECD report, nearly two centuries earlier, prominent economist Thomas Robert Malthus (1766–1834) recognized the impact of natural resource scarcity on economic growth (Mebratu, 1998), suggesting if humankind did not keep their numbers in check, war, environmental crises, or natural resource scarcity would accomplish the task (Malthus, 1798). The prognostications of Malthus would be echoed 150 years later by Ernest F. Schumacher in his 1959 lectures at London University entitled *The Crucial Problems of Modern Living*, and his seminal environmental critique *Small Is Beautiful* (1979). Young and Dhanda (2013) suggested the current sustainability movement has occurred because of a perfect storm of increased energy costs, numerous natural and human-made environmental calamities, increased attention being paid to the green movement, and the Great Recession.

In Chapter 6, the argument was made for sustainability at the individual level as a factor in success. The corporate scandals at the turn of the twentieth century, combined with increasing concern about the impact of business on the environment, have positively influenced the literature on responsibility within management careers (Khurana & Nohria, 2008; Waddock, 2007; Walck, 2009). Responsible careers are defined as those in which workers seek to affect positive impact on social justice and environmental sustainability through their employment (Tams & Marshall, 2011), demanding the ability to recognize the interconnectedness of business, environmental, and social systems, coupled with the ability to interface multiple stakeholder groups (Alvord et al., 2004; Ospina & Foldy, 2008; Waddock, 2008).

The field of sustainability has expanded significantly since first appearing in literature in the 1980s. Careers in the field of sustainability are diverse and evolving, with students challenged to prepare for jobs that do not yet exist (Kross, 2012). In addition to careers in the fields of environmental science and engineering, sustainability-related careers exist in the fields of accounting and auditing, cost estimating, occupational health and safety, human resources, regulatory compliance, logistics, and business operations (Hamilton, 2012). Likewise, career opportunities are expanding in the skilled and semi-skilled disciplines, with workers in the new constellation of opportunities identified as the green-collar workforce (Gregson, 2010). The emerging green-collar workforce will require sustainability literacy, not necessarily in the areas of environmental science and engineering, but in more traditional areas such as manufacturing, materials, agriculture, and construction (Gregson, 2010).

Harman (1992) suggested twenty-first-century business is reflecting a "change of mind" in competitive, exploitive materialism and consumerism will be replaced by a new business paradigm with alternative values of relationship quality, the oneness of humanity, cooperation, caring, nurturing, and spiritual values. Worthwhile societal change begins at the individual level, because an individual cannot accomplish for society what cannot be accomplished individually (Pappas & Pappas, 2014). While studies have examined leaders who engage in sustainability (Rimanoczy, 2014), limited academic research has addressed how sustainability initiatives provide meaning or fulfillment at the individual level (Visser & Crane, 2010). According to Pappas and Pappas (2014), sustainable individuals are described as individuals who create harmony and interconnection, and possess relatively high levels of self-awareness of their values, thoughts, behaviors, and actions. The determination of individual sustainability is dependent upon thorough assessment and evaluation of a range of human factors—emotional, social, physical, economic, and intellectual (Pappas & Pappas, 2014).

The topic of Chapter 7 was sustainable business. While the traditional business model described a company providing shareholder return on investment (Balestrero & Udo, 2014), the emerging sustainable business model incorporates the environmental definition, suggesting a sustainable business provides goods and services of value to the current generation while ensuring goods and services can also be provided to future generations (Beehner, 2018). Progressive businesses are responding to the noticeable disconnect between financial and environmental performance, strengthening the belief businesses can "do well by doing good" (Molnar & Mulvihill, 2003). While many have argued capitalism may be the cause of our current environmental state, others argue capitalism is a powerful means to create value while solving our environmental problems (Dean, 2014). While the primary goal of capitalism may be profit maximization, Dean reminds us that the overarching goal of an economic system is providing value to society, not capital accumulation. However, Dean (2014) argued against rejecting capitalism due to the apparent adverse effects of the current capitalist approach, instead requiring markets work for the environment and not against it. Natural capitalism is a model recognizing the dependence of the global economy on natural resources and systems, suggesting the long-term existence of humankind requires the recognition and proper valuation of natural capital (Hawken et al., 2008). Areas discussed in which businesses are capitalizing on sustainable business opportunities included clean energy and sustainable buildings.

The emerging sustainable business model was compared with the traditional business models. While many have argued that capitalism may be the cause of our current environmental state, others maintained that capitalism is a powerful means to create value while solving our environmental problems. The systems perspective and the stakeholder approach were discussed to support the necessity for achieving and the interconnectedness of the UN SDGs. The transition from capitalism solely as a means for profit maximization to newer models of conscious capitalism, the circular economy, environmental social and governance (ESG) investing, and social entrepreneurship were also topics of this chapter. The chapter's case study illustrated the dark side of performative attempts at greening.

Chapter 8 is new to this edition and explores indigenous sustainability. Creation is conceived as a living process wherein all inhabitants are members of a living universe. Most Indigenous traditions and belief systems regard nature with deep respect. They have a strong sense of place and belonging which sustains knowledge and ways of life that promote nature conservation and sustainable natural resource use. Common Indigenous cultures and their respective spiritual beliefs and practices were explored within the context of the role of sustainability in individual and collective success. The absence of a spiritual-secular binary in Indigenous cultures added an important perspective to the discussion about sustainability.

An Indigenous cosmology is relational and understands that relationships require time to develop and includes reciprocal responsibilities. From an Indigenous perspective, commerce occurs inside, not outside of the natural environment and the community (Bansal, 2021). Earth is more than a planet, she is "Mother Earth", who provides for and receives from everything that exists (Bansal, 2021). Therefore, when business activities harm the community or the environment, those activities harm themselves (Bansal, 2021). This relational worldview is also temporal because past, present, and future are connected; therefore, the interests of ancestors and descendants are as important as the interests of people today (Bansal, 2021). Meanwhile, a Western business perspective considers people, objects, activities, and communities as detached with transactions administered by markets and contracts.

Indigenous peoples have existed for millennia as independent and unique nations within difficult and demanding environments because their cultural values are compatible with sustainability (Tsosie, 2014). Indigenous Peoples are unique because they have inhabited their lands for millennia, and their intergenerational presence and relationship with their lands is deeply engrained within their cultures and societies (Tsosie, 2014). For most Indigenous peoples, sustainability is the result of a conscious and deliberate activities intended to maintain harmony between humankind and nature for the benefit of future generations (Tsosie, 2014). Indigenous communities recognize themselves members of their communities, and the natural environments as interconnected through an attached spirit or energy (Robison, 2020).

The concept of considering future generations is common in most Indigenous cultures, with one common representation being the seventh-generation principle. The seventh-generation principle involves considering the seventh generation of descendants, and remembering the seventh generation of ancestors in decision-making, speech, and action (Haley, 2021). "The seventh-generation principle is based on an ancient philosophy of the Haudenosaunee Confederacy (Iroquois), which is recognized as the oldest democracy in the world and believed to be the model of the American Constitution" (Haley, 2021). Goodman (2015) describes the principle as "choosing our responsibility to the seventh generation over quarterly earnings, regeneration over economic growth, and the pursuit of well-being and harmony over wealth and financial success" (p. 29).

Climate change poses significant threats to Indigenous Peoples' livelihoods and traditional knowledge because most Indigenous Peoples live in areas heavily impacted by climate change and modern development that damage the natural environment (Tsosie, 2014), and are dependent upon, and closely connected with the environment and natural resources (Jerez, 2021). The homes of Indigenous Peoples are being destroyed by flooding and they are having trouble maintaining their traditional, subsistence lifestyles because of the loss of sea ice and the impacts on their food sources (Tsosie, 2014). Other negative impacts include diseases, drought and desertification, excessive rainfall, increased flooding, melting snow, glaciers and sea ice, increased insect infestations, and erosion (Jerez, 2021). The increased frequency and intensity of climate disasters are destroying their land and homes causing many Indigenous peoples to become environmental refugees (Jerez, 2021). Indigenous Peoples are stewards of the world's biodiversity and cultural diversity and essential stakeholders for natural resource and biodiversity protection (Jerez, 2021). Although Indigenous Peoples only represent approximately five percent of the global population, they effectively manage approximately 20–25% of the Earth's land surface. Their traditional lands possess 80% of the planet's biodiversity and approximately 40% of all protected and ecologically intact areas (Jerez, 2021).

Understanding how Indigenous Peoples manage natural resources offers a foundation for developing resource management policies that benefit Indigenous Peoples and perpetuate their cultural beliefs (Chunhabunyatip et al., 2018). The relationship between Indigenous Peoples and sustainability policy is generally approached in one of two ways: placing them inside sustainability or at the perimeter. The sustainability dialogue must occur within Indigenous and Western thought systems, in a platform of mutual respect engagement. This knowledge sharing between and among diverse peoples will provide new opportunities to unlock our potential as human beings in a dynamic natural world (Tsosie, 2014). Indigenous practices and knowledge, which coexist harmoniously with the natural environment, can teach humankind how to achieve UN SDGs which is critical for the survival of the estimated 370 million Indigenous People globally, because their traditional lifestyles and livelihoods are increasingly at risk (Acciona, n.d.).

Chapter 9 is also new to this edition and includes research and perspectives on sustainability in the post-pandemic era. The increase in work from home (WFH) employment during and following the COVID-19 pandemic demonstrated that many business and organizational activities can be performed remotely, in a more sustainable manner. The brief pause in atmospheric CO_2 rise gave hope that meaningful climate change mitigation was possible. This chapter explored sustainability research, initiatives, and topics in the aftermath of the COVID-19 pandemic to provide perspective on achieving sustainability during or despite unexpected global crises.

The long-term consequences of the pandemic on the attitudes about sustainability among government leaders and their constituents are uncertain (Dalsace, 2021). The long-term impact of the pandemic on sustainability efforts will depend on the common narrative that is currently being developed. This narrative may be country-specific and influenced by two important criteria: the extent to which humankind collectively believes the pandemic was either an isolated or recurring event, and our collective post-pandemic attitude toward institutions and governments (Dalsace, 2021). The combination of these two variables leads to four very different potential scenarios: little or no change, bigger government, a shift in mindset, and authoritarian changes (Dalsace, 2021).

There will be little or no change if the pandemic is considered an isolated crisis that was properly managed by institutions. If citizens decide that the pandemic was not an isolated incident but the first of many crises and view the performance of governments during the pandemic favorably, the collective mindset may change significantly (Dalsace, 2021). This is the optimal scenario for sustainability because citizens and NGOs will become change agents, collectively questioning the existing development model and demanding change. If citizens believe the pandemic signifies the beginning of a series of crises for which established institutions are ill-prepared, the opportunity for change might be the greatest (Dalsace, 2021). In this scenario, extensive changes would be required, with citizens possibly willing to exchange some individual freedoms for improvements in health and safety. While this scenario might offer the most significant opportunity to achieve sustainability, any success would be dependent on the commitment of governments and constituents (Dalsace, 2021).

Morrissey and Heidkamp (2022) proposed five "pillars" from which to rebuild the global economy, based on the principles of a shared sustainable prosperity: an ecological prosperity; a decarbonized economy; a shared cost burden; a governance new deal; and, a just resilience. The premise of the five-pillar model is that sustainability must extend beyond being an environmental concern by including social and economic dimensions which are essential for a stable and prosperous society. Achieving just and sustainable growth will depend on effectively and holistically addressing the conditions and interdependency of our economies and societies. Schwab and Sternfels (2022) offer three suggestions for moving forward:

1. The public and private sectors must have a broad view of the resilience agenda.
2. Strategies and structures must be designed for agility and speed.
3. The public and private sectors must supplement business and economic resilience with social resilience.

Economic and social issues such as labor shortages, transitioning to a digital economy, supply-chain disruptions, inflation, and inequality are currently managed in isolation with discipline-specific responses. We must prepare for disruption and uncertainty and approach these issues with internal adaptability and flexibility. The pandemic demonstrated the need for timely information, timely strategic agendas, and faster decision cycles (Schwab & Sternfels, 2022). Leaders must focus on anticipating and predicting disruptions and trends instead of preparing detailed budgets and plans (Schwab & Sternfels, 2022).

In Chapter 10, the argument was made for workplace spirituality and organizational spirituality as factors in organizational success. According to the literature, spirituality contributes to employee well-being and quality of life and provides employees with meaning and purpose at work, along with a sense of community interconnectedness (Karakas, 2010). Positive relationships have been demonstrated between workplace spirituality and job satisfaction (Altaf & Awan, 2011; Chatterjee & Naqvi, 2010; Giacalone & Jurkiewicz, 2010; Gupta et al., 2013; Pawar, 2009), job involvement (Chatterjee & Naqvi, 2010; Kolodinsky et al., 2008; Word, 2012), organizational commitment (Affeldt & MacDonald, 2010; Fry & Slocum, 2008; Marschke et al., 2009; Pawar, 2009; Rego & Pina e Cunha, 2008), and organizational identification, while a negative relationship was found between workplace spirituality and organizational frustration (Kolodinsky et al., 2008). Organizations fostering workplace spirituality have achieved higher productivity and performance (Mehta & Joshi, 2010; Mitroff & Denton, 1999; Reave, 2005; Valasek, 2009), and managers embracing spiritual leadership are more effective managers (Fernando & Jackson, 2006). Employee turnover and turnover intention were found to be lower among organizations with higher levels of workplace spirituality (Chawla & Guda, 2010; Crawford et al., 2009; Giacalone & Jurkiewicz, 2010; Hong, 2012; Milliman et al., 2003; Riasudeen & Prabavathy, 2011).

Workplace spirituality programs have been implemented in organizations in multiple industries, with most programs producing positive organizational results (Dhiman & Marques, 2011; Han et al., 2010; Kinjerski & Skrypnek, 2008; Pawar, 2008; Yong et al., 2011). Although numerous organizations have successfully implemented workplace spirituality programs, the existence of a workplace spirituality program is not necessary for workplace spirituality to exist within an organization (Pawar, 2008). Empirical evidence indicates workplace spirituality programs influence beneficial individual outcomes such as increased joy, peace, serenity, job satisfaction, and commitment, along with beneficial organizational outcomes such as improved productivity and reduced absenteeism and turnover (Case & Gosling, 2010).

Case and Gosling (2010) challenged the framework of workplace spirituality as an instrument for achieving organizational goals. Moreover, other researchers argued the anti-materialist characteristic of spirituality may introduce challenges in the scientific investigation of links between spirituality and financial performance (Dent et al., 2005; Fornaciari &

Lund Dean, 2001; Lund Dean et al., 2003). Further, concerns also exist concerning spirituality being used as an administrative tool for employee behavior manipulation (Brown, 2003; Case & Gosling, 2010; Cavanagh & Bandsuch, 2002; Fernando, 2005; Mirvis, 1997). It is argued that spirituality should be seen as an end in and of itself, not be used as a managerial tool for organizational performance improvement (Cavanagh & Bandsuch, 2002; Fernando, 2005).

The corporate world recognizes that spiritual values are essential to both personal well-being and organizational success (Dhiman, 2017). While businesses often exclude spirituality from the business model, researchers suggest that doing so threatens to separate employees from moral integrity (Brophy, 2015). Spirituality should not be viewed as external interference, but rather as internal embodiment, and should be included in a business to the extent these values are shared by leadership (Brophy, 2015). However, based upon both legal and cultural factors affecting employer-sponsored workplace spirituality program implementation, Lund Dean and Safranski (2008) suggested a non-interventionist approach in workplace spirituality implementation, allowing voluntary employee participation in programs, absent supervisory sanction or pressure for nonparticipation (Lund Dean & Safranski, 2008).

In Chapter 11, the argument was made for sustainability as a factor in organizational success. The contributions and roles of religious and spiritual NGOs and IGOs were also examined. While the goal of traditional capitalism is with making money, there is growing concern within and without industry about how that money is made (Soyka, 2012). Business sustainability is increasingly understood to be both the right thing and the smart thing to do (Soyka, 2012). While at the beginning of the current century, business managers viewed sustainability as adding nothing but cost to their organization, contemporary business managers recognize as beneficial to maintaining a long-term competitive advantage (Hind et al., 2013).

Several methods were introduced for implementation of sustainability at the business or organizational level. Systems thinking is a management discipline with a focus on understanding a system by examining the linkages and interactions between the components and subsystems comprising the entirety of the defined system (Tate, 2009). Enterprise thinking is strategically focused, recognizing the business as a connected system, not merely individual, disconnected components (Rainey, 2006). Life cycle thinking (LCT), and the related life cycle assessment (LCA), tool presents a creative methodology for the examination, assessment, and improvement of products, processes, and technologies, and is operationally focused (Rainey, 2006). According to the value proposition, the primary purpose of business is creation and maximization of value (Rainey, 2006), necessitating any sustainable business strategy be approached from a value-creation perspective (Soyka, 2012).

Benefits that have been identified to having a sustainable business strategy: gaining competitive advantage from goodwill; preference of green brands by consumers; recruiting and retaining good employees; saving money from efficiency and waste reduction; making money from creative forms of waste regeneration; sustainability as a point of differentiation; shaping future of industry; becoming preferred supplier; providing competitive edge to customers; and, changing image and brand (Senge, 2008). On the surface, sustainability might seem to be a "feel good" notion for successful businesses who want to give something back to society, or perhaps look better in the eyes of one or more stakeholder groups. A deeper look reveals sustainability to be a business process for increased revenue and profitability, and reduced costs, in addition to the favorable view that some might have of a business that has "gone green". Companies that do not have a sustainable approach within their strategy risk missing opportunities influenced by the increasingly "green" consumer (Esty & Winston, 2006). Rather than joining a movement that is well underway, many businesses have pioneered the shift toward sustainable business practices, creating a competitive advantage. These smart companies get ahead of the curve and take sustainable actions to lower both financial and operational risk by providing added degrees of freedom to operate, profit, and expand (Esty & Winston, 2006).

High sustainability businesses have outperformed low sustainability businesses in terms of both stock market performance and profitability, demonstrating stock market performance 4.8% higher than low sustainability businesses over one 18-month period (Eccles et al., 2012a). However, sustainability strategy implementation can be difficult because it requires large-scale change, something few companies desire or do well (Eccles et al., 2012b). Sustainable business leaders develop a competitive advantage by accepting a long-term decision-making horizon, accept greater risk when pursuing sustainability, and demonstrate a contagious personal commitment to sustainability (Eccles et al., 2012b). Successful sustainable business requires transparency, openness, and accountability. While accountability is usually mandated or pressured by outsides sources, openness and transparency are voluntary, and as such may stimulate trust (Rainey, 2008).

In Chapter 12, the case was presented for both spirituality and sustainability as individual success factors. Because limited existing literature examines both variables in terms of individual success, much of the content of this chapter addressed the proposed theoretical and conceptual framework for the proposed hypothesis. It can be argued that one's inner world and outer world are not only interconnected, but reflections of each other. This interconnectedness is so intense that the human community is incomprehensible absent the entire planetary community, suggesting the proper role of human intelligence is to elevate and not exploit the natural world (Carroll, 2004). Thus, an interconnected system necessitates all members recognize their relationship with the whole and interact with other members accordingly.

While it may seem intuitive that spirituality and sustainability would contribute to the success of an individual science, perhaps originating with intuition requires a theoretical foundation or framework which can be researched and proven. The mutual dependence of spirituality and sustainability was discussed in Chapter 1 of this text, with scholars suggesting spirituality enhances efforts to act in a sustainably responsible manner, and sustainability reinforces the connectedness of all life (Marques et al., 2010). Several frameworks exist for examination of the relationship among and benefits of spirituality, sustainability, and success.

The title of this text contains three terms this author and others believe to be interrelated: spirituality, sustainability, and success, terms which share ingredients with the three Ps of the triple bottom line (Elkington, 1998). One of the Merriam-Webster definitions of spirituality that was introduced in Chapter 2 was "an animating or vital principle held to give life to physical organisms". Hence, *spirituality* may be considered the principle that gives life to *people*. Because *sustainability* refers to the preservation of natural resources for future generations, sustainability may be considered the principle that gives life to the *planet*. Finally, the success of a business organization is measured in terms of *profit,* while it can certainly be argued that an individual may profit from achieving success in terms of material rewards as well as personal and professional recognition.

Eco-spirituality was introduced as a framework for combining spirituality and sustainability, defined as "the direct consciousness and experience of the Sacred in the ecology which may serve as a sustained source for communities' and individuals' practical search to live sustainably from the Earth's resources" (van Schalkwyk, 2011, p. 77). If we are consciously aware of our connection with nature, and the impact of our actions on the well-being of the planet, we can begin to modify our lifestyles and actions in a manner than producing a sustainable relationship with nature (van Schalkwyk, 2011). The Earth must be understood as a total community or system, one in which we participate, not dominate (van Schalkwyk, 2011).

Systems thinking and system leadership are new topics in this edition. Integrating spirituality and sustainability requires the ability to think systemically because both concepts are systemic in nature. Systems thinking offers a perspective for understanding complex economic, social, and environmental systems (Holling, 2001). The advantage of applying this perspective to sustainability lies in understanding the dynamic interplay among multiple actors and broad social, economic, and ecological systems (Lozano, 2008; Valente, 2012; Williams et al., 2017), which is beneficial to scholars and practitioners when addressing major social problems (Whiteman et al., 2013). Systems thinking is beneficial for developing a better understanding of comprehensive structures, patterns, and cycles in systems (McNamara, 2006). Because sustainability involves a complex economic, social, and environmental system, systems thinking provides an important method for solving sustainability problems (Beehner, 2019).

System leadership is defined as leadership that attempts to achieve transformation across multiple organizations in which the individual leading does not have direct control or responsibility (Timmins, 2015). The term first appeared in literature at the beginning of the twenty-first century within the discipline of education but has since expanded to multiple fields. System leadership is an emerging process constituting a broad range of responsibilities that are developed locally or within individual systems or programs, and when combined, promote systemic change (Hopkins & Higham, 2007). Senge et al. (2015) suggested that the broad changes required to expedite progress against society's most unmanageable problems necessitate "a unique type of leader – the system leader, a person who catalyzes collective leadership" (p. 27).

In Chapter 13, the case was made for both workplace spirituality and sustainability as factors in organizational success. Because limited existing literature examines both variables in terms of organizational success, much of the content of this chapter addressed the proposed theoretical and conceptual framework for the proposed hypothesis. Several frameworks for examination of the relationship among and benefits of spirituality, sustainability, and success were considered in this chapter.

Acknowledging the historical legacy of social technologies intended to extract employee commitment and control, Case and Gosling (2010) introduce a theoretical framework of a spiritual organization that may be useful in understanding recent, and possibly future organizational developments. The spiritual organization constitutes a new category in Etzioni's model of complex organizations to be designated the spiritual organization. Etzioni classified complex organizations according to the "forms of relationship", "member involvement" and "types of power" that predominate in them (1961). The proposed additional category of spiritual organization is characterized by member involvement leading to hope for revelation or enlightenment, where power is exercised pastorally through conscience, willing obedience, self-inspection of inner thoughts, and spiritual discipline (Bell & Taylor, 2003; Foucault, 1978; Mitchell, 2009).

According to Guillory (1997), an organization operates most efficiently when spiritual principles are combined with sound business practices. Guillory further proposed spirituality is inevitable, and a spiritually sourced system is a model for high-performance organization creation. While we are currently operating in the Knowledge Age, which both followed and overlapped with the Industrial Age, both will be replaced by the Spiritual Age and ultimately an Age of Oneness. Guillory (1997) suggested organizations that succeed in these last two, perhaps overlapping ages, will employ quantum thinking, anticipate the next paradigm, and create products and services meeting the spiritual needs of the next group. The only organizations that have the potential to continue to be successful will be those aware of the potential of human spirit (Guillory, 1997), living organizations capable of adapting to change in much the same way as evolving, living organisms (Guillory, 1997).

Systems thinking, the Quadruple Bottom Line for Sustainability, and Man-Environment-Organism (M-E-O) were introduced as frameworks through which to understand the proposed relationship. Flourishing, conscious capitalism, and spiritual entrepreneurship were explored within the context of the chapter theme. The chapter concluded with an examination of Laloux's proposed model of organizational evolution and the emerging evolutionary "teal" organization. The chapter included a continuation of the personal interview summaries from Chapter 12, of two individuals who applied both spirituality and sustainability to achieve success in their organizations.

14.3 Discussion

In this concluding chapter, I would like to expand upon the overlapping characteristics of both concepts. Several of my colleagues have questioned whether spirituality, sustainability, and success are compatible bedfellows. The notion that the three terms can coexist in one relationship may indeed seem preposterous to some. However, recent findings and practical examples support both a positive relationship between spirituality and success, and between sustainability and success. Moreover, the established compatibility of spirituality and sustainability as complementary sojourners supports the proposition that when combined, the two may significantly enhance both individual success and organizational success.

The premise of this book has been that spirituality (individual and workplace) and sustainability are beneficial for individual (and organizational) success. I previously proposed that the commonalities of, and interconnection between spirituality (both individual and workplace) and sustainability support the hypothesis: ***A combination of spirituality and sustainability positively impacts both individual and organizational success***. Within the pages (or digital content) of this book, I have introduced research, models, and testimonials supporting the notion of positive individual and collective results resulting from the amalgamation of spirituality and sustainability.

Granted, by traditional capitalist measures, any discussion of spirituality and sustainability within the context of success may appear irrelevant or contradictory. However, contemporary society appears to be demonstrating a greater acceptance of and demand for spirituality and sustainability within the context of organizational and individual success. Moreover, traditional capitalism does not exist in its pure form in an era of quantitative easing (QE), bank and industry bailouts, and tax reform skewed toward corporations and the wealthy. Perhaps spirituality and sustainability provide the foundation for a form of capitalism in which the success of one individual or organization is not achieved at the expense of another, whether in the present or at a future date.

Numerous researchers and writers echo the error in thinking that humankind could somehow function independently of nature, with Nunez (2011) lamenting the rationalizing of nature and life as mere objects as nothing short of tragedy. Spirituality and sustainability are linked by a common characteristic of connectedness among people with each other and the planet (Nunez, 2011). Education may provide the key to a spiritual, sustainable, and successful future for humankind. Somphone (2011) proposed a holistic model of sustainable education and development emphasizing uniformed improvement of the head, hands, and heart. The proposed model must balance economic development, environmental harmony, cultural integrity, and spiritual well-being. Spirituality is the heart of education, and education and sustainable development are both interrelated and interdependent. For education to be truly transformative, it must foster values for spiritual, ethical, and emotional well-being, which form the true foundation for wisdom, contentment, and happiness.

Economists such as Tim Jackson suggest people and economies can succeed without growth, suggesting the existing economic model of growth as an economic necessity being invalid. Jackson refers to the current state of consumerism and associated environmental consequences as a dilemma of growth. Jackson has been frequently quoted saying that people are "being persuaded to spend money we don't have, on things we don't need, to create impressions that won't last, on people we don't care about" (Jackson, 2009). In referring to the latest gadget or novelty, Jackson notes that we can't live with it, and we can't live without it. The choices society faces in addressing the current human-made environmental condition are to "trash the system or crash the planet" neither of which appears to be a desirable option (Jackson, 2009).

Tim Jackson (2009) uses systems dynamics to explain the circular flow of the economy. In a circular flow, companies produce products and services, and provide workers with incomes enabling them to purchase those products and services. Increased production equals increased income, enabling increased purchase of goods and services. A key component of this economic model is investment. While investment accounts for approximately one-fifth of the economy of most developed nations, it plays the vital role of consumption growth stimulation. One of the benefits of investment is increased productivity, which reduces prices, encouraging consumers to purchase more products (Jackson, 2009).

Jackson describes Joseph Schumpeter's (1942) "process of creative destruction" in which the production and reproduction of novelty grow, as companies continually chase expanding consumer markets, because consumers by nature have an appetite for novelty, delivered by companies in the form of an ever-increasing volume of new consumer goods (Jackson, 2009). The materiality of consumerism has been noted by anthropologists, who interpret material possessions as a symbolic form of language that societies use to tell stories about us, and of our importance. However, this status-driven, conspicuous consumption has created a socioeconomic system driving an engine of growth, consisting not only of economic value, but the consumption of material resources driven by our own insatiable appetites, and a sense of anxiety. Our economic appetite has expanded from the beginning of the Industrial Revolution in which Adam Smith (1776) defined a life without shame as possessing simple creature comforts, to an era of insatiable needs including the latest technology, the newest automobile, and several annual vacations.

This pattern of consumption and growth has created a system which will crash if we reduce consumption, necessitating an ever-expanding supply of credit and debt to maintain system operation (Jackson, 2009).

Jackson suggested we have a responsibility to help the poorer members of society out of poverty by making room for growth where growth matters. This requires a redefinition of prosperity in which the wealthy nations participate in a more meaningful, less materialistic economy. This philosophy of prosperity as a shared endeavor, expanded upon in Jackson's *Prosperity without Growth* mirrors the traditional African concept of *ubuntu*, simply stated "I am because we are" (Jackson, 2009).

The concept of the circular economy, mentioned in Chapter 6, provides an alternative to the traditional linear economy wherein resources remain useable for longer periods of time, maximizing utility, while minimizing waste (Waste & Resources Action Programme, 2018). David Pearce introduced the circular economy in 1990, to address the interconnectedness of the four economic functions of the environment: providing amenity values, is a resource base for economic activities, a sink for economic activities, and is an essential life support system (Andersen, 2007). The circular economy has conceptual roots in industrial ecology, which envisages a material symbiosis between otherwise unrelated companies and production processes. Industrial ecology emphasizes recycling surplus waste materials and by-products, along with resource minimization, and clean energy technology adoption (Andersen, 1997, 1999). Proponents of industrial ecology suggest the circular economy will be beneficial to society and to the economy, through reduced use of the environment as a residual storage receptacle and reduced use of virgin materials for economic activity (Andersen, 2007).

According to Andersen (2007), the assumed benefits of the circular economy are based on the minimization of physical material loss. However, the circular economy also raised the question of how far society should go in the recycling of materials. While initial recycling options provide measurable, and often substantial benefits, as recycling activities increase, subsequent benefits gradually become more difficult to achieve. While 100% material recycling is an admirable goal, at some point, additional recycling efforts will become too difficult and burdensome to provide a net benefit, suggesting the circular economy cannot promote recycling ad infinitum.

Many circular economy proponents note the environmental and ethical foundation of material reuse and recycling. However, in a market economy, the natural resource and material prices may primarily reflect the costs associated with mining and short-term values, not with depletion or environmental costs, and as such may be artificially low (Andersen, 2007). Therefore, in a conventional capitalist economy, recycling will only be attempted when desirable from a profitability viewpoint. Opponents argue that if businesses are rational and profit-seeking, recycling and reuse options would likely have already been realized. Anderson suggests architects of public policy must transcend such narrow perspectives, instituting mechanisms to ensure recycling and reuse occurs whenever socially desirable and efficient.

The field of environmental economics offers an analytical approach, helpful in the identification of material streams and recycling options which may provide the greatest benefits to the economy, if open-ended principles are replaced with circular principles (Andersen, 2007). Public policy environmental economic analysis presumes an in-depth understanding of the environmental consequences of individual and collective choices, resulting in an interdisciplinary approach to the circular economy. Environmental economics also prepares a foundation for introduction of "externality adders" to market prices in the form of environmental taxes and fees, resulting in more complete resource valuation, and influencing market actors to consider the real costs of mutual transactions.

Kasser (2002) showed materialistic values not only undermine personal well-being, but adversely impact the health and happiness of both the individual and others. Material pursuits lead to emptiness, a void which can only be filled with more material possessions. Kasser (2002) further argues materialistic pursuits conflict with close interpersonal relationships, and betterment of the community and the world. Materialism is a poor coping strategy for feelings of insecurity and does not produce an optimally meaningful and high-quality life.

14.4 Future Trends

The social, political, and economic environments have become more dynamic in the twenty-first century. The departure of the United States from the Paris Climate Accord under the Trump administration created a void which may likely be filled by China, or a consortium of concerned nations. Civil unrest has grown in developing nations impacted by environmental changes related to climate change, rising seas, oil spills, military conflict, and natural resource exploitation by developed nations. The demand for sustainable products and services may not only increase but create increased competitive edge among businesses seeking to create a competitive advantage, or possibly differentiate from American businesses labeled as unsustainable due to political actions by the current administration.

The COVID-19 pandemic reminded individuals of the frailty of human life and offered a mandatory, and much needed pause for reflection. There is a high likelihood that society will return to the pre-pandemic behaviors that contributed to our current unsustainable trajectory. The recession that occurred during the pandemic was minimized in many nations through government fiscal stimulus. Many industries suffered during the pandemic (e.g., travel and hospitality), while others were overwhelmed by demand (e.g., health care, home entertainment products, food, and grocery suppliers). The post-pandemic economic environment has been characterized by higher-than-normal inflation, increased demand for travel and leisure products and services, and increased economic activity. The long-term consequences of the pandemic on the attitudes about sustainability among government leaders and their constituents are uncertain (Dalsace, 2021). The long-term impact of the pandemic on sustainability efforts will depend on the common narrative that is currently being developed. This narrative may be country-specific and influenced by two important criteria: the extent to which humankind collectively believes the pandemic was either an isolated or recurring event, and our collective post-pandemic attitude toward institutions and governments (Dalsace, 2021).

The spiritual environment may become more dynamic as religious participation continues to decline in developed nations, while demands for genuine spirituality may increase. The growth in interest in alternative spiritualities was discussed in Chapter 2. The idea of a Spirituality 2.0 as an overlaying platform intended to unite adherents of all major religions in a common understanding (Targowski, 2012) was discussed in Chapters 2, 7, and 13. However, Targowski recognized the likelihood of enforcing a new, wise civilization through Spirituality 2.0 is low, but feasible, requiring several generations to implement. While the future direction of spiritual inquisition remains uncertain, clearly greater numbers of religious adherents are seeking alternatives to religious institutions with which they have become increasingly disenchanted. The question will be in what form and with what level of organization and cooperation will future spirituality become manifest.

While some individuals and cultures remain skeptical of sustainability and the motives of sustainability proponents, an increasing number of individuals and cultures are recognizing the benefits of, and necessity for a sustainable lifestyle. In the personal interview summary in Chapter 13, TerraCycle CEO Tom Szaky suggested the world faces more challenge—environmental, such as climate change, deforestation, or the global garbage crisis, and political, with the United States, and many other countries more divided. Our environmental and political challenges are driven by internationalism, nationalism, or tribalism, as well as selfish or self-focused decision-making. Decisions are being made without consideration of the true costs. Concerning the future direction of sustainability, Tom believes the challenges we face will get worse before they get better. He used the analogy of an alcoholic who is functioning well, and therefore it is hard to convince that person that he or she is an alcoholic because things are going well. However, when things start falling apart it becomes obvious there is a problem, and that something needs to be done. Unfortunately, Tom may be correct that things will become worse before getting better. Hopefully, within the context of the alcoholic analogy, our environment does not completely fall apart before enough individuals and organizations recognize and act upon the problem.

Many individuals act to address the symptoms of the problem, rather than identifying and seeking solutions for the root cause of problems. While it may be appropriate to take aspirin for a headache, if the headache returns daily, or becomes more severe, the headache may be a symptom of a deeper problem. Humankind is facing an increasing number of problems which may not be alleviated by repeated dosages of superficial responses. A deeper investigation will reveal behaviors, values, and lifestyles to be the cause, and solution to our collective problems. Kasser (2009) suggests it may be necessary to address the significant social challenge of modifying individual values and lifestyles, and enacting policies to promote both happiness and environmental sustainability. Addressing the problems of our era may lead to a new era in which humankind benefits from both improved behavior, values, and lifestyles, and an improved relationship with the vessel in which we all travel the universe. While the future may sometimes appear dark and dangerous, out of the darkness may emerge a new era of human excellence.

14.5 Future Recommendations

Despite growing acceptance of workplace spirituality as a significant field of inquiry, research conducted at the intersection of spirituality and organizational performance has not been consolidated and systematically reviewed (Karakas, 2010). Moreover, future research is necessary to understand how workplace spirituality may be implemented in a manner mutually beneficial for both employer and employee. Because of the declining interest in established religion, a continued corresponding increase in interest in spirituality is likely, at both the individual and organizational levels. Future research is needed on the expectations of individuals seeking spirituality individually and collectively, how the organization may meet those expectations, and how individual and workplace spirituality may further enhance performance and well-being.

While nearly two-thirds of participants in a study conducted by *MIT Sloan Management Review* and the Boston Consulting Group rated social and environmental issues as significant, less than ten percent indicated their organizations were properly addressing these issues (Schein, 2015). The researchers attributed this gap to a "disconnect between thought and action" (Kiron et al., 2013, p. 3). While one study has examined this gap, future studies are needed using new sample populations: how ecological worldviews differ between sustainability and "non-sustainability" leaders; how a better understanding of ecological worldviews may enhance the effectiveness of sustainability leaders; how ecological worldviews of sustainability leaders vary across cultures, age groups, and gender; the correlation of ecological worldviews with individual sustainability success; and, how ecological worldviews are expressed at specific developmental stages (Schein, 2015). Moreover, existing sustainability literature has not sufficiently focused attention on corporate sustainability at the individual level (Schein, 2014).

There is currently a lack of a consensus definition of sustainable entrepreneurship, and limited research on the scope and application of sustainable entrepreneurship (Gast et al., 2017). Future research is needed to develop a convergent definition of sustainable entrepreneurship (Gast et al., 2017; Schaltegger & Wagner, 2011), and to further develop the concepts of sustainable entrepreneurship and green entrepreneurship (Gast et al., 2017). Moreover, researchers should examine how sustainable entrepreneurs and their ventures influence communities and society, the specific values that drive sustainable entrepreneurs, and whether these values differ in various contexts (Gast et al., 2017). Further, because business schools will play an important role in teaching sustainable entrepreneurship, a better understanding how ecological sustainable entrepreneurship can be taught, and how to increase awareness of sustainable development, and the corresponding market opportunities is necessary (Gast et al., 2017).

More research is needed on sustainable business models to further develop more integrative theories of sustainability management supportive of sustainable development of the economy and society (Schaltegger et al., 2016). Research is needed concerning how theories at the organizational level, the individual level, and at both levels explain the transformation of business models of established firms (Schaltegger et al., 2016). Moreover, the management tools and instruments, such as design thinking, the Natural Step framework, and biomimicry, should be examined to determine which best enables the management of, or transition to sustainable business models (Schaltegger et al., 2016). Finally, a better understanding is needed of how to manage and measure performance and societal impacts within the business model (Schaltegger et al., 2016).

International frameworks to protect Indigenous knowledge are urgently needed. However, despite national and regional regulations that protect traditional knowledge and encourage cooperation in treatment of traditional knowledge, communication, and collaboration among Indigenous peoples and policymakers, these laws have limited impact (Jerez, 2021). Jerez (2021) offered the following recommendations for governments, representative bodies, United Nations organizations, industry, and other stakeholders (Jerez, 2021):

- Ensure that the UN Declaration on the Rights of Indigenous Peoples is the primary framework for planning and implementing climate change mitigation, adaptation, and finance programs, and include full participation of Indigenous.
- Develop policies that conform with the UN Declaration on the Rights of Indigenous Peoples to prevent misappropriation of Indigenous traditional knowledge and acknowledge Indigenous Peoples as equal participants, and legitimate custodians of their knowledge.
- Provide technical support to improve the adaptive capacity and mitigation ability of Indigenous Peoples, including inclusive sector-specific programs based upon gender, values, and economic conditions of the communities.
- Conduct genuine gender analyses to understand which aspects of Indigenous natural resource stewardship are performed by men and women respectively, or the extent that Indigenous environmental knowledge is gender-specific (Jerez, 2021).

Indigenous wisdom would likely suggest that the climate crisis be conceptualized as an intimately personal crisis connected with emotional well-being (Robison, 2020). The climate change dialogue must validate Indigenous knowledge by including the voices of those peoples for whom environmental sustainability is a measure of individual and community well-being (Robison, 2020).

Indigenous Peoples must participate in the development of natural resource management policies to retain the right to manage and conserve their land through incorporation of traditional knowledge and rights in the policies to preserve their cultural and spiritual traditions (Devereux, 2000; Swamy et al., 2003). Because Indigenous wisdom intimately connects humans and nature, some suggest that "the human mind is not separate from the natural world but an aspect of the larger psyche of nature" (Kapfhammer, 2012, p. 147). Research continues to demonstrate and support the effectiveness of Indigenous approaches to sustainable environmental rehabilitation (Jerez, 2021). Traditional knowledge serves an important role in preserving biodiversity and maintaining entire ecosystems. However, abuse and exploitation of Indigenous knowledge can cause irreparable harm to custodians of the knowledge and entire communities or Peoples (Jerez, 2021). The U.N. Declaration on the Rights of Indigenous Peoples advises governments to acknowledge that Indigenous Peoples are the owners and custodians of their traditional knowledge, and they should control the circumstances in which that knowledge is shared (Tsosie, 2014). Indigenous voices can provide non-Native thinkers with an alternate perspective to understand the impacts of industrial systems on the environment through deforestation, pollution, and fossil fuel dependency and assess the underlying thinking that preserves those systems (Robison, 2020).

Because limited research exists concerning the antecedents and benefits of the combination of spirituality and sustainability at both the individual and organizational levels, the subjects are open for broad depth and breadth of empirical study. While this author has suggested both spirituality and sustainability combined are beneficial for individual and organizational success, the propositions are hypothetical, supported by a small sample of interview participants. Future research could confirm the relationship, examine the antecedents and outcomes of the relationship, and identify potential pitfalls of synthesizing the two constructs individually and within organizations. Many individuals combine spirituality and sustainability in their worldview, regardless of whether benefits are being sought in the process. Likewise, spiritual, sustainable organizations exist, and are thriving. Future research is necessary to quantify and qualify how, to what extent, and in what manner the phenomena occur.

Achieving just and sustainable growth will depend on effectively and holistically addressing the conditions and interdependency of our economies and societies. Schwab and Sternfels (2022) offer three suggestions for moving forward:

1. The public and private sectors must have a broad view of the resilience agenda.
2. Strategies and structures must be designed for agility and speed.
3. The public and private sectors must supplement business and economic resilience with social resilience.

Maintaining the social change necessary to support a transition to environmental sustainability requires a precise, straightforward political structure that includes private investments and behavioral change (Lehmann et al., 2021). Progress toward environmental sustainability by reducing environmental degradation and achieving socio-techno-ecological resilience may create strategies beneficial for preventing and managing future pandemics (Lehmann et al., 2021). Swilling (2020) recommended transformational change comparable to the Neolithic agricultural revolution or the Industrial Revolution (Morrissey & Heidkamp, 2022).

To create a more promising future, our focus must change from short-term and reactive measures and goals to a more just and sustainable growth agenda (Schwab & Sternfels, 2022). Such an agenda would focus on growth that strengthens the health and rehabilitation of the natural environment while enhancing the livelihood of the overall population. We must find avenues to a genuinely improved society so that our actions create a more resilient and secure planet and economy (Schwab & Sternfels, 2022).

Efforts to reduce wealth inequality are urgently needed, including reforms to guarantee that taxes, prices, and subsidies consider the real ecological and social costs of present consumption behavior (Ripple et al., 2017). Meeting necessary emission reductions will require extensive infusions of public sector funding. Green New Deal (GND) proposals would enact an ecological restructuring of the economy through continuous investment (Bauhardt, 2014), including radical commitment to major economic restructuring and public (Galvin & Healy, 2020). Major investments will be needed to build the extensive and systemwide infrastructure necessary for a zero-carbon economy (Morrissey & Heidkamp, 2022). These investments will be less expensive than the longer-term consequences of inaction.

Ethical decision-making in career and business requires thinking beyond traditional financial formulas such as cost-benefit analysis and return on investment (ROI). Individuals must develop the habit of seeking the moral issues and ethical implications involved in each decision and analyze them from multiple philosophical viewpoints. The Earth Charter was introduced in several chapters as an ethical framework for achieving sustainability. The document contains four pillars and sixteen principles for establishing a "a sustainable global society founded on respect for nature, universal human rights, economic justice, and a culture of peace" (Earth Charter International, n.d.). The Earth Charter document neatly overlaps and complements the UNS SDGs. The Earth Charter International provides online and onsite training about the Earth Charter Principles and how to apply them in business, leadership, and academic settings at their Education Centre located at the UN-mandated University for Peace in San Jose, Costa Rica.

14.6 Concluding Thoughts

We have concluded our journey together, although I hope we will continue separate but parallel journeys. Everyone who reads this book may not accept the proposition that spirituality and sustainability result in individual or organizational success. Moreover, everyone who applies spirituality and sustainability in their life, career, or organization may experience success in a different manner, or regrettably, perhaps not at all. Each participant in a dietary or exercise program will experience differing results, depending on genetics, metabolism, willpower, belief, or attitude. Likewise, each individual and organization is unique, and must follow a unique path, experiencing life in a unique manner, with unique outcomes. The intent in writing this book was not to contribute to the existing body of "get rich" or "self-help" literature proliferating bookstores and the Internet. The intent was to consolidate existing literature about the individual and organizational benefits of spirituality and sustainability and begin a practical and scholarly dialogue about the combined benefits of spirituality and sustainability for individuals and organizations. As promising as I believe my argument and proposition to be, future research and dialog is still necessary.

Nearly two centuries ago, Karl Marx described capitalism as having developed such immense means of production that capitalists have become "like the sorcerer, who is no longer able to control the power..." (Marx & Engels, 1844, p. 24). This analogy may accurately describe the current environmental and social conditions faced by humanity. However, although the sorcerer may no longer be able to control the contemporary system, the collective actions of planetary inhabitants may be capable of controlling and harnessing the power for the betterment of society and the environment. A spiritual and sustainable worldview may be the antidote for the current societal and environmental illness. While Marx described religion as the opiate of the masses (Marx & Engels, 1844), spirituality may become the vitamin of the masses.

Major events and catastrophes often trigger religious and spiritual participation and movements. However, those events and behaviors are often temporary and acquiesce to the overarching trend of secular modernism and postmodernity. Events that occurred concurrently with the pandemic such as the economic recession, police brutality, and racial inequality may have influenced the willingness of individuals and groups to embrace change influencing their sense of spirituality. Spirituality is more than a belief, philosophy, or theme, but is also a method for dealing with unexpected and uncertain events in an equanimous manner. Perhaps the pandemic has sufficiently reminded humankind of our mortality that we will embrace and retain our spiritual compass, with all individuals doing so either present or absent any formal religious dogma.

While significant action is required, Kasser (2009) suggests it is plausible for humanity to move away from our current environmentally destructive, and personally alienating lifestyles and organizations to a way of existence that is both more sustainable and satisfying. In an era of "fake news", negative news, social and environmental catastrophes, spirituality, and sustainability offer hope that individuals and organizations can not only succeed and flourish but contribute to the success and flourishing of all of society. This hope has become more important and necessary in the post-pandemic era. Perhaps, regardless of religion or creed, we may all follow Pope Francis' calling for an "ecological conversion" recognizing that "the world is God's loving gift" (Vatican Insider, 2015). Perhaps we will understand and accept the words of Mahatma Gandhi: "The world has enough for everyone's need, but not enough for everyone's greed". Humankind may find common ground in the preservation of something from which we all receive benefit and cannot exist without—planet Earth.

Reflection Questions

1. While the future direction of spiritual inquisition is uncertain, clearly greater numbers of religious adherents are seeking alternatives to religious institutions with which they have become increasingly disenchanted. In what form, and with what level of organization and cooperation do you believe future spirituality will become manifest?
2. Does the practice of sustainability activate or improve the development of ecological worldviews, or do individuals with advanced ecological worldviews self-select work in sustainability (Schein, 2015)? Explain why.
3. Technology has been described as both the cause of and solution for many of society's problems. How might technology contribute to sustainability, thereby resulting in both organizational success and individual success? How might the application of technological advances to create a sustainable planet indirectly create or magnify a future, yet unseen societal problem?

4. How do you believe spirituality and sustainability will have impacted individual and organizational success 10–20 years from now? Visualize and describe how you believe the relationship between spirituality, sustainability, and success will or will not be defined and framed in 10–20 years.

References

Accenture. (2019). *Accenture technology vision 2019*. https://www.accenture.com/_acnmedia/pdf-94/accenture-techvision-2019-tech-trends-report.pdf

Acciona. (n.d.). *How do Indigenous peoples contribute to sustainable development? Sustainability for all*. https://www.activesustainability.com/sustainable-development/Indigenous-peoples-sustainable-development/?_adin=02021864894

Affeldt, D. L., & MacDonald, D. A. (2010). The relationship of spirituality to work and organizational attitudes and behaviors in a sample of employees from a health care system. *Journal of Transpersonal Psychology, 42*(2), 192–208. https://www.atpweb.org

Alomar, A., Mydin, A., & Alaklabi, S. (2022). A review of authentic leadership and workplace spirituality and campus sustainability in educational institutions. *International Transaction Journal of Engineering, Management, y Applied Sciences y Technologies, 13*(2), 1–13. https://tuengr.com/V13/13A2O.pdf

Al-Qutop, M. A. Y., & Harrim, H. (2014). Spiritual organization: A path to organizational sustainable excellence. *International Business Research, 7*(8), 168. http://www.ccsenet.org

Altaf, A., & Awan, M. A. (2011). Moderating effect of workplace spirituality on the relationship of job overload and job satisfaction. *Journal of Business Ethics, 104*(1), 93–99. https://doi.org/10.1007/s10551-011-0891-0

Alvord, S. H., Brown, L. D., & Letts, C. W. (2004). Social entrepreneurship and societal transformation. *Journal of Applied Behavioral Science, 30*, 260–282. https://doi.org/10.1177/0021886304266847

Andersen, M. S. (1997). *Evaluation of the cleaner technology programme, environmental review no. 14*. Environmental Protection Agency.

Andersen, M. S. (1999). Governance by green taxes: Implementing clean water policies in Europe 1970–1990. *Environmental Economics Policy Studies, 2*(1), 39–63. https://doi.org/10.1007/BF03353902

Andersen, M. S. (2007). An introductory note on the environmental economics of the circular economy. *Sustainability Science, 2*(1), 133–140. https://doi.org/10.1007/s11625-006-0013-6

Ashar, H., & Lane-Maher, M. (2004). Success and spirituality in the new business paradigm. *Journal of Management Inquiry, 13*(3), 249–260. https://doi.org/10.1177/1056493604268218

Balcomb, A. O. (2022). Indigenous religions as antidote to the environmental crisis: Surveying a decade of reflection. In *Ecotheology-sustainability and religions of the world* (pp. 123–142). IntechOpen. https://doi.org/10.5772/intechopen.105209

Balestrero, G., & Udo, N. (2014). *Organizational survival: Profitable strategies for a sustainable future.* McGraw-Hill Education.

Bansal, T. (2021). What business leaders can learn from an Indigenous worldview. *Forbes.* https://www.forbes.com/sites/timabansal/2021/06/15/what-business-leaders-can-learn-from-an-indigenous-worldview/?sh=5780d1eb5c2f

Barrero, A. F. (2023). *Max Weber on disenchantment: Is religion obsolete?* https://www.thecollector.com/max-weber-disenchantment-world-religion/

Barrett, R. (2009). What's right and wrong with spirituality in the workplace. *Journal of Management, Spirituality & Religion, 6*(3), 261–268. https://doi.org/10.1080/14766080903069372

Bauhardt, C. (2014). Solutions to the crisis? The Green New Deal, Degrowth, and the Solidarity Economy: Alternatives to the capitalist growth economy from an ecofeminist economics perspective. *Ecological Economics, 102*, 60–68. https://doi.org/10.1016/j.ecolecon.2014.03.015

Bazzano, A. (2014). *After mindfulness.* Palgrave Macmillan.

Beehner, C. G. (2018). Expanding sustainable business education beyond business schools. In S. Dhiman & J. Marques (Eds.), *Handbook of engaged sustainability.* Springer Nature. https://doi.org/10.1007/978-3-319-53121-2_51-1)

Beehner, C. G. (2019). *System leadership for sustainability.* Routledge.

Bell, E., & Taylor, S. (2003). The elevation of work: Pastoral power and the new age work ethic. *Organization, 10*(2), 329–349. https://doi.org/10.1177/1350508403010002009

Biberman, J., & Whittey, M. (1997). A postmodern spiritual future for work. *Journal of Organizational Change Management, 10*(2), 130–188. https://doi.org/10.1108/09534819710160790

Brophy, M. (2015). Spirituality incorporated: Including convergent spiritual values in business. *Journal of Business Ethics, 132*(4), 779–794. https://doi.org/10.1007/s10551-014-2337-y

Brown, R. B. (2003). Organizational spirituality: The sceptic's version. *Organization, 10*, 393–400. https://doi.org/10.1177/13505084030100020l3

Carroll, J. E. (2004). *Sustainability and spirituality.* State University of New York Press.

Case, P., & Gosling, J. (2010). The spiritual organization: Critical reflections on the instrumentality of workplace spirituality. *Journal of Management, Spirituality and Religion, 7*(4), 257–282. https://doi.org/10.1080/14766086.2010.524727

Cavanagh, G. (1999). Spirituality for managers: Context and critique. *Journal of Organizational Change Management, 12*(3), 186–195. https://doi.org/10.1108/09534819910273793

Cavanagh, G. F., & Bandsuch, M. R. (2002). Virtue as a benchmark for spirituality in business. *Journal of Business Ethics, 38*(1–2), 109–117. https://doi.org/10.1023/A:1015721029457

Chatterjee, A., & Naqvi, F. (2010). Spirituality in organizational life: An empirical study of spirituality and job attitudes. *Abhigyan, 28*(3), 18–29. http://www.freepatentsonline.com/article/Abhigyan/249137536.html

Chawla, V., & Guda, S. (2010). Individual spirituality at work and its relationship with job satisfaction, propensity to leave and job commitment: An exploratory study among sales professionals. *Journal of Human Values, 16*(2), 157–167. https://doi.org/10.1177/097168581001600203

Chippendale, P. (2001). On values, ethics, morals & principles. *A Values Inventory. Etik Tanımı, 28,* 1–6. https://www.researchgate.net/profile/Paul-Chippendale/publication/242758616_On_Values_Ethics_Morals_Principles_By/links/5a98d19445851535bce0dbfe/On-Values-Ethics-Morals-Principles-By.pdf

Chunhabunyatip, P., Sasaki, N., Grünbühel, C., Kuwornu, J. K., & Tsusaka, T. W. (2018). Influence of Indigenous spiritual beliefs on natural resource management and ecological conservation in Thailand. *Sustainability, 10*(8), 2842. https://doi.org/10.3390/su10082842

Conger, J. A. (Ed.). (1994). *Spirit at work: Discovering spirituality in leadership.* Jossey-Bass.

Crawford, A., Hubbard, S. S., Lonis-Shumate, S. R., & O'Neill, M. (2009). Workplace spirituality and employee attitudes within the lodging environment. *Journal of Human Resources in Hospitality & Tourism, 8*, 64–81. https://doi.org/10.1080/15332840802274445

Creighton-Smith, B. A., Cook, M., & Edginton, C. R. (2017). Leisure, ethics, and spirituality. *Annals of Leisure Research, 20*(5), 546–562. https://doi.org/10.1080/11745398.2017.1295873

Dalsace, F. (2021). *Sustainability post pandemic: The four scenarios for change.* Institute for Management Development. https://www.imd.org/ibyimd/sustainability/sustainability-post-pandemic-the-four-scenarios-for-change/

Dean, T. J. (2014). *Sustainable venturing: Entrepreneurial opportunity in the transition to a sustainable economy*. Pearson.

Dent, E. B., Higgins, M. E., & Wharff, D. M. (2005). Spirituality and leadership: An empirical review of definitions, distinctions, and embedded assumptions. *The Leadership Quarterly, 16*(5), 625–653. https://doi.org/10.1016/j.leaqua.2005.07.002

Devereux, P. (2000). *The sacred place: The ancient origins of holy and mystical sites*. Cassell.

Dhiman, S. (2017). *Holistic leadership: A new paradigm for today's leaders.* Palgrave Macmillan.

Dhiman, S., & Marques, J. (2011). The role and need of offering workshops and courses on workplace spirituality. *Journal of Management Development, 30*(9), 816–835. https://doi.org/10.1108/02621711111164312

Earth Charter International. (n.d.). *Turning conscience into action.* https://earthcharter.org/

Eccles, R. G., Ioannou, I., & Serafeim, G. (2012a). *The impact of a corporate culture of sustainability on corporate behavior and performance* (No. W17950). National Bureau of Economic Research.

Eccles, R. G., Miller Perkins, K., & Serafeim, J. (2012b). How to become a sustainable company. *MIT Sloan Management Review, 53*(4), 43–50. https://sloanreview.mit.edu

Edginton, C. N., & Kangas, K. E. (2014). World heritage sites as sacred places. *International Leisure Review, 3*(1), 53–74. https://doi.org/10.6298/ILR.2014.3.3

Elkington, J. (1998). *Cannibals with forks: The triple bottom line of 21st Century business.* New Society Publishers.

Esievo, F. K., Oshi, J. E. O., Hettey, H. D., & Tende, F. B. (2019). Workplace spirituality and organizational resilience of shipping companies in rivers state. *Scholarly Journal of Business Administration, 8*(3), 45–51. http://www.scholarly-journals.com/SJBA

Esty, D. C., & Winston, A. S. (2006). *Green to gold: How smart companies use environmental strategy to innovate, create value, and build competitive advantage*. Yale University Press.

Etzioni, A. (1961). *Comparative analysis of complex organizations.* Collier-Macmillan.

Fernando, M. (2005). Workplace spirituality: Another management fad? In M. Adams and A. Alkhafaji (Eds.), *Business research yearbook: Global business perspectives* (Vol. XII, No. 2). International Academy of Business Disciplines.

Fernando, M., & Jackson, B. (2006). The influence of religion-based workplace spirituality on business leaders' decision-making: An inter-faith study. *Journal of Management & Organization, 12*(1), 23–43. https://doi.org/10.1017/S1833367200004144

Foucault, M. (1978). Governmentality. In G. Burchell, C. Gordon & P. Miller (Eds.), *The Foucault effect: Studies in governmentality*. Harvester.

Fornaciari, C., & Lund Dean, K. (2001). Making the quantum leap: Lessons from physics on studying spirituality and religion in organizations. *Journal of Organizational Change Management, 14*(4), 335–351. https://doi.org/10.1108/EUM0000000005547

Fry, L. W. (2003). Toward a theory of spiritual leadership. *The Leadership Quarterly, 14*(6), 693–729. https://doi.org/10.1016/j.leaqua.2003.09.001

Fry, L. W., Matherly, L. L., & Ouimet, J. R. (2010). The spiritual leadership balanced scorecard business model: The case of the Cordon Bleu-Tomasso Corporation. *Journal of Management, Spirituality, & Religion, 7*(4), 283–314. https://doi.org/10.1080/14766086.2010.524983

Fry, L., & Nisiewicz, N. (2013). *Maximizing the triple bottom line through spiritual leadership.* Stanford University Press.

Fry, L. W., & Slocum, J. W. (2008). Maximizing the triple bottom line through spiritual leadership. *Organizational Dynamics, 37*(1), 86–96. https://doi.org/10.1016/j.orgdyn.2007.11.004

Fry, L. W., Vitucci, S., & Cedillo, M. (2005). Spiritual leadership and army transformation: Theory, measurement, and establishing a baseline. *The Leadership Quarterly, 16*, 835–862. https://doi.org/10.1016/j.leaqua.2005.07.012

Galvin, R., & Healy, N. (2020). The Green New Deal in the United States: What it is and how to pay for it. *Energy Research & Social Science, 67*, 101529. https://doi.org/10.1016/j.erss.2020.101529

Gast, J., Gundolf, K., & Cesinger, B. (2017). Doing business in a green way: A systematic review of the ecological sustainability entrepreneurship literature and future research directions. *Journal of Cleaner Production, 147*, 44–56. https://doi.org/10.1016/j.jclepro.2017.01.065

George, B. (2003). *Authentic leadership: Rediscovering the secrets to creating lasting value.* Wiley.

Giacalone, R. A., & Jurkiewicz, C. J. (2010). The science of workplace spirituality. In R. A. Giacalone & C. J. Jurkiewicz (Eds.), *Handbook of workplace spirituality and organizational performance* (2nd ed., pp. 3–26). M. E. Sharpe.

Goodman, D. (2015). Deep in the Amazon, a tiny tribe is beating big oil. *Yes Magazine*, Spring 2015, 28–32.

Graham, J. (1998). Servant-leadership and enterprise strategy. In L. Spears (Ed.), *Insights on leadership: Service, stewardship, spirit, and servant-leadership* (pp. 145–156). Wiley.

Greenleaf, R. K. (1970). *The servant as leader.* The Robert K. Greenleaf Center.

Greenleaf, R. K. (1977). *Servant leadership: A journey into the nature of legitimate power and greatness.* Paulist Press.

Gregson, J. A. (2010). A conceptual framework for green career and technical education: Sustainability and the development of a green-collar workforce. *Journal of Technical Education and Training, 2*(1), 123–137. http://penerbit.uthm.edu.my

Guillory, W. A. (1997). *The living organization—Spirituality in the workplace.* Innovations International.

Gupta, M., Kumar, V., & Singh, M. (2013). Creating satisfied employees through workplace spirituality: A study of the private insurance sector in Punjab (India). *Journal of Business Ethics, 122*(1), 79–88. https://doi.org/10.1007/s10551-013-1756-5

Haley, M. (2021). *Introducing the seventh generation principle—To promote true sustainability.* The Seventh Generation Tours. https://theseventhgeneration.org/blog-the-seventh-generation-principle/

Hamilton, J. (2012). *Is a sustainability career on your green horizon*? U.S. Department of Labor, Bureau of Labor Statistics. http://www.bls.gov/green/sustainability/sustainability.htm

Han, Y., Lu, X., & Li, Z. (2010). In search of excellence: Spiritual training program and junior managers counterproductive work behavior in China.

Human Resource Management International Digest, 18(2), 10–12. https://doi.org/10.1108/09670731011028401

Harman, W. (1992). 21st century business: A background for dialogue. In J. Renesch (Ed.), *New tradition in business: Spirit and leadership in the 21st century* (pp. 11–24). Berrett-Koehler.

Harvey, G. (2012). Indigenous spiritualities. In *Oxford textbook of spirituality in healthcare* (pp. 49–54). Oxford Academic.

Hawken, P., Lovins, A., & Lovins, L. H. (2008). The next industrial revolution. In M. V. Russo (Ed.), *Environmental management: Readings and cases* (pp. 3–14). Sage Publications.

Hawley, J. (1993). *Reawakening the spirit in work.* Berrett Koehler.

Heifetz, R. (1994). *Leadership without easy answers.* Harvard University Press.

Henson, G. (1991). Towards a spiritual perspective on behavior at work. *Management Education and Development, 22*(3), 201–207. https://doi.org/10.1177/135050769102200307

Hicks, D. A. (2002). Spiritual and religious diversity in the workplace: Implications for leadership. *The Leadership Quarterly, 13*(4), 379–396. https://doi.org/10.1016/S1048-9843(02)00124-8

Hind, P., Smit, A., & Page, N. (2013). Enabling sustainability through an action research process of organizational development. *Journal of Corporate Citizenship, 49*, 137–161. http://www.jstor.org/stable/jcorpciti.49.137

Holling, C. S. (2001). Understanding the complexity of economic, ecological, and social systems. *Ecosystems, 4*(5), 390–405. https://doi.org/10.1007/s10021-001-0101-5

Hong, Y. J. (2012). Identifying spirituality in workers: A strategy for retention of community health professionals. *Journal of Social Service Research, 38*(20), 175–186. https://doi.org/10.1080/01488376.2011.615275

Hopkins, D., & Higham, R. (2007). System leadership: Mapping the landscape. *School Leadership and Management, 27*(2), 147–166. https://doi.org/10.1080/13632430701237289

Hotchkiss, L., & Borrow, H. (1990). Sociological perspectives on work and career. In D. Brown & L. Brooks (Eds.), *Career choice and development: Applying contemporary theories to practice* (2nd ed., pp. 137–68). Jossey-Bass.

Jackson, T. (2009). *Prosperity without growth: Economics for a finite planet.* Earthscan.

Javanmard, H. (2012). The impact of spirituality on work performance. *Indian Journal of Science and Technology, 5*(1), 1961–1966. http://www.indjst.org

Jerez, M. M. (2021). *Challenges and opportunities for Indigenous peoples' sustainability* (UN/DESA Policy Brief #101). UN DESA. https://www.un.org/development/desa/dspd/2021/04/Indigenous-peoples-sustainability/

Kahnweiler, W., & Otte, F. L. (1997). In search of the soul of HRD. *Human Resource Development Quarterly, 8*(2), 171–181. https://doi.org/10.1002/hrdq.3920080210

Kapfhammer, W. (2012). Amazonian pain. Indigenous ontologies and Western eco-spirituality. *Indiana, 29*, 145–169.

Karakas, F. (2010). Spirituality and performance in organizations: A literature review. *Journal of Business Ethics, 94*(1), 89–106. https://doi.org/10.1007/s10551-009-0251-5

Kasser, T. (2002). *The high price of materialism.* MIT Press.

Kasser, T. (2009). Psychological need satisfaction, personal well-being, and ecological sustainability. *Ecopsychology, 1*(4), 175–180. https://doi.org/10.1089/eco.2009.0025

Kauanui, S. K., Thomas, K. D., Sherman, C. L., Waters, G. R., & Gilea, M. (2008). Exploring entrepreneurship through the lens of spirituality. *Journal of Management, Spirituality & Religion, 5*(2), 160–189. https://doi.org/10.1080/14766080809518698

Khurana, R., & Nohria, N. (2008). It's time to make management a true profession. *Harvard Business Review, 86*, 70–77. http://www.hbr.org

King, S., & Nicol, D. M. (1999). Organizational enhancement through recognition of individual spirituality: Reflections of Jaques and Jung. *Journal of Organizational Change Management, 12*(3), 234–243. https://doi.org/10.1108/09534819910274026

Kinjerski, V., & Skrypnek, B. J. (2004). Defining spirit at work: Finding common ground. *Journal of Organizational Change Management, 17*(1), 26–42. https://doi.org/10.1108/09534810410511288

Kinjerski, V., & Skrypnek, B. J. (2008). The promise of spirit at work: Increasing job satisfaction and organizational commitment and reducing turnover and absenteeism in long-term care. *Journal of Gerontological Nursing, 34*(10), 17–25. https://doi.org/10.3928/00989134-20081001-03

Kiron, D., Kruschwitz, N., Rubel, H., Reeves, M., & Fuisz-Kehrbach, S. (2013). Sustainability's next frontier: Walking the talk on the sustainability issues that matter most. *MIT Sloan Management Review Research Report.* https://sloanreview.mit.edu/projects/sustainabilitys-next-frontier/

Kolodinsky, R. W., Giacalone, R. A., & Jurkiewicz, C. L. (2008). Workplace values and outcomes: Exploring personal, organizational, and interactive workplace spirituality. *Journal of Business Ethics, 81*(2), 465–480. https://doi.org/10.1007/s10551-007-9507-0

Krishnan, V. (2008). The impact of transformational leadership on followers' duty orientation and spirituality. *Journal of Human Values, 14*(1), 11–22. https://doi.org/10.1177/097168580701400103

Kristensen, M. L. (2018). Mindfulness and resonance in an era of acceleration: A critical inquiry. *Journal of Management, Spirituality & Religion, 15*(2), 178–195. https://doi.org/10.1080/14766086.2017.1418413

Kross, K. (2012). *Sustainability offers variety of career opportunities.* Worcester Polytechnic Institute. https://web.wpi.edu/Images/CMS/Business/SustainabilityCareerOpp.pdf

Kumari, N. (2014). Spirituality at work place: A macroscopic shift from business to ethics. *Abhinav National Monthly Refereed Journal of Research in Commerce & Management, 3*(12), 1–5. https://doi.org/10.110119217

Lehmann, P., Beck, S., de Brito, M. M., Gawel, E., Groß, M., Haase, A., Lepenies, R., Otto, D., Schiller, J., Strunz, S., & Thrän, D. (2021). Environmental sustainability post-covid-19: Scrutinizing popular hypotheses from a social science perspective. *Sustainability, 13*(16), 8679. https://doi.org/10.3390/su13168679

Leider, R. J. (1997). *The power of purpose: Creating meaning in your life and work.* Berrett-Koehler.

Lips-Wiersma, M. (2002). Analysing the career concerns of spiritually oriented people: Lessons for contemporary organizations. *Career Development International, 7*(7), 385–397. https://doi.org/10.1108/13620430210449911

Lips-Wiersma, M., Dean, K. L., & Fornaciari, C. J. (2009). Theorizing the dark side of the workplace spirituality movement. *Journal of Management Inquiry, 18*(4), 288–300. https://doi.org/10.1177/1056492609339017

Liu, C. H., & Robertson, P. J. (2011). Spirituality in the workplace: Theory and measurement. *Journal of Management Inquiry, 20*(1), 35–50. https://doi.org/10.1177/1056492610374648

Long, B. S., & Mills, J. H. (2010). Workplace spirituality, contested meaning, and the culture of organization: A critical sense-making account. *Journal of Organizational Change Management, 23*(3), 325–341. https://doi.org/10.1108/09534811011049635

Lozano, R. (2008). Envisioning sustainability three-dimensionally. *Journal of Cleaner Production, 16*, 1838–1846. https://doi.org/10.1016/j.jclepro.2008.02.008

Lund Dean, K., Fornaciari, C. J., & McGee, J. (2003). Research in spirituality, religion, and work: Walking the line between relevance and legitimacy.

Journal of Organizational Change Management, 16(4), 378–395. https://doi.org/10.1108/09534810310484145

Lund Dean, K., & Safranski, S. R. (2008). No harm, no foul? Organizational intervention in workplace spirituality. *International Journal of Public Administration, 31*(4), 359–371. https://doi.org/10.1080/01900690701590751

Malthus, T. R. (1798). *An essay on the principle of population as it affects the future improvement of society, with remarks on the speculations of Mr. Goodwin, M. Condorcet and other writers* (1st ed.). J. Johnson in St Paul's Church-yard.

Marcos, S. (2010). Spirituality; Perspectives from the first Indigenous Women's Summit of the Americas. In F. Wijsen & S. Marcos (Eds.), *Indigenous voices in the sustainability discourse. Spirituality and the struggle for a better quality of life* (pp. 49–70). LIT Verlag.

Marques, J., Dhiman, S., & King, R. (2005). Spirituality in the workplace: Developing an integral model and a comprehensive definition. *The Journal of American Academy of Business, 7*(1), 81–91. https://www.researchgate.net

Marques, J., Dhiman, S., & King, R. (2010). Exploring the link between spirituality and sustainability. *Business Renaissance Quarterly, 5*(1), 19. https://www.proquest.com

Marschke, E., Prezioni, R., & Harrington, W. (2009). Professionals and executives support a relationship between organizational commitment and spirituality in the workplace. *Journal of Business and Economics Research, 7*(8), 33–48. https://doi.org/10.19030/jber.v7i8.2320

Marx, K., & Engels, F. (1967 [1844]). *The Communist manifesto.* Penguin.

McClaughry, J. (1989). Preface. In E. F. Schumacher (Ed.), *Small is beautiful*. Harper Perennial.

McDaniel, J. (2002). Spirituality and sustainability. *Conservation Biology, 16*(6), 1461–1464. http://www.jstor.org/stable/3095400

McNamara, C. (2006). *Field guide to consulting and organizational development: A collaborative and systems approach to performance, change and learning.* Authenticity Consulting.

Mebratu, D. (1998). Sustainability and sustainable development: Historical and conceptual review. *Environmental Impact Assessment Review, 18*(6), 493–520. https://doi.org/10.1016/S0195-9255(98)00019-5

Mehta, Y., & Joshi, S. (2010, August 22). Impact of workplace spirituality on organization culture through improved employee productivity. In *AIMS International Conference on Value-based Management*. Presented at the meeting of Association of Indian Management Scholars, Houston, TX. http://www.aims-international.org

Milliman, J., Czaplewski, A. J., & Ferguson, J. (2003). Workplace spirituality and employee work attitudes: An exploratory empirical assessment. *Journal of Organizational Change Management, 16*(4), 426–447. https://doi.org/10.1108/09534810310484172

Mitroff, I. I., & Denton, E. A. (1999). A study of spirituality in the workplace. *Sloan Management Review, 40*, 83–92. https://sloanreview.mit.edu

Mirvis, P. H. (1997). "Soul work" in organizations. *Organization Science, 8*(2), 193–206. http://www.jstor.org/stable/2635311

Mitchell, L. (2009). *Cyrus the Great and the obedience of the willing*. University of Exeter.

Molnar, E., & Mulvihill, P. R. (2003). Sustainability-focused organizational learning: Recent experiences and new challenges. *Journal of Environmental Planning and Management, 46*(2), 167–176. https://doi.org/10.1080/0964056032000070990

Moore, T. (1992). *Care of the soul: A guide for cultivating depth and sacredness in everyday life*. HarperCollins.

Morrissey, J., & Heidkamp, P. (2022). Sustainability after COVID-19: Pillars for a just transition. *Environmental Sustainability, 5*, 261–269. https://doi.org/10.1007/s42398-022-00231-y

Neck, C. P., & Milliman, J. F. (1994). Thought self-leadership: Finding spiritual fulfillment in organizational life. *Journal of Managerial Psychology, 9*(6), 9–16. https://doi.org/10.1108/02683949410070151

Neeganagwedgin, E. (2013). Ancestral knowledges, spirituality and Indigenous narratives as self-determination. *AlterNative: An International Journal of Indigenous Peoples, 9*(4), 322–334. https://doi.org/10.1177/117718011300900404

Northouse, P. G. (2018). *Leadership: Theory and practice* (8th ed.). Sage.

Nunez, M. C. (2011). Sustainability and spirituality: A transdisciplinary perspective. *Transdisciplinary Journal of Engineering & Science, 7*, 74–80. https://www.atlas-journal.com

Ospina, S., & Foldy, E. (2008). Building bridges from the margins: The work of leadership in social change organizations. *Integrative Leadership Conference,* University of Minnesota, October 5–7.

Pappas, J. B., & Pappas, E. C. (2014). The sustainable personality: Values and behaviors in individual sustainability. *International Journal of Higher Education, 4*(1), 12. https://doi.org/10.5430/ijhe.v4n1p12

Pawar, B. S. (2008). Two approaches to workplace spirituality facilitation: A comparison and implications. *Leadership & Organization Development Journal, 29*(6), 544–567. https://doi.org/10.1108/01437730810894195

Pawar, B. S. (2009). Individual spirituality, workplace spirituality and work attitudes: An empirical test of direct and interaction effects. *Leadership & Organization Development Journal, 30*(8), 759–777. https://doi.org/10.1108/01437730911003911

PC Magazine. (n.d.). *Post-digital era.* https://www.pcmag.com/encyclopedia/term/post-digital-era

Philips, S. (2023). *Five COVID-fueled shifts in our religious and spiritual landscape.* Fetzer Institute. https://fetzer.org/blog/five-covid-fueled-shifts-our-religious-and-spiritual-landscape

Polley, D., Vora, J., & SubbaNarasimha, P. N. (2005). Paying the devil his due: Limits and liabilities of workplace spirituality. *International Journal of Organizational Analysis, 13*(1), 50–63. https://doi.org/10.1108/eb028997

Rainey, D. L. (2006). *Sustainable business development: Inventing the future through strategy, innovation, and leadership.* Cambridge University Press.

Rainey, D. L. (2008). Transparency, openness, and accountability: A new imperative. In M. V. Russo (Ed.), *Environmental management: Readings and cases* (pp. 228–242). Sage Publications.

Reave, L. (2005). Spiritual values and practices related to leadership effectiveness. *Leadership Quarterly, 16*(5), 655–687. https://doi.org/10.1016/j.leaqua.2005.07.003

Rego, A., & Pina e Cunha, M. (2008). Workplace spirituality and organizational commitment: An empirical study. *Journal of Organizational Change Management, 21*(1), 53–75. https://doi.org/10.1108/09534810810847039

Riasudeen, S., & Prabavathy, R. (2011). Relationship of workplace spirituality and work attitude in manufacturing organization. *Global Management Review, 5*(4), 29–37. http://web.a.ebscohost.com

Rimanoczy, I. (2014). A matter of being: Developing sustainability-minded leaders. *Journal of Management for Global Sustainability, 2*(1), 95–122. https://doi.org/10.13185/1902

Ripple, W. J., Wolf, C., Newsome, T. M., Galetti, M., Alamgir, M., Crist, E., ... & 15,364 Scientist Signatories from 184 Countries. (2017). World scientists' warning to humanity: A second notice. *BioScience, 67*(12), 1026–1028. https://doi.org/10.1093/biosci/bix125

Robbins, S. P., & Coulter, M. (2012). *Management* (12th ed.). Pearson Prentice-Hall.

Robbins, S. P., & Judge, T. A. (2010) *Organizational behavior* (14th ed.). Pearson Prentice-Hall.

Robison, C. (2020). *Decolonizing climate discourse and legitimating Indigenous wisdom: Toward an ecosystemic episteme* (Master's Theses). Rollins College. https://scholarship.rollins.edu/honors/112

Royce-Davis, J., & Stewart, M. (2000). *Addressing the relationship between career development and spirituality when working with college students.* University of the Pacific. Retrieved from ERIC Database (ED452444).

Schaltegger, S., Hansen, E. G., & Lüdeke-Freund, F. (2016). Business models for sustainability: Origins, present research, and future avenues. *Organization & Environment, 29*(1), 3–10. https://doi.org/10.1177/1086026615599806

Schaltegger, S., & Wagner, M. (2011). Sustainable entrepreneurship and sustainability innovation: Categories and interactions. *Business Strategy & Environment, 20*(4), 222–237. https://doi.org/10.1002/bse.682

Schein, S. (2014). *The ecological world views and post-conventional action logics of global sustainability leaders* (Doctoral dissertation, Fielding Graduate University).

Schein, S. (2015). Ecological worldviews: A missing perspective to advance global sustainability leadership. *Journal of Management for Global Sustainability, 3*(1), 1–24. https://doi.org/10.13185/JM2015.03102

Schumacher, E. F. (1959). *Small is beautiful*. Harper Perennial.

Schumpeter, J. A. (1994 [1942]). *Capitalism, socialism and democracy*. Routledge.

Schwab, K., & Sternfels, B. (2022). *3 keys to a resilient post-pandemic recovery.* World Economic Forum. https://www.weforum.org/agenda/2022/02/3-keys-to-a-resilient-post-pandemic-recovery/

Senge, P. (with Smith, B., Kruschwitz, N., Laut, J., & Schley, S.). (2008). *The necessary revolution: How individuals and organizations are working together to create a sustainable world*. Random House Digital.

Senge, P., Hamilton, H., & Kania, J. (2015). The dawn of system leadership. *Stanford Social Innovation Review, 13*(1), 27–33. https://ssir.org/articles/entry/the_dawn_of_system_leadership

Shinde, U. S., Shinde, J. S., & Lytle, L. (2010). The impact of organizational spirituality on employee outcomes. *International Journal of the Academic Business World, 4*(2), 123–130. https://s3.amazonaws.com

Singh, M. (2018). The cultural evolution of shamanism. *Behavioral and Brain Sciences, 41*(e66), 1–17. https://doi.org/10.1017/S0140525X17001893

Smith, A. (1776). *An inquiry into the nature and causes of the wealth of nations.* W. Strahan and T. Cadell.

Somphone, S. (2011). *Exploring the heart of education through spirituality and sustainability: The way we live and the way we educate dictate the future*. Participatory Development Training Centre (PADETC). http://www.padetc.org

Soyka, P. A. (2012). *Creating a sustainable organization: Approaches for enhancing corporate value through sustainability*. Pearson Education.

Sulmasy, D. P. (2013). Ethos, mythos, and thanatos: Spirituality and ethics at the end of life. *Journal of Pain and Symptom Management, 46*(3), 447–451. https://doi.org/10.1016/j.jpainsymman.2013.03.016

Swamy, P. S., Kumar, M., & Sundarapandian, S. M. (2003). Spirituality and ecology of sacred groves in Tamil Nadu, India. *UNASYLVA-FAO-*, 53–55. http://www.fao.org/tempref/docrep/fao/005/y9882e/y9882e10.pdf

Swilling, M. (2020). *The age of sustainability*. Routledge.

Tams, S., & Marshall, J. (2011). Responsible careers: Systemic reflexivity in shifting landscapes. *Human Relations, 64*(1), 109–131. https://doi.org/10.1177/0018726710384292

Targowski, A. (2012). Spirituality 2.0—A condition for a wise civilization. *Dialogue and Universalism, 22*(2), 133–143. https://www.researchgate.net

Tate, W. (2009). *The search for leadership: An organisational perspective*. Triarchy Press.

Taylor, S., & Pearse, N. (2009). Creating sustainable organizations through servant leadership. *The International Journal of Interdisciplinary Social Sciences: Annual Review, 4*(4), 223–234. https://doi.org/10.18848/1833-1882/CGP/v04i04/52885.

Thompson, W. (2001). Spirituality at work: People want to work in a spirited place. *Executive Excellence, 18*(9), 10. https://www.worldcat.org/title/executive-excellence/oclc/67041208

Thompson, D. (2019, February 24). Workism is making Americans miserable. *The Atlantic*.

Thompson, D. (2023). *On work: Money, meaning, identity*. Atlantic Editions.

Timmins, N. (2015). *The practice of system leadership: Being comfortable with chaos*. The King's Fund. https://www.kingsfund.org.uk/sites/default/files/field/field_publication_file/System-leadership-Kings-Fund-May-2015.pdf

Tourish, D., & Tourish, N. (2010). Spirituality at work, and its implications for leadership and followership: A post-structuralist perspective. *Leadership, 6*(2), 207–224. https://doi.org/10.1177/1742715010363210

Tsosie, R. (2014). Indigenous peoples and sustainability policy: Exploring the politics and practice of "Indigenous sustainability". *Sustainability News*.

Arizona State University. https://sustainability-innovation.asu.edu/news/archive/Indigenous-peoples-sustainability-policy-exploring-politics-practice-Indigenous-sustainability/

Vaill, P. B. (1996). *Learning as a way of being*. Jossey-Bass.

Valasek, A. J. (2009). *Examining the relationships of spirituality and religiosity to individual productivity in the United States* (Doctoral dissertation, Northcentral University).

Valente, M. (2012). Theorizing firm adoption of sustaincentrism. *Organization Studies, 33*(4), 563–591. https://doi.org/10.1177/0170840612443455

Van Schalkwyk, A. (2011). Sacredness and sustainability: Searching for a practical eco-spirituality. *Religion and Theology, 18*(1–2), 77–92. https://doi.org/10.1163/157430111X613674

Vatican Insider. (2015). *Pope Francis' encyclical: This "wounded world" needs "an ecological conversion"*. The Vatican. http://www.lastampa.it/2015/06/17/vaticaninsider/eng/the-vatican/pope-francis-encyclical-this-wounded-world-needs-an-ecological-conversion-VIDiWxrhCcCwmSDen1R9yI/pagina.html

Visser, W., & Crane, A. (2010). *Corporate sustainability and the individual: Understanding what drives sustainability professionals as change agents* (SSRN Paper Series, No. 1). https://doi.org/10.2139/ssrn.1559087

Waddock, S. (2007). Leadership integrity in a fractured knowledge world. *Academy of Management Learning & Education, 6*, 543–557. https://doi.org/10.5465/AMLE.2007.27694954

Waddock, S. (2008). The difference makers. *Greenwood*.

Walck, C. (2009). Integrating sustainability into management education: A dean's perspective. *Journal of World Business, 33*, 384–390. https://doi.org/10.1177/1052562908323091

Waste and Resources Action Programme. (2018). *WRAP and the circular economy*. Author. http://www.wrap.org.uk/about-us/about/wrap-and-circular-economy

Weber, M. (1918). *Science as a vocation* (pp. 129–158). H. Gerth and C. Wright.

White, M. (2013). *Building a resilient organizational culture*. UNC Kenan-Flagler Business School.

Whiteman, G., Walker, B., & Perego, P. (2013). Planetary boundaries: Ecological foundations for corporate sustainability. *Journal of Management Studies, 50*(2), 307–336. https://doi.org/10.1111/j.1467-6486.2012.01073.x

Williams, A., Kennedy, S., Philipp, F., & Whiteman, G. (2017). Systems thinking: A review of sustainability management research. *Journal of Cleaner Production, 148*, 866–881. https://doi.org/10.1016/j.jclepro.2017.02.002

Word, J. (2012). Engaging work as a calling: Examining the link between spirituality and job involvement. *Journal of Management, Spirituality & Religion, 9*(2), 147–166. https://doi.org/10.1080/14766086.2012.688622
World Commission on Environment and Development. (1987). *Our common future*. Oxford University Press.
Yin, E., & Mahrous, A. (2022). Covid-19 global pandemic, workplace spirituality and the rise of spirituality-driven organisations in the post-digital era. *Journal of Humanities and Applied Social Sciences, 4*(2), 79–93. https://doi.org/10.1108/JHASS-11-2021-0177
Yong, J., Kim, J., Park, J., Seo, I., & Swinton, J. (2011). Effects of a spirituality training program on the spiritual and psychosocial well-being of hospital middle manager nurses in Korea. *Journal of Continuing Education in Nursing, 42*(6), 280–288. https://doi.org/10.3928/00220124-20101201-04
Young, S. T., & Dhanda, K. K. (2013). *Sustainability: Essentials for business.* Sage Publications.
Zellars, K. L., & Perrewe, P. L. (2003). The role of spirituality in occupational stress and well-being. In R. A. Giacalone & C. J. Jurkiewicz (Eds.), *Handbook of workplace spirituality and organizational performance* (pp. 300–313). M. E. Sharpe.

Index

C. G. Beehner, *Spirituality, Sustainability, and Success*, Palgrave Studies in Workplace Spirituality and Fulfillment, https://doi.org/10.1007/978-3-031-47643-3

I

J

U

SPRINGER NATURE

GPSR Compliance

The European Union's (EU) General Product Safety Regulation (GPSR) is a set of rules that requires consumer products to be safe and our obligations to ensure this.

If you have any concerns about our products, you can contact us on ProductSafety@springernature.com

In case Publisher is established outside the EU, the EU authorized representative is:

Springer Nature Customer Service Center GmbH
Europaplatz 3
69115 Heidelberg, Germany

The manufacturer's authorised representative in the EU is Springer Nature Customer Service Centre GmbH, Europaplatz 3, 69115 Heidelberg, Germany. If you have any concerns regarding our products, please contact ProductSafety@springernature.com

Printed and bound by CPI Group (UK) Ltd, Croydon, CR0 4YY
01/10/2026
02225894-0018